INTERNATIONAL SOCIA
MOVEMENT RESEARCH

Volume 2 • 1989

ORGANIZING FOR CHANGE:
SOCIAL MOVEMENT ORGANIZATIONS
IN EUROPE AND THE UNITED STATES

Voor Brechtje

INTERNATIONAL SOCIAL MOVEMENT RESEARCH

A Research Annual

ORGANIZING FOR CHANGE:
SOCIAL MOVEMENT ORGANIZATIONS
IN EUROPE AND THE UNITED STATES

Edited by: **BERT KLANDERMANS**
Department of Social Psychology
Free University of Amsterdam

VOLUME 2 • 1989

JAI PRESS INC.

Greenwich, Connecticut   *London, England*

CONTENTS

LIST OF CONTRIBUTORS

M. Helen Brown

The Tavistock Institute of
Human Relations,
London, England

Sherry Cable

Department of Sociology
University of Tennessee

Ton Duffhues

Department of Sociology
Catholic University of Nijmegen,
Nijmegen, The Netherlands

Albert Felling

Department of Sociology
Catholic University of Nijmegen,
Nijmegen, The Netherlands

Roberto M. Fernandez

Department of Sociology
Northwestern University

Mark Furman

Department of Sociology
University of Wisconsin,
Madison

Peter Gundelach

Department of Political Science
University of Aarhus,
Aarhus, Denmark

Jean Hartley

Department of Industrial Psychology
Birkbeck College
University of London

Leo W. Huberts

Institute for Public Administration/
Policy Consultants
The Hague, The Netherlands

Bert Klandermans

Department of Social Psychology
Free University of Amsterdam,
Amsterdam, The Netherlands

David Knoke

Department of Sociology
University of Minnesota

Doug McAdam

Department of Sociology
University of Arizona

Joyce Marie Mushaben

American Institute for Contemporary
German Studies,
Washington, D.C.

Pamela Oliver

Department of Sociology
University of Wisconsin,
Madison

Karl-Dieter Opp

Department of Sociology
University of Hamburg,
Hamburg, West Germany

Naomi Rosenthal

Department of American Studies
State University of New York,
College at Old Westbury

Dieter Rucht

Wissenshaftszentrum Berlin
Berlin, West Germany

Michael Schwartz

Department of Sociology
State University of New York,
Stony Brook

Gerrita Van der Veen

Department of Social Psychology
Free University of Amsterdam,
Amsterdam, The Netherlands

Edward Walsh   Department of Sociology
Pennsylvania State University

Hajo Weber   Department of Sociology
University of Bielefeld,
Bielefeld, West Germany

INTRODUCTION:
SOCIAL MOVEMENT ORGANIZATIONS AND
THE STUDY OF SOCIAL MOVEMENTS

Bert Klandermans

Social movements have traditionally been distinguished from other types of collective behavior by their higher levels of organization. As Wilson (1973) argued, social movements inevitably develop more durable structures than other forms of collective action. People in the movement try to regulate and routinize their lives, and, over time, they develop an orientation toward solidary relations within the movement and toward more direct benefits from their participation. From a different angle, Tilly (1982) demonstrated in his study of collective action in France and Great Britain, that over the last two centuries voluntary associations become the typical vehicle of protest behavior. Since Zald and Ash (1966) introduced the distinction between social movements and social movement organizations (SMOs), social movement literature directed its attention more to SMOs than to social movements as objects of study.

International Social Movement Research, Vol. 2, pages 1-17.
Copyright © 1989 by JAI Press Inc.
All rights of reproduction in any form reserved.
ISBN: 0-89232-964-5

Despite the concentration on SMOs over the last decade, literature on them *as organizations* is still scarce. In particular, empirical studies of the organizational characteristics of SMOs are lacking. This anthology, however, brings together papers that examine SMOs as organizations. Contributors from such different countries as Denmark, Germany, The Netherlands, Great Britain, and the United States draw upon research into such varied movements as the civil rights movement, the labor movement, the peace movement, the women's movement, the environmental movement, and the antinuclear power movement. In the individual introductions to each section of the book, I develop a theoretical framework for the study of SMOs as organizations. In this first chapter, I introduce this framework and explicate its use in the design of the book. Before elaborating the theoretical framework, however, three questions must be considered: How are SMOs defined? How organized are social movements? and How are SMOs appreciated in the different theoretical approaches in social movement literature?

DEFINING SOCIAL MOVEMENT ORGANIZATIONS

Most definitions of social movements refer in some way or another to the organizational characteristics of a movement. For instance, Wilson (1973, p. 8) defined a social movement as "a conscious, collective, organized attempt to bring about or resist large scale change in the social order by non-institutionalized means." Wood and Jackson (1982, p. 3) described social movements as "unconventional groups that have varying degrees of formal organization and that attempt to produce or prevent radical or reformist type of change." Other definitions, such as Turner and Killian's (1987, p. 223), refer to organizational characteristics implicitly: "A social movement is a collectivity acting with some continuity to promote or resist a change in the society of which it is a part."

Although there is general agreement on the relevance of organizational structures as a distinguishing feature of social movements, opinions differ on the significance of organizations for social movements. At the one extreme are those who contend either that organizations are symptoms of institutionalization and that institutionalization marks the terminal stage of a social movement (cf. Wood and Jackson 1982) or that organization is detrimental to movements (cf. Piven and Cloward 1979). At the other extreme are those who like McAdam (1982), believe that, in order to survive, a social movement must develop enduring organizational structures. Much of the scholarly discussion is based on differences in the *kind* of organization that is referred to. In a response to Piven and Cloward, Morris (1984) argued that they wrongly present the civil rights movement as a case supporting their argument. What Piven and Cloward mistakenly described as a weak organizational structure, Morris said, was in fact a very effective coalition of indigenous organizations. We can say that Piven and Cloward have taken a restricted definition of movement organization. What they are referring to are bureaucratic organizations, but bureaucratic organizations are not typical of social movements (Gamson and Schmeidler 1983; Jenkins 1979; Knoke and Prensky 1984). Several authors have pointed to the particular character of organizational structures within social movements (Gerlach and Hine 1970; Morris 1984; Neidhardt 1985). Movements are organizations of organizations; loose network structures of organizations that have a broad variety of characteristics.

But there is a problem with including organizational characteristics in a definition of social movements: It is difficult to decide how much organization is required to make a social phenomenon a social movement. McCarthy and Zald (1976) were the first to disentangle, in their definitions, the movement and organization aspects. They defined a social movement (1976, p. 1217) as "a set of opinions and beliefs in a population representing preferences for changing some elements of the social structure or reward distribution, or both, of a society." SMOs, for their part (1976, p. 1218), were defined as "complex, or formal, organizations that identify their goals with the preferences of a social movement and attempt to implement those goals." Useful as McCarthy and Zald's separate definitions are, their identification of a social movement with a set of beliefs and opinions is problematic. Beliefs and opinions are of course important elements of every social movement but ultimately it is individuals and their activities, not ideas that constitute a movement (cf. Marwell and Oliver 1984).

A social movement can, therefore, be defined as a set of interacting individuals who attempt to promote, control, or prevent changes in social and cultural arrangements. The two essential elements in this definition merit elaboration.

A. *Social movements consist of interacting individuals.* Social movements encompass a variety of interactions: contacts between representatives of the movement and representatives of the media or authorities; mobilization attempts, during which attitudinal and material support for the movement is solicited; contacts with other activists in meetings, gatherings, demonstrations; contacts between leaders and rank-and-file members; confrontations with the representatives of opponents and countermovements. These interactions can be peaceful and cooperative, or contentious and disruptive.

B. *Social movements try to promote, control or prevent social and cultural change.* Social movements are always engaged in changes: changes in the societal position of social categories such as women, workers, homosexuals, or immigrants; or cultural changes, for example, the promotion of values such as health, peace, or freedom of speech. Social movements do not always *promote* change. The environmental movement, among other, grew by opposing change. And many social movements have been fueled by the awareness that important values or rights are being threatened.

SMOs can be defined, following McCarthy and Zald, as complex organizations that identify their goals with the preferences of a movement and then try to implement those goals. SMOs are open systems that obtain resources (including members) from an external environment, and reallocate funds for various objectives, both internal and external to the organization (Knoke 1985; Knoke and Prensky 1984).

How Organized Are Social Movements?

Social movements are *more* than the sum of the organizations that identify with the movement. Moreover, the component SMOs vary greatly according to their organizational strength. They can have very loose structures, as do many organizations in the women's movement, or very formal hierarchical organizations, as do labor unions. Both extremes can be present within the same movement. The environmental movements in the United States and Europe, for example, include both very formal, traditional organizations and informal grass-roots organizations (Diani and Lodi 1988; Rucht in this volume; Wood 1982). Different organizations within the same movement can be loosely linked by informal networks or by formal overarching structures. Quite a few organizations within the same movement may have no direct link to each other at all. Like SMOs, social movements differ tremendously in organizational strength. Together these characteristics raise the question of how organized social movements are. Clearly SMOs are organizations and do have organizational characteristics, but what does their organization say about the movement as a whole?

Spontaneity and Organization

The considerable variation in organizational strength within, and between, movements has recently led several authors to reconsider the sharp distinction between social movements and collective behavior as drawn by resource mobilization theory (Killian 1984; Neal 1987; Turner and Killian 1987). In his hotly debated article in the *American Sociological Review,* Killian (1984, p. 770) concluded "that while organization and planning are key variables, social movement theory must take into account spontaneity and emergence, and the transformation of pre-existing structures." Presenting evidence from the civil rights movement in Tallahassee, Florida, Killian argued that analyses of social movements cannot ignore the role of spontaneous, unplanned, and unforeseen events, which must be acknowledged as essential aspects of social movements. In an attempt to overcome the limitations of the case-study approach, Neal (1987) compared a sample of nine SMOs with nine other instances of collective behavior on emergent norms, emergent structures, and spontaneity. Although limited, his study demonstrated that SMOs and other forms of collective behavior, such as disaster groups, have more in common than is often believed. As Turner and Killian (1987) argued, there are natural limits to the extent to which social movements can be organized. The members' impatience, the tactical need to respond promptly to dramatic events, and the leadership's limited control over the actions of adherents or affiliated organizations make the organization of movements tenuous. In their contribution to this volume, Rosenthal and Schwartz discuss the spontaneity organization issue at length and in detail. Distinguishing different levels of organization, they try to solve the apparent paradox that the course of social movements is determined by both planned actions and spontaneous events.

Organizations of Organizations

The question as to what extent social movements are organized, is impressed upon the observer by the peculiar form of organization that social movements take on. The kind of formal, bureaucratic organizational structure sought by many an observer trying to ascertain a social movement's level of organization, is not the structure social movements characteristically adopt. As Gerlach and Hine (1970) noted, social movements are characterized by decentralized, segmented, and reticulate structures. As noted earlier, social movements are organizations of organizations, a fact Morris (1984) convincingly demonstrated in his description of the southern civil rights movement. The organizational structure of the southern civil rights movement consisted of local movement centers, which were networks of local black organizations, and overarching structures, of which the Southern Christian Leadership Conference (SCLC) was the most important. This structure illustrates very well Neidhardt's (1985) characterization of social movements as networks of networks. Social movements are conglomerates of national and local formal organizations and informal grass-roots organizations. The papers in this volume confirm the validity of this characterization for such different movements as the Dutch Catholic movement (Duffhues and Felling), the German and French environmental movements (Rucht), and the German peace movement (Mushaben). Some of these organizations are existing organizations that identify with the movement's goals, such as the black churches in the case of the civil rights movement, the Catholic and Protestant churches in the case of the peace movement, or the traditional natural conservation organizations in the case of the environmental movement. Some of them are temporary organizations set up for no other reason than to organize a specific collective action, for example, the peace platforms in the case of the Dutch peace movement. Hartley's discussion (in this volume) of the Rotherham strike committee shows that, despite their temporary character, such organizations can be very sophisticated. The peculiarities of SMOs will be examined in much greater detail in Part I. Here, however, it is enough to emphasize that the absence of formal organization does not mean that social movements are not organized.

Internal and External Pressure to Organize

Despite their natural tendency to adopt nonbureaucratic structures, internal and external pressure can force movements to set up formal organizations. As Gamson (1975) asserted, bureaucratization helps to prevent factionalism. Formal organization—that is a division of labor, an elaborated set of rules, rights, and duties—provides tools to help the ideologically-heterogeneous collectivities which social movements usually are to survive (Wilson 1973). Especially in situations in which organizational discipline is required, strong organizational structures are indispensible (Schwartz 1976). A common inducement to routinization in social movements is the wish to ensure more reliable and predictable funding and support for the movement. As Wilson (1973) observed, the "fundraising" committee is usually among the first committees to be installed. The need for external funding leads to strong external pressure to erect formal organizations. Funding institutions prefer to transfer their money to organizations that look "serious;" in other words, that look like the organizations they are used to (see Knoke in this volume). Tax regulations can also force a collectivity to adopt formal organizational characteristics (McCarthy and Britt, 1989).

Inclusive and Exclusive Organizations

Social movements differ according to the forms of organization they develop. Apart from structural characteristics, such as size and external funding, social movement culture plays an important role in determining the kind of organization a movement develops. Lofland (1985, p. 219) defines a social movement's culture as "the package of collective ways of approved and fostered member emotions, beliefs and actions." A movement's culture can differ in three aspects: elaboration, expressiveness, and compassion. Lofland did not expressly relate his cultural differentiations to organizational characteristics, but we can assume they do influence organization. Curtis and Zurcher (1974), in their attempt to explore organizational forms of social movements, did relate movement culture to organizational characteristics. Constructing a taxonomy based on two aspects of a movement's culture—expressiveness versus instrumentality of the movement's goals and inclusiveness versus exclusiveness of the movement's membership—they distinguished types of movements that are more or less inclined to develop formal organizational structures. Inclusive-instrumental movements are the most likely to develop formal organizational structures, whereas exclusive-expressive movements are more likely to develop sect-like organizations.

Social movements *are* organized. Clearly the organizational forms they adopt very often, although not always, differ from the bureaucratic, formal structure we are used to thinking of as an "organization." But this difference does not mean that role differentiation, decision making, management, or coordination do not occur in social movements. This volume is intented to provide a more detailed picture of the organizational aspects of social movements than any currently available. First, however, it is necessary to examine the significance of SMOs in social movement theory.

SOCIAL MOVEMENTS ORGANIZATIONS AND SOCIAL MOVEMENT THEORY

Each of four different theoretical approaches in social movement literature attributes different meanings to SMOs. Traditional breakdown theory sees SMOs as the symptoms of institutionalization; resource mobilization theory values organizations as resources, that is, means to goal-achievement; new social movement theory studies SMOs as goals in themselves; and constructionist approaches describe SMOs as sponsors of meaning. In this section, I will briefly discuss social movement organizations in the context of these four major theoretical approaches to social movements. I will confine myself to a discussion of the place of organizations in a theoretical framework and refrain from evaluating the approaches as such (but see Cohen 1985; Klandermans 1986; Klandermans and Tarrow 1988; McAdam 1982; Troyer 1984 for critical comparisons of social movement theories).

Organizations as a Symptom of Institutionalization

Traditional breakdown theories hold that social movements emerge as responses to specific grievances in a society. McAdam (1982, p. 7) gives the following general account of breakdown theories: Structural strain leads to a disruptive psychological state (such as alienation, cognitive dissonance, or relative deprivation). When this psychological disturbance reaches the aggregate threshold required to produce a social movement, the causl sequence is completed. Social movements are the collective response to a society in disarray. Movement organizations do not play a prominent role in breakdown theories. Not that proponents of this theory would deny that social movements

are organized. Movement organizations become the new institutions that
alienated individuals can identify with. But too much organization, especially
formal organization, is considered a symptom of institutionalization. Sooner
or later bureaucratization, centralization, and oligarchization of movement
organizations will mark the end of the movement. In their contribution to this
volume, Duffhues and Felling provide a critical evaluation of this view of
SMOs. In line with Zald and Ash (1966), they conclude that bureaucratization
and oligarchization are not the inevitable fate of SMOs.

Organizations as Resource

Resource mobilization theory take a completely different view of SMOs
(Jenkins 1983). According to resource mobilization theory, social movements
emerge not so much because grievances increase, but because there is an
increase in the availability of resources in an aggrieved population.
Organization, especially indigenous organization, is one of these resources,
and, in the eyes of scholars such as McAdam (1982), Morris (1984), or Schwartz
(1976), a resource of crucial importance. Movement organizations are means
to goal-achievement. Without lasting organizations, movements will not
survive (McAdam 1982), and only if a subordinate group is able to form and
maintain organizations can it develop the power to change societal and cultural
arrangements (Schwartz 1976). SMOs accumulate and allocate resources
(Knoke 1985). Individual and institutional supporters provide resources to the
SMO, and the organization decides how to allocate them. Individual and
organizational decisions to support an SMO are rational decisions based on
an evaluation of the costs and benefits of participation. Centralization and
bureaucratization are seen neither as inevitable developments nor as symptoms
of institutionalization (Gamson 1975; Zald and Ash 1966).

Organizations as Goals in Themselves

The European new social movement approach (Klandermans 1986) differs
from resource mobilization theory in that it does not study SMOs primarily
from a rational—instrumental, strategic viewpoint. SMOs are seen, not as
means to realizing external goals, but as goals in themselves: democratic niches
in a society in which autonomous social action creates new identities (Cohen
1985). The new social movement approach, developed over the last decade in
Europe, is an attempt to explain the emergence of contemporary movements
such as the women's movement, the environmental movement, and the peace
movement (Offe 1985). In its analyses, it stresses the impact of industrialization
and modernization on the growth of the new social movements. It argues that,
unlike the "old" labor movement, contemporary movements are no longer
rooted in the classical labor-capital contradiction. New mobilization potentials,

such as professionals and governmental officials, are identified as the core constituencies. New problems, connected to the shifting boundaries between public, private, and social life, and the struggles against old and new forms of domination in these areas, are believed to fuel the movements. New organizational structures such as decentralized, antihierarchical organizational designs are thought to be typical of social movements.

Both Cohen (1985) and Melucci (1984, 1985) criticized resource mobilization theory for taking for granted the very phenomenon that social movement theory must explain, namely, the existence of SMOs. As long as the existence of movement organizations can be assumed, the rational-instrumental viewpoint can satisfactorily account for the *development* of social movements. The *emergence* of SMOs, however, can be explained only by looking at these organizations from a nonstrategic viewpoint. The new social movement approach adopts, what Cohen (1985) described as the "identity-oriented paradigm." According to Cohen, this paradigm enables the new social movement approach to accomplish what resource mobilization theory has failed to do: It examines the processes through which collective actors create the identity and solidarity they are defending. In other words, SMOs are not simply instruments to change society; but they are networks of groups and individuals sharing and adhering to a conflictual culture and a group identity within a general social identity whose interpretation they contest (Melucci 1985). Creating and defending new identities, an SMO is, to its members, an end in itself.

Organizations as Sponsors of Meaning

Several authors have criticized resource mobilization theory for neglecting the role of grievance interpretation (Ferree and Miller 1985; Klandermans 1986; Klandermans and Tarrow 1988; Snow et al. 1986). To some extent, the controversy between resource mobilization theory and the traditional collective behavior apporoach to the role of grievances in the emergence of social movements goes back to the neglect of grievance interpretation by both currents. Both have a tendency to see a direct link between objective circumstances and individual behavior without taking into account the intervening processes of defining and interpreting the individual's situation. One's interpretations, rather than reality itself, guide political actions. The definition of the situation can make an obnoxious situation justifiable in the eyes of the victim. If authorities are perceived to be legitimate, coercion is not defined as oppression, but as legal enforcement of the law. According to scholars who emphasize the role of grievance interpretation, the crucial variables in movement mobilization are not anger or frustration but the belief that one's interests are common interests, as well as the perception of injustice— that is, the belief that these interests are legitimate yet are not being met.

Despite its interest in identity formation, the new social movement approach also neglects grievance interpretation (Klandermans 1986; Klandermans and Tarrow 1988). This approach assumes that the emergence of contemporary social movements is related to the detrimental impact of modernization and industrialization on the social, political, and ecological environment, but how structural change are transformed into grievances is never elaborated.

Recently, a number of students of social movements focused on the role of SMOs as sponsors of meaning (see Klandermans et al. [1988] for a collection of papers on this aspect of the construction of meaning). Through the use of such labels as frame alignment (Snow et al. 1986), and consensus mobilization (Klandermans 1988), they explored the role of movement organizations in diffusing specific interpretations of the situation that the movement organization wants to change. In a way, these analyses revert to earlier work by scholars such as Gusfield (1970), Lauer (1972), and Spector and Kitsuse (1973). In his introduction to the section, "The Development of Collective Meanings" in his reader in social movements, Gusfield (1970, p. 309) argued that "felt discontents, judgments of possibility, interpretations of official actions, and other aspects of collective action are deeply affected by the way experience is interpreted and given meaning. . . . What comes to be seen as injustice must be pointed to, named, and described from among the logically possible interpretations for the potential adherents' sense of discontent." Elaborating an "interactionist analysis" of social movements, Lauer (1972) argued that, through interactional processes, a symbol system and the meaning of the movement develop. Spector and Kitsuse (1973, p. 146), in their constructionist approach to the study of social problems, stressed that social problems are not objective conditions but "activities of groups making assertions of grievances and claims to organizations, agencies, and institutions about some putative conditions." SMOs are among the groups involved in these "claims-making processes."

Each of the four theoretical approaches described above illuminates a different aspect of SMOs. Institutionalization, instrumentality, identity formation, and the construction of meaning are all facets of the same phenomenon. Thus, it does not make much sense to regard the four approaches as competing paradigms; they are, to a large extent, complementary.

A FRAMEWORK FOR THE STUDY OF SOCIAL MOVEMENT ORGANIZATIONS

A theoretical framework for the study of SMOs must include four core concepts: grievances, resources, opportunities, and meaning. Each of these four concepts is related to a different body of literature and is associated with a different theory. From a movement organization's pragmatic perspective, they are related to different practices and tactics. Traditional social movement theory and the new social movement approach have focused primarily on the grievance component. Resource mobilization theory has concentrated on resources and opportunities. The fourth core element—meaning—has not received much systematic attention until recently.

The construction of meaning is an important element in every mobilization campaign. Grievances, resources, and opportunities are not objective entities. Grievances must be interpreted. People must be convinced that the resources they provide can be employed effectively. Opportunities must be evaluated before strategies and tactics can be chosen. Whether the results of an SMO's efforts are successful is similarly a matter of interpretation. Interpretations and definitions of a situation are problematic, and the interpretations of one actor may well be attacked by other actors. SMOs thus engage in the construction of meaning by interpreting grievances and evaluating opportunities, and through interactions with an external environment with a specific opportunity structure. The construction of meaning is accomplished in part by deliberate attempts of social actors (SMOs, countermovement organizations, opponents) to mobilize consensus; in part, it comes about through unplanned consensus formation within friendship networks, primary bonds, and so on.

In my own treatment of SMOs, and throughout this volume, these four core concepts outlined above are referred to again and again, both explicitly and implicitly.

The theoretical framework developed in this anthology can be summarized in the following way: Organizational characteristics of SMOs are determined by both the external and internal environments they must deal with. Interactions with the external environment can be analyzed in terms of the accumulation and allocation of resources and organizational effectiveness. In the internal environment of an SMO, leadership functions and decision-making processes regulate the input, throughput, and output of resources. In the external environment, allies and opponents determine the political opportunity structure. Organizational characteristics and characteristics of the external environment together determine organizational effectiveness.

These conceptual principles also serve as the organizing principles for the five parts of this book. The organizational characteristics of SMOs are the topic of the first part. The next three parts examine the external and internal environments of SMOs: The second part, on management, focuses on the acquisition of resources from the external environment; the third part looks at leadership and decision-making processes internal to the movement organization; and the fourth part, on interorganizational networks, analyzes an SMO's external environment. The concluding part discusses organizational effectiveness. I will now briefly summarize the contents of each part, highlighting the essential points discussed at greater length in the individual introductions.

Structure and Change

Movement organizations characteristically manifest a variety of organizational structures. Part I describes these several different forms of organization. More characteristic of social movements, however, is the fluidity of their organizational structures. Expansion and contraction give the career of social movements a cyclical character. A distinction can be made between long-term and short-term cycles. Long-term cycles are contingent on the availability of resources in a society and on changes in the opportunity structure (Tarrow 1983). The movements of the 1960s provide an example of such a long-term cycle. Short-term cycles are dependent on managerial decisions. No single movement organization is capable of maintaining its constituency in a constant state of mobilization. The vitality of SMOs thus depends on a core of officials and volunteers whose task it is to be alert and to mobilize support for mass action if necessary. After the action is over, movement activities inevitably contract and return to their base level. Because social movements are cyclical, the number of participants fluctuates and so depends on mobilization, the force that sustains and revitalizes a movement.

Management of Social Movement Organizations

The management of SMOs consists of formulating strategies to acquire resources and of choosing between alternatives in allocating them. Management of social movements requires interaction with two types of actors: supporters, who are needed to provide resources, and authorities, who are approached to exert influence. While the supporters decide whether they will provide the requested resources, it is the movement organization that determines how the accumulated resources will be used. Resources can be obtained from individuals and from other organizations. Decisions to grant resources to an SMO are rational decisions based on an evaluation of the costs and benefits of the support given. In deciding how to allocate resources, SMOs have to choose between four possible areas of deployment: organizational maintenance, incentive systems to secure the influx of resources, public relations, and attempts to influence authorities.

Leadership and Decision Making

Movement leaders are key figures in the management of a movement organization. They are the managers of the incentive system, and they have the authority to take binding decisions on the allocation of resources. But leadership and authority in SMOs are uncertain. Because movement organizations are voluntary associations, in cases of disagreement with the leadership, members, as a rule, prefer to leave the organization rather than make the effort to criticize the leadership. This is not to say that the legitimacy of the movement leadership is questioned very often. Members expect that their leaders will care for the organization, and as long as they feel that the leadership is doing so well enough, they do not really care about democratic decision making. Democracy in voluntary organizations is not an issue as long as the organization produces results relevant to the membership. Nevertheless, many movement organizations are egalitarian simply for ideological reasons. Democratic, egalitarian values have generated such structural arrangements as rotating, distributed, or multiple leadership, even at the expense of organizational effectiveness.

Interorganizational Networks

An SMO's multiorganizational field has both sectors with organizations and institutions that support the movement organization and sectors with organizations and institutions that oppose it (including opposing authorities and countermovement organizations). These sectors can be conceptualized as the SMO's alliance and conflict systems. Almost every kind of organization or institution can become involved in either of the two systems. Alliance systems serve to support the movement organization by providing resources and creating political opportunities. Conflict systems work to deprive the movement organization of its resources and opportunities. Within conflict systems, bargaining relations develop sooner or later between representatives of SMOs and authorities, either at the initiative of the movement organization or of the authorities. Alliance systems link SMOs to the political system, connecting elites and political parties with the social movement sector. Conflict systems tend to develop an ingroup-outgroup dynamic. Proponents and opponents come to see each other and the events relevant to their antagonism in exaggerated terms of black and white.

Organizational Effectiveness

An SMO's effectiveness concerns the efficacy of the organization in its interactions with its external environment; its efficacy in accumulating and employing resources in order to produce desired effects in its environment. Of course, an SMO's activities may also produce unintended or even undesired effects. Although every organizer remembers some such unintended, undesired effect that diverted the career of his or her organization, students of movement organizations have neglected this aspect of organizational effectiveness. Because an SMO is not the only actor that tries to exert influence, evaluations of the organization's impact on its external environment should be made in relation to the effectiveness of influence attempts by other actors in the field. Whether outcomes of an SMO's efforts are defined as a success or a failure is a matter of interpretation and depends on who is making the judgment. Movement success is multidimensional. Apart from achieving its goals, a movement organization can succeed in such different ways as gaining societal and political recognition, setting political agendas, and undermining societal consensus. An additional measure of success of an SMO's activities is whether they provide resource for the future. In this regard, successful consensus mobilization can become the foundation for successful action mobilization. Characteristics of the environment (the political opportunity structure) interacting with characteristics of the movement organization (organizational structure, membership commitment, and strategy and tactics) determine organizational effectiveness. Both success *and* failure can impair *and* improve the chances of a movement organization's survival, depending on how the situation in which it was achieved is interpreted.

THE STUDY OF SOCIAL
MOVEMENT ORGANIZATIONS

SMOs are intriguing phenomena to study. Systematic empirical studies of SMOs would benefit not only social movement theory but also more general organizational theory. Although students of social movements have conducted quite a few studies of SMOs, analyses of these organizations, as organizations, are still scarce. As a consequence, many questions regarding the organizational aspects of SMOs remain unanswered. I do not pretend that this volume has been able to answer them all, despite the wide range of topics covered by the different contributors. In concluding this general introduction, let me briefly mention the five general questions that provide the guidelines for this anthology.

1. What are the organizational characteristics of SMOs, and what causes organizational change or decline? Assuming that organizational characteristics result from the interaction between the organization and its internal and external environments, what factors in the internal and external environments are of influence, and with what effects?
2. How are SMOs managed? Assuming that many SMOs do not conform to the formal organizational model, in what way are they governed? How are decisions made? What leadership functions are operating, and how are they distributed? How are leaders of movement organizations recruited? What incentive systems are in operation for leaders as well as for the membership?
3. What dynamics are operating in an SMO's multiorganizational field? What determines the make-up of and changes in alliance and conflict systems?

4. What makes an SMO effective? How can we evaluate intended versus unintended consequences. What is the impact of an SMO in the field of actors trying to influence the external environment?

5. What functions do SMOs have in the construction of meaning? What makes SMOs effective sponsors of their definition of the social and political situation in relation to rival definitions sponsored by "neutral" experts, competing movement organizations, countermovement organizations, or opponents?

None of these questions is answered in a conclusive way in this book. Indeed, the discussions often raise as many questions as they answer. But I hope that these questions serve to stimulate future research.

REFERENCES

Cohen, J.L. 1985. "Strategy or Identity: New Theoretical Paradigms and Contemporary Social Movements." *Social Research* 52:663-716.

Curtis, R.L. and L.A. Zurcher. 1974. "Social Movements: An Analytical Exploration of Organizational Forms." *Social Problems* 21:356-370.

Diani, M. and G. Lodi. 1988. "Factions, Recruitment Networks and the Ecological Movement in Milan." Pp. 103-125 in *From Structure to Action: Comparing Movement Participation Across Cultures,* edited by B. Klandermans, H. Kriesi, and S. Tarrow. Greenwich, CT: JAI Press.

Ferree, M. and F.D. Miller. 1985. "Mobilization and Meaning: Toward an Integration of Social Psychological and Resource Perspectives on Social Movements." *Sociological Inquiry* 55:38-61.

Gamson, W.A. 1975. *The Strategy of Social Protest.* Homewood, IL: The Dorsey Press.

Gamson, W.A. and E. Schmeidler. 1983. "Organizing the Poor." Unpublished Paper. Chestnut Hill, Boston College.

Gerlach, L. and V.G. Hine. 1970. *People, Power, Change: Movements of Social Transformation.* Indianapolis, IN: Bobbs-Merrill.

Gusfield, J.R., ed. 1970. *Protest, Reform and Revolt: A Reader in Social Movements.* New York: Wiley.

Jenkins, J.C. 1979. "What Is To Be Done: Movement or Organization?" *Contemporary Sociology* 8:222-228.

———. 1983. "Resource Mobilization Theory and the Study of Social Movements." *Annual Review of Sociology* 9:527-553.

Killian, L.M. 1984. "Organization, Rationality and Spontaneity in the Civil Rights Movement." *American Sociological Review* 49:770-783.

Klandermans, B. 1986. "New Social Movements and Resource Mobilization: The European and the American Approach." *International Journal of Mass Emergencies and Disasters* 4/2:13-39. Special Issue on Comparative Methods and Research on Collective Behavior and Social Movements, edited by Gary T. Marx.

———. 1988. "The Formation and Mobilization of Consensus." Pp. 173-197 in *From Structure to Action: Comparing Movement Participation Across Cultures,* edited by B. Klandermans, H. Kriesi, and S. Tarrow. Greenwich, CT: JAI Press.

Klandermans, B., H. Kriesi, and S. Tarrow, eds. 1988. *From Structure to Action: Comparing Movement Participation Across Cultures.* Greenwich, CT: JAI Press.

Klandermans, B. and S. Tarrow. 1988. "Mobilization into Social Movements: Synthesizing the European and American Approaches." Pp. 1-41 in *From Structure to Action: Comparing Movement Participation Across Cultures,* edited by B. Klandermans, H. Kriesi, and S. Tarrow. Greenwich, CT: JAI Press.

Knoke, D. 1985. "The Political Economies of Associations." Pp. 211-242 in *Research in Political Sociology,* vol. 1, edited by R.D. Braungart. Greenwich, CT: JAI Press.

Knoke, D. and D. Prensky. 1984. "What Relevance do Organization Theories Have for Voluntary Associations." *Social Science Quarterly* 65:3-20.

Lauer, R.H. 1972. "Social Movements: An Intractionist Analysis." *The Sociological Quarterly* 13:315-328.

Lofland, J.F. 1985. *Protest, Studies of Collective Behavior and Social Movements.* New Brunswick, NJ: Transaction Books.

McAdam, D. 1982. *Political Process and The Development of Black Insurgency.* Chicago: University of Chicago Press.

McCarthy, J.D. and D.W. Britt. 1989. "Adapting Social Movement Organizations to External Constraints in the Modern State: Tax Codes and Accredition." In *Research in Social Movements, Conflict and Change,* vol. 11, edited by L. Kriesberg. Greenwich, CT: JAI Press.

McCarthy, J.D. and M. Zald. 1976. "Resource Mobilization and Social Movements; A Partial Theory." *American Journal of Sociology* 82:1212-1241.

Marwell, G. and P. Oliver. 1984. "Collective Action Theory and Social Movement Research." Pp. 1-27 in *Research in Social Movements, Conflict and Change,* vol. 7, edited by L. Kriesberg. Greenwich, CT: JAI Press.

Melucci, A. 1984. "An End to Social Movements? Introductory Paper to the Sessions on New Social Movements and Change in Organizational Forms." *Social Science Information* 24: 819-835.

———. 1985. "The Symbolic Challenge of Contemporary Movements." *Social Research* (Winter):789-816.

Morris, A. 1984. *The Origins of the Civil Rights Movement: Black Communities Organizing for Change.* New York: Free Press.

Neal, D.M. 1987. "The Relationship Between SMOs and Other Forms of Collective Behavior: An Empirical Examination." Paper presented at the annual meeting of the American Sociological Association, Chicago.

Neidhardt, F. 1985. "Einige Ideeen zu einer allgemeinen Theorie Sozialer Bewegungen" (Some Ideas on Social Movement Theory). Pp. 193-204 in *Sozialstruktur in Umbruch,* edited by S. Hradil. Opladen: Leske Verlag und Budrich GmbH.

Offe, K. 1985. "New Social Movements: Challenging the Boundaries of Institutional Politics." *Social Research* 52:817-868.

Piven, F.F. and R.A. Cloward. 1979. *Poor People's Movements: Why They Succeed, How They Fail.* New York: Vintage Books.

Schwartz, M. 1976. *Radical Protest and Social Structure.* New York: Academic Press.

Snow, D.A., E.B. Rochford, Jr., S.K. Worden, and R.D. Benford. 1986. "Frame Alignment Processes, Micro-Mobilization and Movement Participation." *American Sociological Review* 51:464-481.

Spector, M. and J.I. Kitsuse. 1973. "Social Problems: A Re-formulation." *Social Problems* 21:145-159.

Tarrow, S. 1983. *"Struggling to reform: Social Movements and Policy Change during Cycles of Protest."* Western Societies Paper No. 15. Ithaca, NY: Cornell University.

Tilly, C. 1982. "European Violence and Collective Action Since 1700." Paper presented at the Conference on Political Violence and Terrorism, Instituto Carlo Cattaneo, Bologna.

Troyer, R.J. 1984. "Birds of a Feather or Different Species? Social Movement and Constructionist Approches." Paper presented at the annual meetings of the SSSP, San Antonio.

Turner, R.H. and L.M. Killian. 1987. *Collective Behavior.* 3rd ed. Englewood Cliffs, NJ: Prentice-Hall.

Wilson, J. 1973. *Introduction to Social Movements.* New York: Basic Books.

Wood, J.L. and M. Jackson. 1982. *Social Movements, Development, Participation, and Dynamics.* Belmont, CA: Wadsworth Publishing.

Wood, P.A. 1982. "The Environmental Movement: Its Crystallization, Development, and Impact." Pp. 201-221 in *Social Movements, Development, Participation, and Dynamics,* edited by J.L. Wood and M. Jackson. Belmont, CA: Wadsworth Publishing.

Zald, M.N. and R. Ash. 1966. "Social Movement Organizations: Growth, Decay and Change." *Journal of Social Forces* 44:327-341.

PART I

STRUCTURE AND CHANGE

INTRODUCTION

Bert Klandermans

Movement organizations are marked by patterns of stratification and role differentiation, patterns that change over time and under the influence of factors internal and external to the movement. Part I focuses on the various modes of organization encountered within the social movement sector of a society and on the way organizational structures change over time. In this introduction, I first describe the several different modes of organization, but, except in the case of ideology, I do not discuss at length the determinants of these different modes. I then address organizational change, and examine trends and developments within social movement organizations (SMOs).

ORGANIZATIONAL STRUCTURE

The structure of SMOs are often ad hoc, the roles within them often ephemeral (Zurcher 1978). In the social movement literature, this ephemeral nature of structures and roles within social movements became the focus of a debate in the social movement literature on organization versus spontaneity (Killian

International Social Movement Research, Vol. 2, pages 21-32.
Copyright © 1989 by JAI Press Inc.
All rights of reproduction in any form reserved.
ISBN: 0-89232-964-5

1984). In their contribution to this volume, Rosenthal and Schwartz provide an extensive review of the literature related to this controversy, so I shall not go into it here. From their discussion, it can be concluded that there is no necessary contradiction between organization and spontaneity. From the viewpoint of an SMO however, there is a real dilemma. As Jenkins (1985) pointed out, formalization and centralization can easily dampen the enthusiasm of the first hour. But Jenkins also sees a solution to the dilemma: Establishing multiple structural levels, a movement organization can enjoy the advantages of both centralized and decentralized structures. The centralized organization operates at the national level, coordinates actions, and formulates global demands. At the same time, the relatively independent grass-roots locals are loosely linked to the national organization and can maintain their spontaneity and diversity. Thus, the degree to which organization kills spontaneity in movements depends on the mode of organization. This point brings us to the patterns of organization to be found within social movements.

Modes of Organization

Several typologies have been suggested to categorize the numerous modes of organization that can be found among SMOs: McCarthy and Zald's (1976) distinction between isolated and federal structures is as simple as it is fundamental. An isloated SMO has no branches, and relies on direct contact with its membership, usually through direct mail, sometimes through travelling organizers. A federal structure does have local branches. Contact with the constituency can be either direct or through the locals; occasionally, contact can take place only through the local movement organization. This distinction is akin to the two forms of organization distinguished by J.Q. Wilson (1973 p. 216): caucus, "an organization in which one or a few leaders carry out the work of the organization, supported by funds or other kinds of support contributed by persons who rarely, if at all, are brought into meetings," and primary organization, "in which whatever the role of officers, members regularly come together to act in concert and to discuss associational affairs or are otherwise mobilized to carry on group activities." This short description makes it clear that the two patterns of organization are completely different. In the following pages, I elaborate on each one in greater detail.

Isolated Movement Organizations

Professional SMOs as described by McCarthy and Zald (1973) are good examples of isolated SMOs. Professional movement organizations have a full-time, paid leadership, are supported largely by external sources, have a paper membership, and attempt to influence poltical decision making on behalf of their constituencies. As I will discuss later in this introduction, McCarthy and

Zald have argued that, over the last decades, SMOs have undergone a process of professionalization. This is true at least in the case of many organizations from the environmental movement in Europe and the United States. Many of these organizations have been very effective in mobilizing public support primarily through direct mail campaigns, as Godwin and Mitchell (1984) demonstrated was true for the American ecology movement.

Federal Movement Organizations

Contrary to McCarthy and Zald's argument, federal structures are still the primary mode of organization within social movements. Different structures can be distinguished according to degree of decentralization and autonomy of the local movement organizations. Three different types of federal structure are noteworthy: the loosely-coupled network structure, the pyramid structure, and the centralized structure.

The *loosely-coupled network structure* was described in detail for the first time by Gerlach and Hine (1970). These authors sought recognition for the peculiar organizational characteristics of many social movements. These characteristics are so different from those we are accustomed to finding in formal organizations in modern society that many observers have failed to recognize them as a mode of organization. According to Gerlach and Hine, the following features are typical of the loosely-coupled network structure: segmentation, that is, a multitude of different groups and organizations with different goals and ideologies; a polycephalous structure, that is, a structure with several leaders, in which no single leader controls the whole movement; a reticulate structure, or a network of bonds and linkages that connects the various groups and organizations. Linkages can be defined as friendship or kinship bonds, overlapping membership, and activities or gatherings where representatives of different groups are present. Gerlach and Hine felt that the loosely-coupled network structure has many advantages: It makes the movement more resistant to repression and social control; it allows a movement to penetrate different sectors of society more easily; it promotes innovation; and, it is less easily damaged by failures, because the failure of one group does not impair the effectiveness of the others. This structure, of course, also has disadvantages. In such a structure, it is difficult to maintain ideological unity, so the movement may be plauged by splits and factionalism. Because of a lack of coordinated action, the movement will have little political impact. The women's movements in Europe and the United States provide many examples of this type of federal movement organization (Katzenstein and Mueller 1987).

With greater integration into and coordination within a community, the loosely-coupled structure can evolve into what Morris (1984, p. 40) called a "local movement center," that is, "a social organization within the community of a subordinate group, which mobilizes, organizes, and coordinates collective action aimed at attaining the common ends of that subordinated group." Local movement centers comprise local leaders, and organizations and their adherents who come together to define goals, discuss tactics and strategies, and engage in collective action. As Morris demonstrated, the existence of local movement centers was decisive in the development of the southern civil rights movement.

In his study of the New York State tenants movement, Lawson (1983) described the *pyramid structure* this movement adopted. In time, the tenant movement developed a structure with three levels: building organizations, neighborhood organizations, and federal (city-wide and at the state level). A similar multilevel structure can be found in other movements. Unions and the Dutch peace movement (Klandermans and Oegema 1987) are cases in point. In a pyramid structure, the links between the various levels are weak. Interaction with the local level usually takes the form of top-down communication: Higher-level organizations provide services, give advice, and define common goals. In doing so, they promote unity within the movement. Local organizations are relatively autonomous, maintaining their diversity and spontaneity. The intermediate-level organizations have some very important functions. They link the state or national level with the local level, provide resources for the state-level organizations, and recruit participants. According to Lawson, the pyramid structure is particularly useful to movement organizations committed to mobilizing grass-roots participants. A multiple-level structure has several clear advantages. The existence of local organizations facilitates mobilization, and, since local organizations are small, they are not usually troubled by free riding. Because they are relatively autonomous, local organizations are better able to relate to the ideological and tactical preferences of their constituencies than are higher-level organizations. The multiple levels make it easier to recruit and educate leaders. Functional specialization of the different levels makes it possible to select positions and strategies suited to the level in question.

It is perhaps no accident that the two examples of *centralized federal movement structures* I found in the literature are religious movements. Beckford (1975) and Snow (1986) focused attention on the centralized federal structure of the Watch Tower movement, and Nichiren Shoshu of America, respectively. Within both movements, local organizations were coordinated by a highly-centralized national organization. Loosely-coupled units were bound together by a strictly hierarchical overarching strucutre. Trained cadres, licensed to act on behalf of the central leadership, reduced the distance between the local and national levels. In both movements, this centralized control guaranteed ideological unity and prevented factionalism and disaffection.

Movement Locals

Federal movement organizations differ not only in their overarching structures but in the characteristics of their local organizations. Until recently, the subject of local organizations has been neglected in the literature on social movements. Lofland and Jamison (1985) were the first to focus on social movement locals as a specific feature of social movements organizations. Adding to this analysis, Oliver and Furman's contribution to this volume discuss frictions that arise between national and local movement organizations in the effort to acquire resources.

Social movement locals are staffed by volunteers. The central task of volunteers is to contribute to the movement organization. Lofland and Jamison distinguish five different levels of engagement in local movement organizations, all dependent on four variables: the amount of time participation requires, the psychological significance of the local, the nature of the claims the local lays on several aspects of a person's life, and the frequency with which high-risk activities are undertaken. Together these four variables produce the five levels of mobilization: study groups (groups of people who meet to study or discuss issues of mutual concern), fellowships (locals with adherents who undertake collective action), congregations (organizations with a broad spectrum of activities, specialized branches, their own buildings, and so on, operating on a long-term perspective), sects (similar to congregations but more exclusive), cells (locals with conspirator members; they are usually small, sometimes underground).

This description of isolated and federal movement structures should make it clear that SMOs can have many different manifestations. Factors in both the external and internal environments of the SMO are responsible for this variation in organizational characteristics. Factors in the external environment include the structure of social and political opportunities, the availability of discretionary resources, funding and tax regulations, and existing organizational experience and networks. In the internal environment, ideology, leadership, strategy, and size are all relevant. Although a full account of the impact of all the determinants of movement organization is beyond the scope of this introduction, some of these factors are presented in greater detail in the following discussion on organizational change, others in chapters throughout the volume. But first I will conclude this examination of organizational structure by calling attention to the role ideology plays in determining modes of organization.

Ideology and the Structure of Social Movements Organization

Ideology has always played an important role in determining organizational characteristics of SMOs and is one of the principle factors that shape the differences between inclusive and exclusive movement organizations (Zald and Ash 1966). Movement organizations are built on principles and are often the result of attempts to put the ideals of the movement into practice. Movements of the 1960s, such as the women's movement or the antinuclear power movement, both in Europe and the United States, have provided many examples of organizations developed in accordance with movement ideology. The new social movements, as they are called by many European scholars (Klandermans 1986; Klandermans and Tarrow 1988; Melucci 1980), were seen by a good many observers and participants as experiments in social organization. Rothschild-Whitt (1979) in her work on the collectivist organizations, has tried to give an analytical account of these experiments. She depicts collectivist organizations as the organizational counterparts of the value-rational orientation to social action, the fourth orientation Weber distinguished, in addition to the traditional, the affective, and the instrumental orientation. Rothschild-Whitt specified the following characteristics of collectivist organizations: no hierarchical structure, decision making by consensus; no rules or central authority; a sense of community; recruitment based on friendship relations and sociopolitical values; primary purposive incentives, secondary solidary incentives, and only in the third place material incentives; egalitarian organization, task sharing and job rotation to maintain the organization's egalitarian character; minimal task and role differentiation. Although ideal-typical, this specification reveals many of the actual organizational characteristics of contemporary SMOs, especially at the local level (cf. Ferree and Hess 1985, and several contributions to this volume, e.g., those by Brown and Mushaben). Many SMOs, or parts of SMOs, are collectivist organizations, and the values and ideology of the participants motivate them to keep it that way. This tendency was illustrated in an excellent way in Baker's (1982) case study of a lesbian-feminist organization, which deliberately decided to replace a more formal alliance structure by a set of small collectives.

ORGANIZATIONAL CHANGE

Perhaps, fluidity, more than any other quality, characterizes SMOs. Locals and branches come and go, and organizational structures and principles change in the course of time as the movement grows, or as it responds to success or failure, internal conflict, or external pressure. In order to impose some system on this changing reality, scholars have proposed that SMOs go through specific phases in the course of their existence. Blumer (1969), for example, suggested that social movements develop in four phases: social unrest, popular excitement, formalization, and institutionalization. There is however, little reason to expect that every SMO goes through the same developmental states. SMOs are open systems in continuous interaction with their environment for the purpose of acquiring and allocating resources. Organizational changes have to be viewed as responses to environmental contingencies (Knoke 1985; Schutt 1986; J.Q. Wilson 1973). Uncertainty about the acquisition of resources, and scarcity or abundance of resources, all produce organizational change. I now examine four different trends prominent in the literature on organizational change in social movements: oligarchization, professionalization, structural differentiation, and a trend toward collectivist modes of organization.

Oligarchization

No single theory on the development of movement organizations is so widely debated as Michels' theory of oligarchization (Michels 1962). Briefly summarized, Michels' argument is that, in the course of their existence and as a consequence of organizational growth, originally democratic political or SMOs shift their attention to organizational maintenance and undergo processes of goal transformation and oligarchization. Michels held that rank-and-file inactivity and functional specialization within growing organizations, each complementing and reinforcing the other, were the dynamics behind this development. In numerous publications, students of SMOs have attempted to verify or refute Michels' iron law of oligarchization. All these attempts have led to the conclusion that goal transformation, a shift to organizational maintenance, and oligarchization are not the necessary fate of SMOs. In the course of time, SMOs can develop in many different ways (Lipset and Raab 1978; Schwartz 1976; Zald and Ash 1966; see Duffhues and Felling's contribution to Part I in this volume for a more full account of Michels' argument). A preference for more modest tactics does not always signify oligarchization or a shift to organizational maintenance, nor does institutionalization or a tendency to organizational maintenance necessarily make a movement organization more conservative (Fine and Stoecker 1985; Gillespie 1983; J.Q. Wilson 1973). More generally, Schutt (1986) has argued that transformation of movement organizations is not determined by internal organizational characteristics, as Michels' theory seems to suggest, but that organizational change must be explained in terms of an organization's relationship with its external environment. Membership inactivity can be rational and need not indicate apathy or alientation. Moreover, since SMOs are voluntary associations, members have a forceful sanction against a neglect of their interests by the leadership: They can resign as members or withdraw their contributions (Barber 1965; McMahon and Camileri 1975; Perrow 1970; Schwartz et al. 1981; see also Oliver and Furman, and Van der Veen and Klandermans in this volume).

Professionalization

McCarthy and Zald (1973) pointed out that, over the last decade, SMOs have become more and more professionalized. They attributed this development to the increased availability of discretionary resources. On the one hand, these resources enabled movement organizations to hire full-time staff personnel, thus making the organization less dependent on the efforts of volunteers. On the other hand, these funds made it easier to mobilize financial support from groups other than the beneficiaries and so allowed the leadership to become less dependent on financial support from the beneficiaries. Consequently, the adherents' control over the leadership declined, and the membership turned more and more into paper membership. Mass media became the main communication channel between the movement organization and its constituency. As a result, a membership that was originally exclusive became more inclusive. Professionalization of SMOs also meant the creation of movement careers. But because SMOs are dependent on the ebb and flow of funding, positions easily vanish. The result is frequent transfers of professionals between SMOs and between SMOs and governmental institutions or universities. In their discussion of McCarthy and Zald's argument, Turner and Killian (1987) remarked that professionalization, as a trend, is not restricted to the so-called professional movement organizations but can be found to a greater or lesser extent, in other SMOs as well. In fact, they argued that outside funding is not a necessary condition for professionalization.

Structural Differentiation

Structural differentiation is the counterpart of organizational growth. According to J. Wilson's (1973) distinction, patterns of growth may be centripetal and centrifugal. A centripetal pattern involves the merger or coalescence of previously independent groups or organizations. For a discussion on coalition formation among SMOs, see the introduction to Part IV in this volume. A centrifugal growth pattern refers to the expansion of a movement through an influx of new members, as a result of the establishment of new branches and local chapters. The following discussion concerns this kind of growth.

When an SMO grows, its membership base and accumulated resources expand, and more distinct organs emerge to fulfill more distinct functions. The establishment of fund-raising committees, the appointment of recruitment officials, and the introduction of an administrative staff are among the first steps toward a more sophisticated organization. Organizational growth is not necessarily a blessing. A rapid influx of new members creates problems of integration and socialization, which, if ineffectively handled, can easily break a movement organization apart, as happened in the case of Students for a Democratic Society (Ross 1983). A rapidly growing movement organization inevitably becomes more inclusive, as a consequence, the membership becomes ideologically more heterogeneous. Thus ideological quarrels and factionalism develop, unless membership growth is accompanied by a process of centralization, which is rarely the case.

In movement organizations with a federal structure, differentiation often takes the form of a division of labor among different groups. Carden (1978) described how the feminist movement proliferated through the establishment of hundreds of groups with different aimes, values, and ideologies. The advantage of such differentiation is, of course, that the organizational network is able to embrace a wide variety of ideologies, objectives, and interests. But it has important disadvantages as well. As Ferree and Hess (1985) pointed out, in the feminist movement ideological differences were easily pushed to extremes, and time and again it turned out to be very difficult to coordinate the diverse constituencies of different groups into taking concerted action. Moreover, all the different groups need resources and can begin to compete among each other for the scarce resources available. Mushaben's contribution to this volume, an examination of the German peace movement, provides a lively description of the problems of this kind.

Structural differentiation can be enforced by strategic decisions. Dwyer (1983) showed that the antinuclear power movement in the United States continually changed its structure. In an ongoing process of splits, coalitions, and mergers, the composition of the movement constantly changed. Reviewing its history, Dwyer concluded that the movement became more complex organizationally as it revised its ideas of what the most effective strategy would be. Its initial strategy of legal appeals required only modest coalitions. When it turned to lobbying in the Congress and participating in national hearings, a more extended organization became necessary. Civil disobedience, its latest strategy, again demands small affinity groups, necessary for supporting and training activists. Both goal-achievement and the failure to achieve important movement goals are also significant determinants of organizational change. For further discussion of this topic, see the introduction to Part V in this volume.

The Trend Toward Collectivist Modes of Organization

New social movement literature has signaled a trend toward collectivist modes of organization among contemporary SMOs (Donati 1984; Klandermans 1986; Klandermans and Tarrow 1988). Rejecting the instrumentally rational pattern of organization of modern capitalist society, participants in contemporary SMOs have attempted to develop new modes of organization. In a discussion of organizational changes within the Italian social movement sector, Donati (1984) noted the transformation of politically- and instrumentally-oriented movement organizations into organizations oriented toward the gratification of immediate needs. Participants were no longer motivated by a long lasting struggle for social change, but by the opportunity to realize a new lifestyle in the context of new movement organizations. The political symbols and the politically experienced leaders of the 1970s were replaced by cultural symbols, and culturally-oriented leaders. The same tendency was observed in West Germany (Brand 1985) and The Netherlands (Van der Loo et al. 1984), although both these authors relativize their observations by noting that the shift away from a political orientation was definitely not a general trend in contemporary SMOs in their countries.

THE CONTRIBUTIONS TO PART I

The contributions to Part I elaborate different aspects of the structure and change of SMOs.

Rosenthal and Schwartz discuss at length the organization versus spontaneity controversy. More significant, however, is their sophisticated account of different levels of organization and decision making at the local level.

Rucht describes the structure and conflicts within a social movement industry. His study of the environmental movement in West Germany and France illustrates how complex the social movement industries—these organizations of organizations—are.

Duffhues and Felling present a picture of the Dutch Catholic movement. Borrowing from the framework established by Zald and Ash, they use the evidence they have collected to argue that Michels' iron law of oligarchization is not pertinent in the case of this movement. Data from network analyses underlie their description of the growth and decline of a social movement industry.

REFERENCES

Baker, A.J. 1982. "The Problem of Authority in Radical Movement Groups: A Case Study in Lesbian-Feminists Organization. *The Journal of Applied Behavioral Science* 18:323-341.

Barber, B. 1965. "Participation and Mass Apathy in Associations." Pp. 477-504 in *Studies in leadership*, edited by A.W. Gouldner. New York: Russell and Russell.

Beckford, J.A. 1975. "Organizations, Ideology and Recruitment: The Structure of the Watch Tower Movement." *The Sociological Review* 23:893-909.

Blumer, H. 1969. "Social Movements." In *Studies in Social Movements. A Social Psychological Perspective*, edited by B. McLaughlin. New York: The Free Press.

Brand, K-W, ed. 1985. *Neue soziale Bewegungen in West Europa und den USA. Ein internationaler Vergleich*. New York and Frankfurt: Campus Verlag.

Carden, M. 1978. "The Proliferation of a Social Movement: Ideology and Individual Incentives in the Contemporary Feminist Movement." Pp. 179-196 in *Research in Social Movements, Conflict and Change*, vol. 1, edited by L. Kriesberg. Greenwich, CT: JAI Press.

Donati, P.R. 1984. "Organization between Movements and Institutions." *Social Science Information* 23:837-859.

Dwyer, L.E. 1983. "Structure and Strategy in the Antinuclear Movement." Pp. 148-161 in *Movements of the Sixties and the Seventies*, edited by J. Freeman. New York and London: Longman.

Ferree, M.M. and B.B. Hess. 1985. *Controversy and Coalition: The New Feminist Movement.* Boston: G.K. Hall & Comp.

Fine, G.A. and R. Stoecker. 1985. "Can the Circle be Unbroken? Small Groups and Social Movements." Pp. 1-28 in *Advances in Group Processes*, vol. 2, edited by Edward Lawler. Greenwich, CT: JAI Press.

Gerlach, L. and V.G. Hine. 1970. *People, Power, Change: Movements of Social Transformation.* Indianapolis, IN: Bobbs-Merill.

Gillespie, D. 1983. "Conservative Tactics in Social Movement Organizations," Pp. 262-275 in *Movements of the Sixties and Seventies*, edited by J. Freeman. New York and London: Longman.

Godwin, R.K. and R.C. Mitchell. 1984. "The Impact of Direct Mail on Political Organizations." *Social Science Quarterly* 66:829-839.

Jenkins, J.C. 1985. *The Politics of Insurgency.* New York: Columbia University Press.

Katzenstein, M. and C. Mueller, eds. 1987. *The Women's Movements in the U.S. and Western Europe: Feminist Consciousness, Political Opportunity and Public Policy.* Philadelphia, PA: Temple University Press.

Killian, L. 1984. "Organization, Rationality and Spontaneity in the Civil Rights Movement." *American Sociological Review* 49:770-783.

Klandermans, B. 1986. "New Social Movements and Resource Mobilization: The European and the American Approach." *International Journal of Mass Emergencies and Disasters*, 4/2:13-39. Special issue on comparative methods and research on collective behavior and social movements, edited by Gary T. Marx.

Klandermans, B. and D. Oegema. 1987. "Campaigning for a Nuclear Freeze: Grassroots Strategies and Local Government in The Netherlands." In *Research in Political Sociology*, vol. 3, edited by R.G. Braungart. Greenwich, CT: JAI Press.

Klandermans, B. and S. Tarrow. 1988. "Mobilization into Social Movements: Synthesizing the European and American Approaches." Pp. 1-41 in *From Structure to Action: Comparing Movement Participation Across Cultures*, edited by B. Klandermans, H. Kriesi, and S. Tarrow. Greenwich, CT: JAI Press.

Knoke, D. 1985. "The Political Economies of Associations." Pp. 211-242 in *Research in Political Sociology*, vol. 1, edited by R.D. Braungart. Greenwich, CT: JAI Press.

Lawson, R. 1983. "A Decentralized but Moving Pyramid: The evolution and Consequences of the Structure of the Tenant Movement." Pp. 119-132 in *Movements in the Sixties and the Seventies*, edited by J. Freeman. New York and London: Longman.

Lipset, S.M. and E. Raab. 1978. *The Politics of Unreason. Right-wing Extremism in America 1790-1977.* 2nd ed. Chicago: University of Chicago Press.

Lofland, J.M. and M. Jamison. 1985. "Structures of Movement Organization Locals. Pp. 201-219 in *Protest, Studies of Collective Behavior and Social Movements*, edited by J.M. Lofland. Brunswick, NJ: Transaction Books.

McCarthy, J.D. and M.N. Zald. 1973. *The Trend of Social Movements in America.* Morristown, NJ: General Learning Press.

————. 1976. "Resource Mobilization and Social Movements: A Partial Theory." *American Journal of Sociology* 82:1212-1241.

McMahon, A. and S. Camileri. 1975. "Organizational Structure and Voluntary Participation in Collective-good Decisions." *American Sociological Review* 40:616-644.

Melucci, A. 1980. "The New Social Movements: A Theoretical Approach." *Social Science Information* 19:199-226.

Michels, R. 1962. *Political Parties.* New York: Free Press.

Morris, A. 1984. *The Origins of the Civil Rights Movement: Black Communities Organizing for Change.* New York: Free Press.

Perrow, C. 1970. "Members as Resources in Voluntary Organizations." Pp. 93-116 in *Organizations and Clients,* edited by W.R. Rosengren and M. Lefton. Columbus, OH: Merrill.

Ross, R.J. 1983. "Generational Change and Primary Groups in a Social Movement." Pp. 177-189 in *Movements of the Sixties and the Seventies,* edited by J. Freeman. New York and London: Longman.

Rothschild-Whitt, J. 1979. "The Collectist Organization: An Alternative to Rational-Bureaucratic Models. *American Sociological Review* 44:509-527.

Schutt, R.K. 1986. *Organization in a Changing Environment. Unionization of Welfare Employee's.* Albany: State University of New York Press.

Schwartz, M. 1976. *Radical Protest and Social Structure.* New York: Academic Press.

Schwartz, M., N. Rosenthal, and L. Schwartz. 1981. "Leader-Member Conflict in Protest Organizations: The Case of the Southern Farmers Alliance." *Social Problems* 29:22-36.

Snow, D.A. 1986. "Organization, Ideology and Mobilization: The Case of Nichiren Shoshu of America." In *The Future of New Religious Movements,* edited by D.G. Bromley and Ph. E. Hammond. Macon, GA: Mercer University Press.

Turner, R.H. and L.M. Killian. 1987. *Collective Behavior.* 3rd ed. Englewood Cliffs, NJ: Prentice-Hall.

Van der Loo, H., E. Snel and B. Van Steenbergen. 1984. *Een wenkend perspectief? Nieuwe sociale bewegingen en culturele veranderingen* (New social movements and cultural change). Amersfoort: De Horstink.

Wilson, J. 1973. *Introduction to Social Movements.* New York: Basic Books.

Wilson, J.Q. 1973. *Political Organization.* New York: Basic Books.

Zald, M.N. and R. Ash. 1966. "Social Movement Organizations: Growth, Decay and Change." *Journal of Social Forces* 44:327-341.

Zurcher, L.A. 1978. "Ephemeral Roles, Voluntary Action, and Voluntary Associations." *Journal of Voluntary Action Research* 7:65-74.

SPONTANEITY AND DEMOCRACY
IN SOCIAL MOVEMENTS

Naomi Rosenthal and Michael Schwartz

Like Athena, sprung full-grown from the head of Zeus, social movements often seem to blossom without any period of gestation. This phenomenon has entranced and bewildered observers, confounding the most elaborate categorical descriptions and theoretical paradigms. Yet, it is the moment of spontaneous action that often provides the "spark" by which the "'mass" crosses "the threshold of organizational life" (Lowi 1971, p. 41).

Demonstrations, massmeetings, protest marches, sitdowns, wildcats, and even riots—those volatile and unpredictable actions that appear to take place outside of, and sometimes in the absence of, any apparent organizational context—play substantial and definitive roles in the history of a protest movement. They are often unplanned and unanticipated, and sometimes they are undocumented. But even a planned demonstration may develop into something quite different from its original conception, providing a spontaneous starting point for crucial strategic directions and dramatic movement growth. In fact, often, no one is more surprised than organizers when an impromptu

International Social Movement Research, Vol. 2, pages 33-59.
Copyright © 1989 by JAI Press Inc.
All rights of reproduction in any form reserved.
ISBN: 0-89232-964-5

event suddenly triggers an explosion of activism, support, and public discussion.

Spontaneity has become the crucial concept in what has been chracterized as a "complex controversy in [the] theory of social movements" (Killian 1986, p. 1). In one view "continuity and emergence, planning and impulse, organizational strategy and individual spontaneity are polar tendencies" in social movements (Killian 1984). In the other, spontaneity and structure are neither discontinuous nor opposed. In this paper, we take the latter position. We argue, moreover, that spontaneity is often indicative of a particular organizational form—the primary movement group, and of a characteristic mode of decision making—direct democracy.

To some degree, the debate appears to emerge from the ongoing and somewhat stale conflict between the two main schools of social movement theory: the resource mobilization and collective behavior perspectives. However, the lines drawn between the two schools are not, in our view, the main delimiters of opinion.

Recent work in social movements has been dominated by the resource mobilization paradigm. This perspective emphasizes "the organizational factors that both shape the emergence of social movements and are critical determinants of their outcomes" (McCarthy and Zald 1977; see also Marwell and Oliver 1984). It treats social movements in the same way as organization theory treats its objects of study; the choices made by individuals and organizations in a movement are regarded as purposive and rational within the constraints imposed by environment and available resources.

Resource mobilization theory has produced many important propositions about the dynamics of social movement organizations (SMOs) and processes, and a number of enduring insights into the role of both organizations and externally supplied resources in determining the character and outcome of social protest. But the applicability of the paradigm to the class of events that we are concerned with here (spontaneous actions), has been increasingly questioned by a number of scholars from both schools.

The very existence of spontaneity, they suggest, is an indicator of unstructured and expressive elements in social movements that cannot be explained by the rationalist logic and structural analysis that is so powerful when applied to well-organized and/or routinized movements and movement organizations. Insofar as spontaneity is a significant factor in social movement trajectories, then, the resource mobilization approach appears to be, at best, incomplete, and at worst, seriously flawed.

Killian (1984, p. 782) a promiment collective behavior theorist, specified the parameters of this issue:

> . . . while organization and rational planning are key variables, social movement theory
> must take into account spontaneity and emergence and the forces which generate them.

It must treat as important, not as irrational, the feeling states and the cognitions which sometimes cause individuals to throw caution to the winds and act in the face of great or unknown odds. It must include as an essential part of its analysis how social movement organizations and their leaders deal with the changes in the course of a movement which unpredictable, spontaneous action introduce, and how they themselves are transformed or even superseded in the process.

Killian's discussion (1986) clarifies the fundamental differences between structural theories, which stress the primacy of organization and collective decision making, and collective behavior theory, which stresses the primacy of spontaneous or "unplanned and impromptu" action in the context of extra organizational, decentralized movements. Killian thus identifies the likely context for what Turner (1981) called "weak rational and/or expressive behavior—the emergent, unstructured conditions of spontaneous social action."

Significantly, however, this critique comes not only from collective behavior theorists (who have been consistently dubious about the explanatory power of the resource mobilization paradigm) but also from within the resource mobilization school itself.

Obserschall and Farris (1985), for example, examine protest diffusion in loosely-structure collectivities "as a way of handling and operationalizing spontaneity." They stress that there are no "crucial differences" between themselves and Killian, although they prefer the terminology of "uncertainty" to that of spontaneity.

Oberschall and Farris present an analysis that specifies the conditions under which spontaneity becomes a significant factor in the spread of protest activity. They propose a continuum of action similar to Killian's, arguing that the degree of prior organization "within the collectivity susceptible to protest mobilization" can be seen as moving from "absent" to "tight" structure.[1] Tight structure is most effective for the realization of movement goals because it allows for careful planning and effective coordination. Tight structures, therefore, behave according to the principles developed by resource mobilization theory. The absence of routinized organizational structures (1985, p. 13) on the other hand, makes action problematic and uncertain because mechanisms for communication, effective allocation of resources and agreement on goals and strategies are underdeveloped or nonexistent. In this context, spontaneity takes on a significant role in determining the orientation, focus, and dynamics of protest.

Oberschall and Farris develop their argument using the spread of the sit-in movement among students at black colleges in 1960 as an example of the proliferation of protest in the context of loose structure. In their view, the key feature of the insurgency was the absence of overarching organizations that united students at different campuses. The spread of protest, therefore, required sources of communication external to the movement itself, and this created significant uncertainty (Oberschall and Farris 1985, p. 23) because:

> ... information is costly to obtain and thus often inaccurate and incomplete, ... decisions are made in finite time before all relevant information is collected and processed, ... actors make errors of judgment even when they possess accurate information, and, most important ... a confrontation decision involving two or more parties is by its very essence fraught with uncertainty since the actions of each party are contingent on other's actions.

In this context, spontaneity can develop, and the impromptu decisions made, may well be based on criteria other than rational calculation of risks and opportunities. In the case of the sit-in movement, Oberschall and Farris (1985, p. 27) focus on the mass media and college basketball rivalries as the (imperfect) mechanisms for communication among North Carolina students. They maintain that the characteristics of the information transmitted by these mechanisms account for what they call a "curious blend of seriousness of purpose and faddishness in the spread of the student sit-ins."

While it seems to us that Oberschall and Farris may be underestimating both the density of structural ties among North Carolina students and the efficiency of information transmission among student activists, it is not our purpose here to challenge the factual foundation of their argument. We are more interested in their ideas about the impact of loose structure on movement processes. Such circumstances certainly occur, even if the sit-in movement in 1960 may not be as clear an example as they claim.

For our purpose, the important contribution of their analysis is its demonstration that there is no necessary contradition between resource mobilization analysis and collective behavior theory in their approach to spontaneous protest. Resource mobilization theory rests on the existence of an organizational rubric capable of mobilizing and harnessing needed resources. Oberschall and Farris argue that spontaneity, and the movement dynamics associated with it, plays a critical role in precisely those circumstances in which there is no encompassing organizational structure. They thus designate two separate realms of analysis: tight structures, that are susceptible to one sort of analytic calculus, and loose structures, that obey different laws and therefore require a different analytic framework. This view also echoes Turner's (1981) call for reintegration of the resource mobilization and collective behavior perspectives.[2]

Insofar as attention to spontaneity as an analytic concept attacks the tendency of some recent work to view social movements as mechanical extensions of organizationally congealed resources, they have considerable analytic merit. Social movements are both much more than—and far less than—bureaucratic formal organizations. They grow on previously fertilized soil (Freeman 1979), take place in "multi-organizational fields," (Curtis and

Zurcher 1973), consist of "complex aggregates of collective actions or events" (Marwell and Oliver 1984), involve networks activism (Rosenthal et al. 1985), and transform "the meaning of objects and events" beyond the confines of formally organized groups (Gusfield 1981). Centralized SMOs are, in our view, results of, as well as causal factors in the history of any given movement.

The reintroduction of spontaneity as a central analytic variable, in our view, is promising. It offers the potential for a clearer understanding of those processes that make social movements qualitatively different from other institutions—their unique role in developing new forms of collective action and their impact on society as a whole. However, we think that two issues, in particular, need to be addressed before the concept of spontaneity can be usefully integrated into a broader analytic framework.

The first problem is the assumption that spontaneity and structure are opposite poles of social action: that is, that planned actions undertaken by tight organizational structures lie at one end of a continuum and that spontaneous actions undertaken in the context of loose or absent structures lie at the other. We contend that such a formulation occludes our understanding of social movements, and that it is the *intermingling* of spontaneous and planned action that is central to the unique dynamics of social movements. Tightly organized structures do sometimes engage in action that is spontaneous by any definition and, conversely, loosely organized structures are capable of premeditated action based on elaborate (collective) strategic thinking.

The second problem is intimately connected to the first. There is a tendency to associate spontaneity with expressive (and sometimes irrational) behavior. This assumption contributes little to our understanding of movements because it directs our attention away from the structural context of all collective action and the processes of collective decision making that operate during mass action.

We would argue that events that are described as spontaneous are neither as disorganized nor as unstructured as analysts from both schools have claimed.[3] We would further argue that even in cases where existing structures are unimportant, or are eclipsed at the moment of protest, there is an organizational backbone to collective action. That is, spontaneity reflects the existence and dominance of a particular structural milieu in which previously existing primary groups utilize direct democracy to develop and sustain group unity and coordination.[4] Moreover, we contend that ongoing primary group involvement and direct democracy are essential elements in the growth and vitality of protest organizations and social movement, even when they are large, established, and apparently institutionalized.

We suggest that even the most spontaneous events are consistent with Morris' (1981, p. 746) conclusion that "collective action is rooted in organizational structure and carried out by rational actors attempting to realize their ends." That is, the impulsiveness and "individual spontaneity" Killian (1984) and others detect are, in fact, a result of rational, and often accurate, calculations about the chances of success for a new action in the context of existing networks of organized support systems. To support our argument, we turn now to a detailed exploration of the current use of spontaneity as an analytic concept.

THE CONCEPT OF SPONTANEITY

We begin with two descriptions that illustrate the current application of the concept of spontaneity to social movement analysis. The first comes from Bordin's (1981) history of the Woman's Christian Temperance Union (the WCTU) and the second from Killian's (1984) reexamination of the civil rights movement in Tallahassee, Florida. Because Bordin's presentation is unselfconscious and contain elements common to such depictions, we use her discussion as paradigmatic and then show its consistency with Killian's more theoretically explicit formulation.

Bordin (1981, p. 15) discusses the generative moment in the history of the WCTU as follows:

> The Woman's Christian Temperance Union grew out of a spontaneous women's crusade against saloons and retail liquor sellers which began in Ohio, swept the Midwest like a prairie fire and spread through the West and parts of the East during the winter of 1873-1874. . . .

The spark which ignites this configuration was a lecture given by Dr. Diocletian Lewis in Hillsboro, Ohio on December 22, 1874. It was, more or less, the same lecture that he had been delivering for 20 years on the national lecture circuit. In his speech, he related how his mother, "sorely distressed by his father's regular patronage of a local saloon . . . prayed in the saloon with several of her friends and actually succeeded in getting the saloonkeeper to close his business." Over the years, occasional audiences had emulated Lewis' mother, but with little success. In Hillsboro, listeners were similarly moved; 50 women pledged themselves to action and many men in the audience said they would back them (Bordin 1981, pp. 19-20):

> The Crusades made their way next day with solemn steps to the hotels and saloons where the liquor trade was a major part of the business . . . They walked singing down the streets . . . Throughout the day songs and prayers were heard at establishments selling liquor . . . In a few weeks businesses dispensing intoxicating liquors were reduced from thirteen to four, and those four sold their wares with considerable trepidation.

According to Bordin (1981, p. 22), the success of those actions was a result of the tenacity of the protesters. Previous efforts had ended after a day, but these temperance advocates sustained the protest for several weeks. Their accomplishment, moreover, inspired others, and temperance crusades spread throughout the region. Within three months, 250 villages and cities in Ohio, Michigan, Indiana, Pennsylvania, and New Jersey were, at least temporarily, dry.

Our second example of the use of spontaneity in describing a social movement phenomenon is contained in Killian's (1984, p. 777) analysis of civil rights activity in Tallahassee, Florida in 1960:

> Events which followed arrests during a major sit-in demonstration on March 12, illustrate the mixture of planning and spontaneity. These sit-ins were carefully planned following the [CORE] manual . . . After the arrests, which took place about 11:30 a.m., the president of CORE returned to the Florida A and M campus, entered the cafeteria, and said to the lunch-time crowd, "The police have arrested Florida A and M University (FAMU) and Florida State University (FSU) students at Woolworth's. Let's march on Woolworth's and McCrory's to fill the jails if necessary." This impromptu action, taken without the consent of other members of the executive committee or other organizations . . . resulted in a march of about 100 students to the downtown area, the arrest of 17 more, and a confrontation with a group of clubwielding whites . . . Later in the afternoon, however, a march of from 800 to 1,000 students was stopped by the police, who attacked the marchers with tear gas and then began indiscriminately . . . arresting students . . .

Both of these descriptions discuss the fact that action occurred outside of the context of a formal organization. Killian (1984, p. 777) presses this point, saying that the action (1) was taken without the prior approval or planning of the local National Association for the Advancement of Colored People (NAACP) or other civil rights organizations in Tallahassee, (2) was a "direct violation of [Congress on Racial Equality (CORE)]," and (3) was an "impromptu" (meaning extraorganizational) response to events. Bordin's (1981, p. 26, 31) analysis is remarkable in its similarity. Her analysis underscores Killian's emphasis. She argues that "the Crusade leadership included many women who had no previous experience outside the home or their local parish church." and that the women involved acted in a militant style "that at first glance seem(s) out of character."

Though Killian says that spontaneity does not imply irrationality, a sense of emotional impulsiveness pervades both of these descriptions (particularly in Killian's [1984, p. 777] discussion of the violation of the CORE rules for nonviolent action and in Bordin's [1981, p. 21] judgment that saloon invasions were "out of character"). We think this implication typifies the use of spontaneity as a concept in social movement analyses. In this context, spontaneity becomes more than a concept—it is a perspective about social movement behavior that maintains a view of spontaneous action as having several enduring characteristics across contexts and historical epochs:

1. Events are *rapid*—a short time period elapses between first advocacy and final execution.

2. They *lack structure*—occurring outside (and even in antagonism to) the framework of existing SMOs and include previously uninvolved or undisciplined protesters.
3. They are *emotional*—those involved are angry and excited, and therefore resistant to changing their minds and/or actions.
4. Participants are *impulsive*—they are not inclined to consider changing their chosen course in favor of less dramatic alternative actions.

The first two propositions imply lack of organizational structure; the second two speak to the capacity for careful planning.

Turner (1981) offers the most explicit and theoretically modulated version of this perspective. The most important facet of his argument for our analysis is his discussion of the relation between what he calls expressive behavior and rationality. He first identifies a "weak type" of rationality (vitiated rationality) that leads movements to "become fixated on courses of action that are dramatically counter productive" or even self-destructive. He argues (1981, p. 11) that even this vitiated rationality:

> does not incorporate the acknowledged need by people who are aroused over a cause to act, and to act conspicuously and dramatically for the cause. We call this *expressive* behavior because its importance to the actor is in expressing support for the cause, regardless of whether it produces the desired visible consequences. The question is not one of acting rationally or irrationally: the advocate wants to "do something," to "go on record," to "strike a blow" for the cause. Demonstrations, published mainfestos, violence, and even terrorism are sometimes ways of expressing commitment. Even when sophisticated leaders are immune to this concern, which is probably rarely, they must satisfy adherents' demands for action.

Turner thus makes explicit a central proposition in the spontaneity perspective: Spontaneous protest is often the expression of emotional needs rather than strategic thinking and they therefore produce behavior that may even contradict instrumental movement goals.

We believe that this usually unexplored assumption has led to a systematic misunderstanding of many social movements actions. This misunderstanding occurs because analysts demonstrate the existence of spontaneity and/or emotionality and then assume that the action is therefore extraorganizational, unstructured, and/or expressive as well. Spontaneous action with characteristics not predicted by this perspective—such as strategic insight or conscious selection among competing alternatives—is, therefore, ignored or, in our view, misunderstood.

We offer a definition of spontaneity that avoids such assumptions in order to provide a starting point for the reconsideration of the phenomenon of spontaneous action: Spontaneity in social movement refers to an *impromptu* action or series of actions undertaken by a collectivity. Neither the organizers of the collectivity (if any), nor the mass of participants in the action, have planned for or even anticipated the course of events (even if some individuals or small groups may have advocated some similar strategy). This definition makes no presuppositions about emotionality, impulsiveness, or expressivity (which may or may not be present) and allows for reassessment of the structural context of action).

Consider the two examples discussed above. They are both instances of action taken without the leadership, planning, or formal support of any organization. Indeed, both actions also involved high levels of emotionality. But we would argue that they also demonstrated considerable collective discipline, strategic thinking, and structure. Moreover, we think the descriptions, themselves, show that organizations did frame the course of events. We think these examples demonstrate that impromptu action is not necessarily without prior impetus, that extraorganizational action is not necessarily disorganized, and that emotional action is not necessarily impulsive (or expressive in Turner's sense).

Bordin's and Killian's descriptions of events, in fact, can easily be accommodated within our definition of spontaneity—they were unplanned and unanticipated (impromptu). The temperance crusaders attended Dr. Lewis' lecture without thought of active protest; they left with a commitment to direct intervention in the saloon trade. Similarly, the students at Florida A and M went to the cafeteria for lunch and left with the intention of confronting the local segregationist establishment.

In the case of the temperance crusade, for example, Bordin's history (1981, p. 16) notes that Dr. Lewis appeared in Hillsboro as "part of the regular winter course of lectures sponsored by the local lecture association" and extended his stay at the request of a local magistrate who was also a temperance advocate. A constituency favoring temperance already existed in that town and the most vociferous attended his lecture. Organized protemperance groups had existed in the United States (1981, p. 18) since the great evangelical crusades of the 1820s and 1830s. Moreover, the tactic employed was not a new one; in fact, Lewis had been urging its employment for twenty years and "instructed the women precisely how to proceed." Finally, the crusaders organized themselves for action (1981, p. 19) in the Presbyterian church and held a mass meeting in the Methodist Episcopal church. They sustained their protest over several weeks, altering foci and modifying demands and strategy in light of their experience. It is difficult to argue that they were either disorganized or impulsive. Their success was not a mere (or perhaps accidental) by-product of expressive action designed to "do something." It was a consequence of instrumental thought enacted through a developing organization. Spontaneity and emotionality played significant (perhaps even critical) roles, but they were not accompanied by disorganization or thoughtlessness.

It is useful in this context to identify what the elements of spontaneity contributed to an idea for action that, within a few days, had matured into a well-organized and highly-structured campaign. The change that took place at Dr. Lewis' lecture could be described as a change in identity, in which a group of individuals began thinking collectively. The audience was already committed to temperance, but they were moved by the event to think of how they might act *as a group* instead of thinking only in terms of their roles as individual advocates of prohibition. This is the basic ingredient in what Fantasia (1987) has called a culture of solidarity and which he argues is one necessary condition for all protest activity. This solidarity is also the necessary ingredient for the creation of an organization—the willingness of members of a group to make and honor collective decisions.

Turning to the Tallahassee example, we note a quite similar process. Before the spontaneous demonstration, as Killian (1984, p. 733) notes in the article, there was elaborate prior organization (including a full array of civil rights groups), a range of effective strategies (sit-ins, demonstrations, and mass arrests), and an already supportive constituency (FAMU and FSU students). Students at FAMU had a previous record of activism (including independent mobilization for a bus boycott in 1956). An organizational link between black students at FAMU and white students at FSU had been forged through CORE. Preexisting local organizations provided a communications network, a cadre of potential supporters was known to exist, and the expectation of adult aid to students was justified by direct contact and previous experience. The Greensboro sit-ins (generally seen as the immediate precursor of the Tallahassee movement) had taken place in late January—two weeks earlier. Sit-ins began in Talahassee (1984, p. 777) after the national CORE contacted the local organization and informed it of a "region-wide sympathy sit-in" to be held on February 13th. The CORE chapter continued the sit-ins beyond February 13th and arrests of demonstrators began on February 20th (1984, pp. 775-777).

Here again, the spontaneity and emotionality of events were not symptoms of disorganized expressivity. These impromptu demonstrations represented the moment when previously inactive (but partisan) students came together as a group and then acted in a perfectly reasonable fashion, even if we apply the most rigorous calculus of strategic effectiveness.

On the other hand, structure and planning do not preclude emotionality or disorganization. The following description (Barkan 1979, p. 27) illustrates the latter situation:

> ... At the May 1977 Seabrook occupation where 1,414 were arrested, the Clamshell Alliance had expected everyone to be taken into custody as soon as they tried to enter the construction area. When, surprisingly, the occupiers were allowed onto the plant's parking lot, they sat down to discuss what to do next. Many thought they should remain where they were, while others criticized the passivity of the occupation and wanted to stop cars

containing personnel of the utility constructing the plant from entering the site. The latter group of protesters also wished to move into the construction area itself by cutting through the fence separating the area from the parking lot. Both these suggestions were condemned as acts of violence by those wishing to remain in the parking lot . . .

After the 1977 Seabrook occupiers were arrested, hundreds were detained in National Guard armories for up to thirteen days . . . The Clamshell Alliance had failed to prepare for the possibility of lengthy incarceration, and ideological differences made for prolonged and often heated tactical debates during the course of the next two weeks.

When the authorities did not immediately arrest them, the impasse occurred in which an inadequate plan was mechanically followed. Leaders had failed to develop an appropriate strategy for the contingencies that the demonstration faced. The arrests revealed an even more profound strategic failure: Despite the expectation of incarceration, the Alliance organization had no useful action to sustain the protesters in jail.

Thus, while we agree that spontaneity is a concommitment element and, indeed, crucial element in social movement activity, we maintain that the evidence shows that impromptu actions are not necessarily disorganized or expressive and that conversely, planned actions are not necessarily strategically sound or well thought out. This analysis challenges a set of assumptions about the components of spontaneous action in social movements. In the next part of this paper, we offer an analytic context for understanding the characteristic structural forms of spontaneous action.

LEVELS OF MOVEMENT ORGANIZATION AND THE ISSUE OF DEMOCRACY

Marwell and Oliver (1984, p. 4) correctly point out, that the "concept 'social movement' is, itself, a theoretical nightmare." They (1984, p. 6 emphasis ours) suggest the following definition:

> . . . social movements are most usefully understood as complex aggregates of collective actions or events . . . conducted by different kinds of people, for different reasons, using *different organizational forms.*

We think that it is precisely the lack of clarity about different organizational forms that promotes the equation of spontaneity with disorganization and expressivity. We propose, therefore, to distinguish between different levels of social movement activity, to identify the characteristic and defining forms of organization at each level, to argue that the nature of rank-and-file involvement in movement decision making is quite different at different levels, and then to utilize these distinctions in discussing the role of spontaneity in social protest.

The term social movement organization may be applied to three very different kinds of organizational forms and the controlling distinction among these distinct forms relates to the role of rank-and-file participants. The most frequently analyzed type, the *federal movement organization,* coordinates activity in more than one locale, from a headquarters that is not proximate to all of the local activities.[5] It usually has a constitution (or the equivalent), a defined purpose, a hierarchy of governance, and a routinized method of acquiring the resources necessary for survival—in short, all the attributes of a formal organization. We use the term "federal movement organization" for this type because its multigeographical scope usually involves a set of local SMOs, which function quasi-independently of the national body. The NAACP, the Farmers Alliance, National Organization of Women (NOW), WCTU, and the San Francisco Regional Young Democrats are all examples of this type. As Turner notes (1981), this type of organization has been the subject of most resource mobilization studies.

In a federal organization, movement participants who are not full-time employees are rarely involved in day-to-day operations or decision making for the headquarters (though they might be very active in affiliated local groups). Democratic processes in federal organizations, where they exist, usually include either the election of officers and/or representatives to policy-making conventions, or referenda on major proposals, such as union contracts or structural reforms.[6] This allows full-time officials substantial decision-making power. If (some or many) members become unhappy or disillusioned with the actions, policies, or behavior of leadership, they must usually mount expensive and often unproductive insurgent campaigns to remove them.

A second movement form, the *local movement organization* is characterized by direct contact between members and leaders and reliance on the labor and monetary contributions of the rank-and-file. Popular programs attract new recruits and increase the commitment (and the contributions) of existing members. Unpopular actions, on the other hand, generate easily-heard complaints, drive away the base, and reduce membership involvement. The survival and success of local movement organizations, therefore, depend much more visible and immediately upon the actions and satisfaction of the membership and this makes organizational responsiveness to membership will (i.e., democracy) much less problematic. The Tallahassee chapter of the NAACP, Huntington NOW, the Poughkeepsie WCTU, and the Port Jefferson Committee to Save the Harbor are examples of local SMOs.

Though they retain some of the attributes of formal organizations, local movement organizations are rarely bureaucratic or coordinative, almost always do without routinized fundraising, and have few, if any, full-time paid staff members. While federal movement organizations generally work with local affiliates of this type—whose activities they influence and coordinate—local movement organizations do not necessarily belong to a federated structure.[7] Many local movement organizations, particularly those responding to purely local conditions, never affiliate with a larger organization. Insofar as local organizations are allied with federal, multilocal organizations, however, they may take on some of the more formal attributes of the national organization. This may be more likely if the federal organization charters the local, provides it with resources and/or staff, and oversees policy. Alternately, insofar as a federal organization is dependent on locals for resources and action, the greater responsiveness of the locals will constrain and moderate the formal hierarchical aspects of the larger organization.[8]

Local groups are not inevitably democratic, but the processes which produce democracy and oligarchy are very different from those which operate in federal organizations. The personal contact between leaders and members, the lack of resources and the great dependence on volunteer labor make local leadership positions less attractive and more vulnerable to popular protest compared to federal leadership positions, where the rewards of power and office may be substantial and where the cumbersome processes of representative elections limit rank-and-file attempts to replace incumbents.[9]

The third organizational type, the *primary movement group,* has received the least scholarly attention. Such groups are best described in Lawson's (1983) examination of the Tenant Movement. He discusses three functionally differentiated levels of organization: city, neighborhood, and building. We would characterize the city level of organization as federal (consisting of a federation of geographically—diverse local organizations), and the neighborhood level of organization as local (official chapters of the federal organization that were the locus of decision making and action for the neighborhood). We apply the term primary group to the lowest level of organization—the building organization. Founded in informal face-to-face interaction, among people who knew each other personally, building groups were "organized around the immediate needs of tenants," typically "formed in respose to inadequate heating during winter by women who know one another." More fluid in structure than the groups normally subjected to scholarly attention, building organizations had shorter life spans than the relatively permanent neighborhood organizations (Lawson 1983, pp. 128-129). Lawson (1983, p. 128) argued that these groups were primary loci of membership participation, facilitated the emergence of leaders, aided in the adoption of strategies that suited each level, and facilitated the development and acceptance of long-term goals.

We suggest that while most primary movement groups (unlike federal or local movement organizations) have little apparent similarity to formal organizations, they should be recognized as distinct organizational types. Leadership exists, although it may be diffuse and situational. Membership— mobilized through personal contact, friendship, and organizational networks as well as common grievances—can be identified, although it may be transitory and inconsistent.

It is precisely because primary movement groups are fluid, informal, and dependent on continual reassessment of personal commitment, that their internal processes are directly and organically democratic.

Direct democracy is more than the principle of "one person, one vote." It is the process by which choices are framed and emerge as well as that by which decisions are made. In a social movement setting, democracy exists insofar as the actions taken reflect the collective (or majority) will of the rank-and-file. This typically occurs when a large number of movement participants gather together in a single place and undertake an interchange of ideas about the immediate or ultimate direction of the movement. The process (explicitly or implicitly) involves consideration of alternative actions, and is sometimes concluded by the group as a whole making a collective decision, either through consensus or a formal vote.

Primary movement groups, because they intermingle a common protest purpose with friendship relations, are the principle loci for discussion of strategic and tactical alternatives. Individuals voice doubts, and raise new ideas, and (most often) change their views in the context of such interchange.

Ultimately, the participatory unit in social movements are primary groups. People rarely attend a demonstration or join a group alone—they do so with one or several (new or old) friends, relatives, or neighbors. Even if such groups have no formal stakes in the organization, individuals filter their decisions to support or join a movement or a particular action through the posture of these primary ties.[10]

Primary movement groups sometimes organize and function independently of local organizations, as in the case of consciousness-raising groups in the modern Women's Liberation Movement (Rosenthal 1984). They also exist as faction, tendencies, or cadres within local organizations and as networks and cliques of potential activists.

We would identify primary groups as the growth sector of social movements and, in many instances, as the source of experimentation, vitality, and excitement in organized efforts for change. They are also the frequent incubators of innovative ideas and strategies. Local organizations frequently adopt and act on such agendas, yet the influence of primary groups may remain invisible to or undocumented by post hoc observers.

PRIMARY MOVEMENT GROUPS
AND DIRECT DEMOCRACY

This leads to the central point we are trying to establish. There is a fundamental link between direct democracy and spontaneity. To see this, we distinguish between direct democracy and representative democracy. The difference is most clearly expressed in the imagery of the New England town meeting which defines direct democracy as the gathering together of all (eligible) town citizens and a decision-making process, involving reasoned debate followed by collective choice based on majority rule or consensus. If we probe this imagery, we realize that such debates and decisions could have involved—without compromising the definition of democracy—a huge amount of emotionality and hot-tempered discussion, resulting in significant changes in individual and collective opinion during the meeting. The policy outcome of a New England town meeting, therefore, could have been quite different from any policy envisioned by any of the participants before the meeting began, both because minds were changed and because compromises were engineered on the spot.

A second feature of this imagery involves the enactment of the agreed-upon policy. In our mind's eye, the duly constituted authorities were required to enact the democratically developed policy, even when it was unanticipated by (or even objectionable to) those authorities. Though such execution of popular will would, at least sometimes, involve considerable discretion and perhaps real decision making, it would always remain within the constraints of the formal expression of popular will. Orderly enforcement by representatives of the group insured, at least in principle, that the new policy would not take on a disruptive and impulsive aspect.

Consider, on the other hand, the decision-making process in social movements. We take as our example here the occupation of the administration building during the Harvard University strike of 1969 (Eichel et al. 1970). Much like a New England town meeting, the Students for a Democratic Society (SDS) meeting that decided upon the sit-in had been talked about for many days in advance. It was well-known that two different proposals for action would be presented: one calling for an occupation that evening, and the other advocating a month of intensive organizing followed by a second vote on the advisability of a sit-in.

This was by far the largest SDS meeting ever held at Harvard, attracting at least 200 people more than at any previous time. The group in attendance developed and voted for a third course of action—a series of daily demonstrations leading up to a sit-in, with the exact date set by the SDS executive committee without recourse to another membership meeting. To no one's surprise, the SDS executive committee scheduled the sit-in for the following day, since the majority of that group had advocated same-day action at the general meeting.[11]

Parallels with the traditional New England town meeting are quite striking. The discussion in the SDS meeting was highly emotional. It included vicious denunciations by both sides, spontaneous development of third, fourth, and fifth proposals, and an outcome that had not been envisioned prior to the meeting. A majority of the members involved in the decision probably had thought very little about the relative merits of potential actions before they arrived, and yet it is clear that, at least for those in attendance, the meeting was democratic in both form and essence. Though emotions ran high, accounts of the meeting make clear that the decision-making process involved reasoned debate and was far from impulsive. The winning proposition, developed at the meeting itself, was not impulsively or thoughtlessly endorsed, and though it represented a commitment to take militant action (a choice that most participants understood to be personally and politically risky), it is hard to make a case for expressivity (in Turner's sense) as constituting a principle component in the ultimate choice. The executive committee's decision, one day later, was certainly an act of leadership discretion, but the participation of over 1,000 students (including virtually all of the SDS membership) in the sit-in that followed demonstrates that it fell well within the broad mandate laid down by the membership.

Once it began, however, the sit-in did not conform to the enactment process associated with New England town democracy. The student rank-and-file did not delegate continuing discretion to leadership; it maintained control through direct democracy. For some 16 hours, until the building was cleared by the poice at about 4:00 a.m. the following day, there was a continuous mass meeting inside the administration building that made virtually all relevant decisions. These included strategic choices, such as policies toward violence and inspection of confidential university files; ad hoc decisions on incidental developments, such as the expulson of a dean who appeared to be compiling a list of participants; and responses to official university actions, such as an offer to negotiate if the building was vacated. In effect, the mass meeting directly administered the enforcement of its sit-in decision, instead of delegating it to a set of official representatives, as would be expected in a town meeting democracy. This sort of direct democracy is often found in large, disruptive, mass demonstrations.

Here we see the difference between representative democracy and rank-and-file enactment of policy. Social movement participants frequently mandate their leadership to undertake action, particularly when negotiations are underway or the movement gains representation in an official decision-making structure. But they sometimes act directly on their own behalf. Whether or not an activity is organized through democratic processes, mass action often infuses events with high degrees of emotionality, volatility, and, in direct consequence, democracy. It is never certain, as in the case of the Harvard strike, the Seabrook demonstration, the Hillsboro temperance crusade, or the Tallahassee sit-in movement, that a mass action will unfold precisely in the way it was planned. But unpredictability does not imply that the decisions are impulsive or expressive rather than rational and goal-oriented. In fact, planning for all contingencies may be unnecessary or even counterproductive. Particularly in militant actions against powerful institutions or groups, only a general strategic outline may be possible, with most choices worked out in the process of action, when the reaction of authorities can be observed and assessed.

We are not arguing that a social movement group always arrives at sensible decisions in the context of mass militant actions. Certainly, in many situations, the choices made by rank-and-file are less well thought out than they might be if participants were given time and calmer circumstances. However, the inefficiency and error inherent in these pressurized situations operates with equal force on movement leaders (when they are delegated such decisions) and on institutional authorities (under similar circumstances).[12] Direct democracy is no more, and perhaps considerably less, likely to degenerate under the pressure of circumstances than any other decision-making process.

Moreover, even in the midst of spontaneous events, rank-and-file participants tend to rely on tactics that are part of an existing strategic repertoire (Tilly 1978). This is the burden of much of Morris' (1984) analysis, and we believe it applies even in the most impromptu circumstances. Actions are deemed appropriate or inappropriate in such situations according to past experience in similar situations, the reliability and credibility of their proposers, and how well they stand up to debate and criticism.

It is in this context that primary movement groups, based as they are on face-to-face relationships, play their most critical role in shaping mass protest. Since unanimity and trust are the foundations upon which a set of individuals form a collectivitiy capable of making joint decisions and acting together, the personal relationships that characterize these groups facilitate the construction and maintenance of a culture of solidarity.

The processes involved in actions generated by such movement groups are rarely studied directly. Primary group actions are usually unanticipated, short-lived, and poorly documented, even in retrospect. Participants rarely write about them analytically, and their nature generally precludes observation by interested researchers. For this reason, Fantasia's study (1987) of two wildcat strikes that occurred in 1975 at the Taylor Casting Company of northern New Jersey, is a precious resource for understanding the structure of primary group action. Fantasia stresses the longstanding sociability in the plant, expressed in joking and teasing, that served to break down the ethnic and skill divisions among workers and to provide a personal unity upon which collective action was constructed. The first strike, was thoroughly spontaneous by any definition: It took place barely two hours after the precipitating incident (the firing of a maintenance worker), and took form outside of the recognized union. It was, nevertheless, preceded by a criticial period of debate in which the incipient leadership, drawn from more experienced and respected workers, convinced the less committed that the strike was necessary and viable. The successful conclusion of this debate brought the entire Taylor workforce into the courtyard of the plant and produced the sense and the reality of collective action. This collectivity was embodied in a continuous mass meeting which constituted itself "as the union," and made all decisions during the strike, including repudiation of the official union leadership. The strength of collective discipline was illustrated by a decision to return to work, vigorously debated and carried by only a small majority, but nevertheless honored by even its most militant opponents. Fantasia (1983, p. 84) says of the first strike:

> The strike at Taylor, while seemingly a spontaneous outburst, actually had an orderly, deliberate and 'rational' character to it. As the action unfolded . . . unity and solidarity were created in the process of interaction with the company and between the participants . . . The solidarity that was achieved was not inherent in the workers (although the conditions of work and day-to-day interaction provided a firm basis) but was to a considerable extent created in the course of the collective action itself.

Fantasia's (1987, Chapter 3, pp. 42-44) more general analysis of the strike speaks directly to the issues we address here:

> The first wildcat was a relatively spontaneous affair. However, it was also an action which relied on mutual trust based on preexisting shop floor relationships. Moreover, while the participants were faced with spontaneous shifts and decisions at various states of the wildcat, their collective negotiations were a crucial element, so though spontaneous in the sense that it was not preplanned, the wildcat was an action which was structured in important ways. By posing a dualism between spontaneity and the planned, rational calculation of collective action, the presence of the structure elements *within* spontaneous action may be missed.

Like the Harvard strike, this mass meeting that characterized the wildcat at Taylor continually made choices in response to an emerging set of developments. We contend that the protoorganization that prececded the facilitated Taylor wildcat is a common feature of spontaneous actions, including those that Killian has analyzed in Tallahassee. If they are not noted in other accounts, it may be because most analysts have neither been participant observers, nor have sought out the evidence that would illuminate these processes. However, continuous mass meetings are regular features of many sustained militant actions (see especially, Kraus 1949; Heirich 1966; Fine 1969). While such raw democracy is certainly spontaneous, it can hardly be callled unorganized. Whether or not it is impulsive in the sense that the decisions are not clearly thought through is always a matter of judgment. Those who disagree with the options chosen many well see the actions as impulsive (even if they ultimately work well), while those who agree with decisions made in this way may interpret them as quite rational (even if they ultimately fail to achieve the desired result). But such disagreement also occurs in every decision-making context.

It is critical to reiterate that leadership also faces such emergent conditions. Returning to the example of the New England town meeting, we note that duly constituted authorities seeking to enforce democractically determined policy had the authority to act on their own discretion and their best understanding of the popular will. In so doing, they may often face unpredictable and confusing circumstances that demand on-the-spot decision making. The adequacy of their choices is a subject for research, but it is almost never brought under the rubric of what we have called the spontaneity perspective. Instead, leadership decisions are most often assumed to be reasonable and rational, not expressive or irrational.

For this reason, it is very important to understand that the aura of impulsiveness, irrationality, and disorganization that pervades descriptions of movements in which the rank-and-file makes and enforces decisions contains the inherent danger of condemning democracy. The degree of impulsiveness, irrationality, and disorganization in a particular situation is variable, but is independent of the form of decision making. Acknowledged leaders, as well as rank-and-file, are prone to impulsive actions in certain circumstances.[13] On the other hand, rationality, thoughtfulness, and planning are possible and sometimes even probable in spur of the moment rank-and-file decisions, depending on the context and circumstances.

PRIMARY GROUPS AND MOVEMENT TRAJECTORY

Mass gatherings are the incubators of spontaneity: the locus of mobilization for demonstrations, protest, and direct action. They also create occasions for the development of new tactics and strategies and for the beginning of new movements and organizations. Sometimes mass gatherings occur outside of the context of formal organizations, but at others, they are generated within formally constituted movement organizations.

Democracy is inherent in mass gatherings because the choices made must be honored collectively. Those who disagree with the outcomes of the decision making process cannot be easily coerced (or persuaded) to cooperate in later actions. In fact, it is commonplace for a considerable proportion of potential activists to withdraw from subsequent participation in a movement because of disagreement. The prospect of losing a substantial number of followers imposes the need for leaders and members to arrive at a choice that will be acceptable to as large a constituency as possible.

Even movements with ongoing organizational structures sometimes require (or encounter) mass meetings. The leadership may not intend to subject the organization's policies to a popular referendum but such events may force reconsideration, since large groups of people are capable of, and frequently willing to alter the basic trajectory of the organization in light of movement efficacy, leadership policies, and the opportunity for collective decision making. Such junctures may occur and recur in the history of a particular organization or movement, and each represents a significant infusion of popular democracy into the group decision-making process (however wise or foolish the decision may prove to be). The mass gathering is thus a time of reckoning both for movements in embryo and for movement organizations.

Primary groups are the constituent building blocks of the mass meeting. They are also the most basic elements of formally constituted movements, but their operation is more apparent in the context of a mass gathering. Individuals rarely go to, or participate in, mass demonstrations, meetings, or protests alone. For example, returning to Killian's description of the Tallahassee sit-ins, we suggest that the students in the cafeteria, deciding whether or not to join in the protest, were (if they follow the pattern of other student populations) most likely sitting with friends and, consequently, were likely to make their decision in concert with others in their immediate circle. Similarly, in the context of the mass gathering, primary groups arrive together, hang together, are likely to choose similar sides in debate, and act as units within the larger population convened. The ultimate choices of the larger body are made, then, not so much by individuals, as by primary groups acting (implicitly or explicitly) as collectivities.

Primary movement groups are also ubiquitous in expanding movements, and play a crucial role in developing movement direction. This is aptly illustrated by the ideological transformations within the NOW, the first breath of resurgent organized feminism after 1920. Founded in 1966 by a leadership group of women from the State Commissions on the Status of Women, the goal of its initiators was to create a civil rights group for women that would function on the national level, pressing for legal reform and for an end to sex discrimination. National task forces were set up to carry out the major goals of the organization and a national board was elected to direct the organization between yearly conventions. Soon after the initial organizing effort, NOW decided to develop local chapters to aid in its campaigns, and within a year had established 14 local groups and a communications network. (Hole and Levine 1971; Rosenthal 1976). By 1970, four years later, the organization had only 3,000 members in 30 local chapters and a reputation for conservatism. NOW's leadership disassociated itself from lesbian, radical feminist, and consciousness-raising groups, and the federal organization continued to maintain control over local activities and goals, concentrating on court cases, nationally-oriented political action, and lobbying campaigns. But in less than two years, the national NOW had reversed its position on excluding lesbians and their issues from the organization and its local chapters were organizing consciousness-raising groups—all previously anathema to the leadership (Rosenthal 1976). What was responsible for this change? After a highly-successful national women's strike and demonstration coordinated by a coalition of feminist organizations in 1970 (including NOW), women poured into the organization. Some swelled the ranks in established locals, but many collectively affiliated as new primary groups sought local charters. Those local groups took the initiative away from the federal organization. The new members had come to NOW because it was the best-known group (Rosenthal 1976), and they refused to accept distinctions between various shades of feminism (Hole and Levine 1971). They undertook a wide range of actions, notably mass protest and consciousness-raising, which the national leadership had previously opposed. Eventually, approval of these new activities filtered upward, but only through the strenuous efforts of local activities, rooted in primary groups.

Primary groups may come to life in established federated movements, bringing new life to the organizations. The national NAACP, for example, benefitted from the southern sit-in movement, though the national leadership did not support sit-ins until after 1960. Even when the federal organization endorsed them, it still referred to them as "extra-legal" and refused to participate in organizing them. Sit-ins were never part of the overall strategy of the federal organization leadership (Marger 1984). Yet Morris (1981) shows that local NAACP groups (acting in conjunction with CORE chapters) played key roles in initiating sit-ins in seven out of fifteen pre-1960 cities.

Movement organizations do live on even after primary group activity has largely ceased. But no matter how large they appear, or how much grass-roots support they may have had commanded in the past, they persist only as echoes of a former existence. Some are institutionalized, as for example, in political parties (Heberle 1951), others continue for a time as mere shells, lacking the viable and active constituency that brought them and their agendas into the public eye. This apparently happened to the Farmers' Alliance and Populsit Party in the 1890s. Even at the zenith of its electoral strength, in 1892-1896, the vitality of the local clubs had already atrophied in most areas, making it vulnerable to both leadership manipulation and rapid collapse (Schwartz 1976; Goodwyn 1976). In Kansas, the inability of the Populists to mobilize around any issue except elections appears to have been a consequence of the absence of viable local organizations and primary groups, that may have itself been a reflection of a rapid top-down organizing strategy (McNall 1986).

CONCLUSION

We have said elsewhere (Schwartz 1976; Schwartz et al. 1981), that democracy is a critical ingredient in social movement success, although of course, democracy does not guarantee movement viability. We conclude with a summary of related propositions about the relation between spontaneity, primary movement groups, and movement trajectory, that emerge from this analysis:

1. Spontaneity is a central phenomenon in social movements.
2. Spontaneous action in social movements is not incongruent with or in opposition to structure.

3. Primary movement groups are the smallest participatory units of viable
    social movements.
4. Primary movement groups constitute the growth sector of social
    movements; they are ubiquitous in expanding movements and play a
    crucial role in developing and reorienting movement direction.
5. Direct democracy is the characteristic mode of operation in primary
    movement groups.
6. Spontaneity is often an indicator of democratic decision making and
    this is particularly likely when primary movement groups are the locus
    of action.

In our view, spontaneity infuses one important category of social movement
actions, but we content that, like spontaneous combustion, such activities
reflect the presence and interaction of certain properties that produce the
appearance of an uncaused conflagration. Under certain circumstances,
internal chemical action generates sufficient heat in oily rags to produce fire.
Similarly, on occasion, groups of people will engage in actions that are largely
unpremeditated, but nevertheless mediated by identifiable forces and
preexisting structures. In these circumstances, spontaneity is the symptom of
two related phenomena: the moment when an assembly of individuals form
themselves into a group capable of collective thought and action, and the
process of direct democracy through which the group develops and enacts its
collective will. Thus, the fact that militant action sometimes appears to come
out of nowhere, generated by the internal heat of high emotion, should not
blind us to the presence of elements conducive to reaction.

As we have noted, actions taken by leadership within formal organizations
are not generally described as spontaneous; the designation is usually reserved
for militant rank-and-file action that is seemingly extraorganizational. What
we have attempted to show here is that careful unpacking of the context of
such events usually reveals preexisting organizational structure (though not
always formally constituted) that provides leadership, resources, ideas,
strategies, and often, occasion for mass action. Even in those instances where
such action is not directed or initiated by a formal organization (as in the case
of the first temperance crusade, the Tallahassee demonstrations, or the first
Taylor wildcat), the action itself creates organizational structure based on
primary movement groups.

Spontaneity is, indeed, a crucial variable in social movement analysis. But
the existence of spontaneity does not threaten the rationalist paradigm. Quite
the contrary, a rationalist approach to the phenomenon is necessary. Protest
action is guided by a logic of *collective* rationality that seeks to understand
how the collectivity can produce its goals with minimal resource expenditure
and personal harm. But this rationality is different from that of an individual
who evaluates an action in terms of individual gains and losses.

When spontaneous events are examined in the light of rationalist theory, rank-and-file actors take centerstage. The actions taken and the structures created in the context of spontaneous mobilization influence the course of movement development, sometimes changing the character of preexisting organizations and, on occasion, creating the base for new organizational formation. Catching fire in the public imagination, burning through the underbrush of habit, the conflagration that marks the appearance of mass movements is frequently sparked, not by expressivity, but by a volatile combination of long held grievances, emotionality, and direct democracy exploding into solidary spontaneous action.

NOTES

1. This position is similar to that enunciated by Freeman, another resource mobilization theorist, who offers "fads, trends and crowds,' as the prototypes of one end of a continuum of social action characterized by "contagious spontaneity and lack of structure," (though such action may later lead to more "mature" forms of social action . . .)" (Freeman 1983, p. 1).

2. Turner, writing in *Research in Social Movements* (1981, vol. 4, p. 20), argued (for the collective behavior school) that the collective behavior and resource mobilization positions could be reconciled so long as advocates refrained from: "an optimizing rationality model of decision making;" the assumption that "decision making is rather effectively centralized in movement organizations;" the treatment of "goals as relatively stable and unproblematic;" the contention that "levels of grievance and relative deprivation are generally irrelevant to the rise and decline of movements;" "the assessment of movement successes strictly in terms of tangible accomplishments;" and the conception of "movement dynamics as the mobilization of measurable and exchangeable resources." These provisos seem, at first, to cut the heart out of resource mobilization theory, but, on closer scrutiny, they do not differ fundamentally from certain criticisms raised from within the rationalist camp. They could be seen as a call to abandon "resource determinism" which has plagued resource dependence on occasion. Assumptions that the amount of resources, perhaps measured in dollars, determines the size of the movement (regardless of the amount of oppression and/or discontent), and that these resources will be used in the most effective manner to redress the motivating grievances of the movement without inventory shrinkage or goal displacement, has indeed been a problem in some resource mobilization work (Schwartz 1976; Morris 1981).

Turner advocates an amalgamation of resource dependency and collective behavior logic, based on Olsen's (1965) free rider dilemma. In Olsen's logic, nonparticipants may reap the benefit of movement success without taking risks or expending their own resources. There is, therefore, a considerable disincentive for rational individuals to participate in collective action. In Turner's (1981, p. 15) view, this disincentive can be overcome in two situations: when so little is demanded of most adherents that costs of support are trivial, (as, for example, small donations or votes), or when the movement derives from previously organized groups that can offer selective inducements and exercise coercive power over potential adherents, (as for example a union with a closed-shop contract).

This argument implies that the conditions in which "the distinctive theoretical position of resource mobilization is weakened" include those mass demonstrations involving previously uncommitted or quasicommitted people in militant, disruptive, or potentially dangerous actions. In these circumstances, Olson's argument operates with full force. Participation is more "expressive of the need to act" than rational in terms of movement goals, even if the action ultimately succeeds in those goals.

3. Our contention, in part, rests on Morris' demonstration that the sit-ins, and other apparently spontaneous events in the Civil Rights movement, were constructed upon ongoing and sometimes venerable community organizations.

4. Our argument reflects the analyses of recent researchers who stress the unique and multiple role played by movement members in determining the structure and orientation of social movement organizations, the type of resources that will be developed and recruited, and the uses to which tangible and nontangible resources will be put (see for example Morris, 1981, 1984; Schwartz 1976; Barkan 1979; Schwartz et al. 1981; Rosenthal et al. 1985; Klandermans 1984; McAdam 1982). In this view, since people inside a movement determine its goals and actions, they are the agency for mobilizing external resources. People are thus, a unique movement resource, more important than, and fundamentally different from, all other resources (Barkan 1979; Useem 1979; Schwartz et al. 1981; Morris 1984).

5. A federated group could operate in a relatively tiny area, for example, a small city, if there was more than one local group (see below) and more than one geographic locus of activity.

6. This distance has claimed the attention of social movement theorists for nearly a century and has led to an insightful (but recently neglected) body of literature, deriving from Michels' work, on the conditions under which democracy persists in what we call federal movement organizations. The strong possibility of oligarchy always exists in such organizations (Michels 1962) but it is neither inevitable or irreversible (Schwartz et al. 1981). An active rank-and-file can overcome these tendencies. Internal dissent and insurgency is, therefore, generally a sign of both democracy and organizational strength (see, for example, such different authors as Lipset 1956, and Prickett 1975, 1981).

7. Patterns of affiliation and nonaffiliation influence the internal dynamics of local organizations in very different ways and they cannot be ignored in analysing movement dynamics. Nevertheless, all local SMOs have similar underlying dynamics that flow from the direct involvement of the rank-and-file in determining the policies and activities of the group. A small, dissatisfied membership severely constrains organizational options, while a large enthusiastic base increases both choices and leverage.

8. Local-federal organizational affiliation can arise in a number of ways. We are accustomed to assuming that federated organizations create locals as part of an expansionist impulse, but such expansion is by no means inevitable, as the sporadic commitment of the American labor movement to organizing the unemployed makes amply clear (Guerin 1979; Prickett 1975, 1981). The opposite process, in which local organizations develop and then create or join federal organizations, may be equally important. The success of one local organization sometimes leads to the formation of others. The formation of the National Consumers League (which sought to mobilize the female buying public on behalf of the underpaid and exploited women employed in retail establishments) (Flexner 1975 p. 213) illustrates this process:

> The New York Consumers League, founded in 1890, turned its attention to arousing this group. Similar Leagues followed shortly in Philadelphia, in Massachusetts, and elsewhere. In 1899 the National Consumers League was established.

Previously independent local movements have also created a federal organization to coordinate their actions. This was the process by which the Southern Christian Leadership Conference was created (Morris 1984). Particular local groups may attempt to "go national." Such was the method chosen by New York and Chicago tenant rights organizations which sponsored a 1969 meeting that "began the National Tenants Organization" and oversaw its formation in other cities (Gillespie 1983, p. 265). Finally, a local group may affiliate with an existing federal group, a pattern common in the union movement when locals join national unions as part of organizing drives (see, for example Fantasia 1987). Schwartz (1976) described a combination of all these processes in the early period of the Southern Farmers' Alliance.

9.   The distinction between federal and local movement organizations has been fruitfully (though often implicitly) used in a number of studies. Gamson (1975, p. 93) analyzed the component structures of 53 nationally-oriented movements and found that almost half had "chapters or divisions . . . that maintain substantial autonomy and the freedom to decide whether or not to support the collective action of the group as a whole." Lawson (1983), observed "multiple levels" of organization in the Tenant Movement and concluded that a pyramidal structure is typical of movements mobilizing grass-roots participants. Schwartz (1976) and Barnes (1984) found that the trajectory of action in the Southern Farmers' Alliance reflected, to a considerable degree, the changing relationship between local and federal structures. Rosenthal and her collaborators (1985) observed that in the 19th century Women's Movement, the network of local organizations was denser and more integrated than the network generated by leaders of federal organizations. Gerlach and Hine (1970) argued that movements that are "segmentary" (composed of a range of diverse groups or "cells"), "polycephalous" (consisting of local leaders who are rivals for control), and "reticulate" (organized into a network through "cross-cutting" links of people, ideas and activities) have better prospects than centrally organized, top-down movements.

These diverse results have not yet been articulated as a coherent portrait of the symbiotic and contradictory relations between local and federated organizations, but they indicate that the processes at the two levels are quite distinct. This implies the necessity to systematically distinguish them and to focus research attention on their different dynamics. We suspect that a certain proportion of the controversy in the field results from the fact that an analysis that focuses on local organizations produces a very different picture from one that centers on federal groups. A forthcoming article on women's networks in Rochester, Poughkeepsie, and Wellsville, New York will examine these differences in detail.

10.   Flexner (1975), a historian, for example, recounts the experience of a farmer's daughter who attended the first womans' rights convention in Seneca Falls, N.Y. in 1848 (the generally acknowledged trigger of movement growth). The woman said that she saw the notice for the convention in the county newspaper, and ran immediately "from one neighbor to another, to find that others had already read it . . . with the same excitement as herself." "She and half a dozen of her friends" decided to go to the convention, fearing that they would be the only ones present. In fact, through similar circumstances, over 300 people attended the convention (called a week earlier and announced in only one newspaper serving a primarily rural constituency).

11.   This discussion is based mainly on Eichel et al. (1970 particularly Chapter 4, pp. 77-95). Their account omits the decision to leave the timing of the sit-in to the Executive Committee and the subsequent Executive Committee vote (see *Harvard Crimson* April 9, 10, 1969).

12.   The flurry of research interest in group think, a form of irrational and expressive decision making which some psychologists think is widespread among American political leadership, demonstrates the necessity of assessing the rationality of all decision making, democratic or otherwise.

13.   Spontaneity is not the exclusive preserve of the unorganized. Leadership in highly-centralized bureaucratic organizations may also engage in spontaneous action, although it is rarely described as such. For example, in 1946 after a long period of organizing and an equally long tug-of-war with the national leadership of the United Automobile Workers (the UAW), the local UAW chapter at North American Aviation in Los Angeles began a strike for union recognition. Subsequent events included a notable four-cornered struggle among the employer, the local union, the national union, and the National Labor Relations Board, with the ultimate outcome being the destructionof the local and its replacement with one more acceptable to the national union leadership. In the course of this struggle, the national UAW leadership engaged in several ad hoc actions, including a public call for the end of the strike and a threat to recruit strikebreakers if the local did not capitulate (Prickett 1981). It is clear that these actions were impromptu and possibly impulsive, yet they would never be so characterized in the social movement literature

as such. The actions of established leadership, even when they occur in a very short time span and can be shown to be highly emotional, are simply not seen in the same context as similar actions taken by large groups of people in a potentially disruptive or violent demonstration.

We raise these examples in order to illustrate a particularly important point about the role of spontaneity in social movement activity. The characterization of spontaneity as impulsive, potentially irrational, and disorganized is almost always applied to circumstances with the potential for disruption that are part of militant action. Alternately, activities that do not threaten large-scale disruption of the ongoing social structure are not generally analyzed within the rubric of the spontaneity perspective.

REFERENCES

Barkan, S.E. 1979. "Strategic, Tactical and Organizational Dilemmas of the Protest Movement against Nuclear Power." *Social Problems* 27:19-42.

Barnes, D.A. 1984. *Farmers in Rebellion: The Rise and Fall of the Southern Farmer's Alliance and the People's Party in Texas.* Austin: University of Texas Press.

Bordin, R. 1981. *Woman and Temperance: The Quest for Power and Liberty 1873-1919.* Philadelphia, PA: Temple University Press.

Curtis, R. and L.A. Zurcher. 1973. "Stable Resources of Protest Movements: The Multiorganizational Field." *Social Forces* 52:53-61.

Eichel, L.E., K.E. Jost, R.D. Luskin, and R.M. Neustadt. 1970. *The Harvard Strike.* Boston: Houghton Mifflin.

Fantasia, R. 1983. "The Wildcat Strike and Industrial Relations." *Industrial Relations Journal* 14:75-86.

———. 1987. *Cultures of Solidarity: Studies in Consciousness and Action Among Contemporary American Workers.* Berkeley: University of California Press.

Fine, S. 1969. *Sit-downs: The General Motors Sit-down Strike of 1936-1937.* Ann Arbor: University of Michigan Press.

Flexner, E. 1975. *Century of Struggle: The Woman's Rights Movement in the United States.* New York: Athaneum.

Freeman, J. 1979. "Resource Mobilization and Strategy: A Model for Analyzing Social Movement Organization Actions. Pp. 167-189 in *The Dynamics of Social Movements,* edited by J.D. McCarthy and M.N. Zald. Cambridge, MA: Winthrop.

———. 1983. *Social Movements of the Sixties and Seventies.* New York: Longman.

Gamson, W.A. 1975. *The Strategy of Social Protest.* Homewood, IL: Dorsey Press.

Gerlach, L.D. and V.H. Hine 1970. *People, Power, Change: Movements of Social Transformation.* Indianapolis, IN: Bobbs Merrill.

Gillespie, D.P. 1983. "Conservative Tactics in Social Movement Organizations. Pp. 262-276 in *Social Movements of the Sixties and Seventies.* New York: Longman.

Goodwyn, L. 1976. *The Populist Movement.* New York: Oxford University Press.

Guerin, D. 1979. *100 Years of Labor in the USA,* translated by Alan Adler. London: Ink Links.

Gusfield, J.R. 1981. "Social Movements and Social Change: Perspectives of Linearity and Fluidity." Pp. 317-339 in *Research in Social Movements, Conflict and Change,* vol. 4, edited by L. Kriesberg. Greenwich, CT: JAI Press.

Harvard Crimson, April 9, 10, 1969.

Heberlé, R. 1951. *Social Movements: An Introduction to Political Sociology.* New York: Appleton-Century-Crofts.

Heirich, M. 1966. *The Spiral of Protest.* Chicago: University of Chicago Press.

Hole, J. and E. Levine. 1971. *The Rebirth of Feminism.* New York: Quadrangle.

Killian, L.M. 1984. "Organization, Rationality and Spontaneity in the Civil Rights Movement." *American Sociological Review* 49:770-783.

_____ . 1986. "Courage or Calculation? Theories of Social Movements." Paper presented at the Southern Sociology Meetings, New Orleans.

Klandermans, P.G. 1984. "Mobilization and Participation: Social Psychological Expansions of Resource Mobilization Theory." *American Sociological Review* 49:583-600.

Kraus, H. 1949. *The Many and the Few.* Los Angeles: The Platin Press.

Lawson, R. 1983. "A Decentralized but Moving Pyramid: The Evolution and Consequences of the Structure of the Tenant Movement." Pp. 119-132 in *Social Movements in the Sixties and Seventies,* edited by J. Freeman. New York: Longman.

Lipset, S.M. 1956. *Union Democracy: The Internal Politics of the International Typographical Union.* New York: Free Press,

Lowi, Th.J. 1971. *The Politics of Disorder.* New York: Basic Books.

Marger, M.N. 1984. "Social Movement Organizations and Response to the NAACP 1960-1973." *Social Problems* 32 (1):16-30.

Marwell, G. and P. Oliver. 1984. "Collective Action Theory and Social Movements Research." Pp. 1-27 in *Research in Social Movements, Conflicts, and Change,* vol. 7, edited by L. Kriesberg. Greenwich, CT: JAI Press.

McAdam, D. 1982. *Political Process and the Development of Black Insurgency, 1930-1970.* Chicago: University of Chicago Press.

McCarthy, J.D. and M.N. Zald. 1977. "Resource Mobilization and Social Movements: A Partial Theory." *American Journal of Sociology* 82:1212-1241.

McNall, S.G. 1986. "The Failure of the Agrarian Protest Movement in Kansas." Paper delivered at the Southern Sociological Society meetings, New Orleans.

Michels, R. 1962. *Political Parties.* New York: Free Press.

Morris, A. 1981. "The Black Southern Sit-in Movement: An Analysis of Internal Organization." *American Sociological Review* 46:744-767.

_____ . 1984. *The Origins of the Civil Rights Movement: Black Communities Organizing for Change.* New York: Free Press.

Oberschall, A. and L. Farris. 1985. "The 1960 Sit-ins: Protest Diffusion and Movement Take-off. Paper presented at the Eastern Sociological Association Meetings, Philadelphia.

Olson, M. 1965. *The Logic of Collective Behavior: Public Goods and the Theory of Groups.* Cambridge, MA: Harvard University Press.

Prickett, J.R. 1975. "Communists and the Communist Issue in the American Labor Movement, 1920-1950." Ph.D. Dissertation, University of California, Los Angeles.

_____ . 1981. "Communist Conspiracy or Wage Dispute?: The 1941 Strike at North American Aviation." *Pacific Historical Review* 50:215-233.

Rosenthal, N.B. 1976. "Consciousness Raising: Individual Change and Social Change in the American Women's Liberation Movement. Unpublished Ph.D. dissertation, State University of New York, Stony Brook.

_____ . 1984. "Consciousness Raising: From Revolution to Reevaluation." *Psychology of Women Quarterly* 84:309-326.

Rosenthal, N.B., M. Fingruthd, M. Ethier, R. Karant, and D. McDonald. 1985. "Social Movements and Network Analysis: A Case Study of Nineteenth-century Women's Reform in New York State." *American Journal of Sociology* 90:1022-1054.

Schwartz, M. 1976. *Radical Protest and Social Structure.* New York: Academic Press.

Schwartz, M., N. Rosenthal, and L. Schwartz. 1981. "Leader-member Conflict in Protest Organizations: The Case of the Southern Farmer's Alliance. *Social Problems* 29:22-36.

Tilly, C. 1978. *From Mobilization to Revolution.* Reading, MA: Addison-Wesley.

Turner, R.H. 1981. "Collective Behavior and Resource Mobilization as Approaches to Social Movements: Issues and Continuities. Pp. 1-24 in *Research in Social Movements, Conflicts and Change,* vol. 4, edited by L. Kriesberg. Greenwich, CT: JAI Press.

Useem, M. 1979. *Protest Movements in America.* Indianapolis, IN: Bobbs-Merrill.

ENVIRONMENTAL MOVEMENT ORGANIZATIONS IN WEST GERMANY AND FRANCE:
STRUCTURE AND INTERORGANIZATIONAL RELATIONS

Dieter Rucht

In Europe, social movements have traditionally been seen in close relationship to political parties and interest groups. However, with the ongoing institutionalization and oligarchization of the labor movement, analysts were inclined to contrast institutions and social movements. The spontaneous, informal aspects of social movements became stylized and exaggerated. Organization was no longer considered to be a genuine element of a social movement but an indicator of its stagnation or demise (Rammstedt 1978).

In the United States, the general perspective was rather the opposite. Mass psychology, while remaining marginally important in the European context,

International Social Movement Research, Vol. 2, pages 61-94.
Copyright © 1989 by JAI Press Inc.
All rights of reproduction in any form reserved.
ISBN: 0-89232-964-5

had a considerable impact on the early American theories of collective behavior. Here, social movements were seen as fluid and amorphous social entities, stemming from irrational sources and motivational forces. With the rise of the civil rights movement and the following protest movements however, this view became untenable. In the 1970s, the resource mobilization approach was established (McCarthy and Zald 1977; Jenkins 1983) in reaction to these movements. Empirical studies showed that social movements often emerge from preexisting networks, and that broad actions and campaigns require systematic organization. Further, proponents of the resource mobilization approach pointed out that social movements generally rely on a complex "social movement industry," a network of cooperating, competing, and antagonistic social movement organizations (SMOs) (Zald and McCarthy 1980).

Such networks rarely have been analyzed, and the preconditions, forms, and problems of interorganizational relations have been neglected.

This article is intended to help to fill this gap.[1] After pointing out some characteristics and contextual conditions of the present environmental movements with special reference to the Federal Republic of Germany and France, the analysis focuses on the organizational elements and the interorganizational relations of social movement industries in these countries.

ENVIRONMENTAL MOVEMENTS AND THEIR CONTEXT

Contemporary environmental movements are embedded in a relatively long-lasting protest cycle and, with respect to their social environment, to a broader congeries of supporting, competing, and conflicting movements. Such a complex, seen in a synchronic perspective, is termed a social movement sector by proponents of the resource mobilization approach (see McCarthy and Zald 1977; Garner and Zald 1981, 1982). In Europe, this sector of social movements have been given the label "new social movements" (Klandermans 1986). Despite its vagueness, this term, as a conceptional tool, implies a qualitative distinction from "old" movements, and a common denominator among "new" movements.

Organizational Aspects of New Social Movements

Phenomenologically, the label "new social movements' refers to a broad variety of protet groups, the student movement, the new women's movement, citizen initiatives, the environmental movement, the so-called alternative movement and the new peace movement (Brand 1985). The answer to the question whether a common content or demand is represented by all these groups, however, remains ambiguous and questionable. Although this is not the place to attempt to give an adequate answer, it is important to know that "new social movements" is not just a catch-all term for the whole variety of present social movements, nor is it synonymous with "movement-sector." For instance, the term does not include countermovements and counterforces to the groups mentioned above.

Despite the disagreement about terminology and conceptionalization, there seems to be a far-reaching consensus on the organizational characteristics of these movements. Emphasis is usually placed on their loose, heterogeneous, decentralized structure (Rucht 1984), definable as a complex of "SPIN-organizations" (segmented, polycephaleous, interaction networks) (Gerlach and Hine 1970) or as "grass roots organizations" (Gundelach 1984). In addition, some observers emphasize the absence of binding decision-making systems and/or outstanding leaders.

It is important to note how new social movements deal with organizational questions. Organization is not considered to be a neutral means to an end: "The new organizational form of contemporary movements is not just 'instrumental' for their goals. It is a goal in itself" (Melucci 1984, p. 830). In its democratic forms, the organization of the movement is taken as an admittedly still restricted and preliminary state of a different and better society. Therefore, organizational questions, as a subject of constant, and generally fundamental controversies, are highly politicized (Narr 1980). Within the movements, there is a clear tendency to contrast sharply a specific notion of social movements shaped by participatory, antihierarchical and anti-institutional emotions, on the one hand, with formalized, hierarchical andoligarchic organizations, on the other.

Though the decentralized network structures of new social movements have been often emphasized, there is no clear evidence that such structures are always present. Simply because of more complete historical documentation and relatively easier access to official data, the role of hierarchic, formal organizations in earlier social movements may well be overestimated (Vester 1983) Further, there is a risk that the self-image of new social movements as grass-roots organizations can be too easily adopted by external observers.

Significance and Political Spectrum of Environmental Movements

By the end of the 1960s and the early 1970s an awareness of the destructive side-effects of technological and industrial progress developed in virtually all advanced capitalist states. After two historical waves in Europe of cultural criticism—bourgeois romanticism and utopian socialism at the beginning of the 19th century and agrarian romanticism, life reform movement, and youth movement in the first part of the 20th century—a new wave of criticism could be observed over the last decades (Mayer-Tasch 1982; Brand 1987). The environmental movement was a spin-off of this wave. Of course, this "new" movement did have roots in the past, and as it developed over time and incorporated a variety of political and ideologic tendencies, it has, to some extent, ambiguous features. Nevertheless, it is clearly related to the third wave of cultural criticism. Compared to its predecessors, this wave has a much more rational-scientific and political foundation.

Various attempts to resist serious interference with the natural environment can be distinguished. They are marked by a specific ideological background and a set of values, by a corresponding perception of problems, definition of aims, and choice of strategies and actions. For analytical purposes, I suggest a threefold typology of conservationism, enviromentalism, and ecologism.

Conservationism refers to the protection of nature for aesthetic, ethical, and/ or religious reasons. Nature, that is, particularly the rich variety of flora and fauna and the beauty of idyllic landscapes, is considered as a gift to human beings, a place for leisure, recuperation, and contemplation that should be respected in its originality and with its own "rights." The preferred methods of conservationism are aesthetic and moral education, public instruction, and support for the establishment and maintenance of nature parks.

By *environmentalism* I mean a pragmatic attitude to the preservation or improvement of the human environment in a very broad sense, focusing on the exploitation of natural resources, problems of noise, pollution of air, soil and water, healthy food, and so on. Scientific arguments, cost-benefit analyses, and the claim for quality of life are points of reference in order to convince and mobilize people. In contrast to conservationism, environmentalism recognizes the political arena as an important battleground in influencing concrete policies that may or may not guarantee a healthy and clean environment.

Ecologism goes far beond a certain range of environmental problems and their corresponding policies. This concept implies a holistic vision of a decentralized, democratic, and egalitarian society existing in harmony with nature. The range of means in order to attain such an utopian state is very broad. It includes changes on an individual level (life style), activities in small groups, public information and mobilization, pressure group politics, civil disobedience, and militant action.

Individuals, groups, and organizations within the environmental movements can be assigned more or less clearly to one of these categories. They may also represent a mixture of different elements, and they may move from one category to another. Since the beginning of the modern environmental movement, the emphasis shifted from conservationism through environmentalism to ecologism, and this marked different stages of development. But this is not to say that these tendencies simply superseded each other; rather they indicate different discourses that eclipsed and influenced each other over time.

Focusing on the environmental movement, one should not forget that considerable impulses and support came from the sciences and official political institutions. They delivered cognitive as well as material resources which proved not only to be very useful to autonomous groups often critical of the government, but which also strengthened public awareness of environmental problems. During the 1970s, the urgency and the public rise of the environmental issue stimulated a real boom in newly-established groups and organizations. Beside this, there were also traditional groups and associations for environmental protection which were newly invigorated, increased in significance or shifted in their orientation. Thereby a complex network of "old," "rejuvenated," and "new" environmental groups developed. The structure, the interaction, and the strategic pattern of such a network, however, has rarely been investigated in depth.[2]

The Structural Setting of Environmental Movements in West Germany and France

Though the horizon of problem consciousness as well as the activity radius of environmental groups may extend beyond national frontiers, it is fruitful to analyze environmental movements as national entities. National parameters (administative structure, federal law and policies, party system, stucture of mass media, political culture, and the like) are crucial to the mobilization capacities, strategies, and outcomes of social movements.

Of course, social movements are very fluid phenomena. In view of the fast rhythms of issue attention cycles and waves of mobilization, the difficulties in grasping latent, internally-directed movement activities, and the problems in separating social movements clearly from their environment, it does not make much sense to register the strength and mobilization capacity in exact figures. But if one refers to indirect indicators (such as lists of initiatives and organizations, representative polls on the willingness to participate in movement activities, the scale of mass demonstrations, documentation of environmental groups in given areas), there is little doubt that it was in West Germany, in the second half of the 1970s, that one of the most powerful and the most active environmental movements developed. In contrast, the environmental movement in France remained relatively weak.

My thesis is that these differences do not primarily stem from internal factors such as the choice of strategies or the quality of leadership but from an external structural setting which, at least in the short- or medium-term, is imposed on the respective movements. Here I refer to three sets of variables:

- the objective level of strains on the environment
- the political opportunity structure (for this concept, see Tarrow 1983; for an application in a comparative study, see Kitschelt 1985) that helps or hinders the movement in placing its issues on the political agenda, in forming alliances with political forces, and in influencing concrete policies

- sociocultural conditions, in particular common values and traditional social forces to which the movement can appeal and which, so to speak, provide a more or less receptive sounding-board for the movement's claims, cultural codes, and modes of action which may reach far beyond the realm of politics.

With regard to the first criterium, Germany evidently suffers from severe ecological problems. In particular, there exists a high degree of industrialization, an intensive exploitation of natural resources and lands, and an unusually high population density (about 240 inhabitants per km^2; France: about 100). Due to the geographic distribution of the population, industry, and infrastructure, Germany has at its disposal very few natural reservations and recreation areas, and these only on a small scale. Even if the objective degree of overdevelopment, regional lack of space, traffic noise, air, water, and soil pollution is high, these conditions per se are not sufficient to explain the strength of the German environmental movement.

Secondly, in Germany there is a relatively favorable political opportunity structure. This is true, among other things, for access to the political system. Compared to France, the German system offers quite a range of leverage points and opportunities for expressing social dissent and political protest. Favorable factors are, for instance, the federalist structure, the possibility of formal participation in political procedures and of litigation in Administrative Courts cases (Nelkin and Pollak 1982), the openness towards participatory democracy and political reforms which existed at least in the first years of the social-liberal coalition, and the balance of power between conservative and progressive forces that allowed third parties a relatively important position. In addition, the social and political elites were mostly divided over the issues that concerned the protest movements. In this way, opposing groups had the chance to form alliances with sections of the elites and to build bridgeheads within the political institutions. In France, on the other hand, the chances of participation, coalition building, mobilization, and resistance are much more limited. Restrictive effects are due to closed systems of recruiting political and administrative elites, the centralized state structures, the absence of administrative courts, the repressive use of police forces against disruptive actions, the existence of left-wing parties which are largely able to absorb critical issues and groups, and finally, the dominant consensus on modernization, industrialization, and economic growth policies.

Thirdly, the environmental movement in West Germany is favored by sociocultural conditions. Among these are the existence of a broad and active movement sector (Roth 1985; Rucht 1985) with an infrastructure spanning the various groups and organizations, the widespread awareness of the negative effects of the "productivist" model of progress, the traditionally firmly entrenched romantic view of nature (Bergmann 1970; Linse 1986) and—in connection with this—the strength of conventional environmental protection organizations.

Origins and Dynamics

The beginnings of the environmental and ecology movement in West Germany are closely linked to the activities of the autonomous *citizen initiatives.* These groups emerged in the late 1960s, aiming at preventing or abolishing specific projects in areas of grave concern in the reproductive sphere (i.e., housing, urban traffic, social services). Moreover, they struggled for more influence on political and adminstrative decisions. At first these groups perceived environmental issues as contingent and mainly local problems. As a consequence, groups and activities were isolated from each other. Only in the second phase a closer cooperation, and regional and national networks developed. Protests got more fundamental. Activities became directed against centralized "big technology," technocratic and bureaucratic decision-making procedures, and the side effects of progress. From 1976 on, in a third phase, massive countermobilization of the "modernization cartel," sophisticated governmental strategies in dealing with protest groups, and conflicts within the movement about questions of organization and the use of violence, led to a search for alternatives for the mostly defensive forms of protest used at the time. Depending on previous experiences and ideological orientation, preference was given to the extension of legal participation, the parliamentarization of protest, actions of civil disobedience, or the realization of a "new life style" or "soft" paths of scientific and technical development.

Ironically, the breadth and the relative success of the environmental movement caused the movement's decline from 1980 onwards. The already existing centrifugal tendencies were intensified by the broad diffusion of the environmental debate, its considerable, though often purely rhetorical resonance in all political camps, and, finally, the concentration of political energies on concrete policies and problem solving attempts. This trend could not be halted in the end by the rise of the Green Party. Thus we have today the picture of a largely fragmented environmental movement whose subunits, focused on specific themes and organizational patterns, seem to be drifting apart (Brand, Büsser, and Rucht 1986).

In *France,* there was no comparable reservoir of citizen action groups. However, the short but violent revolt of May 1968 gave a vital impetus to the relatively early emergence of the environmental movement. Here too, comparably to West Germany, activities in the first phase were mainly individual protests directed at specific environmental problems or at large industrial projects.

Together with the emerging ecological debate (on "limits of growth," effects of urbanization, economic exploitation, and ecological destructions in the third world) these protests very soon became generalized and embedded in the context of a global critique of society (Vadrot 1978; Journes 1979). In a second phase, significantly earlier than in Germany, there blossomed a network of ecological groups, partly connected to the regional movements. Relatively early compared to Germany, ecological journals were started (*La gueule ouverte* in 1972; *Le sauvage* in 1973). From 1974 onwards, the antinuclear protests gained momentum (Garraud 1979). The small but innovative left-wing party, PSU (Parti Socialiste Unitaire), eagerly seized these initiatives. Somewhat later— particularly in reaction to the official policy of "tout nucléaire" (nothing but nuclear energy)—there followed cautious and restricted concessions on the part of the socialist labor union (CFDT) and the socialist party towards the ecologists (Nicolon and Carrieu 1979). But most noteworthy is the fact that the ecological groups, because of their poor chances of extraparliamentary intervention, pressed for electoral participation as early as 1973-1974.

Despite the modest success of the ecological presidential candidate, Réné Dumont, in 1974 and in some cases spectacular results of the ecological lists in the communal elections in 1977 (Samuel 1978, p. 138 ff.), the impact of the left-right-polarization proved to be stronger. The vexed question, if and how closely the environmental movement should ally with the parties of the left, caused rifts which have not been bridged to this day. Also disagreement between various ideological factions as well as mistrust of local and regional groups of all attempts to form centralized organizations, foiled any unified action by the ecologists (Nullmeier and Schulz 1983).

Other factors contributed to the paralysis of the movement, that is, the deep demoralization caused by the violent repression of a mass demonstration in 1977 against the fast breeder in Creys-Malville (Touraine et al. 1983), its partial integration and pacification induced by the left-wing opposition and later Mitterand government (Fagnani and Moatti 1982), and finally, the economic and distributional conflicts that overshadowed the antinuclear debate. Under these circumstances, the birth of the Green Party, which came about in 1984 after a long period in labor, could not prevent the movement's decline. At any rate, on the eve of the European election in 1984, the party "Les verts" came under pressure through the formation of a second ecological group ("Entente radicale écologiste"). In the meanwhile "Les vertes" have consolidated themselves somewhat. Nonetheless, they remained on the fringe of the political arena. From a general perspective, it is evident that the utopias of a "soft" ecological society have faded away. They are being increasingly replaced by pragmatic intervention, directed at concrete policies and instruments.

ORGANIZATIONS AND INTERORGANIZATIONAL RELATIONS

Proponents of the resource mobilization approach tend to overlook the fact that social movements cannot be reduced to their movement organizations. Nevertheless, the focus on social industries has a certain legitimacy. Social movement industries are, so to speak, the skeleton formed by the various stable components; they hold the movement together and allow for coordination between groups, instruments and tactics. Both central and peripheral parts, strong and weak links can be distinguished within this skeleton. However, vitality and power is more likely to depend on physiological processes than on the anatomy of the movement.

The German Environmental Industry

Organizational Components

The "backbone" of the West German environmental movement is basically formed by those organizations which rely conceptually on environmentalism and ecologism. Outstanding national organizations corresponding to these orientations are the Bund für Umwelt- und Naturschutz Deutschland (German Alliance for Environment and Nature Conservation), Greenpeace, "Die Grünen" (Green Party), the Bundesverband Bürgerinitiativen Umweltschutz (Federal League of Citizen Initiatives for Environmental Protection), the Öko-Institut (Institute for Applied Ecology), and the mostly informally-structured antinuclear groups. The conservationist sector is not a driving force within the environmental movement. However, conservationism takes up a supporting role. Here it is worth mentioning organizations like the Deutscher Bund für Vogelschutz (German Association for Bird Protection), World Wildlife Fund/ Deutschland, and the Schutzgemeinschaft Deutscher Wald (Alliance for the Conservation of German Forests). A somewhat more specific role has been adopted by the Deutscher Naturschutzring (German Association for the Protection of Nature) which can be positioned between the conservationist and environmentalist sectors.

Moreover, there exists a whole host of relatively small organizations and networks which are centered on conservationism, environmentalism, and ecologism, respectively (Rucht 1987). Finally, a large group of organizations is only secondarily concerned with environmental issues (associations against cruelty to animals, for consumer interest, for native culture, for alpinism, and so on, on the one hand, and protest groups of the women's movement, the alternative movement, the peace movement, and the like, on the other). Because of the considerable number of their adherents and their resources, these organizations are potentially significant allies for the "primary" environmental organizations.

Only the most important of the primary organizations are briefly described here.

The *Deutsche Bund für Vogelschutz* (DBV, the German Association for Bird Protection), founded in 1899, is one of the oldest conservation associations in Germany. Despite its narrow range of interests, the organization relies on an extensive membership and a relatively large staff of professionals (see the corresponding tables in the appendix). The DBV has a federal structure with subdivisions at the state and district level including about 1,000 local chapters. In addition to the DBV, there is an independent association for the protection of birds in Bavaria. Although these associations originally had a conventional and conservative orientation, in the last few years—whilst maintaining their limited range of interests—they have tended towards a broader perception of environmental problems and their causes, and a more aggressive pursuit of their aims.

The *World Wildlife Fund* (WWF) is a renowned foundation with a global radius of action. Its basic aim is to save species of animals from extinction. After a sluggish consolidation phase, the German section of the WWF, founded in 1961, appointed a highly professional management. Since then, the WWF has been able to attain a significant expansion in support, money, and staff. The securing of a large number of sponsors, including industrial enterprises, has ensured that the WWF activities remain completely within the scope of a constructive and nonpolitical effort to conserve nature. Thus it seeks to avoid disputes with political demonstrations. Instead of engaging in conflict, the WWF usually prefers financial means (i.e., the acquisition of land in order to establish nature reserves).

The *Schutzgemeinschaft Deutscher Wald* (SGW, the Alliance for the Conservation of German Forests) was established in 1947 in order to prevent the destruction of large forests by the allied occupation powers. Later the focus of concern shifted to the conservation and the protection of forests in the face of the boom in building and road construction as well as the damage caused by hunters and tourists. Like the DBV, the SGW is a national federation, subdivided into state, district, and local chapters. Closely connected, but formally independent is the Deutsche Waldjugend (German Youth for Forests). Membership has been at a standstill for many years. At least at the management level, the SGW presents itself as a nonpolitical, moderate association of dignitaries. Because of its financial dependence on state agencies and its institutional integration into regional planning authorities, the SGW is geared to cooperation with the state. Even the violent debate on "Waldsterben" (the dying forests) has not really changed the cumbersome character of the association.

In terms of numbers, the *Deutscher Naturschutzring* (DNR, the German Association for Protection of Nature) is probably the world's largest national organization on environmental issues. It is an umbrella organization including

94 associations with a total of 3.3 million individual members. However, these figures do not reflect the organization's real impact. The organizations associated with the DNR have very different orientations, and they partly pursue contradictory interests and concerns (e.g., prevention of cruelty to animals versus hunting). Thus the DNR is largely incapable of taking a determined stand, to say nothing of implementing any form of aggressive action. Whereas, in the past, the chronic conflict between the "defenders" and "users" of nature within the DNR was regularily resolved in favor of the latter group, recently, the relative weight of these two factions has changed as a consequence of new statutes. In relation to the concerns and aims of the DNR, the growing importance of environmentalism and ecology is resulting in a programmatic reform reflecting a shift from conservationism to environmentalism.

In 1975, partly as a reaction to the impotence of the DNR, the *Bund für Umwelt- und Naturschutz Deutschland* (BUND, the German Alliance for Environment and Nature Conservation) was founded, aiming at the establishment of an environmental organization with a broad scope, unifying the various issues and covering the whole area of West Germany, and intending to play a powerful role in the political arena. Even though the BUND was a member of the DNR from the beginning, it is, in fact, a competitor. Because of its homogeneous organizational and membership structure and its skillful and singleminded leadership, the BUND has meanwhile attained a strong position relative to other environmental organizations. Its programmatic and organizational model as well as it strongest component has been the Bund Naturschutz in Bayern (League of Nature Conservation in Bavaria), which has a long tradition and is powerful in terms of both membership and financial resources.

The German section of *Greenpeace* was not founded until 1980, but because of its spectacular activities calculated in terms of mass media resonance, the organization quickly became well-known. The German section has at its disposal considerable financial resources and a powerful apparatus. The organization is extremely centralized. Local chapters remain totally dependent on the goodwill and the decisionmaking of a small, exclusive leadership group at the national and international level. They have virtually no chance to play an initiating role. Criticism of this structure led to a significant split-off in 1981, leading to a new organization known as "Robin Wood."

Within the sector of ecologism, the *Bundesverband Bürgerinitiativen Umweltschutz* (BBU, the Federal League of Citizen Initiatives for Environmental Protection) is one of the oldest and, at certain phases of its history, one of the most important organizations. It was founded in 1972. Together with the expanding citizen initiatives and the antinuclear movement, the League experienced a rapid rise. With respect to its structure and program, the BBU is contradictory: On the one hand, it claims to be a radical grass roots organization of the ecology movement, and, on the other, the BBU seeks to operate an efficient lobby, oriented and adapted to the mechanisms of political administration. A characteristic of the BBU is the fact that instead of individual membership there is only a group membership. In the period following the mid-1970s, the organization claimed to represent—however without offering any proof—about 1,000 groups with 300,000 adherents. In the early 1980s, however, it entered a state of crisis (see below). Currently the BBU is engaged in a process of basic restructuring, trying to increase the number of its membership groups which have dwindled during the crisis to a total of 300.

Antinuclear groups were the driving force and the focus of interest of the ecology movement of the 1970s. Some belonged to the BBU, but a much greater number did not, and often had reservations about the established enviromental associations. These autonomous groups combined resistance to the civil use of nuclear power with fundamental opposition to the technocratic and bureaucratic control of power. The anti-institutional affect of those groups was reflected in their deliberate maintenance of informal, decentralized structures of organization and decisionmaking. Because such an organization is hard to delimit, and has a strongly varying level of mobilization, it is difficult to present any quantitative data. During the golden age of the antinuclear mobilization (1977-1981), it is estimated that more than 1,000 such groups existed in West Germany. Later their number declined rapidly—a tendency which was reinforced by the absorbtion capacity of the rising peace movement. Not until the conflict over the nuclear reprocessing plant under construction near the Bavarian town of Wackersdorf and with the Tschernobyl disaster could a reactivation of old as well as a mushrooming of new antinuclear initiatives (the so-called "becquerel-movement") be observed.

Procedural conflicts, in which the environmental groups and particularly the antinuclearists were engaged, demonstrated the urgency of solid scientific and juridical support. In reaction to this need, the *Öko-Institut* ("Institute for Applied Ecology") was founded in Freiburg in 1977. It is associated with the Arbeitsgemeinschaft ökologischer Forschungsinsitute (AGÖF, the "Working Group of Ecological Institutes"). Financially, the Institute relies mainly on the fees of about 4,400 individual members, on donations, and on payment for the research studies it undertakes. Under the auspices of the Institute, studies of energy scenarios and risk situations were carried out which were the subject of intensive discussion. Of course, their results generally differed greatly from those preferred by government and industrial enterprises.

During the last few years, the national party *Die Grünen* ("The Greens")— nolens, volens—has taken up positions on a broad range of themes and concerns extending far beyond ecological issues. But because of its roots, its ecological bias and its strategic position within the environmental movement, the party cannot be ignored. Even though its organizational forms and procedures for generating positions and making decisions are still shaped by the claims of grass-roots democracy, one cannot deny the party's tendency to adapt more and more to the structures of its conventional competitors. Owing to the reimbursement of electoral campaign expenses, regulated by federal law, combined with the facilities and resources available to parliamentary parties and the monetary contributions of a substantial percentage of the wages of members of parliament, the Greens have considerable financial resources and staff at their disposal. In this respect, they put the resources of all other environmental organizations in the shade. Further, if one takes into account the publicity machinery of the Greens and the chances of impact which accompany political mandates and offices, the key role of the Greens, within the German environmental movement, becomes evident.

Taking an overall view of the above mentioned organizations the following observations can be made:

- The organizations of the West German environmental movement represent a great variety of forms. These extend from patterns of conventional interest associations and foundations through unconventional associations based on autonomous membership groups and informal networks with specific interests, to an "alternative" party which, at least up till now, is clearly distinct from the established parties.
- There are no uniform and definite correlations between particular issues and structures. However, organizations which are located in the ecologist sector—with the exception of the Green party—are likely to have semiformal or informal structures.
- The resources of the organizations mentioned above vary to a high degree both in scale (see the Appendix) and type. Informal, autonomous groups lack financial means and professional staff to a great extent, but may have, at their disposal, considerable capacity for mobilizing mass rallies and other protest actions. With regard to the number of members, activists, finances, and staff, the nationwide organizations of conservationism and environmentalism can be located in the midfield. The largest financial and personnel pools can be found in organizations like WWF, Greenpeace, Bund Naturschutz in Bayern and, above all, the Green Party. Political power, however, cannot be measured directly by such criteria. While the DNR, with its enormous nominal membership, is not only largely unknown but also virtually incapable of acting in the political arena for structural reasons, financially less well-off organizations such as the BBU or the network of independent antinuclear groups may mobilize masses of people and thus influence public opinion. Further, one must take into account the extent to which financial resources stem from public administration sources. These resources however are reserved for specific tasks, leaving them virtualy outside the environmental organizations' control.

• The catalogue of aims and the repertoire of actions of environmental organizations is broadly diversified. It includes scientific expertise, purchase and management of nature parks, litigation, participation in administrative and parliamentary procedures, lobbying, party politics and electoral campaigns, the informing and agitation of the public, and the mobilization of protest actions and physical resistance. Even though environmental organizations may be specialized with respect to one of these forms, usually they rely on several kinds of action. As a rule, it holds true that organizations in the conservationist and environmentalist sector tend to concentrate on activities considered to be more conventional (e.g., purchase and management of nature reserves, lobbyism, participation in formal procedures). In contrast, organizations within the ecologist sector are likely to undertake more unconventional activities such as mass protests and civil disobedience.

Networks and Interorganizational Relations

The organizations referred to above are interlinked in many ways, for example, informal contacts, alliances, or institutionalized memberships. The global network formed by all these links, however, has no homogeneous structure, but is subdivided into several sectors which are only loosely connected to each other. Each of these sectors can be seen as a distinct network, characterized by a high level of interaction, particular political and ideological orientations, and specific structural features.

The geographical range of these networks, but not of all their single components, extends from the local to the international level. But in terms of everyday practice, primary is placed in the regional and national spheres.

All the large organizations maintain international relations. They are members of international leagues (e.g., the European Environmental Bureau), and some of them also participate in international campaigns, conferences, and resolutions.[3]

Beside these networks, stabilized and/or shaped by formal organizations, and partly in a close relation to them, there are other networks composed of small, locally-based, and mostly informally-structured face-to-face groups. The coherence of these networks is due to a concrete concern (e.g., a national-working group dealing with questions of nuclear waste management and nuclear reprocessing, parent groups concerned about a children's disease caused by air-pollution), a particular activity or service (e.g., the League of Ecological Institutes), or a multi-issue alliance whose common denominator may be the quality of life in a given region (e.g., Rhein-Ruhr campaign against the destruction of the human environment). These networks are likely to operate on a regional or national level. In part, they have intensive contacts with foreign partners. Finally, there exist cross-frontier alliances

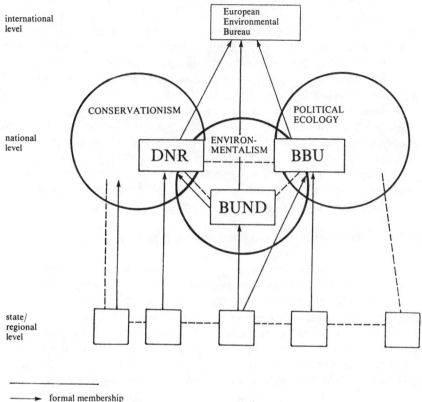

Figure 1. Networks of the Environmental Movement Industry
in West Germany

(Internationale Rheinaktion, Badisch—Elsässische Bürgerinitiativen, Internationale Arbeitsgemeinschaft gegen das Nuklearzentrum Cattenom, Aktionsgemeinschaft Nordsee, and the like) and far-reaching informal networks like Ecoropa.[4]

In total, the organizations and networks of the environmental movement represent a complex, geographically-staggered structure composed of various overlapping sectors. These sectors differ considerably in their organizational structure (formal/informal), scope (local/international), interests (content and degree of specialization), resources (quality and quantity), and preferred modes of action (conventional/unconventional).

A brief, simplified sketch, reduced to a few important protagonists, will be presented in order to give an idea of the complexity of this network structure.

Starting from the basic political and ideological patterns, the framework of the West German environmental movement can be outlineu as a combination of three distinct networks. The cores of those networks are represented by conservationist, environmentalist, and ecologist organizations, respectively. The (DNR) can be categorized within the intersection of the two first segments, the (BBU) within the intersection formed by the latter two. In the center of environmentalism is BUND.

Whereas the international contacts of the small ecological organizations are likely to be informal and sporadic, the three large national environmental organizations—BBU, BUND, and DNR—maintain relatively stable and institutionalized international contacts. In addition, the three networks have a very solid basis at the local and regional levels. Here we sometimes find direct and close links between different components, which do not necessarily exist in this form (or ever at all) on a national level.

Patterns and Problems of Interorganizational Relations

With reference to the status and quality of interorganizational relations, one can discern for analytic purposes four basic patterns. These are neutrality, cooperation, competition, and conflict. On the empirical level, however, a mixture or a succession of these patterns can usually be found.

Neutrality rarely stems from a principal ignorance or apathy per se but is more likely to arise from a need for organizational self-protection, in the face of the arduous and often desperate processes of coordination and bargaining. One of the rare examples of such structural indifference towards other organizations is that of the Weltbund zum Schutze des Lebens (World League for Protection of Life). This association has a right-wing background, including some racist tendencies. Since the late 1970s, it has completely retired from the public sphere.

In contrast, the broad spectrum of forms and fields of interorganizational coordination and *cooperation* proves to be essential for the environmental movement as a whole. It includes reciprocal information, joint press conferences and resolutions, ad hoc actions, and longer-lasting alliances. The latter can presumably only be established on the basis of certain prerequisites for example, (a) nonconflictive public information campaigns; (b) highly dramatic situations and grievances in combination with the absence of a well-defined cause and/or enemy (e.g., the "Alliance Against the Dying Forests"); (c) regional conflicts having a symbolic function for the whole environmental movement and suited to popular and low-risk forms of resistance (e.g., public referenda; and (d) evident abuse of power or strategical errors of political administrations in implementing policies, large-scale projects, and the like.

Forms of intensive cooperation, based on identical or similar interests and ending with a relatively harmonious division of labor, are not typical. For self-evident reasons, it's rare that one environmental organization gives financial aid to another (as for instance, in the 1978 case in which the WWF contributed funds enabling Greenpeace to buy a trawler). Usually we observe more or less manifest interrelations of competition and conflict.

In this context, the term *competition* refers to a zero-sum-game where structurally-comparable participants (having equal or similar means and ends0 struggle for the same pool or resources and thus for a position better than that of the competitors. This is the case, for instance, with the two great national associations DNR and BUND: Both try to represent the whole variety of environmentalist issues on the national level.

By *conflict,* I mean the situation where actors, despite their common interest, oppose each other because they disagree about preferred means and/or ends. In the environmental movement, tensions related to diverging ideological orientations and corresponding preferences for specific actions and strategies are virtually unavoidable. The gap between the nonpolitical conservationists, relying on argumentative means and on cooperation with established forces on the one hand, and the conflict-oriented political ecologists, tending to disruptive actions, on the other, is particularly wide. Whilst the former formulate a moderately-presented, constructive critique of particular failures of environmental policies, the latter aim at fundamental changes in society. The more dramatic and catastrophic the perception of ecological problems, the more radical and impatient are the claims. Differences between the opposite tendencies cannot be simply eliminated, and thus are leading to a mutual neutralization of the two wings. We can thus assume that the networks crystallizing the two poles are only indirectly linked together by the intermediate position of a third network, that of the environmentalists.

Closely connected to political and ideological gaps are tensions based on different organizational preferences. Organizations of the ecologist sector tend to keep their distance from the well-established alliances of conservationism because they reject hierarchical and bureaucratic structures that are often to be found in the conservationist organizations. The latter, in their turn, tend to criticize informal ecological groups because of a lack of clear-cut responsibilities and systematic internal control. Conflicts that focus on organizational structure were particularly intensive with respect to, and within, Greenpeace. The critique articulated by a minority of the national leadership and by local activists led to a severe controversy which ended with a split-off. This gave impetus to the foundation of a new organization in 1982, named Robin Wood. It has a strong commitment to political ecology and to grass roots democracy, underlining its structural differences to Greenpeace. Robin Wood has hitherto remained rather small. Basically, it relies on the same forms of action as Greenpeace; however, its main concern is the problem of air pollution. At first, both organizations treated each other with hostility. But, in the meantime, their relationship seems to have normalized.

Hardly visible, but nonetheless crucial for the mutual relations of organizations and networks is the competition over the pool of resources (sympathizers, adherents, members, donations, public subsidies), access to administrative and political procedures, and public attention. It is true that some organizations have a firm hold on specific market shares. Owing to their predetermined ideological orientations and the choice of related strategies and actions, they can count on a stable core of adherents. However, the three sectors mentioned above constitute the scene for an ongoing fight over resources, alliances, programs, and modes of action. Organizations located in one of these sectors typically imply elements diverging from each other. These organizations are subjected to contradictory requests and offers, risking being torn to pieces. An example of such a situtation is the DNR. Up to the early 1970s, it was unchallenged as the umbrella organization of the existing nature conservation associations. But with its conservative background, and its hesitating policy of small steps, the organization fell behind the newly-emerged groups of environmentalism and ecologism. The BBU, however, was no direct rival to the DNR, because, from its very beginning, its activities were outside the realm of conservationism. The BBU considered itself to be a collection of autonomous, politicized citizen groups. The DNR was neither willing nor could represent these groups. Another part of the conservationist associations, however, was strongly influenced by the fierce debate on the state of environment and "the limits of growth." These organizations attained a new quality resulting in more outspoken requests, more aggressive actions, and a receptiveness to ecological orientations, without their radicality. Because these associations were traditionally members of the DNR but were neutralized by organizations with incompatible interests (i.e., hunters and fishermen) or by organizations with explicitly nonpolitical positions (i.e., folk culture associations), they tried to form an independent national alliance. As a result, the BUND was established on the initiative of some officials. The BUND became, and remains, a member of the DNR. Moreover, it is represented on the DNR's executive board. However, tension continues between both organizations. The BUND criticizes the "policy of the least common denominator" of the DNR, and, from time to time, it threatens to withdraw from the umbrella organization. This threat carries weight, because within the space of only a few years the BUND has become very important. It is relatively homogeneous and relies upon a strong leadership able to lend the association a clear profile respected by its allies as well as by its enemies. Thus the BUND succeeded in conserving its independence without becoming isolated from the sectors of conservationist and ecologist organizations.

Analogous to the DNR, the BBU, situated within the second significant sector, became more and more weakened by internal tensions and frictions. On issues of organization (grass-roots structure versus efficient and strong leadership), of relations to potential alliances (for example the Greens, Social-

Democrats, autonomous antinuclear movement), of priorities of activity (mass mobilization, civil disobedience, and/or lobbyism), the BBU was deeply split. But in contrast to the DNR, cleavages within the BBU are not a consequence of predefined interests and organizationally clearly separated subunits. The conflicts are rather the result of unsolved programmatic and structural ambivalences. One single organization is expected to integrate a whole range of opposites: a pragmatic, constructive policy and fundamental opposition, a decentralized structure with totally independent membership groups and a powerful leadership, disruptive forms of mass mobilization and lobbyism, close ties to parties that are sensitive to ecological issues (Greens and sections of the Social-Democrats), and an alliance with radical autonomous groups. No wonder such a concept failed. The internal contradictions led to a grave crisis in 1982-1983 resulting in the collective withdrawal of a succession of member groups, the dissolution of employment contracts and other agreements, and an almost complete replacement of the leadership.

By and large, the competitive and conflictual relations between and within the environmental organizations did not so much paralyze the whole movement as, in a fruitful and creative manner, keep it in a state of suspense. Not only the mediating sector of environmentalism but also the organizations within its zones overlapping with the conservationist and the ecologist sectors form important bridges and transmission areas to prevent the movement from falling apart. The results of this constellation are broad campaigns which are widely supported, though usually with the exclusion of the most extreme factions.

The French Environmental Movement Industry

During the first half of the 1970s, the French environmental movement was, if not in its range, then at least in its perception of problems and its vitality, more advanced than its West German counterpart. At any rate, the French environmental movement, at its peak, was estimated to include about 15,000 groups with more than two million adherents (Vallet 1978, p. 201). Despite a few victories (e.g., the prevention of a great tourist project in the Vanoise/ Alps, of a military training camp in the Larsac/Southern plateaus, and a nuclear power station in Plogoff/Bretagne), and some impressive electoral results, the movement floundered, in particular because of both the attractiveness and the intransigence of the organized Left. Above all, cherished expectations as to the dynamic power of the antinuclear opposition (Touraine et al. 1983; Kiersch and Von Oppeln 1983) proved to be groundless. This movement never attained weight, either quantitatively or qualitatively, comparable to that found in West Germany. Given such noticeable differences in France, the "model" of the West German Green Party could not be imitated on the parliamentary level either.

Organizational Components

The distinctions drawn between conservationism, environmentalism, and ecologism is also applicable to the French situation. Moreover, there are structural parallels, for example, between associations and groups concerned with protecting birds, with establishing and maintaining conservation areas, with avoiding or reducing specific environmental problems (pollution of food, noise, and so on), or controlling the effects of high-risk technologies. This is still more true for the branches of Greenpeace and the WWF in both countries. In contrast, there are considerable differences between the green parties in both countries.

A survey of the present situation of the most influential environmental organizations is presented by Vadrot (1986). Some basic data on selected organizations are offered in the Appendix B. However, it is worthwhile to introduce two associations on the grounds of their outstanding political and strategic position.

The *Fédération Francaise des Societés de Protection de la Nature* (FFSPN, French Federation of Associations for the Conservation of Nature), founded in 1968, is the successor of a venerable umbrella organization dating back to the 19th century. The FFSPN became the most wide-ranging umbrella organization of conservationist and environmentalist organizations in France. In the beginning of the 1980s, the association's nominal membership expanded considerably (1979: 500,000; 1985: 850,000). At present, the FFSPN consists of 1,100 associations and groups located on a national, regional, and/or local level. But one should not forget that the FFSPN is not a homogeneous corpus with standardized subdivisions. In particular, the main regional associations (i.e., in Alsace, Bretagne, South-West and Rhône-Alpes) each have their own tradition and structure. Originally, the FFSPN could be placed within the conservationist sector. In the last few years, however, the organization has gradually moved towards the environmentalist position, including more issues, and deliberately entering the realm of politics. The FFSPN enjoys a high reputation with respect to the state administration. This is reflected by the flow of public subsidies (about one-quarter of the annual budget—more than a third of all direct subsidies which the Environment Office spent on environmental associations). It is true that the FFSPN has only a quarter of the nominal membership of the West German DNR, but, in contrast to its German counterpart, it scarcely suffers from contradictory interests and politico-ideological positions.

Les Amis de la terre (AT, Friends of the Earth) is probably the first as well as the most important French organization in the ecologist sector. Formally, it is a national branch of the international association Friends of the Earth (see Lowe and Goyder 1983, p. 124ff.). In reality, it has an almost complete organizational and political autonomy. The number of membership groups of

AT has levelled off since 1977 at about 100; the number of activists has clearly decreased. The organization is mainly based on fairly informally-structured and loosely-linked local groups. Not until November 1977 did these groups realize a structure on a national level (the so-called "reseau"): a bureau in Paris. This was expected to be a mere coordination point but it has, since, taken on an important role. Prominent and influential ecologists (such as Pierre Samuel, Réné Dumont, Brice Lalonde, Yves Lenoir, Alain Hervé, André Gorz) were, or still are, closely connected with AT. Thus the organization had an impact that exceeded its modest material resources. From very early on, AT agitated against the civil use of nuclear energy and thereby became an important component of the French antinuclear energy movement. Certainly it is not part of the extreme wing of political ecologism.

The following points could be made regarding the most important French environmental organizations:

- Although the picture drawn above clearly shows some fundamental restrictions for the French environmental movement, the decline of the movement since the late 1970s did not imply its disappearance.
- The resources of French environmental movement organizations (see Appendix B) are relatively poor compared to those of West Germany. However, at least the conservationist and environmentalist organizations show considerable growth rates during the last years. At present, Greenpeace France has, at best, one-sixth of the annual budget of Greenpeace in West Germany. The pool of professionals of Les Verts is about one-hundredth of the German Die Grünen. Also, if one compares AT and the BBU, or the national associations for the protection of birds, a better financial basis and a larger number of members can be observed on the German side. The opposite is true if one compares the traditional umbrella associations on a national level. The FFSPN has more money and a larger staff than the DNR. The relatively high budget of the Société Nationale pour la Protection de la Nature, an organization rich in tradition, is primarily due to public subsidies that are destined for the maintenance of national parks and other nature reserves. Thus the money cannot be used for public mobilization. If one takes into account the considerable resources of the BUND, which has no equivalent in France, there is still more reason to underline the fact that the German environmental organizations, at least at the national level, do have more resources.
- Similarly to their German counterparts, the French environmental organizations do not show any significant correlation between ideological position and organizational structure. On the basis of my own impressions and investigations, I conclude that some ecologist organizations (Les Verts, AT) and Greenpeace France are less formalized

and hierarchized than analogous organizations in West Germany (Die Grünen, BBU, Greenpeace Deutschland). The reason for this situation is not only to be found in differences of organizational size. Presumably it is the outspoken anticentralistic attitude characterizing French ecologism (Trilling 1981) which, until now, has blocked the formation of the strong apparatus assumed to imply a centralistic tendency. As a consequence, Greenpeace France, because of its lower degree of centralization, succeeded in avoiding the massive internal criticism and significant split-offs which seemed inevitable for its German partner organization.

● With the exception of Greenpeace, all organizations in the sector of conservationism and environmentalism remain within the spectrum of conventional political activities whereas organizations of the ecologist sector tend to adopt forms of mass mobilization and disruptive techniques of political opposition and civil disobedience. Even though there is some acceptance of this kind of aggressive action by environmental organizations in France, it does not seem to occur as often as in Germany, and when it does, it is often linked to regionalist protests. The reasons for these national differences may be the low response by the French public to the form and content of offensive ecological protest, and a lower level of tolerance towards civil disobedience in general.

Networks and Interorganizational Relations

In contrast to Germany, the French environmental movement is composed only of two great networks which, in addition, are not closely interconnected. Environmentalism in France could not establish itself in terms of a broad sector with a particular profile and a relatively independent organizational basis. It rather tended to be an enlargement of conservationism.

The uncontestable core of the first network is the FFSPN.[5] This umbrella association, which arose from a conservationist position, is much more homogeneous, but also more flexible, than the DNR. Thus it could be receptive to the environmentalist tendencies, integrating these organizations without suffering from massive internal friction or splits between conservationism and environmentalism.

The network of French ecologist organizations is not only much smaller but also does not demonstrate a centripedal force analogous to that of the FFSPN. Within the ecologist sector, two tendencies, albeit without a clear-cut profile, can be distinguished. The one is formed by "autonomous" and "libertarian" groups which aim at a radical concept of "autogestion" (self-government). Partly they keep distance from party politics, and partly they support minor parties (Parti Socialiste Unieé, Les Verts, and the like). The other wing, even though it may be somewhat dissillusioned by political parties, is still attracted to the Socialist Party, to a very small extent to the Communist Party, and by their respective trade unions. Owing to the strong anticentralist impulses of the French protest movements and to the absorption capacity of left-wing parties and unions, there was only a narrow scope for the organizational formation of ecologism. Firstly, compared to Germany, there is a greater organizational fragmentation of the ecological groups. Secondly, the ecologist sector seems to lack, in terms of pure quantity, a "critical mass" which, if focused, could promise significant political impact. Given these conditions, relatively small organizations such as AT and particular individuals could attain prominent positions within the ecologist spectrum, without being capable of forming a real center.

Because of this overall constellation, the two networks developed fairly independently from each other. It is striking that in France there is already a sharp terminological contrast involved in referring to the "mouvement de protection de la nature" (with FFSPN as a main point of reference) or to the "mouvement écologique" (without a real organizational focus). One of the very few institutionalized links which, however, in fact has no real consequence, is the membership of Les Amis de la Terre of FFSPN. Moreover, both organizations, together with eight other French associations, are members of the European Environmental Bureau. Finally, on the local level, there are some links between members of FFSPN and those of AT. But generally the French movement lacks the broad intermediate sector and corresponding intersections which can be found in the German social movement industry.

Figure 2 offers a sketch of the basic organizational relations.

Patterns and Problems of Interorganizational Relations

The marked gap between conservationists and environmentalists, on the one hand, and of ecologists, on the other, implies advantages as well as disadvantages.

One effect of the juxtaposition of two networks is that many of the internal ideological and strategic quarrels of the German environmental movement can be avoided. The two camps act independently from each other; their particular viewpoints do not allow for close and permanent cooperation. Because these networks rely both on a distinct clientele and on distinct strategies, there is less direct competition between them; the relationship is more one of indifference, or, to put it more positiely, the two sides are complementary. In particular, the FFSPN remains unchallenged in its fundaments: The tensions between its membership organizations are relatively moderate (i.e., in contrast to the DNR, the FFSPN does not include the hunters' organizations that are engaged in a permanent conflict with the environmental groups). Moreover, during the last couple of years, the FFSPN has shown a considerable growth in members and financial resources. Its reservations towards the ecologist

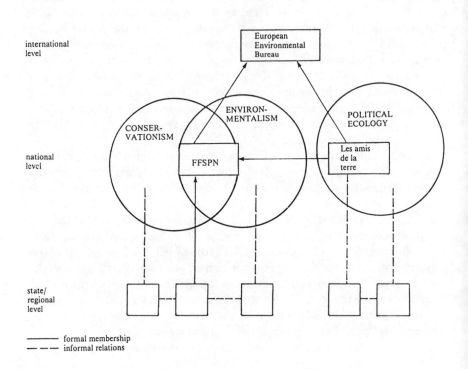

Figure 2. Networks of the Environmental Movement Industry in France

organizations are so fundamental that attempts to formulate compromises or to form alliances have not been very successful. Paradoxically, it is the distance and contradiction between these networks which reduces both the level and the opportunities to engage in conflicts.

On the other hand, there is a price to be paid for such a low-conflict juxtaposition. Firstly, the organizations in both sectors prevent each other from carrying on a fruitful discourse and of learning from each other. In addition, there is no basis for broad coalitions and effective campaigns as long as the French environmental movement reacts to many problems by speaking two languages, or by one-half remaining silent.

Of course, the opponents of the environmental movement can, both passively and actively, profit from such a latent schism. Thus the state administration rewards the seriousness and the pragmatism of conventional conservation and environmental organizations while it denigrates the ecologists as "utopians" and "sectarians," sometimes with more or less explicit approval of traditional conservationists. Under these circumstances, the French environmental movement cannot exercise strong political pressure. This explains why external observers often ask whether or not an environmental movement in France actually exists.

CONCLUSION

Even though organizations aimed at the conservation of Nature can be traced back to the last century, it was not until the early 1970s that genuine environmental movements emerged in Western Europe. These movements can be seen as a part of the "new social movements" which are assumed to rely on informal organization and loose networks. In fact, little research was done to investigate the structure and coherence of their SMOs.

The comparative analysis of the environmental "movement industries" in West Germany and France reveals common features as well as differences.

Obviously, the German environmental movement, in general, and the "movement industry," in particular, are much more significant and powerful than those in France. These differences can be explained by a threefold set of external parameters that clearly favors the German "movement industry:" the objective degree of environmental problems, the political opportunity structure, and sociopolitical conditions.

A closer look at the social "movement industries" in both countries reveals a similar spectrum of tendencies and types of organizations. With regard to politico-ideological orientations, a typology of conservationism, enviromentalism, and ecologism has been constructed and applied to the movements' organizations. These tendencies imply a certain division of labor, marked by different aims and activities. The various activities, however, are generally performed by organizations which differ widely in their historical roots, structural profiles, and pools of resources.

The French environmental movement organizations—presumably as a negative reaction to the political and administrative centralization—tend towards a loose and decentralized structure. For the most part, this is true for both the "old" and the "new" environmental organizations. The German movement, on the other hand, is characterized by the coexistence of more heterogeneous organizational forms: Organically developed traditional associations focused on specific regions and/or concerns, informal networks of loose groups and tendencies that did not exist before the 1970s, and associations with an established organization, both "old" and "new," whose structure has been adopted from the administrative apparatus. Thus the global assumption of the informal organization status and the grass-roots structure of new social movement industries has to be qualified.

In both countries, interactions at, and below, national level play a crucial role. The large (umbrella) organizations, however, do have more or less institutionalized contacts with foreign partners. Some of these associations are national sections of international organizations or associated with international institutions. Here the decisive competence may be located on the supranational level (e.g., Greenpeace), on the national level (e.g., Friends of the Earth), or reltively balanced between both (e.g., WWF). Further, there exist very loose international networks which imply virtually no formal structure.

In counting organizations and networks as parts of one movement, there is a tendency to overemphasize their common interests. In fact, the interorganizational relations of the environmental movements can be qualified in terms of indifference, cooperation, competition, and conflict. Of course, without a certain cooperation, no network and no movement could be established and maintained. However, not only a fierce competition for the same pool of resources but also severe conflicts are found. The most fundamental differences within the environmental movements are marked by the contrast between nonpolitical conservationism and political ecologism. General matters of dispute that are related, but not restricted, to this contrast are usually sparked off by the following alternatives:

- pragmatism versus radicalism
- influence on the political administration exerted by experts and lobbyists or by public media, mass mobilization, and disruptive actions
- cooperation with established parties/formation of green parties/broad alliances versus organizational and political autonomy
- formalized, hierarchical structure versus grass roots organization

One of the really striking results of this analysis is the structural difference between the two movements. In West Germany, at the national level, three influential networks can be identified. They intersect and have intensive institutional and informal links. In France, in contrast, there are only two networks. These are highly polarized, generally acting independently from each other; they have only weak ties and rarely join together for common actions and campaigns.

Within the German environmental movements, the above mentioned matters of conflict are the subject of ongoing struggles. They lead to disputes over basic orientation not only between various sectors but also between and within organizations. This is particularly true of organizations located in the overlap of two sectors. That is why two of the three main national associations, although for different reasons, are dominated by structural contradictions and conflicts, and, therefore, can hardly act as a unit. In the course of these differences, split-offs and the foundation of rival organizations have occurred. Regardless of these quarrels, in the German movement, discourse between the various tendencies and camps is still intensive. This is supported by organizational links, multiple memberships, and broad sections of overlapping areas. Because of these interacting structures, the German environmental movement is capable of forming broad alliances and carrying out joint campaigns.

As a whole, the French environmental movement lacks strong mediating links and common institutions. Thus there are two internally compact, but rather polarized camps, whose dividing lines are marked by the above mentioned alternatives. Because of their well-separated clientele and addressees, these camps are, however, rarely involved in direct competition and conflict. Moreover, French environmental movement organizations seem to be internally more homogeneous and suffer less manifest tensions. The foci of concern and the ideological orientation of the two basic networks as well as of their most influential national organizations are internally and externally unambiguous. Such a constellation may be advantageous to the stabilization of specific organizations and networks. On the other hand, it enforces "camp mentality" and organizational patriotism; it prevents the establishment of joint campaigns, and is thus particularly favorable to the opponents of the movement.

(Appendices follow)

Appendix A. Data of Selected Organizations of the Environmental Movement Industry (West Germany)

Organization	Foundation	Members (1985)	Budget in thousand DM (1985)	Professionals (1985)	Organizational Structure
Deutscher Naturschutzring (DNR—German Association for the Protection of Nature	1950	3,300,000	701	4 full-time; several part-time[a]	national umbrella organization; 94 associated leagues
Bund für Umwelt-und Naturschutz Deutschland (BUND—German Alliance for Environment and Nature Conservation)	1975	140,000	3,170	12 full-time; 4 part-time[a]	national federation with 11 state sections and chapters on the district and local level; autonomous youth organization
Bund Naturschutz in Bayern (Bavarian League for Nature Conservation)	1913	66,000	6,926	11	since 1975, state chapter of the Bund, 75 district chapters and 650 local groups
Deutscher Bund für Vogelschutz (DBV—German Association for Bird Protection)	1899	140,000	2,600	60[b]	national federation with chapters on state and district level, about 1000 local groups; independent organization in Bavaria
Schutzgemeinschaft Deutscher Wald (SGW—Alliance for the Conservation of German Forests)	1947	21,000	550	5[a]	national federation with chapters on state, district, and local level; independent youth organization
Greenpeace Deutschland	1980	40 groups; 80,000 supporters	7,458	22	centralized, hierarchical structure, dependent on the International Council

Organization	Year	Membership	Bureaus/level	Structure
World Wildlife Fund Deutschland (WWF)[d]	1961	50,000 supporters	42[c]	foundation with professional management and supporters that are isolated from each other
Bundesverband Bürgerinitiativen Umweltschutz (BBU—Federal League of Citizen Initiatives for Environmental Protection)	1972	300 groups; 300,000 supporters	3[c]	loose federation of largely independent and heterogeneously structured organizations on the state, regional, and local level
Die Grünen (The Green Party)[d]	1980	40,000	120[a]	national party with state, district, and local chapters
Öko-Institut (Institute for Applied Ecology)	1977	4,400	20[c]	association based on individual members
Robin Wood	1982	750 members; 19 action groups	459	8[c]	decentralized, egalitarian association

Notes: [a] only national bureau/level
[b] national and state bureaus, including persons doing community service and employees financed by a national labor support programme (ABM)
[c] including part-time jobs and persons doing community service and employees financed by a national labor support program (ABM)
[d] With the exception of the Green Party and the World Wildlife Fund, all the above listed organizations have the status of an officially-registered association

Source: Interviews and annual reports.

Appendix B. Data of Selected Organizations of the Environmental Movement Industry (France)

Organization	Foundation	Members (1985)	Budget in thousand FF (1985)	Professionals (1985)	Organizational Structure
Fédération française des sociétés pour la protection de la nature (FFSPN—French Federation of Associations for the Conservation of Nature)	1968	850,000	4,500	10	national umbrella organization with largely autonomous member associations
Société nationale de protection de la natue (SNPN—National Association for the Conservation of Nature)	1855	6,000	7,480	15	national association based on individual members
Ligue française pour la protection des oiseaux (LPO—French League for Bird Protection)	1912	5,000	4,476	17	national federation based on individual members
Fonds mondiale pour la nature (World Wildlife Fund, France)	1973			8	foundation
S.O.S. Environnement	1977	15,000	300	0	centrally-managed association based on individual members

Greenpeace France	1977	750 members; 25,000 supporters	3,500 members	8	association based on individual members
Les verts (The Green Party)	1984	1,500	500	1.5	national party with a strong federative structure
Les amis de la terre (Friends of the Earth)	1971	3,000 members; about 100 groups	600	3	decentralized league of local groups and individual members

Source: Interviews, annual reports, and Vadrot (1986).

NOTES

1. This article is based on (a) a secondary analysis of studies on the organization of environmental movements, (b) on documents and reports of various organizations, and (c) on interviews the author had during spring and summer 1986 with representatives and officials of 18 environmental movement organizations in West Germany and France. These investigations are part of a larger comparative project on "Modernization and Political Protest" (West Germany, France, United States).

2. Studies on environmental "movement industries" in various countries are available (Great Britain: Lowe and Goyder 1983; United States: Mitchell 1985; The Netherlands: Von Moltke and Visser 1982; West Germany: Ellwein et al. 1985; Rucht 1987). Moreover, a group directed by Russell J. Dalton (Florida State University, Tallahassee) is working on a comparative study on environmental associations in Europe (Dalton et. al. 1986).

3. Here one should mention the European Environmental Bureau (EEB) in Brussells (for its history and structure see Lowe and Goyder 1983, p. 163 ff). West German members of the EEB are the BBU, the DNR, the West German WWF, the DBV, Greenpeace Deutschland, the Öko-Institut, and Robin Wood, The DNR is a member of the International Union of Conservation of Nature (IUCN) in Geneva. It is also the national contact organization of the European Information Center for Nature Conservation of the Council of Europe, and it is associated with the United Nations Environment Programme (UNEP) in Nairobi. The Greens, through institutions such as the European Parliament, international conferences and workshops, and/or personal relations, are also in contact with foreign partners.

4. Ecoropa is an informal network based on personal contacts, supported by ecologists and adherents of the peace movements from about 15 European countries and the United States. Well-known exponents of Ecoropa were, or still are, Denis de Rougemont (the former president), Edouard Kressmann, Johan Galtung, Edward Goldsmith, Amory Lovins, Robert Jungk, Carl Amery, and Rudolf Bahro.

5. But see Leggewie (1985, p. 116) who states that the FFSPN includes "the largest part of the ecologist spectrum and is also receptive to the ecological movement which defines itself in more political terms." Here the author refers to a specific conception of ecological movement. In my investigations, I could not find signs of FFSPN open-mindedness with respect to ecologism.

REFERENCES

Bergmann, K. 1970. *Agrarromantik und Grossstadtfeindschaft* (Agrarian romantic and city enmity). Meisenheim: Anton Hain.
Brand, K.-W. ed. 1985. *Neue soziale Bewegungen in Westeuropa und den USA. Ein internationaler Vergleich* (New Social Movements in Western Europe and the USA: An International Comparison). Frankfurt am Main: Campus.
Brand, K.-W. 1987. "Neue soziale Bewegungen—ein neoromantischer Protest?" (New Social Movements—A Romantic Protest?). In *Alternativen zur alten Politik. Neue soziale Bewegungen in der Diskussion* (Alternative Politics. Debates on New Social Movements), edited by U. Wasmuht. Frankfurt am Main: Campus.
Brand, K.-W., D. Büsser, and D. Rucht. 1986. *Aufbruch in eine andere Gesellschaft. Neue soziale Bewegungen in der Bundesrepublik* (Opening to another society. New social movements in the Federal Republic of Germany). 3rd ed., rev. Frankfurt am Main: Campus.
Dalton, R.J., C. Bourdouvalis, E. DeClair, and E. Rohrschneider. 1986. "Environmental Action in Western Europe: A Preliminary Report of Findings." Environmental Movements in Western Democracies: Project Report 2. Tallahassee: Florida State University, Department of Political Science.

Ellwein, T., M. Leonhard, and P.M. Schmidt. 1985. "Umweltschutzverbände in der Bundesrepublik Deutschland" (Environmental Organizations in the Federal Republic of Germany). Forschungsbericht 101 01 131/02 im Auftrag des Umweltbundesamtes Berlin (Unpublished research report).

Fagnani, J. and J.-P. Moatti. 1982. "France: The Socialist Government's Energy Policy and the Decline of the Anti-Nuclear Movement." Paper presented at the conference of the European Consortium for Political Research on "Comparative Research on Nuclear Energy Policy: The State of the Art," Berlin, December 14-16.

Garner, R. and M.N. Zald. 1981. "Social Movement Sectors and Systemic Constraint: Toward a Structural Analysis of Social Movements." Working Paper No. 238. Ann Arbor: University of Michigan, Center for Research in Social Organization.

————. 1982. "The Political Economy of Social Movement Sectors." Unpublished manuscript. Ann Arbor: University of Michigan, Department of Sociology.

Garraud, P. 1979. "Politique électro-nucléaire et mobilisation" (Nuclear politics and mobilization). *Revue francaise de science politique* 29: 448-474.

Gerlach, L.P. and V. Hine. 1970. *People, Power, Change: Movements of Social Transformation.* Indianapolis, IN: Bobbs-Merrill.

Gundelach, P. 1984. "Social Transformation and New Forms of Voluntary Associations." *Social Science Information* 23: 1049-1081.

Jenkins, J.C. 1983. "Resource Mobilization Theory and the Study of Social Movements." *Annual Review of Sociology* 9:527-553.

Journes, C. 1979. "Les idées politiques du mouvement écologique" (The political ideology of the ecological movement). *Revue francaise de science politique* 29:230-254.

Kiersch, G. and S. Von Oppeln. 1983. *Kernenergiekonflikt in Frankreich und Deutschland* (Nuclear Conflict in France and Germany). Berlin: Wissenschaftlicher Autoren-Verlag.

Kitschelt, H. 1985. "Political Opportunity Structures and Political Protest: Anti-Nuclear Movements in Four Democracies." *British Journal of Political Science* 16:57-85.

Klandermans, B. 1986. "New Social Movements and Resource Mobilization: The European and the American Approach." *Journal of Mass Emergencies and Disasters* 4(2):13-39.

Leggewie, C. 1985. "Propheten ohne Macht. Die neuen sozialen Bewegungen in Frankreich zwischen Resignation und Selbstbestimmung" (Prophets without Power. New Social Movements in France between Resignation and Self-Determination). Pp. 83-139 in *Neue soziale Bewegungen in Westeuropa und den USA* (New Social Movements in Western Europe and the USA), edited by K.-W. Brand. Frankfurt am Main: Campus.

Linse, U. 1986. *Ökopax und Anarchie. Die Geschichte der ökologischen Bewegungen in Deutschland* (Eco-peace and Anarchy. History of the Environmental Movement in West Germany). München: Deutscher Taschenbuch Verlag.

Lowe, P. and J. Goyder. 1983. *Environmental Groups in Politics.* London: Allen & Unwin.

McCarthy, J. and M.N. Zald. 1977. "Resource Mobilization and Social Movements: A Partial Theory." *American Journal of Sociology* 82:1212-1241.

Mayer-Tasch, P.C. 1982. *Die Welt als Baustelle. Fragen an die Politische Ökologie* (The World as a Construction Site. Questions about Political Environmentalism). Zürich: Interfrom.

Melucci, A. 1984. "An End to Social Movements?" *Social Science Information* 24:813-835.

Mitchell, R.C. 1985. "From Conservation to Environmental Movement: The Development of Modern Environmental Lobbies." Discussion paper QE85-12. Washington, DC: Resources of the Future.

Narr, W.D. 1980. "Zum Politikum der Form." *Leviathan* 8:143-163.

Nelkin, D. and M. Pollak. 1982. *The Atom Besieged. Antinuclear Movements in France and Germany.* Cambridge, MA and London: MIT Press.

Nicolon, A. and M.-J. Carrieu. 1979. "Les partis face au nucléaire et la contestation" (Political Parties, Nuclear Energy and Protest). Pp. 79-159 in *Nucléopolis. Materiaux pour l'analyse d'une société nucléaire* (Nucleopolis. Materials for the Analysis of the Nuclear Society), edited by F. Fagnani and A. Nicolon. Grenoble: Presses Universitaires de Grenoble.

Nullmeier, F. and H. Schulz. 1983. "Politische Strategien der Ökologiebewegung in Frankreich" (Political Strategies of the Environmental Movement in France). Pp. 11-78 in *Umweltbewegungen und Parteiensystem*, edited by F. Nullmeier, F. Rubart, and H. Schulz. Berlin: Quorum.

Rammstedt, O. 1978. *Soziale Bewegung* (Social Movements). Frankfurt am Main: Suhrkamp.

Roth, R. 1985. "Neue soziale Bewegungen in der politischen Kultur der Bundesrepublik—eine vorläufige Skizze" (New Social Movements and the Political Culture in the Federal Republic of Germany. A Preliminary Analysis). Pp. 20-82 in *Neue soziale Bewegungen in Westeuropa und in den USA* (New Social Movements in Western Europe and the USA), edited by K.-W. Brand. Frankfurt am Main: Campus.

Rucht, D. 1984. "Zur Organisation der neuen sozialen Bewegungen" (The Organization of New Social Movements). Pp. 609-620 in *Politische Willensbildung und Interessenvermittlung* (Political Education and Representation), edited by J.W. Falter, C. Fenner, and M.T. Greven. Opladen: Westdeutscher Verlag.

———. 1985. "Social Movement Sectors in France and West Germany Since 1968." Paper presented at the Fifth International Conference of Europeanists, Washington, DC, October.

———. 1987. "Von der Bewegung zur Institution? Organisationsstrukturen der Ökologiebewegung" (From Movement to Institution. Organizational Structures of the Environmental Movement). In *Neue soziale Bewegungen in der Bundesrepublik* (New Social Movements in the Federal Republic of Germany), edited by R. Roth, D. Rucht, and S. Berthold. Frankfurt am Main: Campus.

Samuel, L. 1978. *Guide pratique de l'écologiste* (A Practical Guide to Environmentalism). Paris: Belfond.

Tarrow, S. 1983. "Struggling to Reform: Social Movements and Policy Change During Cycles of Protest." Western Societies Program, Occasional Paper No. 15. Ithaca, NY: Cornell University, Center for International Studies.

Touraine, A., A. Hegedus, R. Dubet, and N. Wieviorka. 1983. *Anti-Nuclear Protest: The Opposition to Nuclear Energy in France*. Cambridge: Cambridge University Press.

Trilling, J. 1981. "French Environmental Politics." *International Journal of Urban and Regional Research* 5:67-82.

Vadrot, C.-M. 1978. *L'Écologie, histoire d'une subversion* (Environmentalism, a history of subversion). Paris: Syros.

———. 1986. "Faut-il protéger les derniers écolos?" (Do we have to protect the last environmentist?). Pp. 186-202 in *Les natures du vert* (The Green Nature), edited by T. Grillet and D. le Conte de Floris. Paris: Autrement.

Vallet, O. 1978. "La force des écologistes" (The Ecologists' Force). *Projet* 122:201-206.

Vester, M. 1983. "Proletariat und neue soziale Bewegungen" (The Proletariat and the New Social Movements). Pp. 1-21 in *Grossstadt und neue soziale Bewegungen* (The City and New Social Movements), edited by P. Grottian and W. Nelles. Basel: Birkhäuser.

Von Moltke, K. and N. Visser. 1982. *Die Rolle der Umweltschutzverbände im politischen Entscheidungsprozesss der Niederlände* (The Role of Environmental Organizations in Political Decision Making in The Netherlands). Berlin: Schmidt.

Zald, M.N. and J.D. McCarthy. 1980. "Social Movement Industries: Competition and Cooperation among Movement Organizations." Pp. 1-20 in *Research in Social Movements, Conflict and Change*, vol. 3, edited by L. Kriesberg. Greenwich, CT: JAI Press.

THE DEVELOPMENT, CHANGE, AND DECLINE OF THE DUTCH CATHOLIC MOVEMENT

Ton Duffhues and Albert Felling

INTRODUCTION

The roots, growth, and decline of the Dutch "pillars" is a theme that has been discussed in The Netherlands for years. The different segments of the Dutch population, divided according to their beliefs into Catholics, orthodox Protestants, and Socialists, became active in the second half of the 19th century. Each group developed its own set of motivations and justifications or, better yet, ideologies, that corresponded to its own particular situation. A first justification, particulaly with reference to Catholics and orthodox Protestants, involved the preservation and protection of their own identity in Dutch society. Each group was attempting to emphasize its distinctness and to isolate itself from the outside world. At the same time, an attempt was made to gain respect and power, and to play an active role in Dutch society. A second justification,

International Social Movement Research, Vol. 2, pages 95-114.
Copyright © 1989 by JAI Press Inc.
All rights of reproduction in any form reserved.
ISBN: 0-89232-964-5

particularly for the Catholics and Socialists, had more of an international character and was related to notions of social reform (McSweeney 1980).

Once they were set into motion, these movements of emancipation gradually established themselves as organizational frameworks and institutions, and developed The Netherlands into a "pillarized" society. During this period, each pillar gradually created a highly differentiated and interrelated complex of organizations and institutions, covering almost every conceivable area of life.

This pillarized system acquired a political and social base around 1920. Political cooperation between the leading elite groups of the various pillars manifested itself in the mutual tolerance of the other's rights and claims, as well as on the effective separation of the pillarized segments of the population (Lijphart 1968). The political decision-making process became dominated by coalitions and compromises between the elites. In spite of the strict social divisions between the various segments of the population and the isolation they themselves had chosen to maintain, a relatively stable political system was thus established.

It was precisely because of the mutual recognition of political claims that it became extremely important for each movement to promote and sustain the unity among its own members, keep them segregated from other groups, and emphasize the ways in which it differed from the others.

It is striking that in a country as densely populated and undergoing modernization as rapidly as The Netherlands, social life of the individual was, until 1960, constrained by the boundaries of these very rigid pillars. The majority of the country's Catholics belonged to Catholic social clubs, voted for the Catholic political party, read Catholic newspapers, consulted Catholic general practitioners, married a Catholic, had Catholic friends, and would not even dream of patronizing a Protestant shopkeeper. The same held true for orthodox Protestants and Socialists. The fundamental and rapid transformation of this pillarized system was set in motion after 1960, resulting in an era of depillarization (Thurlings 1971; Coleman 1978).

An elite was responsible for the inception of the Catholic movement around the year 1880. Strategies were developed, organizational structures crystallized, the faithful mobilized, and steps were taken towards centralization and uniformity. By 1920, there was a differentiated concatenation of Catholic organizations at the local, diocesan, and national levels. Guidelines for the organization and the expansion of this pillarized complex had been established by the bishops shortly before then. According to Thurlings (1979, p. 84) "in 1916 the Catholic pillar was given a big boost by an episcopal letter launching a program to further the proliferation and integration of Catholic organizations." The enormous proliferation of the pillar during the 20th century is striking. With the German occupation (1940-1945) as a temporary interruption, the pillarized system and Catholic organizations grew until approximately 1960, when the actual decline of the Catholic movement began.

The aim of this article is to present a description and analysis of how the Catholic movement evolved in The Netherlands from 1945 to 1985, a period when it progressed through successive stages of proliferation, consolidation, and decline. The main focus will be on the structural organizational developments that took place on a national level, without, however, losing sight of the impact of ideological processes. On the contrary, the central notion will be that the evolution of social movements is shaped by the interaction between ideology, mobilization, and organizational development (Schreuder 1981).

In their extensive criticism of the Weber-Michels model of the transformation of social movements, Zald and Ash (1966) formulated a number of hypotheses pertaining to the growth, decay, and change of social movements. These hypotheses will be used here as a frame of reference for our description and exploration of the development of the Catholic movement in The Netherlands.

It will be shown, that the evolution of this Dutch Catholic movement cannot be accounted for by using the Weber-Michels model (Zald and Ash 1966, p. 327). The key issue is the existence of an increasing gap between organizational developments and structure, on the one hand, and ideology, on the other. As long as the ideology functions as a unifying principle, somehow the complex of organizations can be held together as a corporate body that represents the movement. Loss of the ideological framework and withdrawal of the traditional leadership, however, gives way to new and diversified developments. From that time on, a movement, or social movement organization (SMO), dissolves in different ways. Some groups of organizations undergo processes of bureaucratization, others of professionalization and secularization, and some (groups of) organizations disappear or merge with other organizations.

The central thesis of this study then is as follows: The gap between ideology and organizational structures increased because of several structural and cultural processes. On the structural level, there was an evolution of increasing functional differentiation and centralization. These processes went hand in hand with assimilation on the cultural or ideological level. The highly-differentiated and hierarchical structure of the Catholic pillar could no longer be held together by common ideology, but only by means of technical organizational tools. One of the most important tools in this sense was the creation of the tight *networks of organizations and functionaries.* The structure and composition of these networks of "interlocking directorates" was highly responsible for the continuation of the Catholic movement as an organizational whole in the period from 1945 to 1960. The growing number of ideological conflicts, and the lack of agreement on goals, remained concealed underneath this stable structure. A reconstruction and analysis of these networks teaches us how the organizational structure survived the ideological backbone of the movement. It also shows how the Catholic movement fell apart after 1960. Further, it shows that centralization, in a structural sense, failed because the center of the network loosened control of the numerous organizations and functionaries located at the basis of the Catholic movement.

PILLARIZATION AND SOCIAL MOVEMENTS

Dutch scientists have left their mark on the study of pillarization and depillarization. In the 1950s and 1960s, the descriptive approach was popular. In the numerous studies on pillarization and depillarization, little mention was made of theories of social movements (a bibliography on pillarization can be found in Van Schendelen 1984). At the end of the 1960s, political scientists started to place pillarization within the context of cross national theories of consociational democracy (Lijphart 1968; Daalder 1966), while sociologists employed theories on pluralism, assimilation, state formation, and modernization (Thurlings 1971; Steininger 1975). More recently they have also turned to theories of social movements (Duffhues et al. 1985). The study and discussion of pillarization has thus been placed in a broader context, making international comparisons possible.

In this study on the evolution of the Catholic movement, a definition is used that emphasizes structural, organizational aspects. Pillarization refers to the commencement, growth, and consolidation of organizational complexes in all areas of life that are separated along lines of belief. Depillarization refers to the opposite process, in which boundaries become more vague and the groups break up, dissolve, and disband.

The Evolution of Social Movements

In the literature, four different theories on the evolution of social movements are available: the natural history approach, Smelser's value-added model, the Weber-Michels model, and the resource mobilization approach (Schreuder 1981).

According to the *natural history approach,* movements pass through the successive stages of germination, growth, and decay. Decay sometimes leads to a new beginning. The life course of every movement is determined by an inevitable, and possibly cyclical, rhythm. Related to this approach is the generation model of movement cycles (Riley 1978). The first generation starts the movement and cultivates it, the second generation expands the movement and picks the fruits of the progress, and the third generation become organizational parasites leading to the premature, dissolution of the movement. Ideology and individual involvement develop correspondingly. The first generation lights the divine fire, the second generation keeps it going but with moderation, and the third generation fails to supply fuel, so that the ideological fire is extinguished.

Smelser's value-added theory defines structural strains and concomitant dissatisfactions as the decisive links in the causal chain leading to the emergence of a social movement. His model contains the following six irreversible stages: "structural conduciveness, structural strain, growth and spread of a generalized belief, precipitating factors, mobilization of participation for action and the operation of social control" (Smelser 1962, p. 15).

According to the *Weber-Michels model* of the transformation of social movements, every social movement goes through the stages of goal transformation, goal adjustment, and oligarchization. Goal transformation takes place when the goals of the movement become modified to fit the norms or demands of the environment, thus stripping them of their more radical elements. Initial goals which have proved to be unfeasible are replaced by more realistic ones, and the movement focusses more on concrete goals. Goal adjustment is the process by which organizational maintenance gain priority. By means of oligarchization, the controling power within the movement winds up in the hands of a small elite of bureaucrats and functionaries.

The resource mobilization approach stresses the importance of an enterprising elite. Next to Jenkins (1983, p. 528), this approach emphasizes "the continuities between movement and institutionalized actions, the rationality of movement actors, the strategic problems confronted by movements, and the role of movement as agencies for social change." The continuing existence of a movement mainly depends on the decisions of an elite. As long as an elite sees some reason for continuing the movement, as long as careers are promoted, as long as the movement is a healthy financial enterprise and as long as there is a sufficient demand for its services, it will continue to exist.

Summarizing, it can be noted that a natural history approach provides a descriptive deterministic framework; the value-added model and the Weber-Michels model provide an analytic deterministic framework; and the resource mobilization approach provides a nondeterministic framework for the analysis of a movements' evolution.

The Weber-Michels model has been selected here as a theoretical frame of reference for the study of the Catholic movement in The Netherlands. Based on the criticism and comments by Zald and Ash (1966), amendments to this framework are formulated. The essence of Zald and Ash's criticism was that movements can develop in any number of directions. Growth and institutional consolidation are possibilities, as are decay, deliberate discontinuation, splitting into factions, or modifications in the original goals.

Zald and Ash's hypotheses on the transformation of social movements and the external and internal factors of influence will be discussed later.

Goals and Organizational Structure

According to Zald and Ash, external factors influence the possibility of success; they determine whether or not goals are realistic and whether members are willing to participate. Not every organization is equally responsive to external influences. Especially requirements for membership and goal directedness determine to what extent movement organizations are responsive. Organizations that are very demanding of their members, subject them to strict codes of conduct and are focused on changing and educating individual members, are less open to external influences than organizations that make few demands of their members and are primarily focused on social reform. According to Zald and Ash, in the effort to retain their members, organizations of the latter type have a greater tendency to follow the Weber-Michels model and adjust to the external environment.

With respect to the further evolution of a movement, they argue that irrespective of movement success or failure in the cours of time, members become less committed and increasingly indifferent about the movement's goals and ideas. The survival of a movement, or of organizations within a movement, depends on the extent of the ties that can be maintained with the members.

A number of different forms of success should be distinguished. One form of success consists of the recognition or tolerance of the outside world, and of the movement's access to sources of power. A second form of success is the realization of the movement's goals. According to Zald and Ash, recognition can easily lead to the loss of idealism and to pragmatic behavior (assimilation), whereas goal achievement leads to the establishment of new goals or to the discontinuation of the entire movement. If, for example, membership has certain social and material advantages, new goals will be endorsed. If members do not endorse new goals, leaders have no choice but to disband the organization. This is more likely to be the case, according to Zald and Ash, in organizations that have few members and limited membership requirements, in specialized organizations, or in organizations focused on social reform, where idealism is the only motivation for membership.

The evolution of a movement that is neither really successful nor unsuccessful is marked by apathy, exhaustion, and indifference. There is usually a self-satisfied leadership, ideological anaemia, and the absence of any revival of the spirit of the movement. As time passes, the only reasons left for joining any of the organizations in the movement are materialistic ones. The members have few obligations to the movement and can be viewed as consumers that make use of certain services as cheaply as possible. This type of context is fertile ground for the growth of conservatism and oligarchy. Hence, the Weber-Michels model seems to be quite applicable here. The same holds true for a movement that achieves the first form of success and then devotes all its energy to preserving this success and taking advantage of the opportunities it provides.

These internal factors are mentioned by Zald and Ash and are noted as being important for the evolution of a movement: disputes between purists and pragmatists about means and ends; heterogeneity of members or organizations; and the power of authorities. Factionalization occurs if heterogeneity is not adequately counterbalanced by a strong central authority capable of settling the dispute about means and ends. This does not hold true for all organizations to the same extent. According to Zald and Ash, pragmatic organizations, whose members have few obligations to them, are less likely to have ideological disputes. If there is, nevertheless, some kind of split, then there is a chance that the organization will abandon its conservatism and tendency towards self-preservation and become more radical.

In the remaining part of this chapter, we will explore whether Zald and Ash's propositions are applicable to the Dutch Catholic movement.

STRUCTURAL DEVELOPMENTS AND NETWORKS

In our description of the Dutch Catholic movement, the following themes will be dealt with: functional differentiation, centralization, and networks of organizations and functionaries.

Functional Differentiation

Differentiation can be measured by the total number and the diversity of national Catholic organizations. Results on both measures are displayed in Table 1.

The peak year was 1960. Between the end of World War II and 1960, a record number of organizations was founded. By 1978, however, almost 100 of the 161 national organizations had disappeared. On the other hand, about 20 new organizations had been founded, most of them in the 1970s. The goal of some of these organizations was a revival of the ideals of the past. Another category of these new organizations consisted of centers of study and contemplation.

Table 1 shows that not all sectors share the upward and downward trend in the years after 1945. There were considerable discrepancies among the eight sectors in which the pillarized organizations were active. In the period from 1945 to 1980, the size of the education sector remained unaltered. As a consequence, this sector's share rose from 20% in 1948 to 50% in 1980. Apparently, the religion, health care, social welfare, youth, and culture sectors were more susceptible to depillarization than the educational sector. Nearly all of the organizations in these sectors disappeared either by disbanding or merging.

The legal form of an organization gives an indication of its relation to its members. Associations are organizations that have members (individuals, legal bodies), and foundations are organizations that do not. As Table 2 shows, the share of the associations rapidly fell from 85% to 65% in the period between 1940 and 1960, and then gradually fell further to 60% by 1980. Further, proportionately speaking, the associations with institutional members increased.

Table 1.   Number of National Catholic Organizations

Sector	1948	1960	1970	1978
Religion	1	2	1	—
Social welfare	17	25	21	13
Health care	15	23	19	7
Education	23	35	35	31
Culture	22	30	20	14
Youth organizations	8	10	10	3
Corporate associations; trade unions	25	32	20	16
Politics	5	4	2	4
Total	116	161	128	88

Table 2.   The Legal Form of Catholic Organizations

Year	Association	Foundations	Total Number of Organizations (%)
1920	38 (91)	4 (9)	42
1940	70 (85)	12 (15)	82
1948	88 (76)	28 (24)	116
1960	104 (64)	57 (36)	161
1970	82 (64)	46 (36)	128
1978	54 (61)	34 (39)	88

After 1940, there was thus increasingly less room for individual members, while the distance between the members and the functionaries increased. The members of numerous organizations were no longer ideologically-motivated, but were mainly interested in goods and services.

To conclude, functional differentiation was at its peak in 1960, followed by a subsequent decrease in the number of national Catholic organizations. The developments after 1960 went in three different directions. Some of the organizations continued to exist, a large number of them were disbanded, sometimes after merging with non-Catholic organizations, and new organizations were founded.

In view of the membership requirements, it was mainly associations that managed to keep members loyal on the basis of social and material incentives, that were able to survive, as evidenced by the continued existence of associations of farmers or farmers' wives, rural women or youth, and the elderly. Many of the organizations providing specialized and professionalized services (social welfare and health care) had already been working in conjunction with similar organizations in the other pillars at a relatively early stage, and merged with them in the 1960s and 1970s.

Organizations with membership based on ideology also experienced severe difficulties. Religious organizations reached a critical stage in the 1950s. The incipient crisis subsequently intensified in the early 1960s. At the same time, the number of members of the Katholieke Volkspartij (Catholic People's Party) dropped. After 1963, the party's electorate declined as well (Bakvis 1981). A decade later, the Catholic People's Party was no longer an independent party on the ballot for the parliamentary elections.

Although the crisis arose in the "ideological" core sectors of the Catholic pillar (religion and politics) and spread to the other sectors, several orthodox Catholic organizations with an ideologically-motivated following first came into existence in the years after 1960. However, the numbers of followers remained relatively small.

Centralization

Processes of differentiation go hand in hand with processes of integration and centralization, or are followed by them.

Particularly in the period from 1945 to 1960, the rise in the number of national Catholic organizations led to the foundation of agencies specifically involved with coordination and cooperation: internal federations or umbrella agencies (see Table 3). This integration took place within the various sectors as well as between them. Cooperation, coordination, and external communication became formalized and centralized through these new agencies and the new legally-regulated relations among the various organizations. By 1960, an umbrella agency had been set up to represent each sector. Further, these umbrella agencies were incorporated in the *Katholieke Maatschappelijke Beraad* (Catholic Social Council) and the *Katholieke Raad van Overleg voor sociaal economische aangelegenheden* (Catholic Consultation Council for Social Economic Affairs). In addition to representatives from the various umbrella agencies, there were also representatives from the corporate associations, the political party, and the church in these all-encompassing councils. In essence, these corporate, political, and religious categories of organizations played a leading and coordinating role in the original Catholic ideology. A structure was created in which the clergy functioned as guides, the corporate groups as a social base, and the political party as a Minister of Foreign Affairs, providing a gateway to the outside world (Duffhues et al. 1985).

Centralization did not stop at this vertical integration. Prior to 1960, a wide range of specialized activities had already been transferred from more general organizations to independent service organizations within the pillar (see Table 3). Examples of this kind of horizontal integration were manifold in the fields of vocational guidance, publishing, and health care (Duffhues et al. 1985).

Table 3. Number of Catholic Organizations Specialized in
Vertical Integration (Umbrella Agencies) or in
Horizontal Integration (Service Organizations)

Year	Umbrella Agencies	Service Organizations	Total (%)
1940	3	1	4 (5)
1948	5	8	13 (11)
1960	7	20	27 (17)
1970	5	16	21 (16)
1978	2	9	11 (13)

Until 1960, the expansion of the Catholic movement went hand in hand with the growth of organizations solely involved with cooperation and communication problems. In the period from 1945 to 1960, the initiation of a joint program, and the necessary interorganizational cooperation, apparently already required increasing technical organizational tools. It was in this period that the power base of the Catholic authorities began to disintegrate (Thurlings 1971; Coleman 1978).

After 1960, the Catholic organizations that were to bring about horizontal integration within the pillar soon began to work together with similar organizations in the other pillars. They subsequently went so far as to merge with them, and became part of the state's welfare network. The internal federations and umbrella agencies also gradually disappeared, with the exception of the *Nederlandse Katholieke Schoolraad* (Dutch Catholic School Council), the umbrella agency for the educational sector. It still existed in 1985. The various umbrella agencies that had originally functioned as policy-making and coordinating agencies, and monopolized the contact with the government and with other movements, gradually lost these functions. Coordination and preservation of uniformity were replaced by contemplation and study. Membership in these umbrella agencies was no longer binding and did not involve any obligations. In the 1970s, these umbrella agencies found themselves in a vacuum, since most of the member organizations had been disbanded. The Dutch Catholic School Council was able to escape the consequences of this development, as it had legally authorized official competence in the financial as well as the policy-making field.

The question is whether the above forms of vertical and horizontal integration were sufficiently able to safeguard the structural hierarchic unity within the Catholic movement, despite the ideological struggles. In other words, were these forms of integration able to prevent segregation and secession? In order to arrive at an answer to this question, it is necessary to discuss the overall structure and development of the national network of Catholic organizations and functionaries.

Table 4.   The Ratio of Functionaries to the Number of
Functions They Fulfilled in One Year

Number of Functions	1948	1960	1970	1978
1	76	72	81	82
2	16	18	13	14
3	5	5	4	3
4	2	3	1	—
5 or more	1	2	1	1
Total number of functionaries	100	100	100	100
(N = 100%)	N = 744	N = 1182	N = 964	N = 696

Table 5.   The Multiplicity of Relations between Organizations
(In percent)

Multiplicity	1948	1960	1970	1978
1	76	75	75	73
2	14	16	15	18
3	7	5	5	5
4 or more	3	4	5	4
Total number of relations	100	100	100	100
(N = 100)	N = 270	N = 634	N = 325	N = 159

Networks

The mutual dependence of Catholic organizations took shape by means of interlocking directorates between the various organizations. One of the channels used to promote and consolidate common Catholic interests was that of Catholic functionaries who were involved in more than one organization at a time.

Table 4 depicts the number of functions that functionaries held in national Catholic organizations. Networks of organizations and of functionaries can be induced from this information.

In order to give an impression of the size and composition of these networks, Table 5 shows the number of relations between the organizations, classified according to multiplicity. A multiplicity of 3 means that 3 functionaries create a relation between two specific organizations. A high multiplicity stands for a strong relationship.

Table 6.   The Percentages of Organizations With and Without
            Relations in the Network of Organizations

	1948	1960	1970	1978
Isolated organizations	22	9	23	22
Organizations connected to others (the greatest component)	73	89	77	73
Other organizations (in small components)	5	2	—	5
Total number of organizations	100	100	100	100
(N = 100%)	N = 116	N = 161	N = 128	N = 88

Table 7.   The Proportion of the Clergy and the National Politicians
            of Functionaries With at Least Two Different Functions

	1948	1960	1970	1978
Clergy	21	18	11	77
Politicians	11	6	4	1
Other functionaries	68	76	85	92
Total number of functionaries (N = 100%)	176	331	185	122

Table 6 shows the proportions of organizations connected versus not connected to other organizations.

From the combination of Tables 4, 5, and 6 we can infer that, in 1960, 331 of the 1182 functionaries (± 28%) created 634 different relations between 147 (91%) organizations. The smallest component existed of three organizations and three relations. The percentage of isolated organizations was the lowest in 1960.

Ideally, the network of Catholic organizations and individuals should be arranged as an organic unit with central positions for the clergy, the representatives of the corporate groups, and the politicians. In this way, at least in a structural sense, the general Catholic values could dominate the specific secular ones. Table 7 reveals a decrease in the percentages of the clergy and the national politicians (members of parliament, ministers), that had functions in at least two different organizations.

Clearly the possibilities for "clerical" and "political" control declined from 1948 onward.

The question that arises is whether the decreasing proportion of politicians and clergy had consequences for their position within the network of Catholic

Table 8. The Development of the Number of Relations between Catholic
Organizations, Induced by 5 Categories of Functionaries

	1948 (%)	1960 (%)	1970 (%)	1978 (%)
Functionaries with four or more functions	142 (53)	428 (68)	190 (58)	74 (47)
National Politicians	36 (13)	92 (15)	25 (8)	—
Political leaders	51 (19)	156 (25)	66 (20)	5 (3)
Clergy	78 (28)	143 (23)	54 (17)	13 (8)
Functionaries of the corporate organizations	73 (27)	216 (34)	111 (34)	44 (28)
Total number of relations	270 (100)	634 (100)	325 (100)	159 (100)

organizations. The number of relations between organizations that could be induced by these two categories gives an indication of the actual clerical and political control.

Table 8 shows the number of induced relations, not only for the clergy and the national politicians, but also for the political leaders (the national politicians and the board of the Catholic People's Party), the functionaries of the six main corporate organizations (workers, farmers, employers, intellectuals, officers, and shopkeepers or tradespeople), and all the functionaries with at least four different functions.

In proportion to the functionaries with four or more functions or the functionaries of the six corporate organizations, the "network-control" of the clergy declined from 1948 on. The political control declined after 1960, first with respect to the national politicians and later, with respect to the board of the Catholic People's Party. The share of the elite with at least four functions increased until 1960 and has remained at a relatively high level. The functionaries of the corporate organizations, on the contrary, lost some of their control in the years after 1970. In 1978, only the corporate organizations of the farmers and the laborers were left.

With the so-called "2-rush" an aspect of centrality of organizations can be measured. More specifically the 2-rush is a measure for the intermediate position of an organization within the network. It gives the number of contacts along shortest paths of length two via the organization (the intermedium) as a fraction of the total number of such contacts (Zijlstra 1982, p. 160).

Table 9 shows that the two general umbrella agencies, the Catholic Social Council and the Catholic Consultation Council for Social Economic Affairs, had an important intermediate position. This was also true for the more specialized umbrella agencies. In 1978, the Dutch Catholic School Council was an intermediate organization in 35% of all the contacts. The 2-rush of the Catholic People's Party and the six main corporate organizations was relatively low during the period examined.

Table 9.   The 2-rush of Four Categories of Catholic Organizations

	1948	1960	1970	1978
Catholic People's Party	2	5	3	1
Corporate organizations	7	4	2	2
General umbrella agencies	10	10	15	8
Specialized umbrella agencies	25	21	27	35

A combination of the information presented thus far, leads to the following conclusions:

- The degree of oligarchization was highest in 1960, due to the large number of functions held by a small minority of functionaries and the various relations that this minority was responsible for.
- The degree of organizational centrality was high: A small number of organizations (especially the umbrella agencies) controlled a great deal of the network.
- The integration of the network was at its highest level in 1960: In this year, isolated organizations were relatively scarce.
- The presupposed organic unity with central positions for the clergy, politicians, and representatives of corporate groups was best approached in 1948. After this year, the clergy and the politicians lost control over the network. Their dominating position was taken over by the umbrella agencies and functionaries with four or more functions. In 1978, the organizational network was especially centered around the educational sector and the Dutch Catholic School Council.
- The specialized umbrella agencies formed the centers of the organizational networks within the different sectors.

This all leads to the conclusion that the network of Catholic organizations has gradually drifted away from the ideal monocentric structure, and developed in the direction of a more polycentric structure (Duffhues et al. 1985). More specifically the following conclusions can be drawn:

- The network of Catholic organizations exhibited a relatively stable pattern throughout the period from 1945 to 1980.
- The existence of a fragmented hierarchical structure was observed throughout the years examined, but fragmentation increased after 1948. The hierarchical aspect was evident up until 1978, so that even in the final year of observation, no completely segregated or polycentric network was in existence. A significant feature of this *loosely-joined hierarchical system* was the role of several specific network organizations

and network specialists (Aldrich 1974): the umbrella agencies and their functionaries. Together they constituted the cores of the organizational and supervisory networks and kept the functionally-separated sectors and specialists united. The sectors became increasingly less directly linked to each other. Contacts between the sectors took place through general umbrella agencies, which are all part of the core of the network of the totality of Catholic organizations.

- It was not until the 1980s that a complete segregation took place, due in part to the fact that all the central organizations and the hard core of diehards had ceased to exist.
- In 1948, the relations between the core of the network and the other organizations and functionaries were of a hierarchical, authoritarian nature. This made it possible to exact a consensus regarding goals and methods. Later, this was increasingly less the case. The autonomy of specialized organizations and functionaries increased, and the relations among the various parts of the Catholic movement became more vague.
- By 1960, only the umbrella agencies adhered to and monopolized Catholic values and interests. Although, in practice, these agencies appeared to be hybrid constructions themselves, the ideal of an integrated organism remained as long as they continued to exist.
- After 1960, an aging, shrinking group of functionaries maintained contacts among specialists. By then, the clergy and the politicians had almost completely withdrawn. Circulation of the managing elite, so indispensable to a dynamic movement, no longer occurred.

In summary, by assuming the structure of a loosely-joined hierarchical system, the Catholic movement prevented itself from sinking into mere organizational structures and conservatism, and created the conditions for a cautious, limited and many-sided sequel. The autonomy of the organizations gradually increased, thus creating room for new loyalties and ideas. It would be equally plausible, however, to contend that the creation of these kind of networks made it possible to prevent the deterioration of the power base of the Catholic authorities, and the chronic lack of consensus regarding goals.

The networks show that the Catholic pillar continued to exist as a more or less integrated structure, at a time when a coherent ideology and an unanimous leadership were lacking. The developments after 1960, however, reveal the friction between ideology and organization.

IDEOLOGY AND ORGANIZATION

External developments have direct effects on internal disputes regarding goals and methods (Freeman 1979). The Catholic ideals of a corporative society based on Christian principles were under a great deal of strain from the very beginning (McSweeney 1980). It suffices to note the importance of several social developments in Dutch Society (Goudsblom 1967; Duffhues et al. 1985):

- Given their numerical minority situation (the Catholics constituted ± 40% of the total population of The Netherlands, the competition with the other movements (orthodox-protestants and socialists), and the necessity of functioning within the framework of a parliamentary democracy, the possibilities for the Catholic movement were limited. In addition, the various movements were forced to behave instrumentally, to form coalitions, and to accept compromises.
- Due to several aspects of modernization and state formation, regional, religious, and class differences were becoming less important throughout The Netherlands and, at the same time, national integration increased. The expansion of the welfare state also implied a gradual reduction in functions of the church.
- Life styles, culture, and value patterns of most Catholics conformed to the generally-accepted bourgeois ones (Felling, Peters and Schreuder 1983).

New ideas and views took root within the Catholic segment of the popualtion. The Catholic authorities attempted to keep these new ideas under their control. Since it was difficult to prohibit them, they opted for an opportunistic policy of acceptance, adjustment, and control via their own functionaries and organizations.

In the long-term, however, this implied that little remained of an exclusive Catholic identity in various activities and in the ideology behind them. In practice, the ideological differences become more vague between the Catholic, the Protestant, and the Socialist organizations, especially since they were all increasingly incorporated into the networks of the state.

External developments also promoted the heterogeneity within the movement, in general, and within many Catholic organizations, in particular. A wide range of opinions, ideas, and attitudes took shape inside the Catholic movement. Many of them suggested that the movement had successfully fulfilled its purpose, and made itself superfluous. Prior to 1960, the church authorities were convinced that this was not the case. Together with an elite of functionaries and politicians, they repeatedly appealed to a sense of Catholic unity. Every effort was made to suppress the "breakthrough" movement that was formed in 1945 as a result of the shared war experiences of Catholics, Protestants, and Socialists (Thurlings 1979). After 1945, all the pillars revived, expanded, and centralized their ranks. In 1954, the bishops wee still prohibiting Catholics to listen to the programs of the Socialist radio broadcasting company, or to join Socialist trade unions.

Many Catholic intellectuals viewed the bishops' standpoints as being outdated and unrealistic, and they no longer supported episcopal proclamations and views.

There was, however, another side to the coin. The internal emancipation of the laity was yet to begin. The toll the country's Catholics had paid for the external success of the movement was the patronization by the clergy. After 1960, the latent crisis within the church became a manifest one, especially for the clergy and the Catholic intellectuals. Even the episcopate abandoned obsolete points of view and ideas, thus giving the laity and the organizations more autonomy. The heterogeneity that held gradually crept into the movement, but which had been kept under control by technical organizational means and a strong central authority, acted as a catalyst and the movement soon disintegrated.

What has been said here of the Catholic movement also holds true for many of the separate Catholic organizations. They also experienced recurrent policy and management problems, some of which resulted from the considerable success and the increasing heterogeneity of ideas and interests. An increasing amount of friction between secular and Catholic values came to the surface, and the majority of the organizations did not adjust their view and goals, at least that was not the case up until 1960. They basically coped by means of a pragmatic course focused on self-preservation and expansion. Moreover, this pragmatism turned out to be a Trojan horse, as the threshold for working with non-Catholic organizations was lowered. Much against the will of the Catholic organizations, government interference increased and the orientation of many specially-trained functionaries and professional people became less Catholic and more professional. Around 1960, when the hidden crisis could no longer be concealed and internal authority relations underwent rather abrupt changes, a public discussion pertaining to the matter of Catholic identity was introduced in many organizations, a discussion that was to continue into the 1980s. The establishment of various study and contemplation centers was one of its direct effects. Many organizations moved towards depillarization, but by establishing their own study centers they could still preserve a modern version of the Catholic element.

DISCUSSION

The example of the Dutch Catholic movement clearly shows that more than one script can be utilized to describe the evolution of a social movement. This reinforces Zald and Ash's (1966) general criticism of the deterministic Weber-Michels model.

The Catholic movement in The Netherlands comprised a conglomerate of organizations with very different goals, methods, and membership requirements. Each organization has had its own functionally distinct, specific goals, but they were subordinate to the ideological framework. In a structural sense, centralization and coordination was accomplished by "interlocking directorates." A superficial examination of organizational structures and networks suggests that the Dutch Catholic movement was very cohesive until the 1980s. A more in-depth study, however, shows that the general ideological backbone was deteriorating long before. After 1960, the complex of organizations could no longer be viewed as a collective actor.

Zald and Ash do not elaborate the relationship between a movement and its constituent organizations. As the study of the Catholic movement in The Netherlands has shown, it seems only logical to take this relationship into account.

With regard to the ideas of Zald and Ash on the degree of success as a condition for the further evolution of the movements, the case of the Dutch Catholic movement demonstrates that the opinions on significance of the movement's results will vary. Consequently, views on the future, on the goals, and on the necessity of the continued existence of the movement, differ. In this sense, the hetergeneity within the Dutch Catholic movement grew after 1920, when the movement achieved its first success. Following the Weber-Michels model, the next period would then bring a continuous effort to preserve the organization, leading to the acceptance of conservatism and oligarchy as tradeoffs. The sudden changes in the Catholic Movement after 1960, are not in line with this model.

On their part, Zald and Ash argue that after the first milestone, a movement can adjust its goals to fit the needs of the times. Once that has been done, it can either formulate new goals or disband. They view these aspects as being dependent on the degree of financial autonomy and on the opportunities available to retain strong ties with the members.

After 1920, concerted efforts were made to adjust the goals to fit the times. This was evidenced by the enormous rise in the number of both organizations and members. In a structural organizational sense, as well as in a financial sense, ample use was made of the opportunities at hand. In an ideological sense, the movement moved further away from its original goals. In the course of time, this discrepancy proved to be destructive. Many felt that the Catholic movement had already reached a point of saturation in the 1930s, and this was even more the case by the 1950s. Many also argued that there were no specific Catholic ideals left to fight for because the integration of Catholics into Dutch sociey had been completed in various ways. A growing number of individuals were in favor of eliminating the rigid boundaries dividing the segments of the population according to their beliefs. At the same time, they were also in favor of greater pluralism within their own circles.

This conception of the success and the future of the Catholic movement was not generally accepted until approximately 1960. In spite of the discrepancy noted above, the episcopate and many prominent Catholics continued to adhere to their goals and their authority. The anachronism of this situation became painfully evident around 1960. The authorities had miscalculated the effects and results of the development they had originally given their full support:

- The laity had become more articulate, less dependent, and had developed new loyalties and ideas.
- There was dissensus among the higher and lower clergy.
- Many of the organizations were already autonomous, had intensive contacts with non-Catholics and were financially heavily dependent on the state.
- Catholic ideas about the social order and the political unity were outdated and no longer served any useful purpose.
- The efficiency of the organizational framework now facilitated the spread of new ideas and points of view.

As a result, friction rapidly intensified, providing an excellent climate for pluriformity and polarization. The sudden change in policy guidelines of the Dutch bishops in the 1960s underscored the crisis within the religious core of the Dutch Catholic movement. All these factors were responsible for a number of developments in contradictory directions: Some Catholics and organizations simply wanted to continue as before and remained within the movement, others opted for a brand of "open Catholicism" and even for anti-Catholicism, and others wanted a return to orthodoxy.

The history of the Dutch Catholic movement makes clear that structural, organizational, and ideological developments have to be combined if we want to explain the fate of a social movement.

REFERENCES

Aldrich, H. 1974. "The Environment as a Network of Organizations: Theoretical and Method-oligical Implications. International Sociological Associations Meeting, Toronto, Canada.

Bakvis, L. 1981. *Catholic Power in the Netherlands.* Kingston: McGill-Queen's University Press.

Coleman, J.A. 1978. *The Evolution of Dutch Catholicism, 1958-1974.* Berkeley and London: University of California Press.

Daalder, H. 1966. "The Netherlands: Opposition in a Segmented Society." Pp. 99-136 in *Political Opposition in Western Democracies,* edited by R.A. Dahl. New Haven, CT: Yale University Press.

Duffhues, T., A. Felling, and J. Roes. 1985. *Bewegende patronen. Een analyse van het landelijk netwerk in katholieke organisaties en bestuurders 1945-1980* (Moving Networks. An Analysis of Networks of Catholic Organizations and Elites 1945-1980). Nijmegen, Baarn: Ambo.

Felling, A., J. Peters, and O. Schreuder. 1983. *Burgerlijk en onburgerlijk Nederland. Een nationaal onderzoek naar waardenoriëntaties op de drempel van de jaren tachtig* (Conventional and

Unconventional Netherlands. A National Survey of Values Orientations at the Turn of
    the Eighties). Deventer: Van Loghum Slaterus.
Freeman, J. 1979. "Resource Mobilization and Strategy: A Model for Analyzing Social Movement
    Organization Actions." Pp. 167-189 in *Dynamics of Social Movements. Resource
    Mobilization, Social Control, and Tactics*, edited by M.N. Zald and J.D. McCarthy.
    Cambridge, MA: Winthrop Publishers.
Goudsblom, J. 1967. *Dutch Society*. New York: Random House.
Jenkins, J.C. 1983. "Resource Mobilization Theory and the Study of Social Movements." *Annual
    Review of Sociology* 9:527-553.
Lijphart, A. 1968. *The Politics of Accommodation: Pluralism and Democracy in The Netherlands*.
    Berkeley: University of California Press.
McCarthy, J.D. and M.N. Zald. 1977. "Resource Mobilization and Social Movements: A Partial
    Theory." *American Journal of Sociology* 82:1212-1242.
McSweeney, B. 1980. *Roman Catholicism. The Search for Relevance*. Oxford: St. Martins.
Riley, M.W. 1978. "Aging, Social Change, and the Power of Ideas." *Daedalus* 107:39-52.
Schreuder, O. 1981. *Sociale bewegingen. Een systematische inleiding* (Social Movements. A
    Systematic Introduction). Deventer: Van Loghum Slaterus.
Smelser, N.J. 1962. *Theory of Collective Behaviour*. London: Routledge & Kegan Paul.
Steininger, R. 1975. *Polarisierung und integration. Eine vergleichende Untersuchung der
    structurellen Versäulung der Gesellschaft in den Niederländen und in Österreich*
    (Polarization and Integration. A Comparative Study of Pillarization in The Netherlands
    and Austria). Meisenheim an Glan: Verlag Anton Hain.
Thurlings, J.M.G. 1971. *De wankele zuil. Nederlandse katholieken tussen assimilatie en pluralisme*
    (The Weak Pillar. Dutch Catholics between Assimilation and Pluralism). Nijmegen: Van
    Loghum Slaterus.
_____. 1979. "Pluralism and Assimilation in the Netherlands, with Special Reference to Dutch
    Catholicism." *International Journal of Sociology* 20:82-100.
Van Schendelen, M.P.C.M. 1984. "Systematic Bibliography on Consociationalism. *Acta Politica*
    19:161-175.
Zald, M.N. and R. Ash. 1966. "Social Movement Organizations: Growth, Decay and Change."
    Social Forces 44:327-340.
Zijlstra, G.J. 1982. *The Policy Structure of the Dutch Nuclear Energy Sector*. Groningen:
    University of Groningen.

PART II

MANAGEMENT OF
SOCIAL MOVEMENT ORGANIZATIONS

INTRODUCTION

Bert Klandermans

Social movement organizations (SMOs) are, like any other organizations "Goal-directed, boundary-maintaining, activity systems" (Knoke 1985, p. 221). Management of organizations centers on the acquisition and allocation of resources, such that the goals of the organization may be realized. To the extent that the movement's goals are not limited to personal growth but aim at social change (Turner and Killian 1987), the resources include those of political power. Not all the resources available to a social movement are intended for external use; a relatively large proportion goes toward maintaining and strengthening the organization as such. As Knoke demonstrates in his contribution to Part II of this volume, the decision to apply the available resources externally or internally is crucial in the management of social movements.

Management of SMOs consists of formulating strategies to procure resources and of choosing between alternatives in allocating them. In this process, Knoke (1985) speaks of an organization's "political economy." In Knoke's analysis, SMOs—like all other influence associations—are confronted with two types of actors: potential supporters and authorities. *Interaction with supporters* must lead to the acquisition of resources. A social movement has

International Social Movement Research, Vol. 2, pages 117-128.
ISBN: 0-89232-964-5

basically three sources of "income": the support of individual sympathizers, support from organizations and institutions, and proceeds from sales of the organization's product. Usually the movement's income derives from these three sources in combination. Through *interaction with authorities,* the organization exerts its influence. Because a particular SMO is not alone in its attempts to exert influence, it must compete with other organizations and pressure groups.

The movement's supporters decide whether or not they will provide the required resources. How the acquired resources are to be put to use is determined by the organization: what portion will go to the interaction with authorities, what part will be used to maintain the organization, and what part will be reserved for legitimizing the goals and methods of the movement and for securing a continued influx of resources (by way of public relations, informative and persuasive communication, membership services, and so on). In these decision-making processes, adequate leadership is indispensable. Sophisticated appeals that encourage support will cause the movement's revenue to rise, while coordination, timing, and strategic choices enhance the effectiveness of the accumulated resources. Leadership will be the topic of Part III. Part II focuses on the accumulation and allocation of resources.

MOBILIZING SUPPORT

SMOs draw on their resources from individuals and from other organizations. In neither case is support given automatically; it must be gained through sometimes lengthy mobilization campaigns. Granting support to a social movement may be seen as a process of exchange and as the outcome of a rational decision. An individual or organization is prepared to support a movement in exchange for forthcoming profits, advantages, and services. The literature on the relative significance of individual support and organizational support is not conclusive. It has been argued, on the one hand, that organizational sponsorship is indispensable because individual sympathizers are unable to achieve sufficient power (Zald and McCarthy 1979), and, on the other, that a movement cannot expect organizational backing before it has achieved a certain status in its own right (McAdam 1982). There is evidence to corroborate both viewpoints, as the following two examples illustrate. For evidence of the effect of organizational support, one can turn to the Dutch peace movement, which would not have expanded as greatly as it ultimately did without the support of the churches (Schennink 1988). But the American civil rights movement, as McAdam (1982) and Morris (1984) demonstrate, did not acquire external organizational support until it had already gained considerable status. The literature does make clear that both kinds of support are necessary; depending on the circumstances and the developmental phase of an SMO, however, either the one or the other may predominate. As long as we lack systematic research into the origins of a social movement's resources in relation to its phase of development and the circumstances surrounding it, it is impossible to go much farther than this general observation. In his contribution to Part II, Knoke demonstrates that individual support is the major source of income for all voluntary associations, especially among less bureaucratized associations. As most, SMOs can be located at the lower end of the bureaucratization scale, it is safe to assume that the largest part of their resources stem from individual supporters.

In this introduction, I will emphasize the ways in which a movement gains the support of individual sympathizers. The acquisition of organizational support will be discussed in Part IV of this volume.

Enlisting Individual Support

Perrow (1970) distinguishes four basic ways in which individuals can contribute to a social movement. They can lend their names to an organization, for instance, by signing a petition; they can give money; they can agree to participate in activities or demonstrations; they can help in building bridges to other organizations or persons. It should not be assumed that individuals, prepared to support a movement in one way, will automatically support the movement in other ways as well. This selective support is illustrated by Oliver an Furman's contribution to Part II of this volume: Willingness to contribute financially to a national movement organization does not make people willing to participate in activities of a local movement chapter. Recruitment of individual support in any form is a complex affair, its outcome fraught with uncertainty.It is a process entailing a number of stages, each with its own determinants, each requiring a different sort of effort on the part of the SMO. Acquisition of support includes the creation of mobilization potential, formation and activation of recruitment networks, stimulation of motivation to participate, and removal of barriers to participation (Klandermans and Oegema 1987). To create a mobilization potential, a movement must gain the sympathy of a segment of the population. To form and activate recruitment networks, it must join forces with other organizations and establish ties with existing formal and informal networks. To stimulate the motivation to participate, it must influence the perceived costs and benefits of participation. To remove barriers, an SMO must be aware of possible obstacles and must have the means to remove them or else be able to motivate an individual to overcome them. From the viewpoint of the individual, entering into participation in a social movement may be seen as a process comprising four steps: One first becomes part of the mobilization potential, then a target of mobilization attempts; next, one becomes motivated to participate, finally overcoming the barriers to participation. Steps one and two are necessary prerequisites for stimulating the motivation to participate. Motivation and barriers in mutual interaction determine whether a person will participate; the greater an individual's motivation, the more likely it is that he or she will surmount any obstacles.

I have dealt with this theory of participation at some length elsewhere (Klandermans 1984, 1988; Klandermans and Oegema 1987), so a brief sketch of the four steps will suffice here.

Mobilization Potential

The term "mobilization potential" refers to those members of a society who may possibly be enlisted in some way or other by an SMO. It includes everyone who envinces a positive attitude toward the movement; hence its boundaries need not coincide with those of the group whose interests it defends or represents (cf. McCarthy and Zald 1976; Jenkins and Perrow 1977). People who do not stand to profit directly from the activities of a social movement may yet become sympathetic to the organization and thus also become part of the mobilization potential. The mobilization potential defines the limits within which a mobilization campaign may be successful. Someone who does not belong to the mobilization potential of an organization will not consider participating in it, even if solicited to do so. The mobilization potential is the reservoir from which the social movement can draw. It is the result of often long-term campaigns in which the movement's organization disseminates its views. Such campaigns may be referred to as "consensus mobilization" (Klandermans 1988) or "frame alignment" (Snow et al. 1986).

A crucial element in the formation of mobilization potential, is the interpretation of grievances (Gurney and Tierney 1982; Klandermans 1988). The concept in question here, that is, the construction of meaning, has recently received much attention in the literature (Ferree and Miller 1985; McAdam 1988; Snow et al. 1986; Taylor 1986; see Klandermans, Kriesi, and Tarrow 1988, for a collection of papers on the topic). These various studies discuss both the beliefs conducive to movement participation and the structures that support the formation of mobilization potentials. In the process of grievance interpretation, casual attribution is of special importance. As an illustration, the distinction between the interpretation of an individual's situation in terms of individual factors (individual blame) and the interpretation in terms of situational factors (system blame) (Gurin et al. 1969); with regard to grievance interpretation, Ferree and Miller (1985) suggested that system blame is a necessary condition for movement participation. Gamson (1988) asserted that within societal discourse there are different "ideological packages," that proffer interpretations of important social events and which are sponsored by certain media and social actors. Taylor (1986) showed the degree in which "political entrepreneurs" can be effective in promoting definitions of the situation.

McAdam (1986, p. 15) pointed to the significance of the micromobilization context, "that small group setting in which processes of collective attribution are combined with rudimentary forms of organization to produce mobilization for collective action."

The (scant) empirical material that is available suggests that a broad range of communication forms, from interpersonal communication to communication via the mass media, may be used successfully for the mobilization of consensus (Klandermans 1988; McAdam et al. 1987). Defining meanings and choosing the symbols and communication channels through which to convey them is an essential aspect in the management of an SMO (Snow et al. 1986; Snow and Benford 1988).

Recruitment Networks and Attempts at Mobilization

No matter how successful a social movement is in mobilizing consensus and however large its mobilization potential may be, if it does not possess a network for recruitment it will be unable to activate its potential. The recruitment network of an SMO determines the reach of its mobilization attempts. The broader the network, and the more closely it is tied to other organizations and networks, the greater the number of people that fall within the scope of a mobilization attempt.

An individual can be reached via one of the following channels: the mass media, direct mail, ties with organizations, and friendship networks. The mass media are not very effective in reaching individual sympathizers, especially not when it is unclear which segment of the medium's audience belongs to the mobilization potential of a social movement. But even if the organization can choose a medium frequently used by individuals who are part of the organization potential, there are no guarantees that individual members of that potential are in fact exposed to the mobilization drive. Direct mail, ties among organizations, and friendship ties offer better guarantees of successful contact.

Building up and activating a recruitment network requires that the organization be developed at the national and the local level and demands the formation of coalitions with other organizations (Wilson and Orum 1976; Ferree and Miller 1985). Those who hold positions within these networks are both object and subject of mobilization: Object in that they need to be mobilized in order to work in the mobilization campaign; subject because, once mobilized, they become active in mobilizing others. Kriesi and Van Praag (1987) describe this dual role in relation to the campaign for the People's Petition initiated by the Dutch peace movement: Before the signatures could be collected, tens of thousands of people had to be recruited simply to undertake that task.

To be effective in reaching the mobilization potential is not the same as effectively motivating the potential. Obviously, the latter process cannot be isolated from the kind of support requested. The mass media and direct mail are reasonably effective means of motivating sympathizers of a social movement to offer symbolic or limited support (Oliver and Furman in this volume; McCarthy 1987; Godwin and Mitchell 1984). But they function poorly when the projected activities involve high costs or great risks (Briet et al. 1987; McAdam 1986). In such cases, links with organizations and especially friendship ties are of decisive significance.

Motivation to Participate

The motivation to participate is a function of the perceived costs and benefits of participation (Oberschall 1980; Klandermans 1984). An important distinction here is that between collective and selective benefits (Olson 1968). Collective and selective benefits together determine the motivation to participate. Selective benefits can be divided into social benefits (the reactions of significant others) and nonsocial ones. The relation of participation to collective benefits is fundamentally different from the relation of participation to selective benefits. While selective benefits are directly linked to one's own behavioral choices, collective benefits depend in part on the choices of others. Thus the perceived *collective* benefits of participation depend on expectations regarding the behavior of others. Two other expectations are also important in determining perceptions of collective benefits: the anticipated chances of success when many people participate and the assessment of one's own contribution to success. These three kinds of expectations jointy determine the subjective relation between one's own choices of behavior and the collective benefits. A multiplicative relation obtains between the value collective benefits have for an individual and the subjective expectation of success. Even when a person estimates the value of a collective benefit as extraordinarily great, his or her behavior will not be strongly influenced unless he or she expects participation to realize that benefit.

An SMO, seeking to create the motivation to participate, must find ways to influence the perceived costs and benefits of participation. Three possible approaches present themselves: (a) increasing the selective benefits of participation; (b) enhancing the value of collective benefits; and (c) reinforcing the subjective relation between participation and the realization of collective benefits. Once more, each of these three approaches places specific demands on the organization.

To begin with, manipulating the selective benefits can make participation more attractive or nonparticipation less attractive. To this end, either the social or the nonsocial benefits can be emphasized. If the former are stressed, the organization seeks to influence the social environment such that significant others encourage participation. If the emphasis is on nonsocial benefits, participation is represented as leading to advantages or nonparticipation to disadvantages. Oliver (1980), however, points out that the manipulation of selective benefits exacts a price. When activities involve a great many persons, it is costly indeed to reward every participant. On the other hand, it may be difficult or undesirable to punish nonparticipation, if one can expect that a relatively large proportion of the mobilization potential will not participate. Oliver concludes that positive and negative measures are effective in different situations. Rewards are most effective when only a small part of the mobilization potential must be activiated; negative sanctions are essential when unanimous participation is needed.

Enhancing the value of collective benefits calls attention to the significance of consensus mobilization in the context of action mobilization, that is, to activating sympathizers. After all, from the viewpoint of those sympathetic to the movement, the concrete goals, for which support is solicited, need not necessarily be related to those which evoked sympathy in the first place. Hence, it must be argued that those concrete goals are instrumental to eliminating the dissatisfactions or realizing the aspirations at the root of the movement's mobilization potential (Klandermans 1988). In passing, it should be noted that enhancing of the value of collective benefits will have no effect unless it is possible to establish at least a minimal connection between participation and the realization of such benefits.

In view of the limits of the preceding two strategies, the third approach to influencing perceived costs and benefits—strengthening the participation-realization connection—is the most important. At stake here is the legitimization of the kind of support requested. That is, one must convince the person appealed to that a sufficient number of others participate, that participation is a meaning-ful contribution to the chance of success, and that the strategy chosen by the SMO is an effective one. Clearly, these are sensitive matters: Too strident an optimism reduces the motivation to participate, but so does extreme pessimism. This danger of alienating possible supporters explains why SMOs work hard to persuade individual sympathizers that their contributions are criticially significant. A movement organization's previous successes also play an important part in legitimizing a chosen strategy (Browne 1983; Schwartz 1976).

SMOs that make use of these three mobilization tactics in combination are, relatively, the most effective in acquiring resources. This view is shared by Knoke and Wright-Isak (1982). They point out that organizations can make use of different systems of benefits in which the emphasis may be on utilitarian benefits (wages, goods, services), on normative benefits (appealing to values and convictions), or on affective benefits (interpersonal relationships). Depending on the kind of benefit system used by a social movement organization, the ties between individuals and the organization may be purely utilitarian, purely normative, purely affective, or some mixture of all three. The authors hypothesize that, in the long run, mixed benefit systems are the more effective, and will facilitate survival of the organization.

Barriers to Participation

Motivation is indicative of willingness to participate. Such willingness, however is not a sufficient condition for participation. It will lead to participation only to the extent that intentions can be acted upon. The interaction of motivation and barriers determines whether a motivated person will actually participate. Hence, in this final phase, an SMO has two strategies at its disposal: (1) maintaining or reinforcing motivation, and (2) eliminating obstacles. Significant others play an important role in sustaining the motivation to participate (Klandermans and Oegema 1987; McAdam 1986).

THE ALLOCATION OF RESOURCES

Once a social movement has acquired resources, it is faced with the question of how to use them. At issue here is the strategy chosen by the SMO. Following Van Noort (1987, p. 91), I define strategy as "the manner in which an actor deploys the available resources in view of a specific goal." The organization must allocate its available resources to four possible ends: influencing authorities, legitimizing the goals and methods by way of public relations, securing the influx of resources by fostering participant involvement, and maintaining the organization (Knoke 1985; McAdam et al. 1987). Perrow (1970) observed that SMOs differ in the freedom they have to allocate resources. Organizations that primarily collect money have more flexibility in the usage of resources than organizations that mobilize manpower, because inlike manpower, money is storable and can be employed when useful.

The priority given to these four areas of resource allocation differs from one SMO to another. Nevertheless, the priorities of most social movements coincide insofar as they invest the lion's share of their resources in promoting participant involvement (Knoke, in Part II of this volume). The same is true of bureaucratized, formalized organizations such as trade unions. Contrary to a suggestion presented in the literature (Michels 1962), there are no indications that, as SMOs become more bureaucratic, they invest a relatively greater part of their resources in the maintenance of the organization.

In the literature on social movements, the allocation of resources for the purpose of exerting influence has received the most attention. The other three possible areas of expenditure have received far less. This emphasis is the more remarkable when we note that the majority of SMOs spend only a modest proportion of their resources on attempts to exert influence (see Knoke, in Part II of this volume). Studies of communication campaigns conducted by SMOs, of the media used in such campaigns, of their effectiveness, and so on, are simply not available. Except for the literature on conversion processes in religious movements (Lofland 1985; Snow and Machalek 1983), little is written (and thus known) about the strategies that SMOs apply in order to intensify participant involvement. A great many studies deal with joining a social movement as participant, very few treat the matter of ceasing to participate (see, however, Van der Veen and Klandermans, in Part II of this volume). Moreland and Levine (1983) developed a process-model of temporal changes in individual—group relations that might be useful in this context. Distinguishing four stages—entry, acceptance, divergence, and exit—they described the transformations in commitment to groups.

The empirical material regarding the maintenance of SMOs, scarce as it is, indicates a tendency to evolve toward professionalization (McCarthy and Zald 1973; Turner and Killian 1987). One of the causes for this evolution is that volunteers are not highly motivated to assist with the necessary maintenance tasks, as Oliver and Furman argue in their contribution to Part II of this volume). The usual solution to lack of volunteer help is to hire paid officials, frequently recruited from the movement's constituency.

To influence authorities, an SMO can have recourse to a number of options. Various typologies are presented in this literature. On the basis of a review of this literature, Van Noort (1987) distinguishes: persuasion, argumentation, demonstration, litigation, and protest. This list incorporates the two dimensions in terms of which Gamson (1968) distinguishes the means of influence used by SMOs: change in the authority's situation (persuasion, litigation, and protest) versus change in the authority's orientation (argumentation and demonstration), and the addition of disadvantages (litigation, protest) versus the addition of advantages (persuasion).

The choice of strategies is determined by a number of factors within and without the organization. Knoke (1985) refers to the importance of the degree to which members are involved in decisions on strategy. The greater the scope for participation in decision making, the stronger the participants' commitment to the organization (Knoke and Wood 1981). In an organization's choice of tactics to implement the proposed strategies, either strategic or expressive principles may predominate (Turner and Killian 1987). If an organization's choice is determined by the strategic principle, it relies on a given tactic to *realize* the social movement's goals. An organization that favors the expressive principle will choose its tactics according to their power to represent these goals *symbolically*. The greater the competence of the leadership and the more disciplined the rank and file, the more consistently the SMO will operate on strategic principles.

Finally, the choice of strategies depends on the perceived strength of the opposition, the system of alliances among SMOs, the resources at their disposal, the movement's ideology, the turn of events and the movement's familiarity with certain strategies (Turner and Killian 1987). Several of these factors are at work in the strategic dilemmas of SMOs described in Walsh and Cables contribution to Part II of this volume. The allocation of resources is guided by the prevailing analysis of the situation within the movement organization. Accurate analyses are of great importance to the organization's survival. A faulty analysis leads to failures and makes the SMO die (Schwartz 1976).

THE CONTRIBUTIONS TO PART II

Resource acquisition and allocation are the focus of the four contributions in Part II. All four address problems of management of SMOs but from different angles.

Knoke's chapter provides extensive empirical data on resource accumulation and allocation in relation to organizational characteristics such as bureaucratization and centralization and environmental characteristics such as complexity and uncertainty. Although his observations are most pertinent to voluntary associations generally, they hold as well for the subset of voluntary associations we are concerned with, that is, SMOs.

Oliver and Furman's contribution discusses the well-known contradiction within SMOs between national and local organizational strength. They argue that contributions to a national organization usually are forms of symbolic solidarity by people who want to *be* paper members and nothing more. Consequently, these people are not the ones who will be easily motivated to become involved in local movement organizations which need people who actually *do* things.

Although "exit"-behavior is a serious problem in the management of every SMO, it is almost completely neglected in the literature. Van der Veen and Klandermans, using empirical evidence from labor unions, attempt to develop theoretical models for the explanation of "exit"-behavior in SMOs.

Walsh and Cable describe some of the strategic and tactical dilemmas confronting organizers of the movements around Three Mile Island in their attempts to secure popular and institutional support. Their examples suggest that, on many occasions, a structural solution to management dilemmas is chosen. In three of the four cases they present, the emergence of new organizations helped to solve the dilemma.

REFERENCES

Briët, M., B. Klandermans, and F. Kroon. 1987. "How Women Become Involved in the Women's Movement." Pp. 44-64 in *The Women's Movements in the U.S. and Western Europe: Feminist Consciousness, Political Opportunity and Public Policy,* edited by M. Katzenstein and C. Mueller. Philadelphia, PA: Temple University Press.
Browne, W.P. 1983. "Mobilizing and Activating Group Demands: The American Agricultural Movement." *Social Science Quarterly* 64:19-34.

Ferree, M.M. and F.D. Miller. 1985. "Mobilization and Meaning: Toward an Integration of Social Psychological and Resource Perspectives on Social Movements." *Sociological Inquiry* 55:38-61.

Gamson, W.A. 1968. *Power and Discontent.* Homewood, IL: Dorsey Press.

_____. 1988. "Political Discourse and Collective Action." In *From Structure to Action: Comparing Movement Participation Across Cultures,* edited by B. Klandermans, H. Kriesi, and S. Tarrow. Greenwich, CT: JAI Press.

Godwin, R.K. and R.C. Mitchell. 1984. "The Impact of Direct Mail on Political Organizations." *Social Science Quarterly* 66:829-839.

Gurin, P., G. Gurin, R. Lao, and M. Beattie. 1969. "Internal-external control in the Motivational Dynamics of Negro Youth." *Journal of Social Issues* 25:29-53.

Gurney, J.N. and K.J. Tierney. 1982. "Relative Deprivation and Social Movements: A Critical Look at Twenty-Year Theory and Research. *Sociology Quarterly* 23:33-47.

Jenkins, J.C. and C. Perrow. 1977. "Insurgency of the Powerless Farm Workers Movements (1946-1972)." *American Sociological Review* 42:249-268.

Klandermans, B. 1984. "Mobilization and Participation: Social Psychological Expansions of Resource Mobilization Theory." *American Sociological Review* 49:583-600.

_____. 1988. "The Formation and Mobilization of Consensus." In *From Structure to Action: Comparing Movement Participation Across Cultures,* edited by B. Klandermans, H. Kriesi, and S. Tarrow. Greenwich, CT: JAI Press.

Klandermans, B., H. Kriesi, and S. Tarrow. eds. 1988. *From Structure to Action: Comparing Movement Participation Across Cultures.* Greenwich, CT: JAI Press.

Klandermans, B. and D. Oegema. 1987. "Potentials, Networks, Motivations and Barriers: Steps Toward Participation in Social Movements." *American Sociological Review* 52:519-532.

Knoke, D. 1985. "The Political Economies of Associations. Pp. 211-242 in *Research in Political Sociology,* vol. 1, edited by R.D. Braungart. Greenwich, CT: JAI Press.

Knoke, D., and J.R. Wood. 1981. *Organization for Action, Commitment in Voluntary Associations.* New Brunswick, NJ: Rutgers University Press.

Knoke, D. and C. Wright-Isak. 1982. "Individual Motives and Organizational Incentive Systems. Pp. 209-254 in *Research in the Sociology of Organizations,* vol. 1, edited by S.B. Bacharach. Greenwich, CT: JAI Press.

Kriesi, H. and Ph. van Praag, Jr. 1987. "Old and New Politics: The Dutch Peace Movement and the Traditional Political Organizations." *European Journal of Political Science* 15:319-346.

Lofland, J.M. 1985. *Protest, Studies of Collective Behavior and Social Movements.* New Brunswick, NJ: Transaction Books.

McAdam, D. 1982. *Political Process and the Development of Black Insurgency.* Chicago: University of Chicago Press.

_____. 1986. "Rercruitment to High-Risk Activism: The Case of Freedom Summer." *American Journal of Sociology* 92:64-90.

_____. 1988. "Micromobilization Contexts and Recruitment to Activism." *From Structure to Action: Comparing Movement Participation Across Cultures,* edited by B. Klandermans, H. Kriesi, and S. Tarrow. Greenwich, CT: JAI Press.

McAdam, D., J.D. McCarthy, and M.N. Zald. 1988. "Social Movements and Collective Behavior: Building Macro-Micro Bridges." Pp. 695-737 in *Handbook of Sociology,* edited by N.J. Smelser. Beverly Hills, CA: Sage.

McCarthy, J.D. 1987. "Pro-life and Pro-choice Mobilization: Infrastructure Deficits and New Technologies." Pp. 49-67 in *Social Movements in an Organizational Society. Collected Essays,* edited by M.N. Zald and J.D. McCarthy. New Brunswick, NJ: Transaction Books.

McCarthy, J.D. and M.N. Zald. 1973. *The Trend of Social Movements in America.* Morristown, NJ: General Learning Press.

————. 1976. "Resource Mobilization and Social Movements: A Partial Theory." *American Journal of Sociology* 82:1212-1241.

Michels, R. 1962. *Political Parties.* New York: Free Press.

Moreland, R.L. and J. Levine. 1982. "Socialization in Small Groups: Temporal Changes in Individual-Group Relations." *Advances in Experimental Social Psychology* 15:137-192.

Morris, A. 1984. *The Origins of the Civil Rights Movement: Black Communities Organizing for Change.* New York: Free Press.

Oberschall, A. 1980. "Loosely Structured Collective Conflicts: A Theory and an Application." Pp. 45-68 in *Research in Social Movements, Conflict and Change,* vol. 3, edited by L. Kriesberg. Greenwich, CT: JAI Press.

Oliver, P. 1980. "Rewards and Punishments as Selective Incentives for Collective Action: Theoretical Investigations." *American Journal of Sociology* 85:1356-1375.

Olson, M. 1968. *The Logic of Collective Action. Public Goods and the Theory of Groups.* Cambridge, MA: Harvard University Press.

Perrow, C. 1970. "Members as Resources in Voluntary Organizations." Pp. 93-116 in *Organizations and Clients,* edited by W.R. Rosengren and M. Lefton. Columbus, OH: Merrill.

Schennink, B. 1988. "Dynamics of the Peace Movement in The Netherlands." In *From Structure to Action: Comparing Movement Participation Across Cultures,* edited by B. Klandermans, H. Kriesi, and S. Tarrow. Greenwich, CT: JAI Press.

Schwartz, M. 1976. *Radical Protest and Social Structure.* New York: Academic Press.

Snow, D.A. and R.D. Benford. 1988. "Ideology, Frame Resonance, and Participant Mobilization." In *From Structure to Action: Comparing Movement Participiation Across Culotures,* edited by B. Klandermans, H. Kriesi, and S. Tarrow. Greenwich, CT: JAI Press.

Snow, D.A. and R. Machalek. 1983. "The Convert as a Social Type." Pp. 259-288 in *Sociological Theory,* edited by R. Collins. San Francisco: Jossey-Bass.

Snow, D.A., E.B. Rochford, Jr., S. Worden, and R.D. Benford. 1986. "Frame Alignment Processes, Micro-Mobilization and Movement Participation." *American Sociological Review* 51:464-481.

Taylor, D.G. 1986. *Public Opinion and Collective Action.* Chicago: The University of Chicago Press.

Turner, R.H. and L.M. Killian. 1987. *Collective Behavior.* 3rd ed. Englewood Cliffs, NJ: Prentice-Hall.

van Noort, W.J. 1987. "Actievoeren: Strategieën en tactieken." Pp. 91-106 in *Protest en pressie. Een systematische analyse van collectieve actie* (Taking Action: Strategies and Tactics in Protest and Pression: A Systematic Analysis of Collective Action), edited by W.J. van Noort, L.W. Huberts, and L. Rademakers. Assen: van Gorcum.

Wilson, K. and A.M. Orum. 1976. "Mobilizing People for Collective Political Action." *Journal of Political and Military Sociology* 4:187-202.

Zald, M.N. and J.D. McCarthy, eds. 1979. *The Dynamics of Social Movements, Resource Mobilization, Social Control and Tactics.* Cambridge, MA: Winthrop.

RESOURCE ACQUISITION AND ALLOCATION IN U.S. NATIONAL ASSOCIATIONS

David Knoke

Social movements and associations share many characteristics that set them apart from other forms of social organization. In contrast to corporations and government bureaus, whose participants are remunerated for full-time work, movements and associations rely heavily upon voluntary labor, with perhaps a few dedicated activists and salaried leaders. They induce participation largely through normative and affect-based incentive systems (Knoke and Wright-Isak 1982). They both depend upon members and external constituents for the bulk of their sustaining resources, rather than upon taxes or sales in the marketplace. Associations and movements typically lack the large-scale, complex internal divisions of labor, and hierarchical authority patterns of corporate and governmental entities. Instead, democratic ideologies and collegial decision making are modal. Indicators of effective performance are more ambiguous and diffuse for associations and movements than for firms, where quantified

International Social Movement Research, Vol. 2, pages 129-154.
ISBN: 0-89232-964-5

measures of goal attainment (e.g., profits, sales, growth) are more prevalent (see Knoke and Prensky 1984, for extended discussion of these contrasts).

Associations and movements converge chiefly in their organizational components. Associations are always formally named collectivities which have either a clearly delimited mass membership or consist only of an elite cadre, such as Nader-Raider and other public interest groups (Berry 1977). Social movements embrace not only mass membership organizations, but also more spontaneous and ephemeral forms such as rallies, marches, protest demonstrations, and other confrontations with authorities. Some social movement analysts pay special attention to social movement organizations (SMO's) and industries (SMI's) (McCarthy and Zald 1977), and investigate movement dynamics through the careers of their organizational components (Gamson 1975). Indeed, many current associations are the organizational precipitates of various challenging social movements, for example, labor unions (steel and auto workers), health fund-raising associations (Planned Parenthood, March of Dimes), civil rights organizations (National Association for the Advancement of Colored People, National Organization For Women), professional societies (American Association for the Advancement of Science, American Nurses Association), and even some recreational associations (Audubon Society, National Wildlife Federation).

In successfully competing for acceptance by established political actors, movement organizations are frequently incorporated into the polity as pressure group associations (Schlozman and Tierney 1985). As institutionalized organizations, such social movement descendants often have an easier time pursuing their collective objectives, since their organizational stability socially validates them. The transition from social movement to association is blurred, as the creation of more enduring structures and routinized practices need not entail a sharp discontinuity with former objectives. In any event, the following study of associations will illuminate many common problems encountered by social movement organizations (SMOs).

ORGANIZATIONAL POLITICAL ECONOMIES

Like all organizations, associations confront substantial problems in managing essential organizational resources. Their organizational political economies are not financially self-sufficient, but must continually acquire funds either from their members or from external constituents (social movements typically have more porous and ambiguous membership boundaries than associations). A small proportion may be generated by market sales to the general public, for example, the Sierra Club's calendar and nature book business, or by public fund-raising campaigns such as charitable disease-treatment associations' telethons. Potentially lucrative external revenue markets include sympathetic nonmember "conscience constituents" (McCarthy and Zald 1977), who do not personally benefit from the association's activities (Walker 1983), and organizational sponsors such as private foundations and government agencies that provide grants or contracts to an association for specific tasks (e.g., manpower training programs run by the Urban League chapters under Democratic administrations). Associations try to tap these external revenue markets to supplement the bulk of their membership-derived incomes (occasionally, contributors may be unaware that their donations automatically enroll them as "members," e.g., in the Red Cross).

Acquiring resources is only one side of the budget ledger. Resource management includes expenditures of funds in various categories, most importantly for those activities involving maintenance and those involving goal attainment. Some theorists simply equate organizational effectiveness with its ability "to exploit its environment in the acquisition of scarce and valued resources," regardless of the subsequent uses to which these funds might be put (Yuchtman and Seashore 1967). But, to understand adequately an association's political economy, distinctions must be made among the collective goals to which resources may be allocated. Three generic headings provide a useful classification for subsuming the wide diversity of specific goals (see Knoke 1985, for an elaboration):

1. *Member servicing goals* are all goods and services, mainly of a material nature, delivered to organizational members for their private consumption. For example, magazines and journals, insurance, travel plans, sociable and recreational activities, marketing information and employment services, and so forth.
2. *Legitimation goals* involve acceptance by the general public and relevant elites of an association's right to exist and to pursue its affairs in its chosen manner. Obtaining the prestige and goodwill of public acceptance is both an end in itself and an adjunct to other goals. "Public education" campaigns typically aim to bolster an organization's image or to change public attitudes and behaviors to become consistent with an association's values.
3. *Public policy influence goals* also involve external interactions, aimed at getting governmental authorities to apply *their* resources to change laws and practices that will gain or preserve advantages enjoyed by an association's members and nonmember beneficiaries. Formal lobbying expenditures and the development of political capacity comprise major public policy goal allocation decisions. Political capacity consists of distinct roles and activities with implicit or explicit obligations to monitor and intervene in the political system, for example, a grass-roots mobilization program or a political action committee. Enlarged political capacity allows an organization to take rapid advantage of opportunities

offered and to avoid constraints imposed upon it by the national political subsystem.

Clearly, all associations do not pursue these three broad types of goals to the same degree. Many associations concentrate solely on member services, to the exclusion of other purposes, for example, antique auto enthusiast or stamp clubs. SMOs, by definition, concentrate significant effort on legitimation and policy influence, typically spending their limited funds on member services only when necessary to maintain sufficient income flows to continue pursuing these external objectves.

This paper examines how mass-membership American national associations manage their political economies, acquiring financial resources from various sources and subsequently allocating them to alternative goals. The following is a discussion of the organizational features that are expected to affect these budgetary decisions.

BUREAUCRACY AND CENTRALIZATION

To develop an explanation of association resource management decisions, the concepts or bureaucracy and centralization of decision making are fundamental. They are durable structural components of any organization's political economy, and jointly shape the way associations obtain and use their funds. In addition, organizational goals and environments provide important contexts that mediate the bureaucratic-centralization relationships. Following a review of the pertinent theoretical and empirical literatures, the hypotheses to be tested are summarized.

Organizational theorists have variously viewed bureaucracy as a rational structure or as a symbolic form, but the implications for resource management are similar. Under the rational model, bureaucracy is a purposeful design to maximize collective efforts toward explicit objectives (Scott 1987, pp. 40-45). The Weberian image of bureaucracies—comprising circumscribable authority, specified roles, procedures, and rules—is alleged to be technically superior to other forms of imperative coordination and control (Weber 1947). An elaborated vertical and horizontal division of labor permits more effective cultivation of both internal and external resource exchanges, since specialists are assigned to deal with members, constituents, and organizational sponsors. Similarly, bureaucratized associations have enlarged capacities to handle many expenditures, as specialized units again deal with the diverse internal and external objectives.

Under the natural systems approach, organizational structures reflect unplanned and spontaneous processes that enhance organizational success and survival. Most associations do not face the technical efficiency constraints or the market mechanisms of control encountered by production organizations. They are freer to adopt shared, institutionalized structures that reflect prevailing social norms about what organizations should look like and how they should operate (Pfeffer 1982, pp. 244-246). A bureaucratic facade is displayed in order to satisfy dominant cultural values and expectations—a ceremonial conformity to symbols that obscures the real decoupling between formal structure and actual activities (Meyer and Rowan 1977). Associations conforming to bureaucratic principles should be more successful in acquiring funds from external constituents and sponsors, who have come to take such elements for granted as signs of fiscal competence, accountability, and effectiveness. Thus, both the rational and the institutional approaches converge, for different reasons, to an expectation that bureaucratically-organized associations will enjoy improved resource management capabilities.

Centralization of decision making concerns the way that an organization reaches binding decisions to allocate its collective resources to various goals. These objectives may be dictated by one powerful actor, be negotiated within a dominant coalition, or be decided consensualy among all participants (Scott 1987, p. 275). These different cleavage patterns within an association's polity imply different resource management decisions concerning member- versus external-revenues and -expenditures. Freeman's (1979, p. 183) analysis of the resource mobilization efforts within the feminist movement exemplified the problems. She pointed to the dilemma of using scarce resources for group maintenance or goal attainment. A "centralized movement devotes minimal resources to group maintenance needs, focusing them instead on goal attainment," while a "decentralized movement on the other hand, is compelled to devote major resources to group maintenance." Centralized movements can often better attain short-range institutional change goals but at the cost of organizational survival. Decentralized movements can achieve person-oriented attitude changes "through recruitment and conversion in which organizational survival is a dominant concern." (Freeman 1979, p. 183). The older branch of women's liberation (such organizations as the National Organization for Women and Women's Equity Action League) tended toward centralization, while the younger branch rejected national structure, hierarchy, and division of labor. Freeman argued that, although organizational structures were not specifically created to accomplish goals, once in place they constrained the strategic alternatives open to movement organizations.

Almost universally, associations purport to be organizational democracies whose constitutions enshrine the priority of member preferences in collective decision making. In practice, oligarchy seems the likelier fate (Michels 1962; Lipset et al. 1956; Schmidt 1973; Berry 1977), although instances of genuine member control do occur (e.g., the League of Women Voters: Tannenbaum 1968; Gouldner 1960; a crisis center: Mansbridge 1980). Organizational size, member apathy, and absence of formal mechanisms to reinforce participation (e.g., local chapter meetings, referenda, open communication channels) can conspire to restrict the scope of member decision participation. The more that power is concentrated in a few hands, the less reliably can an association depend upon its mass membership to supply essential resources. Widespread member involvement in collective decision making promotes commitment and attachment to an association, which, in turn, increases the collectivity's ability to obtain members' personal resources for collective use (see Knoke and Wood 1981, pp. 70-90; Knoke 1981, for evidence on these dynamics in social influence associations). However, associations with more centralized decision-making processes may be judged as trustworthy and accountable by external constituents and sponsors, such as foundations and government agencies, according to the "myths of the institutional environment" perspective described above. Thus, centralized associations will acquire larger proportions of their funds from nonmember sources and will allocate them to goals other than member services, such as information-public relations, lobbying, and enhanced political capacity.

Bureaucracy and centralization are well-known to covary positively for work organizations: Larger corporations are more differentiated but less bureaucratized and centralized in decision making than smaller ones, contrary to the Weberian model (Scott 1987, pp. 243-245). In large corporations, economies of scale reduce bureaucratic administration, decentralization increases to prevent overwhelming of top administrators, and standardization promotes routine decision making. Whether this relationship occurs in nontechnical associations is unknown. Gamson's (1975, p. 94) study of 53 historical American SMO's found bureaucracy and centralization to be unrelated, though both structural dimensions were positively related to organizational success in winning acceptance and new advantages from the polity. Both dimensions appeared to interact with factionalism, such that bureaucratic groups were better able to overcome the debilitating effects of internal dissidence, while the combination of centralization with bureaucracy produced the most successful outcomes. Whether bureaucracy and centralization interact to affect resource management decisions in contemporary associations remains to be seen.

The effects of bureaucracy and centralization on resources decisions must take into account how association goals enter into the process. As discussed above, associations differentially emphasize member-serving, legitimation, and policy-influence goals. Expenditures vary positively as functions of organizational commitments to these objectives. For example, groups that do not seek to affect government decisions, such as hobby clubs, will spend nothing for lobbying. Associations that hold stronger policy-influence interests, such as trade associations and labor unions, will spend greater proportions of their budgets on lobbying and will develop greater political capacities. The magnitude of covariation between goals and expenditures may be attenuated due to differing commitments to achieving multiple goals. Similar concerns apply to the effect of espoused legitimation goals upon spending for information and public relations programs. Allocations to member services should be greatest among associations that are least concerned about external goals.

Similarly, resource management decisions depend upon an organization's external environment, particularly its location along both the scarcity and information-flow dimensions (Aldrich 1979, pp. 110-135). Common to most approaches to organizational environments is variation in resource scarcity. Where organizations operate in rich resource environments—for example, when potential membership populations are large or have high discretionary incomes—they can more readily try to satisfy diverse constituencies and meet many goals than under scarcity conditions. Total revenues are not only an object of explanation, but, in turn, revenues index an association's position within the rich-lean environment, and that may help to explain how it acquires and allocates resources. Less commonly, an organization's environment is viewed as "a source of information used directly by decision makers as one basis for maintaining or modifying structures and activities (Aldrich 1979, p. 122). The flow of information about external conditions across the organizational boundaries to relevant decision makers comprises a perceptual dimension of the environment that may be just as significant as resources in shaping organizational behaviors. In the literature on information flow, uncertainty has received the most attention (Duncan 1972, Legblebici and Salancik 1981; Argote 1982), but a strong case can be made that complexity constitutes a second dimension in the information-flow environment (Child 1972; Dess and Beard 1984). Uncertainty reflects unpredictable relationships and low constraint among elements, while complexity implies that many varied elements are intricately interconnected, though not necessarily in unpredictable fashion. An uncertain environment feeds unreliable information into decision makers, while a complex environment generates huge volumes of data that overwhelm the organization's capacity to assimilate it usefully. Both uncertainty and complexity may independently pose serious problems for organizational decision makers because of the limited information-processing capabilities of people and organizations (Anderson 1983). When organizational decision makers perceive complex or unpredictable information-flow environments, they are likely to respond by trying to improve their access to more reliable data and to exert greater control over these problematic factors. Thus, we can anticipate a greater effort by such associations to tap revenues from external sources, to spend resources on external objectives, and to enhance the organization's political capacity to deal with its external exigencies.

HYPOTHESIS

The preceding discussion suggests several propositions relating bureaucracy and centralization to resource management decisions that can be tested with data on mass-membership associations' revenue and expenditure decisions.

The greater the bureaucratization and the more centralized the decision making, the larger the total amount of revenue that an association generates. Both bureaucratic and centralized organizations acquire larger proportions of their revenues from external sources, such as nonmembers, foundations, and governments. Less bureaucratic and centralized groups are more dependent upon their memberships for income. Finally, bureaucracy and centralization jointly interact to generate larger revenues and more external income than either dimension produces independently.

On the expenditure side, bureaucratic and centralized structures induce proportionately smaller spending on direct services to members and larger allocations to external programs (i.e., lobbying, information-public relations, and political capacity development). As with revenues, bureaucracy and centralization interact to enhance spending on external programs.

In both revenue and expenditure decisions, association goals and environments exert independent effects, as well as possible conditional (interaction) relationships. In particular, associations spend larger shares of their budgets on activities that reflect important organizational goals. Richer resource environments and less calculable (complex and uncertain) information-flow environments will boost total revenues, acquisition of funds from nonmembers, expenditures on external programs, and development of larger political capacity.

DATA

Three compendia were used to compile a master list of all national mass-membership associations in the United States (Colgate and Fowler 1983; Colgate and Evans 1981; Akey 1983). Organizations were sorted into five strata: trade associations, professional societies, labor unions, recreational associations, and a residual category. This latter category contains most of the traditional SMOs (e.g., civil rights, feminist, peace, antinuclear, and others), but these associations are only a small percentage of the stratum. The residual category also includes religious, fraternal, service, scientific, medical, occult, entertainment, and miscellaneous organizations not classified into the four main strata. Insufficient numbers of SMOs were drawn in the sample, preventing their analysis as a separate category.

After eliminating duplicates, nonassociations, and defunct groups, approximately 13,000 organizations remained in the population. Based on directory information about annual budgets, the trade, professional, and recreational categories were each subdivided into small and large sizes, with the latter containing about a fifth of each type. Random samples of 50-60 associations were drawn from each of the eight categories. In January and February 1984, hour-long telephone interviews were conducted with the executive director or chief elected official from each organization. Interviews were completed with 459 informants, for an overall response rate of 92.7%. In analyses reported below, cases are weighted to preserve the relative proportions of the sampling strata in the entire population of American national associations.

MEASURES

Associational *bureaucracy* is measured as a three-level classification of the internal formal structure of the national organization:

- three or more hierarchical levels or horizontal departments—(3);
- employs a full-time chief staff officer or at least three other managerial and professional staff—(2);
- lacks internal differentiation and full-time, managerial-professional staff—(1).

Centralization of decision making uses Tannenbaum's (1968) "control graph" technique for assessing the influence of positions. Informants were asked, "Taking all areas of decision making into account, we would like you to estimate how much influence each of the following groups or persons actually have in the [organization's name]." A five-point rating scale from "little or no influence" to "a very great deal of influence" was used. Because almost every association has a board of directors, the difference in influence ratings between the board and the general membership was calculated, with positive scores indicating a greater concentration of decision-making power in the board's hands. For subsequent analyses, four ordinal categories of roughly equal frequency were created:

- The board is three or four levels more powerful than the membership—(4);
- The board is two levels higher—(3);
- The board is one level higher—(2);
- The board is equal to, or less powerful than, the membership—(1).

Total association *revenues* for the current year's budget were obtained from the informants, from budget documents mailed to us (by about a third of the sample), or estimated from the directories. Only 1% of the sample had missing data on total revenues. Informants were also asked to estimate the amounts or percentages of revenues obtained from four sources:

(a) membership dues and assessments;
(b) contributions from corporate or individual nonmembers;
(c) government grants and private foundations;
(d) sales of services and merchandise.

On the *expenditure* side, three allocation categories were used:

(a) direct services to members;
(b) public relations and information programs;
(c) lobbying activities.

All revenue and expenditure categories were transformed to percentages of total revenue, not necessarily totalling to 100% of an association's annual budget.

Political capacity is operationalized as a simple tally of the number of distinct roles or programs in an association that are potentially relevant to political action. Associations were assigned one point for having each of the following:

• persons who "monitor national policy matters of interest" to the organization;
• persons whose main job is "to lobby government and legislative bodies for favorable decisions;
• a political action committee;
• a program "to activate its members in local areas to lobby their own Congressmen and Senators on national issues of interest;"
• a person responsible for public relations
• in-house legal counsel;
• outside lawyers retained by the association;
• staff members who gather "systematic technical data."

The political capacity index thus ranges from 0 to 8 points, with higher scores indicating greater potential for political activation. Note that only four of the eight index components above refer explicitly to political functions, while several reflect formal roles within the organizational structure. However, previous research on monitoring capacity of major interest groups in Washington indicated that the variety of staff available to an organization is an important indicator of its potential for political activity (Laumann et al. 1985; Laumann and Knoke 1987). Unlike other dependent variables, the political capacity index is not measured by financial costs to the association, although there may be an underlying monotonic relation.

Table 1. Items Comprising Environmental Complexity and
Environmental Uncertainty Scales

Scale Items	Percentage Agreeing
Environmental Complexity	
1. Without this organization to defend their interests, the members would be much worse off than they are.	60.5
2. To achieve our goals, it is essential to work formally with many other organizations.	60.3
3. This organization's members face strong pressures from a difficult environment.	46.9
4. The techniques, skills, and information needed to conduct this organization's business are changing very rapidly.	46.1
5. The political climate of the country right now is very favorable to our goals.[a]	36.7
6. Our relations with other organizations are sometimes marked by conflict.	32.5
7. This organization responds rapidly to new opportunities, making it a leader in several areas.[a]	21.5
Environmental Uncertainty	
1. This organization takes few risks, and mostly reacts to environmental pressures[a]	53.4
2. This organization is not at the forefront of new developments, but concentrates on doing the best job in a limited area.	51.4
3. Making long-range plans for this organization is hindered by difficulty in predicting the nature of future events.	43.5
4. It is frequently difficult to obtain adequte information about what is going on outside of the organization.	17.9

Note: [a] Item reverse coded.

Organizational *size* is computed as the total number of association memberships, counting each natural person or organization as one member.

Two scales measuring organizational goals were based on factor analyses of the informant's indications on a list of eight types of goals: "which ones are not goals, minor goals, moderate goals, or major goals?" (coded 0 to 3). *Social change goals* averages responses from two items: "to change the values and beliefs of a larger society" and "to affect the lives of non-members." The *policy influence goal* is the response to one item: "to influence public policy decisions of the government."

Two scales were constructed to measure the *uncertainty* and *complexity* aspects of each association's information-flow environment. During the interview, informants were read 22 statements about perceived external conditions. They were asked how strongly they agreed or disagreed that each statement applied to their associations (strongly agree, agree, neither agree nor disagree, disagree, strongly disagree, or inapplicable; this latter response was recoded to neutral). Exploratory factory analysis, using principal components, uncovered two dimensions whose contents seem to tap the complexity and uncertainty dimensions discussed above (see Knoke and Adams 1987, for more details). Table 1 shows the items in each scale and the percentage of sample associations agreeing that the conditions exist for the organization. Scale scores were calculated by assigning numerical values to item responses (strongly disagree = 1 to strongly agree = 5), then averaging the association informant's responses to the seven complexity items and the four uncertainty items, respectively. (Note that the first, and possibly the second, uncertainty scale items refer to risk-taking, implying an organizational response to external conditions.) High scores mean that an association is perceived to face more complex and more unpredictable information-flow environments. The two scales each achieved respectable levels of internal-consistency reliability (Cronbach's alpha = .69 for complexity and .68 for uncertainty).

FINDINGS

Because national associations are rarely the object of cross-sectional surveys, the initial findings report greater detail on their attributes than might otherwise be warranted.

Characteristics of Associations

For all associations combined, roughly equal numbers fell into the low (37%), medium (33%), and high (30%) levels of the bureaucratization variable. The distributions across types of associations diverged, however. A majority of labor unions (58%) and a plurality of trade associations (41%) were highly bureaucratized, but a large majority of recreational organizations (72%) were least bureaucratized. Both the professional and residual types closely followed the overall distribution. On the centralization scale, all five categories were skewed relative to the overall equiprobable distribution across the four levels. Majorities of trade associations (51%), professional societies (53%), and labor unions (79%) fell into the two most centralized categories, while majorities of the recreational (56%) and residual (52%) associations occupied the two least centralized categories. As most of the SMOs are in the residual category, these groups appear to be decentralized and nonbureaucratized.

As Tables 2 and 3 show, the measures of bureaucratization and centralization in U.S. national associations vary in expected directions with many of the conventional attributes of nonvoluntary organizations. The more bureaucratized an association, the more likely it is to put into writing its rules for staff members (i.e., to be formalized), to have a larger number of local chapters

Table 2. Characteristics of Associations by Level of Bureaucratization

Level of Bureaucratization	Written Rules for Staff (%)	Local Chapters (Mean)	Standing Committees (Mean)	Members (Mean)	Highly Centralized (%)
3. High	79.4	62.9	9.9	67,118	53.6
2. Medium	61.1	13.7	5.2	11,068	52.0
1. Low	40.5	6.6	3.9	1,489	44.4
Average	60.8	29.6	6.5	28.547	50.1
(p)	(.001)	(.001)	(.05)	(.01)	(.01)

Table 3. Characteristics of Associations by Level of Centralization

Level of Centralization	Board Elects President (%)	Uses Referendum (%)	Convention Makes Many Decisions (%)	Election Turnout (%)	Member Influence Scale (Mean)	Leader Influence Scale (Mean)
4. High	41.1	53.8	28.3	38.5	3.56	4.06
3.	45.1	43.2	27.5	39.1	3.76	3.71
2.	31.1	20.9	53.6	50.2	4.00	3.35
1. Low	21.5	37.6	53.5	52.5	4.01	3.48
Average	34.8	38.6	40.8	44.8	3.84	3.64
(p)	(.001)	(.001)	(.001)	(.002)	(.001)	(.001)

and branches, to maintain more standing committees, and to have a greater number of members. Centralization varies inversely with several indicators of formal democratic procedures: The more powerful the board of directors, the less likely are members to elect the president, to have a referendum for policy matters, to make many policy decisions at a national convention, or to turn out for national elections. Two multi-item scales were created from a series of statements about the locus of decision making (e.g., "power over major policy decisions is concentrated in the hands of a few people;" "major policy decisions are made only after wide consultation at all levels of the organization"). As Table 3 shows, both scales strongly covary with the degree of board control. Indeed, centralization alone explains almost one-tenth of the variance in both the member power and the leader power scales. Finally, bureaucracy is only weakly correlated with centralization, as shown in the last column of Table 2 (gamma = +.09), consistent with Gamson's (1975) historical finding. Thus, these two structural dimensions can reasonably be treated as variables that may independently affect resource acquisition and allocation decisions.

Table 4 displays the average revenue and expenditure distributions for all associations, as well as for four of the five main sampling strata (the residual

Table 4. Annual Revenue and Expenditures by Types of Associations

Category	All Assns	Trade Assns	Professional Societies	Labor Unions	Recreational Assns
Total Revenues ($000)					
Mean	2,695	1,255	707	14,412	1,290
Median	72	175	80	2,001	18
Revenue Sources (%):					
Member dues	64.6	62.0	58.8	83.8	66.2
Sales	18.0	22.8	23.3	2.6	17.9
Nonmembers	5.1	1.7	4.4	1.5	5.7
Govt & Foundations	1.8	1.1	1.6	1.1	1.4
Other	10.5	12.4	11.9	11.0	8.8
Total	100.0	100.0	100.0	100.0	100.0
Expenditures (%):					
Member services	69.8	62.5	67.9	70.9	77.8
Info-public relations	7.6	10.4	6.0	4.2	5.4
Lobbying	2.9	3.7	1.7	6.5	1.5
Other	19.7	23.4	24.4	18.4	15.3
Total	100.0	100.0	100.0	100.0	100.0
(N)	(439)	(104)	(105)	(54)	(123)

Note: Miscellaneous associations not tabulated separately.

category is too heterogeneous to be meaningful). Total annual revenues average almost $2.7 million per association, due mainly to the exceptionally large budgets of labor unions. Median values show that half of all associations have incomes below $72,000 per year, with the median recreational association making do on less than $18,000. Revenue sources exhibit relatively little variation across types, although unions again stand out in being more dependent on member dues. About two-thirds of associations' incomes are generated from membership dues and assessments, and almost another fifth from sales of services and merchandise (some proportion of which also comes from members). About 7% of revenue is externally generated (from corporate and individual nonmembers, government grants, and foundations), and about a tenth from various unspecified sources (such as rents, endowments, and so forth). On the other side of the ledger, members are the direct beneficiaries of the large majority of association expenses. Recreational groups are the most likely to spend their money on member services and trade associations are the least likely. In formation programs and public relations aimed at external audiences account for one dollar in 13, with trade associations as the leader. Direct lobbying expenses comprise less than 3% of expenditures, and unions and trade associations account for more the bulk of these funds (given the large budgets of unions, their 6.5% average translates into almost $1 million yearly

Table 5. Relation of Association Revenues and Expenditures
to Bureaucratization and Centralization

	Total Revenue ($000)	Member Dues Revenue (%)	External Sources Revenue (%)	Member Services Expend. (%)	Info-PR Expend. (%)	Lobby Expend. (%)	Political Capacity Index (Mean)
Bureaucratization							
3. High	2,753	50.9	16.1	62.9	12.5	3.9	3.59
2. Medium	202	60.1	9.8	70.3	8.1	1.7	2.51
1. Low	23	70.8	6.3	69.8	8.3	3.3	1.82
Average	1,075	60.5	10.9	67.4	9.8	3.1	2.62
Eta-square	.037	.071	.031	.014	.026	.009	.149
(*p*)	(.001)	(.001)	(.001)	(.05)	(.01)	(N.S.)	(.001)
Centralization							
4. High	646	60.6	6.2	68.9	6.5	2.1	2.33
3.	1,067	56.7	17.3	70.1	11.5	2.7	2.96
2.	1,110	57.1	9.4	70.0	8.6	2.4	2.98
1. Low	1,403	69.7	9.7	62.9	11.9	4.7	2.73
Average	1,058	60.9	10.8	68.1	9.7	3.0	2.76
Eta-square	.001	.028	.030	.011	.030	.012	.018
(*p*)	(N.S.)	(.01)	(.01)	(N.S.)	(.01)	(N.S.)	(N.S.)

each on lobbying). Recreational clubs and professional societies are least prone
to lobby.

The income and outgo accounts in Table 4 are category averages that conceal
much variation at the individual association level. The following sections try
to explain this variation in terms of the bureaucratic and centralized features,
in conjunction with other organizational variables.

Main Effects

The main relationships of bureaucracy and centralization to revenue,
expenditure, and political capacity measures appear in Table 5. Bureaucracy's
effect on total revenue is striking: Moderately bureaucratized associations take
in almost 10 times, and heavily bureaucratized organizations more than a
hundred times, the incomes of the least bureaucratically-structured groups. Of
course, this relationship is to some extent causally reciprocal—with larger
resource bases, associations can afford to hire sufficient numbers of staff that
must be bureaucratically-organized. Still, the trilevel measure of bureaucracy
accounts for less than 4% of the total revenue variation among associations
(eta-square = .037).

Membership dues account for a decreasing proportion and external revenue sources for an increasing percentage of association revenues as the level of bureaucracy increases. The presence of full-time specialized staff enables an organization more effectively to seek out and cultivate alternative income sources. Expenditures are less clearly related to bureaucracy: Only information-public relations spending is clearly concentrated at the highest bureaucratic level, although spending for member services falls off slightly. However, spending on lobbying does not vary significantly across the three levels. The political capacity index varies strongly with bureaucracy, with twice as many activities carried out at the highest level compared to the lowest. Bureaucracy accounts for one-seventh of the total variation in political capacity (eta-square = .149). At first glance, this covariation may appear tautologous, inflated by the operationalizations of the two variables. Bureaucratized associations tend to assign their employees to the political functions. But nonbureaucratized associations arrange for unpaid members to perform these tasks. And many highly bureaucratized organizations do not develop extensive political capacities because they do not have external influence goals. Hence, the strong relationship observed in Table 5 is neither a definitional tautology nor a measurement artifact. Indeed, later analyses show that the relationship is spurious, arising through common covariation with political influence goals.

Centralization bears fewer strong monotonic relations to revenues and expenditures. Despite the smaller average budgets of most centralized compared to least centralized associations, so much within-level variance remains that a significant difference does not obtain. Both internal and external revenue sources vary nonmonotonically with centralization: The lowest percentage from dues and the highest percentage from outside sources occurs at the second highest level of board control, rather than among the most centralized groups. Among expenditures, only information-public relations spending has a significant relationship, and it is also nonmonotonic. Even the political capacity index is spread almost uniformly across all levels of centralization. In sum, at least at the zero-order level of covariation, centralization is much less related to national association resources than is bureaucratization. As the next section shows, these main effects obscure some important joint interactions.

Interaction Effects

Table 6 reports a set of regression equations in which the various dependent variables are regressed upon bureaucratization, centralization, and an interaction term (the total revenues measure is logged to reduce its skew). The interaction was created by first dichotomizing centralization into high and low categories (board is two or more levels more powerful than members), and by dichotomizing bureaucracy into the highest level versus the lower two. Then,

Table 6. Standardized Coefficients for Multiple Regressions of Budgetary and Political Capacity Measures on Bureaucracy and Centralization

Independent Variables	Dependent Variables						
	Total Revenue (log $)	Member Dues Revenue (%)	External Sources Revenue (%)	Member Services Expend. (%)	Info-PR Expend. (%)	Lobby Expend. (%)	Political Capacity Index (Mean)
Bureaucracy	.78***	-.21***	.04	-.13*	.11	-.06	.34***
Centralization	.06	-.05	-.11*	.06	-.15**	-.16**	-.13**
Interaction	-.17***	-.09	.25***	.03	.07	.18**	.09
R^2adj	.482***	.074***	.058***	.010*	.029***	.019**	.154***

Notes:
  * $p < .05$
  ** $p < .01$
  *** $p < .001$

the 83 organizations that were both highly bureaucratized and centralized were coded 1, and all other combinations were coded 0. By entering both main effects as well as the interaction term into the equation for each dependent variable, the presence of net significant main an joint effects can be assessed. As Table 6 shows, the interaction term was significant in three instances: total revenues, percentage from external sources, and percentage spent on lobbying.

As might be expected from Table 5, bureaucracy exerts a substantial impact on revenues (standardized $b^* = .78$), accounting for most of the multiple R-square of 48.2%. Centralization has no significant main effect, but the sign of the interaction term is negative, meaning that net of bureaucracy's main effect, a highly centralized bureaucracy tends to acquire lower overall income than other types. Inspection of tabulated cell means (not shown) localizes this interaction effect in the combination of highly bureaucratized but *less-centralized* associations (some 72 organizations). These associations reported mean annual revenues of $3.6 million, compared to only $2.0 million for the highly centralized bureaucracies and about $110,000 for all others. This unexpected finding suggests that bureaucratic associations, in which members have relatively greater influence, provide the best structural combination for maximizing total revenues. Perhaps these organizations are more successful at appealing to their members for large contributions (or in persuading members to help collect money for the organization), to judge from the negative (though not significant) coefficient in the equation predicting membership dues in Table 6.

The interaction involving external sources of revenue is exactly the reverse pattern. The positive coefficient indicates that, net of bureaucracy (which is

Table 7. Interaction of Bureaucratization and Centralization
with Percentage of Revenue from External Sources

		Centralization		
		High	Low	Total (*N*)
Bureaucratization	High	22.6 (79)	10.0 (68)	16.7 (147)
	Low	6.3 (127)	9.9 (129)	8.1 (256)
	Total (*N*)	12.5 (206)	10.0 (197)	11.3 (403)

not significant) and centralization (which has a small negative effect),
associations which are both highly bureaucratic and centralized acquire a larger
percentage of their revenues from nonmembers, governments, and
foundations, Table 7 shows exactly how strong this combination is. Centralized
bureaucracies obtain nearly 23% of their revenues from outside, compared to
10% or less for all three other types of associations. A similar relationship
occurs for expenditures on lobbying, net of a significant inverse relationship
for centralization (i.e., groups where member control is greater, spend more
on lobbying). In particular, the combination of a less-bureaucratized group
with high board control is much less likely to engage in lobbying (1% spent),
compared to the high-high combination (4.5% spent).

The relationships identified in Table 6 do not take into account other important
dimensions of associations. Table 8 reports a series of expanded regression
analyses in which two goals measures, two information flow environmental scales,
and membership size and total revenues as indicators of resource environment
are added to the basic equations. The control variables substantially alter several
of the bureaucratic and centralization coefficients that were significant in Table
6. Specifically, taking association goals into account eliminates the negative effects
of bureaucracy on member dues and member services, and erases the effect of
centralization on information-public relations. Both centralization and
bureaucracy are now found to have insignificant relations to political capacity,
once policy influence goals are inlcuded. This finding indicates that political
capacity depends upon the purposes sought by an association, and is not a
tautologous function of formal organizational structure.

Table 8. Standardized Coefficients for Multiple Regressions of Budgetary and Political Capacity Measures on Organizational Characteristics

Independent Variables	Dependent Variables						
	Total Revenue ($000)	Member Dues Revenue (%)	External Sources Revenue (%)	Member Services Expend. (%)	Info-PR Expend. (%)	Lobby Expend. (%)	Political Capacity Index (Mean)
Bureaucracy	.66***	-.01	.01	-.10	.29***	-.06	-.03
Centralization	.08*	-.01	-.08	-.03	-.05	-.07	-.03
Interaction	-.17***	-.13*	.22***	.09	-.02	.13*	.10*
Societal Change Goals	-.05	-.20***	.21***	-.08	.20***	-.02	-.04
Policy Influence Goals	.15***	.11	.05	-.31***	.16**	.30***	.40***
Environmental Complexity	.07	.11*	-.04	-.01	-.05	.04	.13***
Environmental Uncertainty	.01	-.06	.01	-.04	.06	-.02	-.04
Size (log)	.26***	-.02	.13*	.04	-.11*	.01	-.02
Revenue (log)	—	-.27***	-.06	-.02	-.19***	-.04	.42***
R^2adj	.552***	.134***	.111***	.119***	.123***	.090***	.472***

Notes:
* p < .05
** p < .01
*** p < .001

In Table 6, the only main bureaucratic effects remaining significant occur in the total revenues and information-public relations equations. However, not only are the bureaucracy-centralization interactions still significant, but two others become marginally significant (a negative interaction in the member dues equation and a positive coefficient in the political capacity equation). These results suggest that the combination of bureaucracy with centralization remains a potent force in association budgeting practices, net of goals and environmental characteristics.

The effects of the control variables are interesting in their own right. Societal change and policy influence goals affect revenues and expenditures in generally expected directions. The more important that policy influence is to an association, the more total revenues it acquires, the larger the percentage that it spends on lobbying and information-public relations, the greater its capacity for political action, and the less it spends on direct services to its members. In other words, organizational budgetary practices are geared towards achieving its ostensible external goals. These findings are particularly relevant to SMOs, as most of these groups consider governmental policy influence to be a major goal. The absence of significant policy goal effects on member or external sources of revenue, however, contrasts with recent revisionist accounts of the U.S. civil rights movement arguing that indigenous resources were critical (McAdam 1982, pp. 120-125; Morris 1984). A future sampling design that separates conventional interest groups from challenging SMOs might resolve the question of the financial bases of insurgencies.

Societal change goals, which need not involve governmental influence objectives (the two are correlated only .43), generally exhibit a different pattern of effects. Societal-change oriented associations acquire fewer resources from member dues and more from external constituents. They spend larger percentages of their funds on information-public relations, but not on lobbying or members services. Significantly, they do not develop larger political action capabilities than do nonchange associations, presumably because their efforts are direct substantially at nongovernment changes such as public opinion or personal behavior.

The environmental complexity and uncertainty measures do not attain substantial net effects in most equations. Complexity is slightly related to increased dues revenues. However, as expected, complexity is strongly related to developing greater political capacity. Part of the perceived complexity of the environment may lie in difficulties posed by the external political situation (see scale items in Table 1). Finally, the resource environment (logged members size and total revenues) have only a few significant effects. More members mean greater total revenues (certainly true within organizations, but also between them as well, despite varying dues structures). The strong negative effect of logged revenues in the member dues equation suggests that the negative bureaucracy coefficient in Table 6 is really a spurious relationship. That is, more bureaucratized groups do not obtain smaller proportions of their revenues from their members, once one takes into account that associations operating in more resource-rich environments tend to acquire larger proportions of their revenues from nonmember sources. When both bureaucracy and total revenue are included in the same equation, the true effect emerges. Similarly, in the information-public relations equation, Table 8 reveals a suppressor effect: Bureaucratized associations allocate larger percentages of their budgets to these expenditures, controlling for the net tendencies of larger and wealthier associations to spend less on these activities. Finally, the strong positive effect of total revenue on political capacity emphasizes the obvious point that performing extensive political functions costs a lot of money.

The preceding multivariate equations generally support the importance of bureaucratic and centralized structures, particularly their interaction on resources. But, except for the total revenue and political capacity equations, the amounts of variance explained in the dependent measures are disappointingly small. Clearly, much room remains for specifying other factors that enter into resource management decisions. Before discussing some possibilities, the next section examines three conditioning relationships of some interest.

Conditional Effects

The preceding analyses treated the entire sample of associations as coming from a single population experiencing uniform processes. The possibility arises that substantial heterogeneity within the national association population may mask different underlying processes. The bureaucratic-centralization combination may condition the effects of organizational goals, particularly societal change and governmental policy-influence objectives. To examine this possibility, the sample was divided according to the four bureaucratic-centralization conditions, and separate regression analyses were run within each subsample. Unlike that univariate distributions, the joint distribution of bureaucracy and centralization are similar across types of associations. Only labor unions are heavily concentrated, with a majority in the high-bureaucratized, low-centralized combination (62%). The four other strata exhibit only small departures from the overall sample distribution, suggesting that social movement organizations may differ little from other associations in their degree of bureaucratization and centralization.

As Table 9 shows, the process of acquiring funds from external sources varies across the four levels of bureaucratic centralization. Among the two least bureaucratized types of associations, virtually none of the predictor variables achieve significance: only environmental uncertainty in the low-low combination and policy influence goals in the low-high combination. All the

Table 9. Standardized Coefficients for Multiple Regressions of External Revenue, Within Levels of Bureaucratization and Centralization

Independent Variables	Percentage of Revenue from External Sources				
	All Assns	Bureauc=Low Central=Low	Bureauc=Low Central=High	Bureauc=High Central=Low	Bureauc=High Central=High
Societal Change Goals	.22***	.13	.15	-.01	.35***
Policy Influence Goals	.06	.15	-.37**	.43***	.04
Environmental Complexity	-.02	.17	-.05	-.31***	-.01
Environmental Uncertainty	.01	-.23*	-.09	.30***	.02
Size (log)	.15**	.18	-.02	.08	.40***
Revenue (log)	-.01	.01	.10	.13	-.42***
R^2adj	.079***	.157**	.075**	.337***	.201***
(N)	(453)	(129)	(127)	(68)	(79)

Notes:
* p < .05
** p < .01
*** p < .001

150

action resides within the two subsamples of highly-bureaucratized associations, and the processes are strikingly complementary. Highly-bureaucratized organizations whose members have greater influence are more likely to obtain a greater percentage of external funds if they stress policy influence goals, operate in less complex environments, but face greater uncertainty. In contrast, for highly-bureaucratized associations that have stronger boards, none of these variables are significant. Instead, greater external funding comes when societal change goals are major, membership size is larger, but total revenues are smaller. These findings strongly suggest that two distinct markets exist for associations that attempt to augment their resources from external constituencies. One set appeals to supporters by stressing nongovernmental social changes and conforms to the popular image of a mass-membership but board-run bureaucracy. The other set is a member-directed bureaucracy operating in a turbulent environment while seeking to influence government policy decisions.

DISCUSSION

Bureaucracy and centralization are distinct dimensions of American national associations that exert important impacts upon resource acquisition and allocation decisions. Bureaucratized associations depend less upon their members for financial support and engage more in nonservice activities such as information and public relations programs, lobbying, and political capacity. The direct effect of centralization on revenues and expenditures is less clear, but its joint interaction with bureaucracy is strong. The largest total revenues are generated by a combination of high bureaucracy with low centralization, implying that revenues are maximized when members maintain control over a complex association. Much of this money may come from the members themselves, although the coefficient in that equation is not statistically significant. However, the combination of high bureaucracy and high centralization is most conducive to obtaining money from external sources (corporations, nonmember constituents, governments, and foundations), and to spending it on lobbying activity.

Association goals may also affect the selection of a revenue strategy. Societal change goals seem to attract more resources from external constituents when the organization exhibits a board-dominated bureaucratic structure. But, public policy influence goals help to generate greater external revenues when the members retain more power. Presumably, this divergence in structural responses to resource acquisition arises from differences among the types of external sponsors whose contributions are being solicited. Unfortunately, the data do not provide enough detail on the identities of the associations' sponsors to test this proposition.

The findings in this chapter are based on U.S. national associations in the 1980s. SMOs comprise only a small part of this population—perhaps 2%, at most. Any generalization of results to this type of association really requires a large oversample of SMOs. However, to the extent that national movements display organizational characteristics similar to the associations in this study, the findings may have some bearing on their resource problems. As collectivities committed to changing governmental policy decisions and to altering societal values, SMOs confront the classic dilemma of how best to organize without sacrificing their ultimate objectives through adoption of dysfunctional structures. How much effort should go into organizational maintenance and how much into external goal attainment, which might jeopardize organizational survival? The perpetual tension between bureaucratic-centralization and member control lies at the heart of debates between movement purists and organizational partisans, whether one looks at the Cultural Revolution of Chinese Maoists or the Equal Rights Amendment strategies of the National Organization for Women (Mansbridge 1986).

With initial movement successes, imperatives to consolidate and extend the organization's impact become compelling for many leaders. As more supporters rally to the movement's cause and an influx of resources must be effectively managed, the case for formalization, division of labor, hierarchy, and discretion becomes increasingly hard to resist. Preventing the drift of decisions into the hands of organizational specialists becomes problematic, despite loud avowals that the membership ultimately decides policy. When outside sponsors increase in importance because they can provide funds, media attention, power, and legitimacy, an SMO may confront a crisis. Perhaps some of the mass membership falls away, either withdrawing from participation altogether, or following a disaffected cadre into a purist splinter movement. The parent organization may seek renewal, or may become even more dependent on an alternative constituency. Its strategies, tactics, and goals may shift to accommodate the new exigencies. When new leadership ascends, as bureaucracy and centralization become entrenched, and as resource dependencies solidify, an aging SMO comes increasingly to resemble other interest groups in the polity. How frequently such life cycle stages typify SMOs, and whether oligarchy is their inevitable fate, cannot be answered definitively until detailed comparative data on SMO histories are gathered.

The analyses reported above mostly accounted for small percentages of the variance in resource acquisition and allocation, with the exception of total revenue and political capacity. Perceived environmental complexity and uncertainty were conspicuously absent. Considerable opportunity remains for examining other factors. During budget making, what trade-offs among goals and resources are consciously considered? What constraints operate among collective goals, member interests, and leader discretion? How does the content of environmental conditions shape organizational behavior—for example, governmental regulations and legal stipulations (e.g., statutory requirements for nonprofit status), and oppositional coalition activities? What impact do organizational incentive systems have upon the interplay of member services and external objectives? How does the political economy between national headquarters and local chapters shape the flow of financial resources among various budgetary categories? To answer these and other questions will require a knowledge of resource decisions at a substantially more detailed level than is yet available for wide range of associations and SMOs.

ACKNOWLEDGMENTS

Thanks to Bert Klandermans for many helpful suggestions. Data collection and analysis was made possible through grants from the National Science Foundation (SES82-16927 and SES85-08051). Data were collected by the Center for Survey Research at Indiana University, Kathryn Cirkensa, Field Director.

REFERENCES

Akey, D. ed. 1983. *Encyclopedia of Associations.* 18th ed. Detroit, MI: Gale Research.

Aldrich, H.E. 1979. *Organizations and Environments.* Englewood Cliffs, NJ: Prentice-Hall.

Anderson, P. 1983. "Decision Making by Objection and the Cuban Missile Crisis." *Administrative Science Quarterly* 28:201-222.

Argote, L. 1982. "Input Uncertainty and Organizational Coordination in Hospital Emergency Units." *Administrative Science Quarterly* 27:420-434.

Berry, J.M. 1977. *Lobbying for the People: The Political Behavior of Public Interest Groups.* Princeton: Princeton University Press.

Child, J. 1972. "Organization Structure, Environment and Performanc: The Role of Strategic Choice." *Sociology* 6:1-22.

Colgate, C. and L.A. Evans, eds. 1981. *National Recreational, Sporting and Hobby Organizations of the United States.* 3rd ed. Washington: Columbia Books.

Colgate, C. and R.L. Fowler, eds. 1983. *National Trade and Professional Associations of the United States.* 18th ed. Washington: Columbia Books.

Dess, G.C. and D.W. Beard. 1984. "Dimensions of Organizational Task Environments." *Administrative Science Quarterly* 20:613-629.

Duncan, R.B. 1972. "Characteristics of Organizational Environments and Perceived Environmental Uncertainty." *Administrative Science Quarterly* 17:313-327.

Freeman, J. 1979. "Resource Mobilization and Strategy: A Model for Analyzing Social Movement Organization Actions." In *The Dynamics of Social Movements: Resource Mobilization, Social Control and Tactics,* edited by M.N. Zald and J.D. McCarthy. Cambridge, MA: Winthrop.

Gamson, W.A. 1975. *The Strategy of Social Protest.* Homewood, IL: Dorsey Press.

Gouldner, H.P. 1960. "Dimensions of Organizational Commitment." *Administrative Science Quarterly* 4:468-490.

Knoke, D. 1981. "Commitment and Detachment in Voluntary Associations." *American Sociological Review* 46:141-158.

_____. 1985. "The Political Economies of Associations." *Research in Political Sociology* 1:211-242.

Knoke, D. and R.E. Adams. 1987. "The Incentive Systems of Associations." *Research in the Sociology of Organizations* 5:285-309.

Knoke, D. and D. Prensky. 1984. "What Relevance do Organization Theories Have for Voluntary Associations?" *Social Science Quarterly* 65:3-20.

Knoke, D. and J.R. Wood. 1981. *Organized for Action: Commitment in Voluntary Associations.* New Brunswick, NJ: Rutgers University Press.

Knoke, D. and C. Wright-Isak. 1982. "Individual Motives and Organizational Incentive Systems." *Research in the Sociology of Organizations* 1:209-254.

Laumann, E.O. and D. Knoke 1987. The Organizational State. Madison: University of Wisconsin Press.

Laumann, E.O., D. Knoke, and Y. Kim. 1985. "An Organizational Approach to State Policy Formulation: A Comparative Study of Energy and Health Domains." *American Sociological Review* 50:1-19.

Leblebici, H. and G. Salancik. 1981. "Effects of Environmental Uncertainty on Information and Decision Processes in Banks. *Administrative Science Quarterly* 26:578-596.

Lipset, S.M., M. Trow, and J.S. Coleman. 1956. *Union Democracy.* Glencoe, IL: Free Press.

McAdam, D. 1982. *Political Process and the Development of Black Insurgency 1930-1970.* Chicago: University of Chicago Press.

McCarthy, J.D. and M.N. Zald. 1977. "Resource Mobilization and Social Movements: A Partial Theory. *American Journal of Sociology* 82:1212-1241.

Mansbridge, J.J. 1980. *Beyond Adversary Democracy.* Chicago: University of Chicago Press.

_____. 1986. *Why We Lost the ERA.* New York: Free Press.

Meyer, J.W. and B. Rowan. 1977. "Institutionalized Organizations: Formal Structure as Myth and Ceremony." *American Journal of Sociology* 83:340-363.

Michels, R. 1962. *Political Parties.* New York: Free Press.

Morris, A. 1984. *The Origins of the Civil Rights Movement: Black Communities Organizing for Change.* New York: Free Press.

Pfeffer, J. 1982. *Organizations and Organization Theory.* Boston: Pitman.

Schlozman, K.L. and J.T. Tierney. 1985. *Organized Interests and American Democracy.* New York: Harper & Row.

Schmidt, A.J. 1973. *Oligarchy in Fraternal Organizations.* Detroit, MI: Gale Research.

Scott, W.R. 1987. *Organizations: Rational, Natural and Open System.* 2nd ed. Englewood Cliffs, NJ: Prentice-Hall.

Tannenbaum, A.S. 1968. *Control in Organizations.* New York: McGraw-Hill.

Walker, J. 1983. "The Origins and Maintenance of Interest Groups in America." *American Political Science Review* 77:390-406.

Weber, M. 1947. *The Theory of Social and Economic Organization.* New York: Oxford University Press.

Yuchtman, E. and S. Seashore. 1967. "A System Resource Approach to Organizational Effectiveness." *American Sociological Review* 32:891-903.

CONTRADICTIONS BETWEEN NATIONAL AND LOCAL ORGANIZATIONAL STRENGTH:

THE CASE OF THE JOHN BIRCH SOCIETY

Pamela Oliver and Mark Furman

Earlier in this decade, there was a flurry of debate about whether "strong" organizations help or hinder the efforts of aggrieved populations to achieve social change. As Jenkins (1983) said in his review, the answer to this question clearly depends on who is being organized for what. But even Jenkins' review implies that all organizations can be arrayed on a single dimension, with "no organization" at one pole, "strong organization" at the other pole, and "weak organization" somewhere in the middle. "Strong organizations" are seen as those which develop a stable resource base, have a coherent organizational structure capable of unified action, and control a large mass base of members who are mobilized for action.

International Social Movement Research, Vol. 2, pages 155-177.
Copyright © 1989 by JAI Press Inc.
All rights of reproduction in any form reserved.
ISBN: 0-89232-964-5

But "organizational strength" is not really a single dimension. Our thesis is that the features which make for a strong national organization with a sound financial base are different from those which foster active mobilization of the membership. The problems of mobilizing *money* is very different from the problem of mobilizing *action*, and there are inherent organizational tensions created by trying to do both. These tensions can be overcome and some "very strong" organizations manage to do both, at least for a while, but the two kinds of mobilizations really pull organizations in different ways. These tensions can be especially acute for the local chapters of national organizations.

Our thoughts on these matters began with Furman's research on the John Birch Society (JBS), an organization that would be characterized as either "strong" or "weak" depending on the perspective from which it is examined. Looking from the top, the organization has a strong administrative structure, a large financial base derived principally from member contributions, an active publishing operation, and roughly 80,000 members organized into perhaps 4,000 local chapters which are supported by professional field staff. But looking from the bottom, one sees struggling chapters desperate for active members, an absence of a national program for action, and little or no local activity. In seeking to understand this case, we have employed our more unsystematic observations gleaned from years of participation and obsevation in a variety of movement organizations, and from our reading of published accounts of other organizations. Thus, we end up not with definitive proof for our arguments, but with an empirically and theoretically plausible thesis which can be confirmed or refuted with systematic research.

THE JOHN BIRCH SOCIETY

Sources and Limitations of Data

Furman was a participant observer in a local chapter of the JBS in 1983-1984. He joined the organization, collected literature, interviewed the few members he could find, attended the few meetings and events that were held, and toured the national office. We should stress that the secrecy of the JBS prevents us from knowing whether his experiences in one city may be generalized to chapters in other cities. His experiences are consistent with other published accounts of the JBS (for example Westin 1964; Broyles 1964; Ericson 1982; Forster and Epstein 1964, 1966, 1967; Griffin 1975; Hefley and Hefley 1980; Scott 1980), and we believe that they are probably more typical than not, but we can be relatively certain of the empirical facts only for the geographic area studied. Thus, the case study should be viewed more as an instance illuminating an important feature of movement organizations rather than as a definitive empirical report on the JBS.

It is also important to note that the data may already be outdated concerning the actual status of the JBS, since they were collected during a significant watershed in JBS history. In 1983, Robert Welch, the founder of JBS, stepped down as chair and chose replacements who were expected to continue his course. Congressional Representative Larry McDonald (Georgia), a New Right leader, became the chairman, and long-time staffer Tom Hill became President. In their acceptance speeches, neither Hill nor McDonald indicated any plans to vary from Welch's set course. McDonald died when Korean Airlines flight 007 was shot down by the Soviets, and was replaced by long-time Council member William Grede. Welch himself died in 1985. We do not know whether the deaths of two key leaders have produced major changes in the national organization, and the participant observation did not continue past 1984.

Overview and Background

Despite at least some published speculation that the JBS was nothing more than a media creation which disappeared when the soptlight shifted (Lipset in Crawford 1980, p. 46), the JBS as a national organization is alive and well, even though it has been virtually ignored by the mass media since 1980. In 1983, it claimed between 60,000 and 100,000 members nationwide and a six million dollar budget. It operates two magazines with worldwide distribution, oversees the operation of many local chapters and bookstores in the United States, and is computerizing its operations at its national headquarters.

The JBS is the organizational embodiment of Robert Welch. Welch became known in the early 1950s for accusing Dean Acheson and others of being Communist agents. He developed his own version of conspiracy theory in which socialists, proponents of the welfare state, and big capitalists are all agents of a conspiracy to bring all economic power under the control of one world government; this theory was circulated privately in a manuscript called *The Politician.* Welch believed that his own failed primary campaign in 1949, the failed Taft campaign, and McCarthy's downfall showed the importance of a strong and disciplined movement organization independent of the contraints of electoral politics (Griffin 1975, p. 152). In late 1958, Welch founded the JBS at a two-day seminar in Indianapolis attended by 11 friends and potential supporters (Welch 1969, p. viii; Broyles 1964, p. 11-12; Schomp 1970, pp. 34-35). The structure, ideology, and future goals and tactics of the JBS outlined by Welch at that meeting, and now codified in *The Blue Book of the John Birch Society* (Welch 1969), remain the blueprint for the organization.

The organization grew quickly. A national headquarters was rapidly set up, and local chapters were organized around the country (Broyles 1964, Griffin 1975, pp. 275-296). Initial projects included petition drives to impeach Chief

Justice Earl Warren and to have the United States withdraw from the United Nations, and the CASE Project (Committee Against Summit Entanglements) which placed newspaper advertisements and circulated petitions to protest Khrushchev's visits with Eisenhower (Griffin 1975, p. 278).

The Society and Welch became a news "story" when *The Politician* reached the mass media (Griffin 1975, Ch. XIV). Most newsworthy were his claims that Milton Eisenhower and Dean Acheson were Communist sympathizers, that there were outright Communist agents in the State Department, and that President Eisenhower condoned this situation. Suddenly the press wanted to know everything about Welch, the Birch Society, and its members. Before 1961, the *New York Times* carried no articles on the JBS or Robert Welch. Beginning in March of that year, over 130 articles, letters, and editorials appeared referring to the JBS and its leaders and actions. Much of this coverage was negative. Those accused of being Communist sympathizers defended themselves and vilified Welch and the JBS. Most conservative politicians struggled to avoid JBS endorsements, although a few aligned themselves with the JBS. There was a great deal of publicity when John Rousellot, a California politician, publicly announced his affiliation and became director of field relations for JBS. Its campaigns to impeach Earl Warren, to get the United States out of the United Nations, and to elect Barry Goldwater, were heavily publicized. Other big stories included the forced resignation of Army General Walker, allegedly a Bircher, for showing his young recruits films and literature alleging Communist infiltration in high government positions and hinting at treason in the State Department (Broyles 1964, pp. 104-105; Forster and Epstein 1967, p. 35), and the revelation that JBS Executive Council member Dr. Revilo Oliver was a rabid anti-Semite and author of many racist tracts.

By 1962, most reading Americans knew that the JBS was an extreme right-wing organization that espoused a conspiracy theory of history, saw Communists all over the Federal government, and was prone to wild accusations. Even though the JBS officially opposed the Nazis and the Ku Klux Klan (KKK), it was widely perceived as a repository for anti-Semites, racists, and other kooks. There was even a popular song lampooning it. JBS became a national symbol for right-wing extremism.

Although much of this coverage was negative, the JBS was able to use this attention to its own advantage. It was already expanding when the media blitz began and it was ready to handle the influx of inquiries and new members. In 1960, the JBS expanded office space and staff (largely with funds from Welch and a few major donors including Nelson Baker Hunt), organized the first Executive Council meeting, and sent Welch on a speaking tour promoting new chapters (Griffin 1975, p. 275). The organization grew rapidly, with membership approaching 100,000 by 1963.

The "issue attention cycle" (Downs 1972) ran its course and coverage of the JBS declined precipitously after 1967. As this was happening, Welch and others broadened their version of the conspiracy, believing that both Communists and Capitalist Internationalists were controlled by The Insiders (Allen 1971; Smoot 1962, 1973; Griffin 1964, 1971, 1975). Their ideology was similar to Fascist anti-Semitic conspiracy theory, except that the Insiders are not equated with Jews. This shift widened the gap between traditonal conservatives and the extreme right when, for example, Welch argued that the United States should pull out of the Vietnam war because it was really being fought to enrich the American power structure. The change was unpalatable to many key leaders, including Gerald Schomp, Tom Davis, and the most externally-visible member, John Rousellot, who left with a vocal public denunciation (Schomp 1970, pp. 137-140, 174-177).

It is responsible to suppose that many rank-and-file members left during this period as well, but they were replaced by new members who were attracted by the new ideology. The JBS broadened its grievance base beyond patriotic anticommunism and tapped into an ideological and cultural current developing in the radical right in this period. The Society now appealed not only to good patriots, but to those opposed to a large federal government, taxes, civil rights and student movements, loose lifestyles, crime, and anything that contributed to a world government.

The National Organization of the John Birch Society

The JBS is organized like a business (Schomp 1970, p. 175). Welch's role was like that of a president and chief executive officer, advised by a board of directors called the Executive Council. Different divisions reporting to the national leadership carry out the separate functions of the organization. One division produces and disseminates *The Birch Bulletin, American Opinion,* and *Review of the News,* which are sent to members and subscribers. Another produces and sells books by Western Islands Press and other right-wing publishers. A third division operates a warehouse in Belmont, Massachusetts which supplies American Opinion bookstores across the country with literature and books. The bookstores themselves are somewhat independent. Their managers have some discretion, although they cannot carry books banned by the JBS, such as Nazi, KKK, racist, or anti-Semitic literature. They operate on thier own budgets, but are subsidized, if necessary, by the national organization.

Another division is in charge of membership services and recruitment. The country is split into several regions, each having a full-time paid regional cordinator. The regional coordinator supervises a staff of paid field coordinators who organize and support the local chapters in their region. Each chapter has no more than 30 members; chapter leaders are unpaid. The chapter structure was modelled after the cellular organization of the Communist Party as Welch understood it.

Another concept borrowed from the Communists was front organizations, single-issue organizations created by the parent organization. Front organizations, which hide their ties to the parent organization, can attract potential recruits who would be afraid of the extremeism of the parent organization, and can influence public opinion by avoiding the parent organization's stigma. Major JBS front groups in the 1960s were TRAIN (supporting U.S. withdrawal from the United Nations), the Committee to Impeach (Chief Supreme Court Justice) Earl Warren, and SYLP (Support Your Local Police). In recent years, however, most of these front groups have been dissolved. Only TRIM (Tax Reform Immediately) is active now, and it openly acknowledges its links with the JBS.

Although it no longer forms fronts of its own, the JBS still attaches itself to various causes such as opposition to the Equal Rights Amendment for women, tax reform, prayer in schools, opposition to trade with the Eastern Bloc nations, and the demand to continue searching for those Missing in Action from the Vietnam war. New members are still brought in through particular issues. For example, the leader of the local chapter studied became involved in the JBS by looking for a tax reform group. After reading their literature and seeing the whole picture, he became more involved with the JBS as a whole entity, but he still was mainly interested in tax reform and most of his activities addressed this issue.

Mobilizing Money at the National Level

The JBS claims an annual budget of $6 million. Members pay yearly dues of $24 for men and $12 for women. With the maximum membership estimate of 100,000, this means that no more than $2 million (and probably closer to $1 million) is accounted for by member dues. The JBS does not permit inspection of their financial records, but it is possible to make some guesses about their budget. Everyone in the JBS says that the bulk of the money comes from members. This would imply average donations on the order of $60 to $100 per member, a plausible figure, given that some members are extremely wealthy. Actual average contributions could be much lower than this. Although the publishing and bookstore operations do not seem to be making large profits, many of the materials are sold, rather than given away, and their cash flows could account for a significant portion of the claimed operating budget, even if they only break even or are subsidized by dues and donations.

It is reasonable to suppose that the JBS has other sources of income, as well. It thrived through nearly 20 years of media neglect, during a time when public opinion ebbed and flowed and competing New Right organizations grew up. This fact strongly suggests some organizational mechanism for dampening out the effects of the volatility of "marketlike" sources of income for a movement organization (McCarthy and Zald 1977; Oliver 1983). Memberships, donations, and literature sales are all likely to be very uneven from year to year, due to factors like recent political events and the state of the economy. The fact that the JBS cites its membership figures with a very large range, 60,000-100,000, is evidence that they experience some of these problems.

It is known that Welch put a great deal of his own money into the JBS and that there were other major financial backers of the organization. It is also known that most of the national leaders of JBS are independent businessmen who, presumably, know how to keep business solvent. It is logical to infer that some portion of past revenues were invested, either in capitalizing the business operations or in creating endowments for the organization, to permit it to ride out lean periods. Saving and investing are widely regarded in the world of charitable and political contributions as highly unethical. But this norm is unlikely to deter the JBS, since it zealously guarded its administrative secrets, never filed for tax-exempt status, was always tightly controlled by Welch (a businessman who repeatedly stressed the importance of forming a strong organization), and was negatively regarded by the public at large, anyway.

To say that we suspect the JBS of being organizationally rational is not to say that it is nothing more than a business venture. The sale and distribution of literature appears at best to break even, and is probably subsidized. The JBS seems fundamentally to be an ideological organization whose goal is to get its message out to as many people as possible. Attempts are made to make the message pay for itself, but getting it out is what is most important. Its literature cleaves to its ideological line, and does not pander to the mass market. Our speculation is that it has behaved rationally to preserve itself as an organization that can disseminate its ideology, not that it has placed profit above ideology.

Recipe for Survival of a National Organization

Although out of the public and academic eye for nearly 20 years, the JBS has not faded away. It is not IBM, but in the world of social movement organizations (SMOs), it looks solid. We can identify some of the reasons for its persistence. Like prior right-wing organizations, the JBS was dominated by its founder (Lipset 1964; Lipset and Raab 1970; Redkop 1968; Schoenberger 1969), but unlike his predecessors, Welch believed in the importance of organization and devoted a great deal of attention and resources to creating an organizational structure. When the spotlight turned on the JBS in 1961, it had the structure in place to capture the people and resources flowing in its direction. Even though it was popularly portrayed as dangerous and extreme, it was not damaged by external attacks. Even though "kooks and zanies" were attracted to the organization by the publicity (Schomp 1970), Welch never lost control of the organization to them. This may be contrasted with Giltin's account (1980) of how the Students for a Democratic Society was changed, disrupted, and ultimately destroyed by the publicity it received. When the spotlight turned away, the JBS had a genuine membership base, a coherent organizational structure, and solid finances. It was in a position to endure.

If it had relied solely on media attention for members, the JBS would have declined through sheer attrition. This appears not to have happened, at least not to the extent that one would expect. Despite its absence from the popular press, the JBS continued to attract new members. The explanation is straightforward. For many years, until the late 1970s, the JBS was the only real organization on the radical right, and thus it attracted and held many members who wanted more than the Republican Party offered but disdained the violence and hatred of the KKK or Nazis. The JBS was the major organized presence in a largely disorganized social movement environment. In its own way, it played the role of what Morris (1984) calls a "movement halfway house," that is, an organization which provides a home for a movement and nurtures adherents to the cause during those periods when it is otherwise dead. The period of intense publicity contributed to this role. Twenty years later, most Americans still know that the JBS is a radical right organization, even if they know little beyond that. People with a right-wing ideology knew where to go if they wanted to join an appropriate organization. This fact, coupled with the more usual process of recruitment through acquaintance networks, provided a continual source of new memberships.

Trouble in the Chapters

This rosy picture of organizational health is not what one sees at the chapter level. There was actually very little to observe in a year's participant observation of a local JBS chapter. Nobody did much of anything except read books, attend speeches or meetings, and distribute leaflets. Only a handful of members did even this much, and even they did these things infrequently.

A leaflet opposing the election of a liberal congressman signed by the Chapter showed it existed, but no one in town (including the College Republicans) had heard of it. A phone call to the national office in Belmont elicited the name of the chapter leader. Once found, the leader hemmed and hawed about when the chapter meetings were, finally admitting that there had not been any for a while due to a lack of interest. The first two meetings scheduled during the observation year were cancelled because the chapter leader and the observer were the only ones planning to come. When there finally was a meeting, only three people attended: the observer, the chapter leader, and one other person. The leader said that there had been about 12 members in the chapter during the previous few years, but no more than four had ever come to a meeting at one time.

The activitiy at the one meeting was writing letters to Congress on various pieces of New Right legislation suggested by an "action alert" mailing from the Belmont office. Writers were provided with carbonless paper so that copies could be sent to local newspapers.

It turned out that the election leaflet had been the chapter leader's project; he was assisted by some friends and family members who were not members of the JBS. Another project was an antitax billboard paid for by the leader and a friend who was not a JBS member. In short, all the "actions" of the chapter were really the work of one person and his personal acquaintances. Both projects probably would have been done anyway, whether or not there was a JBS chapter.

The manager of the regional JBS bookstore in a larger city in the region told a story which painted a very similar picture of chapters with very small proportions of active members. When he initially joined at age 18, ten years before, he was "assigned" to one of his city's chapters that was not near his home. Nevertheless, he became friendly with the six other active members. This chapter became inactive when the others all left town due to life changes (marriage, the armed forces, school). After a period of inactivity, this man was reactivated by attendance at a JBS youth camp. This time he was a major chapter leader, and even ran two chapters for a while, another indication that leaders are in short supply. He accepted the part-time job of managing the bookstore, even though he also owns a gasoline service station, because he saw it as a step towards a full-time field organizing position with the JBS. As further evidence of the region-wide ennui in JBS, this bookstore had to close during the observation year for lack of customers.

Only two events generated more widespread participation. These were lecture-seminars given by two JBS speakers sent into the state, one on the general philosophy of the JBS and the other on the issue of accounting for American military personnel missing in action in the Vietnam war. Attendance at each was between 50 and 100 members and their guests drawn from the host city, a larger city about an hour's drive away, and surrounding rural areas. This showed that there was a pool of members and sympathizers in the region, despite their inactivity.

In sum, the JBS barely existed at all as an organization in the area. There was an identifiable pool of adherents, but they did almost nothing. Probably there are a few regions of the country in which significant numbers of JBS members actively participate. However, there is reason to believe that this inactive region is more typical than not. Schomp's (1970) account of his years as a regional coordinator for the JBS during its heydey in the 1960s paints a very similar picture. He says that the members he knew did little but write strange letters to Congress and the media, wave flags, and occasionally march in parades on Independence Day. They rarely went to meetings, even more infrequently recruited new members, and never managed to undertake an effective political action.

Chapter Troubles and Organizational Mistakes

Passivity at the base of a large organization is often taken as a symptom of a "weak" organization, or of an oligarchical national leadership uninterested mobilizing member participation. Such an inference would be wrong for the JBS. It is organizationally quite strong, and it devotes organizational resources to an extensive network of paid field staff who recruit members and aid local leaders. It appears that virtually every potential member receives the personal attention of paid staff.

The two active members interviewed had both been subject to personalized recruitment experiences. The bookstore manager had been recruited by his employer, who insisted that he read Allen's *None Dare Call it Conspiracy*. After his period of inactivity, he was reactivated by attendance at a JBS Youth Camp in the region. These camps are a cross between a recreational summer camp and religious revival-style retreat with daily lectures about the JBS. After being an active chapter leader, he was offered the bookstore position.

The local chapter leader began with an interest in tax reform and collected literature from a wide variety of organizations. He contacted the JBS himself after reading their literature and deciding he liked an organization which had local chapters, rather than just a national mailing list. He was personally visited by a field coordinator who discussed JBS ideology with him, giving special emphasis to tax issues, and left *None Dare Call it Conspiracy* for him to read. The field coordinator also encouraged him to become a chapter leader.

The researcher's experience was very similar. Just for asking questions and being interested, he was approached three months after he was joined by the regional coordinator and asked to become a local chapter leader. (He declined.) Schomp (1970) reports having the same experience in the early 1960s.

These recruitment stories are very telling. It appears that every person who expresses an interest in the JBS receives the personalized attention of a paid field coordinator. In part, this says that the JBS is not overwhelmed with inquiries, a sign of trouble at the base which is reinforced by the fact that local activists are clearly in such short supply that anyone who expresses an interest is asked to be a leader. But it is also clear that the organization is alive and well and functioning from the top down. Any organization that can provide a personalized recruitment experience from a paid staff member for every potential recruit and that can run a summer camp has resources and, further, directs those resources toward nurturing activism, not just collecting dues for national projects.

The problem in the chapters is not due to a lack of organizational commitment to member involvement. Rather, it seems to be due to a serious error in Welch's organizational plan, an error the organization seems to have been unwilling or unable to detect and correct. Welch modelled the chapter structure on his understanding of the cellular structure of the Communist Party. Chapters are limited to 30 members, and their membership is secret, so that members of different chapters do not know each other. All contact is hierarchical, through the field coordinators, not lateral. It appears that this structure in the Communist Party permitted intense levels of activity while protecting the identities of members, and Welch wanted to emulate this success. But he overlooked a central feature of the Communist Party, which is that it was an *activist* organization. Potential members had to be active to be permitted to join, and they were subject to strong sanctions if they stopped being active. Thirty *active* members makes for a very strong local organization. But the JBS does not require activism, it merely encourages it. Chapter rosters are made up of a very high proportion of "paper" members, and the upper limit on roster size means that very few chapters have more than a handful of active members.

This problem is exacerbated because the secrecy rule prevents interchapter cooperation. Evidence of the effect of secrecy was seen at one of the speeches. Two men who obviously knew each other from business connections outside of the JBS were seen greeting each other. Each was clearly very surprised to discover that the other was a JBS member. It was determined later that both were active members of their own chapters, but because of the secrecy rule, they had been prevented from cooperating in any joint JBS ventures. In many movement sectors, collective actions are undertaken by loose ad hoc coalitions of different organizations connected by informal linkages (see Gerlach and Hine 1970). This is prevented in the JBS.

NATIONAL VERSUS LOCAL ORGANIZATION: TENSIONS AND CONTRADICTIONS

We believe that the troubles in the JBS are an extreme case of tensions and contradictins that are widespread in movement organizations, especially in the United States. The problem of mobilizing a mass constituency to support national-level programs for social change is fundamentally different from the problem of mobilizing local groups to action. Individual motivations and incentives for supporting national movement organizations are different than those for pariticipating in local action. These differences arise from intrinsic differences in the organizational problems at different levels, and they inevitably produce tensions and contradictions in the local chapters of national organizations. A few large movement organizations have charted a path that permits the organization to function at both levels, but finding such a path is difficult and depends somewhat on the organization's goals and ideology: It is not simply a matter of correct understanding or personal will.

It is widely understood that the incentives for participation in movement activities are solidary (deriving for interaction with others) and purposive (deriving from gratifying one's self-esteem), not material. (See Wilson 1973 for an explanation of this typology of incentives.) In examining the effects of incentives, we need to consider the kind and magnitude of contribution being solicited (i.e., its cost), and the kinds and magnitudes of incentives which encourage people to make those contributions and bear those costs. Briefly, national organizations require different kinds of contributions with different incentive structures than do local activist organizations. We will discuss the two types of organizations in turn, and then show how these differences create troubles for chapters. At each step, we will talk about movement organizations in general (as we understand them from our unsystematically-observed experiences and from the literature) and about the JBS in particular.

National Organizations: Mobilizing Money and Paper Members

In the United States, national policy is largely determined on one edge of a continent that is 3,000 miles wide. It is physically impossible for the vast majority of Americans to participate actively in tactics focused on the national government. Most demonstrations in Washington are essentially local actions of local organizations in Washington or nearby cities. Massive demonstrations involving vast numbers of people coming long distances to Washington, or involving coordinated simultaneous protests in numerous locations around the country, are rare. Thus, most movement *participation* necessarily has a local organizational focus, and even the rare massive "national" protest is necessarily organized through local organizational structures.

But many movement organizations address goals and issues that are national in character, wholly or at least in part, such as nuclear weapons, legal rights for minorities or women, international Communism, taxes, and social welfare policy. National organizations attempt to influence Congressional legislation and administrative policies, or to publish "educational" materials which are distributed nationally. To do so, they require a national organizational presence. The national offices of such organizations conduct research, prepare reports and educational materials, conduct press conferences, and lobby. In the case of the JBS, the major national activity appears to be publishing books and magazines. These are the sorts of activities for which skill and experience matter, and they are most effectively accomplished by a committed staff of paid professionals and their paid assistants.

For national organizations performing such activities, the most important resource is money: money to pay the staff, money to publish educational materials and distribute them, money to pay for typewriters (or microcomputers) and supplies, money for office rent. As McCarthy and Zald (1973) stressed, there are many "national" organizations which rely on financial support from large individual, corporate, or foundation donors and which may have no genuine membership base of any kind.

However, there are other national organizations which rely heavily on small contributions solicited through the mail from "paper members." It is movement organizations with large paper memberships which are our concern here. Such organizations *do* have a genuine mass base, but we need to investigate clearly just what its character is. The central offices of these "mass" national organizations are not democratically controlled from below. It is not that paper members have no control, but their control is indirect. Paper members vote with their checkbooks: An organization which has lost legitimacy loses money. But this "exit" option is their only source of power; paper members cannot directly influence the policy or strategy of a national organization.

The active members of organizations with strong active chapters may exert some control over the national organization's overall policies and strategies through national conventions and elections, although, even in these cases, the national office often functions autonomously, rather like a special kind of chapter.[1] It should be stressed that the claim that national offices of SMOs tend to be autonomous is *not* a claim that they "dominate" the chapters, since strong active local chapters tend also to be quite autonomous (see Carden 1978 and the discussion below). Rather, the two levels seem to operate almost independently of one another.

Paper Members and Symbolic Solidarity

There has been a fair amount of attention paid to the question of why professionalized movement organizations find it desirable to have paper members, but little to the question of why people would want to *be* paper members. Only by investigating such motivations can be we understand the dynamics of such organizations. We take it as given that very few people find it intrinsically pleasant to write a check or give up money, so we rule out the possibility that people donate money simply to donate. Paper membership is inherently an isolated act and is thus incapable of providing solidary incentives. Apart from those organizations (such as Consumer's Union) whose "members" are really subscribers or customers, paper members receive no material benefits.

Thus, the motivation for making a financial contribution is clearly in the realm of purposive incentives. People give money to "causes" because it makes them feel good to do so. By writing a check, they vicariously experience the rewards of doing the right thing by paying someone else to do it. National causes are inherently distant and out of the reach of the individual who cannot personally argue a case before the Supreme Court, lobby in Congress, provide weapons to guerrillas, or defeat an international conspiracy. One cannot choose between contributing money and contributing time to a national organization: One contributes money or nothing at all. Although some people are active in local organizations and also contribute to national organizations, the rolls of national organizations are principally made up of those who have chosen to contribute money as a form of vicarious participation.

These contributions are "cheap." A donation typically represents a tiny portion of the contributor's income, an amount that is usually virtually unnoticeable and represents little, if any, sacrifice or opportunity cost. Although the thrill or satisfaction of vicarious participation may be small, it can easily exceed the cost of the donation, and the entire transaction could have quite minor importance in the person's life. These are the sorts of contributions othat are especially vulnerable to volatile "market" and public relations cycles and events (McCarthy and Zald 1977).

There is another purposive incentive which can be of considerably greater importance to the contributor, a phenomenon that we may call "symbolic solidarity." The act of joining (i.e., paying dues to) certain movement organizations can satisfy a desire to affirm a self-identity as a movement member: One can be a card-carrying feminist by joining the National Organization for Women, a card-carrying socialist by joining the Democratic Socialists of America, or a card-carrying true American by joining the JBS.

For its members, joining the JBS is an important symbolic political act. Simply by joining the Society, a person asserts his or her radical right-wing politics and participates in notoriety. Its image as a secret extremist organization is so strong that the fact that one is a member can be stigmatizing in itself, leading a person to be treated as unstable or deviant. There is some true risk of material consequences if the secret is discovered by the wrong people, although the risk is probably great only for people who aspire to politics, government service, or university professorships.

With the rise of the New Right in America in the 1980s, one might expect the JBS to lose members to the new organizations. However, since the JBS does not demand much loyalty beyond paying dues, its members can still belong to other national SMOs on the New Right while not relinquishing their ties to the JBS. For example, the chapter leader was on almost every New Right mailing list in the country, and sent many other organizations money.[2] Since the JBS is still viewed as much more "radical" than the New Right organizations, members can retain their symbolic self-identity while also contributing to other organizations which accomplish more.

To summarize, most dues-paying members of large national organizations are motivated to make a low-cost contribution to a worthy cause in exchange for the purposive incentive of vicarious participation in activities they deem important. Additionally, they may be motivated to affirm their self-identity as "members" of a particular movement.

Local Organizations: Mobilizing Active Participation

Local organizations are very different.[3] Direct participation is the currency of local mobilization. Even those local organizations whose principal goal is to raise money for a charitable or artistic purpose are dominated by members who engage in activities to pursue that end. Local organizations need people who will actually *do* things, that is, people who will incur much higher costs than those involved in making a small financial contribution. Such activists are mobilized by purposive incentives supplemented by solidary incentives and the intrinsic pleasure of the activity. That is, they are most motivated by the prospect of feeling that they have personally accomplished some social good, and this motivation is supplemented by the attraction of the activity itself and the people one works with.

Carden (1978, p. 184) argues that ideological incentives are the predominant incentive for member participation in a social movement, but the purposive incentive of "the satisfaction of working for a just cause is of a different order from other selective incentives." She argues that when people are motivated by ideological or purposive incentives, it matters to them *what* they are accomplishing. Projects are not interchangeable, and different individuals will be motivated to work hard on different projects. One corollary of this argument is that decentralization is essential for mobilizing member participation. Carden argues that the decentralization of the women's movement in the 1970s accounted for its efflorescence. Even the National Organization for Women, which appears hierarchical on an organization chart, functions at the local level as issue-specific task forces chosen by members on the basis of personal interest.

It is also important to recognize that even the healthiest of local organizations rarely mobilize intense levels of participation from very large numbers of people across a long period of time. Healthy local organizations typically have a small number (less than 20, often less than 10) members who form the activist cadre and make large sustained contributions. These very active members do things with "decelerating" production functions (Oliver et al. 1985; Oliver 1984), that is, activities which can provide general benefits from the efforts of a few. They lobby, give speeches, write newsletters, distribute leaflets, counsel recruits, and so forth. They also create the conditions that permit others to make smaller contributions. For example, a task force leader may organize a project and plan a division of labor that permits others to participate meaningfully in contributing a few hours of their time. Solidary incentives and smaller purposive incentives can motivate "lesser participants" to attend meetings when enough of the background work is taken care of by the activist cadre. And, of course, the activist cadre may plan occasional "mass" events which draw in very large numbers of people for vey short periods of time.

Thus, the key organizational problem for a local organization is the motivation of the activist cadre, those people who will make large contributions. Sustaining a local organization requires not only an aggregated pool of individuals with activist motivations, but a shared collective willingness to combine those motivations into an ongoing organization. All communities have local activists who devote a great deal of time and energy to local collective issues, but who work individually, pulling together ad hoc groups of supporters for various projects, while making no sustained commitment to any organization. Instead, they are intensely motivated to accomplish each successive goal in whatever way they can. Many local organizations are formed around a small number of activists working on a particular problem, and begin to dissipate when the initial burst of activity has passed.

Organizational maintenance is always a problem for local organizations. Although people differ greatly in the kinds of activities they find satisfying, organizational maintenance activities are not on most people's lists. Activists view them as diversions from their goal orientations, and nonactivists simply find them boring. Treasurer's reports, minutes of past meetings, changes in by-laws, reports from committees, and discussions about how to increase attendance at meetings are all viewed as intrinsically unpleasant and worthless by most people. Activist organizations survive by constantly replacing old goals and projects with new ones, while minimizing organizational maintenance activities and concentrating them in the hands of those few members who are committed to preserving the organization.

To remain vital over time, a local organization requires a source of new recruits and a structure that provides purposive and solidary incentives by involving them in satisfying goal-oriented projects and creates satisfying personal ties within the organization. There are certainly many local organizations that have done this, but it is very difficult, and, most commonly, local organizations formed around specific issues turn into empty shells after the initial ranks are thinned by attrition, leaving behind a few survivors committed to maintaining the organization in memory of what it once was.

In short, the lifeblood of local movement organizations is active participation. The problems of maintaining and sustaining this participation are great and involve very different personal incentives and organizational dynamics from those that arise for national organizations.

The Problem of Chapters

Local chapters of national organizations are caught in the middle between the organizational imperatives of national and local organizations. National organizations encourage chapters as a way of providing a locus of participation for their members, and common membership in a national organization can provide a reason for activists to come together to form a local organization. Membership rolls, provided by the national office, give local activists the hope that there is a ready-made pool of potential recruits already committed to the cause, needing only notice of the times and places of meetings to pull them into a life of active participation.

The reality is usually very different. As we have argued, sustaining any local activist organization is difficult. Chapters of national organizations have one advantage, but they also have two special disadvantages. The advantage is, of course, that the national organization answers the question "Why have an organization?" There is a built-in rationale for forming and sustaining an ongoing local organization that transcends any particular goal or project. This can be a real advantage for a local organization if the organization's ideology implies goals and projects which are likely to be shared by significant numbers of members. This advantage can be large, but so are the disadvantages faced by chapters.

The first disadvantage is that chapter members must be recruited from national members, or at least from those who are willing to become national members. But the incentives and motivations for national membership are different from, and almost incompatible with, those for local participation. The incentives for national membership are vicarious participation and symbolic soidarity. Paying national dues is attractive precisely because it is a low-cost *substitute* for active participation. Many of the members of national organizations *want* to be paper members, and they have participated as much as they want to (or feel they physically can) by writing a check. The roster of national members mailed to the chapter leader from the national office is a mirage. Anyone on that list who wants to be active almost certainly already is; even a national member who just moved to the area probably took the initiative to find the chapter instead of waiting for a call. Active chapter members can become unnecessarily self-critical and dispirited if they believe they ought to be able to turn those paper members into active members with the right program or the right recruitment strategy.

Chapters can and do recruit active members, but they do it the same way other local organizations do: They have projects and activities which attract people motivated by purposive incentives, and which create or strengthen the social ties that provide solidary incentives. Just as for any other local organization, new recruits are pulled in mostly from social network ties to existing chapter members. Ties to the national organization can give the chapter visibility which may promote inquiries from people who want to be active and feel themselves in sympathy with the known goals of the national organization, but these inquirers can be turned into recruits only if the chapter is viable as a local activist organization. In short, chapters can be successful local organizations only by essentially ignoring their apparent membership base of national members, and seeking to sustain themselves by persuading local people with activist tendencies to become members of the national organization.

In recruiting and maintaining an activist membership, chapters must overcome a second disadvantage. Their links to the national organization increase the burden of organizational maintenance activities. Chapter leaders receive directives and information from the national office which are supposed to be communicated to and discussed with members. Chapters are supposed to file reports with the national office on their activities, finances, and membership and recruitment efforts. It is extremely difficult for any chapter to absorb this much organizational overhead and survive as a viable local activist organization. Meetings devoted to these activities will drive away goal-oriented activists and potential members who want to participate in small ways. Taken seriously, the requirements of the national office could absorb all the energies of a small activist cadre in a struggling chapter, leaving them no time for goal-oriented projects which might attract local recruits. Even those who are personally oriented to organizational maintenance become despairing when recruitment efforts fail and meeting attendance dwindles to a dispirited handful.

Money is another source of conflict. Activists with local orientations often view national dues as a worthless tax. Viable chapters often have intense debates about whether individuals must pay dues to the national organization, and about whether the local chapter should devote time and energy to fundraising activities to benefit the national. In the early 1970s, many chapters of the National Organization for Women had "local members" who paid no national dues, and there were heated debates within the organization about whether this was acceptable. This same debate was a major issue at a recent convention of the Nuclear Freeze Campaign and in the nuclear disarmament movement of the 1950s and 1960s (Robert Kleidman personal communication). The authors have participated in such debates in virtually every local chapter of a national organization they have ever been involved in. No such debates were observed in the local chapter of the JBS, which was not a viable local organization.

The local chapter of the JBS is an extreme case of the problems of chapters in national organizations. This SMO exacerbated the chapter problem by fragmenting its paper membership into "chapters" which were statistically unlikely to have more than a couple of potential activists. This was compounded by secrecy rules which prevent the few true activists, scattered across these chapters, from even being aware of each other's existence. It also appears that the national staff do not trust the members enough to let them act autonomously, judging by the accounts of former members, such as Schomp (1970), who says that most members were apathetic, and the activists were "kooks and zanies" who set off bombs, made insance threats to media personalities, or wrote strange letters to newspapers. The JBS seeks to be a respectable organization in an ideological field that attracts a lunatic fringe, and is ever vigilant to prevent the fringe from speaking for the organization. But, if Carden (1978) is right, decentralization and local autonomy are essential to provide incentives for activists. Finally, the conspiracy ideology itself does not seem to provide an obvious local referent for activism. This last point is less important than the others, however, since JBS members who want to be active do involve themselves in a variety of local single-issue campaigns.

Chapters of national organizations have problems with local mobilization, but these problems are not insoluble. Chapters are viable when they find a strategy for keeping the maintenance demands of the national organization within bounds, either by ignoring them or by isolating them in coordinating committee or business meetings which can be avoided by all but the committed few. Success is especially likely in those areas with large pools of potential activist members, so that maintenance activities can represent a very small part of the total person-hours available to the organization.

Based on Carden's (1978) work, Ferree and Hesse' account (1985), and our own more superficial impressions, the National Organization for Women appears to be a national organization which found a successful strategy for combining local activism and a strong national organization. The keys seem to be a loose ideology which tolerates diversity, organizational decentralization, and the task force model. Like the JBS, the National Organization for Women, at the national level, is supported by a very large base of paper members. The National Organization for Women has long been the largest and most visible feminist organization in the United States, and many women and men pay dues symbolically to express their feminism. Also like the JBS, its visibility provides it with a stream of new recruits who turn to it first when they become interested in feminism. But unlike the JBS, chapters have no maximum size, and are allowed to define their own geographic limits to take in a large enough pool of potential activists. Its task force structure fosters activism by allowing members to select the issue that is most worthwhile to them. Large chapters delegate organizational maintenance to a small committed cadre who meet separately as an executive committe, and devote their occasional chapter meetings to programs of general interest. Although it will doubtless collapse eventually, as all movement organizations do, the National Organization for Women has survived a number of bitter disputes in which major factions left the organization.

CONCLUSIONS

Movement organizations cannot be arrayed on any simple strong-weak dimension. Organizations may successfully mobilize monetary resources and have stable sources of funding that permit them to endure as entities and pursue social change goals for a very long time without ever being able to foster widespread mobilization of active participation. Conversely, organizations may succeed in mobilizing widespread active participation while failing to mobilize the resources necessary to achieve financial or organizational stability. But organizational stability and mass mobilization are not opposites, either: Some organzations achieve both, and many neither. They are simply distinct problems which require very different resolutions. Participation mobilization is not a means to financial solvency, and financial resources contribute little to mobilization of action.

To influence policy at a national level, a movement almost requires a national-level organization to argue lawsuits, to formulate policy proposals or demands, to deal with the mass media, or to lobby with politicians for their support.[4] It is physically impossible, at least in the United States, for these tasks to be performed by grass-roots volunteers, unless they happen to reside in Washington. Political realities almost "force" organizations addressing national issues into creating a professionalized staff to perform these taks. In this circumstance, money is the key resource that needs to be mobilized. As McCarthy and Zald (1973) argue, many organizations obtain their money from foundations, corporations, or wealthy individuals and never even try to create any sort of mass base.

But many national organizations with professional staff mobilize money year after year by collecting dues and contributions from a loyal base of small "grass-roots" contributors. McCarthy and Zald aptly called these people "paper members," because they do not actively participate in the national organization's activities. However, they imply that this is one (increasingly popular) alternative, that it is somehow possible to have nonpaper, that is "real," members at the national level. Our thesis is that, at the national level, virtually *all* members are "paper," that is, unable directly to influence or participate in the organization's choice of strategy and tactics.

There are "real" members of movement organizations, members who participate at the "grass-roots," that is, outside the national office. But their activities are tied to local organizations. They may sometimes work locally to organize local protests timed to coincide with other local protests, all coordinated through the national organization, or to arrange for local people to travel together to a major protest in Washington. Most often they work autonomously on projects which address the larger concerns of the movement organization in some local context. They may direct protest at some visible local embodiment of the movement's "enemy," seek passage of relevant legislation at the municipal or state level or, perhaps, work to educate the local population about the national issue.

In most American movement organizations, the national organization has virtually no control over local activities. National staff and officers make suggestions and seek to persuade local members to pursue certain activities rather than others, but they have absolutely no way to compel obedience.[5] The only sanction they may have available is expulsion for violating the organization's principles, and this merely protects the organization's identity without effectively altering local behavior. Local activism (and, by implication, virtually all grass-roots activism) is locally generated and locally controlled. Although the national organization may provide the initial idea or spark, local mobilization is built on local social networks invoking locally-available incentives for participation. If the local base is lacking, there can be no active grass-roots mobilization.

In short, the nationals cannot exert much control over the locals, and the locals cannot exert much control over the nationals, beyond choosing among contestants in an election or passing general policy resolutions. National mobilization of money cannot create local mobilization of activism, and widespread local mobilization cannot ensure a stable financial base for a national organization. The organizational dynamics and the incentives for individual contributors or participants are entirely different. National organizations, if they wish to operate in the national policy environment, cannot rely solely on active members for financial support because there are too few of them (and they are not likely to be particularly wealthy). Thus they rely on external support or paper members, and develop a power base outside their active membership. To be viable, local organizations must *do* something, they must engage in activities that are meaningful to the members or meet the members' needs for social interaction. The simple existence of a prosperous and successful national organization does not fulfill this need for local social networks and a local base of action.

There are national organizations without local branches or chapters, and local organizations which are independent of any national organization. Such organizations can proceed "naturally" to resolve their organizational needs. But those organizations which combine both levels, which seek to join national policy-influencing activities with genuine active participation in local chapters, suffer conflicts and contradictions. The fundraising, paperwork, and appeals for expressions of support for national legislation which support the national organization can hinder the development of meaningful local projects which are central to the motivations of local activists. The goal-specific or project-specific orientations which tend to motivate local activists lead them to give low priority to supporting the distant activities of the national organization.

In the JBS, we see an organization in which a dominant and successful national office blocks the conditions which could give rise to viable active local branches. In other movement organizations, we find other specific patterns of relation between the national and local levels, some producing strong nationals and weak locals, some producing strong activist locals but weak underfunded nationals, some producing strong mobilization on both levels, and some producing deadlock and failure. In movements, as a whole, we often see a kind of division of labor between professionalized national organizations with no active membership and decentralized local mobilizations with no centralized national presence. We believe that identifying the different ways in which the local and national levels of a movement or movement organizations relate to each other, and the ways in which these relations affect movement trajectories and outcomes, will greatly further our overall understanding of the dynamics of social movements.

NOTES

1. National movement organizations which also have strong activist chapters may have substantive elections which actually affect the organization's national policy and strategy, for example of the widely-publicized campaigns for the presidency of the National Organization for Women (see Ferree and Hess 1985 for a brief overview). Such events are rare. It would be interesting to see a study of whether the election results affected behavior in the national office.

2. The chapter leader said he remained loyal to the JBS for two reasons. First, the all-encompassing ideology of the JBS helped to integrate the messages of all other groups into a coherent and more simple whole. Second, the JBS emphasis on local chapters made him feel more a part of an organization than a name on a mailing list. We suspect that even for this active member, "symbolic solidarity" was also important.

3. In this section, we are not distinguishing independent local organizations from chapters of national organizations. Rather, we believe that there are important dynamics involved in local mobilization that are common to both types of groups.

4. This is not to deny that unorganized mass protest or rebellion can produce policy changes, but, in this case, those in power devisse policy strategies to deal with the crisis without directly consulting the protestors for their policy inputs.

5. This statement is true for ordinary volunteer movement organizations whose members can, and do, freely quit whenever they want to. There are, of course, a small number of coerceive cult-like organizations which do compel obedience through physical threats and psychgological intimidation. The dynamics of such coerceive organizations are entirely outside the scope of the arguments advanced in this paper. These arguments also do not apply to organizations which successfully operate under "democratic centralism" or other hierarchical principles in which members become so committed to the organization that they bind themselves to follow the directives of the national organization whether they agree with them or not. Such organizations are rare and attract few members, at least in the United States.

REFERENCES

Allen, G. 1971. *None Dare Call It Conspiracy.* CA: Concord Press.

Broyles, J.A. 1964. *The John Birch Society: Anatomy of a Protest.* Boston, MA: Beacon Press.

Carden, M. 1978. "The Proliferation of a Social Movement." Pp. 179-196 in *Research in Social Movements, Conflicts and Change,* vol. 1, edited by L. Kriesberg. Greenwich, CT: JAI Press.

Crawford, A. 1980. *Thunder on the Right.* New York: Pantheon.

Downs. A. 1972. "Up and Down with Ecology—The Issue-Attention Cycle." *Public Interest* 28:38-50.

Ericson. E.L. 1982. *American Freedom and the Radical Right.* New York: Frederick Ungar.

Ferree, M.M. and B.B. Hess 1985. *Controversy and Coalition: The New Feminist Movement.* Boston, MA: Twayne.

Forster, A. and B.R. Epstein 1964. *The Radical Right.* New York: Random.

_____. 1966. *Report on the John Birch Society: 1966.* New York: Random.

_____. 1967. *The Radical Right: Report on the John Birch Society and Its Allies.* New York: Random.

Gerlach, L. and V. Hine. 1970. *People, Power, Change.* New York: Bobbs-Merrill.

Gitlin, T. 1980. *The Whole World is Watching: Mass Media in the Making and Unmaking of the New Left.* Berkeley: University of California Press.

Griffin, G.E. 1964. *The Fearful Monster: A Second Look at the United Nations.* Belmont, MA: Western Islands.
————. 1971. *The Capitalist Conspiracy.* Thousand Oaks, CA: American Media.
————. 1975. *The Life and Worlds of Robert Welch, Founder of the John Birch Society.* Thousand Oaks, CA: American Media.
Hefley, J. and M. Hefley. 1980. *The Secret File on John Birch.* Wheaton, IL: Tyndale House.
Jenkins, J.C. 1983. "Resource Mobilization Theory and the Study of Social Movements." *Annual Review of Sociology* 9:527-553.
Lipset, S.M. 1964. "Three Decades of the Radical Right: Coughlinites, McCarthyites and Birchers." Pp. 373-446 in *The Radical Right,* edited by D. Bell. Garden City, NY: Anchor Books.
Lipset, S.M. and E. Raab. 1970. *The Politics of Unreason: Right Wing Extremism in America 1790-1970.* Chicago: University of Chicago Press.
McCarthy, J.D. and M.N. Zald. 1973. *The Trend of Social Movements in America: Professionalization and Resource Mobilization.* Morristown, NJ: General Learning Press.
————. 1977. "Resource Mobilization and Social Movements: A Partial Theory." *American Journal of Sociology* 82:1212-1241.
Morris, A. 1984. *The Origins of the Civil Rights Movement.* New York: Free Press.
Oliver, P. 1983. "The Mobilization of Paid and Volunteer Activists in the Neighborhood Movement." Pp. 133-170 in *Research in Social Movements, Conflict and Change,* vol. 5, edited by L. Kriesberg. Greenwich, CT: JAI Press.
————. 1984. "If You Don't Do It, Nobody Else Will: Active and Token Contributors to Local Collective Action." *American Sociological Review* 49:601-610.
Oliver, P., G. Marwell, and R. Teixeira. 1985. "A Theory of the Critical Mass, I. Interdependence, Group Heterogeneity, and the Production of Collective Goods." *American Journal of Sociology* 91:522-556.
Redkop, J.H. 1968. *The American Far Right: A Case Study of Billy James Hargis.* New York: Eerdmans.
Schoenberger, R.A., ed. 1969. *The American Right-Wing: Readings in Political Behavior.* New York: Holt, Rinehart, and Winston.
Schomp, G. 1970. *Birchism Was My Business.* New York: MacMillan.
Scott, J. 1980. "Keeping Up With The Birchers." *Boston Magazine* (June).
Smoot, D. 1962. *The Invisible Goverment.* Belmont, MA: Western Islands.
————. 1973. *The Business End of Government.* Belmont, MA: Western Islands.
Welch, 1969. *The Blue Book of the John Birch Society.* Belmont, MA: Western Islands.
Westin, A. 1964. "The John Birch Society." Pp. 239-268 in *the Radical Right,* edited by D. Bell. Garden City, NY: Anchor.
Wilson, J.Q. 1973. *Political Organizations.* New York: Basic Books.

"EXIT" BEHAVIOR IN SOCIAL MOVEMENT ORGANIZATIONS

Gerrita Van der Veen and Bert Klandermans

INTRODUCTION

Participation in social movements has long been a topic enjoying the attention of social scientists. Usually it is assumed that different forms of participation can be placed on a single activity-dimension. The degree of participation is held to equal the sum of distinct activities undertaken separately. Several authors (Nicholson et al. 1981; McAdam 1985; McShane 1986; Klandermans 1986) however, have pointed out recently that participation in a social movement in multidimensional. Its specific forms derive from distinct motivations and produce different results. Discussing participation in trade unions, Regalia (1986) and Kalndermans (1986) distinguish three types of voluntary participation:

1. membership—without engagement in organizational activities;
2. active membership—participation in day-to-day activities;
3. participating in collective actions initiated by one's union.

International Social Movement Research, Vol. 2, pages 179-198.
Copyright © 1989 by JAI Press Inc.
All rights of reproduction in any form reserved.
ISBN: 0-89232-964-5

Similar distinctions may be applied to participation in social movements, even if not every movement displays each of the three types. In the feminist movement in The Netherlands, for instance, there is no formal membership; hence, only the second and the third type of participation are found (Briët et al. 1985). In the squatters' movement, participation in the movement equals direct action: The very act of squatting defines one as a participant in the movement (Huberts and Van Noort 1986).

Although a great deal of attention is being paid to participation, there is little literature on systematic, comparative research into its distinctive forms, while another aspect of it—that of ceasing to participate in the movement— has been neglected altogether. Theory and research focus on how people join a movement and, to date, have hardly been concerned with people leaving.

Each of the types of participation mentioned allows for the option of leaving. One can terminate one's membership, discontinue active participation or disengage oneself from collective action. Declining participation in any one of these categories is critically significant to the functioning of social movement organizations (SMOs). A sizeable exit of members is likely to affect the organization dramatically and may ultimately mean its demise (Messinger 1955; Obserschall 1978). In this respect, SMOs and voluntary associations are unlike work organizations in which, as a rule, departing employees are easily, person for person, replaced. While such turnover may adversely affect the stability of the staff, the size of the organization remains the same. In SMOs, however, where the recruitment of new members often is a struggle to start with, a decline in membership makes for serious difficulties. Once a certain critical point is reached, the organization simply ceases to exist, on account of, first, the lack of material and immaterial means (these organizations depend heavily on material and immaterial contributions by members); second, because of the dwindling potential manpower that can be called upon for collective action; and, third, in view of the fact that a meagre constituency reduces the credibility and, hence, the impact of the movement in society at large.

When the number of active members decreases, the internal functioning of the organization is affected first of all. The continued existence of social movement organizations stands or falls with the efforts exerted by volunteers, who often invest a significant amount of free time. As a consequence, the movement's scope of action diminishes as well. Actions that depend on a dedicated cadre are no longer securely rooted, nor are actions requiring mass support, since the infrastructure needed for mass mobilization is no lonter in place.

A downward trend in the number of participants in a given collective action initiates a spiral effect leading to its termination. The notion of "production function" developed by Oliver et al. (1985) can help to clarify this. In their view, some actions proceed such that the initial participants contribute most to the realization of the goals; once a given threshold is crossed, action will succeed and the influx of additional participants will have relatively little effect. In other actions, only if a certain threshold is crossed do new participants enhance the chances for success. In the former case, Oliver et al. speak of a "decelerative function" between the input of contributions and the output of collective goods; in the latter situation, of an "accelerative function."

The same functions come into play when the number of participants shrinks. When individuals quit, the effect on the results of the action varies with the production function. In case of an accelerative function, individual withdrawal will soon put into motion a downward spiral, while, in the case of a decelerative function, it may take some time before the effects of "exit" behavior become visible. In either case, once the critical point is reached, the action comes to a halt.

In this article, we limit ourselves to just one type of "exit" behavior: membership resignation. Not because this is the most important type, but rather because we can build on research results available from neighboring fields of investigation, such as the literature on employee turnover in work organizations (Buchanan 1974; Steers 1977), data on membership turnover in voluntary associations (Knoke 1981; Wilson 1973), and trade unions (cf. Klandermans 1986). The literature regarding employee turnover provides us with the concept of "commitment," which has proved to be the best predictor of turnover in work organizations. Although up to now no relation has been established between turnover and commitment in voluntary associations, the data suggest that here, too, the concept may be of service (Gordon et al. 1980; Knoke 1981).

Since trade unions are, in many ways, similar to SMOs, literature on membership turnover in unions merits special attention. Further, prompted by declining membership in trade unions in The Netherlands, research has, of late, been undertaken on their membership turnover. In this paper, we make use of data provided by some recent Dutch Studies in this field. After presenting a discussion of studies on membership turnover in unions, we outline two theoretical approaches to the investigation of "exit" behavior. We conclude with an attempt to apply our findings to SMOs in general.

MEMBERSHIP DECLINE IN TRADE UNIONS

In 1980, the industrial workers union of the Federation of Dutch Trade Unions (Industriebond-FNV) conducted a large-scale study among 723 exmembers. In 1985, 85 former members of the hotel-workers union (Horecabond-FNV) were asked, upon resigning, why they no longer valued their union membership (Van der Veen 1985). Teulings (1983) compared 64 members and 64 exmembers of the food-workers union (Voedingsbond-FNV)—a union comprising both food industry and service). Teulings made use of a "matched sample:" Every former member in the sample is paired with a current member with a number of similar characteristics. In the other two studies, persons were contacted who were deleted from the membership file at their own request. Only exmembers who withdrew for subjective reasons, such as objections to policy, comlaints regarding service facilities, concerns about the financial burden of membership, and the like, were included. Members withdrawing for objective reasons (like moving to another job, retiring, and so forth) were not included. For each study, data were gathered by way of structured interviews.

Who are these exmembers? What induced them to leave the trade union? The two principal causes of diminishing membership turn out to be: (a) doubt as to the usefulness of continued union membership because of one's specific position in the labor market and (b) the lack of positive experiences with union activities. Let us take a closer look at each of these.

Position in the Labor Market

Many exmembers find themselves outside of the labor process either because of unemployment or because of injury. From the group of former members of the Industriebond-FNV, one-fourth are out of work; two-thirds of those interviewed in the hotel-workers study were without work and one-third of the exmembers from the Voedingsbond-FNV consists of non-working people.

Being out of work, as such, need not be a reason to terminate one's membership. This depends on union rules. For example, some unions in the United Kingdom do not allow the unemployed to be members. In The Netherlands, unions claim to serve the interests of jobless people as well, and many of those who lose their job simply continue their union membership. Nonworking former members of the Horecabond-FNV, however, looked upon unions as organizations mainly for workers and did not think that continued membership would help much. Congruent with this attitude, many announced that they would reenlist once they found work again.

Young people and women are two other categories overrepresented among leavers. The high percentage of unemployed among youth (32% of the registered unemployed are under 24 years of age) show that, for young people, the Dutch labor market is far from favorable. The same is true of women, who represent 35% of the total number of unemployed. Moreover, women and young people frequently hold jobs with built-in disadvantages: irregular working hours, fluctuating tasks, a poorly-regulated legal status. Traditionally, trade unions have been reluctant to represent the interests of certain subgroups. Hence, they have paid scant attention to the special problems of women and youth. Consequently, neither group is attracted to the labor movement and, since there is little specific concern for them, many of them quit. In the reviewed studies, more than one-third of the exmembers are less than 25-years-old, while the total membership stands at 25% young people. For women, the same scores are obtained. Here, then, the problem is compounded: Young people and women are not only poorly represented among the membership, but also, having become a member, they are more prone to leave.

Experiences

The bleak expectations concerning their own future notwithstanding, many young people, women, and nonworking individuals are members of a trade union. Evidently, reference to vulnerability in the labor market does not provide a sufficient explanation of diminishing membership. The experiences of members with the union services (in the event of reorganization or dismissal, or similar) constitute an additional explanation. Those who experienced positive dealings with the trade union will stay; those for whom such experiences were unfavorable or who had no union experience at all will leave. A weak position in the labor market combined with poor experiences with the trade union provides many with a strong motive to terminate their union membership.

In our study among hotel workers, a comparison of male and female exmembers reveals that women leave, not so much because of negative experiences, but because they lack union experience altogether. Women are less active in the union than men are. They are less concerned with collective protection of interests and are less familiar with union policy. The study undertaken by the Industriebond-FNV leads to the same conclusion.

A comparison between younger and older exmembers among the hotel workers shows that negative expectations regarding the possible benefits of membership induce younger members leaving the union and causes them to lack positive experiences with the union. They fail to see that, in today's situation, the trade union can be instrumental.

The nonworking exmembers in the horeca study also proved to lack union experience. Loss of work implies loss of the context within which contact with the union habitually takes place. Becoming jobless or injured often means that contacts with one's trade union and colleagues fade away.

It appears, then, that among youthful, female, and nonworking former union members, resigning is closely linked to a lack of (positive) experience with the union, in combination with a poor position in the labor market.

On the other hand, negative experiences with union work may itself be sufficient to cause quitting. This proved to be so among job-holding exmembers. In this group, negative experiences with various types of union services was the most frequently stated motive for membership termination.

THEORETICAL APPROACHES TO "EXIT" BEHAVIOR

There are two theoretical ways in terms of which one can embark upon the study of "exit" behavior. A first approach is to view leaving as the process of joining, in reverse. The very model used to explain enrollment can *then* be applied to resignation *now*. Many authors implicitly acted upon this assumption (cf. Toch 1965; Van de Vall 1963). This may explain why the literature on social movements has paid little attention to "exit" behavior. It was presumed that with the answer to the question as to why people join, the key was given to an explanation as to why they leave. The second approach assumes enrolling and resigning to be distinct processes. During the period that people are associated with a movement, qualitatively new dimensions are added to being a member, so that the reasons for quitting are not the same as those for joining. In the following discussion, these two approaches will be elaborated.

Joining Equals Leaving

If enrollment is predicted on the same process that leads one to resign, it would mean that theories of joining may also be used to explain "exit" behavior.

Bain and Price (1980) define membership turnover in unions as ". . . the outcome of a mass of individual decisions to join and to leave trade unions." This definition presupposes that joining and leaving follow upon one's individual decision. In the literature on social movements, the decision to participate is taken to be a calculation of the costs and benefits of participation as perceived by the individual (Oberschall 1980; Klandermans 1984a; Muller and Opp 1986). If the benefits outweigh the costs, the individual decides to participate This decision is made at a specific time however, and one does not stop balancing costs against benefits once one has joined. When a single process is assumed to underlie both joining and leaving, resigning will be explained in terms of events having occurred during one's involvement with the movement on account of which a negative balance resulted: Costs have outrun gains. Particularly in cases where the balance is only just positive, the slightest alteration may have drastic consequences. Perhaps this serves to clarify why, in many trade unions, membership turnover is so large (in The Netherlands union membership is based on voluntary participation). Most likely a good many members consider the balance to be only just favorable. Relatively insignificant events such as a minor increase of the membership fee will suffice to tip the scales and people will leave. Conversely, there are those to whom the balance is only just negative. Here, too, a little nudge, for example, an acquaintance citing a positive experience, adds sufficient weight, and the union gains a member. Obviously there is a fair amount of "border traffic" in the area where the advantages and the disadvantages of membership pretty well cancel each other out.

In terms of theory, membership termination may be prompted by one of four developments:

1. The costs of participation increase while the benefits decrease (see a in Figure 1);
2. The costs increase while the benefits remain as before (see b in Figure 1);
3. The benefits decrease while costs remain unchanged (see c in Figure 1);
4. The costs increase more quickly than the benefits (see d in Figure 1).

These functions indicate that alteration has occurred in the assessment process of the costs and benefits gained. It will be clear that not every change will bring about the same consequences. Whether an increase in costs will lead to "exit" behavior or not depends on the degree of compensation offered by the benefits. Diminishing returns lead to "exit" behavior only when the costs remain constant.

In the literature on participation, a distinction is customarily made between "collective" and "selective" costs and benefits (Olson 1965; Wilson 1973; Carden 1978; Oberschall 1980; Klandermans 1984a). Collective costs and benefits are related to the expectation that participation will help the movement to realize its goals. They provide a collective motive for participation. Selective costs and benefits refer to the individual advantages or disadvantages of participation, and constitute a selective motive for doing so.

It seems reasonable to assume that these distinctions are relevant for "exit" behavior as well. Membership retention is linked to a favorable outcome of the collective and selective cost/benefit calculation, while membership termination is related to an unfavorable result. Table 1 lists, for either type of motive, the possible combinations, three of which can induce resigning. Further, Table 1 represents the distribution of the possible combinations among the exmembers in our study of hotel workers.[1]

The first quadrant (+ +) contains those participants who are convinced that membership helps to realize collective goals, and for whom, further, since the selective gains outweigh the costs, the selective motives are positive. They continue their membership in the movement. This cannot be said of the remaining categories. In the fourth quadrant (− −), we place those whose collective motivation has disappeared and in whose estimation selective gains accruing to membership no longer equal the costs. These people will leave. In the second quadrant (+ −), we put those for whom collective motivation to participate does exist, but the selective loss seems to them greater than the profit. They will quit once the point is reached at which the collective gains no longer compensate for the selective costs of membership. Participants who lack collective motivation, but who feel that the selective benefits of membership are greater than the costs, are assigned to the third quadrant (− +). They cease to be members once selective benefits fall short of selective costs.

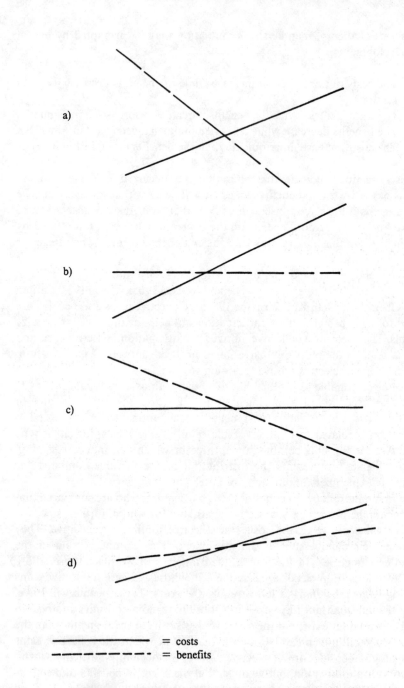

Figure 1.   Exit as a Function of Costs and Benefits

Table 1.   Motivation of Exmembers to Leave the Union
(Percent)

		Selective Motives		
		(+)	(−)	
	(+)	10.3	41.2	51.5
Collective Motives				
	(−)	13.2	35.3	48.5
		23.5	76.5	100.0

Of the former members of the union of hotel workers, 10.3% considered the balance of costs and benefits to be favorable, both with respect to collective and selective items. Closer inspection reveals that these persons are nonworking exmembers. They still subscribe to the goals of the trade union and do not doubt the efficacy of the union in attaining them. We cannot explain their leaving in terms of the approach sketched here. "Exit" behavior of the remaining 89.7%, however, can be accounted for. The majority turns out to have an unfavorable balance of selective benefits (76.5%). Among more than half of these exmembers, the negativity of the selective benefits combine with positive collective benefits (quadrant 2), but these do not seem to compensate. One can understand this in the light of Olson's suggestion (1965) that membership is not necessarily a prerequisite for sharing in collective benefits. Therefore, positive collective benefits do not preserve people from leaving.

The significance of selective benefits readily fit into a development in union membership to which various authors have called attention. Several authors claimed that union membership has become more instrumental and less ideological over the last few decades (Van de Vall 1963; Goldthorpe et al. 1968).

Such shifts in motivation will affect the relative weight assigned to motives at the moment of leaving. In suport of this view, Van de Vall (1963) noted that, in the heydey of the welfare state, the union was confronted with an exodus of members occasioned by doubts regarding the instrumentality of membership. The seeming lack of selective gains motivated "exit" behavior. These findings point to a development from an ideological orientation towards union membership to a more instrumental one. Van Ham et al. (1985) found that this development spread in the course of the 1970s. Self-realization and individual autonomy were now emphasized. Partly on account of technological progress, and its incessant demand for greater specialization, the requirements and interests of individuals also tended to diverge, for the most part prompted by materialistic and pragmatic considerations. Consequently, people are prone to join or leave on pragmatic grounds, rather than for ideological reasons.

This line of argument is supported by the trade union studies already referred to. The inquiry among hotel workers revealed that only 13% of the former members interviewed had joined for the sake of collective benefits. Most of them enrolled because of selective incentives, ranging from immediate needs to future threats (dismissal, reorganization).

Against this background, it is understandable that the cost/benefit approach does a fair job of elucidating exit-behavior in the labor movement.

Joining Does Not Equal Leaving

Some authors have reacted to the markedly individualistic approach to participation in social movement organizations of the cost/benefit model, and instead they have focused on interaction processes among individuals within a movement. They hold that, in deciding to (continue to) participate, members are not lone individuals, unrelated to others. They argue that during one's stay in a movement, new dimensions of affiliation develop. Within this frame of reference, leaving is not merely the reverse of joining; consequently, exit is qualitatively different from entering.

While Regalia (1986) also takes it that anticipated benefits motivate people to participate, she points to a different type of satisfaction from participation. People do not participate merely because of perceived benefits, but also because they seek social recognition and affirmation of their identity. They join a social movement if its collective identity reflects their own expectations, values, and needs. Identity affirmation occurs in the interaction among members. Regalia borrows the term "collective identity" from Pizzorno (1978), for whom the concept refers to the shared values, needs, and expectations on which the social movement is based and in terms of which it acts. She calls these benefits, accruing to participation, "identity incentives." To her, joining may largely be explained from benefits anticipated, but, in addition, people see their identity affirmed in interactions with the movement and this determines whether or not they continue to participate. She explains "exit" behavior in terms of the interaction of both factors.

Like cost/benefit theorists, Regalia presupposes that at the moment of joining, the individual already has values, needs, and expectations in common with other members. However, this assumption has been subjected to repeated criticism (Ferree and Miller 1985; Melucci 1985). Shared values, needs, and expectations result from interaction, rather than precede it. Ferree and Miller argue that the way a movement presents itself is based on expectations and attitudes developed jointly in the interaction of individuals in the movement. The ideology thus developed, shapes the expectations individuals have, rather than the other way around.

In Melucci's eyes, a social movement is more than the sum of its separate individuals. Melucci is prepared to use the term "collective identity"—unlike

Pizzorno, however, he does not assume it to be ready-made; he regards it as a shared, negotiated definition of the situation. Participation, then, not only affirms identity, it shapes it as well. According to Melucci, the resultant collective identity provides the basis on which cost/benefit calculations are possible.

The weakness of concepts such as "ideology" and "collective identity" is their lack of empirical referents. Conceptualization and operationalization still leave much to be desired, so that their usefulness remains difficult to ascertain. Nevertheless, the recent emphasis on processes of interaction within social movements, and on their cognitive counterparts, indicates a need for concepts and theories that can do justice to the dynamics of movement participation.

Commitment

The process of identity-formation within SMOs seems to us akin to that of developing commitment to the organization. "Commitment" stems from the literature on work organizations, and is defined as the degree of identification with the aims of the organization, willingness to expend extra effort in its service, loyalty towards it, and the intensity of the desire to continue participation in it (Buchanan 1974; Porter et al. 1974; Steers 1977; Gordon et al. 1980). Commitment to the organization on the part of its employees makes for staff-stability, enhancing the enterprise's functioning.

Commitment proves to be a better predictor of employee turnover in work organizations than "job satisfaction" (Porter et al. 1974). Far less is known about commitment to voluntary organizations and social movements. Knoke (1981) attempted to measure commitment to voluntary organizations. He found that commitment and detachment are influenced by the degree to which the organization's policy-structure allows for communication and participation in decision making on the part of the members. Gordon et al. (1980) studied commitment to trade unions. They describe four dimensions of union commitment: (1) loyalty to the union; (2) responsibility for the union; (3) willingness to be active in it; and (4) belief in unionism, that is, a sturdy faith in the values and goals of the union. Loyalty turned out to be the most important factor. They describe it as consisting of a feeling of communality, together with the conviction that the union is able to satisfy the needs of its members. This community-feeling arises in one's socialization as a member of the union. This socialization, one's integration in the organization, comes to fruition in the experiences of members with the union; passively, as when one attends the meetings, or actively, through engagement in extra union activities such as becoming a branch official. The socialization process, as an aspect of loyalty, seems similar to the process in which identity is established. The other side of commitment, the conviction regarding the union's ability to fulfill needs, reminds one of the cost/benefit equation.

Commitment and Exit

Hirschman (1970) states that, when individuals are dissatisfied and faced with the choice of staying or leaving, loyalty will decide the issue. Basically, a member has a choice: to quit or to critique, to exercise his "exit-option" or his "voice-option." If commitment to the movement is low or nonexistent, a member's dissatisfaction will induce him to leave; if he does feel a measure of commitment, he is more likely to vent his criticism within the organization.

Yet there is another alternative: a third option combining "exit" and "voice." Individually departing members seldom make use of it. As a rule they leave anonymously, sometimes without any reasons stated. But situations do occur where members leave *en masse* or in small, organized groups, by way of protest against (aspects of) union policy. This can be undertaken with the promise of reentry (Hirschman 1970), but a situation of no return is also possible (Schuyt 1972). While trying to predict "exit" behavior from commitment scores, the second author accidentally came across an example of en bloc withdrawal. A group of union members, in a specific section of a company, left the union in protest against union policy regarding reorganization of the section. Each member of this group was highly committed to the union, so, against our expectations, commitment was positively related to exit (Klandermans 1984b). Another example is provided by the British miners' strike in which a new miners' union arose (Adeney and Lloyd 1986). The term "oppositional exodus" (Teulings 1983) seems quite suitable here. The combination of exit and voice is a particularly potent weapon in the case of a fairly organized walkout (Schuyt 1972).

In some circumstances, however, exit is very difficult or impossible. For example, to leave one's work organization is a less than attractive option when the labor market is satiated and jobs become scarce. Voluntary organizations are different in this respect: One may not stand to lose a great deal upon leaving; in fact, nonmembers share in a good many movement-procured benefits (Olson 1965). In the case of trade unions, this holds to a lesser degree, since, next to protecting collective interests, the union also provides selective incentives. Hence, like employees in a work organization, may trade union members hardly have their individual interest represented (Weiss 1963). In unions where membership is mandatory (closed shops), as in the graphics industry in The Netherlands, members have no exit option at all. In that case, if to critique is too costly in the eyes of the individual, the only thing left is to exercise the "silence option" (Barry 1979): One continues to be a member but does not lift a finger in any union activity.

In addition to the choices recounted by Hirschman, then, there are in fact more alternatives. Noncommitted members may decide to retain membership, when exit costs are too high, and settle for the silence option. Committed members can leave the movement in order to underline their criticisms and carry out a combination of exit and voice.

Table 2.   Participation in Union Activities
(Percent)

Participation	Industry	Food Industry	Horeca
Never	76	64	88
Passive	19	27	11
Active	5	9	1

All things considered, commitment proves to be a key concept in the explanation of the exit behavior. The study conducted by the Industriebond-FNV, that of the Voedingsbond-FNV, and our own research among hotel workers each showed that the majority of exmembers was not enrolled for very long. These people were written off before the integration process that leads to commitment had a chance to take hold. In addition to this, it turned out, in each of these studies, that a sizeable portion (about 75%) of these one-time members were never actively engaged in union matters (Table 2). This allows us to conclude that at issue here is the departure of members with a low degree of union-commitment. This explains why cost/benefit theory did so well in accounting for "exit" behavior. As we argue later in this paper, the cost/benefit approach does especially apply among members with a low degree of union commitment.

Even so, among a sizeable 25% of the membership, some degree of integration into union activities did take place. The exit-voice theory predicts that they will become vocal when dissatisfied. Stil, they too left the union. Since, as far as could be traced, no combination of exit and voice was exhibited here, we can surmise that for these people union-commitment has waned. Their leaving must be clarified in terms of factors that adversely affect such commitment. The attitude of workers towards their union is known to be subject to change due to changed working conditions. Lieberman (1965) has shown, for instance, that employees become anti-union after they adopted a management position in the company. Conversely, it is also possible to understand why so many nonworking people leave the union. One of the reasons for their "exit" behavior appears to be that, with the loss of their job, they became estranged from the social framework in which union contract is maintained. Loss of the job and its context, then, is a change of position that leads to loss of contact with the union, so that detachment is a possible consequence.

On the other hand, change in the employment status is not the sole cause of alienation. In this connection, it is relevant to recall that unions show a tendency towards bureaucratization, as a result of which contact with members is becoming more formal and regulation-prone. For instance, dues and donations used to be collected person-to-person by a local representative.

Today, membership fees are often withdrawn automatically. These and similar organizational changes have induced a shift from personal contact to bureaucratic administration. No wonder, then, that commitment to the union is evaporating.

The above leads us to conclude that, in explaining "exit" behavior in trade unions, one cannot do without commitment as a factor.

We have sketched two ways of elucidating "exit" behavior in SMOs. The scope of these approaches was illustrated in relation to empirical data on trade unions in The Netherlands. One approach is predicted on the assumption that joining and leaving rest on the same principles. Cost/benefit theory may be taken to represent this approach. On its tenents, "exit" behavior follows from alterations in the cost/benefit ratio taking place during the period of membership, such that the balance becomes a negative one. These shifts occur when new costs or benefits arise or when the relative weight of "known quantities" is being reconsidered.

The second line presupposes that, in the course of membership, new qualities develop through interaction between the individual and the movement, in virtue of which considerations other than those that led to joining will now underlie one's decision to leave. Although a number of authors hint that much happens once one has enrolled in a movement, little has been done in the way of investigating this. We therefore turned to commitment theory as developed, for the most part, in the context of work organizations. According to this theory, the integration of individuals in the organization takes place while they are members, such that commitment to the organization develops. When integration in the movement has occurred, the grounds for leaving must be sought, then, in factors that put into motion the opposed process of detachment.

The empirical data in union studies show that either the cost/benefit theory or the commitment theory are able to explain exit in unions. The two approaches do not conflict. The concept of commitment can be used as a complement to the cost/benefit theory. When little or no integration has been achieved, the cost/benefit theory offers an adequate explanation for exit. When commitment has developed, the decision to leave involves more than a mere calculation of costs and benefits. Leaving the organization, then, is due to factors influencing commitment.

RELEVANCE FOR OTHER MOVEMENTS

Since both approaches to "exit" behavior are based on data derived from the study of trade unions, one should not generalize them to social movements uncritically. On the other hand, cost/benefit theory and commitment theory are not elaborated in the literature on trade unions alone. Hence, one may justifiably expect them to be of use in the explanation of "exit" behavior in other social movements as well. However, this is more difficult to ascertain, as the reasons for joining and leaving other social movements are often elusive. In the labor movement, membership is relatively well-defined. Joining and leaving are determined by whether one starts or ceases to pay membership dues. In order to arrive at a generalization, we have to take into consideration similarities and differences between social movements, and the implications of these, for "exit" behavior. Comparing the labor movement, the peace movement, and the feminist movement, Klandermans (1984c) lists three dimensions—organizational structure, mobilization potential, and strategy—in which social movements differ and which affect their members' propensity to participate. With regard to "exit" behavior, two questions should be dealt with:

1. To what extent does a movement appeal to individual instrumentality of membership? Organizations which offer much in the way of services expect to recruit and retain members on the basis of cost/benefit calculation.
2. To what extent does an organization allow for interaction among members, such that a degree of commitment to the organization will develop?

Organizational Structure

The structure of a movement's organization directly influences the degree of commitment and detachment of its members. The more opportunities there are for communication with the members and for their participation, the stronger the bond will become (Knoke 1981). This means that a decentralized structure will more readily elicit membership commitment than a centralized organizational structure can. In The Netherlands, the peace movement depends on local groups that execute actions independently. The feminist movement is also concentrated in a variety of small, autonomous groups (therapeutic, activist, educational). Small, independent groups provide ample opportunity for interaction on a personal level, and individual members are able to directly influence decision making.

In contrast, the Dutch trade union is organized into a markedly centralized structure. Both decisions, and the implementation of decisions, are undertaken at the top. In a centralized organizational structure, members have but marginal influence on policy. This is why they are seldom strongly motivated to attend union meetings (Klandermans 1984d; Klaassen 1986). There is little point to seeking contact with the union, unless one has problems which require union assistance. We also pointed to the development that, today, the union is being organized along more bureaucratic lines. This implies that contact between the union and its members is becoming less personal.

Compared with other movements, then, the organizational structure of the Dutch trade union allows for little interaction and, consequently, for little commitment to develop.

Mobilization Potential

Social movements differ from each other with respect to the composition of their mobilization potential. The paying members are the union's potential mobilization force. Membership, however, is unequal: Some are "ordinary" members while others are activists. An ordinary member is one who does nothing more than pay his fees. Interaction is not sought and integration will not occur. An activist is one who participates in organization activities. As a consequence, integration and commitment will inevitably develop.

In the peace movement, the feminist movement, and other less ridigly-structured movements, the mobilization potential consists of an unidentifiable group of sympathizers who may occasionally come together. One becomes a member of such organizations by actively participating in it. Membership without integration, is, therefore, inconceivable. We may assume that "exit" behavior, as in the case of the activists of a trade union, it to be attributed to factors affecting commitment. Since many sympathizers and ordinary union members do not go through a process of commitment development, their "exit" behavior is more likely to be a matter of cost/benefit calculation.

The mere fact that unions exact membership fees already means that the calculative aspects of membership are stressed. Among 70% of the former members of the Horecabond-FNV, an important reason for resignation was that membership fees were too steep. The amount of the contribution, as such, need not be the reason for leaving: It depends on whether one gets one's money's worth.

In short, with the paying membership, the union invites people to consider (continued) participation more in terms of cost/benefit calculations than other SMOs do.

Strategy

Collective bargaining is central to union strategy in The Netherlands. Negotiations proceed within a highly institutionalized framework. Some theorists (Wood and Jackson 1982) do not look upon the trade union as a social movement, precisely in view of its high degree of institutionalization. However, unions move outside of regulated bargaining when they organize collective action (strikes, demonstrations, and so on). To this extent, trade unions are similar to other social movements.

The Dutch labor movement sets itself three tasks: emancipation—the promotion of social consciousness in society as a whole; protection of the collective interests of anyone employed in The Netherlands; and, protection of the individual interests of union members.

While the first two are goals pursued to a greater or lesser degree in every social movement, the third is more specifically characteristic of trade unions, setting them apart from the others. It certainly affects the manner in which unions conduct their affairs; they must expend a large portion of their resources on providing individual services. In fact, in the new union strategy, facilities of this sort (legal aid, schooling) will soon come to play a central part. As we mentioned earlier, this is a result of a restructuring of the labor market which, in combination with a tendency towards individualization in society at large, encourages an attitude such that enrollment in the union is motivated less by ideological considerations than used to be the case, and more by pragmatic and materialistic considerations. Therefore, many people do not join until they personally need the union; hence, membership means little to them once their problem is solved. They simply leave again. Union strategy today is converging on this escalating tendency toward calculation on the part of employees.

The more important a movement considers service to individual members, the stronger the movement is appealing to instrumental motives to be a member (Regalia 1986). Contrary to other movements, this is the case for trade unions.

CONCLUSION

Depending on the characteristics displayed by a social movement, "exit" behavior is explicable in terms of either cost/benefit theory or commitment theory. The answers to questions as to how the organization is built up, what type of membership it has, and what its strategy is, indicate which approach is the more effective. The more a movement is open to interaction on the individual level in each of these areas, the more scope for factors influencing commitment to explain "exit" behavior. The more a movement gravitates to the individual benefits of membership, the more exhaustive the explanation of exit-behavior in terms of the cost/benefit theory.

Given the linkage between membership and the paying of fees, together with increased attention to "person-directed" services, trade unions appeal strongly to instrumental motives for joining. The markedly centralized organizational structure and the possibility of merely passive membership conspire to curtail interaction among members of a trade union. Hence, one can expect the cost/benefit theory to be able to explain more "exit" behavior in case of the trade union than in other social movements.

NOTES

1. A cost/benefit ratio is obtained by individual exmembers assigning a value of -1, 0, or 1 to any possible cost or benefit, and by averaging these values per category (collective or selective).

Possible costs are assigned to the following values:
-1 = a strong reason for leaving
 0 = a weak reason for leaving
 1 = no reason

Possible benefits are scored as follows:
-1 = considered highly important
 0 = considered of some importance
 1 = unimportant

It is assumed that any single cost or benefit is of a weight equal to any other cost or benefit entering into the calculation. In spite of the fact that some objections cling to this procedure, we think that, in the context of this article, the score obtained may offer a reasonable approximation of one's individual cost/benefit ratio.

REFERENCES

Adeney, M. and J. Lloyd. 1986. *The Miners' Strike: Loss without Limit.* London: Routledge & Kegan Paul.
Bain, G. and R. Price. 1980. *Profiles of Union Growth.* Oxford: Blackwell.
Barry, B. 1979. "Exit, Voice and Loyality." *British Journal of Political Science* 4: 79-107.
Briët, M., F. Kroon, and P.G. Klandermans. 1985. *Vrouwen in de vrouwenbeweging* (Women in the Women's Movement). 's Gravenhage, The Netherlands: Ministerie van Sociale Zaken en Werkgelegenheid.
Buchanan, B. 1974. "Building Organizational Commitment: The Socialization of Managers in Work Organizations." *Administrative Science Quarterly* 19: 533-546.
Carden, M.L. 1978. "The Proliferation of a Social Movement. Ideology and Individual Incentives in the Contemporary Feminist Movement." Pp. 179-196 in *Social Movements, Conflict and Change,* edited by L. Kriesberg. Greenwich, CT: JAI Press.
Ferree, M.M. and F.D. Miller. 1985. "Mobilization and Meaning: Towards an Integration of Social Psychological and Resource Perspectives on Social Movements." *Sociological Inquiry* 55: 38-61.
Goldthorpe, J.H., D. Lockwood, F. Bechhofer, and J. Platt. 1968. *The Affluent Worker: Industrial Attitudes and Behavior.* Cambridge: Cambridge University Press.
Gordon, M.E., J.W. Philpot, R.E Burt, C.A. Thompson, and W.E. Spiller. 1980. "Commitment to the Union: Development of a Measure and an Examination of its Correlates." *Journal of Applied Psychology Monograph* 65: 479-499.
Hirschman, A.O. 1970. *Exit, Voice and Loyality, Responses to Decline in Firm, Organizations and States.* Cambridge, MA: Harvard University Press.
Huberts, L.W. and W.J. van Noort. 1986. "Participation in Radical Social Movements in The Netherlands: Description and a Possible Explanation." Paper presented at the International Workshop on Participation in Social Movements. Amsterdam.
Industriebond-FNV. 1981. Verslag onderzoek ex-leden (Research report exmembers). August-September 1980.
Klaassen, R. 1986. "Participatie van kaderleden in besluitvormingsprocessen van de vakbond" (Participation in Decision Making within Unions). Amsterdam: Vrije Universiteit.
Klandermans, P.G. 1984a. "Mobilization and Participation, Social Psychological Expansions of Resource Mobilization Theory." *American Sociological Review* 49: 583-600.
_____. 1984b. "Een sterke bond bij Polysar?" (A Strong Union at Polysar?). Amsterdam: Vrije Universiteit.

_____. 1984c. "Unionists, Feminists, and Pacifists, Comparisons of Organization, Mobilization and Participation." Paper presented at the ASA Meeting, Washington, D.C.

_____. 1984d. "Membership Meetings and Decision Making in Trade Unions. Paper presented at the Egos Colloquium on Trade Unions in Europe: The Organizational Perspective." Amersfoort, The Netherlands.

_____. 1986. "Psychology and Trade Union Participation: Joining, Acting, Quitting." *Journal of Occupational Psychology* 59:189-204.

Knoke, D. 1981. "Commitment and Detachment in Voluntary Associations." *American Sociological Review* 46: 141-159.

Lieberman, S. 1965. "The Effects of Changes in Roles on the Attitudes of Role Occupants." In *Basic Studies in Social Psychology,* edited by H. Proshansky and B. Seidenberg. New York: Holt, Rinehart and Winston.

McAdam, D. 1985. "Macro Political Process and Individual Activism: Building Micro-macro Bridges." Paper presented at the CES Conference on Participation in Social Movements. Ithaca, New York.

McShane, S.L. 1986. "The Multidimensionality of Union Participation." *Journal of Occupational Psychology* 59: 177-187.

Melucci, A. 1985. "Multipolar Action Systems. Sytemic Environment and Individual Envolvement in Contemporary Movements." Paper presented at the CES Workshop on Social Movements. Ithaca, New York.

Messigner, S.L. 1955. "Organizational Transformation: A Case Study of a Declining Social Movement." *American Sociological Review* 20: 3-10.

Muller, E.N. and K.D. Opp. 1986. "Rational Choice and Rebellious Collective Action." *American Political Science Review* 80: 471-487.

Nicholson, N., G. Ursell, and N. Blyton. 1981. *The Dynamics of White Collar Unionism: A Study of Local Union Participation.* London: Academic Press.

Oberschall, A. 1978. The Decline of the 1960's Social Movements." Pp. 257-289 in *Research in Social Movements, Conflicts and Change,* edited by L. Kriesberg. Greenwich, CT: JAI Press.

_____. 1980. "Loosely Structured Collective Conflict: a Theory and an Application." Pp. 45-68 in *Research in Social Movements, Conflicts and Change,* edited by L. Kriesberg. Greenwich, CT: JAI Press.

Oliver, O., G. Marwell, and R. Texeira. 1985. "Group Heterogenity, Interdependence and the Production of Collective Action: A Theory of the Critical Mass." *American Journal of Sociology* 91: 522-556.

Olson, M. 1965. *The Logic of Collective Action: Public Goods and the Theory of Groups.* Cambridge, MA: Harvard University Press.

Pizzorno, A. 1978. "Political Exchange and Collective Identity in Industrial Conflict." Pp. 277-298 in *The Resurgence of Class Conflict in Western Europe since 1968,* edited by C. Crouch and A. Pizzorno. New York: Holmes & Meier Publishers.

Porter, L.W., R.M. Steers, R.T. Mowday, and P.V. Boulian. 1974. "Organizational Commitment, Job Satisfaction, and Turnover among Psychiatric Technicians." *Journal of Applied Psychology* 59: 603-609.

Regalia, I. 1986. "Evolving Patterns of Participation in the Trade Union Movement: Membership, Strikes and Militancy in Italy." Paper presented at the International Workshop on Participation in Socal Movements, Amsterdam.

Schuyt, C.J.M. 1972. *Recht, orde en burgerlijke ongehoorzaamheid* (Law, Order and Civil Disobedience). Rotterdam: Universiteitspers.

Steers, R.M. 1977. "Antecedents and Outcomes of Organizational Commitment." *Administrative Science Quarterly* 22: 46-56.

Teulings, A.W.M. 1983. "Strijd en zekerheid, een onderzoek naar ledenverlies en ledenbinding van de vakbeweging in crisistijd" (Conflict and Security. A Study of Membership Turnover in Unions in a Period of Economic Recession). Amsterdam: Universiteit van Amsterdam.

Toch, H. 1965. *The Social Psychology of Social Movements.* Indianapolis, IN: Bobbs-Merrill.

Van de Vall, M. 1963. *De vakbeweging in een welvaartsstaat.* Meppel, The Netherlands: Boom.

Van der Veen, G. 1985. "Leden winnen en leden binden: een onderzoek naar mogelijkheden voor een vakbond om leden te winnen en het ledenverloop te verlagen" (Gaining Members and Membership Commitment: A Study of Opportunities to Gain Members and to Reduce Membership Loss). Amsterdam: Vrije Universiteit.

Van Ham, J.C., J. Paauwe, and A.R.T. Williams. 1985. "De vakbeweging in Nederland: van leden naar klanten." (Unions in The Netherlands: From Members to Customers). *Economisch Statistische Berichten:* 468-473.

Weiss, R.F. 1963. "Defection from Social Movements and Subsequent Recruitment to New Movements." *Sociometry* 26: 1-20.

Wilson, J. 1973. *Introduction to Social Movements.* New York: Basic Books.

Wood, J.L. and M. Jackson. 1982. *Social Movements, Development, Participation, and Dynamics.* Belmont, CA: Wadsworth.

REALITIES, IMAGES, AND MANAGEMENT DILEMMAS IN SOCIAL MOVEMENT ORGANIZATIONS:

THE THREE MILE ISLAND EXPERIENCE

Edward Walsh and Sherry Cable

Political social movement organizations (SMOs) are often assumed to be relatively stable and autonomous entities constructed by mobilized constituencies to press their collective demands on the state. Subject to the routine constraints imposed by the particular social movement in which they are embedded, these protest organizations are portrayed as being geared to the pressuring of political elites and to the expansion of their own popular support base. Although we currently lack sufficient information on the actual functioning of a representative sample of SMOs to say how typical such a portrait really is, there is reason to believe that the more common situation

International Social Movement Research, Vol. 2, pages 199-211.
Copyright © 1989 by JAI Press Inc.
All rights of reproduction in any form reserved.
ISBN: 0-89232-964-5

is one in which managers of protest organizations find themselves manipulated, confused, and forced into awkward political situations by a confluence of conflicting interests, values, ideologies, and tactics.

The realities of vibrant social movements are doubtlessly more complex than either their public images or their typical profiles in the scientific literature suggest. Earlier analysts who assumed homogeneity of attitudes on the part of participants—what Smelser (1963) labelled "generalized beliefs"—mistook such simplifications for the more messy realities of collective action. Careful research on functioning SMOs reveal more fragile and changing structures (Lofland and Fink 1982) as well as numerous difficulties involving attitudinal frame alignment processes between protest organizations and potential constituents (Snow et al. 1986).

Dilemmas for SMO decision makers often derive from tensions between the complex internal dynamics of a protest organization and its necessarily more simplified public image. Grass-roots movements commonly include personality conflicts among contending leaders, ideological disputes over both goals and means, disagreements between advocates of relatively radical and more mainstream repertoires of collective action, and the practical constraints of a limited resource pool (Tilly 1978; Zald and McCarthy 1979; Morrison 1986). Without selective incentives for participants, most movement organization managers must settle for sporadic cooperation from the relatively few sympathizers who transcend the free-rider temptation (Olson 1965).

In contrast, the images which social movement leaders typically communicate to potential supporters, the press, and their adversaries are considerably less complicated. Although opponents of protest movements frequently attempt to homogenize participants by exaggerating the extent of dictatorial outside leadership and irrational membership docility, the press also contributes to an overly-simplified image of such movements by relying on interpretations from movement activists. The public images which these spokespersons promote, of course, tend to portray a unified collectivity with reasonable demands.

Social movement analysts need to examine more systematically the dilemmas faced by leaders of movement organizations in balancing the enthusiasm of active participants against the norms of outside sympathizers. The former are the wellsprings of life and support for organized collective action, while the latter cannot be antagonized without serious risk to any sustained challenge. Contemporary perspectives on social movement phenomena emphasize the role of protest organizations as mobilization agents which frame structural discontents and coordinate individual responses (Oberschall 1973; Gamson 1975; McCarthy and Zald 1977; Klandermans 1986), but they tend to ignore the internal tensions and dynamics occurring within and between these organizations themselves.

This chapter addresses such issues by examining some presumably typical management dilemmas faced by leaders in the SMOs that formed after the

Three Mile Island (TMI) accident in 1979. Following the public emergency precipitated by the partial meltdown at Unit 2, a number of community protest groups were formed to monitor the cleanup procedures and to block the restart of the Unit 1 reactor, coincidentally shut down for refueling at the time of the accident. Movement organization leaders encountered problems in obtaining funding, in setting goals, and in tactic selection, which are not uncommon for such protest organization (Freeman 1979; Tilly 1979). We focus specifically on the management dilemmas created by the disparities between activists and other collective actors in their environment.

METHODS AND DATA

This report draws upon field observations, systematic surveys, taped interviews with activists, and files of newsletters from SMOs from 1979 to 1985.

The survey instruments were only constructed after 18 months of initial fieldwork immediately following the accident. Extensive details on the fieldwork (Walsh 1981), the surveys of activists and sympathizers (Walsh and Warland 1983), and the file data (Cable 1985) are available elsewhere.

Field visits continued over the course of the seven-year struggle. Systematic surveys including 149 activists and 288 sympathizers were carried out during the second and third years, and comprehensive files of newspapers and movement newsletters were compiled over the six-year course of the struggle. These various sources are used selectively in the following discussion and analysis.

POPULATION PROFILES

The TMI nuclear reactors, bordered on both sides of the Susquehanna River by small towns and farms, are located approximately 12 miles south of Harrisburg, Pennsylvania. The local population is generally quite conservative on political issues, but protest organizations emerged after the 1979 accident in Middletown and in Newberry Township, on the east and west shores, respectively, within a five-mile radius of the island. Other protest organizations developed in the larger cities of Harrisburg and Lancaster, the latter approximately 22 miles southeast of the reactors. While more detailed analyses of the evolution and development of these various groups are available elsewhere (Walsh 1981; Cable 1985), it is adequate for our purpose to distinguish three relatively distinct populations of TMI opponents within the area. A fourth collective actor, outside funders, also enters the following discussion of management dilemmas.

The first two groups consist of activists from the smaller towns and those from the larger cities. The former, in the communities closer to the reactors,

Table 1.   Comparisons of Ideology Among Activist Cosmopolitans,
Activist Localites, and Sympathizers

		Cosmopolitans	Localites	Sympathizers
	N:	77	72	288
A.	Opposition to nuclear weapons after TMI accident	5.0	3.9	3.5
B.	Support for nonviolent civil disobedience as protest tactic	4.8	4.1	2.8
C.	Liberal vote in the 1980 presidential election (%)	91	58	23

Notes: Item A and B used five possible response categories, with the middle category neutral and the direction
of the scale indicated by the item wording. Thus, a higher mean score signifies more opposition in
the first item and more support for civil disobedience tactics in the second. All differences are significant
at the .01 level or beyond. Readers wishing more details on the cosmopolitan/localite comparisons
may consult the Cable et al. (1986) article, and those interested in additional information on the activist/
sympathizers comparisons may consult Walsh and Warland (1983).

tended to be older and more conservative than those from Harrisburg and
Lancaster. Adopting Merton's venerable conceptual distinction, we labelled
the latter "cosmopolitans" and distinguished them from the "localites" who
predominated in the SMOs from the smaller towns (see Cable et al. 1986).
The cosmopolitans were more likely to have been involved in prior protest
movements, and also more inclined to generalize their opposition to other
nuclear issues. The localites, on the other hand, reported more identification
with their neighborhoods and limited their focus to issues involving the TMI
reactors.[1]

The third relevant population for our purposes is that portion of the local
public generally sympathetic to the activists' protests but themselves having
contributed no time or money to SMOs in any of their respective communities.
This third category was called "free riders" in an earlier paper (Walsh and
Warland 1983), but we label them "sympathizers" here because this was the
audience which activists had to be concerned about in assessing the implications
of the decisions and events discussed below.

Table 1 displays the mean scores of these collectivities on three important
and easily interpreted indicators, providing adequate quantitative evidence of
their ideological differences. We have selected these from a much broader list
of variables to provide a glimpse of the intergroup variation on nuclear issues,
perspectives on nonviolent protest tactics, and electoral preferences in the 1980
presidential elections. While all of the differences between the cosmopolitans,
localites, and sympathizers are statistically significant, the positioning of the
three collectivities is also important. The localites are situated, ideologically,
between the cosmopolitans and the random sample of generally conservative
sympathizers in the four TMI communities.

The fourth group entering the following analysis of management dilemmas in movement organizations is the outside funders insisting on more structural unity and greater cooperation between and among the cosmopolitan and localite activists, as a precondition for their much needed financial assistance.

The interactions between and among these four collective actors form the background for the discussion of management dilemmas occurring at critical junctures in the TMI conflict. The localite activists were more similar to the free riders in their communities than were the cosmopolitans. Consequently, they pressured other activists to conform to community norms regarding protest activities. As a result, the public image of the localite SMOs was consistently more conservative than that of their cosmopolitan peers. The latter, in contrast, were more atypical in their respective communities while their social ties with statewide and national organizations tended to be much stronger.

MANAGEMENT DILEMMAS

Drawing on the TMI conflict, we have selected four examples of management dilemmas and their solutions which involved varying degrees of intramovement conflict and confusion over issues such as institutional funding, goal setting, and tactic selection. In each case, movement leaders were faced with perplexing predicaments involving the challenge of balancing committed activists' dynamism and creative ideas, on the one hand, with the constraints imposed by the movement's need for outside support, on the other.[2]

Funding

The various movement leaders were early confronted with the unattractive alternatives of either competing as independent fundraisers to cope with rapidly mounting expenses or turning to outside funders insisting on organizational consolidation.

Geographical and ideological factors militated against the formation of a single protest organization in the TMI area. The mile-wide Susquehanna River was the major impediment to the fusion of the Middletown and Newberry Township groups, linked only by bridges 10 miles or so upstream and downstream. Ideological differences, personal tensions between and among leaders, and diverse structural constraints were the wedges between the small town groups, which we label "localites," and the "cosmopolitans" from the larger cities of Harrisburg and Lancaster (Cable et al. 1986).

The cosmopolitans were the first to begin accumulating litigation costs deriving from the TMI accident. Harriburg activists hired attorneys to fight the restart of Unit 1 while their Lancaster counterparts incurred debts from legal efforts to prevent the dumping of radioactive Unit 2 water into the Susquehanna

River. Within five months of the accident, leaders from these two organizations began planning their own joint funding appeals at the local, state, and national levels until word of their intentions reached activists from Middletown and Newberry Township. Smoldering interpersonal tensions and ideological differences, between leaders of these small town movement organizations and their counterparts from Harrisburg, were forced to the surface.

Convinced that they were more attuned to the conservative sympathies of most area residents than the more liberal leaders of the Harrisburg citizens' organization (a claim supported by the data in Table 1), the small town activists resisted identification with this urban SMO even though they accepted a limited amount of critical assistance from it on certain early projects. If some of the Harrisburg leaders perceived this reluctance to affiliate as ungrateful and misguided behavior on the part of the localites, the latter were equally disturbed by what they regarded as hegemonic aspirations of the Harrisburg SMO.

The leaders of the Lancaster organization only learned of these tensions after localite leaders expressed concern about being excluded from the cosmopolitans' proposed funding appeal. Lancaster representatives subsequently took the side of the small town activists, refusing to continue cooperating with the Harrisburg organization on this project.

After months of meetings, including one with representatives of national funding organizations where spokespersons of SMOs were constrained to interact in the same hotel room for approximately 12 hours, image requirements eventually came to be viewed as important enough to force the protest group managers to transcend interorganizational differences. Two area-wide coalitions, one focused on fundraising for numerous legal interventions and the other concentrating on community education, were subsequently formed approximately one year after the accident. Funded by outside sponsors, these coalitions were managed by boards of directors comprised of representatives from the various movement organizations.

In seeking the support of institutional funders, protest group leaders were confronted with the dilemma of presenting a credible image of their organizations as cooperative and united forces without denying their differences or surrendering their autonomy. The funding agencies insisted that the organizations coordinate their efforts; they refused to fund several TMI organizations working independently of one another. The solution finally arrived at was to create two new coalitions of existing organizations, thus presenting enough of a unified structure for the funders without forcing any of the community groups into an unwanted merger.

Goal Setting: The Rally Theme

During the late fall of 1979 and through the winter of 1980, other representatives from the TMI citizen protest groups were also meeting.

Frustrated with the internecine strife between and among local SMOs, they circumvented the leadership cadres to plan a cooperative first-year commemorative rally. One of the major decisions confronting the activists involved was the scope of the rally theme. The debates at the first few planning meetings were intense because the significance of the theme went beyond the success or failure of the event itself. The choice of a rally theme was equivalent to a public statement of the goals of the movement organizations.

Although the Nuclear Regulatory Commission (NRC) had ordered hearings on the safety of the Unit 1 reactor prior to any restart, some of the rally organizers viewed their own preparations as somethign of a "dry run" for the massive civil disobedience demonstrations they envisioned after the expected positive vote by the NRC to restart Unit 1. Outside assistance from a variety of groups loosely associated with the antinuclear movement was viewed as critical for the success of any such collective action. Some of the cosmopolitan activists insisted on rally themes broad enough to make such fellow-travellers comfortable by including opposition to all nuclear power plants as well as to nuclear weapons.

Localite activists, on the other hand, insisted that such a wide ideological net would discourage many local residents from attending the rally. Their argument was that most of the people in the area were reluctant even to generalize their TMI opposition to *all* nuclear power plants, much less to nuclear weapons. This was, after all, a very conservative and patriotic audience, as the data in Table 1 reveal. The activists adopting this line of logic insisted that the rally theme focus exclusively on opposition to the TMI plant for the sake of appealing to as broad a base of local residents as possible.

The localite activists were also concerned that, if this rally attracted the 100,000 people some of their cosmopolitan confreres envisioned, the crowds would trample properties in the vicinity of the plant and thus alienate many otherwise sympathetic local residents.

After much discussion and debate, those planning the first year's commemoration decided to limit its scope to an anti-TMI theme and only encourage central Pennsylvanians to attend. Some of the cosmopolitan activists were disappointed with the narrowness of focus, but localites from the small towns closest to the reactors convinced the others that alternatives might very well be counterproductive in the long run. After numerous planning sessions, it was agreed that the wisest course of action would be to have the rally in Harrisburg rather than closer to TMI. Approximately 15,000 people attended this March 1980 rally, regarded by the organizers as an outstanding success. Sympathetic antinuclear groups from around the nation held their own rallies at their neighborhood nuclear reactors on the anniversary of the TMI accident in a show of symbolic support.

The management dilemma here involved the relationships between the activists and their local public sympathizers. The activists knew that in choosing a rally theme they were proclaiming their goals. Localites, more community-oriented than their cosmopolitan counterparts, were concerned with gaining and keeping the goodwill of their generally sympathetic neighbors, even if it was only a passive support. The cosmopolitans, with their weaker orientation to the local community, wanted to set broader goals, placing TMI in a more global context of nuclear weapons, war, and energy conservation. The solution to this dilemma was a compromise whereby the rally theme was restricted to promote local residents' support, but fellow travellers, from across the nation, were encouraged to hold simultaneous rallies of their own on the anniversary of the accident.

Tactic Selection: The Referendum

One of the most important public protests in the protracted struggle emerged in spite of initial opposition by most protest group leaders. Two activists from the Harrisburg organization learned, in early 1982, that a local commissioner was considering the idea of getting an antirestart referendum on the ballot in the upcoming May elections. They volunteered their help and subsequently established a new organization which they named the "Bipartisan Committee to Vote No on the Restart of TMI-1." This newly-formed group was not initially welcomed by any of the existing anti-TMI organizations, primarily because most activists were concerned that such a venture might fail. The existing SMOs' aloofness, however, turned out to be an advantage to the new organization.

After a week or so of random telephone canvassing, the Bipartisan Committee learned that people affiliated with the Harrisburg organization were commonly perceived by outside sympathizers as "the skull and crossbones people" who were too radical in rhetoric and tactics. Even more surprisingly, the Committee discovered that many local residents, who had not previously become actively involved because of this "radical" image, were quite willing to help get out the antirestart vote in their own neighborhoods. Well-dressed volunteers going door-to-door were shocked at the warm receptions they received from people who wanted to talk about their personal experiences during the TMI emergency period a few years earlier. By early May, the Bipartisan Committee had 30 people using phones and door-to-door canvassing in their efforts to mobilize the vote against a Unit 1 restart.

Initially conceived by a Dauphin County commissioner, the referendum item eventually was submitted to the voters in Dauphin, Cumberland, and Lebanon counties, all in the TMI vicinity. The vote, on May 18, 1982, was against a Unit 1 restart in 129 of 130 Dauphin County precincts, 86 of 88 in Cumberland County, and 50 of 55 in Lebanon County. Together, the three counties voted approximately 2-1 against restart, an overwhelming symbolic victory for the anti-TMI forces.[3] The anniversary of this referendum vote became second in importance only to the anniversary of the accident itself among restart opponents in the area.

Movement leaders were confronted with a difficult choice when informed of the establishment of the Bipartisan Committee to Vote 'No' on restart. Despite their political sympathies in favor of such a venture, many were fearful of its prospects for success. If the activists forced the issue to a public vote and then suffered a humiliating defeat in the May election, this tactic would have backfired. On the other hand, the movement leaders could not very easily argue against the project, especially when they were claiming the support of the great majority of people in the area. The referendum initiators solved the dilemma for the existing movement organizations by expressing a preference not to become closely identified with any existing protest organization lest they jeopardize their widespread support base among the sympathetic public. Activists from the various organizations were encouraged to work with the Bipartisan Committee on the latter's own terms.

By the time the public voted in May 1982, the referendum was the major movement project in the TMI area even though none of the established SMOs had allowed themselves to become overtly identified with it.

Tactic Selection: Civil Disobedience Actions

Just as annual commemorative rallies were staged on the anniversary of the accident, so were there civil disobedience actions at the TMI gates on anniversaries of the referendum vote. On the first anniversary, in May 1983, 12 activists blocked the gates to the island and allowed themselves to be arrested as a reminder of the community sentiment against a Unit 1 restart. This form of relatively extreme protest action was, of course, risky in a number of respects. It was not officially endorsed by any of the existing SMOs or coalitions, even though some of their own members were involved. Such nonviolent civil disobedience was precisely the type of "radical" activity that many of the sympathizers responsible for the referendum victory opposed. Managers of the existing movement organizations were understandably reluctant to support publicly these actions by "the TMI Twelve."

By the second anniversary of the referendum vote, however, 51 people allowed themselves to be arrested at the TMI gates. Community reluctance to condemn civil disobedience by this time seemed to be weakening in light of the evidence of increasing incompetence on the part of the utility coupled with a clear enough pro-industry bias by NRC officials to push Governor Dick Thornburgh to a position of strong opposition to any immediate restart (see Walsh 1986). An August 1984 trial of "the TMI Twelve" was used by activists to persuade the jury of the dangers deriving from a Unit 1 restart as well as the futility of relying on the NRC for a fair-handed evaluation of the case. After nominal small fines ordered by a very sympathetic judge, the defendants ultimate victory came when all members of the jury signed a posttrial petition against any Unit 1 restart.

The SMOs were the organizational carriers and official reminders for area residents of both the referendum victories and civil disobedience action successes—even if these same protest organization opposed such projects when they were initiated. When confronted with problematic proposals such as the referendum or direct action by their members, the protest organizations hesitated or refused to endorse them, thus avoiding the alienation of many of their own members as well as the wider sympathetic public. Some activists involved themselves regardless of the SMOs' official position. When it became apparent that the proposed courses of action were favorably regarded by outsiders, the organizations then included them in their official memory banks, so to speak. Movement managers thus find themselves occasionally in positions similar to government bureaucrats who privately encourage individual agents in their illegal activities on behalf of the state's goals while publicly distancing themselves from such ventures as assassinations, bribes, and disinformation campaigns. If the activity succeeds, the state will benefit, but the buffers of nonendorsement are set up as shields against embarrassing official involvements in potential fiascos.

DISCUSSION

This case study of post accident SMOs in the TMI area focused on organizational problems involving the interrelated issues of funding, goals, and tactics. While seldom analyzed in the social movement literature, there are reasons to think that managerial dilemmas deriving from discrepancies between realities and preferred public images in these and kindred areas are quite common.

Precariously perched between a dedicated cadre of activists and less committed outside sympathizers, many SMO managers find themselves vulnerable from two sides. In need of both their loyalists and more casual supporters, they cannot afford to alienate either. Their solution is sometimes to foster the creation of separate organizations, without public links to existing movement organizations. At other times, they can only stand by as such spinoffs emerge. At TMI, the activists who became involved in civil disobedience actions were not publicly identified with any of the existing movement organizations in the area lest their tactics alienate the tens of thousands of citizens opposed to the restart of Unit 1.

Sometimes, however, the existing SMOs themselves are perceived by the sympathetic public as being too radical, and then the challenge is to activate weaker supporters on their own terms (see Ennis and Schreuer, 1987). In the TMI case, this was accomplished by creating a new organization, the Bipartisan Committee, which intentionally distanced itself from the established protest groups.

Such phenomena suggest that, contrary to the common assumption, the existence of multiple SMOs espousing quite different tactics should not automatically be interpreted as an indicator of counterproductive factionalism for a social movement. Only more systematic empirical research can tell us how common it is for such distinct organizations to complement, rather than counteract, one another in recruitment efforts.

Social movement managers had little discretion in the creation of the relatively radical "TMI Twelve" and more conservative "Bipartisan Committee" organizations. Some of their own activists initiated each with little regard for the sentiments of the leaders. The situation was different in the case of the outside funding groups insisting on more interorganizational coordination. Again, of course, the decisionmakers were in a bind, but they had some leverage over their options. This time they decided to create two umbrella coalitions.

The fourth dilemma analyzed in this paper involved a decision about the theme of the first anniversary rally. As in the cases of the Bipartisan Committee and of "the TMI Twelve," the tens of thousands of local sympathizers were again the critical factor. Rather than risk alienating them, the movement decisionmakers limited the rally theme to the TMI issue, even though it necessitated turning their backs on numerous speakers and other forms of support for broader antinuclear themes.

Tensions and disagreements between and among subgroups of different political persuasions are common in social movements. Moderates in the Southern civil rights movement, for example, were not very successful in controlling radical movement organizations intent on introducing the issues of communist participation, the Vietnam War, and black power (Barkan 1986) or in controlling emergent protest groups (Killian 1984).

Although managerial dilemmas have yet to be systematically explored, the literature does reveal some evidence of comparable problems in other social movements. We have already alluded to a few in the civil rights movement. Informal leaders in the women's movement also found it difficult to respond to different age groups, and frequently had to adjust their ideology to emergent strategies in their efforts to enlist new members (Freeman 1979). Likewise, Cesar Chavez's life-threatening fast in the midst of the farmworkers' struggle (Walsh 1978) provides an example of the dramatic efforts sometimes required of managers of SMOs in persuading their members not to turn to more radical tactics. Outside support and funding were certainly critical considerations for Chavez as he put his health on the line in challenging those members of his own organization who were advocating violence.

Managers of mainstream organizations also confront occasional dilemmas somewhat similar to those sketched above. Because mainstream managers are usually equipped with more political and economic power than their movement organization counterparts, however, the former's dilemmas are likely to be less frequent and less critical in their organizational implications. The SMO manager is commonly situated in the midst of conflicting forces, an opportunistic press, and potential supporters. These latter may be organizational, as with funding groups, or individuals whose sentiments are labelled as "public opinion." In the examples we have considered, the solution to the dilemma has involved the creation of new movement organizations in three out of the four cases. Perhaps such structural solutions are much more common than the existing literature suggests. The frequency of the dilemmas themselves, however, probably are a characteristic of SMOs setting them off from more mainstream organizations, but these are empirical questions in need of further research.

ACKNOWLEDGMENT

Grants from the National Science Foundation to the first author were essential for this research and are hereby gratefully acknowledged.

NOTES

1. Careful analysis of the various SMOs newsletters (see Cable 1985) also supports the notion of significant ideological differences between the small town and urban SMOs. the former, for example, were less likely to include items generally opposing all nuclear power plants as well as those opposing nuclear weapons.

2. More complete analyses of these and related episodes, situated in their structural and historical contexts, may be found in *Democracy in the Shadows* (Walsh 1988).

3. Pennsylvania only allows nonbinding referenda, and thus such results merely give decisionmakers a sense of public sentiment without carrying any force of law.

REFERENCES

Barkan, S.E. 1986. "Interorganizational Conflict in the Southern Civil Rights Movement." *Sociological Inquiry* 56:190-209.

Cable, S. 1985. "Differential Paths to Activism: A Study of Social Organizations in Three Mile Island Communities." Unpublished doctoral dissertation, Pennsylvania State University.

Cable, S., Walsh, E. and R. Warland. 1986. "Differential Paths to Political Activism: Comparisons of Four Mobilization Processes after the Three Mile Island Accident. Paper delivered at American Sociological Association meetings, New York.

Ennis, J.G. and R. Schreuer. 1987. "Mobilizing Weak Support for Social Movements: The Role of Grievance, Efficacy and Cost." *Social Forces* 66:390-409.

Freeman, J. 1979. "Resource Mobilization and Strategy: A Model for Analyzing Social Movement Organization Actions." Pp. 167-189 in *The Dynamics of Social Movements*, edited by M.N. Zald and J.D. McCarthy. Cambridge, MA: Winthrop.

Gamson, W. 1975. *The Strategy of Social Protest*. Homewood, IL: Dorsey.

Killian, L.M. 1984. "Organization, Rationality, and Spontaneity in the Civil Rights Movement." *American Sociological Review* 49:770-783.

Lofland, J. and M. Fink. 1982. *Symbolic Sit-Ins: Protest Occupations at the California Capitol.* Washington, D.C.: University Press of America.

McCarthy, J.D. and M.N. Zald. 1977. "Resource Mobilization and Social Movements: A Partial Theory." *American Journal of Sociology* 82:1212-1241.

Morrison, D.E. 1986. "How and Why Environmental Consciousness has Trickled Down." Pp. 187-220 in *Distributional Conflicts in Environmental Resource Policy,* edited by A. Schnaiberg, N. Watts, and K. Zimmerman. Berlin: WZB Publications.

Oberschall, A. 1973. *Social Conflicts and Social Movements.* Englewood Cliffs, NJ: Prentice-Hall.

Olson, M. 1965. *The Logic of Collective Action: Public Goods and the Theory of Groups.* New York: Schocken.

Smelser, N. 1963. *Theory of Collective Behavior.* New York: Free Press.

Snow, D., E.B. Rochford, S.K. Worden, and R. Benford. 1986. "Frame Alignment and Mobilization." *American Sociological Review* 51:464-481.

Tilly, C. 1978. *From Mobilization to Revolution.* Reading, MA: Addison Wesley.

———. 1979. "Repertoires of Contention in America and Britain, 1750-1830." Pp. 126-155 in *The Dynamics of Social Movements,* edited by M.N. Zald and J.D. McCarthy. Cambridge, MA: Winthrop.

Walsh, E. 1978. "Mobilization Theory vis-a-vis a Mobilization Process." Pp. 155-177 in *Research in Social Movements, Conflict, and Change,* vol. 1, edited by L. Kriesberg. Greenwich, CT: JAI Press.

———. 1981. "Resource Mobilization and Citizen Protest in Communities around Three Mile Island." *Social Problems* 29:1-21.

———. 1986. "The Role of Target Vulnerabilities in High-Technology Protest Movements." *Sociological Forum* 1:199-218.

———. 1988. *Democracy in the Shadows: Citizen Mobilization in the Wake of the Accident at Three Mile Island.* Westport, CT: Greenwood Press.

Walsh, E. and R. Warland. 1983. "Social Movement Involvement in the Wake of a Nuclear Accident." *American Sociological Review* 48:764-780.

Zald, M.N. and J.D. McCarthy. 1979. *The Dynamics of Social Movements.* Cambridge, MA: Winthrop.

PART III

LEADERSHIP AND
DECISION MAKING

INTRODUCTION

Bert Klandermans

Leadership and decision making are aspects of social movement organizations (SMOs) which are more often debated than studied empirically. It is clear from the literature that leaders contribute significantly to the development of SMOs, but systematic studies of the way in which movement leaders function are scarce. Similarly, there is an extensive literature on democracy in movement organizations, but studies of actual decision making are rare. One reason for this lack of empirical research is the character of the organizations themselves. How can one study leadership and decision making in organizations that have no clear boundaries, that have distributed, rotating, or multiple leadership or that claim they have no leadership at all? Nevertheless, leadership and decision making are key issues in the internal life of every SMO. Morris' (1984) study of the southern civil rights movement demonstrated, as few other studies have done, the importance of competent leaders and careful decision making for a movement's fate.

Social movement literature tends to focus on the character of the movement leader: A typology is developed and individual leaders are then classified according to type. The problem with this approach is that it is not suited to

International Social Movement Research, Vol. 2, pages 215-224.
Copyright © 1989 by JAI Press Inc.
All rights of reproduction in any form reserved.
ISBN: 0-89232-964-5

those organizations in which there is no single leader, or in which there is some form of distributed or rotating leadership (Brown and Hosking 1986). For the fact that no one person can be identified as *the* leader does not mean that no leadership functions are carried on. To accommodate the several varieties of leadership, Part III departs from the usual approach and analyzes leadership and decision making in the context of the accumulation and allocation of resources. Leaders are the managers of the SMO's incentive systems that guarantee the influx of resources, and leaders have the authority to make binding decisions on the allocation of resources. SMOs differ in the extent to which the membership is involved in decision making. In many movement organizations, leadership and authority are uncertain. SMOs are voluntary associations, and the members of such organizations will prefer to express their disagreement with the leadership by leaving the organization (exit) instead of criticizing the leadership (voice). Because of the organization's voluntary nature, movement leaders cannot use coercion to enforce commitment to the organization. As a consequence, leaders and members have a precarious relationship in which leaders cannot afford to neglect the memberships' interests for long without jeopardizing the survival of the organization.

Leadership functions and decision making procedures are the general subjects of this introduction. More specifically, the first section focuses on leadership-membership relations, leadership and organizational characteristics, ideology and leadership, and changes in leadership; the second section concentrates on the different types of leadership that can be distinguished within SMOs, and, referring to the numerous typologies presented in the literature, draws some basic distinctions among them; and the conclusion explores an almost completely neglected aspect of SMO leadership, the recruitment of movement officials.

LEADERSHIP FUNCTIONS AND DECISION-MAKING PROCEDURES

As managers of movement organizations, movement leaders must deal with both actors external to the organization, such as supporters and authorities, and with those inside the organization, such as the membership. Part II and Part IV examine the movement organization's interaction with the external environment, while Part III focuses on the internal environment of a movement organization, that is leadership-membership relations. Movement organizations traditionally have problematic hierarchical relations because the authority of movement leaders is so precarious. Thus complex structural arrangements can easily develop within organizations. In examining the relationship between leaders and members of a SMO, I first describe the nature of this relationship, then review the ideological underpinnings and the structural counterparts of different forms of leadership. Finally, I discuss how leadership-membership relations change.

Leaders and Members

The relationship between leaders and members of SMOs is complicated and often tense. Like most voluntary associations, SMOs must balance a hierarchical distribution of power with the ideals of democratic participation in organizational affiars. There is an ingrained tendency in SMOs to question leadership positions. Normative authority beliefs stress—at least formally—decentralization and membership participation in decision making, and place strong restrictions on the autonomy of movement leaders (Knoke and Prensky 1984). This is not to say that the legitimacy of the leadership is often questioned. Perrow (1970) argued that democracy in voluntary organizations is not an issue so long as the organization produces results relevant to the membership. Many a member prefers to support a movement organization financially instead of participating actively, as Oliver and Furman demonstrate in their contribution to this volume. Leaders are high-cost investors in a SMO in terms of time, effort, energy, and sometimes money. Members invest much less, and are less concerned with, the day-to-day operations of the leadership (Browne 1983; Oliver 1984). Members expect the leaders to oversee the organization, and as long as they believe that the organization is doing so well enough, they are satisfied. That is, as long as the movement leadership is able to operate effectively in the eyes of the membership, there is no need for internal democracy. On the other hand, Knoke and Wood (1981, p. 94) demonstrated that membership participation in decision making strengthens membership commitment. These authors suggest, however, that the member's belief in leadership legitimacy is a functional alternative to their participation in decision making. Centralized decision making can coexist with a high degree of commitment if members "have been socialized or persuaded to believe that the structure is the proper one for the organization." Referring to Weber's well-known distinctions, the authors identify three types of legitimacy: rational, traditional, and charismatic. Unlike most social movement literature, Knoke and Wood's study does not point to charismatic authority as most typical of SMOs. Instead, they suggest that, in the case of SMOs, a fourth type of legitimacy is relevant: value-rational authority, based on a conscious belief in the values of the movement organization for its own sake. As mentioned in Part I, Rothschild-Whitt (1979) used this same concept in developing a model of collectivist organization.

Precarious as they may be in many SMOs, membership-leadership relations will not be too tense so long as the needs of the membership and the needs of the leadership coincide. When they no longer do, conflicts can develop between leaders and members, which can eventually result in the destruction of the organization, since, in a conflict with the leadership, the last weapon of the members is mass exodus (Schwartz et al. 1981). Conflicts between members and leaders usually erupt after periods of intensive activity, when the movement organization is evaluating its operations. Destruction of the organization is not an inevitable outcome of such conflicts, however. Resolutions depend to a great extent on what Knoke (1985) calls cleavage and influence patterns. "Cleavage patterns" refer to the degree of consensus within a SMO, "influence patterns" to the way in which the positions of influence within an organization are distributed among representatives of its different factions. When opposing factions within a SMO clash, rotating leadership can prevent the organization from breaking apart (for an example involving a union organization, see Lipset et al. 1956), or leaders can be voted out of office (Hemingway 1978). There are also more subtle mechanisms for influencing. Leaders of SMOs are dependent on their members. Every movement leader knows that there will come a time when the membership has to be mobilized in order to put pressure on authorities. A membership that questions the legitimacy of the leadership can simply resist mobilization, thus undermining the leadership's ability to deal with its external actors. Even in an oligarchic structure, a movement leader cannot alienate the membership without risking the loss of his ability to acquire resources. The greater an SMO's dependence on resources provided by the membership, the greater its leaders' dependence on membership approval.

Tension between leaders and members is most likely to develop if the two have different structural and/or ideological backgrounds. Leaders of SMOs quite often come from a different social rank than does the membership, and even if they do not, they eventually attain a different rank because of their position in the movement. As a consequence, members and leaders develop diverging orientations and interests. This is not to say that leaders are necessarily more conservative than members. Naturally, they are more concerned with organizational maintenance, but this concern should not be confused with conservatism. Indeed, movement leaders are often more radical than the rank-and-file, a fact which led Zald and Ash (1966) to hypothesize that radical leadership in an organization with oligarchic tendencies makes the organization more, not less, radical.

Ideology, Leadership, and Organizational Structure

Discussions about leadership in SMOs usually have an ideological undertone. Many SMOs adhere to democratic ideals, and centralized decision making does not fit very well with these ideals. Whatever an SMO's ideological antecedents, the way its leadership is arranged inevitably has an impact on organizational structure.

In many SMOs, democratic, egalitarian values have generated such arrangements as rotating, distributed, and multiple leadership. Many SMOs can be characterized as collectivist organizations (Rothschild-Whitt 1979) in which authority rests in the collectivity as a whole, not in individuals according to the positions they occupy. The structure is that of a direct democracy: All members participate in the collective formulation of problems and negotiation of decisions. In her contribution to Part III, Brown describes forms of distributed leadership in the British women's movement. The women's movement, more emphatically than other movements, has rejected hierarchical relations and personalized leadership. Brown's paper illuminates the ideological justifications for such a position. Rotating, distributed, and multiple leadership are arrangements deliberately designed to prevent SMOs from becoming bureaucratic organizations. Morris (1984), in emphasizing the role of what he described as local movement centers in the southern civil rights movement, provides an example of yet another way of solving the leadership problem without founding formal organizations. Coalitions of indigenous leaders with the power to make decisions on short notice, together with regular mass meetings in the context of existing local networks, turned out to be very effective vehicles for collective decision making. To some extent, the local movement centers Morris described are akin to the organization that developed among the workers of the steel company on strike, described in Hartley's paper in this volume.

Leadership arrangements have their structural counterparts, which can be elucidate by the parallel distinction between closed-access and open-access leadership styles (Eichler 1977; Fine and Stoecker 1985). The former can be found in leader-dominated SMOs; the latter in more egalitarian movement organizations. With closed-access leadership, legitimacy is based on loyalty to the person of the leader. With open-access leadership, legitimacy is based on agreement with a principle or an ideology. (Note the similarity of this distinction to J. Wilson's [1973] distinction between charismatic and ideological leadership.) The two different leadership styles involve completely different organizational structures. In the case of closed-access leadership, decision making is strongly centralized. There are few checks and balances in the form of meetings, committees, or conventions. Delegation of authority, the appointment of secondary leadership, is based on loyalty to the leader. Changes in the movement's policy are announced by the leader, who tries to maintain an element of uncertainty. In the case of open-access, leaders are appointed not because of their personal qualities but because of their merits as interpreters of the movement's ideology. Decision making is decentralized. Delegation of authority is based on ideological reliability. Changes in the organizational policy are extensively discussed throughout the organization. Decisions are made by consensus.

Changes in Leadership

Changes in an SMO's position in society supposedly lead to changes in leadership. For instance, Rothman (1974) argued that two basic types of leadership compete with each other in the course of a movement's development. In periods of protest, militant leadership styles become prominent, whereas, in periods of negotiation, accommodative leadership styles prevail. Blumer (1969) related different leadership roles to the four different phases that, in his view, social movements go through. In the initial stage of social unrest, movement leaders act like agitators. During the popular excitement stage, the leadership role evolves into the role of prophet. During the formalization stage, leaders act like statesmen, and in the final stage, institutionalization, they become administrators.

Although it is clear that leadership roles change in response to changing circumstances, evolutionary models of change are questionable, for roles that are supposed to develop sequentially in fact exist simultaneously in the same SMO, and there is no reason why it should be otherwise. Some movement leaders are agitators, others are prophets, and still others are statesmen or administrators. Leadership changes usually signify the initiation of a new movement policy, not seldom after the acknowledged failure of the old policy (Schwartz 1976; Schwartz et al. 1981). Knoke and Prensky (1984, p. 8) described an organization's leaders as "participants in a dominant coalition that effectively controls the disposition of collective resources." In her contribution to Part III, Mushaben demonstrates how the position of the dominant coalition in the German peace movement is continually challenged by outsiders. Her observations illustrate that different factions within a movement organization compete for leadership positions, and that, depending on events, some faction comes to predominate. And, if a different current takes over, the movement policy consequently changes.

LEADERSHIP TYPES

Many different typologies of movement leadership have been proposed in the literature. Turner and Killian (1987) distinguished symbolic leaders, who symbolize the ideology, the struggle of the movement, from decision-making leaders, who help to direct the movement by their preferences and choices. Gusfield (1966) differentiated articulation and mobilization. Leaders concentrating on articulation focus on the relationship with the external environment; leaders engaged in mobilization try to stimulate and inspire constituencies. J. Wilson (1973) opposed pragmatic leaders to charismatic and ideological leaders. Roche and Sachs (1969) labelled leaders as either "enthusiasts" or "bureaucrats," and Jenkins (1985) stressed the distinction between organizers and formal leaders of an SMO.

All these distinctions acknowledge the two basic aspects of movement organization management: the accumulation and allocation of resources. Apparently, the execution of each of these two management tasks requires different skills, skills that are not often found in one and the same person. Zurcher and Curtis (1973, p. 183), in their study of the antipornography movement, discovered one of those rare movement leaders who combined "enthusiastic and contagious commitment and a knowledge of, experience with, and practical ability in the use of organizing and organizational techniques." They proposed the term "bureaucharisma" as a label for this kind of leader. More often, however, SMOs must face the problem of reconciling the two types of leadership. If the two types are differentially prominent in developmental stages of the movement, or if neither is prominent enough to undermine the other, the problem, in a sense, solves itself. In other cases, an alternating leadership can be a practical solution.

RECRUITMENT OF MOVEMENT LEADERS

As extensive as is the literature on the recruitment of movement participants, so scanty is the research on the recruitment of movement leaders. First, it is clear that recruitment patterns vary according to type of organization and leadership. As indicated above, the way in which an organization recruits its leaders depends on whether it has a closed- or open-access leadership. In organizations with closed-access leadership, it is the leader who recruits secondary leaders from the rank-and-file, basing his choices on the strength of an individual's commitment to him. In SMO's with open-access leadership, it is the collectivity that appoints leaders, and recruitment of leaders is based not on loyalty to the leader but on ideological expertise and reliability (Eichler 1977; J. Wilson 1973). Morris (1984) observed that in movements that are "organizations of organizations," newcomers, among indigenous leaders, have a higher probability of becoming a leader of the movement as a whole. Since they are not yet committed to one of the competing factions within the community, they are better able to bridge existing cleavages.

J.Q. Wilson (1973) forcefully argued that every explanation of entrepreneurial activity in political organizations must begin by acknowledging that the roots of such activity lie in motives and attitudes different from those of rank-and-file members. There is evidence to support Wilson's reasoning. Reviewing studies on union activists—both lay officials, shop stewards, and paid officials—Klandermans (1986) concluded that union leaders, paid and unpaid, have a stronger class-consciousness, more radical political economic ideologies, and a more positive attitude toward radical, political union issues than do ordinary members. Oliver (1983), in her comparison of paid and volunteer activists in the neighborhood movement, arrived at similar conclusions. Paid activists in the neighborhood movement are more likely to have leftist political orientations, as a result of their greater involvement in the social movements of the 1960s. Paid activists are the more committed, experienced, and ideologically-involved participants in the movement. Of special interest in Oliver's data is the evidence that recruitment into leadership positions in social movement organizations is facilitated by previous involvement in social movements. In an intriguing piece on leaders in all-volunteer local organizations, Oliver (1984) demonstrated that, in the case of activities with a decelerating production function (i.e., diminishing marginal returns from contributions), pessimism about the willingness to contribute motivates people to adopt leadership roles. The fact that "nobody else will do it," apparently spurs volunteer leaders to take the lead in organizing.

Some evidence on recruitment for leadership positions is provided by the study of the recruitment of shop stewards in British labor unions. Nicholson (1976) showed that there are several very different ways in which employees become shop stewards. He distinguished between external and internal forces that act on individuals. The internal forces he divided into task-oriented, ideological-oriented, and ambition-oriented forces; the external forces into a crisis (in which the least apathetic employee takes the task upon himself or herself), accidental occupancy (when a person's colleagues elevate him to a leadership position because of his popularity or prestige), and, finally, nomination (when a person is nominated by current stewards or officials). The two latter situations occurred most frequently. Although numerous biographies of movement leaders have been written, systematic studies of the careers of movement leaders are scarce. A rare exception is Jonkergouw's (1982) study of the careers of all-paid officials of the three Dutch union federations from 1906 to 1978. Jonkergouw showed how the leadership of the union federations changed with increased recognition of the Dutch union movement. Professional and technical expertise became more important than ideological inspiration. Higher education, a white-collar career, a career in the union organization, and the *lack* of experience as a lay official became increasingly characteristic of the leaders of the union federations. To apply our earlier distinction between mobilization and allocation of resources: It appears that, as the movement evolved over time, the experts in resource allocation became more and more prominent in the movement leadership.

THE CONTRIBUTIONS TO PART III

The contributions to Part III diverge from the traditional taxonomic approach to movement leadership, emphasizing instead the fluid nature of authority in SMOs.

Distributed leadership in the British women's movement is the subject of Brown's paper, in which she demonstrates the importance of ideology in the structuring of leadership in SMOs.

Hartley's examination of leadership and decision making in a strike organization illustrates the development of temporary organization in collective action. Mushaben's analysis of the complex decision making processes within the German peace movement clearly shows the struggle for leadership among the movement's divergent factions.

REFERENCES

Blumer, H. 1969. "Social Movements." In *Studies in Social Movements. A Social Psychological Perspective,* edited by B. McLaughlin. New York: Free Press.

Brown, M.H. and D.M. Hosking. 1986. "Distributed Leadership and Skilled Performance as Successful Organization in Social Movements." *Human Relations* 39:65-79.

Browne, W.P. 1983. "Mobilizing and Activating Group Demands: The American Agriculture Movement." *Social Science Quarterly* 64:19-34.

Eichler, M. 1977. "Leadership in Social Movements." *Sociological Inquiry* 47:99-107.

Fine, G.A. and R. Stoecker. 1985. "Can the Circle be Unbroken? Small Groups and Social Movements." Pp. 1-28 in *Advances in Group Processes,* vol. 2, edited by E. Lawler. Greenwich, CT: JAI Press.

Gusfield, J.R. 1966. "Functional Areas of Leadership in Social Movements." *Sociological Quarterly* 7:137-156.

Hemingway, J. 1978. *Conflict and Democracy. Studies in Trade Union Government.* Oxford: Clarendon.

Jenkins, J.C. 1985. *The Politics of Insurgency.* New York: Columbia University Press.

Jonkergouw, Th. 1982. "Vakbondsleiders in Nederland: Van indringer tot bondgenoot en steunpilaar" (Union Leaders in The Netherlands: From Intruder, to Ally and Mainstay). Unpublished dissertation, University of Tilburg.

Klandermans, B. 1986. "Psychology and Trade Union Participation: Joining, Acting, Quitting." *Journal of Occupational Psychology* 59:189-204.

Knoke, D. 1985. "The Political Economies of Associations." Pp. 211-242 in *Research in Political Sociology,* vol 1, edited by R.D. Braungart. Greenwich, CT: JAI Press.

Knoke, D. and D. Prensky. 1984. "What Relevance Do Organization Theories Have for Voluntary Associations?" *Social Science Quarterly* 65:3-20.

Knoke, D. and J.R. Wood. 1981. *Organization for Action, Commitment in Voluntary Associations.* New Brunswick, NJ: Rutgers University Press.

Lipset, S.M., and M.A. Trow, and J.S. Coleman. 1956. *Union Democracy: The Internal Politics of the International Typographical Union.* Glencoe, IL: Free Press.

Morris, A. 1984. *The Origins of the Civil Rights Movement: Black Communities Organizing for Change.* New York: Free Press.

Nicholson, N. 1976. "The Role of the Shop Steward." *Industrial Relations Journal* 7:15-26.

Oliver, P. 1983. "The Mobilization of Paid and Volunteer Activists in the Neighborhood Movement." Pp. 133-170 in *Research in Social Movements, Conflict and Change,* edited by L. Kriesberg. Greenwich, CT: JAI Press.

———. 1984. "If You Don't Do It, Nobody Else Will; Active and Token Contributors to Local Collective Action." *American Sociological Review* 49:601-610.

224   BERT KLANDERMANS

Perrow, C. 1970. "Members as Resources in Voluntary Organizations." Pp. 93-116 in *Organizations and Clients,* edited by W.R. Rosengren and M. Lefton. Columbus, OH: Merrill.

Roche, J.P. and S. Sachs. 1969. "The Bureaucrat and the Enthusiast: An Exploration of the Leadership of Social Movements. Pp. 207-222 in *Studies in Social Movements. A Social Psychological Perspective,* edited by B. McLaughlin. New York: Free Press.

Rothman, J. 1974. *Planning and Organizing for Social Change.* New York: Columbia University Press.

Rothschild-Whitt, J. 1979. "The Collectivist Organization: An Alternative to Rational-Bureaucratic Models." *American Sociological Review* 44:509-527.

Schwartz, M. 1976. *Radical Protest and Social Structure.* New York: Academic Press.

Schwartz, M., N. Rosenthal, and L. Schwartz. 1981. "Leader-Member Conflict in Protest Organizations: The Case of the Southern Farmers Alliance." *Social Problems* 29:22-36.

Turner, R.H. and L.M. Killian. 1987. *Collective Behavior.* 3rd ed. Englewood Cliffs, NJ: Prentice-Hall.

Wilson, J. 1973. *Introduction to Social Movements.* New York: Basic Books.

Wilson, J.Q. 1973. *Political Organizations.* New York: Basic Books.

Zald, M.N. and R. Ash. 1966. "Social Movement Organizations: Growth, Decay and Change. *Journal of Social Forces* 44:327-341.

Zurcher, L.A. and R.L. Curtis. 1973. "A Comparative Analysis of Propositions Describing Social Movement Organizations. *Sociological Quarterly* 14:175-188.

ORGANIZING ACTIVITY IN THE WOMEN'S MOVEMENT:

AN EXAMPLE OF DISTRIBUTED LEADERSHIP

M. Helen Brown

INTRODUCTION

In December 1982, 30,000 women surrounded the air base at Greenham Common. Three months later, a journalist writing in The Guardian under the headline "Peace movement without leaders" commented:

> Faced with a demonstration, the first thing a policeman or a journalist is trained to look for is a leader. Any organization begins with a committee, and that provides leaders and, therefore, someone to interview, and, if the situation requires it, someone to arrest. When the peace movement grew, mushroom-like, from the group of dedicated women camped outside the Greenham Common air base, the press began to look for leaders and to create personalities. But the peace camp movement, as distinct from the Campaign for Nuclear Disarmament, appears to have no organization and no leaders. (. . . .) Every woman at Greenham Common starts an interview by making clear she speaks only for herself, and she is not a leader. (. . .) The potential strength of this system cannot be underestimated (Brown 1983, p. 5).

International Social Movement Research, Vol. 2, pages 225-240.
Copyright © 1989 by JAI Press Inc.
All rights of reproduction in any form reserved.
ISBN: 0-89232-964-5

This observer has accurately identified the characteristic form of social organization within the women's movement; that is, one in which leadership in the traditional "focused" sense (Gibb 1969) is absent. Faced with the evidence that social organization can and does occur in these circumstances, there is a need for social movement analysts to examine the processes involved. However, with a few notable exceptions (e.g., Gerlach and Hine 1970), this has not been done. Some writers (e.g., Katz 1981) are content to characterize this form of organizations as "spontaneous," thus removing any sense of the problematic. Others (e.g., Freeman 1984) strongly suggest that a lack of formalized leadership leads inevitably to a situation where there can be unrestricted exercise of power. It will be shown that this argument does not accord with empirical evidence. A third variant is summarized by McAdam (1982, p. 47): "All manner of movement analysts have asserted the importance of leaders or organizers in the generation of movement insurgency." This view, he states, is not a matter for theoretical discussion, but of "common sense." This assertion comes close to suggesting that movement organizations cannot exist without leaders, and again appears angled to exclude this area from examination.

The approach to the understanding of leadership which is advanced in this paper follows from the arguments put forward by Chemers (1984). He identifies (1984, p. 106) a gap in most current leadership theories such that there is "very little understanding of the values, needs and motives which give rise to the observed behaviours." This leads him to the view that instances of leadership behavior should be examined in relation to their cultural context. We shall show that the cultural context of the women's movement contains a strongly-held value for nonhierarchy, and that organizing activity, within the women's movement, is undertaken in a manner which is consistent with that value. As has already been noted, this implies a rejection of focused leadership, but will not be taken as evidence that leadership acts do not occur. Instead, leadership behavior is viewed as a set of organizing skills (Morely and Hosking 1984) which comprise skillful information search, interpretation, influence, and choice. The application of these skills is necessary for the successful accomplishment of organization, but there is no requirement that they be performed by a minority (including a minority of one) of participants. For example, Kerr and Jermier (1978) have suggested that leadership (in the traditional hierarchical sense) may be redundant in certan settings, one of which is when participants find the task intrinsically motivating and have all the skill and knowledge they need. It is not unreasonable to assume that the movement participants have an adequate degree of motivation; it may be more difficult to assume that they have de facto sufficient skills and knowledge. However, what can be shown is that there is a desire on the part of committed participants to seek to acquire such skills, and thus the means to enact a form of organization which more fully approximates to the ideal of distributed leadership (Brown and Hosking 1986).

Following Melucci (1983, pp. 3-4), it is accepted that, in the analysis of social movements, "organization becomes a critical part of observation, an analytical level that can't be ignored." I first establish the widespread advocacy of nonhierarchical organization within the women's movement and then show that, in practice, (a) it is not sufficient to characterize this form of organization as "spontaneous;" negotiative processes are involved in the construction and maintenance of nonhierarchical organization; (b) leadership acts which are other than temporally or task-specific will provoke a reaction from other participants; a component of the negotiative processes is directed towards constraining the unilateral exercise of power; and (c) leaders (or organizers), in the usual hierarchical sense, are not necessary for the achievement of social organization. What is necessary is that participants devise a means of engaging in leadership acts and thus acting as skilled organizers which is legitimate in terms of their shared values. If this condition is met, social movement organizations (SMOs) do not have a choice between "degenerating" into friendship groupings which conceal elites or oligarchies, or of moving in the direction of bureaucratization (see Satow 1975; Freeman 1984). Neither tendency is inevitable. Zald and Ash (1978, p. 260), for example, are clear that, as a statement on the transformation of SMOs, the Weber-Michels model is incomplete. They note that "there are a variety of other transformation processes." This paper examines one such possibility.

Research Settings and Methods

Women's Centers are organizations set up by women to provide services, activities, and social space specifically for women. They are used in a variety of ways such as the advising and supporting of homeless and battered women, as information exchanges and contact points for the locality, and as physical spaces available for group work or more informally—dropping in for coffee. They are a part of the women's movement, which Coote and Campbell (1982, p. 35) characterize as "a loose federation of small groups, linked chiefly by a sense of involvement and a common cause."

Present estimates suggest that there are about 40 women's centers in Britain. The towns and cities which have women's centers are seen to show some variation over time. There are always some projects which are coming to the end of their life and others which are starting up. However, it may be argued with a fair degree of certainty that all population concentrations of any size have the potential to establish a women's center. Other manifestations of women's movement activity will occur to a greater or lesser extent in all population aggregates; only some locations will formalize a section of this activity in the establishment of a women's center. Whether or not this occurs will depend on the value attached to such a provision, and the success of those who hold this value in mobilizing resources towards its attainment. In this context, the specific resources required to establish a women's center are a defined spatial location, and a group of women who are able to create and maintain a viable organization. The first requirement is likely to be achieved when a grant-awarding body, or the local authority in a particular area, is persuaded of the value of women-only organizations. The second requirement is the focus of this paper; the forms of organization which are characteristic of the women's movement.

For this study, participant observation was conducted in five women's centers for periods ranging from one week to two years. The observational material was amplified by semistructured interviews with selected participants in each organization. In addition, an extensive range of first-hand or "grass-roots" accounts of organizing activities which appeared in movement publications and elsewhere was examined.

NONHIERARCHICAL ORGANIZATION IN THE WOMEN'S MOVEMENT

In the early days of the women's movement in Britain, a National Coordinating Committee (NCC) existed and, surprising as it now seems, men were not excluded from the first two national conferences. In 1971, the NCC was dissolved in response to the realization that it had become a sectarian battleground for various groups on the left, and, when the women's liberation workshop opened in London in 1973, a series of meetings decided that men should be excluded from it. "What (the majority of feminists) wanted above all was autonomy" (Coote and Campbell 1982, p. 35). The separation from the broad sweep of left politics which followed this decision meant more, however, than the exclusion of men as individuals. It also rejected forms of organizing which were defined as "male." In particular, rejection of hierarchical forms and of leaders was seen as vital in defining the *differences* of the women's movement. As one women involved in these processes expressed it, "we were opposed to all forms of leaderism, and struggled for equality in all our social relationships" (Segal 1979, p. 167). The following account of setting up a feminist organization reflects the importance of these values in defining appropriate organizing activity within the women's movement (Tyneside Rape Crisis Centre Collective 1982, p. 176).

The Rape Crisis Centre organises along feminist lines. We are nonhierarchical—that is we don't have an executive committee or elect officers, as these functions are shared among members (. . .) The tasks arising outof business meetings (are) undertaken by a member or members volunteering to carry them out (. . .) We also try to pay as much attention to the form and process of our meetings and interactions as we do to the content, ensuring that all women are involved in decision making, and the tasks of the group. Often, those more used to formal structures and hierarchical organisation will query whether feminist principles are compatible with getting things done—but we can say to them that we managed to set up a rape crisis service after only a few months of work.

This description is typical of statements made by individual women's groups. The emphasis on task sharing, temporary task allocation, and distribution of decision making within this group shows some of the organizational strategies which are commonly adopted in the construction of nonhierarchical organization. To an extent, the negotiative processes by which such strategies are implemented are suggested in this account. Taking a longer-term perspective illustrates more clearly the development of processes and the negotiations which are involved in achieving a workable organizational structure which is in accordance with the values of the women's movement. In the following account (Wires 1978, p. 19, emphasis added), the group produced a newsletter for the women's movement. The time period covered is two-and-a-half years.

Collective working was a positive experience (. . .) but there were problems. At the beginning 'leadership' was supposedly non-existent. Everyone was expected to do everything *immediately,* answer letters, file, type, duplicate (. . .) it was pretty chaotic and not everyone could cope.. Sometimes we were expecting far too much of people. It's a question of working out when someone is ready to take something on and then encouraging them to do it.

Sharing skills wasn't always smooth and easy. We had to learn to criticise each other's work constructively, not moan behind backs or secretly correct errors when the person who'd made the mistake had left for the day. Oldtimers had to face their responsibility to teach newcomers, something we all found hard at first as it seemed like giving orders. As time went on some women did necessarily specialise; we only had one woman doing the accounts at one time. Other specialisms weren't so necessary and change involved the specialist letting go her hold and communicating her skill and the others having the confidence and willingness to learn. *In the end,* the necessity to do things made us all able to do them.

What is striking in this account is the amount of learning activity which is not simply directed towards the learning of new tasks. Members of the group who were skilled initially were required to learn as much as those who were less skilled. For example, they saw a need to pace the sharing process appropriately, to make criticism overt, but to label it in such a way that it was not construed as personal attack, and to give instruction without giving orders. This group also found that temporary specialisms—one woman doing the accounts at one time-were organizationally useful, and were acceptable within the general ethos of equality as long as they were defined as temporary. The extent to which time and energy is expended on these processes depends on the importance given to the values of equality and nonhierarchy. As Rothschild-Whitt (1982, p. 36) observes, on the basis of her study of collective organizations, "The time and priority typically devoted to internal education makes sense only if it is understood as part of a struggle against the division of labour." Moreover, the example makes it clear that it is inadequate to characterize this form of organization as "spontaneous." The negotiative processes which are involved in attempts to minimize skill differentials between participants are difficult, and must be motivated by the espousal of values which have salience for all participants. SMOs which reference their activities to the values of the women's movement will seek ways of minimizing differences in skill and influence in their day-to-day interactions, and thus to construct a form of social organization which approaches a condition of nonhierarchy. This, as has already been suggested, is a form of transformation which is contrary to that implied by the Weber-Michels model. For example, Katz (1981, p. 142) has appreciated that his earlier "natural history" model requires revision on the basis of recent empirical evidence. Referring to women's movement groups as an example, he notes that, "some groups (. . .) eschew the stages of Leadership Emergence and Formal Organization." This is in agreement with the findings of the research on which this paper is based, and is to be understood by reference to the importance of the values for equality and nonhierarchy for organizing activity within the women's movement.

The Negotiation of Influence

Running through many current definitions of leadership processes is a component which identifies "acceptable influence" (see, for example, Hunt 1984; Brown and Hosking 1986). To explain: In the course of constructing social organization participants negotiate over the conditions of influence and their acceptance. This is particularly true when participants share a value for equality since, as the example of skill and task learning shows, equality cannot be imposed by fiat, but must be negotiated over time. It is accepted that participants will vary in, for example, verbal skills, self-confidence, access to information, or interest in the task-attributes which commonly lead to inequalities of influence within groups and organizations. However, under conditions of nonhierarchy all members have the right to full and equal participation in the formulation of problems and identification of solutions, and tactics may be introduced which aim to reduce the effects of differences in personal attributes. For example, consensus decision-making processes place a high premium on verbal skills, but, as Mansbridge (1973, pp. 363, 367) suggests:

> The less verbally facile can be assured that the group (. . .) is willing to put up with stumbling or help them with longwindedness, and most important, actually listens to and understands what they are saying (. . .) The more potentially influential can themselves curb their impulses to speak or to try to influence the group.

This attention to the form of group processes in the furtherance of equality echoes the similar remarks of the Rape Crisis Centre Collective. Thus, it is possible for groups to develop ways of managing the effects of seemingly irreducible inequalities.

Distributed Leadership

In the introduction to this paper, leadership was conceptualized as a set of organizing skills which are necessary for the accomplishment of social order; skills which may be confined to one or a few organizational members in the traditional focused sense of leadership, or, in other circumstances, distributed among all participants. As Douglas (1983, p. 3) has observed there is "no such thing as a leaderless group, there are only groups with different degrees of leadership residing in the actions of one person *or of several*" (emphasis added).

The preceeding sections have illustrated Chemers' argument that observation of leadership behavior should be contextualized through reference to the values and motivations of participants. In their attempts to implement a system of nonhierarchical organization which accords with the value of the movement, participants adopt the tactics of task-sharing, temporary task allocation, and consensus decision making. Their intention is to create a social order which permits organizational tasks to be accomplished, but which does not create a hierarchical system. Thus leadership acts must be accomplished in a manner which constitutes acceptable influence. This process involves managing differences between participants with the intention of achieving, ultimately, a situation wherein participants are able to contribute to the organizational tasks on an equal basis. For this to be possible in the sense of a fully enacted system of distributed leadership, *all* participants must become skilled organizers. As has already been suggested, these complex social processes make demands which individual members may or may not be able to meet; on the other hand, it should not be supposed that the difficulties of implementation are so great as to render those involved helpless to resist domination by an elite or increased bureaucratization.

The remainder of this section examines the requirements for skilled organizers in more detail (Morley and Hosking 1984; Brown and Hosking 1986). Skilled organizers are those who:

1. understand the "threats" and "opportunities" which confront their system of values and relationships, and are, in this sense, skilled at information search and interpretation;
2. structure interactions so that the capacities of participants are effectively linked to the demands of their tasks;
3. recognize and act on key "dilemmas" associated with the achievement, maintenance, and dissolution of order; and

4. are, therefore, able to protect and pursue the values and interests seen to be at stake.

The exercise of skill in these areas can be illustrated by events which took place in one women's center. This center was dependent on the financial support of a community project. It became evident that this support would shortly be withdrawn and the center was faced with the threat of closure. At a collective meeting, participants decided they should explore alternative sources of finance. This would involve making contact with, and acquiring information from, other community groups in the area. The process of networking produced a great deal of new information concerning the feasibility of obtaining sufficient funding. This information had always been available; however, until the threat of closure, the group had not perceived it as necessary to search for it. Of particular importance was the discovery that other community groups were in a position to veto any grant application they might make, and further, that they would indeed do so. It therefore became clear that the group would have to "paint" new pictures of the nature of their activities and thereby influence others in their favor. This was successfully done by a number of participants and alternative funding was achieved. In terms of the exercise of skills, it is clear that, in this case, participants reacted effectively to a perceived threat by building relationships with those on whom they were dependent. These were used to gather important information which was used to inform the group's subsequent choices and to influence opinion in their favor. Thus, closure was turned from a "threat" to an "opportunity," that, is financial independence.

The management of key "dilemmas" has particular significance for social movements. These dilemmas arise from (a) managing relationships in the absence of "formal authority;" (b) managing resources (e.g., balancing long and short term considerations); (c) managing activities, (e.g., deciding what to do, when, how, and for how long;and (d) managing values (e.g., negotiating the strategies which connect future outcomes with present-time means) (Brown and Hosking 1986, p. 72). As Freeman (1975, p. 102) has observed, "The major problem a movement organisation faces is to keep from degenerating into solely consummatory activities on the one hand, or rationalising itself into too rigid a structure on the other." In general, the dilemma for participants is to build a sense of social order which is *sufficient*—to provide a basis for action—but not *too much,* (Sherif and Sherif 1969) which would lead to the present order being maintained, unchanged, at all costs. In the latter case, cohesion is achieved, but at the price of failure to create or seek out resources, and of threats and opportunities passing unrecognized. A shortage of participants, who have the skills of leadership necessary to manage this dilemma, provides a likely explanation for situations where "degeneracy" into friendship groupings has been identified.

The following account of a discussion in the women's center provides an example of an attempt to handle the above dilemma. Both the paid workers in the center said they were finding meetings, in general, depressing and that they were just reporting back decisions which had been made anyway. As such, they found them largely a waste of time and suggested that they could be improved by restructuring along more conventional lines with a formal agenda, minutes, and so on. For some participants, the advantages of this kind of change were not so obvious; they said the meetings were good for seeing other people and keeping in touch, and that, if there were any contentious issues, it was assumed that they would be talked through with the collective before any decision was made. It appeared that many members failed to recognize just how clearly they were being told that this kind of general support was not really very useful, and that "decision making" was not normally something which could be deferred; it happened all the time and "if you weren't there, you wouldn't be a part of it." As a strategy for the future, it was decided to alternate business meetings and issue-based discussions.

This example suggests that some participants recognized the need to restructure certain aspects of their social order; in particular, they appreciated the significance of an overemphasis on cohesive aspects and were able to influence others to handle this dilemma. Skillful organizers understand the difference between consensus as the outcome of a process through which differences have been expressed and received, and "complacent unanimity" (Likert and Likert 1976, p. 153); they know that their value for equality does not imply that conflict should be devalued. The key to the effective management of this dilemma lies in the facilitation of a value for a particular mode of conduct; that is, one in which all participants have both the right and the responsibility to contribute to the construction and maintenance of social order. Equally, their mode of conduct must reflect value for the resources and influence of all participants (cf. Rothschild-Whitt 1982). Studies have indicated the probable role of such conduct in obtaining high quality decision making and in securing the commitment of participants (see, for example, Mansbridge [1973, pp. 352-353]).

The following account of consensus decision-making processes in one group illustrates the attention given to both the cohesive aspects of the group and the quality of decisions (Jones 1982, pp. 136-137).

> Through consensus we are working not only to achieve better solutions, but also to promote the growth of community and trust (. . .) Consensus does not mean that everyone thinks the decision made is the best one possible, or even that all are sure it will work. What it does mean is that in coming to that decision, no one has felt that her/his position on the matter was misunderstood or that it wasn't given a proper hearing. Hopefully, everyone will think that it is the best decision; this often happens because when it works, collective intelligence does come up with better solutions than could individuals.

The overt and explicit synthesis of views implied in this process involves participants in an understanding of problems in a way which is not possible within hierarchical structures where decisions may be simply received. Movement groups of the kind described here are at something of an advantage in that the values which promote these forms of conduct are central to their social order.

The skills which have been described here are important for all organizing activity; the particular relevance in this context is that the values which inform organizing activity in the women's movement contain the requirement that leadership be distributed. It has not been argued here that nonhierarchy comprises a situation where leadership is redundant (cf. Kerr and Jermier 1978), and, instead, instances have been described which show the application of organizing skills and some potential consequences of a shortage of such skills. The findings of this research are hence in agreement with Likert and Likert (1976) who have suggested the likelihood of an inverse relationship between the degree of hierarchy present in an organization and the distribution of leadership skills. Thus leadership may be more or less distributed in a social organization to an extent which is: (a) sanctioned by the values which characterize a particular social order, and (b) successfully enacted by skillful participants.

DISCUSSION

It is important for social movement analysts to examine the processes involved in the construction of nonhierarchical organization, and it is particularly so in those cases where this form of organization constitutes an important dimension of the ideology of a social movement, as it does in the women's movement. To explain: It is generally accepted that participants in social movements direct their activities to the achievement of certain goals, that is, political outcomes; more recently (see, for example, Melucci 1983) the importance of the *means* by which such goals are achieved has also been identified. The form of social organization which is preferred by participants will reflect and embody the values of the movement.

Here it has so far been argued that:

1. Leadership behavior is to be understood in terms of "acceptable influence"
2. Participants in SMOs have the capabilities to be actively involved in the process of constructing social order
3. The values which inform organizing activity in the women's movement emphasize equality and nonhierarchy.

Taking these arguments together makes it possible to see that for influence to be acceptable it must also be perceived as legitimate, and that participants are able to actively negotiate the conditions of legitimacy. For groups and organizations which hold the values described above, "distributed leadership" (where every participant has both a right and a responsibility to contribute) is the only form of influence which will be perceived as legitimate, and hence be acceptable.

In the terms of this argument, the solution proposed by Freeman (1984, p. 6) to the difficulties of operating nonhierarchical structures in SMOs (which are not disputed) is unacceptable. Freeman suggests that rules and structures must become formalized, but such an appeal to formal rationality is, as Rothschild-Whitt (1982, p. 26) notes, directly counter to the substantive (or value) rationality of collective organization. Under substantive rationality (1982, p. 27) "only decisions which appear to carry the consensus of the group behind them, carry the weight of moral authority (. . .) Authority resides in the collective as a whole." The fact that Freeman fails to identify the importance of a value for equality in the culture of the women's movement prevents her appreciating that the elitist behaviors she identifies are unacceptable at the level of the group, and may be addressed at that level. (Further consideration of the importance of group processes may be found in Levine's [1984] reply to Freeman.)

Freeman is also unswervingly critical of "the tyranny of structurelessness" in the women's movement. In her view (1984, p. 6-7), the advocacy of "leaderless groups" leads, inevitably, to a situation where a "myth of structurelessness" conceals an informal structure within which elites are able to wield unchallenged power. This point is taken up because the influence of this paper has been such that, for some writers, the arguments it presents have acquired the status of "facts" and are accepted uncritically (see, for example, Carroll 1984). From this perspective, ordinary (i.e., nonelite) members of a group or organization are rendered powerless in the face of the influence exercised by elites (Freeman 1984, p. 9): "Informal structures have no obligation to be responsible to the group at large (. . .) there can be no attempts to put limits on the use of power (. . .) (and) they cannot be directly influenced by the group."

As an aid to understanding the apparent contradiction between these assertions and those which have been put forward in this paper—namely that there is a strong value imperative within the women's movement which acts to counter the emergence of "elites"—it is useful to look at work which has considered the processes of group maturation. Bennis and Shepard (1965), for example, have described a series of stages through which a group may proceed in order to reach a stage—the mature group—which is characterized by (a) the acceptance of individual differences between participants; (b) conflict occurs only over substantive issues relating to groups tasks, rather than over emotional issues; (c) decisions are made through a process of consensus which encourages dissent; and (d) participants are aware of the group's processes and their own involvement in them. This characterization parallels the descriptions which have been provided of group processes within movement organizations. In addition, attention has been given to group processes in relation to the group's organizational environment, through which members of the group seek to acquire information, provide interpretation, exert influence, and exercise choice. It has been argued that the ideology of the women's movement is such that participants will seek to avoid the implementation of hierarchical forms of organization by distributing leadership tasks, and, in so doing, will acquire the characteristics of a mature group. However, sharing tasks and skills is not an easy process, and we will only occasionally expect to find examples of fully enacted distributed leadership in practice. The likely shortages of skills and commitment, in some movement groups, provides a way of understanding why it is sometimes reported (as by Freeman 1984) that informal groups are vulnerable to domination by "elites." In cases such as this, it is to be anticipated that there is a current accumulation of skills in some participants, and that the negotiative learning processes involved in achieving some redistribution of skills have not been successfully implemented, in contrast to the example of a group of women producing a newsletter described above. It's a matter for discussion whether a failure to identify the processes of skill and task-sharing within a group is a reflection of the analytical framework adopted by the researcher or whether it represents a true absence. A resource mobilization perspective (e.g., Freeman 1979), which sees the role played by segments of the elite as crucial in the generation of mass insurgency, is likely to apply the same analytical framework to within group processes as is utilized to explain intergroup relationships. Thus, an analytical perspective which seeks to identify the role of elites in relation to insurgency is also likely to find that elite domination is a characteristic internal to movement groups.

It is important to consider these contradictory viewpoints in the light of empirical evidence. Some of the weaknesses of the resource mobilization model have been well-identified by McAdam (1982, p. 29); in particular, in terms of the present discussion, a "major weakness of the resource mobilization model concerns a consistent failure by many of its proponents to acknowledge the political capabilities of the movement's mass base." ("Political capabilities" are taken to mean the ability to create SMOs which may, for certain issues and at certain times, without any additional resources other than the dissemination of information, amalgamate into mass demonstrations, as at Greenham Common. The issue of political effectiveness is a separate concern which is not considered here.) McAdam's argument is that powerlessness is not an invariant characteristic of ordinary members in social movements, and specifically here it is argued that this applies to the women's movement. The examples which have been given illustrate the possibilities of both mass demonstrations without external sponsorship, and of within-group processes which aim to reduce the effects of differences of influence, and, hence, power. It is not accepted that elite sponsorship is necessary for insurgent acts, nor, conversely that elite emergence is an inevitable outcome of small-scale SMOs.

These last two points should be taken together in the interests of both empirical and analytical consistency. It seems inappropriate to suppose that radically different forms of organization operate within and between movement groups—the "loose federation" to which Coote and Campbell (1982) refer is linked precisely because some values are common to all movement groups, and thus equally common to the temporary coalescences which constitute mass demonstrations. Within women's movement organizations, the values for equality and nonhierarchy act to define a situation where consistent contributions to social order are expected and valued from *all* group members (Brown and Hosking 1986, p. 76), and, therefore, there are strong countertendencies to domination by elites. Any minority which consistently attempts to dominate groups (or movement) processes will be resisted.

Elsewhere (Brown 1986), it has been shown that this emphasis on collective group processes provides a means of understanding the proliferation which is found to exist in the women's movement (cf. Carden 1978). The dilemmas of management described earlier are variously "solved" in different ways by different groups and at different times. Although a full discussion of these ramifications is beyond the scope of this paper, it can be shown that proliferation arises in part, as Carden (1978, p. 186) notes, from the differing political agendas of different movement groups, but it is also found to derive from variation in the presence or absence of skilled organizers (that is those with the capabilities outlined above), and in the strategies by which present time means are legitimately connected to longer term goals. Thus, identification of the proliferation which exists in practice should not obscure the fact that the ideology of the women's movement specifies, in terms of legitimate influence and of distributed leadership, the nature of a characteristic form of social organization. The achievement of this form of social organization represents as much a goal of movement participants as do other items on their political agendas. Thus as Gerson (1976, p. 797) in his discussion of "commitment organization" has commented, "participation in any system (. . .) is simultaneously constraining in that people must make contributions to it, and be bound by its limitations and yet enriching in that participation provides resources and opportunities otherwise unavailable." In drawing attention to the fact that social organization offers participants rewards which are, crucially, a product of interaction, we are able to see that the establishment (or attempted establishment) of a social order with particular characteristics can be valuable in itself in terms of the rewards and opportunities which it offers participants. These considerations may affect the choice of organizational form made by a movement group. For example, Jones (1983, p. 131) has cited the views of the Women's Pentagon Action Groups in America who, "discussed and rejected the idea of 'going national' because we felt that we would not be able to keep the democratic participatory decision-making we value if we were a national organization." The instances which have been discussed in this paper illustrates the fact that the establishment, or attempted establishment, of nonhierarchical forms of organization provides an important motivator for participants in the women's movement. The intention is to create organizational forms which differ from those which characterize much of society.

Further research may show whether similar, or different, but nevertheless characteristic, forms of social organization can be identified in studies of other social movements. Whatever is the case, studies of SMOs, and the associated forms of leadership, require an approach which is cognisant of the value component attached to social organization by participants. So far this area has not been explored to any great extent by social movement analysts. Examples which may be cited include Abrams and McCullough's (1976) work on communes, Thompson's (1973) on religious organizations and Gerlach and Hine's (1970) examination of social movements. In common, these writers draw attention to the role played by values, ideology, and symbolism in organizational structuring. Gerlach and Hine (1970, p. 60) consider that, "the ideology is perhaps the key to the infrastructure of the movement," while Thompson (1973, p. 301) observes that, "religious organizations are judged not only for their efficiency, but also for their symbolic appropriateness." However, while both action and its symbolic referents may be expressed in terms of agreement about a shared set of values, particular attention must be paid to the area of negotiation between the two. To do otherwise is to fall into the trap of determinism which arises from a "Parsonian" sense of consensus values. It is therefore important to follow Thompson's example in explicating the empirical dimension. As he points out (1973, p. 300), "one of the sources of conflict in religious organizations (. . .) is the fact that religious symbols cannot in practice be broken down into specifiable empirical conditions without generating controversy." Thus the strategies, tactics, and actions which are invoked in achieving and maintaining social organization are "political" and involve negotiation. The examples given here have shown some of the negotiative processes which can occur in attempts to reduce inequalities between participants, and to foster a group of skilled organizers who are better able to construct a form of organization which is congruent with the values of the women's movement.

One final point: It must, of course, be emphasized that while it is possible to idenfity agreement about a shared set of values which characterize the organizational form of the women's movement, it is unlikely that participants will share *all* values and the potential for conflict is maintained. It is also to be expected that participants will continue to vary in the skills and resources which they are able (or choose) to bring us to the process of constructing a social organization. Strauss (1978, p. 259) reminds us that the realm of negotiability is mutable with respect to the resources—"time, money, skill, information, boldness or perhaps desperation"—which are brought to bear on it. However, not all applications of resources are equally weighted, equally acceptable, or equally valued in their contribution to the production and maintenance of social order. They must also be identified as valid in terms of the values which characterize the social order in question. Therefore, the political processes referred to above must be extended to include "politics as the management of meaning" (Pettigrew 1985, p. 44). By this means, the cultural and value components of social organizations are linked, via the concept of legitimacy, to processes within the organization. The importance for studies of SMOs of the ideological context within which organization occurs, and the manner in which the ensuing relationship between movement values and the organizational forms which arise through enactment of these values is negotiated, should not be overlooked.

REFERENCES

Abrans, P. and A. McCullough . 1976. *Communes and Society*. Cambridge: Cambridge University Press.

Bennis, W.G. and H.S. Shepard. 1965. "A Theory of Group Development." *Human Relations* 9: 415-457.

Brown, M.H. 1986. "Organisational Aspects of Women's Centres." Unpublished Ph.D. dissertation, University of Warwick, England.

Brown, M.H. and D.-M. Hosking. 1986. "Distributed Leadership and Skilled Performance as Successful Organisation in Social Movements." *Human Relations* 1:65-79.

Brown, P. 1983. "Peace movement without leaders that won't go away." *The Guardian* March 31, p. 5.

Cardel, M.L. 1978. "The Proliferation of a Social Movement: Ideological and Individual Incentives in the Contemporary Feminist Movement. Pp. 179-196 in *Social Movements, Conflicts and Change* vol. 6, edited by L. Kriesberg. Greenwich, CT: JAI Press.

Carroll, S.J. 1984. "Feminist Scholarship on Political Leadership." Pp. 139-156 in *Leadership: Multidisciplinary Perspectives*, edited by B. Kellerman. Englewood Cliffs, NJ: Prentice-Hall.

Chemers, M.M. 1984. "The Social, Organisational and Cultural Context of Effective Leadership." Pp. 91-112 in *Leadership: Multidisciplinary Perspectives*, Englewood Cliffs, NJ: Prentice-Hall.

Coote, A. and B. Campbell. 1982. *Sweet Freedom: The Struggle for Women's Liberation*. London: Pan Books.

Douglas T. 1983. *Groups: Understanding People Gathered Together*. London: Tavistock.

Freeman, J. 1979. "Resource Mobilization and Strategy: A Model for Analyzing Social Movement Organization Actions." Pp. 167-190 in *The Dynamics of Social Movements: Resource Mobilization, Social Control and Tactics*, edited by M.N. Zald and J.D. McCarthy. Cambridge, MA: Winthrop.

————. 1984. *The Tyranny of Structurelessness*. London: Dark Star Press and Rebel Press.

Gerlach, L. and V. Hine. 1970. *People, Power, Change: Movements of Social Transformation*. Indianapolis, IN: Bobbs-Merrill.

Gerson, E.M. 1976. "On 'Quality of Life." *American Sociological Review* 41: 793-806.

Gibb, C. 1969. "Leadership." Pp. 205-282 in *The Handbook of Social Psychology,* vol. 4, 2nd ed., edited by G. Linzey and E. Aronson. Reading, MA: Addison-Wesley.

Hunt, J.G. 1984. "Organisational Leadership: The Contingency Paradigm and its Challenges. Pp. 113-138 in *Leadership: Multidisciplinary Perspectives,* edited by B. Kellerman. Englewood Cliffs, NJ: Prentice-Hall.

Jones, L. 1983. *Keeping the Peace.* London: The Women's Press.

Katz, A.H. 1981. "Self-help and Mutual Aid: An Emerging Social Movement?" *Annual Review of Sociology* 7: 129-155.

Kerr, S. and J.M. Jermier. 1978. "Substitutes for Leadership: Their Meaning and Masurement. *Organisational Behaviour and Human Performance 22*: 375-403.

Levine, C. 1984. *The Tyranny of Tyranny.* London:Dark Star Press and Rebel Press.

Likert, R. and J. Likert. 1976. *New Ways of Managing Conflict.* New York: McGraw-Hill.

McAdam, D. 1982. *Political Process and the Development of Black Insurgency 1930-1970.* Chicago: University of Chicago Press.

Mansbridge, J. 1973. "Time, Emotion and Inequality: Three Problems of Participatory Groups." *Journal of Applied Behavioural Science* 9: 351-368.

Melucci, A. 1983. "An End to Social Movements." *Social Science Information* 24:819-835.

Morley, I.E. and D.-M. Hosking. 1984. "Decision-making and Negotiation: Leadership and Social Skills." Pp. 71-94 in *Social Psychology and Organisational Behaviour,* edited by M. Gruneberg and T. Wall. Chichester: Wiley.

Pettigrew, A.W. 1985. *The Awakening Giant: Continuity and Change in ICI.* Oxford: Basil Blackwell.

Rothschild-Whitt, J. 1982. "The Collectivist Organisation: An Alternative to Bureaucratic Models." Pp. 23-49 in *Workplace Democracy and Social Change,* edited by F. Lindenfeld and J. Rothschild-Whitt. Boston: Porter Sargent.

Satow, R.L. 1975. "Value-Rationale Authority and Professional Organisations: Weber's Missing Type." *Administrative Science Quarterly* 20: 526-531.

Segal, L. 1979. "A Local Experience." Pp. 157-210 in *Beyond the Fragments: Feminism and the Making of Socialism,* edited by S. Rowbotham, L. Segal, and H. Wainwright. London: Merlin Press.

Sherif, M. and C. Sherif. 1969. *Social Psychology.* New York: Harper and Row.

Strauss, A. 1978. *Negotiations: Varieties, Contexts, Processes and Social Order.* San Francisco: Jossey Bass.

Thompson, K.A. 1973. "Religious Organisations: The Cultural Perspective." Pp. 293-304 in *People and Organisations,* edited by G. Salaman and K.A. Thompson. London: Longman.

Tyneside Rape Crisis Centre Collective. 1982. Pp. 170-180 in *Women in Collective Action,* edited by A. Curno, A. Lamming, L. Leach, J. Stiles, A. Wright, and T. Ziff. London: The Association of Community Workers in the United Kingdom.

W.I.R.E.S. 1978. *Spare Rib.* 70: 18-19.

Zald, M.N. and R. Ash. 1978. "Social Movement Organisations: Growth, Decay and Change." Pp. 259-274 in *Collective Behaviour and Social Movements,* edited by L.E. Genevie. Itasca, IL: Peacock.

LEADERSHIP AND DECISION MAKING IN A STRIKE ORGANIZATION

Jean Hartley

INTRODUCTION

This chapter, like the longer case study from which it is drawn (Hartley, Kelly, and Nicholson 1983) is based on a novel approach to the understanding of strikes. It blends an organization perspective with concepts about trade union government, and applies these to understanding the processes of strike leadership and decision making. In this chapter, the modification of a trade union into a temporary organization with a distinct structure, division of labor, goals, and leadership is described.

The case study is based on a major strike in the steel industry, which took place in Britain in 1980. Nearly 100,000 employees of the British Steel Corporation went on strike for 13 weeks. The case concerns the 100,000 strikers in one area (Rotherham in Yorkshire) who established their own fairly autonomous organization for the prosecution of the strike locally.

International Social Movement Research, Vol. 2, pages 241-265.
Copyright © 1989 by JAI Press Inc.
All rights of reproduction in any form reserved.
ISBN: 0-89232-964-5

STRIKES, TRADE UNION GOVERNMENT, AND ORGANIZATION THEORY

Three quite separate literatures are drawn together here to understand the Rotherham strike organization.

First, there is a large literature on strikes but few attempts to develop theory about the social processes of organizing and running strikes. There are a number of case studies, but these have been largely journalistic, chronicling the history and development of key public events in the course of the strike. They have often been partisan, and lacking in analysis (e.g., Karsh 1982; Beck 1974; Dromey and Taylor 1978). There are exceptions; some cases have provided descriptions and theories of processes internal to the strike organization (e.g., Lane and Roberts 1971; Waddington 1986, 1987; Hiller 1928) and there are some attempts to integrate this literature (e.g., Kelly and Nicholson 1980). However, the literature on strikes have largely been divorced from the consideration of trade union government—operation in war rather than peace-time. Also, there has been a failure to use organization theory to understand some of the social processes of strikes. There are significant questions to ask. How does mobilization occur? If an organization is established, how is that done and how does the structure influence its effectiveness? What is the nature of people's involvement during a strike, and is it different from the processes of government during "normal" (strike-free) periods?

The second domain of literature concerns trade union government, about which industrial relations has much to say. It explores mechanisms for reaching decisions and for the expression of democracy. Often this work has detailed the institutional procedures and social processes for internal government and policy-making (e.g., Undy et al. 1981; Martin 1968; Nicholson et al. 1982).

A theme of much of this work has been a concern with the emotive issue of oligarchy (Michel 1962). This has been manifested in concern over the power exercised over policy by elected officials relative to that exercised by the rank-and-file (e.g., Lane 1974; Crouch 1982; Nicholson et al. 1982). However described and however it operates in practice, a central feature of a collective organization such as a trade union is that two-way control over policy is a formal and major aspect. This is because of the nature of members' involvement in the union and the "democracy dilemma" (Hemingway 1978).

The participation of members in their union is multi-dimensional (McShane 1986; Klandermans 1986a, 1986b). Joining a union may or may not be a voluntary act but participating in union affairs is to a significant degree. Unions may try at times to coerce their membership, or to entice them by remunerative means, but these are limited ways of exercising power within a voluntary institution and so more predominant is the encouragement of moral involvement (Etzioni 1975), through symbols, norms, and appeals to values.

The democracy dilemma is essentially about the tension between democracy as an end in itself and as a means to other ends. Hemingway (1978) notes that, on the one hand, trade unions are effective through collective action. Unity is strength, and so the organization needs to be a disciplined body with strong leadership, united in commitment and objectives. In this way, a collective organization can stand up to the employer.

But, on the other hand, trade unions are political institutions in which democratic self-government is an article of faith and a structural imperative. Since the ultimate reference for union action is the interests of the members, the institutions of union government are designed to protect their rights to share in decision making and the selection of leaders. Thus, for many trade unions, democracy is not only a moral but also a structural imperative.

The tension, or democracy dilemma, occurs because of the need for integration, control, and discipline (to be effective against the employer) which implies strong leadership but also the need for member involvement (to create high levels of participation in union activities). Child et al. (1973) discuss this in terms of the conflict between the administrative system (the need for control and integration) and the representative system (the need for members to have influence over leaders).

While the tensions of union democracy have occupied a range of writers, little consideration has been given to its application during "war" rather than "peace." I suggest that the democracy dilemma is likely to be heightened in the circumstances of a strike, where external pressures intensify and where the need for internal cohesion is strong. So there will be additional pressures on the decision-making processes and on the leadership.

Finally, there is the literature about organizations. This has hardly considered voluntary organizations such as trade unions, professional organizations, or charities, focusing instead on employing organizations. While caution is necessary in applying organization theory to a temporary strike organization and to an organization which is formally based on two-way control rather than on authority downwards, nevertheless, there are some valuable concepts. Of course, not all strikes require a special organization and therefore are amenable to organization theory. The majority of strikes in Britain are small affairs involving a handful of people and lasting only a few hours (Edwards 1983). In such strikes, social organization is required to coordinate the withdrawal of labor (Batstone et al. 1978) but may be limited to that. In longer or larger strikes, an organizational structure, however rudimentary or temporary, may be needed if the strike is to be prosecuted effectively. This is to establish and pursue the strikers' objectives and to coordinate and control efforts to that end. A division of labor may well be required. Once differentiation occurs (through the division of labor) then integrating mechanisms are necessary (Lawrence and Lorsch 1967). In employing organizations, integration is achieved through a number of mechanisms but management is a principal one. In trade union parlance, management is not a widely used term but leadership is. Whatever term is used, it can be seen that there are issues to be faced about how a strike is to be directed and lead. How does a strike leadership cope with issues of control, motivation of members, and organizational objectives? Where does leadership lie in a strike organization in any case—is it manifest in authority (legitimate power), or does it lie in other aspects of the organization? How far should the strike organization be considered a bureaucracy and how far a very different type of organization?

The issue of leadership cannot be divorced from questions about decision making. We know from the literature that decision making is a complex process (Hickson et al. 1986; Koopman et al. 1984; DIO 1983). Classical organization theory treated decision making as a process of rational assessment grounded in the careful gathering and evaluation of information. However, the work of March and Simon (1958) and Cyert and March (1963) among others (e.g., Lindblom 1959; Mintzberg et al. 1976) demolished the rationality of organizational decision making, showing that decision makers exhibited bounded rationality and that information search was often based on commitment to a choice rather than vice versa. Empirical studies showed this to be a widespread practice in organizations, even extending to "garbage-can" decision making (Cohen et al. 1972). Recent work has pointed to the importance of understanding interest groups in decision making and the role of incorporating or subduing opposition (Hickson et al. 1986; DIO 1983). However, little attention has been paid to the decisions of trade unions or to everyday decisions rather than simply strategic decisions.

Finally, in relation to organization theory, the importance of a systems theoretical approach in the field is noted. While other frameworks are valuable (especially the political perspective implied in much decision making literature) the systems approach is useful insofar as it emphasizes the importance of the organization as a system interacting with an external environment. We can anticipate that the external environment of a strike is likely to be highly salient to organizational members, since the environment may be characterized as both hostile and rapidly changing. How is organization shaped by such a turbulent environment?

This brief survey of the literature on strikes, organizations, and trade unions has enabled us to identify some concepts with which to explore the steel strike case. We will explore how a temporary organization is spawned and how it functions in the context of a turbulent environment. In particular, we will be interested in how the strike is governed—how the leadership operates and how decisions are made. I turn now to look at the steel strike in more detail.

THE STEEL STRIKE CASE STUDY

The 1980 steel strike lasted 13 weeks and involved approximately 100,000 strikers. This is a long and large strike by any standards. In Rotherham, the area studied, there were 10,000 strikers.

The research was carried out by a three-person team and was based on fieldwork. Having previously established good relations in the steel industry, we approached the steel unions in the first week of the strike to ask if we could conduct a study of the developing strike organization. This proposal was accepted and we were thus in the unusual position of being nonactive but close observers of the strike in the Yorkshire area. A major source of information was the daily meetings of the Rotherham Strike Committee, which we attended as observers. This provided an almost unique opportunity to observe decision making in action, something which, in many other studies, has to be constructed retrospectively. In addition, we attended a range of other meetings and activities, interviewed a broad section of strike activists, often several times, and used documentary material and a poststrike questionnaire.

In 1980, the British steel industry employed steel workers both in the nationalized company, the British Steel Corporation (BSC), and in a number of private companies. The strike occurred in the public sector (with efforts made by BSC workers to draw in the private sector). The predominant union in the steel industry, representing over 50% of the workforce, was the Iron and Steel Trades Confederation (ISTC) although a further eleven unions in the strike had members and negotiating rights in the Rotherham area. These were the general, transport, and craft unions. The full 12 unions were organized into four units for bargaining purposes. However, although each unit negotiated separately, all recognized that the ISTC was the pace setter in wage settlements.

The trigger for the strike was a pay offer in December 1979 by the BSC management to the ISTC of approximately 2%. this was seen as insulting (inflation was running at 17%) and the ISTC issued a strike call for January 2, 1980. The other unions followed suit within a short period. In the background of the dispute was the high level of redundancies which had been and were taking place in BSC. However, the strike was called and prosecuted on the wages issue. Wage negotiations were conducted nationally, while the responsibility for running the strike was based at local level, in this case, Rotherham. (Further details of the background to the strike are available in Hartley et al. [1983]; Upham [1980]; and Docherty [1983].)

The strike call on December 8 gave the unions 3 weeks to prepare for industrial action. The ISTC, which lead the strike, had not had a national strike for 50 years and had a history of cooperative relations with management. Three-quarters of the workforce were going on strike for the first time in their lives. There was no national ISTC advice about how to prosecute the strike and each area had to develop its own plans.

Establishing the Temporary Organization

In Rotherham, the strike organization grew out of the main steel trade union (ISTC) but was by no means identical to it. It was an unofficial body and its leadership consisted both of lay officials and nonofficials. The actual organizational structure was complex and it is remarkable how quickly it was established, by a group of people who had little or no previous experience of strikes.

Initially, it was unclear to the steelworkers what would need to be organized. No one knew much about picketing and they had little idea of the other demands which would be made on them in running a major strike. In fact, in the period running up to Christmas, there was a general feeling that the management's bluff had been called and that the strike would be called off. Overtime continued at a high level in many departments, with the encouragement of branch officials. In short, the steelworkers were inexperienced in how to prepare for a strike.

However, despite the continuance of normal working, some preparations were made in Rotherham for the strike. (Not all areas of the country did this.) Preparations were initiated by the joint branches body of ISTC in Rotherham. The joint branches body had no formal power in the ISTC, but met regularly for mutual information exchange in the Rotherham area. So strike preparations were started by lay rather than full-time officials. The Rotherham joint branches body met a week before the Christmas break and elected six branch officials to sit on the committee they set up to run the strike. This they called the Rotherham Strike Committee (RSC). They did this on the advice of the local area miners' union, which had experience to offer about how to organize a strike. By the time the RSC met for the first time two days later there were 13 people in attendance who considered themselves to be members. The RSC at this time consisted of the more senior (in status) branch officials and, despite its more fluid membership, one can see the strong links with the union from which it developed. The first RSC meeting decided to widen the membership still further to ensure a geographical spread of ISTC branch representation. Before the strike started, over half the RSC members had been coopted rather than elected. Cooptation continued in the first week of the strike when the other unions sent representatives to the RSC (although other unions also had their own strike committees). In fact, as we shall see, the membership of the RSC widened still further during the strike.

From January 2, the RSC met daily to organize activities. It was the central body of leadership and decision making in the Rotherham area. It claimed the right to choose priorities and objectives during the strike, and had beneath it a complex structure to engage in what had been defined by the RSC as the principal activity of the strike: picketing factories and plants which were using steel (with the goal of closing them for the duration of the strike). The "line of command" between the RSC and picketing strikers is indicated in Figure 1. This structure can be briefly explained. Picket volunteers from the branches were divided into small groups (varying in size from 25 to 50 with the average being 30), called picket cells, consisting of people living in the same area. Each

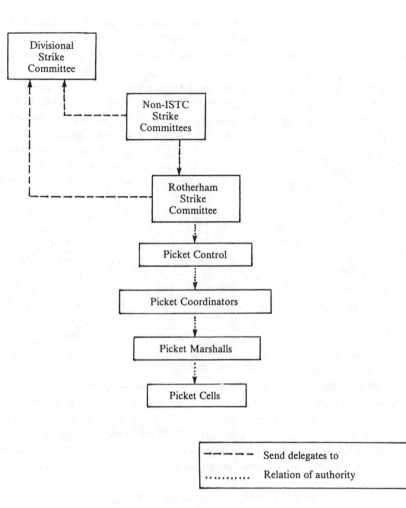

Figure 1.　Strike Organization in Rotherham

cell was assigned a leader or picket marshall whose job was to organize the cell. Picket marshalls consisted of less senior officials (compared to the RSC) and also nonofficer branch activists, a fact which underlines the parallelism between the hierarchy of the strike organization and that of the union. Picket coordinators were appointed by the RSC and were responsible for five to six picket cells. As local picket activity stabilized over the first couple of weeks, the role of coordinators declined and there was more direct communication between the RSC and the picket marshalls. Finally, Picket Control ran the office which directed and provisioned the cells. Consisting of a small group of white collar steel workers, they operated from the strike headquarters.

Finally, it should be noted that flying pickets were not organized within the cell structure but on a roster based at the strike office.

In addition, early in the strike, a body called the Divisional Strike Committee was established (see Figure 1). This covered four strike areas in Yorkshire and was established as a multiunion and multiarea body to "coordinate" strike activities over a wider geographical area. The most senior ISTC members left the RSC to join this body: There was no overlapping membership. Although this later proved problematic, we can see in the structure the development of a bureaucratic organization, with lines of authority and established roles both above and below the RSC.

The RSC, it must be emphasized, was not an official trade union body. Moreover, it did not exist prior to the strike and it had no formal powers of decision making within the ISTC structures. It was not answerable to local branches or to the national Executive Committee of ISTC. Yet it was crucial to the running of the strike, not only in Rotherham but also nationally since the RSC's vigorous and militant prosecution of the strike meant that often they were able to take the initiative in developing activities and objectives, which captured media attention. Within a week of the strike starting, the RSC had led the way nationally by commencing strong and systematic picketing and by calling for a pay rise of 20%, a claim which was rapidly adopted by all steelworkers.

Finally, we note here the importance of organizational choice in the structure of the new temporary organization. The Rotherham branches had chosen a structure which was separate from existing trade union bodies. Also, the structure was relatively complex and apparently hierarchical. These features are in contrast to other areas of the strike (even in Yorkshire) where a more rudimentary organization was slowly established or where existing trade union structures were used to spearhead strike activities.

Leadership: The Rotherham Strike Committee

An indication of the variety of issues dealt with by the RSC is given in Figure 2. While picketing dominated many of the daily discussions, it can be seen that the RSC had a complex internal and external environment to cope with.

The RSC was not a committee of fixed membership, and its numbers grew as the strike progressed. New people came and sometimes stayed. Others would leave for a period as other strike matters occupied their attention. There were no apologies for absence or explanations for a new presence. The RSC did have certain roles however: From the beginning, it had a chairman and a secretary. In assessing the membership, it is useful to make a distinction between core and periphery.

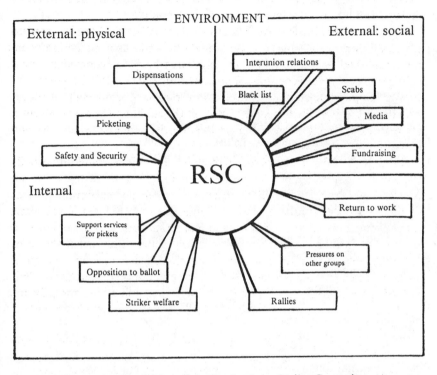

Figure 2. Activities of the Rotherham Strike Committee

Most core members would attend daily, except if urgent business took them away. Core members were mainly ISTC (which in both numbers and values dominated the committee), although other union members were also part of the core.

Peripheral members, on the other hand, were irregular or temporary attenders, who only came for a few meetings or even just part of a meeting. They attended to provide unsolicited ideas—or criticisms—about the running of the strike, or to provide expertise on specific issues. Peripheral members were those who more usually sat on other committees (either locally or in terms of national negotiations), or were picket marshalls (who were in charge of a group of pickets). The marshalls involvement was generally brief and irregular, being more engaged in the day-to-day management of their cell,but they could be prominent and vocal members of the RSC periphery. They tended to communicate picket reactions to particular RSC decisions.

Strikers joined the RSC as their importance in terms of their strike expertise or function increased. For example, Picket Control was drawn into the RSC in the early weeks of the strike.

The RSC had begun as a formally constituted (though unofficial) body, but it quickly displayed some more "organic" features, both in membership and function. In particular, the membership was one with permeable boundaries. Any striker could attend the meetings and give their views. Indeed, this was the expressed policy of the RSC. This gave the RSC the appearance of open government.

However, in reality, there were subtle ideological barriers which prevented some strikers attending RSC meetings. Early in the strike, the RSC had developed a militant outlook, both in terms of their bargaining demand (they had set the tone for the national claim) and crucially in viewing picketing as the central strike activity. Therefore, although the RSC was theoretically open to the views of any ISTC striker, in practice, the memberhsip was drawn from those who held identical or similar views about the importance of picketing, their views about militant action and their perceptions of the main protagonists in the strike.

This political basis for membership is indicated in a number of ways. First, picket marshalls who joined the core tended to be involved in the more vigorous (often flying) picketing. Second, two RSC members dropped out of the daily strike meetings, ostensibly to administer the hardship fund although, in practice, they were older, white-collar branch officials who held a more conservative outlook on the strike. Third, there was an uneven representation of branches on the RSC, with some branches having three members while others had none at all. An early view held by the RSC was that it should have a wide representation of branches, but this did not happen in practice. Fourth, there were hardly any staff branch officials on the RSC. White-collar steelworkers have traditionally been less militant. Fifth, the non-ISTC members of the RSC, who had a greater range of strategies for making the strike effective (beyond and instead of picketing), were hardly listened to, despite their clear seniority and wider experience of trade union activities.

The Significance of the Leadership

The apparent openness of the RSC served a number of functions for the strike leadership, but also more widely for the conduct of the strike. A principal effect was that it provided a means for the RSC's authority to be legitimated since the RSC was not a permanent or official trade union body. Its authority to direct the strike rested less on its position in a hierarchy than on its willingness to be the voice of the strikers. Without support from the rank-and-file strikers it would have been difficult for RSC decisions to carry much weight. Yet by being open to, and apparently accepting of, suggestions and opinions of anyone who came to give their views, the RSC may have increased its authority with the membership. In this way, the democratic ethos of the strike was reinforced.

The openness of the RSC may also have helped to diffuse the responsibility for actions and decisions. This was especially important where the decisions had far-reaching consequences beyond the strike (beyond the jurisdiction of the RSC). The RSC was aware that after the strike it might be held responsible for decisions taken earlier. The permeable boundaries may have helped to generate commitment from the strikers to the major decisions and reduced the burden of responsibility on the RSC.

The openness may also have given RSC members a greater confidence in their militant outlook. By appearing to sample and consider a wide range of views and opinions, the RSC was able to maintain its strike objectives. The RSC was actually able to neutralize criticism by seeming to be open to it. Critics got a chance to air their views, even though the RSC rarely did anything but defend itself against criticism

The features of the strike leadership, notably the existence of a core and periphery, the ideological consistency, and the permeable boundaries all suggest that the RSC did not operate as a bureaucracy despite its location at the head of an organizational structure, and in spite of its formal relationship to the divisional strike committee. In actuality, the RSC was operating more like a political organization, where beliefs, values, and resources were critical to the performance of the organization.

Leader-Member Relations

The leadership of the strike cannot be considered separately from the membership. The relationship between them was particularly salient where picketing is considered. Strikers often use a military metaphor (the strike as a war, battles, the troops, and so on—even the term, picket, has a military origin), which suggests that a strike leadership is able to deploy its human forces in a disciplined manner like troops on a battlefield. In fact, closer examination indicates the essentially voluntary nature of striker involvement and, therefore, the means of encouraging commitment to collective goals had to be largely (though not entirely) moral and persuasive. The RSC had to learn this.

Picketing was the principal method used by Rotherham for prosecuting the strike. It had been pursued with vigor and enthusiasm in the first weeks of the strike and had achieved considerable success in closing down local plants which were using steel. But as plants closed (or alternatively as those workers who crossed picket lines continued to do so day after day), the local picketing became predictable and monotonous. So, as the weeks progressed, "absenteeism" on the local targets increased: Some strikers either did not turn up for their allocated duties (especially at weekends) or had smaller groups on shift working reduced hours. However, flying picketing (daily or weekly picketing to long-distance targets) continued with numbers growing as some strikers transferred to the more interesting, vigorous, and prestigious flying picket groups.

The RSC was initially reluctant to accept the accumulating evidence of the decrease in local picket effectiveness. But, several weeks into the strike, the RSC had to examine the problem in its meetings. The RSC perceived the problems to stem from flagging morale and during the rest of the strike reluctantly considered a number of ways of attempting to deal with it. Sending a "model picket cell" of enthusiastic pickets around the local picket lines was tried but was abandoned when the RSC lost control of its activities.

The RSC decided to organize mass pickets of specified local targets. Mass pickets were initially intended simply to close plants using or making steel. However, within a couple of weeks, their function changed somewhat. It was intended that these large events, bordering on demonstrations, would revive flagging morale (while also serving both the practical function of closing a target plant and the symbolic function of exhibiting Rotherham's power and commitment to the strike to the onlookers of the media, BSC, and government). The RSC commenced, despite complaints from Picket Control who had to implement the plan, by instructing pickets to attend the mass pickets. However, although the mass pickets did have the desired effect on some cells of inspiring and invigorating them, for others the reverse happened. Some pickets complained of the disruption to their routines and were doubtful and concerned about legal and moral aspects of mass picketing. There were a number of complaints, through picket marshalls who attended the RSC expressly to criticize the mass pickets and through complaints received via Picket Control. After this, the RSC accepted that it could not instruct attendance but could only request it. Therein lay the limits to its formal power. Here we see most clearly the limits of the military analogy of control. Persuasion and an appeal to strike commitment was more effective with the rank and file. The picket cells had developed their own fairly autonomous methods of working on local targets and, in some cases, this reinforced their reluctance to be directed.

Later in the strike, the RSC considered paying pickets (beyond the nominal expenses for travel they received). This was debated but not put into effect because there were too many moral objections to rewarding pickets for what it was felt they ought to be doing anyway out of commitment to the strike. It would also create problems of inequity for those strikers who had picketed out of a sense of conviction up till then. (In fact, flying pickets were paid some expenses but this created a number of difficulties for the RSC). Again, we see here an emphasis on moral commitment and persuasion rather than more calculative or coercive means of involving strikers in the strike activities. Also later, punitive militancy was considered by the RSC, under pressure from activists to coerce nonpickets into activity. Consideration was given to a range of poststrike punishments for lack of involvement (for example, distribution of overtime after the strike). Had the RSC failed to discuss such coercive control of inactive strikers, it may well have faced disaffection or revolt by activists and a challenge to its authority greater than that posed by those reluctant to engage in mass picketing. Although poststrike punitive militancy (coercion) was not considered, it was not pursued for very long after the strike because within the ISTC union rules it would have stood little chance of success.

Decision Making in the Strike Organization

From the discussion of leadership, it is clear that decision making and leadership were intimately bound together in the strike organization. We saw above that the openness of the RSC to the membership (at least potentially) was significant in helping to diffuse responsibility for decisions taken. The openness of the RSC pointed to the political features of the strike organization (in the sense of having to coordinate disparate interests and views and to maintain cohension). How was decision making affected by the nature of the organization?

In the Rotherham area, decision making covered a host of activities, including furthering the strike objectives and looking after the welfare of strikers (see Figure 2). Decisions had to be taken about both the internal and external environment for the strike to be prosecuted effectively. While some decisions were delegated to certain strikers (for example, organizing the hardship fund or raising funds through voluntary contributions from the labor movement and public), all activities were discussed within the RSC, especially where matters of policy were concerned. Some issues were also discussed at a range of committees. (In practice, the dividing line between the RSC and the Divisional Strike Committee as well as others was far from clear.) Here, discussion is limited to decisions internal to the RSC rather than those which were shared or contested with other strike committees (though see Hartley et al. 1983 for details of these).

Within the RSC, it was possible to discern different types of decisions, which had different decision making processes associated with them. In analyzing internal RSC decisions, we divided them into three categories of strategic, tactical, and administrative decisions.

Strategic decisions were those concerned with the fundamental objectives of the strike. For the RSC, one aim was paramount—to stop any steel being moved or used by steel producers or steel users (e.g., engineering firms). Stopping steel movement was essentially the mission of the RSC and as such was inaccessible to doubt or scrutiny. Confident of their own power and the moral basis of their strike, the strategy was pursued with little restraint. In this, Rotherham held a different view of stopping steel from the national ISTC office where preventing steel movement was more qualified and secondary to negotiations. The mission was endorsed both by the RSC and by the overwhelming majority of strikers in the Rotherham area (at branch and mass meetings). The consensus over strategy meant that, within the RSC, little discussion took place about alternative strategies. Also, the force of the objective meant that evaluation of the strategy was limited—to whether lorries left plants loaded with steel or not. Success was measured by the quantity rather than type of steel so the focus was on the larger plants regardless of how crucial their use of steel in the economy. The task facing the organization was huge (300 steel producers and users in Rotherham alone and thousands around the country). As the strike progressed, there were serious failures to stem the flow of steel into Britain and into and out of factories around the country. The RSC attributed this failure of its strategy to insufficient resources (of pickets) rather than difficulties with the goal itself. Only later, after major defeats in encouraging the private sector steelworkers to join the strike, and after coming to terms with the scale of the task they had set themselves, was there some slight modification of the objective. At that stage, there was somewhat more emphasis on key plants (seen as having at least symbolic victory if they were closed) and on essential supplies (such as chemicals) needed in the manufacture of steel. There was tacit acceptance that some plants could not be prevented from working.

Tactical decisions concerned how the organizational goals were to be carried out. The RSC discussed two ways of preventing the movement of steel—picketing and the establishment of interunion agreements to prevent the handling of "blacked" steel by other workers sympathetic to the strikers' aims. Tactical decisions tended to follow a similar pattern of commitment to a position and only gradual and reluctant acceptance by the RSC of the need for modification.

Decision making about picketing has already been partly discussed, but here I give more details of the decision making that occurred within the RSC. The principal, indeed crucial, tactic for achieving steel stoppage was seen by the RSC to be picketing. It was seen to be the cornerstone of the strike, without which all other efforts would founder. So hard, consistent, well-directed picketing both locally and in flying picketing was the focus of the majority of RSC meetings. Most of the information flow in and out of the RSC was about steel movement, picket numbers, victories, defeats, and changes of target.

The RSC had taken the lead nationally in organizing both local and flying pickets. The ISTC members were especially enthusiastic about picketing. However, the non-ISTC members (who attended as representatives of the transport, general, and craft unions) were more experienced in industrial action, through their own experience, their involvement in their own unions, and because they were senior lay officials in their own unions. They were already familiar with many of the issues and problems of industrial action (in marked contrast to the ISTC members) and they saw the establishment of interunion agreements as highly valuable. Through discussion and union contacts, workers in other industries might be persuaded to refuse to handle, transport, or work with "blacked" steel. In January, the two craft union members of the RSC, in particular, argued forcefully for interunion agreements which they said would render picketing almost redundant, thus releasing pickets for other locations. There were too many plants for every one to be picketed and there was always the danger that, once pickets had left, the plant would reopen. Interunion agreements would be more effective and longer lasting than pickets and police they suggested. They made out a strong case, with consequent emphasis on the deployment of articulate rather than physically intimidating pickets. However, these arguments, which continued into February, were listened to politely by the rest of the ISTC members— and then passed over without discussion. Even the seniority of the craft officials was insufficient to generate a discussion on this issue. The views of non-ISTC members in the RSC were given less attention than ideas coming from ISTC members. In addition, the non-ISTC members, in effect, were advocating a move away from the central focus of the strike, so this contributed to the failure to win support for alternatives.

The activity and excitement which picketing discussion generated in the RSC meant that little attention was paid to the possibility that the tactic could fail. The interest in the external environment of the strike meant that correspondingly little attention was paid to the internal environment—of picket morale and performance. News of growing picket dissatisfaction, boredom and "absenteeism" on local targets began to filter through informally to RSC members in the first month but was not initially discussed at the RSC meetings. However, after a few weeks, the issue was brought up by Picket Control (who had most ocntact with organizing the pickets). They reported problems of recruitment and deployment but their comments were passed over unheeded because the RSC felt that a breakthrough in the strike was imminent so there was no need to pay attention to cell deterioration. Undoubtedly, the fact that Picket Control was manned by white-collar steelworkers who were thus less central to the struggle (in the eyes of the RSC) contributed to this lack of action. In the middle of the strike, Picket Control continued to inform the RSC of problems but the discussions were generally brief. The RSC merely advocated tighter control of the picket cells by picket marshalls, without specifying how. The RSC argued that it was too late to change or even modify the cell system.

In the midstrike lull, the RSC did have to acknowledge that the cell system was not working as well as it might and it agreed that information should be collected on each cell and its target with a view to reorganization if necessary. However, support for this was not wholehearted and, in fact, it was left to Picket Control to gather information. That collected was brief and ambiguous. "Doing OK" or "good" became the normative comment from picket marshalls to Picket Control. This meagre information was not even utilized by the RSC.

A further indication of the commitment to picketing is given in the RSC response to criticism of its campaign. The RSC drew criticism from a range of activists, lay officials, and trade unionists in engineering firms sympathetic to, but affected by, the strike. Some criticism, as we have seen, was internal to the RSC itself. Comments were often conflicting as might be expected but the RSC was impervious to criticism—even when one meeting was unexpectedly interrupted by a group of six flying picket marshalls who forcefully complained of the handling of the flying picketing campaign—and of the conduct of the RSC itself. After their departure, the RSC returned to its former discussions without comment.

By contrast, administrative decisions, the third category, were handled very differently by the RSC. Administrative decisions were those concerned with keeping the strike organization functioning. As can be seen from the variety of strike activities (Figure 2), there were many issues to attend to, for example, the hardship fund, support for arrested pickets, food and fuel for pickets. Administrative decisions were very different in form and process from the strategic and tactical decisions. Some took a long time to reach and were changed several times as new information came to light.

One example is the decision about how much of a picket marshall's telephone bill should be paid out of strike funds, in recognition of the extra telephoning to members of his picket cell and to the strike office. In March, the RSC changed the decision about the basis of payment three times in a week, in order to ensure that it was fair to all marshalls. On this issue, opinion among picket marshalls was informally canvassed outside the RSC, and arguments for and against particular payment systems were assessed. On this, as on a number of administrative decisions, the RSC was very sensitive to rule-making, precedent, and equity. A further example can be seen in the discussion of how the hardship fund (consisting of donations from sympathetic unions, political groups, and the public) should be distributed. As the ISTC members were not in receipt of strike pay, this was an important issue. The RSC discussed, in detail, who would be eligible for hardship money and also how the money would be distributed. The basis for eligibility changed as the circumstances of particular individuals was brought to the attention of the committee. The basis of payment was also changed several times. Initially, cash was given out but, as cases of abuse came to light, the system was changed to one where recipients were given a voucher to spend on specified items in specified shops. However, the voucher system created such antagonism that it was quickly abandoned. The RSC regularly had to make such administrative decisions, especially as financial hardship deepened, for example rules about car repairs for pickets who travelled to their "place of work" and decisions about the distribution of resources.

Analytically, the concern with equity can be seen as important in reducing or preventing sectional conflict within the strike organization. Decision making here serves an integrative function in the strike organization. However, such decisions about equity issues often took much longer to resolve than other types of decisions.

The administrative decisions are almost a classical example of "rational" decision making. This is generally described as a process involving defining objectives, defining the immediate problem, then evaluating alternative strategies, implementing one and evaluating the outcome, with a change of decision if the feedback indicates a poor choice has been made. The search for, and use of, information is important at all stages. For the strategic and tactical decisions of the RSC, this order was essentially reversed, with a commitment to a decision being folowed by the search for, and evaluation of information to justify that decision. This latter process is characteristic of political decision making, where values guide policy formulation and practice. We will assess the reasons for these differences when we examine the functioning of the organization.

DISCUSSION AND IMPLICATIONS FOR OTHER ORGANIZATIONS

This case study has drawn together concepts drawn from trade union government and from organization theory to understand the behavior of the strikers and the organization they had created. What has been learnt from this—both about the Rotherham strike organization and more widely for other organizations such as other strike organizations as well as for temporary and/ or voluntary organizations more generally? There may even be some pointers for the study of employing organizations (the dominant form within organizational theory). In this section, I present four themes concerning the strike organization: origins, functioning, mission and commitment, and the environment..

Origins of the Organization

The Rotherham strike organization was established very quickly and with little previous experience of being on strike, let alone coordinating one. Additionally, the organization was set up to respond to a crisis—the breakdown of negotiations and the commencement of hostilities. The metaphor of war is not an exaggeration to workers long accustomed to industrial calm. So, it is remarkable in these circumstances how complex an organization was established. A hierarchical structure (apparently) with lines of command, a network of committees (not all of which have been described or indicated here), and a variety of activities which were coordinated through the central committee of the RSC. In operation it was quite different from that which had been envisaged in the strike preparation days. And it continued to develop and change in structure and activity as the strike progressed and as further need for organization occurred.

Of course, the organization did not emerge from nowhere—it was partly derived from the structure of the trade union. Some features of the "old" trade union were evident, for example, some aspects of hierarchy (with more senior trade unionists in more senior positions in the strike organization). However, in the main, it operated rather differently, with little of trade union authority available to the RSC. It was a much more fluid, less rule-bound organization than the local union. It also had to cope with multiunion influences—some members were outside the control of the ISTC in any case.

How far is any organization totally new? How far does any social or voluntary organization build on origins in other organizations or in the experience of individuals derived from other organizations? This is an area we seem to know little about. In understanding the origins and initial structure, the significance of organizational choice is important to remember. Despite the constraints of the environment, people may choose quite different structures to pursue their goals. The Rotherham structure was different from that found in other parts of Yorkshire.

Organizational Functioning: Building Consensus

If we look at the Rotherham strike organization purely in terms of its structure, then we may think that it was a bureaucracy, with a network of committees, lines of authority, and the gradual accumulation of rules. But, in fact, this is rather deceptive. An examination of the processes of the organization reveal that it operated in a much more political way. The basis of activity was a set of beliefs and values. Thus politics pervaded the organization as an activity to build and maintain consensus about the strike. In this sense, politics was an activity to affect the organizational culture. It occurred so pervasively to shape the outlooks of potentially disparate parties and to create a relatively unified and disciplined collective force. This takes us back to the roots of trade union activity, since, in order to prosecute the strike effectively, the organization must be cohesive. Both leadership and decision making were directed implicitly to this end. (At least, they can be analyzed in this way). So, it is partly against the criterion of cohesion that these processes must be judged.

Aspects of politics—consensus—mobilization are evident throughout the case. They can be seen in the permeable boundaries of the RSC, in the ideological barriers to participation at the core of the strike, in the similar views held by RSC members (or a corresponding lack of attention to those who held divergent views), in the adherence to a strategy and a means of implementation regardless of effectiveness of that in meeting the task goals. Further, throughout the case, we see examples of symbols, values, norms, and shared meanings being displayed. The power of the consensus is seen in the failure of either criticism or divergent thinking to gain an effective voice.

The significance of RSC debate for the building of consensus can be seen in the fact that voting in the RSC took place only rarely. During the 13 weeks, there were only four votes taken, and these were never used to develop policy but for symbolic purposes—to communicate to other strike bodies (especially national ISTC) the resolve and determination of the Rotherham organization.

Does the power of consensus mean that the RSC suffered from "group-think" (Janis and Mann 1977)? This is a phenomenon to which cohesive groups are vulnerable, especially in times of crisis. Defensive avoidance is created by the group developing illusions about their invulnerability and hence a restricted range of decision choices is "evaluated" and employed. An inflexible policy is adhered to, despite information from the external environment.

The internal cohesiveness in the RSC and the fervor with which views were held means that the RSC did seem to display some features of group-think. However, that is not the whole story. Divergent views existed—they were simply not heard. Also, administrative decisions did not exhibit inflexibility. So, before making a decision about the existence or not of group-think, it would be wise to consider the effectiveness of the decision making. This has only rarely been undertaken in the decision making literature (Koopman et al. 1984).

It has been traditional to view effectiveness of decision making in terms of its rationality in relation to the task. Given that many organizations fail to display this to any great extent (e.g., Cohen et al. 1972; Hickson et al. 1986), we may need to look for other indicators of effectiveness—for example, implicit goals or the total functioning of the organization rather than just the achievement of its tasks. In this way, it is important that a strike organization is not judged by standards of rationality which even more bureaucratic organizations do not live up to.

In terms of the strategic task it set itself, the Rotherham strike organization was not effective. Steel poured into the country, mass pickets were largely unable to stop plants more than temporarily, the economy was not suffering from a severe shortage of steel.

However, the strike organization was effective in achieving a consensus and commitment to the strike. To keep a strike going for a full 13 weeks is no mean achievement. In addition, there were no strike breakers at all in this period. The attainment of this should not be underestimated when many strikers were severely in debt and vulnerable to information, persuasion, and even hostility by other parties. Further, despite some fall-off in activity, there was a high level of involvement in the strike by pickets. The absenteeism of some should not obscure the considerable efforts of others. Finally, there were no significant splits in the ranks, and, although criticism was voiced, it was not sustained for any length of time. People were largely united about why they were on strike, what they would go back for, and who were the principal protagonists in the strike. Thus, the strike can be seen to have been very successful in certain respects.

There is an increasing recognition that decision making might usefully be considered partly in terms of its success in subduing or incorporating opposition (cf. Hickson et al. 1986). In developing consensus, political, rather than rational, decision making might be a much more effective approach. Coordinating disparate interests in organizations has been an underemphasized part of the literature. It may be more important than has been realized in any organization, but perhaps no more so than in a strike organization where unity is a major source of strength. The importance of the organizational culture may have a strong bearing on the style of decision making.

The value of consensus may be especially salient in the context of a turbulent and hostile environment, where internal weaknesses may be exploited by other parties. Indeed, there may be extra pressures on decision makers to maintain a consistent and unchanging position on external matters, since a change of strategy might signal weakness. In this sense, decision making is not taking place internally only but in the full glare of publicity with the outcomes under scrutiny.

However, we may note a contradiction. Although decision making can be analyzed in terms of its effectiveness in drawing together disparate elements and the development of consensus, the information sought by the RSC did not relate to this. The focus of the data collected and evaluated by the RSC concerned the external environment. Information about consensus such as morale, criticism, and alternative ideas was largely ignored. A contribution to an explanation of this contradiction is discussed in the next section.

Mission and Commitment

Central to the building of consensus in the organization was the strategy, or in this case, the mission of the organization, which was stopping all steel movement. The mission was so strong and commitment to it so great that it influenced decision making as we have seen, and influenced the composition of the RSC leadership. The mission was indeed greater than a mere strategy for the organization. It had a strong and pervasive emotional component.

The mission had further consequences in that the organization could have a flexible structure and the "management' of the organization could be minimal (in terms of the control of subordinates). This was because the basis of strikers' involvement was largely moral rather than calculative or coercive. The strong mission engaged people's hearts.

This is often a feature of voluntary organizations—the basis of people's involvement in their moral commitment means that authority does not need to be very centralized or very strong. However, it can lead to problems of a different kind which is that of "semiautonomous working groups" (of pickets, or other kinds of workers in other organizations). Since commitment inspires activity, it can be hard to control if it happens not to coincide exactly with the leadership's view of appropriate tactics. This happened between the national ISTC leadership and Rotherham, and also between the RSC and some groups of pickets.

I suggested earlier that the democracy dilemma might be heightened in a strike, with the need for unity and leadership and the need for involvement coexisting and creating tensions for the organization. the environment of the strike organization has been seen, in this case, to be creating strong pressures for both. The tension has been partially resolved through the flexible structure. The permeable boundaries, the changing roles, the relationships between the committees (although not described here) all gave a flexibility which many more permanent, less crisis-oriented organizations might find hard to match. The organization was essentially organic, with structures being used to pursue tasks in a fast-changing environment. It was possible to achieve this flexibility through the members' commitment to the mission.

However, there seemed to be a trade-off between consensus, task achievement, and flexibility. It was difficult for the organization to adapt when the mission of the organization became unattainable. Modification of the mission was not easy and indeed was not achieved. This is a feature of many voluntary (and perhaps other) organizations with a powerful mission or internal culture.

The Environment

In this analysis, I have made several references to the environment as turbulent and hostile and a potent force on the organization, constraining choices and inhibiting certain types of change. It is useful to think here in systems terms with the organization interacting with the environment. The environment being the employer, the media, the government, public opinion, other workers, and trade unionists, with the Rotherham organization as the system. The external environment induced in the organization a sense of crisis and turbulence, which affected the initial shape of the organization and the flexibility which it subsequently developed. The environment also powerfully shaped the dogged consistency to the position about stopping steel movement and picketing since change might have signalled weakness to the opposition. However, the environment was not deterministic in the shape or operation of the Rotherham strike organization, as has been noted in comparison to other steel strike organizations. It remains to be seen how far other crisis-induced organizations show the mixture of flexibility and rigidity shown here.

IMPLICATIONS FOR THE ANALYSIS
OF OTHER STRIKES

The case study of a temporary, voluntary organization suggests that the four features described above may be important in other voluntary or temporary organizations. The origins, the functioning, the mission and the commitment base, as well as the impact of the environment may all affect the organization, especially as regards the crucial organizational processes of leadership and decision making.

I would suggest that the organizational processes described in this case are relevant where there is a large or long strike. Certainly these elements were important in the recent miners' strike in Britain. This lasted for a whole year (1984-1985) and initially involved over 100,000 strikers. A number of accounts are available (e.g., Adeney and Lloyd 1986; Beynon 1985) although not from an organizational perspective.

The strike was run at local level (due to the federal structure of the miners' union) although the national leadership of the executive was more prominent than in the steel strike in shaping objectives, policies, and member commitment. Strike committees sprang up in all the coal areas of Britain and were responsible for recruiting and deploying pickets, and for striker welfare. The strike committees were based in the local branch organization although, as with the steel strike, there were some modifications to the structure. For example, there was a strong mining community involvement. Organizational structure had to be adapted to build a temporary organization which included women, who had become involved, as relatives of miners, not only in striker welfare but in picketing duties. Without formal union power, the women nevertheless had a significant influence on local union activities.

The strategy of the local organizations was stopping the use of coal, especially at power stations, and also to prevent strike-breakers. Picketing was the supreme activity for both these aims and generated a lot of commitment, both from the strikers on the ground and from the national leadership. The charisma of the union president was instrumental in generating considerable support initially for this approach to the strike. The mission was maintained even when it became apparent that it was having a contrary effect on working miners and even though it was ineffective in closing power stations. While it appears that internally there was dissent from this policy in the executive, this did not have the effect of changing the overall strategy and tactics.

The maintenance of position, in the face of a changing environment, however, can be seen as contributing to the goal of strike maintenance by building consensus about the strike, its enemies, and goals. Additionally, here as in the steel strike, a change of policy might have been interpreted and used by the strike's opponents as a sign of weakness and defeat. The reluctance of executive members to pursue their criticism of the policy too vigorously may have been due to the awareness both of the danger of changing direction and of a leak of information being exploited to indicate internal strife.

Involvement of strikers in strike activities was demanded by the national leadership, but the demand was not one of formal authority (which was limited by the voluntary nature of involvement) but of moral persuasion and exhortation. This was also true of local leaderships. Coercion and remuneration also played some part but was overshadowed by moral persuasion as a means of encouraging involvement. Working miners did not perceive the argument as persuasive so much as coercive—the commitment of pickets to their task contributed to this in large measure. However, for those on strike, the nature of their involvement in strike activities was essentially voluntary. The tenuous nature of voluntarism in strike participation and even union membership was forcefully brought home to the union leadership when a large segment of miners refused to go on strike and eventually resigned from the union to establish a breakaway trade union. This illustates the democracy dilemma of unions in stark form.

As in the steel strike, we can infer that the striking union existed as a political organization with political decision making and access to the leadership. Maintaining consensus over values and beliefs was a major, if implicit, goal. It was not a method of functioning which appealed to all miners but it was, nevertheless, highly successful in maintaining cohesion and commitment over an astonishingly long period of time.

Wider Implications

The lessons of the steel strike case may be relevant more widely. The steel strike case study has shown an organization where authority cannot be taken for granted and where leadership is shaped both by internal constraints and external pressures. Decision making power apparently lies at the top of the organization but that power is limited to the extent to which the membership are prepared to implement it. Now, it may be that similar processes exist in a wider set of organizations but have not been so recognized by organization theorists (with a few exceptions such as Braverman 1974; Thompson 1983; Pfeffer 1981). Many employing organizations may find leadership, authority, and decision making more problematic than often appears to be the case from many organizational behavior texts (Bryman 1986). The steel strike suggests a need to move away from the study of the formal features of organizations to a greater emphasis on a wider range of informal social processes.

ACKNOWLEDGMENTS

This chapter is based on research undertaken with John Kelly and Nigel Nicholson and described in Hartley et al. (1983). I would like to thank Paul Marginson, John Kelly, and John Coopey for helpful comments on an earlier draft.

REFERENCES

Adeney, M. and J. Lloyd. 1986. *The Miners Strike: Loss without Limit.* London: Routledge & Kegan Paul.

Batstone, E., I. Boraston, and S. Frenkel. 1978. *The Social Organization of Strikes.* Oxford: Blackwell.

Beck, T. 1974. *The Fine Tubes Strike.* London: Stage 1.

Beynon, H. 1985. *Digging Deeper.* London: Verso.

Braverman, H. 1974. *Labor & Monopoly Capital: the Degradation of Work in the Twentieth Century.* London: Monthly Press Review.

Bryman, A. 1986. *Leadership in Organizations.* London: Routledge & Kegan Paul.

Child, J., R. Loveridge, and M. Warner. 1973. "Towards an Organizational Study of Trade Unions." *Sociology* 7:71-91.

Cohen, M., J. March, and Olsen. 1972. "A Garbage-Can Model of Organizational Choice." *Administrative Science Quarterly* 17:1-25.

Crouch, C. 1982. *Trade Unions: The Logic of Collective Action.* London: Fontana.

Cyert, R. and J. March. 1963. *A Behavioral Theory of the Firm.* Englewood Cliffs, NJ: Prentice-Hall.

D10 International Research Group. 1983. "A Contingency Model of Participative Decision Making." *Journal of Occupational Psychology* 56:1-18.

Docherty, C. 1983. *Steel and Steel-workers.* London: Heinemann.

Dromey, J. and G. Taylor 1978. *Grunwick: The Workers' Story.* London: Lawrence & Wishart.

Edwards, P. 1983. "The Pattern of Collective Industrial Action." In *Industrial Relations in Great Britain,* edited by G. Bain. Oxford: Blackwell.

Etzioni, A. 1975. *A Comparative Analysis of Complex Organizations.* rev. ed. Glencoe, IL: Free Press.

Hartley, J., J. Kelly, and N. Nicholson. 1983. *Steel Strike.* London: Batsford.

Hemingway, J. 1978. *Conflict and Democracy: Studies in Trade Union Government.* Oxford: Clarendon Press.

Hickson, D., R. Butler, D. Cray, G. Mallory, and D. Wilson. 1986. *Top Decisions: Strategic Decision making in Organizations.* Oxford: Blackwell.

Hiller, E. 1928. *The Strike.* New York: Arno Press.

Janis, I. and L. Mann. 1977. *Decision making.* New York: Free Press.

Karsh, B. 1982. *Diary of a Strike.* Urbana: University of Illinois Press.

Kelly, J. and N. Nicholson. 1980. "The Causation of Strikes. *Human Relations* 33:853-883.

Klandermans, B. 1986a. "Psychology and Trade Union Participation: Joining, Acting, Quitting." *Journal of Occupational Psychology* 59:189-204.

Klandermans, P.G. 1986b. "Perceived Costs and Benefits of Participation in Union Action." *Personnel Psychology* 39:379-397.

Koopman, P., J. Broekhuysen, and D. Meijn. 1984. "Complex Decision Making at the Organizational Level." *Handbook of Work and Organization Psychology,* edited by P. Drenth, H. Thierry, P. Willems, and C. de Wolff. Chichester: Wiley.

Lane, T. 1974. *The Union Makes Us Strong.* London: Arrow Books.

Lane, T. and K. Roberts. 1971. *Strike at Pilkingtons.* London: Fontana.

Lawrence, P. and J. Lorsch. 1967. *Organization and Environment.* Homewood, IL: Irwin.

Lindblom, C. 1959. "The Science of 'Muddling Through.'" *Public Administration Review* 19:79-99.

McShane, S. 1986. "The Multi-Dimensionality of Union Participation." *Journal of Occupational Psychology* 59:177-188.

March, J. and H. Simon. 1958. *Organizations.* New York: Wiley.

Martin, R. 1968. "Union Democracy: An Explanatory Framework." *Sociology* 2:205-220.

Michel, R. 1962. *Political Parties.* Glencoe, IL: Free Press.

Mintzberg, H., D. Raisinghani, and A. Theoret. 1976. "The Structure of 'Unstructured' Decision Processes." *Administrative Science Quarterly* 21:246-275.

Nicholson, N., G. Ursell, and P. Blyton. 1982. *The Dynamics of White-Collar Unionism.* London: Academic Press.

Pfeffer, J. 1981. *Power in Organizations.* Marshfield, MA: Pitman.

Thompson, P. 1983. *The Nature of Work.* London: Macmillan.

Undy, R., V. Ellis, W. McCarthy, and A. Halmos. 1981. *Change in Trade Unions.* London: Hutchinson.

Upham, M. 1980. "British Steel: Retrospect and Prospect." *Industrial Relations Journal* 121:5-21.

Waddington, D. 1986. "The Ansell's Brewery Dispute. A Social-Cognitive Approach to the Study of Strikes." Journal of Occupational Psychology 59:231-246.

———. 1987. *Trouble Brewing.* Aldershot: Gower.

THE STRUGGLE WITHIN:

CONFLICT, CONSENSUS, AND DECISION MAKING AMONG NATIONAL COORDINATORS AND GRASS-ROOTS ORGANIZERS IN THE WEST GERMAN PEACE MOVEMENT

Joyce Marie Mushaben

> But then are we in order when we are most out of order.
>
> —Shakespeare, *Henry IV*

The "new social movements" have become an integral feature of the political-cultural landscape, gaining in acceptance with each cycle of protest that has sought to transform the foundations of West German democracy since the late 1950s. Studies comparing "old" with "new" protest campaigns reveal that participants in the movements of the 1980s have become more sensitive, if not

International Social Movement Research, Vol. 2, pages 267-298.
Copyright © 1989 by JAI Press Inc.
All rights of reproduction in any form reserved.
ISBN: 0-89232-964-5

more accommodating, to the organizational imperatives of the parliamentary system (Brand 1982; Mushaben 1985; Raschke 1985). Activists have learned from earlier movements that if they are to effect social change, they must conceive of protest not as a spontaneous outburst of public indignation in response to a faulty government decision, but rather as a complex process of resource mobilization, agenda-building, and social action networking. In recognition of "the system's" enormous capacity for manipulating the public trust (i.e., through the media), social movement organizers are today finding it necessary to professionalize their own structures of communication and decision making. The political and managerial sophistication evinced by members of the Coordinating Committee (*Koordinierungsausschuss*) for the West German peace movement, along with their demonstrated success in mobilizing the largest protest coalition ever witnessed in the Federal Republic, transcends the orthodox notion that "the movement is a state of mind" (Freeman 1983, p. 2) or merely a "belief which redefines social action" (Smelser 1962, p. 8). Possessing the "right consciousness" will not automatically result in the spontaneous uprising of the masses intent on radical system transformation (as Marxists and Maoists once presumed). For many of the key activists, protest—like politics—has become a vocation, in accordance with which their social movements are turning (in)to professional organizations.

Certainly a hybrid among the West European peace movement organizations, the evolution, experiences, and effectiveness of the Coordinating Committee (CC), appear to challenge conventional theories about protest mobilization in at least three other important respects. At issue are presumptions about the positive versus the negative effects of (a) movement "institutionalization," (b) movement continuity in relation to personnel and objectives, and (c) the role of factional or intraorganizational conflict. These three aspects of social movements organization (SMO) provide the theoretical parameters for this essay.[1]

Representative of mainstream thinking with regard to the first point is Rammstedt's (1978) argument that groups comprising a social movement are under constant pressure to change; they perceive the current state of affairs as temporary, even if they lack the ability to predict or alter the movement's course themselves. "The movement must be kept moving in constant acceleration, must constantly effect changes" (1978, p. 128). Rammstedt equates formal organization, routinization, the increasing professionalism of activists at the movement's center, and eventual adaptation to the dominant social structures with a "standing still" that inevitably brings the movement's demise. In short, the ideal-typical "end" of every social movement is the phase of institutionalization. I argue in the case of the West German peace movement that formal organization and professionalization processes at the national level compelled grass-roots incentives to undertake similar steps which, in fact, served to sustain and strengthen the movement as a whole; similarly, its adaptation to, and at least partial internalization of, formal parliamentary-democratic values and processes have *saved* the movement from sure and sudden death.

Focusing on the significance of continuity for movement identity, Freeman (1983, p. 4) contends that the "people in movements may change, and the objectives may change, but if both of these factors change, it is not the same movement." Continuity is thus defined in terms of persons or objectives, not in terms of some transcending dynamic. As a collective, interactive social phenomenon dedicated to the fundamental transformation of national security policy and regional defense structures, the West German peace movement represents a convergence of social protest currents that precludes identification of permanent-core participants or exclusive objectives. Yet the "peace movement" is perceived by most as being firmly rooted in the antiarmament/radical democratization campaigns of the 1950s and 1960s (Knorr 1983; Mushaben 1986; Otto 1977; Rupp 1970), the consciousness of which has afforded important "learning experiences" for organizers of the 1980s even though the same actors or goals are not necessarily involved (Buro 1982). My contention with regard to recent and future peace mobilization efforts at the national level is that "continuity" thus defined has served the cause but, in critical respects, has outlived its usefulness. As insistence on allowing the same personalities to determine future strategies or on limiting the campaign's objectives to those adopted in 1981-1984 will likely precipitate the very historical "break" that mobilizers hope to avoid during the second half of the decade.

In relation to the third theme, factionalization is engraved all too often as the "cause of death" upon the tombstones of protests past in the graveyard of SMOs. Internal factionalization can begin to plague an SMO at many different stages in its development; it becomes fatal during the phase where the movement has failed to attain an immediate objective judged critical to its overall strategy. As a massive wave of resignation washes over participants and sympathizers, protest tends to transform itself internally. Less committed or strategically moderate groups may drop out, and "the protest process not only radicalizes itself, as protest becomes an ongoing, escalating questioning of the existing system of domination; it also concurrently rejects the possibility of a compromise" (Rammstedt 1978, pp. 131-132). Intramovement or group conflict is viewed as a disruptive, destructive force, with few exceptions throughout the organization theory literature. I argue, it is not the existence of ostensibly irreconcilable ideological positions per se but rather peace organizers' (in)ability to find appropriate channels for airing and processing conflicts that determines whether it becomes a destructive or a creative force for the movement. The German case allows for a consideration of "conflict" as a mobilization resource in its own right.

The chapter begins with a brief description of the overarching political "spectra" and the fusion of social movements represented in the CC since its founding. It then provides a chronology of key events relative to the evolving functions of the CC, its Executive Committee (EC), and the broader-based Action Conferences (AC). The third segment focuses on the consensus-building and conflict-management orientations that gradually established themselves as standard operating procedures. The fourth section addresses the more important strengths and weaknesses of the CC as in SMO, and offers a few personal reflections on the prevailing political culture of power among the peace movement ranks. The conclusion returns to the questions of institutionalization, continuity, and conflict in relation to future mobilization tasks and capacities. These findings derive from experiences and interview data collected by this author as a participant observer of peace movement developments from July 1983 to January 1984, as well as from follow-up interviews conducted in the Federal Republic from November 1985 to March 1986.

THE COORDINATING COMMITTEE:
CALL TO ACTION AND PREPOLITICIZED FRONTS

The West German peace movement encompasses a kaleidoscope of formal organizations, "citizen initiatives," affinity groups, prominent and not-so-prominent agitators and supporters. Its ranks include 20-30 year verterans, whose antiarmament engagement dates back to the early 1950s, 10-year activists schooled in the student and antinuclear energy movements of the 1960s and 1970s, as well as relative newcomers to the protest scene recruited during the 1980s. Professing membership in the protest coalition are many other SMOs whose primary causes are judged integrally related to the peace issue: feminists, religious laiety and clergy, conscientious objectors, and antinuclear energy groups; punks, squatters, and elements from the "alternative culture" scene; a mixed showing of Old Left, Old Right (conservationists), New Left and Eco-Left cadres; occupationally-linked initiatives (athletes, lawyers, scientists, teachers, nurses, psychologists, and the like), and trade unions; youth organizations, party-political committees, Third World solidarity groups, human rights organizations, and even retired *Bundeswehr* generals. The sole criterion for membership was articulated by Erhard Eppler at the October 1981 demonstration in Bonn, the movement's first mass mobilizational success: "The peace movement will only become capable of mustering a majority when it does not exclude but rather open itself. To this movement belongs everyone who wants to belong to it" (Deile 1981, p. 116).

The catalyst triggering the most recent cycle of German peace protest was the NATO Double-Track Decision of December 12, 1979 opting to deploy 108 Pershing II and 96 ground-launch cruise missiles within the borders of the already nuclear-dense Federal Republic (Mushaben 1985). The completion of the Pershing deployments sounded the deathknell for the (admittedly negative) "minimal consensus" kneading together a panoply of ideological factions and "Eco-pax" initiatives in the face of incredible odds. Best labelled the phase of "manifest latency," developments since 1984 have revolved around a search for a positive, longer-range consensus that will enable the constituent parts to work cohesively towards the reduction of existing arsenals and the adoption of alternative defense concepts.

The peace movement's (PM) kaleidoscopic character notwithstanding, a multitude of participating groups have aligned themselves over the last five years with one of six political spectra that emerged and crystallized with the birth of the CC itself. Its 30 member organizations (26 until 1984) are at best *broadly* representative of the estimated 4,000 grass-roots groups (known as "the Base") found at the local and regional levels. As individual delegates repeatedly stress, however, "The Coordination Committee is not the peace movement," no matter how often the media incorrectly attempt to equate the two (personal interview with Schöffman, March 1, 1986). The member organizations, classified according to their primary constituency type or task domain, are listed in Table 1. Figure 1 denotes each group's affiliation with a particular partisan or ideological spectrum.

According to the CC's own classification, the primary spectra include:

1. The Christians, who actually encompass all religious denominations, stressing nonviolence and reconciliation with the former victims of fascism.
2. The Independents, whose ranks include everything from strictly nonviolent antimilitarists, humanists, feminists, and Third World solidarity groups, to the occasionally violent, oft-masked "Autonomous Ones," support civil disobedience and advocate German withdrawal from NATO.
3. The KOFAZ wing, whose adherents are affiliated with but not necessarily card-carrying members of the Communist party (DKP), stress antifascism, anti-imperialism, and "peaceful coexistence."
4. The Social-Democrats, with a strong youth contingent, call for a return to the détente policies of the early 1970s, favoring disarmament and "ABC"-free zones (atomic, bacteriological, chemical).
5. The ecologist and liberal groups, with a base of over 800 "citizen initiatives" for environmental protection, usually fused their own ecopeace aims with the social-democratic postures—owing to the overlapping memberships of their key spokesperson.
6. The Greens, ecological, socially responsible, grass-roots-democratic and nonviolent in orientation, advocate German withdrawal from NATO and the dissolution of military blocks. (Owing to personality conflicts, Green CC members coalesced more often with Independents than with their "logical" ally, the ecologist spectrum, through 1984.)

Table 1. CC-Member Organizations According to
Primary Constituency, Activity Field, or Task Domain

POLITICAL PARTIES OR PARTY-AFFILIATES (10)

Die Grünen	The Greens
Liberale Demokraten (LD)	Liberal Democrats
Demokratische Sozialisten (DS)	Democratic Socialistis
Arbeitsgemeinschaft	Task Force Social Democratic
Sozialdemokratische Frauen (ASF)[a]	Women
Jungsozialisten (Jusos)	Young Socialists
Jungdemokraten (JD)	Young Democrats
Sozialistische Jugend Deutschlands	Socialist Youth of Germany-
-Die Falken (SJD)	The Falcons
Sozialistische Deutsche	Socialist German Worker Youth
Arbeiterjugend (SDAJ)	
Initiative für Frieden,	Initiative for Peace, international
internationalen Ausgleich und	Balance and Security
Sicherheit (IFIAS)	
Komitee für Frieden, Abrüstung und	Committee for Peace, Disarmament
Zusammenarbeit (KOFAZ)	and Cooperation

CHRISTIAN AND RELIGIOUS GROUPS (6)

Aktion Sühnezeichen/	Action Reconciliation/
Friedensdienste (AS/Fd)	Peace Services
Aktionsgemeinschaft Dienst	Action Community Service
für den Frieden (AGDF)	for Peace
Evangelische Studentengemeinschaft	Evangelical (Lutheran)
(ESG)	Students Association
Initiative Kirche von Unten (IK)	Initiative Church from Below
Aktion "Ohne Rüstung Leben" (ORL)	Action "Live without Weapons"—
Pax Christi (PC)	Pax Christi

YOUTH ASSOCIATIONS (3)

Deutscher Gewerkschaftsbund-	German Trade Union Federation-
Jugend (DGB-J)[b]	Youth Group
Bundesschülervertretung (BSV),	Federation of School Representatives
formerly KdLSV	
Vereinigte Deutsche	Association of German
Studentenschaften (VDS)	Student Governments

COORDINATING, CONFEDERATED OR CLEARING-HOUSE GROUPS (3)

Koordinationsstelle Ziviler	Coordination Office for
Ungehorsam (KZU)[a]	Civil Disobedience
Bundeskonferenz unabhängiger	Federal Conference of
Friedensgruppen (BUF), formerly BAF	Independent Peace Groups
Föderation Gewaltfreier	Federation of Nonviolent
Aktionsgruppen (FÖGA)	Action Groups

(continued)

Table 1. *(continued)*

FEMINIST GROUPS (2)

Anstiftung Frauen für den Frieden (AFfF)	Activating Women for Peace
Frauen in die Bundeswehr-Wir sagen Nein! (FiB-Nein)	Women in the Military—We say NO!

PERSONAL MEMBERSHIP GROUPS (2)

Gustav Heinemann Initiative (GHI)	Gustav Heinemann Initiative
Komitee für Grundrechte und Demokratie (KfGD)	Committee for Basic Rights and Democracy

ECOLOGY MOVEMENT (1)

Bundesverband Bürgerinitiativen Umweltschutz (BBU)	Federation of Citizen Initiatives for Environmental Protection

CONSCIENTIOUS OBJECTORS (1)

Deutsche Friedensgesellschaft-Vereinigte Kriegsdienstverweigerer (DFG-VK)	German Peace Society-United War Service Resisters

ANTIFASCISTS (1)

Vereinigung der Verfolgten des Nazi-Regims—Bund der Antifaschisten (VVN-BdA)[a]	Association of Victims of the Nazi Regime-Organization of Antifascists

THIRD WORLD SOLIDARITY (1)

Bundeskongress entwicklungspolitischer Aktionsgruppen (BUKO)	Federal Conference of Political Development Action Groups

Notes: [a] acquired official membership status in December, 1984.
 [b] observer status
Source: Adapted from Leif (1985)

Status and power differentials were present and obvious within the CC from the start. They have been modified or intensified by specific developments in the movement as a whole or by the nature of the issues confronting the CC as a subset thereof; many have persisted up to the present. What determined the actual "power-position" of each individual organization, as well as the nature and degree of influence exercised, was not the ostensible homogeneity or numerical strength of its respective constituency but rather the organizational image and discipline of each. In particular, it was the degree of protest experience, procedural savvy and public recognition accrued by specific personalities that weighted and reinforced the internal balance of

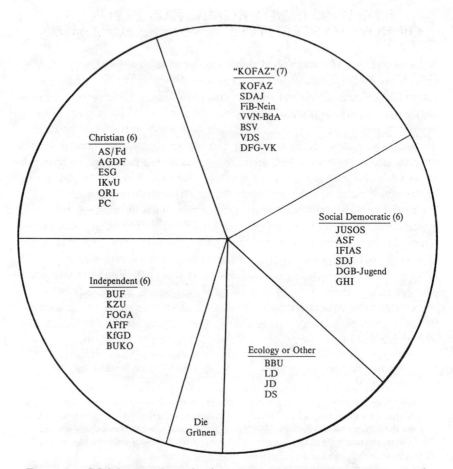

Figure 1. CC-Member Organizations According to Political Orientation[a]

Note: [a] Loosely-defined; does not preclude other coalition possibilities.
Source: Adapted from Leif (1985, pp. 24-30).

power—and contributed to the CC's unprecedented influence vis-à-vis the movement as a whole up to 1984. While not *all* national, regional, and local peace initiatives were adequately represented by this body, the general assessment by members is that 60-70% found *some* representation within the six spectra and among their respective delegate organizations.

Compared with the bitter factionalization characteristic of the late 1960s and the sometimes violent protest turbulence of the early 1970s, the CC's extraordinary success in masterminding a nonviolent mass-mobilization in the millions 1981-1983 merits it a place in the SMO history books as an organizations-theoretical *Wunderkind,* its mistakes and frailties notwithstanding.

"S/HE WHO IS NOT AGAINST US, IS FOR US" OR HOW TO STRUCTURE A NONORGANIZATION

A social movement committed simultaneously to the internal application of grass-roots-participatory principles and the democratic transformation of external political institutions faces a unique organizational dilemma. No social movement can long survive without some form of leadership; nor can it move beyond "spontaneous" protest activity without an identifiable infrastructure to facilitate communication among participant groups. Freeman (1983) suggests that groups must be "linked" if protest is to become generalized and its social base expanded. Linkage functions tend to accrue to "higher level" bodies which claim to have a capacity for presenting "the big picture."

On the other hand, hierarchy, centralized decision making by elites, legitimation by procedure, cooptation, and power-politics are themselves targets of the movement, whether one's own or the system's actors are under review. Hence, judgments about SMO "effectiveness" are subject to two different sets of criteria, one internal, the other external. What happens when a movement's internal structure is simultaneously supposed to avoid "bureaucracy," foster community, avoid specialized roles, allow for tactical flexibility, and personalize concern, while pressurizing the establishment into new policies? As Davidson (1983, pp. 165, 173) discerns, the thrust

> is to routinize, limit uncertainty, increase predictability, centralize functions and control
> .... Typical evaluations of organizational effectiveness such as stability, productivity, and
> adaptability to external environments are only partially applicable to social units
> emphasizing social change, individual actualization, and community .... Though they
> play the organization game by new rules, the alternatives interact with traditional
> organizations which do not .... and they face problems in determining how independent
> they might be of this external environment.

To resist formalization and professionalization is to sacrifice effectiveness and adaptiveness in relation to the external political "targets." The SMO must permit "enough" centralization of structure and create "sufficient" linkages to the external environment that will enable it to enhance its bargaining position without coopting its goals. A less formalized structure, that is, one resembling the decentralized, segmented, reticulate model advanced by Gerlach (1971), seems better suited to servicing SMO-internal needs. A movement held together not by a central control organ but rather by virtue of a network of personal relationships and nonofficial decisional structures enhances the freedom of individual members to define and design the nature of their own involvement; this, in turn, is expected to internalize and intensify their commitment. Of course, determining how much formalization is "enough" or "too much" for a particular movement is inevitably a trial-and-error process.

Not just any linkage system will do. A key prerequisite to effective mobilization is a communications network "that is *cooptable* to the new ideas of the incipient movement, . . . composed of like-minded people whose backgrounds, experiences, or location in the social structure make them receptive" to the new movement (Freeman 1983, p. 9). Personal skill, the compatibility of core groups, and a fertile issue-field are necessary but not sufficient conditions for movement success unless properly combined. For a three-year period at least, German coordinators managed to maintain a productive, though hardly perfect, balance among the three. The following subsections illustrate the degree to which personal skill occasionally got in the way of group compatibility, while an expanding issue-field led into an increasing reliance on role delegation, structural differentiation, and acceptance of a common set of decision-making procedures. In short, the result was an institutionalization that worked but that nobody claimed to want, the pillars of which are the three organs depicted below.

CC—Prototype: The "Bonn Breakfast Club"

Inspired by the "Stop the Neutron Bomb" campaign initiated in The Netherlands (Klandermans and Oegema 1984), two key individuals from the Aktion Sühnezeichen/Friedensdienste (As Fd) and the Aktionsgemeinschaft Dienst für den Frieden (AGDF) (Ulrich Frey and Volkmar Deile) issued a personal invitation to representatives of 22 organizations shortly after the 1981 Hamburg German Protestant Church Convention to discuss the possibility of cooperation with other European peace groups. Meeting informally over a bite to eat at the AGDF's "home" in Bonn, most of the participants were personally acquainted via involvement in earlier/other protest movements. In retrospect, those who assembled maintain that it was never their intention to establish a planning body with firm membership. Rather, it was assumed that each organization would take on a specific preparatory responsibility on an ad hoc or rotating basis, that is, different organizational sponsors and recruiters for each demonstration.

They agreed to convene again in July and August to schedule and plan peace actions for the autumn of 1981. To facilitate discussion in view of time pressures, invitations were circulated requesting that interested organizations send no more than one representative each; delegates from 95 groups attended the July meeting. Invitations to the August session were issued to 340 groups that had already undersigned the "Call to Action" (preformulated by the "Breakfast Club") for the October demonstration, again with the on-delegate-only proviso. Participants focused on the selection of key speakers, plans for a "cultural program" to accompany the "demo" and exchanged information about locally-planned actions. Criticism against the "two dozen functionaries" began to percolate in "independent" circles as news of the two meetings and their outcomes spread. Some 30 initiatives proclaiming their own "base" status protested their "exclusion" from the planning and staged a mid-September countermeeting.

Inclusive or not, the October 10, 1981 demonstration was a success that left the primary coordinators "literally dancing in the streets" (personal interview with Deile, January 6, 1986) once the crowd of 300,000 disspelled. The "Breakfast Club" rejected appeals by some groups to assume a primary coordinators' role throughout the fall, but as Ronald Reagan's visit linked to the June 1982 NATO summit in Bonn drew nearer, there was a perceived need for further small-group discussion in an atmosphere of relative trust, as intergroup differences rapidly emerged. Details were hammered out for the first "AC" of February 1982 in Bonn with the aim of promoting discussion of "action models." Efforts were made to incorporate more "autonomous" elements; roughly 600 delegates from 252 groups brought along 50 "action models," ranging from proposals for peace camps, tax boycotts, to designs for nuclear-free zones, and actions against NATO maneuvers. Moderators rejected efforts to have the CC adopt definitive or binding "policy" resolutions. Discussions in the ad hoc workgroups was particularly heated over what stand the peace movement (FB) ought to assume regarding contemporary political developments, for example, the Polish crisis.

A round of phone calls brought together representatives from 25 organizations in February to organize an Extraordinary Action Conference to "ensure the peace movement's presence" during the NATO summit. The 800 delegates in attendance at the April Conference in Bad-Godesberg hotly debated the text of the proclamation for the June rally, unable to reach a common position on Poland, Afghanistan, and relations with the unofficial German Democratic Republic (GDR) peace movement (the last item would become a permanent source of dissention). The AC resolved to accept 17 organizations as the ex officio sponsors (AS/Fd declined). It moreover created two organs to oversee the June preparations, a Coordinating Committee and an Executive Committee (*Geschäftsführung*).

The newly-formed CC met the day after the Extraordinary Conference to define its own role, as follows:

1. It would assume primary organizational and political responsibility for preparation of the June "demo" with decision-making capability.
2. It appointed to the EC delegates from six organizations who would represent the CC in external dealings with state authorities, the media, and so on.
3. It arranged for office space, equipment, and a budget, each member organization depositing DM 500 into a common account.
4. It worked out a "speaker's principle" for the demonstration ("less is more").
5. The CC agreed on six substantive points for discussion in a press conference to be conducted by the EC.

Each EC organization named one to two staff workers who moved into a rented office in central Bonn which by May "was functioning well but in need of more equipment." The CC met five times prior to the NATO summit. The best empirical gauge of its mobilizational effectiveness was the June 10, 1982 turnout: An estimated 500,000 attended the Bonn demonstration, some 70-80,000 rallied to the cause in Berlin (Weidmann and Meyer 1982). Frey and Deile scheduled another "small circle" meeting for late August ("by personal invitation only") to consider options for future peace work. The "breakfast cartel," consisting then of 20 men and 3 women, came to be recognized—or at least publically labelled—as the hardcore of the *Friedensbewegung,* representing a total of 265 organizations.

The same group came together in January, February, and March to formulate a "minimal statement" for the year ahead, to discuss operational procedures for enhancing mobilizational effectiveness, and to plan for the Third Action Conference (April) in Köln. The inner-circle organizations were asked to provide thematic working papers for these meetings; prospective participants in the Third AC subsequently received a five-page "Statement of Principles" paper, including contrasting positions, mailed with an invitation listing 30 planners by name. Before it could address the main agenda theme, namely, plans for the "Hot Autumn" antideployment protests, the AC was called upon to endorse the 26 organizations who had been involved in coordination from the start for ex officio CC membership. The membership structure prevailed as proposed, because it was supported by the most influential groups—DFG-VK, KOFAZ, BBU, AS/Fd, AGDF (refer to Table 1), and the Social Democrats. The structure worked, in fact, because the individuals at the core knew each other so well, some acquaintanceships dating back 10-12 years (Leif 1985). At this point in its development, the PM could rely upon the personal skill factor to override both group and issue incompatibilities.

The Coordination and Executive Committees:
Formalizing Procedures and Functions

Ten days prior to the June 1982 demonstration, the acting CC resolved that its future meetings would be "open to the peace movement public;" both the frequency and location of subsequent meetings nonetheless put limits on the practice. The delegates who assembled for the first time in May 1983 perceived this CC as a newly-constituted organization, *not* as the legal successor to the 1982 coordinating body. At the high-point of its activity, the CC would have at its disposal 16 advisory work groups, 25-30 staff members and three telephones (eventually tapped by the Federal Chancellor's Office and the Office for Constitutional Protection). Operating out of a "hopelessly full and excessively noisy" new office on the outskirts of Bonn, it distributed 10,000 copies of a 16-20 page newsletter, produced more or less monthly, along with shorter "info" supplements prior to specific events. The CC met 26 times between May 1983 and June 1984 (biweekly) in Bonn. Its character changed considerably following the Autumn Actions and general demobilization of 1984; this owed in part to a conscious decision by the Christian spectrum to abstain from mass actions in favor of grass-roots work. After January 1985, it moved to a much smaller office in central Bonn, staffed by a single, paid, full-time worker.

Neither the CC members nor AC participants evinced strong interest in debating a lasting structure for movement coordination; communication and decision-making procedures were not created, they evolved. Formal work groups set up to consider organizational alternatives attracted few participants. The 1983 CC was established "exclusively to perform tasks of a temporally limited nature," namely to prepare for the October "Action Week" protests (Leif 1985, p. 84).

In May, the CC nonetheless adopted a resolution on "The Organizational Structure for the Autumn Activities of 1983," which defined its own formal competence, limited the functions of the Executive, and laid down basic operational procedures. In this so-called "Principles Paper," the CC assigned itself supraregional responsibility. It would:

a) manage the program, organization, technical equipment, traffic, and stage arrangements for the "Days of Resistance;"
b) distribute invitations and collect signatures supporting the October "Call to Action;"
c) design and produce central materials (buttons, posters) and publish a federal newsletter;
d) consult on financial matters;
e) faciliate contacts with different program organizers and foreign peace movements;
f) provide legal advice and services;
g) rent and staff its own office (based on a DM 300-500 contribution from each member organization), and meet at least monthly; and
h) develop work groups to advice the CC on tactics and to help implement CC resolutions.

Further,

1. All "currents" or representatives were to enjoy "equal" status.
2. All members would accept the "Call" paper as the basis for the fall activities.
3. All actions would be of a nonviolent, peaceful nature.
4. All CC and AC resolutions would be binding on the CC and staff.

5. The CC would pursue an open relationship with the police and state authorities.

6. Members would reject or postcribe attempts to reach a decision by overriding or ignoring minority positions within the CC ranks. Instead it would seek broad consensus on all central decisions.

The paper stressed national/grass-roots division of labor as depicted in Figure 2—responsibility for regional events would be borne by independent preparation bodies. CC functions were to be of a consultative character, for example, promoting discussion, communication, exchange of information, and resolving conflicts between regional groups. The CC stood as a service organ and channel for articulation; lacking direct-democratic legitimation it could not impose political obligations on the whole/parts of the PM, nor could it exercise political functions vis-à-vis the external environment.

Composed of the institutional *crème de la crème* (AS/Fd, BBU, BUKO, DFG-VK, AFfF, VDS, [refer to Table 1]), the Executive brought together a concentration of organizational influence, public recognition, plus many years of political experience and commitment. This combination allowed the EC's "political professionals" (those with years of protest experience) to define their role in spite of ostensible formal limitations. Its delegated tasks were to:

a) give form to the agenda for CC meetings and Action Conferences;
b) guarantee communication and the flow of information within the movement through the CC;
c) formulate preliminary papers, answer inquiries, produce newsletters, and coordinate the work groups;
d) cultivate contacts with the media and other external organizations;
e) politically monitor CC office work;
f) direct finances and revenue-generation.

The Executive's real power lay in the preparation of materials for discussion and in its direct contacts with the media. In theory, all press releases required CC clearance, but this did not prevent the emergence of "media stars," a constant source of irritation from within. The EC and CC sought "transparency" by inviting the media to CC meetings; what it could not control was who got filmed/how often. The "personalization of leadership" did not occur on the basis of over 28 collective, nameless press releases issued between May and December; rather, it resulted from the media's penchant for charismatic, articulate personalities, for example, Jo Leinen, 'the man every mother would love to see as her son-in-law" (personal interview with Deile, January 6, 1986). The CC's own ambivalence towards its executive organ probably added to the EC's influence; member opinions fluctuated between "you know best" and "never trust a professional;" the EC overstepped its

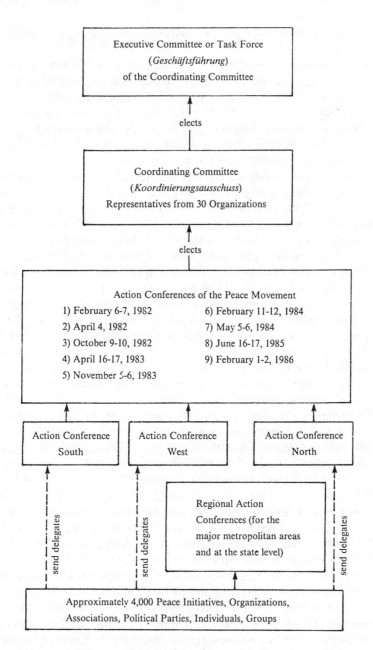

Figure 2. Structure of Representation and Decision Making
(In the West German Peace Movement)

Source: Adapted from Leif (1985, p. 254).

functions because the need for CC control was not recognized early enough. By December 1983 the Executive had generated a "negative coalition" among CC members; harshest critics were the Greens and Independents. It was, therefore, dissolved after a heated, protracted debate at the year's end, replaced by a Task Force (ironically, with more or less the same, albeit slightly expanded, membership) for the June 1984 "People's Referendum" (*Volksbefragung*) campaign. The latter, however, had neither the "clearinghouse" capabilities, nor was it as "publically effective" as the former. Consequently, a new Executive was voted into existence in July 1984.

The CC faced its first internal consensus test in August 1983 pertaining to acts of violent protest against, the then Vice-President, Bush's visit to Krefeld. For the first time, all members were compelled to discuss the use of physical force (*Gewaltfrage*) in concrete terms, placing the credibility and self-image of individual organizations on the line. The CC formally and collectively declared its commitment to nonviolent action, while charging the government with defamation and provocation (Mushaben 1986). (Correctly) anticipating a groundswell of criticism from independent "base" groups, it nonetheless significantly qualified its own role: "We deny anyone the right to define who or what the peace movement is in this land. Even the Coordinating Committee for the autumn actions can only speak for the organizations represented therein, and not for the peace movement as a whole" (CC Press release and Resolution, June 28, 1983).

The CC passed its second critical consensus test with less than flying colors a mere two weeks before its largest rally ever set for October 22, 1983. Over a two-month period, members had been unable to reach agreement on whom to invite as the keynote speaker. Each organization nominated two candidates based on two criteria: The speaker would have to express his/her unqualified opposition to deployments and support withdrawal from the deterrence system. The final decision was tabled several times in the hopes that a consensus would emerge, as had been the case with other highly controversial topics; by early October, the CC began to experience organizational overload, as more and more conflicts began to backlog under imminent "activity pressure." After almost two hours of negotiations between the EC members and Social Democratic Party (SPD) chief executives, the CC majority settled on Willy Brandt, whose actual speech and qualified opposition was a major disappointment to all and left a residual of bitterness among Greens and Independents.

Having successfully mobilized 1.5-2 million supporters, but unable to block the arrival of the missiles, the movement's greatest fear over the following months was that it would "quietly disappear with a whimper or end with a big bang," for example, through violent resistance (*Die Zeit*, December 2, 1983). No longer held together by the "urgency factor" or a "minimal consensus" after the Bundestag's November vote to deploy, the CC faced an existential crisis. Personal exhaustion and "burn-out" exacerbated an already tense atmosphere, publicized ad hominem attacks (e.g., against Leinen) multiplied. The AS/Fd proposed a move away from "actionism" and tried to stimulate discussion of longer-term perspectives with papers on the "Re-Formation and Structure of Tasks for the CC," on "War Fighting Strategies and NATO" *inter alia*. Endorsement for the "People's Referendum" and the "Mass Resistance to War Service" campaigns for June 1984 and beyond was halfhearted and hardly unanimous. The Executive was dissolved, conflict over relations with independent peace groups in the East and reactions to Soviet counterdeployments resurfaced and intensified. The grass-roots, meanwhile, evinced signs of radicalization, as Leinen noted: "The groups on-site are much more action-happy and ready for action than we judged them to be here" (Minutes from the October 28, 1983 CC meeting).

The role of the "Base" in the CC, as represented by the Independent spectrum, had nonetheless taken a peculiar turn. First joining the CC ranks in 1983, BUF (refer to Table 1) delegate, Dieter Schöffmann, declared, "one thing is certain, we reject in principle the structure of the Coordinating Committee and are working to create a structure on the basis of regional associations" (cited in Leif 1985, p. 202). As the group proposing the November "Beisieging of the Bundestag" BUF's speaker warned, "we will organize and carry it out even if we don't get a majority," in a shift "from protest to resistance" (cited in Leif 1985, p. 206).

Later developments rendered this position untenable, however; they also conveyed the critical lesson that mobilizational effectiveness depends upon the extent and intensity of collective consensus, which is the functional equivalent of group compatibility. A demonstrated lack of agreement regarding plans for major "actions," particularly those of a more radical nature, resulted in a reduced degree of mobilization. The "Besieging" effort and autonomous groups' declared intention to violate the "one-mile no-protest zone" surrounding official government buildings produced a turnout of only 3,000. Reaction to the referendum proposal supported by the Christian, Social Democratic, and KOFAZ (refer to Table 1) spectra ranged "from crass rejection to euphoric affirmation," 70% of the February 1984 Conference voting for, 30% against. Key personalities attempting to advertise actively for the event found little media resonance. The results were nonetheless impressive: some 58% of the citizens (5 million) who came out for the European Parliament elections in June at over 18,000 voting locales cast a second ballot, 87% of whom rejected the Pershing II and cruise deployments outright. A third proposal for a national War Service Refusal campaign was accepted by 80%, opposed by 20% of the AC delegates. While Independents' active opposition to the referendum was "crippling," support for the refusal was widespread but passive, also true of other spectra. The third campaign found no media resonance and few organizations willing to assume active responsbility for its execution.

Hence, group consensus regarding the besiegement was *limited but intense;* with respect to the referendum, consensus was *relatively broad* and of *moderate intensity;* the refusal campaign generated *wide acceptance* but *little active enthusiasm.* Of the three, only the second combination resulted in a measure of mobilizational success. By May 1984, Schöffmann was "no longer for breaking off with the majority" (Leif 1985, p. 22). Operating from an "established" position from within the CC (and born-again Executive), Schöffmann became a defender of the CC's existence by December 1984, urging and foreswearing "loyalty and unity" among its constituents" (Leif 1985, p. 23). Having adopted the procedural and organizational style manifested by the original CC "heavies," whom they initially sought to depose, the Independents had witnessed a better coming-together of their own ranks. Consequently, grass-roots groups became more optimistic about securing at least a partial adoption of their own agenda by the whole as of 1984.

No longer facing the "action-urgency" characteristic of CC decision making through June 1984, coordinators at the national and local levels, in theory, had time for a systematic reconsideration of existing organizational relationships and long-term objectives. Reacting to significantly lower turnouts at the Autumn 1984 activities, eight member organizations (CC-Resolution and "Compromise Paper" of December 14, 1984) proposed a modification of CC functions:

> In the year 1985 the CC enters a consultation phase. During this consultation phase, the CC will not decide on any actions or Action Conferences, unless as the result of substantive consultations there emerges the necessity and possibility for jointly conducted, successful Action Conferences or activities. For 1985 and in the period thereafter, the CC is to decide on actions and political positions on the basis of consensus.

In practice, however, individual organizations had less incentive to expedite the consensus-building process by voluntarily compromising their own positions. The more abstract or longer-term the questions raised for substantive discussion, the more "principled" and, hence, irreconcilable, the differences between groups and spectra appeared. Further, the more multifaceted the approach to protest strategy and the more organizations seeking formal inclusion in the national coordination structure (a testimonial to its success), the less coordinators could rely on small-group preparations, responsible for the harmonization of positions at the movement's outset. The alternative was to propose formal mechanisms for securing intergroup agreement (CC-Resolution, approved December 14, 1984):

> If consensus cannot be attained, the CC will render a decision based on the following quorum: A proposal is acceptable when it has the majority of CC members and at the same time is not opposed by more than 15% [5 organizations] of the CC.

The results were disappointing, or cynically stated, "the burial was postponed" (*die Tageszeitung,* November 28, 1984). No fundamental reorganization plan was deliberated, nor did the self-imposed "action abstinence" prevent subsequent CC debates from becoming "an exchange of blows based on well-known arguments" (Leif 1985, p. 239). Local and regional groups could no longer expect to be supplied with carefully-prepared position papers and newsletters, a development that was intended to open and intensify a debate of alternative security policies at local and regional levels but, instead, weakened and fragmented the discussion. In retrospect, spokespersons from competing spectra agree that their failure to dissolve the CC itself immediately after the Autumn 1983 mobilizations was a major organizational mistake. Even more grievous, in my judgment, was the failure to decide the CC's fate before the deployments commenced—this compelled the CC to remain in existence so as not to convey the impression of total movement collapse so shortly after its mobilizational climax.

During the formalization phase of PM development, the personal skills of particular CC and EC members lost their "bridging" function and became a barrier to in- and out-group compatibility. I suggest it was the perceived exclusion of the Independent elements, especially, rather than unreconcilable issue positions, per se, that precipitated opposition to professionalization efforts. As representatives of those groups adapted to the carryover of Breakfast-Club methods, interorganizational compatibility at "the top" was secured, at least until the issue-field was split open once deployments began. The problem of issue cleavages was most clearly manifested by developments at the AC level, depicted below.

The "Jewel" of the Movement: Action Conferences

By 1985, the CC was grudgingly recognized at all levels as the only structure capable of carrying out supraregional mobilization tasks. Yet neither the force of individual personalities nor the influential organizations comprising its membership led to the CC's ultimate acceptance. The key legitimizing agent behind its influence over the movement as a whole was its "highest organ," the AC.

Praised by some for its "really revolutionary progress in the direction of grassroots democracy" (Leif 1985, p. 74), the AC, as a forum for strategic deliberation, has been excoriated by others as "the victory of the buttocks over the spirit" (*antimilitarismus informationen,* November 1982). Attempts to encourage participation in the ACs by all mainstream and marginal PM currents could not guarantee their proportional (or even adequate) representation. The problem was not that there were "too many" communists seeking to gain control, but rather that there were "too few" representatives from the "new social movements." Autonomous groups, recently formed citizen initiatives and even the Greens tended to be less well-organized, and already overburdened with local responsibilities, with the result that their representation was usually limited only to executives or hard-core activists.

AC plenary resolutions were to provide political guidelines and to place limitations on the exercise of power by the CC. However, the 4,000 peace initiatives active at the local levels were themselves hard to integrate and control. Directing changes in course and building consensus were very time-consuming processes, as CC members realized all too well. AC delegates had two days at most to deliberate and decide critical questions; consequently, the CC's practice of circulating its own position papers in advance, along with its ability to redistribute financial resources across regions and direct media access, ensured its preponderant influence.

The significance and self-image of the ACs was already established by the time of the first AC in February 1982. The 600 delegates from 252 groups concurred that the PM can be neither a single-issue movement, nor a political party with clearly defined, stable structures representative of all orientations. The ACs importance rest in its quasipublic demonstration of the willingness among a multitude of potentially competitive groups to seek active cooperation. Some 800 participants at the Extraordinary AC of April 4, 1982, in Bad Godesberg imposed a three-fourths majority rule—never again employed—in order to forge a solid consensus regarding the proclamation for the anti-Reagan demonstration. Sharp disagreements over Poland, Afghanistan, and human rights notwithstanding, the final product refuted the myth of the "minimal consensus" (common NO to Pershing IIs): The six-point appeal signalled, in Kelly's words "that we cannot be an anti-missile movement, nor a disarmament movement, rather we must become a demilitarization movement" (Leif 1985, p. 176).

The second AC of October 1982 in Köln bore witness to a further professionalization on the part of national coordinators. The 700 delegates permitted a division of labor by appending themselves to one of 7 "workgroups;" the group on long-term "Goals and Criteria for the Peace Movement," which emphasized the need for a "mutual understanding" on the most important activities for 1982-1983, attracted 150. Key conflicts revolved around ways to expand the minimal consensus and to radicalize the opposition effort. The third AC of April 1983, convened in Köln, saw 850 participants distributed among 11 workgroups; the plenum considered a five-page "concepts paper" circulated in advance with two contrasting positions, intended to prevent the AC from becoming merely an information-exchange or activities board. By the time the fourth AC met in November 1983, again in Köln, 300 Independents found it necessary to hold their own preparatory strategy meeting prior to the plenary session. The polemics, chaos, and booing that occurred among the 1,500 plenum participants indicated that the internal PM power struggle was now in full swing, while the 16 workgroups testified to an ongoing expansion of the protest agenda to replace the "minimal" consensus.

Only 50 Independents met in Köln to conspire for the fifth AC of February 1984. Representatives from five spectra delivered one 20-minute position paper each on 11 key themes to the 1,300 in attendance. The plenum was further presented with a catalogue of eight "common points" for a final vote, a list of seven explicit "points of dissension" intended to promote dialogue, and a package of centralized activity proposals for 1984. A last minute compromise rescued the AC from (what appeared to outside observers) as a state of absolute chaos.

As a result of "too many meetings in too few weeks," only 40 Independents assembled in Köln prior to the sixth AC in May 1984. Plenum participation dropped to 800, divided into five work groups, indicating a loss of momentum. Fifteen CC organizations supplied conference delegates with a "Reader" outlining contrasting positions on NATO membership, as well as a seven-point package for the Autumn Activities of 1984. The Bundestag vote had clearly taken its toll on the movement—resolutions were passed "in a most tense atmosphere, under great time pressure," based on "a power decision rather than a carefully worked out compromise," with "formal majorities reflecting the will of certain political majors" (delegates cited in Leif 1985, pp. 233-234). Changes in the composition of the coordinating body appeared inevitable as it entered the "consultation phase."

A 13-month pause ensued, before 800 delegates felt compelled to reconvene for a major strategy conference in June 1985. Despite the name change, there was little to distinguish this "Great Deliberation" assembly in composition or style from earlier ACs. The plenum approved an activities package for November 1985, consciously rejecting large-scale demonstrations at the regional or national levels. Discussions were hurried: South Africa, Nicaragua, and the Strategic Defense Initiative (SDI) were added to the agenda. A further conference scheduled for December was, in fact, postponed until February 1986.

As the primary legitimizing agent for the less than democratically-constituted CC, the AC could not escape the horns of its own legitimacy dilemma. The key problem facing the ACs was that the peripheral, usually more radical "wing" organizations mobilized most consistently for these meetings. Spokespersons concur that organizations accounting for 5-10% of the movement's supporters supplied one wing with 40% of the delegates, while 5-10% identifying with a second wing provided another 40%; the remaining 20% in attendance represented some 80%, the "independent middle" or mainstream groups. Location and timing reduced the ACs to "peace conferences for the major metropolitan area Bonn-Köon (personal interviews with Deile and Zumach, January 5, 1983 and January 6, 1986). Grass-roots delegates "better at carrying out actions than strong at public speaking" objected to the influence of the routine coordinators who had dominated "the same podium for the last three years and were proud of it" (Leif 1985, pp. 213, 197), through their own influence was hardly proportional to numerical strength at the "Base."

The degree of AC-level consensus that could be attained was subject to fluctuation. Frequently shifting majorities and temporary, albeit effective coalitions astounded outside observers—and no doubt contributed to the survival of the collectivity. The openly aggressive political style, an apparent carryover from the student-movement era, generated a "functionary atmosphere" that stood in stark contrast to the casual familiarity of the Breakfast Club days. As Lenin held, "discussion with 100 people is group-dynamically impossible" (Leif 1985, p. 213). Many grass-roots mobilizers tended to find on-site activity much less stressful and alienating, especially religious and feminist activists. The ACs primary role also changed depending on the external context, as a center for single-action coordination or informational exchange, as a decision-making body, an organ for action-planning and, least successfully, as a conceptualizer or programmer for long-term movement development. I argue that it was not the "minimal consensus" alone that provided the necessary adhesive for collective action during the periods of greatest internal conflict; equally significant was the fact that no single group or spectrum wished to/could afford to go down in the history book of SMOs as the "splitter" of the movement.

The problem of "legitimacy" must also be interpreted as a question of degree, provoking more/less intramovement tension depending on situational factors. By 1984, the AS/Fd (AS/Fd Draft Resolution for the CC meeting of February 29, 1984), adopted a very critical stance:

> It's not a matter of creating a peace parliament, and it is clear that 100% representativeness in regard to the conferences in a movement as variated as the peace movement cannot be achieved without formal membership. But the present circumstances have become untenable. It cannot go on that spectra which are only a minority within the entire peace movement provide 40-60% of the participants at the Action Conferences. In the past this has already resulted in more groups and individuals putting a halt to their participation in the Action Conferences out of sheer frustration.

AS/Fd's proposal to employ a numerical formula for delegate selection (10 from each CC member organization plus 30% from the individual regions and Bundeslander) was nonetheless rejected.

Although all three structures considered above failed to meet the radical-democratic expectations of national and grass-roots activists, regular participants grudgingly agree that "the coalition is the best that we have at this time," and "at this time there is no realistic alternative" (interviews). Hence, a combination of two factors appears to have saved the PM from imminent "death by interorganizational strife," when the continuity of personnel became an irritant and the continuation of the minimal consensus became impossible:

a) the internalization of formal democratic norms and the acceptance of "structure" by CC members; and

b) the internalization of movement-procedural norms by the more "autonomous" AC factions, undertaken in the hopes of acquiring more influence over collective strategic decisions. While both were necessary, neither has proved sufficient for the generation of a long-term, substantive consensus.

Consensus and Conflict Management Principles: Learning by Doing

What tenets and procedures made it possible for such a wide range of groups, many of which were diametrically-opposed in their political fundamentals, to come together, stick together and stabilize a set of effective communication and decision-making structures? Coordinators successfully mobilized the largest protest coalition witnessed in postwar Germany by adopting as their single, most important premise: "common goals must always take precedence over that which divides." Six corollary precepts, reiterated in press releases and summarized here, laid the foundation for what would become standard operating procedures. Throughout 1982, national coordinators consciously eschewed efforts to have either the CC or ACs adopt definitive resolutions beyond the scope of a specific protest activity under the motto "everyone can learn from others." Initially, strict "boundaries were set by an understanding of politics fixed on a minimal consensus" (Weidmann and Meyer 1982, p. 51). The CC was not to be used to build public opinion, nor would the PM be presented as a single-issue movement. A second guiding principle adopted early on held that "common action leads to more togetherness than common papers." The rotation of planning responsibility and integration-through-implementation practices (potentially conflicting groups sharing concrete tasks, for example, the production of newsletters and posters) employed throughout 1983 were critical to mobilizational success; but 1984 turnouts suggest there is a yet-to-be-defined threshold in social movement development where actionism becomes counterproductive if used as a substitute for substantive and strategic conceptualization.

Increasingly hefty controversies over the location and nature of future mobilizations revolved around the ostensibly contradictory desires of movement coordinators to expand the PM's social base, to extend the "minimal consensus" by incorporating new peace-linked issues, and to radicalize or intensify the forms of opposition. The third AC hit upon a compromise formula that allowed for the simultaneous pursuit of all three objectives, while preserving the autonomy and flexibility of the grass-roots vis-à-vis national coordinators: It agreed to targetgroup-specific "days of resistance," thus establishing the third tenet that "expansion and intensification [radicalization] are not possible on the basis of a single action." While ascribing unanimously to the nonviolence principle, national mobilizers left open the prospects for civil disobedience. This provided an incentive to otherwise obstreperous Independent elements to find ways to influence the CC and ACs from within, for which integration and accommodation to the prevailing operational mode proved the most effective vehicles. This compelled more and better organization at the lower levels which occasionally allowed for an upward flow of creativity from the base and a downward transmission of experiences garnered at higher levels.

The single most important mechanism for "minimizing the Against-Each-Other to strengthen the With-Each-Other," the fourth precept, evolved out of the small-group practices of the Breakfast Club turned coordination body. A unique (by German standards) consensus-building process crystallized during the planning for the 1983 Bonn demonstration and was employed regularly thereafter without ever having been formally adopted. If standpoints on a particular issue appeared to be too far apart or controversy too intense, any decision on the matter was tabled until the next meeting. As the practice evolved, those issues likely to result in polarization were usually subjected to a brief discussion of the overarching questions to solicit the spectrum of possible positions, but detailed discussion was postponed. During the intervals between official meetings, delegates would join informal workgroups to hammer out compromise proposals. The integrative function of the Executive was especially important in this regard, as was the role of the AS/Fd which provided a steady flow of written, "decision-ripe proposals."

The most important decisions were filtered through the work-groups in this manner in the hopes of achieving unanimity through cumulative consensus. The procedure nonetheless had two inherent disadvantages as the movement underwent rapid expansion. First, delaying tactics led to a growing backlog of decisions ultimately subject to the "urgency factor," for example, the Brandt invitation, which resulted in a last-minute consensus with backlash effects. Secondly, there was a tendency to confuse a compromise among CC members with consensus within the movement as a whole.

The fifth principle requiring *active cultivation of relations with "the outside,"* especially with the media, generated internal conflict and projected external consensus simultaneously. Select individuals were harshly criticized for violating the rule that no one could speak publicly for "the movement" without an explicit CC mandate. Through regular press releases and press conferences, coordinators attempted to create their own news focus on substantive issues— as opposed to the media's penchant for "happenings." Calls to individual journalists inevitably resulted in a media concentration on specific "personalities." Direct appeals for personal support addressed to prominent ellites or for cooperation with police and state authorities bestowed a degree of respectability and legitimacy upon national coordinators from without, but led to charges of collusion and opportunism from within. This self-conscious, "taking the initiative" approach nevertheless seems to have been more successful than not in expanding the PM's social base and structuring coalition opportunities.

Last but not least, national coordinators recognized the *importance of feedback and self-evaluation* as a basis for future activity planning. The problem with "imminent threats" such as deployments is that they tend to mobilize support that stands 100 kilometers wide but only one centimeter deep for specific protest events. When a specific action-form proves successful, it may be repeated without a thorough analysis of the context contributing to its initial effectiveness. The "human chains" mobilized in 1983 and 1984 stand as concrete examples. CC members sought to avoid such tactical-judgmental errors by convening evaluation sessions within days of their major undertakings, for example, the 1983 "Action Week" and the 1984 Referendum.

Thus, the guiding principles used to promote movement-internal integration invoked methods not usually associated with radical-transformation movements, that is, a combination of interorganizational integration, incremental decision making, and pragmatic implementation. The political savvy and managerial competence of the national coordinators opened the doors to PM participation by established instutitions (parties, churches, unions)—"Base" disgruntlement notwithstanding. In stark contrast to SMOs and protest campaigns of earlier decades, the CC and the AC have evinced an openness to cooperate with any and all potential sympathizers ("s/he who is not against us is for us"); they are extremely self-conscious of their own integrative, potentially innovative role in the debate over German national security policy. Finally, they have recognized and accepted the need to professionalize and democratize their own communication and decision-making structures—as difficult as it may be to reconcile the two processes.

PEACE MOVEMENT ORGANIZATION AND THE POLITICAL CULTURE OF POWER

Neither the division of labor, the allocation of influence nor the structure of authority characteristic of the West German peace movement by the mid-1980s was implicit or predictable from the outset. As an SMO, the CC assumed form and function based on the combined influences of personal experience, grass-roots pressures, media feedback and politcial externalities. Its organizational self-dynamic reflects a balance of strengths and weaknesses, briefly summarized as follows.

From the developments outlined in the preceding sections, we are able to derive a number of general factors that contributed to the effectiveness of the CC and, therefore, to the strength of the movement as a whole. They include:

a) the regularity of contacts and meetings among key actors;
b) the informal "growing together" of its member organizations into a single structure;
c) the gradual expansion of its functions;
d) the stability of commitment levels and the continuity of mobilization efforts;
e) the guarantee of more-or-less efficient implementation of plans and resolutions by publicly-recognized organizations;
f) the increasing authority allocated on the basis of satisfactory infrastructural performance and increasing public influence;
g) self-directed and improving relations with external institutions (including recognition by GDR-Premier Enrich Honecker and a visit to the Kremlin); and
h) the eventual legitimation of a geographical and functional division of labor within the movement.

The CC's conscious (s)pacing of activities, geographically and temporally, the rotation of responsibility for the planning, and execution of concrete activities had a centripetal and mitigating effect on radical-actionistic factions, such that the truly "irreconcilable conflicts" were waged at the margins.

The primary weaknesses of the organized peace movement lie in its lack of a "comprehensive concept," its almost ritualized love-hate relationship to structure and hierarchy, and its jealousy-ridden fixation with an inherited concept of "power," be it personal or organizational in nature. The PM's character of 1979-1984 was forged on the basis of "action" rather than "program;" its component parts began to converge without a clearly defined framework of means, ends, and stages—for which no one can be directly faulted. As part of the natural dynamic of social movement development, it is easier to be commonly "against" rather than collectively "for" a specific national security policy. The heterogeneity of the movement will make the determination of a comprehensive alternative security policy a difficult, long-term—but not forever impossible—task.

Perhaps some direct criticism is nonetheless in order with respect to coordinators' benign neglect of an "internal successor generations" problem. SMOs, like their establishment counterparts, must plan for the recruitment of new members and facilitate their integration (Perrow 1979). A "movement generation" is characterized by shared experiences, as well as by an intellectual and tactical continuity that results in a common identity (Ross 1983). New recruits are potential agents for movement-change from within, but if not integrated as equals, they are likely to form new cliques or competing power circles vis-à-vis the Old Guard. As experiences with the "Autonomous Ones" have demonstrated, the radical becomes the routine, which might be interpreted outside as an ostensible shift in movement goals as well as strategies. Protest "veterans," such as Deile and Schöffmann, are sensitive to the fact that potential recruits aged 16-18 are turned off by CC members' "too technical" talk about missile ranges and delivery systems. The younger ones fail to realize that the former have only acquired this technical competence based on their own learning experiences of the last six years. The "personal interaction" element has been lost with SMO expansion such that the peace movement itself conveys a "bureaucratic" impression, rather than a grass-roots-democratic one.

Hence, the national coordinators, in particular, have learned a great deal since 1979 but do not yet find themselves in a position to transfer their experiences as a form of collective learning. Nor have the "peace professionals" completed their own learning process. As CC-member Buro (KfGD) (1982, p. 401ff) holds:

> Learning depends not only upon the supply of lessons available from experience but also upon the needs of those who are to learn. Many of these who are suddenly pulled into the social learning process of the peace movement attempt first to protect their contemporaneous beliefs in order to secure their identity. They will repress those aspects that might shatter their own value orientations and take up others that are sooner reconcilable with their current thinking. It is therefore to be expected that only a selective learning process occurs according to one's own needs (a process) which only in crisis situations and with great efforts can move the individuals beyond internally set boundaries. For the extension of the learning process, discussions among people with very different starting points may be helpful, if they succeed in listening to one another. More important, however, as the experiences have taught, is the common practice/implementation which compels them to reflect about what has been experienced.

What coordinators have thus far failed to learn, or at least to demonstrate that they have learned, is that their own movement continues to reflect the prevailing political culture of power. Power is treated within the CC and ACs as a finite sum, whereby a "gain" for one-member organization is perceived as a "loss" by another. The fight for political turf is all too reminiscent of the internal, Machiavellian power struggles of the late 1960s—testifying no doubt to the power of German political culture itself with its innate inability to comprehend that "power with" means more "power for" the movement. This point is best illustrated by the casual remarks (from interviews conducted by the author between July 1983 and January 1984, and November 1985 and March 1986) of various spectrum-affiliated individuals:

- I am for everything that gives us more power. This is also a power struggle within the peace movement (Northrhein-Westphalian Green).
- Some emphasize too much that some actions are unacceptable to their own group and don't look to the needs or imperatives of the movement (Juso).
- There is certainly dissatisfaction with the performance of individual people who appear too often on television . . . because some people say

'we don't get to appear anymore, the others are just trying to make a political name for themselves.' The same can be said of those complaining . . . . This profile neurosis is just a sign that people are dissatisfied with the outcome of [the former's] behavior and with their political success" (AGDF).

● [In regard to the dissolution of the Executive Committee] . . . one was not flexible, one was not tolerant or pragmatic but in essence typically German at the very moment when fundamental questions were being posed . . . which did not result in a better hearing for groups who up to now have been too inadequately represented in the national coordination owing to their substance or to their structure (AFfF).

● The tendency of individual groups who hold their own position to be the only correct one will increase the longer the struggle for disarmament is waged. This threatens to pose a greater danger to the peace movement than the much-feared resignation among the citizens (Social-Democrat).

● Naturally some massive attacks [against individuals] occurred, but ultimately it is a question of power. And that is what's sad about the whole thing . . . . I would take it very seriously, the question of power within the peace movement. It has destroyed the political culture (Independent).

This "typically German" penchant for behaving as if the need to gain internal advantage is as important as the need to gain external acceptance complicates the search for a flexible movement structure. Other SMO studies indicate, however, that the dilemma is actually universal: Transformational movements committed to participatory democracy, equality, communal responsibility, and individual liberty easily adopt the belief that a more formalized delegation of responsibility is "bad because it gives some people power over others and does not allow everyone's talents to develop" (Freeman 1983, p. 200). In light of the peace movement's ultimate aim, namely, the desire to eliminate all possibilities of a nuclear exchange between the superpowers, an acceptance of the internal exercise of power would seem a small price to pay for movement effectiveness and success.

The conclusion that "structure," "leadership," and "standard procedures" are perfidious in and of themselves does not automatically do away with drawbacks inherent to more "participatory democracy." According to McAdam (1983, p. 294), the latter

works well in organizations that are small or in which consensus is high about everything except details. But when powerfully divisive issues arise, the participatory approach lacks means to limit the length or acrimony of the debate or protect the organization from irrelevant or deliberately destructive intrusions. Since it assumes that consensus can be achieved on every issue, it is ill equipped to hold an organization together when factions absolutely fail to agree.

Peace movement structure and strategy are mutually reinforcing. Repeated use of existing structures tends to strengthen them as participants grow accustomed to working within a given framework. Davidson (1983, p. 154) holds that "strategy can create structure, and it can change it. New structures are occasionally created in order to make new strategies possible." Freeman (1983, p. 205), on the other hand, contends that "organizational structure cannot be changed at will. What arises in response to one set of concerns in effect sets the agenda for what the organization can do next." *Both* arguments find confirmation in protest-veteran Deile's prognosis (cited in Leif 1985, pp. 130-131) for the peace movement's future course in the Federal Republic:

> There is a need for long term perspectives if the movement is to survive. One doesn't get these when one extends the life of structures that were developed with an action-orientation and therefore were necessarily pragmatic and used to facilitate compromises; rather, one only gets them in now allowing an open, alternative debate to take place regarding the goals of the peace movement and by allowing a new compromise to evolve out of this [debate] over what we want to undertake in practice, and then one can again reconstitute an executive body. We cannot permit our own structures to stand in the way of necessary change processes within the peace movement.

CONCLUSION

Returning to our three introductory propositions, what general conclusions can be drawn regarding the significance of institutionalization, movement continuity, and intrasocial movement organizational conflict for peace movement developments in the Federal Republic of Germany?

First, movement institutionalization under the auspices of the CC has bestowed a contradictory image if not a split personality upon the PM. As collective representatives of the movement, CC members remain radical in their external, fundamental opposition to the production and deployment of nuclear, chemical, and bacteriological weapons in the FRG; their operational modus is nonetheless internally moderate, committed to consensus-building and the cultivation of direct contacts with the political establishment. The organized peace movement can be simultaneously denounced and applauded for its "state-maintenance function." During the peak mobilization phase, it spared the state an all-out crisis of political legitimacy by assimilating mass protest potential to a degree never before witnessed in postwar Germany; it gave this protest form, guided its entry into the channels of public consciousness, and compelled a debate with key elements of the German political establishment. It has effected at least a partial incorporation of its own arguments and proposals into the agenda of the system actors (e.g., the SPD), and has contributed to a shift in the political balance of forces (e.g., Greens in Bundestag, Lafontaine, and Leinen governing in the Saarland).

Formal organization and professionalization, at the national level, induced parallel processes at the grass-roots level, strengthening their position for the long haul ahead.

Secondly, movement continuity must be defined in terms extending beyond recognizable personalities or a once-and-for-all slate of objectives. The small-circle or protest-professionals approach in the movement's early development played a critical role in the harmonization of short-term objectives and tactics but generated significant internal conflict as mobilization progressed. The openness to a wide range of group types and nonviolent tactics is intended to foster self-mobilization, at the same time an ever-expanding protest agenda is expected to broaden the base of potential supporters (Mushaben 1986; Reuband 1985). Resignation is an individual phenomenon; a social movement needs members to survive, but membership continuity is, to some extent, an interchangeable resource. A loss of members can be offset by an intensification of commitment by remaining supporters or through the recruitment of new groups, made possible by the incorporation of new objectives. It is the consciousness of the campaign's linkages and learning experiences rooted in protests past that will serve as the best guarantor of PM continuity in Germany. It is the mix of conventional and unconventional mobilization tactics that provides a bridge between old politics and new politics, between old and new protests.

Finally, there is question as to the presumedly negative and potentially positive role of factional conflict in relation to the rise and fall of social movements. A protest campaign as heterogeneously composed as the PM is best served when several competitive but cooperative SMOs are permitted to play different roles and are encouraged to pursue different strategic possibilities simultaneously. Personality conflicts have been energy-draining, but ineschewable; programmatic conflicts among representatives of competing political spectra, on the other hand, have resulted in closer monitoring and pressures for accountability than would have occurred had each spectrum attempted to build a movement of its own. The adoption of a two-track strategy, combining parliamentary and extraparliamentary protests, reflects the tension between efforts to integrate at the national level and the need to preserve autonomy at the grass-roots level. In differentiating between "antagonistic" and "nonantagonistic" contradictions among various spectra and levels, the ACs have been an important first step in maximizing creativity, protecting diversity, and promoting tolerance among traditionally inimical factions and organizations. As of this writing, internal conflicts has provided the movement, more often than not, with a constructive impetus rather than a self-destructive dynamic.

Uncertain is whether or not the mass mobilizations for peace over the last five years have induced significant changes in West German political culture, or whether the scope and strength of the PM are the product of political-culture changes that have already taken hold in the postwar era. The relationship between the two, in my judgment, has been a reciprocal one. The degree of movement institutionalization and professionalization witnessed in the FRG supports Perrow's (1979) postulate that radical transformation movements (represented by multiple SMOs) must endeavor to aggregate resources; in so doing, the SMOs themselves ultimately compete and cooperate like formal organizations. In adapting to the structural, political, and procedural requisites of parliamentary democracy, the *Friedensbewegung* has kept alive and contributed to the hope that West German decison makers, in turn, will someday adopt the grass-roots, nonviolent, nonnuclear approach to national security for which it stands. It is a movement gearing up for the "politics of the deep breath" as well as for the long march through the institutions.

NOTES

1. Allow me to clarify three terms that appear intermittently throughout this chapter, the usage of which may not correspond exactly with definitions found in mainstream organizational-theory literature.

By *professionalization,* I mean the increasing tendency towards functional differentiation, a degree of personnel specialization, division of labor, and an accepted delegation of authority, along with the creation of formal, regularly accessible communication structures.

[*Inter*]*Organizational integration* refers to efforts to create regular communication and input channels for the purpose of shared decision making *without* effecting the standardization or harmonization of internal goals and procedures. It is not to be equated with assimilation or the absorption of one organization by another.

I use the term *institutionalization* to include *some* effort to formalize communication and decision-making structures in a way that renders them recognizable as an "organization" (however temporary) to outsiders as well as insiders. I see these efforts as signaling at least a partial internalization of prevailing formal-democratic values, on the one hand, and a selective accommodation or partial adaptation to prevailing structural-procedural rationales, on the other.

REFERENCES

Brand, K.W. 1982. *Neue soziale Bewegungen: Entstehung, Funktion und Perspektive neuer Protestpotentiale* (New Social Movements: Origins, Functions, and Perspectives of New Protest Potentials). Opladen: Westdeutscher Verlag.

Buro, A. 1982. "Was kann die 'neue' von der 'alten' Friedensbewegung lernen?" (What Can the New Peace Movement Learn from the Old Peace Movement?) Pp. 401-417 in *Die neue Friedensbewegung: Analysen aus der Friedensforschung* (The New Peace Movement: Analyses in Peace Research), edited by R. Steinweg. Frankfurt am Main: Suhrkamp.

Davidson, L. 1983. "Countercultural Organizations and Bureaucracy: Limits on the Revolution." Pp. 162-176 in *Social Movements of the Sixties and Seventies,* edited by J. Freeman. New York: Longman.

Diele, V. 1981. *Bonn 10.10.81-Friedensdemonstration für Abrüstung und Entspannung in Europa* (Demonstrations for Disarmament and Détente in Europe). Bornheim-Merten: Laumuv.

Der Stern. 1983. "Angst vor den Raketen" (Fear for the Missiles). October 20, 70-76.

Freeman, J. 1983. "A Model for Analyzing the Strategic Options of Social Movement Organizations." Pp. 193-210 in *Social Movements of the Sixties and Seventies,* edited by J. Freeman. New York: Longman.

Gerlach, L. 1971. "Movements of Revolutionary Change: Some Structural Characteristics." *American Behavioral Scientist* 14: 812-836.

Klandermans, B. and D. Oegema. 1984. "Mobilizing for Peace: The 1983 Peace Demonstration in The Hague." Paper presented at the Annual Meeting of the American Sociological Association, Washington, DC, August.

Knorr, L. 1983. *Geschichte der Friedensbewegung in der Bundesrepublik* (History of the Peace Movement in West Germany). Köln: Pahl Rugenstein.

Leif, T. 1985. *Die professionelle Bewegung: Friedensbewegung von innen* (A Professional Movement: The Peace Movement from Within). Bonn: Forum Europa Verlag.

McAdam, D. 1983. "The Decline of the Civil Rights Movement." Pp. 279-319 in *Social Movements of the Sixties and Seventies,* edited by J. Freeman. New York: Longman.

Mushaben, J.M. 1985. "Cycles of Peace Protest in West Germany: Experiences from Three Decades." *West European Politics* 8: 24-40.

———. 1986. "Grassroots and *Gewaltfreie Aktionen:* A Study of Mass Mobilization Strategies in the West German Peace Movement." *Journal of Peace Research* 23: 109-122.

Otto, K. 1977. *Vom Ostermarsch zur APO.* Frankfurt am Main: Campus.

Perrow, C. 1979. "The Sixties Observed." Pp. 192-211 in *The Dynamics of Social Movements,* edited by M.N. Zald and J.D. McCarthy. Cambridge, MA: Winthrop.

Rammstedt, O. 1978. *Soziale Bewegung* (Social Movements). Frankfurt am Main: Suhrkamp.

Raschke, J. 1985. *Soziale Bewegungen. Ein historisch-systematischer Grundriss* (Social Movements: An Historical-Systematic Analysis). Frankfurt am Main: Campus.

Reuband, K.H. 1985. "Die Friedensbewegung nach Stationierungsbeginn: Soziale Unterstützung in der Bevölkerung als Handlungspotential" (The Peace Movement after Deployment: Social Support among the General Population). *Vierteljahresschrift für Sicherheit und Frieden* 3: 147-156.

Ross, R.J. 1983. "Generational Change and Primary Groups in a Social Movement. Pp. 177-189 in *Social Movements of the Sixties and Seventies,* edited by J. Freeman. New York: Longman.

Rupp, H.-K. 1970. *Ausserparlamentarische Opposition in der Ära Adenauer: Der Kampf gegen die Atombewaffnung in den fünfziger Jahren* (Opposition in the Adenauer Period: The Fight Against Nuclear Armament in the Fifties). Köln: Pahl-Rugenstein.

Smelser, N. 1962. *Theory of Collective Behavior.* New York: Free Press.

Weidmann, B. and H. Meyer. 1982. *500,000 Gegen Reagan & NATO* (500,000 Against Reagan & NATO). Göttingen: Steidl Verlag.

PART IV

INTERORGANIZATIONAL
NETWORKS

INTRODUCTION

Bert Klandermans

Over the last two decades, the significance of support structures for the generation and survival of social movement organizations (SMOs) has become increasingly apparent. Curtis and Zurcher (1973) were among the first to point to the operation of multiorganizational fields in the development and maintenance of protest organizations. According to their definition (1973, p. 53), a multiorganizational field "is the total possible number of organizations with which the focal organization might establish specific linkages." Linkages can be established on the organizational level "by joint activities, staff, boards of directors, target clientele, resources, etc.," and on the individual level "by multiple affiliations of members." Their study of the antipornography movement revealed that antipornography organizations were enmeshed in a network of other community organizations and that participants in antipornography organizations were members of other voluntary associations as well. These linkages were based on common interests, ideologies, audiences, or other shared characteristics.

A few years earlier, Heirich (1968) showed how the Berkeley Free Speech Movement developed out of existing networks of activists and student organizations

International Social Movement Research, Vol. 2, pages 301-314.

at Berkeley. More recently, Morris (1984) observed that the existence of internal social institutions and organizations is a basic requirement for the development of SMOs, as the core of what he called "indigenous perspective." What proved to be true in the case of the antipornography movement and the Free Speech Movement, turned out to be equally true for the civil rights movement (Morris, 1984): SMOs develop out of existing networks of organizations which are necessary both to generate and to maintain them. In the meantime, numerous studies reported the importance of social networks as support structures for such different movements as the feminist movement (Rosenthal et al. 1985), the environmental movement (Taylor 1986), the fundamentalist Right movement (Oberschall 1984), the peace movement (Kriesi 1986), terrorist organizations (Della Porta 1988), and the neighborhood movement (Henig 1982).

Although Curtis and Zurcher (1973) note that the opponents to the antipornography movement also constitute a multiorganizational field, generally, in the literature, surprisingly little attention has been given to the fact that multiorganizational fields need not necessarily be supportive. In an apparently unnoticed part of his book on the Quebec separatist movement, Pinard (1975, p. 186, emphasis added) remarks, "Whenever pre-existing primary and secondary groupings possess or develop an ideology or simply subjective interests *congruent* with that of a new movement, they will act as mobilizing rather than restraining agents toward that movement." The reverse is of course also true, and Pinard hypothesized that intermediary structures will have a restraining, neutral, or mobilizing effect, depending on their position on the "alienation-conformity continuum." This hypothesis was supported by data he presented on the Quebecois movement.

In other words, the multiorganizational field of an SMO has both supporting *and* opposing sectors. These two sectors can be described as (1) an SMO's alliance system, consisting of groups and organizations that support the organization, and (2) its conflict system consisting of representatives and allies of the challenged political systems, including countermovement organizations (Kriesi 1985). The boundaries between the two systems remain vague and may change in the course of events. Specific organizations that try to remain aloof from the controversy may be forced to take sides. Parts of the political system (political parties, elites, governmental institutions) can coalesce with SMOs and join the alliance system. Coalitions can fall apart, and previous allies can become part of the conflict system.

Alliance systems serve to support SMOs by *providing* resources and *creating* political opportunities; conflict systems serve to *drain* resources and restrict opportunities. Within conflict systems, bargaining relations develop sooner or later between representatives of SMOs and target institutions, either at the initiative of the movement organization or of its opponent.

Different SMOs have different but overlapping conflict and alliance systems. The greatest overlap will exist among organizations from the same social movement industry (organizations from the women's movement, from the environmental movement, and so on), but also movement organizations from different social movement industries will have overlapping conflict—and alliance systems. The cleavage between an SMO's alliance and conflict systems may coincide with other cleavages, such as social class, ethnic lines, or Left/ Right affiliation. The proportion of the multiorganizational field that becomes engaged in conflict or alliance systems will vary from situation to situation. Moreover, there will be variation over time. The proportion of the multiorganizational field engaged in one of the two systems expands or contracts according to cycles of protest (Tarrow 1983). At the peaks of protest, almost any organization will be enmeshed in either system; in the valleys, most organizations will belong to neither. The "indifference quotient of the general public" (Terchek 1974) will vary accordingly.

The specific make-up of alliance and conflict systems fluctuates over time, and with the particular movement, situation, and circumstances. For example, Walsh (1981) showed that, in the different communities surrounding Three Mile Island, after the reactor accident, SMOs with different alliance systems developed, depending on existing differences in the multiorganizational field.

A specific SMO can be engaged in an alliance system of modest proportions and an extensive conflict system; or, in contrast, it can belong to an encompassing alliance system and a weak conflict system. Over time, the location of an SMO in its multiorganizational field and the relative significance of the two systems can change dramatically. This fluctuation is clearly illustrated by the fortunes of the women's movement in the United States. (Conover and Gray 1983; Mansbridge 1986): In the absence of a significant conflict system, the movement was able to succeed without developing a solid alliance system. But when the movement's conflict system rapidly gained strength and significance (because of the bonds between the new Right and the conservative government), the lack of an alliance system became a liability. It was only when the women's movement appeared to be on the defensive that it started to build new coalitions—but too late to rescue the Equal Rights Amendment (ERA). In his discussion of the movements of the 1960s in the United States, Jenkins (1987) observed a similar process at work at the level of politics in general. The movements of the 1960s brought a new Center-Left coalition into power, which operated as a part of the alliance system of the new social movements. However, the initial successes of this coalition not only unleashed a broad wave of new social movements but also set off a wave of countermovements. The New Right and its political allies mobilized polity members threatened by the new movements, adopting many of the new movement's strategies and tactics. Eventually, they succeeded in bringing a New Right coalition into power.

ALLIANCE SYSTEMS

Research on the multiorganizational fields of SMOs functioning as alliance systems abounds. Major parts of the alliance system consist of other movement organizations, from the same movement industry or from different movement industries. Kriesi's research (1987) reveals that organizations from a variety of social movements (such as the environmental movement, the squatters movement, and the women's movement) form an important part of the alliance structure of the Dutch peace movement. Diani and Lodi (1988) report a considerable degree of multiple affiliation among activists from different currents of the Milanese environmental movement.

Although coalitions between cognate SMOs seem natural, competition is equally likely (Zald and McCarthy 1980). Wilson (1973) argued that competition between movement organizations is especially likely if an SMO has little autonomy, that is no area of competence distinct from that of other movement organizations. Those organizations which have few resources will, in particular, tend to attack other movement organizations in an attempt to strengthen their own identity. Paradoxically, then, we can expect greater competition among cognate movement organizations appealing to the same mobilization potential than among movement organizations with nonoverlapping mobilization potentials. This phenomenon is exactly what Benford (1984) described in his study of the interorganizational dynamics of the Austin peace movement, and what Rucht reports in his study of the French and German environmental movement in his contribution to this volume. Another example is the conflict within the southern civil rights movement between the Student Non-Violent Coordinating Committee and the Southern Christian Leadership Conference (Morris 1984).

In general, enduring coalitions between SMOs are not very likely. Coalition formation can be threatening for many movement organizations. In Wilson's words (1973), "Resources, autonomy, and purposes can be jeopardized if the organization must share the credit for victory and the blame for defeat." Wilson goes on to argue that coalition formation is stimulated if resources are significantly shrinking or if it is thought that joining a coalition will increase them significantly. In line with this argument, Staggenborg (1986, p. 388) in one of the rare empirical studies of coalition formation in social movements, concluded that organizations are most likely to form coalitions "(1) when individual organizations lack the resources needed to take advantages of opportunities or fend off threats, or (2) when coalition work allows movement organizations to conserve resources for tactics other than those engaged in by the coalition." Examples of coalitions formed to offset shrinking resources are, in The Netherlands, the mergers of socialist and Catholic unions in the wake of the rapid decline of the latter; and, in the United States, the recent merger of Freeze and Sane. An example of a coalition formed for the purpose of resource accumulation is the merger of Three Mile Island protest organizations urged by outside funding institutions (Walsh and Cable, in this volume). Once formed, however, coalitions easily break down, because of ideological conflicts and because the organizational maintenance needs of individual organizations compete with the needs of the coalition. The chance of breakdowns decreases if the coalition requires few resources from the affiliated organizations and concentrates on tasks that are too costly for individual organizations (Staggenborg 1986).

Much more common than enduring coalitions are ad hoc alliances among movement organizations: loose, cooperative bonds between two or more organizations. One example of such an ad hoc alliance is the peace platform in local communities in The Netherlands, several groups and organizations brought together to mobilize mass collective action (Klandermans and Oegema 1987; Kriesi 1987). Since ad hoc alliances usually develop among organizations that agree on substantial goals, similar alliances return over time and in different circumstances.

Although other movement organizations form a major part of the alliance system of an SMO, almost any kind of organization can become engaged in an alliance system: political parties, unions, churches, recreational organizations, youth organizations, student and campus organizations, traditional and new women's organizations, natural conservation organizations, business organizations, consumer organizations, community organizations, and sometimes even governmental institutions. For instance, the alliance system of the Dutch peace movement comprised (apart from other movement organizations) political parties, unions, churches, and a variety of local social welfare, neighborhood, and specialized (youth, elderly, women) organizations (Klandermans 1990; Kriesi 1987). Further, the composition of alliance systems changes in the course of the cycle, as Tarrow's (1989) research on the Italian protest cycle in the 1960s and 1970s shows. Although traditional and institutional actors were absent in the initial phases of this cycle, these actors joined and took over events at the peak of the cycle, either to channel protest into more moderate directions or to use the accumulated political pressure to advance their own interests. At the downturn of this cycle, the alliance system rapidly disintegrated, radical organizations became more dominant, and the alliance system eventually contracted into a network of political radicals (Della Porta and Tarrow 1986).

Because alliance systems provide an SMO with resources and political opportunities, they are indispensable to SMOs, if the organizations are to survive and have any impact. The greater the resources and the more political opportunities an organization in the multiorganizational field can supply, the more attractive an ally it is.

Resources

The resources furnished to a SMO by its allies are both tangible (money, space, equipment, and the like) and nontangible (organizational experience, leadership, strategic and tactical know-how, ideological justifications, and so on) (Aveni 1978). More important, alliance systems provide SMOs with extended communication and recruitment networks. Nonmovement networks turn out to be extremely important for a movement organization in consensus and action mobilization, especially in the earlier stages of mobilization (Klandermans 1988). The strength of ties is similarly an important factor: Rosenthal et al. (1985) conclude from their study of nineteenth-century women's reform in New York that weak ties in the network of organizations function primarily as communication networks, whereas strong ties facilitate the exchange of resources.

Tierney (1982) observed that organizations which sponsor alliances benefit from that sponsorship. They are able to influence SMOs and their support might reinforce a favorable image. Governmental institutions sometimes sponsor moderate claims to prevent the ascendance of more radical claims. Political parties hope to win electoral support from the constituency of the movement organization. In short, collaboration between movements and established organizations is an exchange relationship.

Resource mobilization theorists have stated that external support is a necessary condition for effective movement organizations to develop (McCarthy and Zald 1976). Both McAdam (1982) and Morris (1984) have argued convincingly that indigenous resources are more important than external support, especially in the initial stages of the movement. External support is relevant, but as a rule it will become available only after a movement has had some initial success. External support may even accelerate movement decay. Jenkins and Eckert (1986) present evidence from the civil rights movement in support of this view: Patronage aims at controlling turbulence. They conclude, however, that the social-control effects of patronage are more subtle than a simple cooptation thesis would assume: The professionalized forms into which patronage channelled the civil rights movement were not inevitably counterproductive.

Opportunities

Alliance systems create political opportunities. Interorganizational networks link SMOs with the political system, connecting elites and political parties with the social movement sector. Costain and Costain (1986) and Jenkins (1987) have shown that, in the United States, the social movement sector and the political system have become increasingly enmeshed. Nedelmann (1984) and Rucht (1985) argue that SMOs develop as a separate innovative and propelling level between individual citizens and institutionalized intermediaries such as political parties. Links to political parties and elites are indispensable for political influence. Drawing from Lipsky's and Wilson's models of protest, bargaining and political culture, Terchek (1974) showed that the political influence of the civil rights movement depended not only on public opinion and the level of insurgency, but also on the extent to which movement organizations could activate ideological allies and pragmatic intermediaries with substantial political resources. According to Terchek's definition, ideological allies agree with the goals of the SMO; pragmatic intermediaries, on the other hand, are primarily concerned with pursuing their own interests. If these interests can be satisfied by repressing the SMO, they would not object. If repression does not work, pragmatic allies are prepared to accept compromises, provided that the compromises will end insurgency. Pragmatic allies are effective if they have substantial political resources at their disposal, if compromises do not hurt them—and if continuation of the movement's insurgent action may hurt them. Sophisticated lobbying and ties with the party system and governmental institutions increase an SMO's impact on policy-making considerably (Boender 1985, Costain and Costain 1986; Schenk 1981). In our study of grass-roots mobilization and local government in The Netherlands, the inclusion of some of the local political parties in the alliance system of the peace movement turned out to be decisive in passing freeze motions or peace programs in Dutch city councils (Klandermans and Oegema 1987). Political entrepreneurs occupy strategic positions linking social movement networks with the political system (McCarthy and Zald 1976).

CONFLICT SYSTEMS

Part of the multiorganizational field of an SMO consists of organizations and institutions that are opposed to it. Central to the conflict system are target organizations and institutions: governmental institutions, employer's organizations, business organizations, elites, political parties, and so on. But, just an SMO's alliance system, is open to any kind of organizational ally, so an SMO's conflict system can admit any kind of organizational opponent. Occasionally, the actions of the SMO itself push organizations and institutions into the conflict system. Protests inevitably have spillover effects that penalize people other than the intended target. Consequently, these people may ally themselves with the opponents of the SMO.

Within conflict systems, an "us-them" dynamic tends to develop. Mansbridge (1986) describes this process, frequently discussed in the literature on intergroup relations (cf. Tajfel 1978, p. 179), for the proponents and opponents of the ERA: "Building an organization on belief in a principle, when the world refuses to go along with that principle, produces a deep sense of us against them; when two movements are pitted against each other reality will provide plenty of temptations to see the opposition as evil incarnation." Organizations such as SMOs, which rely on volunteers, can easily become engaged in such ingroup-outgroup dynamics because it "requires an exaggerated, black or white vision of events to justify spending time and money on the cause" (Mansbridge 1986, p. 6). Especially if a countermovement develops, the conflict system easily becomes dominated by such intergroup dynamics.

A countermovement tends to develop if an SMO is successful (Zald and Useem 1982). Countermovements are often (and sometimes openly) supported by elites and the established order. As a consequence, they have extensive financial resources at their disposal. Some examples of countermovements are the antiabortion movement in several countries, the anti-ERA movement in the United States, and the new Christian Right in U.S. churches. Each of these countermovements involves business elites and conservative political parties (Conover and Gray 1983; Mansbridge 1986; Marshall and Orum 1987; Oberschall 1984; Outshoorn 1986), reacting against the achievements of movements such as the feminist movement. Another countermovement is The Netherlands' Interdenominational Committee for Mutual Disarmament (ICTO), established by conservative church members, many of whom have military backgrounds, in rection to the successful mobilization against cruise missiles by the Interdenominational Peace Council (IKV) (Klugkist and Spaargaren 1983; Walravens 1983).

Within conflict systems, bargaining relations develop between representatives of SMOs and target institutions. Social movement organizations and their opponents try to get in touch with each other to negotiate demands, and the termination of disruptions, as well as rules, control measures, and so on. In the literature, bargaining relations are seen as signs of recognition or acceptance and are interpreted as an indicator of movement success (Gamson 1975; Mueller 1978). In this context, it is not the effects of collective actions that we are interested in (see Part V for a discussion of this topic), but rather the observation that conflict systems comprehend both confrontation *and* negotiation.

Draining Resources and Restricting Political Opportunities

Authorities and countermovements and their allies try to deprive an SMO of resources and political opportunities by increasing the costs of participation in the SMO, by undermining its organizational strength, declaring specific tactics illegal, abolishing specific opportunities, criminalizing the organization, offering symbolic concessions, and campaigning to turn the public against it (Griffin et al. 1986; Henig 1982; Terchek 1974). To accomplish these ends, a variety of tactics are used (Griffin et al. 1986; Zald and Useem 1982); opponents attempt:

1. to break the unity of the movement;
2. directly impair the SMO (through infiltration, bribery, penalizing and arresting members and leaders, anti-SMO legislation, restricting resources);
3. increase the costs of mobilization and collective action (by using the police, strong-arm boys, repression, and by threatening activists); and
4. constrain the political opportunity structure (through antipropaganda and litigation, and by undermining the moral and political bases of the SMO.

Well-known examples of exercises in movement control appear in Marx's (1974, 1979) work on external efforts to damage social movements. Police undercover work, agents provocateur, and informants are all used to undermine SMOs. Taking a different angle, Kriesi's (1985) study of political protest movements in Switzerland reveals that commitment to protest organizations in that country was related to the activists' experience of repression. Griffin et al. (1986) demonstrated that, in the 1920s, U.S. employer organizations were very effective in blocking union growth.

Issue definitions play an important role in conflicts over resources and opportunities between opponents. Opponents in a conflict, sponsor different ideological packages and struggle to win acceptance among the public at large. Conover and Gray (1983) and Mansbridge (1986) showed how the anti-ERA forces were able to redefine the ERA issue so that a plea for equal rights came to be seen as a threat to family life. Pro-ERA forces were either too late or unable to undertake a counterattack and so lost the ERA. In The Netherlands, anti-IKV forces, within the churches, were able to transform the nuclear arms issue into a "free speech" issue by arguing that IKV was one-sided and that churches had to allow other-minded organizations to present their views. They succeeded in getting permission, and enough resources to distribute their own materials. As a consequence, the impact of IKV within local church communities decreased. The IKV view was no longer seen as the official view of the churches. In the eyes of many church members, the IKV position was devalued and became simply one of two competing visions (Klugkist and Spaargaren 1983).

Sometimes, however, to impair an SMO can actually work to the organization's advantage, fostering internal cohesion, increasing support from the alliance system, persuading individuals and organizations to become engaged in the alliance system, and sometimes forcing governmental institutions to side with it. (Lyng and Kurtz 1985; McAdam 1983; Tarrow 1988; Terchek 1974).

Bargaining

Sooner or later, SMOs an their targets have to enter into some bargaining relationship. Bargaining can serve the interests of challengers *and* the polity.

As a rule, challengers try to arrive at substantive gains, whereas the polity tries to prevent or put an end to insurgent action. Consequently, the authorities' interests in bargaining increase with the degree of disorder (Morris 1984; Mueller 1978; Terchek 1974). Sometimes challengers and opponents negotiate to reduce the risks associated with collective action (as in agreements between police officials and the organizers of a demonstration to prevent violent confrontations, or negotiations between a strike committee and management on the termination of a complex production process).

In time, more or less elaborate bargaining structures develop as a component of the conflict system. Specialized institutions are created, in which representatives of SMOs and target institutions meet. As a result, parties develop a vested interest in maintaining these bargaining structures. Bargaining structures form a bridge between the conflict and alliance systems. The more they expand, the more the SMOs run the risk of cooptation, that is, of participating in the structures they were fighting against. No wonder SMOs are ambivalent about becoming too engaged in those structures.

Paradoxically, target institutions will be most open to compromises in the quiet periods at the beginning of a protest cycle. At the peak of the cycle, counterforces are mobilized, considerably limiting the room target institutions have for maneuvering (Terchek 1974). Bargaining relationships develop most easily if parties agree on premises defining each other's position, if the issues are suitable for bargaining (are divisible, exchangeable), if SMOs lean heavily on material as opposed to purposive incentives, and if social movement organizations control resources that are of value to the opponents (Wilson 1973). Little empirical work has been done on collective bargaining in conflict systems, but students of movement organization conflict systems can learn much from the literature on collective bargaining in industrial relaions (cf. Stephenson and Brotherton 1979, pp. 155-239).

NEW SOCIAL MOVEMENTS AND MULTIORGANIZATIONAL FIELDS

SMOs emerge from multiorganizational fields. Through interorganizational linkages and overlapping membership they are solidly integrated into the organizational networks of their communities. This conception of SMOs (i.e., as emerging from multiorganizational fields) implies a historical continuity in the generation of social movements. Moreover, it denies that marginality is a distinguishing feature of movement participation and social movements. By partitioning multiorganizational fields into alliance and conflict systems, one is alerted to look for linkages between SMOs and existing organizations and institutions.

Such an approach seems to be at odds with new social movement literature, in which the very use of "new" suggests discontinuity. Indeed, much of the new social movement literature stresses the distinction of new SMOs from traditional organizations such as trade unions, political parties, pressure groups, interest organizations, churches, and so on (cf. Brand 1985; Klandermans 1986). New social movements are presented as developing in the margins of postindustrial society, detached from, and opposed to, traditional organizations of interest intermediation. A closer look, however, reveals that this representation is oversimplified. New SMOs, like any other SMOs, have all kinds of links with organizations and institutions in their sociopolitical environment. Far from being detached from traditional organizations of interest intermediation, they appear to be enmeshed in the sociopolitical networks of the societies in which they develop (Diani and Lodi 1988; Klandermans 1990; Kriesi 1987).

Rather than argue that specific social movements are detached from the political and/or social system, we can more profitably study the multiorganizational fields in which SMOs are embedded. By mapping out and identifying their allies, their opponents, and those who are indifferent, we might improve our explanations of an SMO's ability to mobilize resources, use opportunities, and exert influence.

THE CONTRIBUTIONS TO PART IV

The three contributions to Part IV each elaborate an aspect of the argument developed here.

Fernandez and McAdam demonstrate the importance of multiorganizational fields as support structures. In their study of applicants for the Mississippi Freedom Summer from the University of Wisconsin, multiorganizational fields turned out to be decisive in determining whether an applicant eventually did or did not participate. Of equal importance is the authors' application of network analysis in the study of interorganizational networks.

Opp's contribution illustrates that multiorganizational fields need not necessarily be supportive. Opp shows that the impact of integration of individuals in voluntary organizations, on their participation in the antinuclear power movement, depends on the kind of organization individuals are integrated in and on the rewards and punishments which the organizations provide for participation.

Weber describes how employer organizations in the FRG were able to defeat the unions in a struggle for a shorter workweek, on the one hand, by successfully depriving the unions of resources through legislative action, and, on the other, by maximizing the unions costs of mobilization through lockouts. His chapter provides a clear illustration of how actors in a conflict system serve to drain the resources and restrict opportunities of their opponents.

REFERENCES

Aveni, A.F. 1978. "Organizational Linkages and Resource Mobilization: The Significance of Linkage Strength and Breadth." *The Sociological Quarterly* 19: 185-202.

Benford, R. 1984. "The Interorganizational Dynamics of the Austin Peace Movement." Unpublished thesis. The University of Texas, Austin.

Boender, K. 1985. *Sociologische analyse van milieusolidariteit onder elites en publiek.* Rijswijk: Sythoff Pers.

Brand, K.-W., ed. 1985. *Neue soziale Bewegungen in West Europa und den USA, Ein internationaler Vergleich* (New Social Movements in Western Europe and the USA. An International Comparison). New York/Frankfurt: Campus Verlag.

Conover, P. and V. Gray. 1983. *Feminism and the New Right. The Conflict over the American Family.* New York: Praeger.

Costain, A.N. and W.D. Costain. 1986. "The Decline of Political Parties and the Rise of Social Movements in America." Paper presented at the 81st annual meetings of the American Sociological Association, New York.

Curtis, R.L. and L.A. Zurcher. 1973. "Stable Resources of Protest Movements: The Multi-Organizational Field. *Social Forces* 52:53-61.

Della Porta, D. 1988. "Recruitment into Clandestine Organizations: Leftwing Terrorists in Italy." In *From Structure to Action: Comparing Movement Participation Across Cultures,* edited by B. Klandermans, H. Kriesi, and S. Tarrow. Greenwich, CT: JAI Press.

Della Porta, D. and S. Tarrow. 1986. "Unwanted Children: Political Violence and the Cycle of Protest in Italy, 1966-1973." *European Journal of Political Research* 14:607-632.

Diani, M. and G. Lodi. 1988. "'Three in One': Currents in the Ecological Movement in Milan." In *From Structure to Action: Comparing Movement Participation Across Cultures,* edited by B. Klandermans, H. Kriesi, and S. Tarrow. Greenwich, CT: JAI Press.

Gamson, W.A. 1975. *The Strategy of Social Protest.* Homewood, IL: The Dorsey Press.

Griffin, L.J., M.E. Wallace, and B.A. Rubin. 1986. "Capitalist Resistance to the Organization of Labor Before the New Deal: Why? How? Success?" *American Sociological Review* 51:147-167.

Heirich, M. 1968. *The Spiral of Conflict: Berkeley, 1964.* New York: Columbia University Press.

Henig, J.R. 1982. *Neighborhood Mobilization, Redevelopment and Response.* New Brunswick, NJ: Rutgers University Press.

Jenkins, J.C. 1987. "Interpreting the Stormy Sixties: Three Theories in Search of a Political Age." In *Research in Political Sociology,* vol. 3, edited by R.G. Braungart. Greenwich, CT: JAI Press.

Jenkins, J.C. and C.M. Eckert. 1986. "Channeling Black Insurgency." *American Sociological Review* 51: 812-830.

Klandermans, B. 1986. "New Social Movements and Resource Mobilization: The European and the American Approach." *International Journal of Mass Emergencies and Disasters* 4(2):13-39. Special issue on comparative methods and research on collective behavior and social movements, edited by Gary T. Marx.

————. 1988. "The Formation and Mobilization of Consensus." In *From Structure to Action: Comparing Movement Participation Across Cultures,* edited by B. Klandermans, H. Kriesi, and S. Tarrow. Greenwich, CT: JAI Press.

————. 1990. "Linking the "Old" and the "New": Movement Networks in The Netherlands." In *Challenging the Political Order,* edited by R. Dalton and M. Kuechler.

Klandermans, B. and D. Oegema. 1987. "Campaigning for a Nuclear Freeze: Grassroots Strategies and Local Government in The Netherlands." In *Research in Political Sociology,* vol. 3, edited by R.G. Braungart. Greenwich, CT: JAI Press.

Klugkist, J. and G. Spaargaren. 1983. "Tussen kern en kerk, Een empirisch onderzoek naar de relatie die kernen van het Interkerkelijk Vredesberaad onderhouden met de plaatselijke kerken" (In between peace group and church. An empirical study of the relationship between local peace groups and churches). Unpublished thesis. Landbouwhogeschool, Wageningen.

Kriesi, H. 1985. *Bewegung in der Schweizer Politik, Fallstudien zu politischen Mobilierungsprozessen in der Schweiz* (Movement in Swiss Politics. A case study of political mobilization in Switzerland). Frankfurt/New York: Campus Verlag.

———. 1986. "Nieuwe sociale bewegingen: Op zoek naar hun gemeenschappelijke noemer" (New social movements: A search for a common denominator). Inaugurele Oratie, Universiteit van Amsterdam.

———. 1987. "The Alliance Structure of the Dutch Peace Movement." Paper presented at the workshop "New Social Movements and the Political System", ECPR Joint Session, Amsterdam.

Lyng, S.G. and L.G. Kurtz. 1985. "Bureaucratic Insurgency: The Vatican and the Crisis of Modernism." *Social Forces* 63:901-922.

McAdam, D. 1982. *Political Process and the Development of Black Insurgency.* Chicago: University of Chicago Press.

———. 1983. "Tactical Innovation and the Pace of Insurgency." *American Sociological Review* 48: 735-754.

McCarthy, J.D. and M.N. Zald. 1976 "Resource Mobilization and Social Movements: A Partial Theory." *American Journal of Sociology* 82:1212-1241.

Mansbridge, J.L. 1986. *Why We Lost the ERA.* Chicago: The University of Chicago Press.

Marshall, S.E. and A. Orum. 1987. "Opposition Then and Now: Countering Feminism in the Twentieth Century." In *Research in Politics and Society,* vol. 2, edited by G. Moore and G.D. Spitze. Greenwich, CT: JAI Press.

Marx, G.T. 1974. "Thoughts on a Neglected Category of Social Movement Participants: The Agent Provocateur and the Informant." *American Journal of Sociology* 80:404-442.

———. 1979. "External Efforts to Damage or Facilitate Social Movements: Some Patterns, Explanations, Outcomes and Complications." Pp. 94-125 in *The Dynamics of Social Movements,* edited by M.N. Zald and J.D. McCarthy. Cambridge, MA: Winthrop.

Morris, A. 1984. *The Origins of the Civil Rights Movement: Black Communities Organizing for Change.* New York: Free Press.

Mueller, C. 1978. "Riot Violence and Protest Outcomes." *Journal of Political and Military Sociology* 6:49-65.

Nedelmann, B. 1984. "New Political Movements and Changes in Processes of Intermediation." *Social Science Information* 23:1029-1048.

Oberschall, A. 1984. "The New Christian Right in North Carolina." Paper presented at the annual meetings of the American Sociological Association, San Antonio.

Outshoorn, J. 1986. *De politieke strijd rondom de abortus wetgeving in Nederland 1964-1984* (The political struggle for abortion rights in The Netherlands 1964-1984). Amsterdam: Vrije Universiteit.

Pinard, M. 1975. *The Rise of a Third Party, a Study in Crisis Politics.* Montreal: McGill-Queen's University Press.

Rosenthal, N., M. Fingrutd, M. Ethier, R. Karant, and D. McDonald. 1985. "Social Movements and Network Analysis: A Case Study of Nineteenth-Century Women's Reform in New York State." *American Journal of Sociology* 90:1022-1054.

Rucht, D. 1985. "Parteien und Bewegungen als Modi kollektiven Handelns (Parties and Movements as Collective Actors). Vortrag am Zentralinstitut für sozialwissenschaftliche." Forschung der Freien Universität Berlin, März.

Schenk, M. 1981. "Bürgerinitiativen: Interpersonell Kommunikationen und politischer Einfluss."
    Kölner Zeitschrift für Soziologie und Sozialpsychologie 33:623-641.
Staggenborg, S. 1986. "Coalition Work in the Pro-Choice Movement: Organizational and
    Environmental Opportunities and Obstacles." *Social Problems* 33:374-390.
Stephenson, S.M. and C.J. Brotherton. 1979. *Industrial Relations, a Social Psychological
    Approach.* Chichester: Wiley.
Tajfel, H. 1978. "Intergroup Behaviour." Pp. 401-447 in *Introducing Social Psychology,* edited
    by H. Tajfel and C. Fraser. Harmondsworth: Penguin Books.
Tarrow, S. 1983. *"Struggling to Reform: Social Movements and Policy Change During Cycles
    of Protest."* Western Societies Paper No. 15. Ithaca, N.Y.: Cornell University.
————. 1988. "Old Movements in New Cycles: The Career of a Neighborhood Religious
    Movement in Italy." *From Structure to Action: Comparing Movement Participation
    Across Cultures,* edited by B. Klandermans, H. Kriesi, and S. Tarrow. Greenwich, CT:
    JAI Press.
————. 1989. *Democracy and Disorder;: Social Conflict, Protest and Politics in Italy, 1965-1975.*
    Oxford: Oxford University Press.
Taylor, D.G. 1986. *Public Opinion and Collective Action.* Chicago: The University of Chicago
    Press.
Terchek, R.J. 1974. "Protest and Bargaining." *JPR* 11:133-145.
Tierney, K.J. 1982. "The Battered Women Movement and the Creation of the Wife Beating
    Problem." *Social Problems* 29:207-220.
Walravens, G. 1983. "Recente behoudende vredesorganisaties en hun ideeën" (Contemporary
    Conservative Peace Organizations and their Ideas). *Historisch Vredesonderzoek* 1:7-15.
Walsh, E.J. 1981. "Resource Mobilization and Citizen Protest in Communities Around Three
    Mile Island." *Social Problems* 29:1-21.
Wilson, J.Q. 1973. *Political Organizations.* New York: Basic Books.
Zald, M.N. and J.D. McCarthy. 1980. "Social Movement Industries: Competition and
    Cooperation Among Movement Organizations." In *Research in Social Movements,
    Conflicts and Change,* vol. 3, edited by L. Kriesberg. Greenwich, CT: JAI Press.
Zald, M.N. and B. Useem. 1982. "Movement and Countermovement: Loosely Coupled Conflict."
    Paper presented at the 77th annual meetings of the American Sociological Association,
    San Francisco.

MULTIORGANIZATIONAL FIELDS AND RECRUITMENT TO SOCIAL MOVEMENTS

Roberto M. Fernandez and Doug McAdam

Among the topics that have most concerned researchers in the field of social movements is that of differential recruitment (Jenkins 1983; Zurcher and Snow 1981). What accounts for individual variation in movement participation? Why does one individual get involved while another remains inactive? Traditionally, these questions have been answered by reference to various "personalogical" (Zukier 1982) accounts of movement recruitment. The basic assumption underlying such accounts is that it is some characteristic of the individual activist that either compels them to participate or, at the very least, renders them susceptible to movement recruiting appeals. Among the individual attributes, most frequently seen as productive of activism, is a strong attitudinal affinity with the goals of the movement or a well-articulated set of grievances consistent with the movement's ideology. Some authors attribute the individual's ideological leanings to the effects of early childhood socialization

International Social Movement Research, Vol. 2, pages 315-343.
Copyright © 1989 by JAI Press Inc.
ISBN: 0-89232-964-5

(cf. Block et al. 1968; Lewis and Kraut 1972; Thomas 1971). Others describe them as a by-product of more immediate social-psychological dynamics. For example, relative deprivation theorists see the motivation to activism growing out of the perception—often triggered by a shift in reference group—that "one's membership group is in a disadvantageous position, relative to some other group" (Gurney and Tierney 1982, p. 34). Regardless of these differences, all grievance- or attitudinally-based models of activism locate the motive to participate within the individual actor. This assumption has informed any number of otherwise different accounts of participation in political or religious movements (cf. Block et al. 1968; Braungart 1971; Fendrich and Krauss 1978; Glock 1964; Flacks 1967; Geschwender 1968; Pinard and Hamilton 1984; Searles and Williams 1962; Toch 1965).

However, the emergence and increasing influence over the last decade of the resource mobilization and political process perspectives in the study of social movements has led to growing dissatisfaction with the individual motivational accounts of recruitment. The following statement by Snow et al. (1980, p. 789) cuts to the heart of these objections: "However reasonable the underlying assumption that some people are more (psychologically) susceptible than others to movement participation, that view deflects attention from the fact that recruitment cannot occur without prior contact with a recruitment agent." The argument holds that it is not attitudinal affinity so much as structural availability that accounts for differential involvement in movement activity. It matters little if one is ideologically disposed toward participation if he or she lacks the structural or network contact that would "pull" them into protest activity. Consistent with this argument, a number of recent studies have demonstrated the decisive role of structural, rather than attitudinal factors, in encouraging activism (Bibby and Brinkerhoff 1974; Bolton 1972; McAdam 1986; Orum 1972; Rosenthal et al. 1985; Snow et al. 1980; Von Eschen et al. 1971). A similar argument has been made for recruitment to religious movements (Harrison 1974; Heirich 1977; Stark and Bainbridge 1980).

One of the most important of the structural factors studied has been the role of interconnections among formal organizations in recruitment to social movements (Aveni 1978; Curtis and Zurcher 1973; Rosenthal et al. 1985). The point of this research is that social movement organizations (SMOs) do not exist in a vacuum—in many cases the social environment of SMOs consists of other SMOs. Linkages among these organizations are seen as an important channel through which SMOs mobilize resources, including one of their most valuable resources, personnel (See Perrow 1970).

In this paper, we study the role of interorganizational linkages in recruitment to an incident of high risk/cost activism (McAdam 1986), the 1964 Mississippi Freedom Summer Campaign. We start by adopting Curtis and Zurcher's (1973, p. 53, original emphasis) definition of multiorganizational fields:

The concept of "multi-organizational field" suggests that organizations in a community setting approximate an ordered, coordinated system. Interorganizational processes within the field can be identified on two levels, which conceptually overlap: the *organizational* level, where networks are established by joint activities, staff, boards of directors, target clientele, resources, etc.; the *individual* level, where networks are established by multiple affiliations of members.

Following this definition, we see organizations linked to the Freedom Summer movement as a multiorganizational field, providing a stable recruitment base for the movement. Consistent with this definition, we see linkages among SMOs facilitating recruitment at both levels of analysis, the organizational and individual levels.

At the organizational level, multiorganizational fields can serve as the primary source of movement participants through what Oberschall (1973) has termed "bloc recruitment." In this pattern, movements do not so much emerge out of established organizations as they represent a merger of such groups. Hicks (1961), for instance, has described how the Populist party was created through a coalition of established farmer's organizations. The rapid rise of the free-speech movement at Berkeley has been attributed to a similar merger of existing campus organizations (Lipset and Wolin 1965).

At the individual level, multiorganizational fields can serve to draw individuals into a movement by virtue of their involvement in organizations that serve as the associational network out of which a new movement emerges. This was true, as Rosenthal et al. (1985) note, in the case of the nineteenth-century women's rights movement in New York, with a disproportionate number of the movement's recruits sharing a dense network of multiple memberships in voluntary organizations. Curtis and Zurcher (1973) have observed a similar pattern in connection with the rise of two antipornography groups. In their study, the authors provide convincing data to support their contention that recruits were overwhelmingly drawn from the broad multiorganizational fields in which both groups were embedded.

We hope to contribute to the literature on multiorganizational fields and recruitment to social movements by bringing some of the conceptual and methodological rigor of formal network analysis (see Burt 1980) to bear on the topic of recruitment. Using Breiger's (1974) method of analyzing overlapping organizational affiliations, we examine, at both the organizational and individual levels of analysis, the structure of multiorganizational fields for a set of applicants (both participants and nonparticipants) to the Freedom Summer project. The basic question we seek to answer is whether the structure of the multiorganizational field affected the applicants likelihood of participating in the campaign.

In the next section, we briefly describe the instance of collective action examined in this study. This is followed by a discussion on the various aspects of the measurement of the multiorganizational field for the set of applicants to Freedom Summer that we study in this paper, and the analytical techniques used in this study. The results of the three steps are then presented. First, we discuss the structure of the interorganizational level of analysis. Next, we discuss the results at the individual level of analysis. Finally, we predict activism among the applicants using variables measuring individuals' structural position in the multiorganizational field. In the final section, we conclude by discussing the theoretical implications of our results for the study of multiorganizational fields and recruitment to social movements.

THE MISSISSIPPI FREEDOM SUMMER PROJECT

This paper represents an attempt to study the role of multiorganizational fields on recruitment to a single, highly visible case of high risk/cost activism: the 1964 Mississippi Freedom Summer project. That campaign brought hundreds of primarily white, northern college students to Mississippi for all, or part of, the summer of 1964 to help staff freedom schools, register black voters, and dramatize the continued denial of civil rights to blacks throughout the South. The Freedom Summer campaign was both costly and risky. Volunteers were asked to commit an average of two months of their summer to a project that was to prove physically and emotionally harrowing for nearly everyone. Moreover, they were expected to be financially independent in this effort. Thus, they were not only asked to give up their chance of summer employment elsewhere, but to support themselves as well.[1]

Preliminary to their participation in the campaign, all prospective volunteers were required to fill out detailed applications providing information on, among other topics, their organizational affiliations, college activities, and reasons for volunteering. On the basis of these applications (and, on occasion, subsequent interviews), the prospective volunteer was either accepted or rejected. Acceptance did not necessarily mean participation in the campaign, however. In advance of the summer, many of the accepted applicants informed campaign staffers that they would not be taking part in the summer effort after all. Completed applications for all three groups—rejects, participants, and withdrawals[2]—were copied and coded from the originals which now repose in the archives of the Martin Luther King, Jr. Center for the Study of Non-Violence in Atlanta and the New Mississippi Foundation in Jackson, Mississippi. These applications provide a unique source of archival data for assessing the relative importance of various factors in recruitment to high risk/cost activism. The data used in this study are taken from these applications.

It is important to note that these data are collected during a relatively late phase of the Freedom Summer mobilization. This is important because network factors are usually seen as crucial in the initial phases of the mobilization process (see Snow et al. 1980), drawing individuals into the movement and socializing them to share the goals and ideologies of the movement. Because our data are for individuals who have already applied to participate in the Freedom Summer project, we cannot assess the importance of network or other factors during the early stages of the mobilization process. However, while these data cannot address the factors that attracted individuals to apply to the Freedom Summer project in the first place, these data are ideally suited for studying the network or other factors that maintain commitment to the Freedom Summer Campaign among the set of applicants to the project. Unlike much prior research in the area which study activists *after* the onset of the campaign in question, our study provides data on individuals before their participation or nonparticipation in the movement. Therefore, for this late stage of the process, we are able to identify the factors that distinguish between activists and nonactivists, that is, those who followed through on their intention to participate in the summer program, and those who withdrew from the project.

DATA AND METHODS

We have two goals in this paper. The first is to describe the structure of the multiorganizational fields in which applicants to Freedom Summer were embedded. The second goal is to examine the role of structural position in the multiorganizational field in recruitment to Freedom Summer. Toward this end, we use methods of network analysis to define the multiorganizational field for applicants to Freedom Summer at both the individual and organizational levels of analysis. However, before explaining how network methods can be used to address this problem, we must first clarify some conceptual issues that derive from the use of a network perspective.

When dealing with network structures, an important issue that needs to be addressed is the definition of the boundaries of network structure (Lauman et al. 1982). We define the network boundary as the community containing the university or college that the Freedom Summer applicants affiliate with. There are two reasons for this conception. First, the university or college represents the locus of the recruiting efforts for the project (see McAdam 1987, Chapter 2). Second, it also corresponds to the theoretical definition of a multiorganizational field as given by Curtis and Zurcher (1973), that is, multiorganizational fields are defined within community settings. The first of these two reasons grounds our definition of the community as the network boundary in a "realist" metatheoretical approach to defining network boundaries, that is, where ". . . the investigator adopts the presumed vantage point of the actors themselves in defining the boundaries of social entities" (Laumann et al. 1982, p. 20). At a lower level of abstraction, using the university or college as the operational boundary also corresponds to a positional approach to network boundary definition, that is, where membership "... refers to presence or absence of some attribute, most commonly occupancy of a position in a formally constituted group" (Laumann et al. 1982, p. 23).

In this paper, we have limited ourselves to the 23 applicants from one university—the University of Wisconsin—for which we have complete data. We are still in the process of obtaining and coding the detailed organizational affiliations data that are required to determine the multiorganizational fields for respondents from other colleges and universities. By focusing on just one recruitment site, we buy depth of analysis at the cost of breadth. However, rare among studies of social movements, the small number of subjects in this study has the advantage of allowing us to examine the role of little-studied small group network processes in social movements (see Fine and Stoecker 1985). Note that in future studies we will vary the recruitment context by examining a number of colleges or universities as the data for other sites become available.[3]

We develop measures of multiorganizational fields by recording the organizational affiliations for each of the 23 applicants to Freedom Summer from the University of Wisconsin. It is important to note that, in keeping with the idea of the college or university as the social context of recruitment, we code only those organizations that are locally based, that is, either campus organizations or local Madison organizations (e.g., the University of Wisconsin Chapter of the Friends of the Student's Non-Violent Coordinating Committee or the Madison Wisconsin Chapter of the Congress of Racial Equality). Of the 22 organizations that were named by the applicants to Freedom Summer from the University of Wisconsin, 17 met this criterion. For example, membership in extra-local religious organizations, or national organizations (e.g., the Democratic party) were excluded from consideration. However, campus or local-level affiliates of national organizations (e.g., Young Democrats) were used in these analyses if respondents mention the campus or local-level organizations explicitly.[4]

As a result of these coding decisions, we formed a 23 by 17 people by organizational affiliations matrix. Using Breiger's (1974) method of analyzing overlapping organizational affiliations, we reworked this 23 by 17 matrix to reflect network relations among the set of applicants to Freedom Summer at both the organizational and individual levels of analysis. As we argued above, we see relations at both of these levels as corresponding to Curtis and Zurcher's (1973) notion of multiorganizational fields.[5] At the organizational level, we used Breiger's (1974) procedure to produce a 17 by 17 organization by organization matrix showing the number of people all possible pairs of organizations share. As such, this matrix describes the structure of relations of overlapping memberships among locally-based organizations. Individuals serve to link the various organizations. Note that this relational matrix is by its definition symmetric, that is, the number of people linking organization i to organization j is the same as the number of people linking j and i.

At the individual level of analysis, we derived a 23 by 23 people by people matrix describing the number of organizations that all possible pairs of applicants share.[6] This matrix reveals the structure of common memberships in local organizations. Therefore, organizations serve as the links among individual applicants to Freedom Summer. Unlike past research in this area, which discusses the role of the *number* of social movement organizations that recruits are involved in (McCarthy and Zald 1977, p. 1218), our approach examines the effects of the *pattern* of overlapping organizational membership on recruitment.

Because the organizations at the community level are usually small so that members are likely to know one another, it is reasonable to ascribe social significance to these network relations at both levels of analysis. Although these ties may also reflect friendship or other interpersonal relations, at the very least, the individual-level network relations imply face-to-face encounters, that are likely to be crucial in micromobilization processes (Gamson et al. 1982, pp. 1-12). At both levels of analysis, the multiorganizational field serves as an important resource base for social movements (Curtis and Zurcher 1973). However, multiorganizational fields are not uniform; they vary in the fine texture of their relations, and these variations may have significant implications for resource mobilization. Relations among the actors (either individual or organizations) can serve as communication channels that can be activated in helping SMOs mobilize resources. As we describe below, we test the hypothesis that the structural positon of the Freedom Summer applicants, within the multiorganizational field, facilitates the recruitment of personnel to the Freedom Summer project.

For both levels of analysis (i.e., organizational and individual), we examine various aspects of the structure of relations in the multiorganizational field. We use three measures of network centrality to characterize each organization's and individual's structural position within their respective networks: relative degree, relative betweenness, and prominence. In each case, the indices measure each actors' position in the network relative to every other actor. As such, these measures are not simple attributes of each actor (cf. Fireman and Gamson 1979), but are a function of the structure of the overall network each actor is embedded in (on "embeddedness," see Granovetter 1985).

The *relative degree* measure of centrality is each actor's average strength of relation (Burt 1983). The index measures the average number of ties (shared either by people or organizations) that each actor has with every other actor. The *relative betweenness* measure of centrality is the number of "bridges" each actor forms between all other actors as a proportion of the number of possible bridges in the network (see Freeman 1977, 1979). It measures the extent to which each actor stands between other actors in the network and, as such, measures each actor's potential for brokerage or gatekeeping (Freeman 1980).[7] *Prominence* is a measure of centrality where each actor's centrality is weighted by the centrality of the actors to whom they are linked (Bonacich 1972; Knoke and Burt 1983). The idea is to distinguish among actors that are equally central (i.e., that are tied to the same number of others in the network) on the basis of the centrality of the actors to whom they are tied. Note that because each actor's prominence is weighted by every other actor's prominence, the prominence measure is computed as a routine eigenvector problem where every actor's prominence scores are computed simultaneously (see Knoke and Burt 1983).

In addition to examining the structural position of both organizations and individuals within the multiorganizational field, we also attempt to examine the effects of structural position on individual activism. We are limited in this attempt by the small number of cases in our analyses. Our dependent variable in these analyses is participation or nonparticipation in the summer project. Of the 23 applicants from the University of Wisconsin, only 10 actually participated in the program, and 13 applicants were withdrawals. We coded activism as a dummy variable where a 1 indicates participation and 0 indicates that the applicant withdrew from the program.

We predict activism in two steps. First, we use the three measures of structural position within the multiorganizational field at the individual level of analysis to predict activism. Because we have very few cases in these analyses (i.e., 23) and the three measures are highly interrelated, we examine each of their effects separately. Second, we examine the effects of the measures of structural position after attempting to control for the effects of individual level variables on activism.

More specifically, the individual level variables which we thought might explain activism were applicants' age, years of education, gender (1=male), past level of civil rights involvement, in-state versus out-of-state residence, and major area of study (social science and humanities versus other). Age, gender, and years of education are likely to reflect individual constraints on activism. Because of parental and peer sex-role expectations, we expect females to be less likely to undertake the Freedom Summer project than males. Older individuals are likely to be freer of parental and other constraints, and therefore, are more likely to attend Freedom Summer than younger individuals. On the other hand, subjects who are more advanced in their educational careers are less likely to be able to commit a summer to civil rights activism. We see past civil rights involvement as reflecting either the individual's attitudinal affinity with the goals of the civil rights movement, and/or previous integration into activist networks. Our hypothesis regarding the major area of study variable is that social science and humanities majors are likely to be more socially conscious than business or natural science major, and therefore, will be more likely to attend Freedom Summer. Finally, we distinguish in-state versus out-of-state residence and hypothesize that applicants who are from out-of-state are likely to be freer of parental constraints than applicants attending college in their home state of residence.

With the exception of past civil rights activity, the coding of these variables is straightforward. Both participants and withdrawals were asked to list on their applications any previous civil rights activities they were involved in. We assigned a numeric value to each activity reflecting its intensity relative to other forms of civil rights activism. The idea here was to distinguish between what Oliver (1984) has called token and active contributions to collective action. For example, participation in the Freedom Rides was assigned a score of "7," while contributing money to a civil rights organization was designated a "1." We then assigned each subject the sum of the points for the activities reported on their applications.

ANALYSIS

Our goal in these analyses is to examine the role of multiorganizational fields in recruitment to the Freedom Summer campaign. We begin by presenting descriptive information for the organization-level multiorganizational field.

Organizational-Level Multiorganizational Field

Table 1 shows the organization-level multiorganizational field for the University of Wisconsin applicants to Freedom Summer. Each of the organizations listed has at least one member who was an applicant to Freedom Summer. Casual inspection of the list reveals that the majority of these organizations were clearly SMOs. These included Madison or University of Wisconsin chapters of such groups as the Students for a Democratic Society (SDS), Friends of the Student's Non-Violent Coordinating Committee (SNCC), and the Congress of Racial Equality (CORE).

Although the majority of organizations listed by the Freedom Summer applicants were SMOs, there were some exceptions to this pattern. Two fraternities (Phi Beta Kappa and Psi Epsilon), and five other nonmovement organizations (UW Student Employee Association, Channing-Murray House, UW Contemporary Affairs Forum, Coed's Congress, and the UW Rugby Club) are among the organizations listed by applicants to Freedom Summer. While by virtue of being mentioned by Freedom Summer applicants these organizations are part of the multiorganizational field surrounding the Freedom Summer project, these organizations are clearly in a marginal position in the field. The Rugby Club, Coed's Congress, UW Contemporary Affairs Forum, and Phi Beta Kappa are all isolates (i.e., they do not share any members with other organizations in the network).

Table 1.   Number of Applicants Sharing Organizational Memberships Among the Organizations Named by Applicants to Freedom Summer from the University of Wisconsin

	a	b	c	d	e	f	g	h	i	j	k	l	m	n	o	p	q
a: Anti-urban Renewal		—	—	—	—	—	—	—	—	—	—	—	—	—	—	—	—
b: Student Peace Union			1	1	—	—	—	—	—	—	—	—	—	—	—	—	—
c: CORE-Madison				3	1	1	—	1	—	—	—	—	—	1	1	—	—
d: UW Friends of SNCC					—	—	1	1	—	—	—	—	—	—	—	—	—
e: UW SDS						1	—	—	—	—	—	—	—	—	—	—	—
f: Students for Peace and Disarmament							—	—	—	—	—	—	—	—	—	—	—
g: Psi Epsilon Fraternity								—	—	—	—	—	—	—	—	—	—
h: UW Socialist Club									—	1	1	—	—	—	—	—	—
i: Social Action Comm-Unitarians										—	—	—	—	—	—	—	—
j: UW Student Employee Assoc.											1	—	—	—	—	—	—
k: Channing-Murray House												1	—	—	—	—	—
l: UW Student Peace Center													—	—	—	—	—
m: UW Contemporary Affairs Forum														—	—	—	—
n: Young Democrats															1	—	—
o: Coeds' Congress																—	—
p: UW Rugby Club																	—
q: Phi Beta Kappa																	

Notes: Lowercase letters denote organizations; '—' = Absence of relation.

If we consider the remaining organizations, there are two isolated SMOs, that is, their only ties to the multiorganizational field are through having their members apply to Freedom Summer. These organizations are the Social Action Committee of the Unitarian Church, and the Anti-Urban Renewal organization. The rest of the organizations listed by the applicants to Freedom Summer show a pattern of interlocking memberships. The largest number of overlaps (3) is between the UW Friends of SNCC (at the national level, the organizers of Freedom Summer), and the Madison Chapter of CORE. The remaining organizations share only one member in common.

While the degree of overlap in the network overall does not appear to be very high, the configuration of the overlaps is revealing. In addition to a high degree of overlap among themselves, CORE-Madison and the UW Friends of SNCC both share members with two other organizations: the Student Peace Union, and the University of Wisconsin Socialist Club. Therefore, these four organizations have both direct links (where the various pairs of organizations have overlapping members) and *indirect* links (where each organization shares membership with a common third organization) among themselves. Beyond

Table 2. Network Centrality Indices for Organizations
Named by Applicants to Freedom Summer
from the University of Wisconsin

		Relative Degree[a]	Relative Betweenness[b]	Prominence[c]
a:	Anti-urban Renewal	.000	.000	.000
b:	Student Peace Union	.125	.000	.486
c:	CORE-Madison	.438	.280	1.000
d:	UW Friends of SNCC	.250	.100	.677
e:	UW SDS	.125	.000	.409
f:	Students for Peace and Disarmament	.125	.000	.409
g:	Psi Epsilon Fraternity	.063	.000	.196
h:	UW Socialist Club	.250	.200	.650
i:	Social Action Comm-Unitarians	.000	.000	.000
j:	UW Student Employee Assoc.	.125	.000	.274
k:	Channing-Murray House	.188	.080	.293
l:	UW Student Peace Center	.063	.000	.085
m:	UW Contemporary Affairs Forum	.000	.000	.000
n:	Young Democrats	.125	.000	.409
o:	Coeds' Congress	.125	.000	.409
p:	UW Rugby Club	.000	.000	.000
q:	Phi Beta Kappa	.000	.000	.000

Notes: [a] Relative Degree is the number of organizations each organization is linked to as a proportion of the total number of organizations.
[b] Relative Betweenness is the number of "bridges" each organization forms between all other organizations as a proportion of the number of possible bridges in the network.
[c] Prominence is a measure of centrality where each organization's centrality is weighted by the centrality of the organizations it is linked to.

the Student Peace Union and the UW Socialist Club, CORE-Madison and UW Friends of SNCC are also connected to different sets of organizations. CORE-Madison shares members with UW-SDS, Students for Peace and Disarmament, Young Democrats, and Coeds' Congress, while UW Friends of SNCC only overlaps members with the Psi Epsilon Fraternity.

If we consider indirect links, the UW Socialist Club serves as the bridge between both the UW Friends of SNCC and CORE-Madison and a set of interconnected organizations. The UW Socialist Club is tied to the UW Student Employee Association and Channing-Murray House (a campus-based Unitarian organization), which are also linked to one another. Tracing out the links even further, we find that Channing-Murray House is also connected to the UW Student Peace Center.

Table 2 summarizes various aspects of the overall structure of relations in the organization-level multiorganizational field. As we described above, the three indices presented in this table measure various aspects of each organizations' structural position within the network. Because these are measures of each actors relationship to every other actor in the network, these social structural measures do not simply reflect the attributes of each of the organizations, but reflect the structure of the entire network.

The three measures are highly correlated,[8] but careful inspection shows that there are subtle but important differences among them. if we consider the relative degree measure, we find that CORE-Madison emerges as the most central organization in the multiorganizational field. The average strength of links from other organizations in the field to CORE-Madison is .438. The next most central organizations are the UW Friends of SNCC and the UW Socialist Club, each with average centrality scores of .25 from other organizations in the field. Channing-Murray House is the next most central organization, showing an average linkage strength of .188 from the other organizations in the field.

Turning to the relative betweenness measure, we find that CORE-Madison is again the most central organization. However, where the relative degree measure shows UW Friends of SNCC and the UW Socialist Club to be equally central, the betweenness measure shows the UW Socialist Club as more central than the UW Friends of SNCC. This is because the UW Socialist Club serves as a unique bridge between CORE-Madison and a number of organizations in the field (i.e., the UW Student Employee Association, Channing-Murray House, and through Channing-Murray House, to the UW Student Peace Center). The only other organizations that serve as bridges to other organizations are the UW Friends of SNCC and Channing-Murray House.

Finally, the last column in Table 2 shows the results for the prominence measure of centrality. The prominence measure adjusts each organization's prominence by the prominence of the organizations that each organization is linked to. The results for this measure show only subtle differences when compared to the results using the relative degree measure. This is not surprising because these two measures are very highly correlated.

As with the other two measures, the most prominent organization in the multiorganizational field is CORE-Madison. Whereas the UW Socialist Club emerges as the next most central organization according to the relative betweenness measure by virtue of its bridging function, and the relative degree measure shows the UW Socialist Club and the UW Friends of SNCC as equally central, the prominence measure slightly favors the UW Friends of SNCC over the UW Socialist Club. This is because, although the UW Friends of SNCC and the UW Socialist Club both have the same number of ties to other organizations, the organizations that the UW Socialist Club are linked to tend to be more marginal than the organizations that the UW Friends of SNCC have ties to.

If we consider the rank-orderings, the patterns for the other organizations are similar to the results for the relative degree measure. There are two exceptions, however. First, the Student Peace Union is more central according to the prominence measure than the relative degree measure. This is because it is tied to the two most prominent organizations (i.e., CORE-Madison and UW Friends of SNCC), while the other five organizations with the same relative degree scores (UW SDS, Students for Peace and Disarmament, UW Student Employee Association, Young Democrats, and Coeds' Congress) are all linked with more marginal organizations.

The second difference between the relative degree and prominence measures is the UW Student Employee Association, which is less central according to the prominence measure than the relative degree measure. This is because the organizations that the UW Student Employee Association is linked to are less prominent than the other organizations with the same relative degree scores.

What do these analyses tell us about the structure of the organization-level multiorganization field for Wisconsin applicants to Freedom Summer? The various measures of centrality reveal a center-periphery structure to the multiorganizational field. The two civil rights organizations are clearly at the center of the network. CORE-Madison is the most central organization, with the next closest organization being the UW Friends of SNCC. The UW Socialist Club is also quite important in the network, being relatively close to the center of the network and serving as a bridge to other more peripheral organizations. Moreover, the isolated organizations tend to be far afield from the civil rights movement, for example, the UW Rugby Club or Phi Beta Kappa.

In sum, it appears that the multiorganizational field is structured around a core of organizations that are oriented toward civil rights issues, with other activist organizations linked to those. The least central organizations tend to be of a nonactivist nature. This pattern is a function of the choices of organizational affiliations of individual applicants to Freedom Summer. However, the macro consequence of these individual choices is a stable resource base for the Freedom Summer project that is structured in such a way that those organizations that are most likely to offer assistance and support during resource mobilization are in a better positon to do so. The aggregate structure of these organizational affiliations is what we mean by the organization-level multiorganizational field.

Individual-Level Multiorganizational Field

Table 3 presents the individual-level multiorganizational field. Each entry in the matrix denotes the number of organizations that each pair of individuals share membership in. The individuals labelled A to J all participated in Freedom Summer, while those labelled K to W withdrew from the project.

Two interesting patterns emerge in Table 3. First, the density of ties appears to vary with participation in Freedom Summer. That is, there is a tendency for interrelationships among those who participated in Freedom Summer (i.e., A to J) to be denser than the relations between the set of participants and

Table 3. Number of Organizational Ties
Among the Applicants to Freedom Summer
from the University of Wisconsin

	A	B	C	D	E	F	G	H	I	J	K	L	M	N	O	P	Q	R	S	T	U	V	W
A		—	—	—	—	—	—	—	—	—	—	—	—	—	—	—	—	—	—	—	—	—	—
B			—	—	—	—	—	—	—	—	—	—	—	—	—	—	—	—	—	—	—	—	—
C				—	—	—	—	—	—	—	—	—	—	—	—	—	—	—	—	—	—	—	—
D					—	1	—	1	2	2	—	—	—	—	—	—	1	—	—	1	—	—	—
E						—	—	—	—	—	—	—	—	—	—	—	—	—	—	—	—	—	—
F							—	—	1	1	—	—	—	—	1	—	—	1	—	—	1	—	—
G								—	—	—	—	—	—	—	—	—	—	—	—	—	—	—	—
H									1	1	—	—	—	—	—	—	—	—	—	—	—	—	—
I										2	—	—	—	—	—	—	1	—	—	1	—	—	—
J											—	—	—	—	—	1	1	—	—	1	—	—	—
K												—	—	—	—	—	—	—	—	—	—	—	—
L													—	—	—	—	—	—	—	—	—	—	—
M														—	—	—	—	—	—	—	—	—	—
N															—	—	—	—	—	—	—	—	—
O																—	—	—	—	—	—	—	—
P																	—	1	—	—	—	—	—
Q																		—	—	1	—	—	—
R																			—	—	—	—	—
S																				—	—	—	—
T																					—	—	—
U																						—	—
V																							—
W																							

Notes: Capital letters denote individuals; '—' = Absence of Relation; persons A through J attended Freedom Summer; persons K through W did not attend Freedom Summer.

withdrawals (between A-J and K-W), and the density among withdrawals (K to W). If we compute the density among those participating in Freedom Summer,[9] we find a density of .200 (9/45 = .200), while the density for ties between the set of participants and withdrawals is .077 (10/130 = .077), and the density for withdrawals is .026 (2/78 = .026).

Second, the most dense region of the network is the interrelations among D, F, I, and J. In addition to all being participants in Freedom Summer, persons D, I, and J all share memberships in two organizations. Inspection of the original 23 by 17 people by organization matrix (not presented here) shows that the two organizations linking the three are CORE-Madison and UW Friends of SNCC, the most central organizations in the organization-level multiorganizational field. Person F is also linked to I and J through membership in CORE-Madison.

Table 4 shows the centrality measures for each of the individuals in the individual-level multiorganizational field. As with the organization-level

Table 4. Network Centrality Indices for Applicants to Freedom Summer from the University of Wisconsin

	Relative Degree[a]	Relative Betweenness[b]	Prominence[c]
A	.000	.000	.000
B	.000	.000	.000
C	.000	.000	000
D	.273	.010	.970
E	.000	.000	.000
F	.273	.030	.910
G	.000	.000	.000
H	.136	.000	.549
I	.273	.010	.970
J	.318	.070	1.000
K	.000	.000	.000
L	.000	.000	.000
M	.000	.000	.000
N	.045	.000	.170
O	.000	.000	.000
P	.091	.030	.194
Q	.227	.000	.883
R	.045	.000	.036
S	.000	.000	.000
T	.227	.000	.883
U	.000	.000	.000
V	.000	.000	.000
W	.000	.000	.000

Notes: Capital letters denote individuals; persons A through J attended Freedom Summer; persons K through W did not attend Freedom Summer.
[a] Relative Degree is the number of organizations each organization is linked to as a proportion of the total number of organizations.
[b] Relative Betweenness is the number of "bridges" each organization forms between all other organizations as a proportion of the number of possible bridges in the network.
[c] Prominence is a measure of centrality where each organization's centrality is weighted by the centrality of the organizations it is linked to.

network, the centrality scores are highly correlated.[10]. For all three measures, the centrality scores for those who participated in Freedom Summer tend to be higher than the scores for those who withdrew from the project. In particular, person J shows the highest centrality score on all three measures. If we consider the relative degree measure, persons D, F, and I are all the next most central. Inspection of Table 3 showed that these four individuals were all members of the core organizations in the organization-level multiorganizational field.

It is useful, at this point, to speculate on what it is about network centrality that may account for its relationship with individual activism. In some cases, it may be that structural position in the network serves a crucial communication function, alerting individual actors to planned collective action. Although this may have occurred in this case, as we discussed above, our data cannot offer any evidence for this early phase of the mobilization process. Because an awareness of the summer project was required for one to apply to the campaign, it is clear that it is not this function of network position that accounts for the relationship between network position and activism. In this case, then we must look elsewhere for the role of network position. One very likely possibility, in our view, is that network centrality helps maintain the individual's commitment to the impending collective action by exposing the applicant to a) more social support for participation while b) increasing the social cost of nonparticipation. Isolates or individuals who are only marginally linked to others in the network receive less support for going and face reduced social costs for not going than more popular or prominent individuals.

Whether or not this interpretation is correct, it is clear that participation in Freedom Summer is not *only* a function of structural position in the multiorganizational field. There are many exceptions to the tendency for the participants to be more central than the withdrawals. Persons A, B, C, E, and G are all participants in Freedom Summer, but they are all isolates. On the other hand, actors Q and T are two of the most central actors (at least according to relative degree and prominence measures), and they withdrew from the Freedom Summer project. We will return to the role of the structural position in the multiorganizational field in the next section when we examine the relative importance of individual versus structural factors in predicting participation in Freedom Summer.

Although the three measures are highly correlated, the subtle differences among the measures are informative. If we examine the relative betweenness measure, the second most central people are F, a participant, and P, a withdrawal. Actor P's relatively high level of betweenness is due to his/her role as a bridge to the relatively marginal R (see the relative degree and prominence scores) by means of shared membership in the UW Socialist Club. Actor F shares an organizational membership (i.e., UW-SDS) with the relatively marginal actor N. Finally, Actors D and I, both participants, are the next most central actors in the network. Both these actors share membership in CORE-Madison and UW Friends of SNCC, the two most central organizations in the organization-level network.

The prominence measure is extremely highly correlated with the relative degree measure (.99), but less highly correlated with the relative betweenness measure (i.e., .53). Whereas the relative degree measure shows actor J to be the most central actor in the network, and actors D, F, and I are all tied for next most central, both the relative betweenness and prominence measures distinguish among these latter three actors, albeit in different ways. While the relative betweenness measure favors actor F, the prominence measure favors actors D and I. This is because actor F serves as a bridge to actor N and this is reflected in the relative betweenness measure. In contrast, both D and I are more strongly related to the most central actor in the field (i.e., actor J) than is actor F. Since the prominence measure weights each actor's prominence by the prominence of the actors they are linked to, the prominence measure favors actors D and I.

What do these analyses tell us about the structure of the individual-level multiorganizational field? Like the analyses of the organization-level field, these analyses show that there is a clear core of activists that are highly interrelated in the network. These are actors D, F, I, J, Q, and T. These individuals tend to overlap by means of shared membership in the most central organizations in the organization-level network, CORE-Madison, and UW Friends of SNCC. In fact, the three individuals receiving the highest prominence scores (D, I, and J) all share membership in *both* CORE-Madison, and UW Friends of SNCC. There is nothing inherent in these methods which guarantees this result. The confluence of the most central organizations and most central individuals in their respective networks shows that there is a coherent structure cutting across both levels of the multiorganizational field.

In addition, despite some notable exceptions, there is a tendency for more central individuals in the multiorganizational field to be participants in the Freedom Summer project. Also, network ties among the set of withdrawals to Freedom Summer are less dense than among either the set of participants or between the sets of participants and withdrawals. These results suggest that structural position in the multiorganizational field is likely to predict participation in Freedom Summer. This is consistent with the notion that structural factors are important determinants of participation in social movements; that is, that network contacts are important in maintaining individuals' commitment to protest activity. However, the fact that there are exceptions to the pattern of more central individuals participating in Freedom Summer, suggests that there are other determinants of activism besides structural position in the multiorganizational field. We turn to this issue next.

Models Predicting Activism

Our goal in this section is to examine the role of structural position in the individual-level multiorganizational field in predicting participation in the Freedom Summer campaign. As we discussed in the last section, structural position is unlikely to be the only determinant of participation. Moreover, it is possible that other factors might explain the tendency for individuals who are in a more central position in the multiorganizational field to be more likely to attend Freedom Summer than individuals who are less central. That is, there may be individual background characteristics that explain the relationship between centrality and activism. We attempt to test this hypothesis by controlling for a number of individual background characteristics in a model predicting activism for the applicants from the University of Wisconsin.[11]

Table 5.   Logistic Regression Analyses Predicting
Participation in the Freedom Summer Project
(N = 23; Standard Errors in Parentheses)

	Equation 1	Equation 2	Equation 3
Relative Degree	6.284**		
	(4.023)		
Relative Betweenness		50.501*	
		(42.550)	
Prominence			1.731**
			(1.120)
Constant	-.790**	-.543*	-.763**
	(.553)	(.472)	(.545)
-2Log- Likelihood	28.788	29.180	28.886

Notes: * = T-value > 1.0; ** = p < .20

Tables 5 and 6 show the results of our attempt to assess the independent effects of the structural and individual background variables on participation in the Freedom Summer project. Table 5 shows the total effects of the three centrality measures on participation in Freedom Summer. We study the effects of each of the centrality measures separately because they are highly correlated and we have very few cases with which to try and distinguish their independent effects. In all three equations, the centrality scores meet our weak criterion of statistical significance, that is, in each case, the coefficients exceed their standard errors. Moreover, in the equations for relative degree and prominence, the coefficients reach the .20 level of statistical significance. In each case, the coefficients are positive, indicating that more central individuals are significantly more likely to participate in Freedom Summer than less central individuals. In all three equations, the coefficients for the intercept are negative, indicating that individuals with centrality scores of zero are less likely to attend Freedom Summer than more central individuals. In the case of the relative degree and prominence measures, scores of zero refer to structural isolates, that is, individuals that do not have common memberships with anyone else in the network. In the case of the relative betweenness measure, scores of zero indicate that the individual does not serve as a unique bridge among others in the network. The fact that marginal individuals are less likely to participate in the Freedom Summer campaign is consistent with the idea discussed above that structural isolates have less social support for participation and lower social costs for nonparticipation.

Table 6. Logistic Regression Analyses Predicting
Participation in the Freedom Summer Project
(N = 23; Standard Errors in Parentheses)

	Equation 1	Equation 2	Equation 3	Equation 4
Age	.166	.419*	.135	.446*
	(.302)	(.413)	(.308)	(.441)
Education	-1.408**	-1.764**	-.990**	-2.007**
	(.713)	(1.193)	(.724)	(1.433)
Gender	11.456	13.202	11.985	15.237
(1 = Male)	(50.710)	(44.170)	(49.660)	(42.350)
Past Activism	.265**	.099	.318**	.074
	(.176)	(.239)	(.209)	(.290)
In-State	1.070	1.295	1.199	1.821
	(2.212)	(2.171)	(2.346)	(2.503)
Major	-.354	-.369	-.478	-.707
	(2.113)	(1.944)	(2.248)	(2.126)
Relative Degree		17.857*		
		(14.620)		
Relative Betweenness			-29.088	
			(63.170)	
Prominence				7.025*
				(5.593)
Constant	-5.96	2.573	-1.394	3.475
	(51.150)	(44.930)	(50.140)	(43.360)
-2Log- Likelihood	14.524	12.262	14.310	10.974

Notes: * = T-value > 1.0; ** =p < .20

These results show that the relative degree and prominence conceptions of structural centrality are equally efficacious as sole predictors of participation in Freedom Summer. Apparently, the subtle distinctions between the relative degree and prominence measures we discussed above do not affect these individuals chances of participation in Freedom Summer (recall that prominence distinguishes among equally popular individuals on the basis of the centrality of the people each person is connected to). On the other hand, there is some evidence that the relative betweenness measure is a poorer predictor of participation in Freedom Summer than the other two structural measures for these subjects. It appears that brokers are more likely to attend Freedom Summer, but perhaps because of the lack of variation in the measure for this group, this tendency is less strong than the tendency for more popular and more prominent individuals to participate in the program.

If we consider the goodness of fit for these three equations, we find that each of the centrality scores decreases the log-likelihood statistic.[12] The baseline model with only the intercept in the equation yields a log-likelihood statistic of 31.492. The decrement for the relative degree measure is 2.704 while the corresponding figures for the prominence and relative betweenness measures are 2.606 and 2.312. In each case, the improvement in fit is significant at the .20 level of statistical significance.

We next consider the model for the individual background variables in Equation 1 in Table 6. Only two effects emerge as significant in this model. As we hypothesized, controlling the other variables in the model, individuals with high levels of education are less likely to attend Freedom Summer than less well-educated individuals. We interpret this as indicative of the increased constraints on time that people who are more advanced in their educational careers face. Also as expected, individuals with a higher level of past civil rights activity are more likely to attend Freedom Summer than individuals who have not had a history of involvement in civil rights activity. None of the other variables reach even our weak level of statistical significance. However, if we consider the goodness-of-fit of the model overall, we find that the improvement in fit for the model over the baseline model with just the intercept is highly significant. The log-likelihood statistic decreased by 16.968. With six degrees of freedom, this decrement to chi-square is significant at the .01 level.

These analyses suggest that the total effects of both structural position in the multiorganizational field and individual background characteristics are important determinants of participation in Freedom Summer when each are considered separately. In global terms, the individual background factors and the variables measuring structural position are about equally efficacious predictors of participation in Freedom Summer. This can be seen by comparing the decrement to chi-square per degree of freedom for the model with only individual variables with the models containing only the centrality measures. For the individual background factors, the decrement per degree of freedom is 2.928 ($16.968/6 = 2.868$) compared to decreases of 2.704, 2.606, and 2.312 for the relative degree, prominence, and relative betweenness centrality measures, respectively. However, while the individual background factors and the measures of structural position appear to be equally useful as predictors of participation in the Freedom Summer campaign, the analyses discussed thus far have not addressed the issue of the independent impact of the two sets of variables. We turn to that task next.

If we compare the goodness of fit statistics for Equation 1 with Equations 2 and 4, we find that both the relative degree and prominence centrality measures significantly improve fit over the model with just the individual background variables, but that the prominence measure is slightly better than the relative degree measure. The chi-square for the relative degree measure is significant at the .20 level (i.e., 2.262 with one degree of freedom), while corresponding figure for the prominence measure is significant at the .10 level (3.550 with 1 degree of freedom). This suggests that structural position in the multiorganizational field, conceived as either popularity or prominence, helps to explain participation in Freedom Summer, over and above the individual background variables.

In addition to the question of whether structural position and individual background factors have independent effects, we are also interested in their patterns of interrelations. Equations 2 and 4 in Table 6 show the partial effects of the individual background factors controlling for the three centrality measures. Equation 2 shows the independent effect of structural position as measured by relative degree. Controlling the individual background variables, individuals who are in a more central position in the multiorganizational field are more likely to attend Freedom Summer than more marginal individuals. This same result emerges in Equation 4 which measures structural position by means of the prominence measure. These results also lend credence to the notion that structural position has an effect on individuals' propensities to become active in the Freedom Summer campaign, independent of the individual background factors.

But other effects emerge in these models as well. The effect for education in Equations 2 and 4 remain the same as in the model including only individual background variables (Equation 1 in Table 6): More highly educated people are less likely to attend Freedom Summer than less well-educated people. However, there are some changes from Equation 1. First, the coefficient for age is strengthened in Equations 2 and 4 and becomes significant once the individual's structural position is controlled. We interpret the positive effect of age as suggestive of our hypothesis that, controlling other factors, older people face fewer parental constraints on their summer activities. The fact that the effect of age becomes stronger after controls are introduced suggests that structural position acts as a suppressor variable. That is, initially there appears to be no difference between the tendencies of older and younger applicants to attend Freedom Summer, but when we compare individuals in similar structural positions (as measured by the relative degree measure), we find that older applicants are more likely to attend Freedom Summer than younger applicants. It appears that older people are more likely to participate in Freedom Summer, but this tendency is hidden by the fact that younger people tend to be in more central positions in the multiorganizational network and this centrality serves to encourage these younger applicants to participate in Freedom Summer.

The second change from Equation 1 is that the effect of past civil rights activism on participation in Freedom Summer is explained by the individual's structural position in the multiorganizational field. There are two scenarios that might account for this result. First, past activism might cause structural position in the network. That is, activists may come to occupy central positions in the multiorganizational field by virtue of their prior history of civil rights activism. It appears that people with extensive civil rights histories are more likely to participate in the Freedom Summer project *because* they tend to be in more central positions in the multiorganizational field. This is because individuals who have been highly active in civil rights, but are not structurally central, are no more likely to attend Freedom Summer than less active individuals. If this is the correct scenario, then our resutls indicate that structural position is an intermediate variable, wholly mediating the effect of past activism on the probability of participation in Freedom Summer. Therefore, structural position should be seen as a proximate cause of participation, while past civil rights activity is a distal cause of participation in Freedom Summer. In the second scenario, the individual's past structural position might cause the individual's past civil rights activism. The individuals might have been drawn into civil rights activity by their past structural position in the multiorganizational network.

Whichever of these two scenarios is the correct one, it is clear that structural position in the multiorganizational field plays a critical role predicting participation in the Freedom Summer campaign. Of course, a true measure of structural position at a previous point in time is needed to be able to choose between the two scenarios with any confidence. However, because there is little reason to expect individuals' structural positions to be stable over time, we see the former scenario in which structural position is caused by past activism as the more reasonable of the two. This implies that structural position in the multiorganizational field is a product of individual interests in civil rights, but that those interests are not translated into a propensity to participate in Freedom Summer, except by virtue of these individuals' positions in the multiorganizational network. As such, structural position in the multiorganizational field serves as a crucial recruitment channel for the Freedom Summer campaign.

SUMMARY AND CONCLUSION

In this paper, we have examined the role of multiorganizational fields in recruitment to the 1964 Freedom Summer Campaign for a set of applicants from the University of Wisconsin. We started by examining the organization-level multiorganizational field for these subjects. We found that the field consisted of 17 community or university-based organizations, the majority of which qualify as SMOs.

We then used techniques of network analysis to examine the structure of overlapping memberships among the organizations in the field. We examined each organization's structural position in the field by examining three measures of network centrality: relative degree, relative betweenness, and prominence. Although these indices measure different structural features of the network, there are only subtle differences in the results among the measures. Overall, the three centrality measures show a clear center-periphery structure in this network. The most central organizations in the organization-level multiorganizational field are the two civil rights organizations (i.e., CORE-Madison and UW Friends of SNCC), while the sports club and fraternities (i.e., UW Rugby Club and Phi Beta Kappa and Psi Epsilon) tend to be the most peripheral organizations. With few exceptions, the other politically-oriented organizations (e.g., UW SDS, UW Socialist Club, Young Democrats) show an intermediate level of centrality.

We next examined the structure of the individual-level multiorganizational field. Here too, we found a center-periphery pattern in the network. Moreover, there is a confluence between the organizations and individuals forming the core of their respective networks: The three individuals that make up the core of the field all share membership in the core organizations of the organization-level multiorganizational field.

We then examined the role of structural position in the multiorganizational field in recruitment to Freedom Summer. Although we were limited by the small number of cases in the study, we found that individuals who are more central in the field are more likely to be participants than withdrawals to the Freedom Summer project. However, detailed inspection of each individual's centrality scores showed that there were notable exceptions to this pattern. Several of the Freedom Summer participants were structural isolates, not connected to anyone in the field, and two of the most structurally central individuals did not participate in Freedom Summer. This suggests that there are other determinants of participation in the Freedom Summer campaign besides structural position in the multiorganizational field. We hypothesized that individual background characteristics might also help account for participation in Freedom Summer.

To test this idea, we examined the effects of a number of individual background characteristics on the likelihood of participating in Freedom Summer. We found that more highly educated individuals were less likely to attend Freedom Summer than less educated individuals, and that people with extensive histories of civil rights activity were more likely to participate in Freedom Summer than people with little background in the civil rights movement.

Adding the centrality measures to this model shows that individuals who occupy a more central position in the multiorganizational field are more likely to participate in Freedom Summer, independent of the individual background factors. This lends support to our notion that centrality exposes the individual to more social support for participation and raises the costs of nonparticipation, independent of individual-level determinants of participation in Freedom Summer. This finding accords with the results of several other studies of individual activism (e.g., Bolton 1972). However, adding the relative degree and prominence network centrality measures to the equation with individual background characteristics also changes the effects of some of the individual background variables.

First, the introduction of the measures of structural position temper the effects of some of the individual background characteristics. Controlling for structural centrality strengthens the effect of age on the likelihood of participation. Second, and most important, structural position in the multiorganizational field explains the effect of past civil rights activity on the likelihood of participation in the Freedom Summer project. That is, the effect of past civil rights activity on participation becomes nil when the relative degree and prominence structural centrality measures are controlled. We argued that past civil rights activity is causally prior to both structural position and participation in Freedom Summer, so that the effect of past civil rights activity is wholly mediated by structural position in the multiorganizational field. It appears that people with extensive civil rights histories are more likely to participate in the Freedom Summer project because of their being in more central positions in the multiorganizational field.

At the end of our journey, what can we conclude about the role of multiorganizational fields in recruitment to social movement? Because of the small number of cases and the relatively low level of statistical significance used in this study, our conclusions must be seen as provisional, awaiting further research and replication before they can be seen as definitive. Nevertheless, we may draw some tentative conclusions.

The results lend support to the notion that structural position is an important determinant of participation in social movements: Network contacts are important in pulling individuals into protest activity. Social movement organizations do not exist in a vacuum, and the interconnections among formal organizations inherent in multiorganizational fields serve to facilitate recruitment to social movements. Even at a relatively late stage in the mobilization process, and among individuals who are predisposed to participation by virtue of being applicants to the campaign, we have shown that structural position in the multiorganizational field operates to differentiate between participants and withdrawals to Freedom Summer. We see this as due to a tendency on the part of more central individuals to receive more social support for participation, and experience more social costs for nonparticipation than more marginal individuals.

While prior investigators have shown similar results regarding the importance of structural factors in explaining activism, we go beyond their work in a number of important ways. First, we have extended the work in this area by sharpening the conception of the kinds of structural positions that can have important implications for recruitment. We found that more popular and prominent individuals in the individual-level multiorganizational field are more likely to engage in protest activity than less popular or prominent individuals, but that brokers are no more likely to engage in protest than nonbrokers. Second, while other researchers have shown that activists are often integrated into networks (see e.g., Snow et al. 1980), they have not shown that nonactivists are *not* exposed to network contacts. We have shown that structural factors differentiate between groups of participants and withdrawals, even among individuals that are predisposed to participate in collective action. Third, rare among studies in this area, we have shown that the effects of structural position on participation are independent of a number of individual-level determinants of activism.

Finally our results are suggestive of the complex interrelations between structural and individual background factors in producing activism. The aggregate structure of multiorganizational fields at both the individual or organizational levels is a macro consequence of individual choices for organizational affiliations. That is, each actors' position in the network is a complex function of all the other actors' choices for organizational affiliations. However, in addition to differentiating between participants and nonparticipants to Freedom Summer, the macro structure of the multiorganizational field serves to channel individuals whose personal biographies predispose them to protest activity into participation in the Freedom Summer campaign. Therefore, the multiorganizational field serves as more than a facilitator of protest. It also appears to be the prism that concentrates individual energies and propensities toward civil rights activity, and ultimately converts them into collective action.

ACKNOWLEDGMENTS

The first author gratefully acknowledges the support of the Rockefeller Foundation in undertaking this research. The second author gratefully acknowledges the support of a Guggenheim Fellowship, and a grant from the National Science Foundation. We would like to thank Dick Curtis, Ken Dauber, Debra Friedman, Roger Gould, Charles Kadushin, Edgar Kiser, Bert Klandermans, Jim Shockey, Michael Sobel, and Harrison White for their helpful comments and suggestions.

NOTES

1. For further descriptions of the Mississippi Freedom Summer Campaign, see McAdam (1987).
2. Very few of the applicants to Freedom Summer were rejected. Of the original 1,068 applicants to Freedom Summer, only 55 were rejected; 720 were participants in the program, and 239 were withdrawals. The participation status of an additional 54 applicants could not be

determined and have been coded as missing. All of the subset of applicants we analyze in this paper (i.e., applicants from the University of Wisconsin; see below) were either participants or withdrawals.

3. It is important to note that the applicants from the University of Wisconsin are not typical of the set of applicants to Freedom Summer in that Wisconsin is the only school where the majority of applicants did not participate in Freedom Summer. It is unclear whether this difference between the applicants from Wisconsin and the applicants from other schools has any important implications for the model we present here. Resolution of this issue will have to wait until we have data available for other schools so that we can vary the recruitment context.

4. Including extra-local organizations in the multiorganizational field does not change the results we present here. This is because very few interrelations among people or organizations are due to shared membership in extra-local organizations.

5. It is important to note that the multiorganizational field we derive corresponds to a late phase of the mobilization process (see above), and therefore, is only relevant to the applicants to Freedom Summer. One may imagine a much broader field, of which the one we identify in this paper is a subset, which would correspond to the University of Wisconsin as a whole. The structure of such a field might have been crucial in the early phase of the recruitment process, that is, in getting individuals to apply to Freedom Summer. Unfortunately, our data are not appropriate to study this earlier process and the corresponding broader multiorganizational field that potential applicants were drawn from. For these reasons, it is important not to interpret the field we study in this paper as applicable to the University of Wisconsin as a whole.

6. This is similar to the approach taken by Rosenthal et al. (1985) in their analysis of the 19th-century women's movement. However, the studies differ in two important respects. First, Rosenthal et al. focused on relations of overlapping organizational affiliations among people and did not study, as we do here, the interorganizational structure of the multiorganizational field. Second, because of the method they used to select people for inclusion in their study, they cannot, as we do in this study, compare activists and nonactivists to address the issue of the role of multiorganizational fields in recruitment to social movements.

7. Betweenness is a structural property defined on binary relations, that is, the measure only distinguishes the presence from the absence of a tie (see Freeman 1980). Because the networks studied here are not naturally dichotomous (see tables 1 and 3), we dichotomize the networks (one or greater number of ties $= 1$; zero $= 0$) for the purpose of computing the betweenness measure of centrality.

8. The correlations among the measures at the organizational level in Table 2 are as follows: relative degree-relative betweenness .87; relative degree-prominence.

9. Density is the number of ties among the actors as a proportion of the number of possible ties. As such, all that is distinguished is the presence or absence of a tie, so that the strength of the tie is irrelevant. For this reason, in computing density, the network is dichotomized as one or greater number of ties $= 1$; zero $= 0$. For discussions of the network concept of density, see Burt (1980).

10. The correlations among the three centrality measures at the individual level in Table 4 are as follows: relative degree-relative betweenness .62; relative degree-prominence .99; relative betweenness-prominence .53.

11. Because the dependent variable is dichotomous (i.e., participation at Freedom Summer versus not), we use techniques of logistic regression analysis (see Hanushek and Jackson 1977, Chapter 7). Ordinarily least squares regression estimates would result in estimates that are not minimum-variance because of heteroskedasticity. A logit specification provides a solution to this problem. Because we have only 23 cases in this study, we adopt a weak criterion of statistical significance, that is, a t-value of one, or whether a coefficient is larger than its standard error (for a similar procedure, see Lincoln and Zeitz 1980). Rao and Miller (1971, p. 37) point out that variables whose coefficients are smaller than their standard errors impair rather than improve

the model's goodness of fit. While Rao and Miller (1971, p. 37) discuss this in the context of ordinary least squares regression, the principles are analogous in the case of the logit models we present here (Aldrich and Nelson 1984, pp. 52-65).

12. The goodness-of-fit statistics reported here (i.e., -2Log-likelihood) is asymptotically distributed as chi-square with the number of degrees of freedom equal to the number of parameters fit (see Aldrich and Nelson 1984). Similar to log-linear models, this chi-square can be decomposed for models that are hierarchically-related.

REFERENCES

Aldrich, J.H. and F.D. Nelson. 1984. *Linear Probability, Logit, and Probit Models.* Beverly Hills, CA: Sage.
Aveni, A.F. 1978. "Organizational Linkages and Resource Mobilization: The Significance of Linkage Strength and Breadth." *The Sociological Quarterly* 19:185-202.
Bibby, R.W. and M.B. Brinkerhoff. 1974. "When Proselytizing Fails: An Organizational Analysis" *Sociological Analysis* 35:189-200.
Block, J.H., N. Haan, and B.M. Smith. 1968. "Activism and Apathy in Contemporary Adolescents." Pp. 189-200 in *Understanding Adolescence: Current Developments in Adolescent Psychology,* edited by J.F. Adams. Boston: Allyn and Bacon.
Bolton, C.D. 1972. "Alienation and Action: A Study of Peace Group Members." *American Journal of Sociology* 78:537-561.
Bonacich, P. 1972. "Techniques for Analyzing Overlapping Memberships." Pp. 176-185 in *Sociological Methodology 1972,* edited by H.L. Costner. San Francisco: Jossey-Bass.
Braungart, R.G. 1971. "Family Status, Socialization, and Student Politics: A Multivariate Analysis." *American Journal of Sociology* 77:108-129.
Breiger, R.L. 1974. "The Duality of Persons and Groups" *Social Forces* 53:181-189.
Burt, R.S. 1980. "Models of Network Structure." *Annual Review of Sociology* 6:79-141.
_____. 1983. "Range." Pp. 176-194 in *Applied Network Analysis,* edited by R.S. Burt and M.J. Minor. Beverly Hills, CA: Sage.
Curtis, R.L. and L.A. Zurcher, Jr. 1973. "Stable Resources of Protest Movement: The Multi-Organizational Field." *Social Forces* 52:53-60.
Fendrich, J. and E.S. Krauss. 1978. "Student Activism and Adult Left-Wing Politics: A Causal Model of Political Socialization for Black, White and Japanese Students of the 1960's Generation. Pp. 231-255 in *Research in Social Movements: Conflict and Change,* vol. 1, edited by L. Kriesberg. Greenwich, CT: JAI Press.
Fine, G.A. and R. Stoecker. 1985. "Can the Circle be Unbroken? Small Groups and Social Movements." *Advances in Group Processes* 2:1-28.
Fireman, B. and W.A. Gamson. 1979. "Utilitarian Logic in the Resource Mobilization Perspective." Pp. 8-44 in *The Dynamics of Social Movements: Resource Mobilization, Social Control, and Tactics,* edited by M.N. Zald and J.D. McCarthy. Cambridge, MA: Winthrop.
Flacks, R. 1967. "The Liberated Generations: An Exploration of the Roots of Student Protest." *Journal of Social Issues* 23:52-75.
Freeman, L. C. 1977. "A Set of Measures of Centrality Based on Betweenness." *Sociometry* 40:35-41.
_____. 1979. "Centrality in Social Networks: Conceptual Clarification." *Social Networks* 1:215-239.
_____. 1980. "The Gatekeeper, Pair-Dependency and Structural Centrality." *Quality and Quantity* 14:585-592.
Gamson, W.A., B. Fireman, and S. Rytina. 1982. *Encounters with Unjust Authority.* Homewood, IL: Dorsey Press.

Geschwender, J. 1968. "Explorations in the Theory of Social Movements and Revolution." *Social Forces* 47:127-135.

Glock, C.Y. 1964. "The Role of Deprivation in the Origin and Evolution of Religious Groups." In *Religion and Social Conflict,* edited by R. Lee and M. Marty. New York: Oxford University Press.

Granovetter, M.S. 1985. "Economic Action and Social Structure: The Problem of Embeddedness." *American Journal of Sociology* 91:481-510.

Gurney, J.N. and K.J. Tierney. 1982. "Relative Deprivation and Social Movements: A Critical Look at Twenty Years of Theory and Research." *The Sociological Quarterly* 23:33-47.

Hanushek, E.A. and J.E. Jackson. 1977. *Statistical Methods for Social Scientists.* New York: Academic Press.

Harrison, M.L. 1974. "Sources of Recruitment to Catholic Pentecostalism." *Journal for the Scientific Study of Religion* 33:49-64.

Heirich, M. 1977. "Change of Heart: A Test of Some Widely Held Theories of Religious Conversion." *Americna Journal of Sociology* 83:653-680.

Hicks, J.D. 1961. *The Populist Revolt.* Lincoln: University of Nebraska Press.

Jenkins, C. 1983. "Resource Mobilization Theory and the Study of Social Movements." *Annual Review of Sociology* 9:527-553.

Knoke, D. and R.S. Burt. 1983. "Prominence." Pp. 195-222 in *Applied Network Analysis,* edited by R.S. Burt and M.J. Minor. Beverly Hills, CA: Sage.

Laumann, E.O., P.V. Marsden, and D. Prensky. 1982. "The Boundary Specification Problem in Network Analysis." Pp. 18-34 in *Applied Network Analysis: Structural Methodology for Empirical Social Research,* edited by R.S. Burt and M.J. Minor. Beverly Hills, CA: Sage.

Lewis, S.H. and R.E. Kraut. 1972. "Correlates of Student Political Activism and Ideology." *Journal of Social Issues* 28:131-149.

Lincoln, J.R. and G. Zeitz. 1980. "Organizational Properties from Aggregate Data: Separating Individual and Structural Effects." *American Sociological Review* 45:391-408.

Lipset, S.M. and S. Wolin. 1965. *The Berkeley Student Revolt.* New York: Doubleday Anchor.

McAdam, D. 1986. "Recruitment to High-Risk Activism: The Case of Freedom Summer." *American Journal of Sociology* 92:64-90.

———. 1987. *The Idealists Revisited: The Personal and Societal Consequences of Mississippi Freedom Summer.* New York: Oxford University Press.

McCarthy, J.D. and M.N. Zald. 1977. "Resource Mobilization and Social Movements: A Partial Theory." *American Journal of Sociology* 82:1212-1241.

Oberschall, A. 1973. *Social Conflict and Social Movements.* Englewood Cliffs, NJ: Prentice-Hall.

Oliver, P. 1984. "'If You Don't Do It, Nobody Else Will'" Active and Token Contributors to Local Collective Action." *American Sociological Review* 49:601-610.

Orum, A. 1972. *Black Students in Protest: A Study of the Origins of the Black Student Movement.* Washington, DC: American Sociological Association.

Perrow, C. 1970. "Members as Resources in Voluntary Organizations." Ppp. 93-116 in *Organizations and Clients: Essays in the Sociology of Service,* edited by W.R. Rosengren and M. Lefton. Columbus, OH: Charles E. Merril.

Pinard, M. and R. Hamilton. 1984. "The Motivational Dimensions in a Nationalist Movement: The Quebec Case." Paper presented at the annual meetings of the American Sociological Association, San Antonio.

Rao, P. and R.L. Miller. 1971. *Applied Econometrics.* Belmont, CA: Wadsworth.

Rosenthal, N., M. Fingrutd, M. Ethier, R. Karant, and D. McDonald. 1985. "Social Movements and Network Analysis: A Case Study of Nineteenth-Century Women's Reform in New York State." *American Journal of Sociology* 90:1022-1054.

Searles, R. and J.A. Williams, Jr. 1962. "Negro College Students' Participation in Sit-Ins." *Social Forces* 40:215-220.

Snow, D.A., L.A. Zurcher, Jr., and S. Ekland-Olson. 1980. "Social Networks and Social Movements: A Microstructural Approach to Differential Recruitment." *American Sociological Review* 45:787-801.

Stark, R. and W.S. Bainbridge. 1980. "Networks of Faith: Interpersonal Bonds and Recruitment to Cults and Sects." *American Journal of Sociology* 85:1376-1395.

Thomas, L.E. 1971. "Family Correlates of Student Political Activism." *Developmental Psychology* 4:206-214.

Toch, H. 1965. *The Social Psychology of Social Movements.* Indianapolis, IN: Bobbs-Merrill.

Von Eschen, D., J. Kirk, and M. Pinard. 1971. "The Organizational Substructure of Disorderly Politics." *Social Forces* 49:529-544.

Zukier, H. 1982. "Situational Determinants of Behavior." *Social Research* 49:1073-1091.

Zurcher, L.A. and D.A. Snow. 1981. "Collective Behavior: Social Movements." Pp. 447-482 in *Social Psychology: Sociological Perspectives,* edited by M. Rosenberg and R. Turner. New York: Basic Books.

INTEGRATION INTO VOLUNTARY ASSOCIATIONS AND INCENTIVES FOR POLITICAL PROTEST

Karl-Dieter Opp

INTRODUCTION

The relationship between integration into social groups and political participation has been a subject of concern of social scientists for a long time. Integration or, equivalently, social solidarity is defined here as "the extent to which people participate in organized groups and are objectively and subjectively attached to their community" (Useem 1980, p. 361).

Mass society theory and resource mobilization theory, two intensively discussed theoretical perspectives in the social movement literature, entail different predictions about the relationship between integration and participation.

Kornhauser (1959), the main advocate of the *theory of mass society,* claimed that social groups are, so to speak, a "safety belt" for the elites. Groups protect

International Social Movement Research, Vol. 2, pages 345-362.
Copyright © 1989 by JAI Press Inc.
All rights of reproduction in any form reserved.
ISBN: 0-89232-964-5

the elites from extensive participation of the population. The uprooted, marginal citizens are those participating in mass movements. If this reasoning is correct, high integration should be associated with low participation.

Proponents of the *resource mobilization perspective* argue, in short, that integration into groups "furnishes individuals with a communication network, a set of common values and symbols around which members can be mobilized, a tradition of participation in group activity, and an authority structure" (Useem 1980, p. 357). In general, groups provide resources that make participation easier for their members. Contrary to mass society theory, a positive correlation between integration and participation is thus to be expected (see McAdam 1982, 1983; Morrison 1971; Obserschall 1973; Pinard 1971; Pollock III 1982; Snow et al. 1980).

The results of empirical research are inconclusive. In a study of two antipornography organizations Curtis and Zurcher (1973) found that approximately 90% of the members were affiliated with at least one community organization. The authors show that on the macro level the linkages of the organizations with other groups and organizations enhances the persistence of the antipornography groups. Snow et al. (1980) showed that interpersonal ties, including extramovement networks, played a major role in recruitment. These studies and others indicate that, in contrast to the theory of mass society, integration promotes political participation.

In other studies, however, no relationship or even a negative relationship is found. Useem (1980), for example, reports negative or zero correlations between primary group participation and participation in or support for the Boston antibusing movement. Orbell and Uno (1972) found that taking some remedial actions, if neighborhood problems were present, decreased rapdily with length of residence, which is one of the indicators of integration frequently employed in empirical research. According to Isaac et al. (1980, p. 203) "integration with friends and into the neighborhood all show moderately large, significant negative effects" on protest orientation.

In summary, then, (1) the effects of integration differ, depending on the kind of the group; and (2) the theoretical approaches mentioned above make assumptions about incentives for participation being related to integration into groups. The resource mobilization perspective, for example, points that, in general, integrated people are exposed to positive incentives for participation. If, then, differential integration has different effects on participation, the incentives for participation will be different in different groups.

In this paper, we examine the effects of differential integration focusing on integration into voluntary associations. The effects of integration into the community are dealt with in a complementary paper (Opp 1988). We use data of a survey of opponents of nuclear power in West Germany. Because it turns out that the extent of participation is dependent on the kind of group the respondents are members of, we examine whether these findings can be explained by specific incentives being provided by the groups.

EXPLAINING THE EFFECTS OF INTEGRATION

What are the incentives for participation that may be connected with integration into social groups? We want to distinguish three possible effects of integration that are more or less clearly specified in the literature on political participation:

1. A high degree of integration may provide opportunities for participation and thus may raise perceived political efficacy.
2. The group may exert social control in the sense that it provides positive or negative incentives for participation.
3. Groups may have a socializing effect in the sense that they change values and attitudes of their members.

The paper begins with an elaboration of these three types of effects. We then propose a general model based on these hypotheses linking more explicitly integration, incentives for protest and protest behavior.

Political Efficacy, Social Control,
Preference Change, and Social Integration

Integration and Political Efficacy

One of the main propositions of solidarity theorists, in contrast to adherents of mass society theory, is that integration facilitates mobilization and thus political participation (see McAdam 1982, 1983; Morrison 1971; Oberschall 1973; Oliver 1984; Pinard 1971; Pollock III 1982; Snow et al. 1980; Useem 1980). If this claim holds true, we expect that integration will correlate positively with perceived political efficacy: if groups, in fact, provide opportunities for protest, then the member of a group disposes of a greater amount of resources than a nonmember and is, thus, in fact, more influential than a nonmember. If we assume that the increased influence is also perceived, it is possible that a positive relationship between integration and perceived political efficacy is obtainable.

Social Control and Integration

If integration affects political participation, one would expect that people who are integrated into social networks would be exposed to political stimuli encouraging participation (see, for example, Finifter 1974; Oberschall 1973; Putnam 1966; Wilson and Orum 1976). Reference persons are, to a great extent, members of the network individuals are part of and, therefore, integrated persons will be more strongly exposed to normative expectations of reference persons to participate than less integrated persons. We expect, however, that integrated persons will be confronted more often with positive sanctions and less often with negative sanctions for participation than less integrated groups.

The Socializing Effects of Social Networks

According to mass society theory, intermediate groups socialize members to accept the "rules of the game" (Pinard 1971, p. 183). A rule most groups will subscribe to is to avoid the use of violence for achievement of political goals. Integrated people, therefore should be inclined not to accept violence. Legal participation, however, is part of the "game." We thus expect to find a negative correlation between norms of violence and integration and a positive correlation between norms of protest and integration.

Further, group membership should strengthen preferences for the public good that the group is concerned with. If a member enters a group, he will be faced with new arguments and justifications in favor of the goals of a group and against the aims of the group's opponents. This should lead to more intense preferences for the public goods that the group attempts to provide.

The data set that has been used to test our hypothesis consists of a sample of opponents of nuclear power. Their primary aim is to reduce the utilization of nuclear energy. As casual observations suggest, many antinuclears also seem to reject the present economic and political order, that is, they are alienated from the political system. We surmise that integration affects or strengthens the preference for nonprovision for both these public bads. Therefore, we expect that integration will correlate positively with discontent with nuclear energy as well as with system alienation.

If political actions are rewarded for a long time, these actions will become intrinsically rewarding. We suppose that for individuals who are members of groups where participation is rewarded, political actions will become rewarding per se: they will acquire an entertainment value, and they will be performed in order to displace or eliminate aggression on the part of the group members and, therefore, acquire a catharsis value.

Our data include various indicators of the incentive variables. The sources of the incentives have not been identified. We assume, however, that if people are integrated into a group, at least some rewards and costs for participation will come from the respective group, provided that integration correlates with participation.

Linking Incentives, Integration, and Political Protest

We have argued that if integration is associated with political protest (or with political participation in general), it is because integration is associated with incentives for protest which affect protest behavior.

This is exactly the argument which is provided by rational choice theory. It posits that the choice to be politically active depends on the costs and benefits associated with political action. If, accordingly, groups (or, to be more precise, members of groups) provide relatively strong positive (or negative) incentives for political participation to their members, integration into groups is expected to correlate positively (or negatively) with political participation. Further, there may be groups that provide neither positive nor negative incentives for participation. In this case, expect to find no relationship at all between integration and participation.

In explaining the relationship between integration and participation, it is not enough to look only at the incentives being provided by the respective groups. There may be rewards and costs that an individual obtains from outside specific membership groups. A student, for example, may be faced with expectations of a protest group, in which he is a member, to invest time in order to initiate various actions. He may, however, restrict his activities in the protest group because he wants to pass an examination in the near future and, thus, his opportunity costs for participation are high. It is, therefore, necessary to take into account not only the incentives being provided by members of specific groups, but other incentives as well, if we want to explain effects of integration on participation.

Figure 1 displays the *general model* outlined thus far. The arrows symbolize casual relationships, whereas the line denotes a noncausal relationship. The relationship between integration and political participation may, therefore, be obtained because integration is connected with various costs and benefits for participation, and because these costs and benefits, together with other costs and benefits coming from outside the specific groups, determine participation. If, however, integration and participation are not related, we expect that the respective groups will not provide any incentives for participation.

In sum, then, we contend that the relationship between integration and participation is spurious and can be explained by the presence or absence of incentives for protest provided by the groups.

Given the variety of social groups, we expect that membership in different groups will have different effects on participation. This view converges with a differential socialization hypothesis (see particularly Portes 1971; Isaac et al. 1980) that may be called, in this context, the *differential integration hypothesis* (this term was suggested to us by Bert Klandermans): Groups differ with respect to the ideologies, information, and other stimuli to which members are exposed.

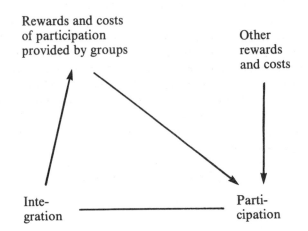

Figure 1. The General Model of Explaining the Relationship
Between Integration and Political Participation

In order to test the rational choice explanation of the relationship between integration and participation, it is reasonable to proceed in four steps.

The starting point and first step is to ascertain the relationship between integration and participation itself. In explaining why this relationship exists or not, we first need to determine whether a positive, negative, or zero correlation between integration and participation exists.

In claiming that integration correlates with protest only if it is connected with incentives to protest, we must examine whether the rewards and costs outlined above correlate with integration. This is the second step of our analysis.

Explaining the correlation between integration and participation by means of costs and benefits implies that these costs and benefits actually are determinants of participation. We thus need to test, in a third step, whether costs and benefits have significant effects on participation.

The final question to be answered is to what extent the rational choice model can explain the relationship at issue. This can be done in a fourth step by computing partial correlations between integration and participation, controlling for the incentive variables.

METHODS

The Sample

One of the objectives of our study of opponents of nuclear power was to explain why only few of those who opposed the utilization of nuclear energy engaged in protest behavior. Our sample consisted of 398 opponents of nuclear power from two different locations: a district of Hamburg (West Germany), where many counterculture people and, thus, supposedly, opponents of nuclear power lived (229 people interviewed), and a small town near Hamburg with an atomic power station to the proximity (169 people interviewed).

A random sample of the population of the two locations comprised 187 respondents. Another 211 respondents stemmed from a snowball sample, with the interviewees of the random sample as a starting point.

Demographic differences between the samples were not large enough to require a separate analysis of both samples.

Dependent Variables

Participation in Legal and Illegal Protest

Respondents were first presented with a list of legal and illegal behaviors, described as actions people may take to protest against the construction of nuclear power plants. The referents of the legal and illegal protest items were: participation in a petition signing campaign; participation in a permitted political demonstration; participation in a citizen initiative; seizing factories, offices, or other buildings; damage of other people's property; use of violence against persons.

Respondents were also asked about their intention to perform the respective action in the future, using five response categories ranging from "in no case" to "quite certain."

Each behavior response (scored "1" for "have not done," "2" for "have done") was multiplied by the respective intention response (scored 1 to 5, where a high score meant that the behavior would be performed with a high probability in the future).

The resulting six product terms were subjected to a principal component analysis. Two factors have been extracted, one exhibiting high loadings of the legal, the other one showing high loadings of the illegal protest product terms. Due to this pattern, a legal and an illegal protest scale were constructed by adding the product terms of the legal and illegal items, respectively.

The possible and observed range of the legal protest scale is from 3 to 30 with a mean of 17.00 and a standard deviation of 6.17. The possible range of the illegal protest scale is from 3 to 30 and the observed range is from 3 to 22.83 with a mean of 6.07 and a standard deviation of 3.67.

Independent Variables

Integration into Voluntary Associations

In order to measure this variable, we used a question from the general survey (ALLBUS) or the ZUMA (Centre for Surveys, Methods, and Analyses—

Zentrum für Umfragen, Methoden und Analysen e. V., Mannheim, West Germany). Each respondent was asked whether he was at present a member of an organization or group. Twenty-two organizations and groups ranging from unions and political parties to environmental groups and hobby clubs were ascertained. Our general measure of integration was the number of groups a person was a member of.

In order to avoid confusion of the independent and dependent variables, membership in groups from the antinuclear movement were disregarded.

Only 31.7% (N = 126) of our 398 respondents were not members of an organization or group. The same percentage of respondents was a member of one group. There were 19.6% reported as being a member of two groups and 17.1% of three to six groups. On the average, each respondent was a member in 1.28 groups (with a standard deviation of 1.20, N = 380).

Incentive Variables

Our questionnaire included, first of all, items measuring perceived influence and the two public good variables "discontent with nuclear energy" and "system alienation." The rational choice model required that the public good variables be weighted by perceived influence. It was, therefore, necessary to construct two multiplicative terms: "discontent with nuclear energy * influence" and "system alienation * influence." As the correlation between both interaction terms was .71, which was due to the common variable "influence," we constructed additive scales of the two public good variables. First, legal protest on the two public good variables was regressed, each variable weighted by its unstandardized regression coefficient, and the products and the constant added. Then illegal protest on both public good variables were regressed and a similar scale was constructed. The scales were called "public good constructs." Each construct was then weighted by the perceived influence scale.

Other items measure expectations of reference persons to protest, positive sanctions, negative sanctions, norms of protest, norms of violence, catharsis value of protest, and entertainment value of protest.

The details of the measurement are described elsewhere (Muller and Opp 1986; Opp 1985, 1986).

RESULTS

Differential Integration and Political Protest

The correlation of our general integration measure, referring to number of memberships in voluntary associations with legal protest, is .21, whereas integration correlates with illegal protest at -.01.

Table 1. Voluntary Associations Promoting, Preventing, and Being Neutral to Protest

Type of Group	Groups Assigned to Each Type	N^2
(1) Promoting *legal protest*	Union (member of German Unions—DGB), youth organizations, environmental/peace/women's groups, other "counterculture" groups, Green Party	183
(2) Neutral to *legal* protest	Civil servants' union, professional organizations, sport and hobby clubs, refugees' and veterans' organizations, groups associated to church	152
(3) Preventing *legal* protest	Trade and employer associations, other hobby and recreational clubs	70
(4) Promoting *illegal* protest	Environmental and other "counterculture" groups, Green Party	105
(5) Neutral to *illegal* protest	Union (member of German Unions—DGB), professional organizations, hobby-type clubs, refugees' and veterans' associations	175
(6) Preventing *illegal* protest	Union of civil servants, trade and employer associations, sport clubs and other hobby clubs, groups associated to church	148

Notes: 1. If the correlation of membership in a group with legal/illegal protest was greater than or equal to .05, we assigned the group to types (1) or (4). If the respective correlation was less than or equal to -.05, a group was assigned to types (3) or (6). The other groups were assigned to types (2) or (5).

2. Number of respondents being a member of at least one of the organizations assigned to the respective types of organizations. N − 398 is equal to the number of nonmembers.

These results are incompatible with mass society theory, that entails only negative correlations, and with the resource mobilization perspective, implying only positive correlations.

It may be argued that these correlations are an artifact due to the lumping together of very heterogeneous groups into the integration measure. It may thus be expected that integration into different kinds of groups has different effects on political protest. This is borne out by our data. Membership in environmental groups, for example, correlates positively with legal protest (r = .24), membership in leisure groups correlates negatively with legal protest (r = -.13), and membership in sport clubs does not correlate at all with legal protest.

Based on the correlations between membership and protest, a typology could be constructed. If there was, for example, a positive correlation—even a small one—between membership in a group and participation, one may conjecture that this group offers more incentives for participation than a group where membership has a negative correlation with participation. Three categories of groups were thus identified for both legal and illegal protest, based on the correlation of membership and (legal/illegal) protest: (1) groups promoting protest; (2) neutral groups; and (3) groups preventing protest.

Table 1 indicates which associations fall under each type of group. It is remarkable that being a member of the more conservative groups such as professional associations and of various groups concerned with recreation promotes neither legal nor illegal protest. Membership in groups pertaining to the "counterculture," however, is positively correlated with legal as well as with illegal protest. Membership in the Green Party promotes illegal protest. The effects of membership in unions depend on the kind of union. There is one result, however, that holds true for all unions: They do not promote illegal protest.

The correlations of membership in the six types of groups with protest exhibit the expected pattern due to the classification, as the second column of Table 3 shows.

Correlations also exist, however, between membership in groups promoting or preventing legal protest with illegal protest. The reason is that the groups assigned to types 1 to 3 and 4 to 6 overlap, because we have two independent classifications. This is consistent with the fact that legal and illegal protest correlate at .46.

Types of Voluntary Associations and Incentives for Protest

We expect the following correlations to hold:

1. For groups promoting legal or illegal protest, most of the correlations between the incentive variables and membership should be positive.
2. For neutral groups, most of the respective correlations should be zero.
3. For those groups preventing legal or illegal protest, most correlations between the incentive variables and membership should be negative.

Table 2 displays the observed correlations. The first column contains the incentive variables. The second column shows the correlations between membership in groups *promoting legal protest* and the incentive variables. All correlation coefficients, with one exception, are positive: the exception is the variable "negative sanctions." The negative sign means that members in groups promoting legal protest expect to a high extent to receive negative sanctions for protesting. This will be discussed later.

There is one coefficient that should be negative. One of our hypotheses was that integration into groups reinforces the "rules of the game" in the sense that integration leads to rejection of norms of violence. This hypothesis is not

Table 2. Membership in Types of Groups and Incentives for Protest: (Bivariate Correlations[a])

Incentive Variables	Membership in Groups						Number of memberships in groups in general
1	Promoting LP	Neutral to LP	Preventing LP	Promoting IP	Neutral to IP	Preventing IP	
	2	3	4	5	6	7	8
(1) Discontent with nuclear energy	.23[d]	-.06	-.20[d]	.19[d]	.08	-.15[d]	.06
(2) System alienation	.22[d]	-.13[d]	-.21[d]	.17[d]	.11[c]	-.25[d]	-.00
(3) Influence	.12[d]	.04	-.02	.12[d]	.05	.02	.09[c]
(4) Public good construct[c] infl.[b]	.24[d]	-.05	-.16[d]	.21[d]	.09[c]	-.13[d]	.08
	.24[d]	-.09[c]	-.18[d]	.20[d]	.10[c]	-.18[d]	.05
(5) Expectations of reference persons[b]	.25[d]	.00	-.17[d]	.17[d]	.16[d]	-.10[c]	.13[d]
	.26[d]	-.04	-.14[d]	.17[d]	.14[d]	-.10[c]	.12[d]
(6) Positive sanctions	.25[d]	.00	-.06	.23[d]	.12[d]	-.05	.14[d]
(7) Negative sanctions	-.12[d]	-.02	.16[d]	-.13[d]	-.05	.10[c]	-.04
(8) Norms of protest	.23[d]	-.00	-.13[d]	.16[d]	.15[d]	-.09[c]	.11[c]
(9) Norms of violence	.14[d]	-.07	-.12[d]	.18[d]	-.03	-.11[c]	.01
(10) Catharsis value	.03	-.07	-.10[c]	.05	-.05	-.09[c]	-.05
(11) Entertainment value	.18[d]	-.07	-.06	.08[c]	.11[c]	-.07	.06

Notes: [a] LP = legal protest; IP = illegal protest.
[b] The first row of coefficients refers to the composite public good variable which was constructed on the basis of a regression analysis for legal protest, whereas the second row displays the coefficients constructed on the basis of a regression analysis for illegal protests.
[c] p < .05
[d] p < .01

355

supported (see line 9, column 2, of Table 2). Membership in groups promoting legal protest correlates positively with norms of violence.

Almost the same pattern of relationships holds for membership in groups promoting illegal protest (column 5), which is consistent with our predictions.

Let us now look at the correlations for groups that are neutral to legal and illegal protest. Our theory implies that most of the correlations of the incentive variables with membership in these groups should be approximately zero or at least lower than the coefficients for groups promoting legal or illegal protest. The third and sixth column clearly confirm this expectation.

The remaining group of correlations concerns membership in groups preventing legal and illegal protest. The expected negative correlations of the incentive variables with membership are clearly borne out by our data (see columns four and seven of Table 2): With two exceptions, all incentive variables correlate negatively with membership. The one exception is again the coefficient for "negative sanctions." The positive sign for the correlation coefficient means that few negative sanctions for protest are expected by members of the respective types of groups. The second exception is that the coefficient for "influence" is zero.

The eighth column of Table 2 shows the correlations between "number of memberships in groups in general" and the incentive variables. As the correlation between this integration variable and protest is low (.21 for legal and -.01 for illegal protest); we expect most of the correlations with the incentive variables to have a positive sign and to be close to zero. This expectation is borne out by the data.

The fact that these correlations are close to zero is also to be expected due to the construction of this variable: Memberships in groups promoting, being neutral to, and preventing protest are lumped together in the variable "number of memberships." The resulting correlations of this composite variable with the incentive variables should thus be close to zero.

There is one result that requires special attention, namely the correlations between *negative sanctions* and membership in the six types of groups. The general pattern of relationships is as follows (see Table 2, line 7):

1. Membership in groups promoting legal or illegal protest is associated with relatively strong and not, as expected, with weak negative sanctions in the case of protest (correlations of -.12 and -.13).
2. The respective correlations with membership in groups that are neutral to legal or illegal protest are close to zero.
3. Negative sanctions correlate positively with membership in groups preventing legal or illegal protest (the correlations are .16 and .10).

The negative correlations probably indicate that the negative sanctions come, to some extent, from outside the membership groups. Analysis of the single-item components of the negative sanctions scale provides some support for this conjecture. The negative sanction with the strongest negative coefficient is the expectation of being registered by the police and the secret service: It correlates at -.17 with membership in groups promoting legal protest and at -.14 with membership in groups promoting illegal protest. On the other hand, the sanction "I am criticized by people whose opinion I esteem" is expected, to a low extent, by members of groups promoting legal and illegal protest (the correlations are .14 versus .11). Although these correlations are low, they suggest that the source of negative sanctions is, in part, the group and, in part, other people or institutions.

Although the data are, in general, consistent with our hypothesis that groups provide incentives for legal as well as illegal protest, it is not possible to prove that the presumed causal relationships are obtainable because we are restricted to cross-sectional data. Our findings cannot rule out the possibility that some of the incentives measured were not provided by the groups but rather were incentives for becoming a member of the groups or were provided from outside of the group.

We collected some data which support our assumption that the source of a great deal of the incentives, members of groups are faced with, is the group. In West Germany, there is a federal association of environmental citizen incentives (Bundesverband Bürgerinitiativen Umweltschutz [BBU]) which is a special type of voluntary group. This association distributes statements that represent the opinion of most of the environmental groups in West Germany. Some of these statements and various pamphlets of protest groups were available to this study. The material reveals that these groups use various types of arguments in order to provide or affect some of the incentives measured in our study. In what follows we delineate some of these arguments.

First, there are attempts to change or influence the *preferences for collective goods,* particularly to foster a negative evaluation of nuclear energy. The arguments put forward pointed to various negative consequences of employing nuclear energy. At the same time, politicians, courts, and the political institutions involved in promoting the utilization of nuclear energy were blamed for not being competent, for trying to act only to achieve their own interests, and for not paying attention to the rights of the people. The strategy employed in the written material is to produce links between nuclear energy, on the one hand, and a variety of phenomena that are valued negatively, on the other. Apparently, the BBU tried to establish such associations in order to increase rejection of the utilization of nuclear energy. As can be seen from the social movement literature (see Klandermans 1984) and from social psychological theory (see, e.g., Ajzen and Fishbein 1980), this strategy basically leads to the intended result of influencing preferences in the desired direction.

Another major concern of the pamphlets and statements apparently is to enhance *perceived influence.* The successes of past actions of protest groups are enumerated, the movement is described as large and powerful, and it is suggested that everyone is important for achieving the movement's goal. We presume that these arguments cause many people to regard themselves as being influential.

The BBU and the protest groups devote much space to *appeals to norms*. They argue that the construction of nuclear power plants is unjust and that there is an obligation to resist them. A slogan reads "where right becomes wrong, resistance becomes a duty." A general norm is thus applied to a specific situation. There are also justifications for civil disobedience, which is defined as nonviolence. It is argued that the authorities employ real violence in constructing nuclear power plants and that they, therefore, have no right to prescribe the forms of resistance of the people. Official restrictions with regard to the means of protest to be chosen are thus considered unjustified.

In the documents, there is also advice about how to behave in case of contacts with the police. This apparently is intended to reduce the *costs of protesting*.

These observations indicate that protest groups consciously and in part effectively provide incentives or try to affect incentives in order to increase the probability of protesting. Thus, if we find that membership in groups is positively associated with incentives for protest, we may be confident—in agreement with the literature on integration—that at least a substantial part of these incentives is provided or influenced by the respective groups.

Explaining the Relationship between Integration into Voluntary Associations and Protest

The relationship between integration into voluntary associations and protest can only be explained by our incentive variables, if these exhibit statistically significant relationships with legal and illegal protest. Regressions of legal and illegal protest on the public good construct, weighted by "perceived influence," and the other incentive variables, showed that each variable—with the exception of the "entertainment value of protest"—significantly affects at least one of the two dependent variables (with explained adjusted R^2's of .47 for legal and .32 for illegal protest).

The fourth step of our analysis can be accomplished in the following way. If a bivariate correlation between an integration variable and protest is statistically significant, we compute a partial correlation coefficient. The incentive variables to be controlled for have to meet two requirements: they have to correlate significantly (at least at the .05 level) with the respective integration items. Further, the incentive variables to be controlled for must have yielded significant regression coefficients as independent variables for legal or illegal protest.

According to our general model (Figure 1), the correlations between integration and protest are spurious. Consequently, the partial correlations

Table 3. Membership in Groups and Political Protest
(Bivariate and Partial Correlations[a])

Membership in Types of Groups	Bivariate r's with LP/IP	Partial r's	Variables Controlled for (Numbers of Variables in Table 2)
Promoting LP			
Legal protest	.39[c]	.24[c]	4, 5, 6, 7, 8
Illegal protest	.16[c]	.01	4, 5, 7, 8, 9
Neutral to LP			
Illegal protest	-.09[b]	-.06	4
Preventing LP			
Legal protest	-.23[c]	-.12[c]	4, 5, 7, 8
Illegal protest	-.17[c]	-.06	4, 5, 7, 8, 9, 10
Promoting IP			
Legal protest	.36[c]	.26[c]	4, 5, 6, 7, 8
Illegal protest	.20[c]	.08	4, 5, 7, 8, 9
Neutral to IP			
Legal protest	.14[c]	.05	4, 5, 6, 8
Preventing IP			
Legal protest	-.12[c]	-.03	4, 5, 7, 8
Illegal protest	-.19[c]	-.10[b]	4, 5, 7, 8, 9, 10
Number of memberships in groups in general			
Legal protest	.21[c]	.13[c]	5, 6, 8

Notes: [a] LP = legal protest; IP = illegal protest; N = 398 for bivariate correlations. N for partial correlations is at least 389.
[b] $p < .05$
[c] $p < .01$

should be zero, if all relevant rational choice variables have been measured without measurement errors. This condition is, of course, not met. Therefore, we can only expect that partial correlations will be smaller than the respective bivariate correlations. The larger the difference, the better our success in explaining the relationship between the integration item and protest.

The results are displayed in Table 3. Each partial correlation is clearly lower than the corresponding bivariate correlation. Six of the eleven partial r's are even statistically insignificant, in contrast to the eleven significant bivariate r's. The incentive variables thus explain, to a substantial extent, the correlations between membership in different types of groups, on the one hand, and legal and illegal political protest, on the other.

SUMMARY AND CONCLUSIONS

The proposition that integration into social life may be an important determinant of political participation will not be debated by any political scientist or sociologist. Major theoretical traditions, however, differ with respect to the kind of effect that social integration is assumed to have. Mass society theory, in particular, implies that integration into groups deters from extensive participation, whereas the resource mobilization perspective hypothesizes the contrary. Results of empirical studies are contradictory. Sometimes positive, sometimes negative, and sometimes no relationships are found between integration and participation. The theoretical models and the results of research led us to conclude that (1) the effects of integration differ for different kinds of groups and that (2) incentives for participation being related to membership in groups determine the extent of participation.

A study of opponents of nuclear power in West Germany is used to test these conclusions. Our analyses indicate that there is no consistent effect of integration into voluntary groups on either legal or illegal protest. Neither the resource mobilization perspective nor mass society is thus confirmed by our data.

Rational choice theory is applied to explain the relationship between integration and participation. If integration is positively or negatively related to protest, then, due to the rational choice model, integration should also be related to incentives or disincentives for protest. We tested various predictions specifying expected relationships between particular integration variables and the costs and benefits measured in our study. We also tested to what extent the rational choice variables are able to explain relationships between integration and protest.

The results of our analyses are clearly in favor of the rational choice explanation: Relationships between integration, on the one hand, and legal and illegal protest, on the other, could be explained to a large extent by the incentive variables.

Many empirical studies have proceeded in this manner: respondents are presented with a list of groups and are asked to state the groups to which they belong. Our research indicates that the results depend heavily on the kinds of groups included on the list.

This, and the fact that we could create different correlations between integration and participation by constructing a typology of groups, suggests that a general hypothesis asserting a relatonship between integration, in general, and participation is questionable.

This is also entailed by the rational choice model. The effects of integration on participation depend, according to this model, on the incentives provided by the respective groups. Unconditional predictions of the effects of integration on participation, as mass society theory and the resource mobilization perspective suggest, are thus not tenable.

The theoretical argument and the empirical results presented in this paper suggest a new research strategy for exploring the relationship between integration and participation. The emphasis should lie on ascertaining the incentives for participation provided by groups and their effects on participation.

ACKNOWLEDGMENTS

Financial support of this research by the Volkswagenwerk-Foundation (Stiftung Volkswagenwerk) is gratefully acknowledged. I would also like to thank Peter Hartmann for his assistance in analyzing the data and for valuable suggestions. I am also grateful to Bert Klandermans and Edward N. Muller for critical comments.

REFERENCES

Ajzen, I. and M. Fishbein. 1980. *Understanding and Predicting Social Behavior*. Englewood Cliffs, NJ: Prentice-Hall.
Curtis, R.L., Jr. and L.A. Zurcher, Jr. 1973. "Stable Resources of Protest Movements: The Multi-Organizational Field. *Social Forces* 52: 53-61.
Finifter, A.W. 1974. "The Friendship Group as a Protective Environment for Political Deviants." *American Political Science Review* 68: 607-625.
Isaac, L., E. Mutran, and S. Stryker. 1980. "Political Protest Orientations Among Black and White Adults." *American Sociological Review* 45: 191-213.
Klandermans, B. 1984. "Social Psychological Expansions of Resource Mobilization Theory." *American Sociological Review* 49: 583-600.
Kornhauser, W. 1959. *The Politics of Mass Society*. New York: Free Press.
McAdam, D. 1982. *Political Process and the Development of Black Insurgency 1930-1970*. Chicago and London: University of Chicago Press.
_____. 1983. Tactical Innovation and the Pace of Insurgency." *American Sociological Review* 48: 735-754.
Morrison, D.E. 1971. "Some Notes Toward a Theory on Relative Deprivation, Social Movements and Social Change." *American Behavioral Scientist* 14: 675-690.
Muller, E.N. and K.-D. Opp. 1986. "Rational Choice and Rebellious Collective Action." *American Political Science Review* 80: 471-487.
Obserscall, A. 1973. *Social Conflict and Social Movements*. Englewood Cliffs, NJ: Prentice-Hall.
Oliver, P. 1984. " 'If You Don't Do It, Nobody Else Will': Active and Token Contributors to Local Collective Action." *American Sociological Review* 49: 601-610.
Opp, K.-D. 1985. "Konventionelle und unkonventionelle politische Partizipation" (Conventional and Unconventional Political Participation). *Zeitschrift für Soziologie* 14: 282-296.
_____ . 1986. "Soft Incentives and Collective Action: Participation in the Anti-Nuclear Movement." *British Journal of Political Science* 16: 87-112.
_____. 1988. "Community Integration and Incentives for Political Protest." In *From Structure to Action: Comparing Movement Participation Across Cultures*, edited by B. Klandermans, H. Kriesi, and S. Tarrow. Greenwich, CT: JAI Press.
Orbell, J.M. and T. Uno. 1972. "A Theory of Neighborhood Problem Solving: Political Action vs. Residential Mobility." *American Political Science Review* 66: 471-489.
Pinard, M. 1971. *The Rise of a Third Party*. Englewood Cliffs, NJ: Prentice-Hall.

Pollock III, Ph.D. 1982. "Organizations as Agents of Mobilization: How Does Group Activity Affect Political Participation?" *American Journal of Political Science* 26: 485-503.

Portes, A. 1971. "Political Primitivism, Differential Socialization, and Lower-Class Leftist Radicalism." *American Sociological Review* 36: 820-835.

Putnam, R.D. 1966. "Political Attitudes and the Local Community." *American Political Science Review* 60: 640-654.

Snow, D.A., L.A. Zurcher, Jr., and Sh.E. Ekland-Olson. 1980. "Social Networks and Social Movements." *American Sociological Review* 45: 787-801.

Useem, B. 1980. "Solidarity Model, Breakdown Model, and the Boston Anti-Busing Movement." *American Sociological Review* 45: 357-369.

Wilson, K.L. and A.M. Orum. 1976. "Mobilizing People for Collective Action." *Journal of Political and Military Sociology* 4: 187-202.

CONFLICT IN INTERORGANIZATIONAL SYSTEMS:
ON THE LOGIC OF TRADE UNIONS AND EMPLOYERS' ASSOCIATIONS IN THE 1984 METAL STRIKE IN WEST GERMANY

Hajo Weber

INTRODUCTION

The relations between workers and employers, in West Germany, passes for relatively peaceful when compared with those of other Western European countries such as, for instance, Great Britain, Italy, and France. A widely acknowledged explanation for this fact is that the industrial relations system in the Federal Republic of Germany (FRG) is especially fitting for dealing with processes of social change and for absorbing the conflicts accompanying these processes (Streeck 1979; Müller-Jentsch 1984; Dittrich and Weber, 1985).

International Social Movement Research, Vol. 2, pages 363-380.
Copyright © 1989 by JAI Press Inc.
All rights of reproduction in any form reserved.
ISBN: 0-89232-964-5

Among the factors accounting for this accomplishment in the West German industrial relations system is the dual character of bargaining structures: "the conditions of sale" of labor power—that is, working time and wages—are negotiated between the respective organizations of labor and capital, that is, trade unions and employers' associations, at the industry level, while "the conditions of the utilization" of labor power—that is, the specific conditions of work—are negotiated between the company's management and a works council ("Betriebsräte"), an institution formally separated from the unions, at the company and plant level. This differentiation between bargaining levels, involving conflicts arising in either of the bargaining arenas, largely remains limited to the bargaining level in question.

However, with the strike action taken in the metal and printing industries pushing for a shorter workweek, the year 1984 brought the FRG not only the most extensive labor disputes in its previous history but also, as it seems, some significant changes in the system of collective bargaining.

The 1984 labor dispute was the most costly and the best prepared in terms of strategies adopted. The outcome of the dispute, however, illustrated the increasing uncontrollability of industrial conflicts in complex industrial societies characterized by the division of labor. The previous form of institutionalization and the previous mechanisms of control appear to have reached a limit.

In this paper, we outline the theoretical perspective adopted for analyzing the conflict between both sides of industry. After delineating the legal and institutional frameworks, the respective strategies pursued by the relevant union and employers' associations are described. We then deal with the settlement of the dispute and, finally, we discuss the theoretical perspective and the contribution to the literature.

RESOURCE EXTRACTION IN INTERORGANIZATIONAL SYSTEMS: A THEORETICAL PERSPECTIVE

Conflicts between trade unions and employers' associations are conflicts between organizations within an interorganizational system.

Evan 1978

Analyses of interorganizational systems have been carried through in a variety of different social and economic fields. The fruitfulness of applying the perspective to the study of the structure and functioning of employers' associations and trade unions has been demonstrated in particular by "neocorporatism research," investigating the role played by interest organizations in modern, market-mediated industrial societies (Schmitter 1979;

Schmitter and Streeck 1981; Grant 1985; Farago and Kriesi 1986).

Applying this research framework to conflicts between unions and employers' associations, in modern societies, draws attention to the structured and specified systems these organizations are acting in. In this framework, the distribution of bargaining power between two or more organizations or between organizations and coordinated systems of autonomous organizations, respectively, becomes of key importance.

The bargaining power of two opposing organizations depends not only on the amount of financial resources they have available but also on the outflow of resources either party can bring about on the side of the opponent. Industrial action thus becomes a problem of the efficient employment of resources. An organization uses its financial resources, then, in a particularly effective way if it achieves, with a minimum of input, a maximum of resource extraction on the opponent's side.

In light of these considerations, it is now possible to investigate the question as to whether there is such a thing as logic of conflict guiding the behavior of trade unions and employers' associations in the case of industrial disputes. Our thesis is that such disputes follow the pattern of interorganizational resource extraction. The strategy pursued by either of the parties involved in such a dispute aims at extracting financial, motivational, and legitimatory resources from the opposing party, the members as well as the social and political environment of that party. Disputes which are broader in scope may generally include the whole spectrum of resources and addressees, with the financial resources, however, undoubtedly having precedence.

It lies in the logic of this strategy of mutual resource extraction that the party which sees itself attacked will, in turn, adopt measures seeking to counteract the opponent's strategy from the very outset. The attacking party, however, will provide for this in its strategy. The parties' strategies thus exhibit a double contingency (Luhmann 1981). One classical example of the double contingency of strategy and counterstrategy is, for instance, the pattern of well-aimed key strikes on the trade union side and rather large-scale lockouts on the side of the employers.

Legal Framework

The conflicting parties' possibility of considering and adopting such strategies is determined by a set of rules. These rules include the various political, legal, social security, and organizational regulations governing the conduct in industrial disputes. They regulate which of the conflicting parties may attack the other side when, where, now, to what extent, and at what cost, and how the party attacked may parry. In this context, the rules regulating which of the workers directly or indirectly affected by an industrial dispute are eligible for financial assistance from the treasury of the Federal Labor Office are of particular strategic importance because they enable unions to ease the strain on its own resources by way of being able to draw on external resources. However, the strain will not be completely removed given the union's liability to pay strike benefits to its members. Nonetheless, these rules have a bearing on the extent to which a union's resources will be drained in the event of strike action.

From the perspective of interorganizational resource extraction, the respective parties' rules regulating the payment of benefits to their members in case of industrial action and the relevant social security legislation, are of central significance in the parties' devising and adopting of strategies of industrial action. In general, trade unions and employers' associations provide the payment of benefits to those among their members whom are directly involved in strikes or lockouts and whom are located within the area covered by the collective agreement. In this connection, it should perhaps be pointed out that, in West Germany, contracts usually cover an industry within the FRG. Those workers or firms located within the area of coverage, which are indirectly affected by industrial action, say, by stoppages of production, as a rule, have no right to payments from the funds of their respective organizations. This also applies to workers and firms outside the area of coverage which suffer indirect effects from industrial action taken within this area. In short, trade unions' and employers' associations' rules provide that only those members who are directly affected by a strike or lockout are eligible for strike benefits.

However, those workers indirectly affected, whom are located outside the area covered by the collective contract over which industrial dispute has arisen, in principle, have access to another source of financial assistance: They receive unemployment benefits or short-time allowances from the treasury of the Federal Labor Office. This option is available to them, although, under the Labor Promotion Law, the Federal Labor Office is not allowed to indirectly intervene in labor disputes by way of granting unemployment benefits. The law, however, contains an escape clause which stipulates that this only applies if the union raises "similar demands in terms of content and scope" in all areas of coverage. Thus, by establishing (formally) different demands in the various areas of coverage, the unions, in general, have always succeeded in circumventing the exclusion provision. Hence, the strategic combination of its own refunding rules, with the provisions of the Labor Promotion Law, enables a union to cut the outflow of its own resources and, at the same time, to secure financial assistance from the treasury of the Federal Labor Office for its members located outside the area of coverage. Given the logic of achieving the highest possible outflow of resources on the side of the opposing party, with the outflow of one's own resources being held at a minimum, it is obvious for a union to adopt a strategy which deploys its effects as far as possible outside the area of coverage. Such a strategy enables the union to achieve both preservation of its own resources and an optimal extraction of resources from the treasury of the Federal Labor Office as well as from the funds of the firms involved.

Moreover, the extent to which the financial resources of a union are drained, in the case of an industrial conflict, is determined by the appropriate rules of the labor dispute legislation. These rules regulate the options available to employers to influence, in their turn, through the use of lockouts, the type and extent of resource overflow on the union side. A Federal Labor Court decision, dating from 1980, stipulates that employers must tune their countermeasures, in consideration of the principle of parity of weapons in industrial disputes, to the scope of conflict delineated by the union in terms of the number of workers called on strike. Lockouts are still considered to be lawful if the employers, in addition to the number of workers on strike, lock out roughly twice that number (Bobke 1985).

Employers are not allowed to extend the lockout to a distinctly larger number of workers than are on strike, or are they given the possibility of using the lockout outside the area of coverage.

Nevertheless, they have other options at their disposal: accelerating the outflow of resources from union funds and increasing the number of workers cut off from regular wage payments as a result of strike action. Employers may shutdown production as a result of being indirectly affected by the industrial dispute. For the workers involved, this measure is tantamount to a lockout. It therefore meets with strong criticism from the unions which designate it as a "cold lockout."

Shutdowns affect both the volume of a union's resources as well as its capacity to take collective action. Certainly, shutdowns do not primarily contrive to accelerate the outflow of a union's financial resources, although this may also be the case. Thus, in the 1984 metal strike, IG Metall, the German metalworkers union, did pay, contraty to its statutes, "special benefits" amounting to the regular strike benefits in order to secure capacity for collective action and enhance solidarity among the strikers in the areas of coverage in which industrial action was taken. But shutdowns tend to undermine the internal loyalty of union members, inside and outside the area of coverage, whom are not eligible for union strike benefits or benefits granted under the Labor Promotion Law. Thus, in addition to the financial and motivational problems caused by shutdowns to the unions, this also increases the union's legitimation problems. Union leaders are forced to explicate their aims and strategies to their social environment which might become questionable in view of the employers' lockout practices.

Institutional Framework

A party's possibility of pursuing and succeeding with the strategy of interorganizational resource extraction, however, is not only determined by the "rules of the game" but, similarly by the structures and characteristics of the "field" in which the industrial conflict is carried out. This not only includes economic factors such as the cyclical and structural situation of the industry and the firms, their market and organizational integration, the degree of dependence on the world market, the level and distribution of unemployment but also the internal differentiation of the collective bargaining system.

As has already been mentioned, collective contracts in the FRG are usually concluded separately for each industry. Each industry is subdivided into different areas of coverage, on the basis of regional criteria. The metal industry comprises, at present, 16 different areas.

Of central importance for the bargaining policies and strategies of industrial action of trade unions and employers' associations in the German metal industry today is that, on the one hand, the sector is rather large and heterogenous in terms of company size, export dependency, and economic situation and on the other, that collective agreements are concluded in a generalized way, with particular circumstances not being taken into consideration.

As labor disputes do take place in interorganizational systems, it is necessary for trade unions and employers' associations to develop the appropriate organizational properties in order that strategies of industrial action be effectively controlled. The distinguishing feature is the extent of interorganization differentiation, for example, the number of autonomous organizations to be coordinated. The ability to take collective action of parties, whose organizational structures are characterized by interorganizational differentiation, depends on its ability to develop organizational stringency, to centralize decision-making competence, to gain sanctioning power, and to pool the financial resources scattered within the system.

It is against this background that the trade unions' and employers' associations' possibility of opting between "centralized" or "decentralized" bargaining gains its relevance. This is illustrated by the fact that, besides the controversies over substantive issues in wage negotiations, there are also controversies over the degree of centralization or decentralization of bargaining, which are obviously informed by stratetic calculations.

These controversies, arising over the choice of bargaining arenas, may be interpreted, on the one hand, in light of the differential organizational structures of the relevant employers' associations and IG Metall. While the employers' associational system is characterized by an interorganizational structure, the organizational system of IG Metall exhibits an intraorganizational differentiation. These differential organizational structures involve a differential potential of internal guidance and control for the two actors (Weber 1987a). On the other hand, these controversies may be interpreted in light of the parties' considerations concerning their strategies aimed at reducing the ability of the other side to increase the outflow of their resources. Thus, from the outset, through decentralized bargaining, the union is given the possibility of limiting the number of its members who are entitled to strike benefits and of cutting the option of the employers to conduct the industrial dispute at the federal level. Its organizational properties of intraorganizational differentiation enabled IG Metall to exert a higher degree of control in decentralized bargaining than was the case with respect to the associational system of the metal manufacturing employers which is characterized by interorganizational differentiation.

As the organizational properties of IG Metall favor decentralized bargaining, the union disposes of the better preconditions for making well-aimed interventions into the "merry-go-round" of collective bargaining. Thus, in the past years, IG Metall could demonstrate, in various collective bargaining rounds, that it was in a position to centrally devise a negotiation design and to guarantee its realization in the various coverage areas. This governing capacity of IG Metall, which is due to its organizational properties, entails a pressure for coordination on the side of the employers. Given the "bargaining mechanism" which involves that once an agreement is reached in one coverage area, it becomes the basis for settlement in all the other coverage areas, employers are forced to prevent agreements exceeding the level previously envisaged by them. The pressure for coordination, within the associational system of the metal manufacturing employers would decrease if the employers were given the possibility of concluding differentiated collective contracts. Until the 1984 labor dispute, this possibility was largely barred because on both the employers' and the unions' side there were forces insisting on industrywide agreements. From the employers' perspective, it is particularly in their interest to avoid imperfect competition. Further, companies with several plants located in different coverage areas, may similarly be interested in industrywide agreements. On the union side, it comes down to the fact that union officials, and members of union bargaining committees, might not wish to appear in a more unfavorable light than their colleagues from other coverage areas achieving better bargaining results. Moreover, the organizational power of IG Metall rests upon the homogeneity and generalizability of industrywide agreements (Streeck 1979).

From the strategic aspect, the question now arises as to whether trade unions and employers' associations are in equal positions to influence the choice of the coverage area in which industrial action is to be taken. The parties' ability to exert influence on this choice depends on their options of being able to use their weapons, that is, the strike or the lockout.

Under the existing labor dispute legislation of the FRG, trade unions and employers' associations, do not dispose of the same parameters of action. Employers are not allowed to start on industrial action: "offensive lockouts" are unlawful. In contrast, the unions dispose of the option of officially opening a labor dispute upon expiration of the peace obligation. Thus, the decision of employers to use "defensive lockouts" has the status of a follow-up action. Under the existing legislation, unions dispose of the better options of intervention in the "merry-go-round" of bargaining as concerns the choice of time and place of the industrial action. They may concentrate the industrial dispute on that "field of action" which is most suitable in terms of economic situation and organizational conditions such as degree of unionization, experience of union members with strike action, and a favorable input-output relation.

The Strategy of the Union

If one retrospectively analyzes the strategy adopted by IG Metall in the 1984 strike action, then it becomes clear that the union did plan this longest and most costly labor dispute from the perspective of organizational policy and strategy of conflict.

In this dispute, IG Metall could resort to an extensive strike fund, which is a central prerequisite to strike action (*Industriemagazin*, August 1984).

In anticipation of this requirement, IG Metall had deliberately desisted from calling strikes to achieve better results in wage negotiations. In doing so, it accepted that the real wages of its members had actually declined over a period of two or three years (Janssen and Lang 1985).

The design of the strike concept of IG Metall clearly shows that the union took advantage of the structure of the collective bargaining system and the mechanism of bargaining in order to determine the area and the most favorable time for industrial action. After several bargaining rounds had been conducted in all coverage areas and after negotiations had reached a deadlock, the executive committee of IG Metall strategically selected the area in which strike action should be taken: It concentrated the dispute in the coverage area of North-Württemberg/North-Baden.

In addition to its own organizational advantages, within this area, such as workers and union officials experienced in industrial action, compactness of area, and the limited possibilities of the opponent of extracting financial resources from union funds through the use of the lockout weapon, IG Metall considered the following in its selection:

- Low levels of unemployment, prospering firms with an above average degree of capacity utilization, and latitude for passing on prices would lower the threshold for workers to take part in collective action and increase the willingness to make concessions on the side of the employers.
- The interpenetration of markets and distributive channels, as well as the integration of concerns to be found in this area, entailed that strike action conducted in this area (as it hardly applied to any other coverage area) would also affect firms located outside this area, thus intensifying the

effects of the strike and transferring the problems it would cause to employers to other regions as well. The union would thus be given the possibility of being able to calculate the dispute and to preserve its financial resources as workers affected by shutdowns outside the area could be assumed to receive (factually or supposedly) financial assistance through the Federal Labor Office. The concentration of some of the major car manufacturing companies and of suppliers to car manufacturers within this area makes it possible to disrupt one of the major industries of the national economy—the automobile industry.

- Finally, the position and attitude of the opponent's organizations, in particular that of the Verband der Metallindustrie (VMI), the regional association of metal manufacturing employers with headquarters at Stuttgart, favored strike action to be taken in this area. Although the VMI is one of the employers' associations in the metal industry which has the greatest experience with strikes and lockouts, it is also the organization which had most frequently broken away from the concerted negotiating concept of Gesamtmetall, the peak organization of German metal employers. It did so in 1981 (Weber 1987a, p. 72).

Moreover, for the first time in the history of labor disputes in the metal industry since 1945, IG Metall started a strike campaign in a second coverage area, Hessen, in order to demonstrate "the new quality of the strike" (Janssen and Lang 1985, p. 20).

The consideration of the above factors obviously led IG Metall to concentrate the strike action on these two coverage areas and to devise a strategy aiming at extracting, with a minimum of input, a maximum of resources on the opponent's side. This strategy, which has come to be known as the "mini-max" strategy, was first praised by the public as a strategic masterpiece but was later met with criticism.

The point of application for this strategy to be successful were the firms manufacturing radiators, pistons, oil pumps, and gaskets, which, on account of the nonsubstitutability of their products in the forward stages of production were likely to cause major disruptions in other firms of the automobile industry (Riester 1984, p. 259).

With its strategy, involving an extremely low number of strikers as compared to other labor disputes, IG Metall intended to achieve a gradually self-reinforcing blockade of the automobile industry and its suppliers. "The concept of the strike was chosen such that if the metal employers continued to asssume their attitude of refusal ... the effects of the strike and the economic pressure it involved would, as time went by, automatically extend" (Janssen and Lang 1985, p. 21). In anticipation of the employers' use of the lockout, the number of workers involved in the strike should obviously have been kept to the minimum. To this end, the executive committee of IG Metall decided to limit the strike action to the aforementioned suppliers of the automobile industry and to start the labor dispute with 15,000-18,000 workers on strike.

The Strategy of the Employers' Associations

The primary strategic aim of the employers was to prevent the union from developing capacity for collective action. In the case that collective action on the union side should occur, it was planned, secondly, to induce the union, through the use of appropriate counterstrategies, to call off the strike in the shortest time possible because of an extensive outflow of resources. In the case that the labor dispute should protract, it was planned to force the union, by way of a compromise, to pay an additional "price," in that it should abandon the principle of the "federal blanket coverage" (Bundeseinheitstarif) equally applying to all firms and to all categories of employees falling under the Collective Agreements Law. A possible compromise would be coupled to an improvement of the status quo for the employers' camp, consisting of giving employers more latitude in scheduling work through the inclusion of flexibilization and differentiation components in a new master agreement on working time.

The introduction of flexibilization and differentiation components, which the employers advanced with some vigor, is of interest to them in a twofold respect: from the perspective of firms, on the one hand, and from the perspective of employers' associations for organizational policy reasons, on the other. Flexibilization regulations would enable firms to better adapt the employment volume to cyclical or seasonal market fluctuations. In addition, the flexibilization of working time would enable them to achieve an economization effect in terms of the capital invested in equipment and stockages. Capacities, which had been considerably augmented in the last few years, would be better utilized and thus the realization of a cost degression effect would be possible. This was the main argument advanced by employers in a public debate for substantiating their demand for flexibilization and differentiation components to be included in collective contracts (VMI 1985; *Der Spiegel* 12, 1984).

Although not an object of public debate, but, nevertheless of equaly great importance is the effect of flexibilization and differentiation for the organizational policy of employers' associations. The advantage of such arrangements for employers' associations resides in the fact that internal tensions, within the system, would be reduced and internal integration would be increased. This is due to the fact that collective agreements, following the pattern of the "federal blanket coverage," constitute a problem to business firms insofar as they have to orient themselves towards a general standard level. An increasing number of firms, however, appear to be in less of a position to meet these standards due to their economic situation and cyclical conditions. As a result, the employers' associational system finds itself confronted with internal turbulences and an increase of centrifugal forces. Hence, the employers' associations' officials obviously assumed that the increase of heterogeneity of interests, within the employers' camp, could best be handled by pushing for collective agreement regulations allowing for greater variety. Thus they saw a possibility of simultaneously solving one of their internal organizational problems.

To be able to achieve their aim, the employers' associations adopted a set of strategies. In the different phases of the conflict, they employed different measures carefully tuned to the union as such, to its members, and to its social environment. First, the employers tried to withdraw its legitimatory and motivational resources from IG Metall through carefully-directed public relations work, either by the associations themselves via the media, or by the management within the firms. In doing so, they drew on surveys commissioned by themselves, and by the unions. The employers at first, obviously believed that IG Metall would fail to organize collective action. This opinion of the employers was based partly on social survey results and partly on their own analyses of the union's situation. They were convinced that the labor dispute would last only for a short duration as the union members would not support their organization (for the surveys, see Engfer et al. 1983). Contrary to this assumption, IG Metall succeeded in obtaining the requisite approval to embark on strike action, in the strike ballots held in the coverage areas North-Württemberg/North-Baden and Hessen, although it met with considerable initial difficulties and had to incur considerable costs (VMI 1985).

Although they were convinced that a labor dispute was unlikely to occur, the employers' associations obviously had made prior arrangements in case IG Metall found, contrary to all prognoses, the requisite approval of its members for strike action. For this event, the employers' associations had developed a concept enabling the strategy of resource extraction to be most effectually put into action. To achieve this end, the metal employers' associations included two innovations in their arsenal of industrial action weapons.

The first of these innovations relates to the provisions of the Labor Promotion Law regulating eligibility for unemployment benefits and short-time allowances in case of industrial disputes. The union's nationwide and uniformly-advanced demand for the introduction of the 35-hour-workweek and the coalition of Christian Democrats and Free Democrats taking over power in Bonn, seemed to render it possible to deny the union to resort to the funds of the Federal Labor Office. Being debarred from securing external resources, the union would be faced with the alternatives to either support the workers concerned by payments from union funds, which inevitably would accelerate the outflow of union resources, or to confront considerable internal turbulences in case it denied support from union funds to the workers concerned. In either case, by calculation of the employers, the union's fighting strength would soon break down.

The second innovation relates to the labor dispute rules in a narrower sense. In case the union called a regionally limited key strike, centering on single firms of the automobile industry, the employers envisaged extending lockouts (nationwide) to other car manufacturing firms located outside of the coverage area in which the strike had been called. The nationwide extension of the lockout, would have entailed, for the union, an accelerated outflow of its resources, since, in this case, the union statutes provide eligibility for strike benefits. In addition, the employers could expect that a nationwide extension of the lockout would enhance intraindustry loyalty among the car manufacturing firms most strongly affected by strike action due to intraindustry competition having been suspended. At the same time, the firms' willingness to take part in industrial action would be enhanced through the provision of financial assistance from the employers' associations' labor dispute funds. This latter effect, however, should not be overrated, because support payments, as a rule, make up for only about 90% of the firms' payroll, which is a relatively small amount in relation to the total costs incurred in a labor dispute due to losses in sales and costs of capital.

The strategy, which was later used by the employers, included both elements of the above concept, although the initially intended practice of nationwide lockouts was replaced by more-or-less carefully-directed shutdowns. This replacement was due to an intervention by the Federal Minister of Labor. Apart from the use of the lockout in the coverage area where the strike had been called, the shutdown device became a central element of the employers' strategy pursued in the dispute. But the shutdown also turned out to be "the most difficult chapter in the dispute" for IG Metall (Janssen and Lang 1985, p. 21).

After the employers had overcome their astonishment that IG Metall had succeeded in developing a capacity to take strike action and had devised a new concept in the form of the so-called "mini-max" strategy, they instrumentalized the "mini-max" strategy for their own benefit. In combination with the interdependence of production in the coverage area where the strike had been called, and the "reorientation" in the Federal Labor Office, they confronted the union with the alternative to face either a rapid extraction of its financial resources or to lose membership support. In this situation, IG Metall apparently had no choice but to opt "for the organization" and, thus, against a part of its members as it would otherwise have jeopardized the organization's survival.

In its response to the "cold lockouts" used by the employers, IG Metall called on its members to perform "plant inspections" (i.e., go-ins), a strategy which proved to be detrimental to the employers. On the other hand, these actions threatened to get out of control because, in some cases, members occupied the plants permanently.

Apart from its creation of a larger number of "secondary theaters of industrial warfare," which were rather difficult to control, IG Metall also pursued an additional politization of the dispute by pointing out to its members the role and function government officials at Bonn played in the conflict. Thus carried the diffuse feeling of loyalty among union members in an attempt to transform their latent motivation—"unionists do not abandon their organization"—into a manifest one. It sought to enhance its members' motivation for taking part in the struggle against the "bleeding" of the trade unions and, thus, against those who, supposedly or factually, had set the course for this development. The conflict over the distribution of work was, therefore, increasingly politicized and, at least rhetorically, turned into a struggle against the "cartel of combines, cabinet, and coalition parties."

The Settlement of the Conflict

The labor dispute in the metal industry was brought to an end after six- and seven-week strikes, respectively. Before the willingness for a compromise could be reached and a result could be achieved, it was necessary for two things to happen: First, it was obviously necessary to obtain a (preliminary) legal settlement of the point at issue, that is, whether workers indirectly affected by the strike action and shutdown, outside of the coverage area, were eligible for benefits from the Federal Labor Office. After this was agreed upon, the strategic position of IG Metall improved.

Second, it was necessary to exceed beyond the "pain thresholds" set by both the trade union and the employers' associations. These thresholds were reached after the labor dispute had protracted over several weeks, IG Metall had called about 47,500 workers on strike in both coverage areas, and after the employers, in their turn, had locked out about 147,000 workers (Bobke 1985).

The willingness to make concessions on the side of IG Metall was increased by the fact, that, in the last week of the dispute, it had to pay strike benefits not only to the more than 100,000 union members affected by the strike and lockout, but also to the workers within the area of coverage which were indirectly affected through shutdowns. In securing ability to take collective action, IG Metall paid the latter group of workers "special benefits" amounting to the regular strike benefits. These were, however, not provided for in its statutes.

The costs incurred by IG Metall due to strike pay, special benefits, public relations, and motivational work are estimated at about 500 million German marks (Bobke 1985). The size of this amount is approximately equivalent to the reserves accumulated by IG Metall over the last three years for the conduct of labor dispute (480 million marks) (*Der Spiegel* 22, 1984).

The employers' side had also incurred considerable costs before a compromise could be achieved. Alone, the VMI puts the amount of the benefits paid to its members, from the centrally-supplied labor dispute fund of the employers, at 472 million marks (VMI 1985). Added to this must be the costs incurred by the employers' association in Hessen for which exact figures are not available.

To these costs accruiung to the organizations conducting the labor dispute, the costs incurred by the members on both sides which were directly or indirectly affected by the dispute must be added.

The labor dispute could not be terminated on the side of the employers until the car manufacturers were no longer willing to accept in favor of the small and medium-sized firms. An end to the conflict came when concessions could be assumed to find support among the membership. Any giving way or drawing back at an earlier time would have increased the tensions within the employers' associational system and turned out an "explosive charge."

Both sides were under an enormous pressure from their organizations to score a success. For reasons of organizational policy, IG Metall also had to go to the limits of its financial and motivational resources. So far, the result of the labor dispute constitutes a compromise, exhibiting positive as well as negative consequences for both parties. Thus, the employers could score as a success the inclusion of flexibilization and differentiation components into collective agreements giving them more latitude in scheduling work, while the trade union could bring about at least a formal drawing away from the 40-hour workweek on the employers' side.

IG Metall, and the employers' associations, in the future, will have to face the problem of securing capacity for collective action in view of the options now available to firms to make company-specific arrangements and the loss of the organizations advantage springing from standard regulations which could be centrally decided upon. Above all, IG Metall will have to rethink its strategy of "mini-max" for several reasons. Conference reports of IG Metall shop stewards (Vertrauensleute) illustrate that union officials, for instance at BMW, met with "hot hatred over the coldly locked out colleagues" (*Handelsblatt* 1984), that union members tried the rebellion against their own organization because they held the union responsible for their financial misery. The union members' discontent with the strategy adopted by IG Metall in the dispute, and the response possibilities it thereby offered to the employers, is said to have induced 1,000 workers of an Opel plant, located outside the coverage area where the strike had been called, to resign membership (*Handelsblatt* 1985). H. Mayr, chief chairman of IG Metall describes the problem of his organization as follows: "Not all things that unions do immediately enter people's heads, even not those of the younger ones. The work of the unions is not always thus plainly understandable that everybody on the spot wants to join the organization" (*Stern* 1984, p. 105).

"Mini-max" which originally had been conceived as a self-reinforcing blockade within the employers' camp, turned into a selfreinforcing avalanche of protest within IG Metall (*Handelsblatt* 1984). Moreover, the firms' new policy of keeping low stocks, in connection with a high degree of interdependence between producers and suppliers, results in labor disputes being even more difficult to control. Thus, the number of 140,000 "controlled" workers involved in the dispute (strikers and locked-outs) contrasted with, depending on the various sources, that of the 200,000 to 300,000 "uncontrolled" workers, indirectly affected by the dispute (Bobke 1985; Riester 1984; *Industriemagazin* 1984). As a consequence, about 200 million marks would have to be raised if these indirectly-affected workers, were found to be eligible for benefits under the Labor Promotion Law—thought this is hardly legitimizable over the long run, given the actual political conditions (Weber 1987b). In case these workers were left emptyhanded, the internal turbulences would increase for the union and, thus, its capacity to take collective action would diminish.

In the last analysis, the 1984 metal strike has demonstrated that, while, as a result of the changes in the interrelationships of production in connection with the companies' new policy of reduced stockkeeping, the need for consensus with respect to a system of industrial interest representation is increasing, the basis for a rational settlement of conflict is strongly eroding.

SUMMARY

The relations between sellers and buyers of labor power have preferentially been treated at the level of the interaction between single, or groups of, employees and employers (Crouch 1982; Weber 1981). Another approach has centered on the level of society, dealing, in particular, with the relationship between "labor and capital." From this perspective, industrial relations conflicts often assume the character of a struggle between the bargaining parties for improving their strategic position on the labor market (Offe and Hinrichs 1984).

Current social research, informed by the theory of public goods, has drawn attention to the fact that "collectively rational strategies" are not "automatically" individually rational strategies (Hinrichs and Wiesenthal 1986; classic in this respect: Olson 1965). While Olson develops "The Logic of Collective Action," Offe and Wiesenthal (1985) formulated their "Two Logics of Collective Action." They argue, that business associations and trade unions have different problems in acting as a collectivity.

Rather than analyzing the conflict between trade unions and employers' associations exclusively in terms of a "problem of transforming rationality," we propose to conceptualize it as a conflict within interorganizational systems. Thus, the focus of analysis is not on the level of the individual, the group, or the class, but on the level of organizations forming part of the industrial relations system (Dunlop 1958). Hence, we would have to deal with differentiated systems developed by either side of industry which are geared to conducting collective bargaining and which comprise several organizations interacting with one another (Clegg 1972).

The problem of generating capacity to take collective action is, thus, no longer exclusively a problem of transforming individual into collective rationality but a question of the resources available to an organization or system of organizations and of the strategic use of these resources.

To the extent that securing of membership support in collective action is no longer primarily a problem of norms of rules but rather of financial gratification, the potential of trade unions and employers' associations to take industrial action becomes dependent on the financial resources available to them and their use of those resources (Streeck 1981).

Bargaining power becomes directly, although not exclusively, connected with the funds which parties can dispose of. They are capable of taking industrial action if they have at their disposal sufficient financial resources to go through a labor dispute without incurring the danger of jeopardizing their organizational functioning and stability (Ross 1970).

This being the case in conflicts, parties are likely to follow the same logic, despite their organizational differences: the strategy of extraction of resources on the opponent's side.

REFERENCES

Bobke, M.H. 1985. "Arbeitsrecht im Arbeitskampf—Der Arbeitskampf 1984 in der Metallindustrie und in der Druckindustrie im Spiegel juristischer Auseinandersetzungen" (Industrial Law in Labor Conflicts. The Conflicts in Engineering and Printing in the Context of Labor Laws). *Wirtschafts- und Sozialwissenschaftliches Institut des Deutschen Gewerkschaftsbundes (WSI), Mitteilungen* (2): 57-59.

Clegg, H.A. 1972. *The System of Industrial Relations in Great Britain.* 2nd ed. Oxford: Blackwell.

Crouch, C. 1982. *Trade Unions: The Logic of Collective Action.* London: Fontana Paperbacks.

Der Spiegel. 1984. "Das ist volkswirtschaftlich ein Wahnsinn" (This is Economically Nonsense). (12).

Der Spiegel. 1984. "Durchstehn, sonst können wir uns abmelden" (Sustain, Otherwise We Will Be Layed Off). (22).

Dittrich, E. and H. Weber. 1985 "Gesellschaftliche Konstitutionsbedingungen von Gewerkschaften, ihre Struktur und Politik in der Bundesrepublik" (Social Determinants of Unions Structure and Policy in the Federal Republic of Germany). Pp. 99-148 in *Zur Gesellschaftsstruktur der BRD. Beiträge zur Einführung in ihre Kritik* (The Social Structure of the Federal Republic of Germany), vol. 2, edited by F. Buer, E. Dittrich, A. Cramer, R. Reichwein, and H.-G. Thien. Münster: Verlag Westfälisches Dampfboot.

Dunlop, J.T. 1958. *Industrial Relations Systems.* New York: Holt.

Engfer, U., K. Hinrichs, C. Offe, and H. Wiesenthal. 1983. "Arbeitszeitsituation und Arbeitszeitverkürzung in der Sicht der Beschäftigten" (Shortening of Working Hours from the Viewpoint of the Employed). *Mitteilungen aus der Arbeitsmarkt- und Berufsforschung* 18: 91-105.

Evan, W.M., ed. 1978. *Interorganizational Relations.* Philadelphia: University of Pennsylvania Press.

Farago, P. and H. Kriesi., eds. 1986. *Wirtschaftsverbände in der Schweiz. Organisation und Aktivitäten von Wirtschaftsverbänden in vier Sektoren der Industrie* (Economic Organization in Switzerland. Organization and Activities of Economic Organizations in Four Industrial Sectors). Grüsch: Rüegger.

Grant, W. 1985. Introduction in *The Political Economy of Corporatism.* London: MacMillan.

Handelsblatt. 1984. "Der Geist der Funktionäre ist stark, das Fleisch der Basis aber schwach" (The Spirit of the Officials is Willing, but the Flesh of the Roots is Weak). November 19.

————. 1985. "Mitgliederverlust ist keine Protestbewegung" (Membership Loss is not a Protest Movement). January 23.

Hinrichs, K. and H. Wiesenthal. 1986. "Bestandsrationalität versus Kollektivinteresse— Gewerkschaftliche Handlungsprobleme im Arbeitszeitkonflikt 1984" (Compromises versus Collective Interests. The Unions' Tactical Problems in the Labor Conflict of 1984). *Soziale Welt* 37: 280-297.

Industriemagazin. 1984. "Minimax hat ausgedient" (Minimax is Warned Out). August.

Janssen, H. and K. Lang. 1985. "Gewerkschaftspolitische Schlussfolgerungen aus dem Arbeitskampf um Arbeitszeitverkürzung" (Union Political Consequences on the Conflict of Shortening the Work Week). Pp. 7-37 in *Existenz sichern, Arbeit ändern, Leben gestalten. Gewerkschaften im Kampf um Arbeitszeitverkürzung* (Secured Existence, Changed Labor, Molded Life. Unions in the Conflict on Shortening of the Work Week), edited by E. Ferlemann and H. Janssen. Hamburg: VSA-Verlag.

Luhmann, N. 1981. "Interpenetration—Zum Verhältnis personaler und sozialer Systeme" (Mutual Penetration. The Relation of Personal and Social Systems). Pp. 151-169 in *Soziologische Aufklärung,* 3rd ed., edited by N. Luhmann. Opladen: Westdeutscher Verlag.

Müller-Jentsch, W. 1984. "Kollektive Interessenvertretung: Das System der 'industriellen Beziehungen' " (Collective Bargaining: The System of Industrial Relations). Pp. 362-392 in *Einführung in die Arbeits- und Industriesoziologie* (Introduction to Industrial Sociology), vol. 2, edited by W. Littek, W. Rammert, and G. Wachtler. Frankfurt and New York: Campus.

Offe, C. and K. Hinrichs. 1984. "Sozialökonomie des Arbeitsmarktes: primäres und sekundäres Machtgefälle" (The Social Economy of the Labor Market: Primary and Secondary Power). Pp. 44-86 in *Arbeitsgesellschaft, Strukturprobleme und Zukunftsperspektiven* (Labor Society, Structural Problems and Perspective for the Future), edited by C. Offe. Frankfurt and New York: Campus.

Offe, C. and H. Wiesenthal. 1985. "Two Logics of Collective Action: Theoretical Notes on Social Class and Organizational Form. Political Power and Social Theory." Pp. 170-220 in *Disorganized Capitalism,* edited by C. Offe. Oxford: Polity Press.

Olson, M.J.R. 1965. *The Logic of Collective Action.* Cambridge, MA: Harvard University Press.

Riester, W. 1984. "Der Kampf um die 35-Stunden-Woche" (The Fight for 35 Hours). *Wirtschafts- und Sozialwissenschaftliches Institut des Deutschen Gewerkschaftsbundes (WSI), Mitteilungen* (9): 526-533.

Ross, A. 1970. "Die Gewerkschaften als eine Institution der Lohnbestimmung" (The Unions as an Institute of Wage Determination). Pp. 181-205 in *Arbeitsökonomik,* edited by B. Külp and N. Schreiber. Köln: Kiepenheuer & Witsch.

Schmitter, P.C. 1979. "Still the Century of Corporatism?" Pp. 7-52 in *Trends toward Corporatist Intermediation,* edited by P.C. Schmitter and G. Lehmbruch. Beverly Hills and London: Sage.

Schmitter, P. and W. Streeck. 1981. *The Organization of Business Interest.* IIM/LMP 81-13. Berlin: Wissenschaftszentrum Berlin.

Stern. 1984: Gewerkschaften: "Wir haben ein paar Schrammen abbekommen" (Unions: We Got a Few Scratches). (28): 105.

Streeck, W. 1979. "Gewerkschaftsorganisation und industrielle Beziehungen. Einige Stabilitätsprobleme industriegewerkschaftlicher Interessenvertretung und ihre Lösung im westdeutschen System der industriellen Beziehungen" (Union Organization and Industrial Relations. Problems of Stability in Interest Representation and their Solution in the German Industrial Relations System). *Politische Vierteljahres Schriften*: 241-257.

_____. *Gewerkschaftliche Organisationsprobleme in der sozialstaatlichen Demokratie* (Organizational Problems of Unions in Social Democracies). Königstein/Ts.: Hain.

Verband der Metallindustrie Baden-Württemberg e.V. (VMI). 1985. *Der Arbeitskampf '84* (The Labor Conflicts of '84). Stuttgart: VMI.

Weber, H. 1981. *Soziologie des Betriebsrats. Managementstrategien und Handlungssituationen betrieblicher Interessenvertreter* (The Sociology of the Workers Council. Management Strategies and Action Context in Company Bargaining). Frankfurt and New York: Campus.

_____. 1987a. *Unternehmerverbände zwischen Markt, Staat und Gewerkschaften-Zur intermediären Organisation von Wirtschaftsverbänden* (Employer Organizations between Market, State and Unions. The Intermediary Organizations). Frankfurt and New York: Campus.

_____. 1987b. "Desynchronisation, Dezentralisierung-und Dekomposition; Die Wirkungsdynamik des Tarifkonflikts '84 und ihre Effekte auf das System industrieller Beziehungen" (Desynchronization, Decentralization and Decomposition: The Dynamics of the Wage Conflict of 1984 and its Consequences for the Industrial Relations System). In *Arbeitsmarkt, Arbeitsbeziehungen und Politik* (Labor Market, Industrial Relations and Politics), edited by H. Abromeit and B. Blanke. Opladen: Westdeutscher Verlag.

PART V

ORGANIZATIONAL EFFECTIVENESS

INTRODUCTION:

ORGANIZATIONAL EFFECTIVENESS

Bert Klandermans

Understanding the effectiveness of social movement organizations (SMOs) is a challenge both to organizers and to students of SMOs. Organizers believe influential organizations capable of changing society; researchers dream of measures and criteria that would be valid indications of an SMO's impact. Organizer's interest in an SMO's effectiveness is easily understandable, for it is not organizing per se which motivates them to establish and maintain an SMO, but the desire for social influence. Students of social movements, for their part, are plagued by the problem of defining and measuring a movement organization's impact and relating social change to efforts of movement organizations. Central to this last part of the volume is the question of what makes SMOs effective. Since Piven and Cloward (1979) took the provocative stand that organizations are detrimental to movement success, this question of effectiveness has become all the more pressing. The two contributions to Part V provide extensive reviews of the literature, and I do not wish to preempt their discussions here. Thus, in this introduction, I touch only briefly on some

International Social Movement Research, Vol. 2, pages 383-394.
Copyright © 1989 by JAI Press Inc.
All rights of reproduction in any form reserved.
ISBN: 0-89232-964-5

of the relevant issues, delineating the subject and raising some theoretical and methodological questions that receive scant attention in the literature.

The effectiveness of an SMO concerns its efficacy in interacting with its environment: its efficacy in accumulating and employing resources in order to bring about desired effects in its environment. This formulation raises several questions that any treatment of SMO effectiveness must answer.

1. What are the effects that SMOs desire to bring about, and to what extent do they coincide with the effects that SMOs actually produce? In other words, what are the intended and unintended consequencees of an SMO's efforts to act upon its environment? Several consequences are discussed in the literature, some—such as getting access to polity of goal achievement—receive much attention, others—such as agenda setting and questioning societal consensus—little or no attention, while unintended consequences are neglected altogether.

2. What influence do characteristics of the environment have on the effectiveness of a movement organization? The impact of multiorganizational fields, political opportunity structures, and climate of opinion will be addressed in this context.

3. What influence do characteristics of the movement organization itself have on organizational effectiveness? Do specific features such as structure and culture, strategy, and tactics have any impact?

4. What are the consequences of success and failure for organizational survival?

5. In an area this complicated, what might be some fruitful research strategies?

EFFECTS

On the whole, SMOs are far from ineffective in acting upon their environment. For example, Gamson (1975) found that 62% of the protest organizations in his study at least partially achieved their goals. Snyder and Kelly (1976) reported that 64% of the strikes in Italy in the period from 1878-1903 ended in success for the workers. O'Keefe and Schumaker (1983) observed that, in the period from 1960-1978, 43% of the protests in Malaysia, 35% of those in the Philippines, and 71% of those in Thailand were in some way effective. Shin (1983) found that, in South Korea between 1945-1972, 36% of the protests had some effect. In his contribution to this volume, Huberts concludes that six out of eight attempts to protest highway construction plans had some influence.

Success Evaluations

Whether outcomes of an SMO's efforts to act upon its environment succeed or fail is a matter of interpretation which depends on the standards used and on who is making the judgment. In order to arrive at an adequate and objective evaluation of the effectiveness of an SMO, possible outcomes of alternative ways of achieving the SMO's objectives should be taken into account, and intended and unintended consequences should be weighed against each other.

Compared to the often lengthy bureaucratic procedures required to influence policy-making, protest can be a very effective way of pushing authorities into action (Daalder 1981). However, systematic comparisons of the effectiveness of SMO pressure with alternative influence strategies, or with pressure from other social actors, are almost completely lacking. Hubert's contribution to this volume is a rare example of a systematic presentation of empirical data on the relative impact of SMOs in the field of other social actors. He concludes from his data that, in comparison to other actors in the decision-making process, SMOs are relatively weak. Equally rare are studies that compare intended and unintended consequences of the influence attempts of SMOs. Exceptions are those studies which reveal the detrimental consequences of the use of violence (Snyder and Kelly 1976; Zimmermann 1987). Another exception is Mansbridge's (1986) study that showed that pro-Equal Rights Amendment (ERA) activists, in their zeal to convince people, actually helped to create the caricature of the ERA so effectively used by the anti-ERA movement.

Thus adequate evaluation of the outcomes of SMO activities requires information about alternative strategies and unintended consequences. Although this information is usually lacking, individuals inside and outside the movement do have opinions about the movement's effectiveness, and, interestingly, these opinions differ depending on the position of the person who is doing the evaluating. Organizers, activists, outside observers, and opponents all differ in their appraisal of a movement's effectiveness. A few examples can serve as illustrations. Knoke and Wood (1981) asked both the associations' members and a panel of individuals, knowledgable of affairs in their community, to evaluate organizational effectiveness of influence associations. Member evaluations stressed, to a greater degree, internal organizational processes, whereas community informants emphasized formal organizational characteristics and financial resources at the organization's disposal. This finding is in line with the conclusion of Demerath et al. (1971), based on longitudinal research among volunteers in the voting registration campaign in southern states in the United States in 1965: Volunteers' success evaluations were strongly related to the experience of social solidarity within groups of volunteers. Finally, in our own research on the Dutch peace movement, we found that opponents of the peace movement estimated the movement to be more effective than did its supporters.

Intended Outcomes

In the literature, much attention has been paid to goal achievement and recognition by authorities as movement objectives (Gamson 1975; Mueller 1978; O'Keefe and Schumaker 1983; Shin 1983). Analyses that are restricted to goal-achievement use an unnecessarily narrow concept of organizational effectiveness. The objectives of SMOs are much more varied than the achievement of some stated goal. Moreover, as Levitas (1977) pointed out, aim-centered models of social movements, which concentrate on the achievement of some desired social change, are not without problems. Such models assume that SMOs have fixed, static goals, which is usually not true. Movement goals change over time; some goals become more important, other goals less important. As both Huberts and Gundelach, in their chapters in Part V, discuss the literature on goal achievement and recognition as movement objectives, I will not elaborate on this topic here. Instead, I will point to some other objectives of SMOs, which are less well-documented.

In addition to goal achievement, several other outcomes of SMO's efforts can be distinguished. One of the strengths of SMOs is their ability to put issues on the political agendaa, as Mazur's (1981) study on technological controversies and Tierney's (1982) study on the battered women's movement illustrate very clearly. Both studies showed how movement activists were able to transform, in the one case, subjects of discussion among experts (Mazur) and, in the other case, private shame (Tierney) into objects of public concern. It is beyond dispute that SMOs not only deliberately aim at putting issues on the political agenda but also take pride in their successes in doing so, sometimes even more than in goal-achievement. These outcomes are closely related to another effect of SMOs, that is, successfully undermining societal consensus. Examples of movement organizations that have been able to change public opinion, especially organized opinion (i.e., the positions of political parties, unions, churches, and the like) are not difficult to find. The Dutch peace movement and the anti-ERA movement in the United States are cases in point. Throughout its campaign, the Dutch peace movement proved to be very effective in questioning official defense, policy and in changing the official stands of churches, unions, and political parties (Everts 1983). In the United States, once the initial unspoken political consensus on the ERA had emerged, the anti-ERA movement was very successful in putting both direct and—by mobilizing public opinion—indirect pressure on lawmakers in states that had not yet ratified the amendment (Conover and Gray 1983; Mansbridge 1986).

Finally, the activities of SMOs can be considered successful if they are able to accumulate resources for future actions, even if they fail in terms of goal achievement. In his study of the southern civil rights movement in the United States, Morris (1984) convincingly demonstrated that episodes of collective action strengthened the movement, although they failed to reach their goals.

In this regard, the mobilization of consensus about the movement's views deserves special attention. Consensus mobilization is a prerequisite for action mobilization (Klandermans 1984, 1988). An SMO's capability to mobilize resources increases in relation to its success in mobilizing consensus. Schennik (1988) demonstrated that, in the 1970s, the Dutch peace movement was able to mobilize the consensus that became the foundation for its successful action mobilizations in the 1980s. Another aspect of effective consensus mobilization was discussed by Barnes (1985, p. 16) in a paper on the Southern Farmers Alliance. According to him, elites have significant control over problem definitions and solutions, but without "grassroots protest organization that allows for widespread transmittal of criticisms of the diagnosis and solutions of the elite, there is little hope for significant reform."

THE ENVIRONMENT

In the preceding discussion of effects, a distinction was made between goal achievement and recognition, on the one hand, and persuasion, changing public opinion, and mobilization of consensus, on the other. The characteristics of an SMO's environment which are relevant to goal-achievement and recognition can be summarized as the political opportunity structure in a society. For persuasion, the most important aspect of the environment is the mass media structure in a society. Multiorganizational fields play a crucial role in both contexts, as the discussions in Part IV demonstrate. Knoke and Wood (1981) concluded that an influence association's position in the multiorganizational field (or the "interorganizational relations system," as they call it), can be more significant in determining its influence than characteristics of its organization or internal organizational processes. Steedly and Foley (1979), in their multivariate analysis of Gamson's (1975) data, concluded that the number of a group's alliances was the next most important factor in the explanation of movement success.

Mass Media

Mass Media are an extremely important element in an SMO's environment. Gitlin (1980) goes so far as to argue that the mass media are able to make and unmake social movements. In his treatment of the media coverage of Students for a Democratic Society (SDS), he makes perfectly clear how important the media are in sponsoring leaders and the frame of reference of a movement organization. The media help to create a "climate of opinion" (Marshall and Orum 1987) favorable or unfavorable to the movement. These authors showed, for example, that different climates of opinion at the end of the 19th century, and in the 1980s, among other factors, determined why the antisuffragette movement failed where the anti-ERA movement succeeded. But the media do much more. Media attention is an asset to a movement, as Mazur (1981) demonstrated in the case of the antinuclear power movement, Gitlin (1980) in the case of SDS, and Tierney (1982) in the case of the battered women's movement. Media coverage gives a movement more visibility, certifies its leaders, and facilitates the recruitment of support.

Political Opportunity Structure

Since the seminal work of Eisinger (1973), McAdam (1982), and Tarrow (1983), the importance of the political opportunity structure for movement success has been widely agreed upon in social movement literature. Alliances with the polity, dissent among elites, electoral instability, and the openness and responsiveness of the political system turned out to be conducive to the effectiveness of movement organizations. Differences in political opportunity structure between countries or changes in political opportunity structure over time were used to explain differential organizational effectiveness (Gelb 1985; O'Keefe and Schumaker 1983; Rucht 1985; Shin 1983). A breakdown of consensus among elites, together with alliance formation between dissident elites and SMOs appeared to be an especially effective combination of factors (Jenkins 1987; Boender 1985). The impact of opportunity structures on movement success varies with movement structure and tactics. In South Asia, democratic regimes were more responsive to moderate demands, larger protest groups, and moderate use of constraints; while authoritarian regimes were more responsive to smaller groups and the use of constraints (O'Keefe and Schumaker 1983).

MOVEMENT CHARACTERISTICS

Movement organizations vary in organizational structure, membership commitment or loyalty, strategy and tactics. Each factor is known to influence organizational effectiveness.

Organizational Structure

The previous chapters revealed that formal bureaucratic structures are not the kind of organizations most frequently encountered in the social movement sector of a society. Much of the literature on the impact that movement organizational characteristics have on success and failure, however, restricts itself to the impact of varying degrees of bureaucratization on movement success. In other words, much of our knowledge is biased toward only one of the possible modes of organization in the social movement sector, and not even the most common mode of organization. Ferree and Hess (1985) suggest, that different modes of organization have been successful in different ways. Comparing bureaucratic and collectivist organizations in the feminist movement, Ferree and Hess concluded that the former kind of organizations was more effective in lobbying and fundraising, whereas the latter was more effective in directly changing institutional patterns. What this observation suggests is that characteristics of bureaucratic organizations facilitate goal achievement and access to polity, whereas collectivist organization facilitates the mobilization of consensus, recruitment, direct changes in life-style, and so on. Available research results indeed seem to indicate that characteristics such as professionalization, availability of full-time staff personnel, centralization, formal organization, and availability of resources are conducive to goal achievement and access to polity (Gamson 1975; Jenkins and Eckert 1986; Knoke 1985; Steedly and Foley 1979). Collectivist organizations are less effective in these areas (Dwyer 1983; Marshall and Orum 1987). Collectivist organizations are often so-called redemptive organizations, that is, organizations that require participants to change their life-style. Stoper (1983) argued that redemptive organizations are not suited for goal-achievement activities, because goal achievement requires willingness to compromise, which is not the strength of this kind of organization. It has been argued, however, that collectivist organizations are more effective in persuasion and recruitment than are bureaucratic organizations (Carden 1978; Dwyer 1983; Gundelach in Part V of this volume).

Membership Commitment and Loyalty

An important requirement for the effectiveness of a movement organization is organizational discipline, that is, a rank and file that knows when to take action and when to stop action (Schwartz 1976). In her study of the value of union sponsorship of strikers, Conell (1980) demonstrated the importance of timing for the success of collective actions. Organizational discipline is an indispensable prerequisite for effective timing. In order to become a disciplined organization, a movement must integrate the multitude of motives and interests individual members harbor—in other words, it must develop something like a movement culture (McNall and Divney 1986) or collective identity (Melucci 1980). In their contribution to this volume, Van der Veen and Klandermans suggest using membership commitment or loyalty as counterparts at the individual level of concepts such as collective identity. Clearly, membership commitment evidently furthers organizational effectiveness (Knoke and Wood 1981).

Strategy and Tactics

Empirical evidence concerning movement strategy and tactics is inconclusive. Gamson's (1975) conclusion that moderate demands and the use

of constraints foster movement success is well known. With regard to the
second of these two factors, Mueller (1978) demonstrated that, in the protest
U.S. ghetto riots, the higher the level of violence to persons, the more successful
the protest. Snyder and Kelly (1976) however, in their study of Italian strikes,
arrived at the opposite conclusion: violence is detrimental to the workers' cause.
Probably O'Keefe and Schumaker (1983) are right in arguing that the
effectiveness of movement tactics depends on the political context in which
these tactics are used. As mentioned above, O'Keefe and Schumaker found
that the use of constraints was not effective under democratic regimes but was
effective under authoritarian regimes. The same rule held true for movement
demands. Democratic regimes were more responsive to moderate demands,
and authoritarian regimes were more responsive to radical demands. Clearly,
controlled comparison is needed to arrive at more definite conclusions (Gurr
1983; Zimmermann 1986).

THE EFFECTS OF SUCCESS AND FAILURE

Up to now I have discussed success and failure as the consequence *of* certain
characteristics of movement organizations, but both success and failure also
have significant consequences *for* movement organizations.

The effects of success or failure on SMOs are ambiguous (Schwartz 1976).
Movement success may threaten the survival of an SMO. First, the necessity
of the organization's continued existence may be questioned if the movement's
principal goals have been achieved. Duffhues and Felling's description (in this
volume) of the Dutch Catholic movement provides a case in point. Second,
initial successes can result in an influx of large numbers of new members, which
the movement may be unable to handle. Miller (1983) and Ross (1983) both
argue that the end of the SDS was rung in when a large group of students
entered the movement after its initial successes and after it received favorable
media coverage. The relation of success to movement growth and decline, is
paradoxical. A movement organization needs a large membership to be
successful, but it needs success to grow. If it is too successful, however,
movement goals may lose their urgency, and, as a consequence, participation
may become less necessary in the eyes of potential participants.

Failure can easily demoralize participants. Moreover, it often leads to
factionalism, which has a debilitating effect on movement organizations and
makes future failures more likely. However, as long as failure does not bring
into question the chances of success for the organization as a whole, it need
not necessarily to have demoralizing consequences. If the failure can be blamed
on target institutions, it can even strengthen a movement organziation.
Nevertheless, in the long run, the impression that a movement organization
is not capable of reaching its objectives is deleterious. Failures, especially

repeated failures inevitably create an image of inefficacy and thus discourages potential recruits, for most people see no sense in sacrificing for a movement organization that is ineffective (Pinard and Hamilton 1986; Klandermans 1988).

METHODS

Studies on organizational effectiveness are seriously hindered by methodological pitfalls. As Huberts devotes an ample portion of his essay to a discussion of this topic, here I will confine myself to some remarks that may stimulate fruitful research in the area. In this introduction, organizational effectiveness has been presented as the result of the interaction of characteristics of the organization and its external environment. It was assumed that there is neither a single effective mode of organization nor a single responsive external environment. Organizational characteristics can be differentially supportive, depending on the context in which a movement organization operates. Such a contingency theory of organizational effectiveness requires adapted research strategies capable of revealing the details of the interaction of characteristics of movement organizations and the external environment. Moreover, because (as Huberts convincingly argues) movement organizations are not the only actors trying to influence political decision making, the effectiveness of movement organizations must be assessed in relation to the other actors engaged in the decision-making process.

Such an assessment may be accomplished through several strategies:

- Controlled comparison of different modes of organization in different environments. Studies such as those of O'Keefe and Schumaker (1983) and Shin (1983), who examined movement organizations in a democratic and an authoritarian political context, can serve as a model. Klandermans and Oegema (1987) similarly compared the effectiveness of local organizations of the Dutch peace movement in influencing local governments.
- Carefully conducted case studies that depict the ways in which characteristics of a movement organization and its environment interact in bringing about, or failing to bring about, specific outcomes. Several good examples of such case studies are already available. To mention only a few: Morris' (1984), study of the southern civil rights movement, Jenkins' (1985), study of the UFW, and Boenders' (1985), study of the environmental movement in the Rotterdam area, that successfully forced the city's government to change its industrial policy.
- Detailed analyses of the decision-making processes that movement organizations—among other actors—attempt to influence. An

elaboration of this strategy is presented in Huberts' contribution to Part V (in this volume).

Each strategy has its particular disadvantages. Controlled comparison necessarily lacks depth. Comparing different organizations in disparate external environments is too extensive an undertaking to collect in-depth information on dynamics and processes. In this respect, case studies and process analyses have the advantage. But case studies and process analyses in their turn, raise questions of generalization. It remains unclear whether findings apply only to the specific movement organization, environment, and decision being studied or whether they can be generalized to other movement organizations and settings. In addition, process analysis, in restricting itself to the impact of movement organizations on specific decisions, does not arrive at an evaluation of the effectiveness of the organization in general. Clearly, the research strategies supplement one another, and solid conclusions have to be rooted in some combination of the three.

THE CONTRIBUTIONS TO PART V

My earlier references to the two essays in this part provide some idea of their contents, but a few additional remarks are necessary.

Huberts' contribution provides an extensive discussion of theoretical and methodological problems in the study of movement effectiveness. The empirical part of the paper presents results from an intriguing study of the impact of movement organizations in relation to the impact of other actors on decision making in the highway construction. Huberts concludes from his evidence that movement organizations have relatively little impact on decision making.

Gundelach discusses the restrictions that structural characteristics of "new social movements" impose on the movements in terms of success. He concludes that the typical mode of organization of new social movements is more effective in mobilizing support than in realizing social change.

REFERENCES

Barnes, D.A. 1985. "Organization and Effective Protest: An Antithesis?" Paper presented at the annual meeting of the American Sociological Association, Washington, D.C.
Boender, K. 1985. *Sociologische analyse van milieusolidariteit onder elites en publiek* (Sociological Analysis of Environmentalism Among Elites and the General Public). Rijswijk: Sythoff Pers.
Carden, M. 1978. "The Proliferation of a Social Movement: Ideology and Individual Incentives in the Contemporary Feminist Movement." Pp. 179-196 in *Research in Social Movements, Conflict and Change*, vol. 1, edited by L. Kriesberg. Greenwich, CT: JAI Press.
Conell, C. 1980. "The Value of Union Sponsorship to Strikers." Unpublished dissertation. University of Michigan.

Conover, P. and V. Gray. 1983. *Feminism and the New Right. The Conflict over the American Family.* New York: Praeger.

Demerath, N.J., III, G. Marwell, and M. Aiken. 1971. "Criteria and Contingencies of Success in a Radical Political Movement." *Journal of Social Issues* 27: 63-80.

Dwyer, L.E. 1983. "Structure and Strategy in the Antinuclear Movement." Pp. 148-161 in *Movements of the Sixties and the Seventies,* edited by J. Freeman. New York/London: Longman.

Eisinger, P.K. 1973. "The Conditions of Protest Behavior in American Cities." *American Political Science Review* 67: 11-28.

Everts, Ph. P. 1983. "Public Opinion, the Churches and Foreign Policy, Studies of Domestic Factors in the Making of Dutch Foreign Policy." Unpublished dissertation, University of Leiden.

Ferree, M. and B.B. Hess. 1985. *Controversy and Coalition: The New Feminist Movement.* Boston: G.K. Hall.

Gamson, W.A. 1975. *The Strategy of Social Protest.* Homewood, IL: The Dorsey Press.

Gelb, J. 1985. "The Impact of Feminist Movements on Governmental Activities in the United States and the United Kingdom." Paper presented at the 13th World Congress of the International Political Science Association, Paris.

Gitlin, T. 1980. *The Whole World is Watching. The Media in the Making and Unmaking of the New Left.* Berkeley: University of California Press.

Gurr, T.R., ed. 1983. "Group Protest and Policy Responses: New Cross-National Perspectives." *American Behavioral Scientist* 26: 283-416 (Special Issue).

Jenkins, J.C. 1985. *The Politics of Insurgency.* New York: Columbia University Press.

————. 1987. "Interpreting the Stormy Sixties: Three Theories in Search of a Political Age." Pp. 269-305 in *Research in Political Sociology,* vol. 3, edited by R.G. Braungart. Greenwich, CT: JAI Press.

Jenkins, J.C. and C.M. Eckert. 1986. "Channeling Black Insurgency." *American Sociological Review* 51: 812-830.

Klandermans, B. 1984. "Mobilization and Participation: Social Psychological Expansions of Resource Mobilization Theory." *American Sociological Review* 49: 583-600.

————. 1988. "The Formation and Mobilization of Consensus." In *From Structure to Action: Comparing Movement Participation Across Cultures,* edited by B. Klandermans, H. Kriesi, and S. Tarrow. Greenwich, CT: JAI Press.

Klandermans, B. and D. Oegema. 1987. "Campaigning for a Nuclear Freeze: Grassroots Strategies and Local Government in The Netherlands." Pp. 305-337 in *Research in Political Sociology,* vol. 3, edited by R.G. Braungart. Greenwich, CT: JAI Press.

Knoke, D. 1985. "The Political Economies of Associations." Pp. 211-242 in *Research in Political Sociology,* vol. 1, edited by R.G. Braungart. Greenwich, CT: JAI Press.

Knoke, D. and J.R. Wood. 1981. *Organization for Action, Commitment in Voluntary Associations.* New Brunswick, N.J.: Rutgers University Press.

Levitas, R.A. 1977. "Some Problems with Aim-Centred Models of Social Movements." *Sociology,* 11: 47-53.

McAdam, D. 1982. *Political Process and the Development of Black Insurgency.* Chicago: The University of Chicago Press.

McNall, S. and J. Divney. 1986. "Bureaucratization and Mobilization in a Third-Party Movement: The Kansas Farmers' Alliance and Populist Movement, 1890-1900." Paper presented at the annual meeting of the American Sociological Association, New York.

Mansbridge, J.L. 1986. *Why We Lost the ERA.* Chicago: The University of Chicago Press.

Marshall, S.E. and A. Orum. 1987. "Opposition Then and Now: Countering Feminism in the Twentieth Century." In *Research in Politics and Society,* vol. 2, edited by G. Moore and G.D. Spitze. Greenwich, CT: JAI Press.

Mazur, A. 1981. *The Dynamics of Technical Controversy*. Washington, DC: Communication Press.

Melucci, A. 1980. "The New Social Movements: A Theoretical Approach." *Social Science Information* 19: 199-226.

Miller, F.D. 1983. "The End of SDS and the Emergence of Weatherman: Demise through Success." Pp. 279-297 in *Movements of the Sixties and Seventies*, edited by J. Freeman. New York/London: Longman.

Morris, A. 1984. *The Origins of the Civil Rights Movement: Black Communities Organizing for Change*. New York: Free Press.

Mueller, C. 1978. "Riot Violence and Protest Outcomes." *Journal of Political and Military Sociology* 6: 49-65.

O'Keefe, M. and P.D. Schumaker. 1983. "Protest Effectiveness in South East Asia." *American Behavioral Scientist* 26: 375-394.

Pinard, M. and R. Hamilton, R. 1986. "Motivational Dimensions in the Quebec Indepence Movement: A Test of a New Model." Pp. 225-280 in *Research in Social Movements, Conflicts and Change*,vol. 9, edited by L. Kriesberg. Greenwich, CT: JAI Press.

Piven, F. and R.A. Cloward. 1979. *Poor People's Movements: Whey They Succeed, How They Fail*. New York: Vintage Books.

Ross, R.J. 1983. "Generational Change and Primary Groups in a Social Movement." Pp. 177-189 in *Movements of the Sixties and the Seventies*, edited by J. Freeman. New York/London: Longman.

Rucht, D. 1985. "Social Movement Sectors in France and West Germany since 1968." Paper presented at the Fifth International Conference of Europeanists, Washington, D.C.

Schennik, B. 1988. "Dynamics of the Peace Movement in The Netherlands." In *From Structure to Action: Comparing Movement Participation Across Cultures*, edited by B. Klandermans, H. Kriesi, and S. Tarrow. Greenwich, CT: JAI Press.

Schwartz, M. 1976. *Radical Protest and Social Structure*. New York: Academic Press.

Shin, M. 1983. "Political Protest and Government Decision Making." *American Behavioral Scientist*, 26: 395-416.

Snyder, D. and W.R. Kelly. 1976. "Industrial Violence in Italy, 1878-1903. *American Journal of Sociology* 82: 131-162.

Steedly, H.R. and J.W. Foley. 1979. "The Success of Protest Groups: Multivariate Analysis." *Social Science Research* 8: 1-15.

Stoper, E. 1983. "The Student Non-Violent Coordinating Committee: Rise and Fall of a Redemptive Organization." Pp. 320-334 in *Movements of the Sixties and the Seventies*, edited by J. Freeman. New York/London: Longman.

Tarrow, S. 1983. *Struggling to Reform: Social Movements and Policy Change during Cycles of Protest*. Western Societies Paper No. 15, Ithaca, N.Y.: Cornell University.

Tierney, K.J. 1982. "The Battered Women Movement and the Creation of the Wife Beating Problem." *Social Problems* 29: 207-220.

Zimmermann, E. 1986. "Political Unrest in OECDCountries, Trends and Prospects, Consequences and Risks of Political Democracy." Paper presented at the 'Global Situation and Political Risks' Seminar on the Finland Committee of the Club of Rome, Helsinki.

_____. 1987. "Political Violence and Other Strategies of Opposition Movements. Going Beyond Simple Case Studies: A Look at Some Recent Evidence." *Journal of International Affairs* 40.

THE INFLUENCE OF SOCIAL MOVEMENTS ON GOVERNMENT POLICY

Leo W. Huberts

INTRODUCTION

Literature on social movements usually states that social movements try to promote or resist societal and/or personal change. But what change do they actually achieve? What is the effectiveness of such movements and/or how successful are they?

Although these questions are difficult questions, I will nevertheless try to provide an answer. In doing so, I will restrict myself to one type of achievements of social movements; the actual influence of social movement actors (SMAs) and activities on political decision making in general, and on government policy, in particular. After having clarified the concept of political influence, I will discuss foreign and Dutch research on the political influence of social movements. The paper continues with a presentation of results from a research

International Social Movement Research, Vol. 2, pages 395-426.
ISBN: 0-89232-964-5

project on decision-making processes about national highway construction in The Netherlands. In a concluding paragraph, some theses are formulated about the political influence of social movement organizations (SMOs).

Concepts of Political Influence

Dahl (1957, p. 202) used the terms power and influence interchangeably. He proposed the following description of power: "A has power over B to the extent that he can get B to do something that B would not otherwise do." Ever since, alternative descriptions and typologies have been proposed (Lukes 1974, 1979; Wrong 1979). Nevertheless, with small amendments, Dahl's initial definition is useful to define the influence of social movements. The first amendment will be that the change A realizes must be in accordance with A's interests or goals. Secondly, the term "influence" is to be preferred since "power" is usually associated with the potential exercise of negative sanctions. Taking this into account, the influence of a social movement can be defined. A social movement exerts *influence* to the extent that its' actors get others to act more in accordance with the movements' goals than these actors otherwise would have done. The *political influence* can be defined as the effects of social movement actors and their activities on the decisions and nondecisions of political authorities. The focus in this paper is directed at the influence on government actors.

This limitation to influence on government policy means that the topic differs from the often discussed overall *success* or significance of movements. Success in reference to a social movement can have different meanings and can be gauged in various ways (Turner and Killian 1972, p. 255). A movement might be judged successful as long as the number of adherents continues to increase. Success is sometimes viewed as the perpetuation of the movement and its organization. And success can be measured by the degree to which the values the movement promotes are achieved. This paper concentrates on the last criterion, that is, the extent to which movement goals and demands are realized. It limits itself to the realization of one type of goals and demands, namely those concerning change in governmental policy. Primarily cultural effects, personal change that might be brought forward by movements, as well as societal effects that might result from that change in the longer run, will not be discussed. Emphasis will be on the political goals and demands that are formulated, the actors that mobilize the support for those demands, and the resulting changes in government policy.

Two questions are important in research on the political influence of SMAs:

- To what extent do political and official authorities change their policies when social movements direct their demands and organize their activities towards them?
- What are the decisive factors for the success or failure of the political action (and nonaction) of social movements?

RESEARCH ON POLITICAL INFLUENCE

My purpose here is to give a brief overview of the research on the political influence of social movements.

Of the major schools of thought in the social movement literature, the resource mobilization approach (RM approach) most closely deals with the issue of influence. In the RM approach, SMOs are seen as rational, political collective actors as indicated by Tilly and Tilly (1981, p. 15):

> taking the definitions and beliefs of the participants seriously; attempting to connect the action with the interests, grievances, and aspirations of everyday; and attaching great importance to the social structures which link the actors to each other as well as to their rivals, enemies, and exploiters.

More traditional approaches interpreted the nonconventional social movements as apolitical expressive actions (Jenkins 1983, 1985; McAdam 1982) and "insofar as success is gauged, it is in terms of the self-defined goals or utopias advanced by charismatic leaders" (Jenkins 1985, p. 21). Research traditionally focused on the development of the movement itself, without paying much attention to the interrelationship between movements and politial system as observed by Jenkins (1983, p. 543):

> Theories of the outcomes of social movements have traditionally been framed in terms of a "closed system" model of development, arguing that movements pass through a standard evolutionary sequence or "life cycle" culminating in either collapse or bureaucratization and institutional accommodation. (—) In contrast resource mobilization theorists have adopted an "open system" approach, arguing that the outcomes of movements are critically shaped by the larger political environment. The outcomes of challenges depend not only on strategic choices but also on the stance of political elites and the support/opposition of established interest organizations and other movements.

The traditional interpretation of success and its "closed system" approach of the development of movements is to a certain extent also recognizable in the so-called "new social movement approach" (NSM approach). In the NSM approach, researchers "attempt to relate the emergence and the development of "new" movements (primarily the environmental, the women's, and the peace movements) to developments in western industrialized societies. New social movements are seen as responses to modernization processes in such societies" (Brand 1985; see also Klandermans 1986). Researchers in the NSM approach concentrate on the extent to which a movement succeeds in realizing radical cultural, political, and social changes. Indicators for the realization of those chances are primarily found in the development or the potential of the movement itself (for example, in the number of members of movement organizations, in the number of participants in movement activities, and in the amount of public support for movement demands). These researchers tend to neglect changes in government policy in appreciating a movement's success. In the interpretation of the "new social movement approach," the state is one of the enemies of the movement rather than a target that can be influenced.

A citation from the work of Brand et al. (1984, p. 256) can serve to illustrate this. Referring to the environmental movement, they stated

> It is clear (—) that the pollution of water, air, soil and food has not decreased but has increased and more species in flora and fauna have become endangered. This is true, even although the measures taken may have prevented an even worse situation. The relative defeat of the movement against nuclear energy seems to be most obvious. Single projects were stopped or delayed, but the main objectives of nuclear energy programs were carried out.

The movements might have prevented the worsening of the environmental situation and might have stopped nuclear energy projects, but this is considered irrelevant given the ultimate goals of the movement. Success is only gauged "in terms of the self-defined goals or utopias" and then "social movements inevitably fall short" (Jenkins 1985, p. 21). The actual influence of movement actors on government policy is ignored.

The RM approach paid much more attention to the relation between movement activity and political decisionmaking. Of key importance was Gamson's *The Strategy of Social Protest* (1975). His empirical results play a major role in most reviews of the literature (Jenkins 1983; Raschke 1985; Schreuder 1981; Tarrow 1982). It is therefore legitimate to focus the discussion on his work and the criticisms it encountered. In this context, other studies pertinent to the topic will also be discussed.

Gamson studied a representative sample of 53 American voluntary groups that, between 1800 and 1945, have challenged aspects of the status quo. One of his aims was to assert conditions of a group's success or failure. He described two forms of achievement: The acceptance of challenging groups by its antagonists as a valid spokesman for a legitimate set of interests and the distribution of new advantages to the group's beneficiaries (acceptance; benefits). Gamson related the success of challenging groups to 39 organizational, tactical, and goal-oriented parameters for each group. Jenkins (1983, p. 543) summarized Gamson's findings in the following way: "In general, successful movements were bureaucratic, pursued narrow goals, employed selective incentives, enjoyed sponsorship, used unruly methods (including violence) and made their demands during periods of socio-political crisis."

In the next paragraphs, the following questions will be reviewed:

1. What is the importance of the use of violence and the presence of a (bureaucratic) organizational structure for success?
2. What is the relationship between success and the presence of allies in the private as well as in the public arena?

3. Which characteristics of the political system are important for movement success?
4. Are challenges in the private sector comparable to challenges directed at government policy?
5. What conclusions can be drawn about the responsiveness of political systems in western industrialized democracies?
6. How can the actual political influence of movement organizations be measured?

Violence and Organization

Vehement discussion was generated by Gamson's conclusions, that the use of constraints, including violence, and bureaucracy and organization favored movement's success.

The effectiveness of using constraints was shown by other studies (Piven and Cloward 1977; van Noort 1984), but Gamson's conclusions about the effectiveness of the use of violence by challenging groups was questioned by many authors. Steedley and Foley's (1979) multivariate analysis of Gamson's data lead them to suggest some moderations. They stressed that violence operates as a double-edged sword. A large and powerful group may be able to withstand the consequences of the response of authorities, but small groups will usually lose the battle in violent confrontations. The findings of Tilly et al. (1975, p. 283) on the other hand, suggested the contrary: "For a powerful group, almost by definition, it will rarely make sense to choose a means of collective action which currently has a high probability of producing violence." For a powerless group, which normally has a very small range of collective actions which can be used, violence will sometimes pay, for example, when their demands are not being heard.

Literature on the effectiveness of violence is inconclusive and points at the importance of distinguishing types of effects. Violence might be suited to attract political attention, while it might, at the same time, be counterproductive when policy changes are at stake.

Fundamental questions were also raised about the relationship between organization and influence (Piven and Cloward 1977; Cloward and Piven 1984). Gamson and Schmeidler (1984, p. 583) opposed the thesis that insurgency would bring more benefits than organized action and that organization would inevitably or usually dampen insurgency. They stressed that it would be necessary to determine what *types* of organization are likely to facilitate insurgency or abandon their oppositional politics under different historical conditions. Cloward and Piven (1984, p. 588) did not contest this point of view: "The dispute is not about organization versus no organization; it is about the political effectiveness of different kinds of organization." At the same time, however, they repeated their conviction that low-income groups only exert influence through disruption. It would, therefore, make little sense to invest resources in building enduring membership organizations of the poor. Jenkins (1985, p. 225) criticized this thesis on the basis of his research on the campaigns of farm workers. Blunting insurgency and diverting dissidence must be seen as strategic choices and not as organizational imperatives: "the powerless can be organized into permanent associations that provide the basis for mass defiance."

Alliances

Gamson hardly touched upon the possibility and effectivity of alliances with private and public actors. Steedley and Foley (1979, p. 10) emphasized that the variable (the number of alliances that a group has) is an important predictor of success: "Generally those groups that were not hindered, especially those who were actually helped by outside groups, were more successful in achieving their goals. This variable measures the protest group's support from nonrival groups." Others stressed that support, and especially hindrance, by an organized opposition seem important for the outcome of challenges (Turk and Zucker 1984).

Even more important, in my opinion, is the possibility of alliances between challenging groups and members of the polity (Tilly 1978). Political systems are not monolithical. Different parties, agencies, and officials represent different interests and opinions. This offers a possibility for social protest groups to ally with parts of the political and bureaucratic system. This possibility cannot be ignored when the political influence of SMOs is studied. Of course, access to members of the polity is a prerequisite for the establishment of alliances.

Research on public interests groups (Berry 1977, 1984; Richardson and Jordan 1979; Wilson 1981)[1] as well as research on social movements (Jenkins 1983) provides evidence for the relevance of alliances with members of the polity. Jenkins (1985, p. 25) concluded about the farm worker movement:

> The success of insurgencies is even more dependent on favorable political alignments than the generation of challenges. At a minimum, success entails changes in public policies. More durable changes require the development of routine political access. The key questions are the strength of the coalitions forged between insurgents and polity members and the access of its reform coalitions to centers of political power.

Similarly, Browning et al. (1984, p. 243), in their work on the struggle of blacks and Hispanics for equality in urban politics concluded: "A group that achieves substantial incorporation—beyond the right to vote and simple representation—is in a strong position to change government policy in areas of special concern to them." Minority protest was important for incorporation in the political system. Minority group participation in the dominant political coalition appeared to be crucial for winning new advantages.

Political Challenges

Gamson did not systematically differentiate between public and private challenging groups. Therefore, his study does not allow unambiguous conclusions concerning the influence of social protest on government policy.

Of the 53 groups Gamson (1975, p. 191) selected, 55% had predominantly governmental targets. Only 34% of them won acceptance and 41% new advantages, against 62% and 58%, respectively for groups with private targets.

Gamson explained the differences between challenges in the private and the public sector by pointing to the higher number of groups with target displacement goals among the challengers with public targets (goals requiring the removal of at least some of the antagonists). He (1975, p. 191) stated:

> when these groups are removed from the analysis, the results disappear or even reverse themselves. Of the nondisplacing groups with public targets, 60 percent win acceptance, compared to 64 percent of the nondisplacing groups with private targets. The figures for new advantages are 80 percent and 59 percent respectively.

Based on this explanation, differences between private and public challenges are ignored in the rest of the analysis. As a consequence, important differences between the two sectors are overlooked. Let me illustrate this by reanalyzing Gamson's data on the relationship between violence and success for different categories of groups.[2] Twenty groups were occupationally-based (e.g., occupational groups, craftsmen, farm organizations), seventeen were in one form or another a "reform group" (e.g., civil rights organizations, peace groups), ten were rooted in the socialist tradition, and six of the groups were some variety of right-wing or navitist group (Gamson 1975, p. 20). The occupational groups were very successful, while the socialist groups hardly ever succeeded (Table 1).

Table 1.   Categories of Groups and Their Success[a]

	Total Number	Full Response		Collapse	
Occupational groups	20	12	60%	2	10%
Reform groups	17	7	41	6	35
Socialist groups	10	0	0	9	90
Right wing groups	6	1	17	5	83
All groups	53	20	38	22	42

Note: [a] Full response: acceptance and new advantages.
Collapse: no acceptance, no new advantages.
Source: Based on Gamson (1975, pp. 187-189).

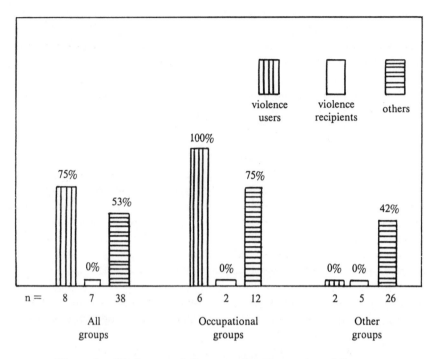

Figure 1.   Violence and Outcome for Categories of Groups:
Percentage of Groups that Won New Advantages

Gamson's conclusion that violence users among the challenging groups were more successful than other groups, appears to be determined by the success achieved by occupational groups (Figure 1). Gamson's data do not confirm the conclusion for the other, most likely more government-oriented groups.

Political System

Goldstone (1980) argued that Gamson's own data show that the success of challengers is independent from organizational and tactical group parameters and that periods of crisis are much more relevant. According to Jenkins (1983, p. 543), Gamson (1980) effectively challenged these contentions: "demonstrating that Goldstone's conclusions are based on an erroneous recoding of cases, a significant narrowing of the meaning of success and an ambiguous interpretation of 'crisis periods.' "

Nevertheless, it can hardly be denied that the social and political environment is important for success as well. Indeed, Gamson (1975, p. 110-129) formulated a similar view in *The Strategy of Social Protest* in a chapter about the historical context of challenges.

It is clear as well that we cannot limit ourselves to the "crisis" variable when the political and social context is discussed. Tarrow (1982, p. 28) hypothesized that three elements of the "political opportunity structure" appear to be the most germane to the outcomes of political protest:

> These are, first, Eisinger's variable of the openness or closure of formal political process; second, the stability or instability of alignments within the political system; and third, the availability and strategic posture of potential alliance partners.

Eisinger (1973) used the variable the "openness or closure of the formal political process" to study the relationship between opportunity structure and the incidence of protest. Information concerning the relationship between the openness of the political system and the success of protest is still lacking (Tarrow 1982, p. 29). To a certain extent, the same holds true for the significance of the stability of alignments, as measured most conveniently by electoral stability. The importance of alliances that protest groups make in support of their policy demands is more evident, as was discussed earlier.

Of course, groups that operate in a favorable political situation will not automatically succeed. Characteristics of the social movement actor and its campaign are important as well (Tarrow 1982, p. 46; Jenkins 1985, p. 228).

Pluralism versus Elitism

McAdam (1982) suggested that interpretations of social movements are directly connected with interpretations of the political system. When the political system is seen as open and responsive (as pluralists do), conventional political participation will be enough to influence decisionmaking. Elitists, on the other hand, see social movements as a tactical response to the harsh realities of a closed and coercive political system. Both institutionalized politics and social movements are seen as rational attempts to pursue collective interests. The RM approach is consistent with this model.

McAdam's thesis is supported by Gamson's remarks about the American political system. Gamson (1975, p. 9) cited Schattschneider (1960, p. 35):

> The flaw in the pluralist heaven is that the heavenly chorus sings with a strong upper-class accent. Probably about 90 percent of the people cannot get into the pressure system.

Goldstone (1980) reanalyzed Gamson's data and criticized Gamson's claim that success was difficult to attain and that only the best-organized groups, after a long struggle, were likely to attain their ends. Goldstone (1980, p. 1942) found a picture of flexibility combined with rigidity. Nondisplacement groups attained their ends, while displacement groups normally failed:

Thus the American social system appears to be willing to accommodate itself to a tremendous range of social protest, provided that destruction or replacement of well-established interests is not sought.

Whether the political decision-making system is open and responsive or is dominated by an elite, cannot be answered on the basis of the available research on movement influence. Further research on different questions is necessary:

1. Which wants and demands of people are converted into movement demands and activities?
2. Which movement demands and initiatives reach political agenda status? (who enters pluralist heaven?)
3. What is the policy outcome of decision-making processes about issues presented by movements?

How to Measure Influence?

Gamson (1980, p. 1043) distinguished two dimensions of success: The provision of tangible benefits that meet the goals of the challenging group and the formal acceptance of the group by its main antagonist as a valid representative of legitimate interests. He knew that this interpretation would be criticized: "There is no more ticklish issue in studying social protest than deciding what constitutes success." The form of success this paper is focusing on is close to Gamson's "winning new advantages." Winning partial advantages could be added to the success score of challenging groups (Goldstone 1980).

More important and problematic, in my view, is the issue of how to measure winning new advantages or influence. Gamson studied the preceptions of historians, the challenging group, its antagonist and the group's level of satisfaction after the challenge. When all observers judged that most of the goals in at least one important aspect were met, the group was considered successful in winning new advantages.

Gamson (1975, p. 34) admitted that the relation between the group's efforts and the winning of new advantages is problematic:

No assumption is made that the challenging group necessarily caused the benefits. We asked only whether the desired results were forthcoming, for whatever reason, during and immediately after the period of challenge.

In other words: influence or success is equated with goal attainment. That poses a serious problem which can be summarized under the heading of "pseudosuccess." Groups can win new advantages and can achieve goals without having caused the effect themselves. A group that joins successful campaigns but, in reality, contributes little of importance to them, is considered successful. This problem was acknowledged by Gamson (1980, p. 1050) but not solved.

In general, pseudosuccess refers to the fact that other actors and factors might have caused the winning of advantages. Earlier changes in public opinion might, for example, be responsible for a review of government policy as well as for the success of an SMA campaign. Thus, when it is known that a social movement has achieved its ends, it still must be shown that changes in government policy were indeed effected by movement actors and activities.

The reverse situation is also possible (pseudofailure). "One cannot conclude that no influence has occurred simply by a failure to achieve a preferred outcome" (Gamson 1968, p. 66). When an SMA does not succeed in achieving his desired ends, influence on government policy may have taken place in the sense that the policy would have been different, without the movements' activity.

Summary

Success of movements and movements' actors have become an often discussed and researched subject during the last decade. Important work has been done and the state of the art is less cumbersome than 10 years ago when Marx and Wood (1975, p. 403) concluded that "most statements about the consequences of movements are primarily descriptive or taxonomic." Information is available about the goal achievement of several SMAs and the same is true for possible reasons for success and failure.

Nevertheless, two fundamental problems are not yet satisfactorily solved.

First, we will have to deal with the problem of describing and measuring influence (the problem of pseudosuccess and pseudofailure). As long as we limit ourselves to influence defined as goal-achievement, serious doubts about the usefulness of empirical results will remain.

Secondly, we will have to be more systematic in defining the factors, variables, or parameters which are relevant for the influence of movements and movement actors. Until now, researchers selected one or more of the following factors:

1. characteristics of the groups and organizations that tried to exert influence;
2. characteristics of the targets of influence attempts (the political authorities and authority structure);
3. characteristics of the historical context the influencer and influencee were operating in (characteristics of the political, social, cultural, and economic context).

However, a theoretical framework, integrating these different factors, is not yet available.

DECISION-MAKING PROCESSES AND
THE STUDY OF MOVEMENT INFLUENCE

In order to tackle the problem of defining and measuring influence, a step-by-step process must be chosen. It is not beneficial to try to answer questions about the overall political influence of a whole social movement. Influence research has to start with questions concerning the relationships between actors. The first step is the specification of the SMAs and activities and the area of government policy they try to influence. Certain SMAs try to influence certain decisions by organizing certain activities aimed at changing the policy of certain political actors.

A second step is delineating the political system and the social movement. Generally, both consist of an interorganizational network, in which various actors represent different opinions and interests.

Further, it will have to be made plausible that policy was influenced by movement existence and/or activity, by presenting what would have been the course of action taken by a political actor when an SMA had been absent ("counterfactual"), and by specifying the means or mechanism by which the SMA has prevented the alternative government policy (Lukes 1974, pp. 41-42).

For the student of social movements, this implies a shift in focus from social movements and its activities, per se, towards the *decision-making processes* in which an SMA is only one of a number of relevant actors.

It all comes down to a reconstruction of the decision-making process. A study of movement influence cannot be movement-centered (Pickvance 1973). Webb et al. (1983, p. 323) stressed the same:

> In most policy decisions, where the issues pose differential costs and benefits to various sectors of the community, there are likely to be a number of other actors involved, both within the institutional political system and without it, and it may be one or more of these other factors that may prove decisive, not the actions of a particular challenging group. It is absolutely essential, therefore, that if strategies of groups are to be evaluated, a detailed interactive study be undertaken wherein the specific linkage between group and outcome is demonstrated.

The reconstruction has to demonstrate whose interests were at stake; who the participants were in the decision-making process; what they were advocating; what means of influence participants employed and to what extent participants were successful.

To show that participants actually were successful in influencing the policy decision, the counterfactual and the mechanism of influence have to be traced. Comparing decision-making processes is very helpful in this respect. When an actor is present and active in one situation but absent in another, comparable situation, it is plausible that differences in outcome can be attributed to the influence attempts by that actor.

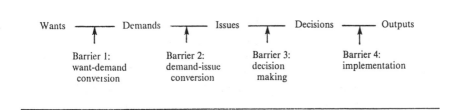

Figure 2. A Barrier-Model of the Political Process

Source: Van der Eijk and Kok (1975, p. 284); adaptation of Bachrach and Baratz (1970, p. 54). Reprinted with the permission of C. Van der Eijk.

In investigating decision making, a barrier model of the political process is useful (Bachrach and Baratz 1970; Van der Eijk and Kok 1975).

Conclusions about the responsiveness of political systems will be premature when they are not based on complex research. Not only the translation of wants and interests of people into movement demands and activities has to be studied, but also the transformation of movement demands into issues that reach political agenda status and the treatment of issues by actors inside the political and bureaucratic system.

Explaining Influence

When the extent to which an SMA has influenced government policy has been established, the question to which factors this influence can be attributed, comes into view.

To answer this question, it is necessary to *compare* decision-making processes with different outcomes. Decision-making processes which were influenced by SMAs will have to be compared with processes in which SMAs failed to exert influence.

On the basis of existing research, at least the following elements must be included in a model to explain the political influence of SMAs:

1. Characteristics of the *SMA* and its activities: ideology, demands, strategy, organization, resources (manpower, money, expertise, contacts/access), media coverage;
2. Characteristics of the social *movement*, the conglomerate of actors and activities of which the SMA is a part;
3. Characteristics of the *decision-making* process:

   a. the responsible political authority involved (policy freedom, stability of the governing coalition)

    b.   the decision-making procedures (including the available time)
    c.   the private actors involved (allies and opponents);
    d.   the public actors involved (allies and opponents);

4. Characteristics of the *context* of that process: political, economical, and cultural developments (including crises).

DUTCH RESEARCH ON INFLUENCE

Research on movement influence on government policy is scarce and it is remarkable that much work was done by Dutch scholars. Two factors seem to be responsible for this:

- the relative openness of the Dutch political system (for movements and researchers on movements); and
- research that has been done on the influence of other than SMAs on government policy.[3]

Braam's (1981) research on the influence business firms exert upon decisions of the Dutch government is an example of the latter. His basic outline is presented in Figure 3.

Braam distinguished three influence aspects:

- the degree to which actors are aware of their problems;
- the degree to which actors turn to the government for a solution of their problems (the degree to which they undertake influence attempts);
- the degree to which the government complies with the influence attempts ("tested influence").

For his empirical investigation, Braam selected 130 firms, dependent upon transport by water (shipyards and other firms). Problems, influence attempts, and decisions were traced in case studies. Once the information was gathered for the single cases, the cases in the sample were used for statistical analysis.

The most remarkable empirical result of Braam's research was that the main hypothesis, that large firms have more influence on government than small ones, was not confirmed for the effectiveness of influence attempts ("tested influence"). Government decisions did not tend to favor large firms. The degree of influence did depend upon the rate of growth of the business firms. "Growers" were found to extract more favorable decisions from the government than "nongrowers."

Braam's research design was also used to establish the influence of other actors on government policy (soccer clubs, for example; Bos and Braam 1980).

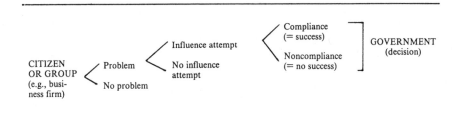

Figure 3. Problems, Influence Attempts, and Decisions

Source: Page 4 in Geert P.A. Braam (1981), *Influence of Business Firms on the Government.* Reprinted with permission from Mouton de Gruyter, Berlin.

Social Movement Actors' Influence

An example of a study looking at the influence of SMAs on policy-making was van Noort's study (1984) of the Dutch *squatters' movement.* In The Netherlands, thousands of young people occupied houses during the 1970s and, in several cities, groups emerged to defend their interests. The squatters' movement protested against the large number of buildings left empty due to speculation and project developments.

Numerous actions were undertaken by this movement in order to change government housing policy, predominantly on the local level. Van Noort did research on squatter groups in four cities and on the responses of local governments to movement demands. He concluded that the squatters' movement did influence decision-making processes.[4] It appeared to be easier to prevent unfavorable policy from being executed than to get political and bureaucratic actors to execute favorable policy.

The squatters' movement in Dordrecht, a city of about 100,000, was the most successful (van Noort 1984, pp. 76-101). Approximately 300 activists squatted 153 buildings between 1977-1982. The Dordrecht Squatters' Association represented the movement's interests although it counted a mere 10-15 active members and could mobilize no more than 70 people at any demonstration. But the Association exerted influence on local government policy. For instance, it arranged the legalization of squatted premises, it was successful in getting the city council to adopt antivacancy laws and in getting the local government to institute policy preventing the sale of regular rental accommodations. The movement's demands were moderate and supported by expert opinion, and although the Squatters' Association had frequent contact with city hall, it did not hesitate to resort to more radical action such as occupying public buildings.

Van Noort (1984, pp. 101-101) accounted for the Dordrecht Squatters' Association's success by pointing to its moderate demands, its expert support, its strategy (both discussion and use of constraints), the absence of organized opposition, and the dominant influence of the social democratic party on the city's housing policy.

Another example of Dutch research is the work of Everts and his colleagues (1985) on the influence of domestic actors on Dutch foreign policy and the study of Everts (1983) on peace movement organization.

Everts (1985, pp. 12-19) assumed that four sets of variables were important for the political influence of actors:

- the *setting* in which decision and policy-making takes place (the degree of autonomy, the degree of domestic freedom to maneuver and the amount of time available for decisions);
- the *stages* through which the decision and policy-making process has to pass,
- the decision and policy-making *structure* (constitutional and political rules, relationships between actors, distribution of responsibilities); and
- the *conditions of influence* (characteristics of domestic groups: character and size of the support received, resources and action strategies, legitimacy and access to decision makers and target groups).

Everts et al. studied 17 controversial foreign policy decisions. In six instances, influence was successfully exerted; in four instances, domestic actors were partially successful, and in seven instances, domestic actors failed. Examples of successful influence were Dutch government action to restore democracy in Greece, the cancellation of an export license for two submarines for Taiwan, the support for Israel during the oil crisis in 1973 despite Arab pressure, and the negative decision with respect to the introduction of the neutron bomb. Examples of decision-making processes in which influence failed were the issue of an export license for Corvettes to Indonesia, the relaxation of export credit guarantees for Chile, the human rights policy with respect to dictatoral Argentina, and the change of the criteria for development aid.

Everts concluded that the Dutch political system seemed to be relatively open to outside influence. Well-organized and strongly motivated groups that advocated reasonable and generally accepted points of view, exerted considerable influence when they undertook timely action. In contrast, the likelihood of success was small when important national economic interests were at stake. Top level bureaucrats usually sided with business interests when there were conflicts between the demands of human rights groups and business interests.

Some years earlier, Everts (1983) used more or less the same framework to study peace movement organizations. He concluded that most "conditions of influence" played a role in the explanation of the relative success of the protest movement against nuclear weapons. Both the size and the character of public support should be taken into account. The legitimacy of the groups, derived from ties to the churches, was another important factor. The demands put forward were not accepted in their entirety but the radical proposals "served to create a considerable space into which others could move with more moderate proposals, which seemed more feasible and hence more attractive" (1983, p. 222). Sympathetic media coverage and personal ties to members of the foreign policy elite helped the interest groups to get direct and indirect access to decision makers. Resources seemed to be a less important variable but the ability to add new strategies to old ones was important for success.

ENVIRONMENTAL MOVEMENT ACTORS AND NATIONAL HIGHWAYS

In this section, some results of a research project on the influence of environmental movement actors (EMAs) on government pollicy on national highways is presented. I start with a brief introduction on the movement and the policy area.

Environmental Movement

The histories of the American and Dutch environmental movements are remarkably similar (Tellegen 1983; Wood 1982). In both countries, the environmental movement emerged at the end of the 1960s and prospered at the beginning of the 1970s. This period brought a sudden shift in public opinion towards the environment in both countries. In the subsequent period, public concern about environmental conservation and protection did not disappear. In The Netherlands, a stable portion of about 90% of the public thinks that the government should take far-reaching measures against environmental pollution (*Sociaal en Cultureel Rapport 1986* [1986, p. 359]). However, at the same time, the relative importance of the environmental issue has decreased since 1971 (Table 2). Other issues became more dominant.

Other points of similarity between the Dutch and American environmental movement were:

- Both sought to influence government policy;
- Special political parties to address environmental isssues were absent (or irrelevant) and;
- The issue of nuclear energy did not get the emphasis it got in a number of West European countries.

Table 2.   Importance of Different Issues
among the Dutch Population[a]

	1967	1971	1972	1977
Unemployment	29	5	6	70
Inflation	6	17	19	21
Environment	1	44	34	13
Energy	0	0	0	6
Housing	21	38	24	14
Law and order	2	8	5	16
Others/miscellaneous	17	34	42	39

Note: [a] Percentage of respondents mentioning a certain problem as "the most important problem in the
country." In 1971, 1972, and 1977 more than one answer was possible.
Source: Wiebrens (1977, p. 54).

The structure of the Dutch environmental movement seems to be less comparable to the structure of the same movement in other countries. Since the beginning of the 1970s, the Dutch environmental movement has consisted of a large variety of groups and organizations, and their respective activities. Most local groups cooperate on a provincial level in a so-called environmental federation. These federations, in turn, participate in the national Foundation for Nature and Environment (FNE), together with some large, traditional conservation organizations (since 1972). Most movement actors see the FNE as the major voice of the movement at the national level.

The FNE is accepted by the government as the most important national represenative of ecological interests. FNE functionaries represent the interests of nature and the environment in approximately 70 advisory bodies of the national government. The FNE and its provincial counterparts receive large funds from national and provincial governments. For instance, in 1983, two-thirds of the FNE's budget was covered by government subsidiaries.

Numerous case studies have demonstrated how the Dutch environmental movement succeeded in embarrassing government officials at local, provincial, and national levels. In some instances, this caused dramatic changes in government policy and the SMAs achieved, at least partially, their goals (Tellegen and Willems 1978). Examples include: the prevention of the construction of large polluting factories in Amsterdam (1969) and Rotterdam (1971); the prevention of highway construction in a number of places; the conservation of Dollard-marshes (1974); and the prevention of the closing of the Oosterschelde estuary (1974).

A systematic analysis of the numerous successful and unsuccessful attempts of Dutch environmental SMAs to influence government policy is lacking. Similarly, no detailed research of the factors that influenced the outcomes of decision-making processes had been conducted. My own research has focused on the decision-making processes with respect to the construction of national highways.

Decision Making About Highways

Decision-making processes about national highways were chosen for several reasons. The most important reason was that the interests involved, as well as the choices made, are easily recognizable and unambiguous when infrastructure is the subject of decision-making processes. Whenever central government plans a national highway, interests of local and provincial governments, private organizations representing business, agricultural and community interests and local, regional, and national EMAs are involved. Decision making about highways is subject to a consultation procedure, in which all actors may propose amendments and alternatives or express their objections. EMAs usually seize the opportunity to (1) question the necessity of the project, and/or (2) propose less damaging alternatives to the plan. At the end of the procedure, the Minister of Transport and Public Works makes the final decision.

Fifteen decision-making processes about national highways were studied. To be able to compare these processes, only projects in one province were selected (Noord-Brabant). Archives of environmental actors and of the local, provincial, and national agencies that were involved, were analyzed (including nonpublic sources). Approximately 75 representatives of private and public actors were interviewed. Whenever necessary, additional information was collected through interviews by telephone (50 respondents). This research was used to write detailed descriptions of the decision-making processes about the 15 highway projects.

Additional information was collected about the political context of the decision-making processes by interviewing the responsible Ministers of Transport and Public Works (1967-1986), leading civil servants, members of parliament, and members of national advisory councils (including representatives of environmental, agricultural, and employers organizations). Information concerning more general economic, cultural, and political developments was added.

Four questions lead the discussion of the results:

1. To what extent did EMAs participate in the decision-making processes?
2. To what extent did participating EMAs achieve their goals?
3. To what extent did EMAs actually influence the outcome?
4. Were there significant differences between cases in which SMAs were successful and cases in which SMAs failed to exert influence?

Table 3.   Environmental Movement Actors
and Decisions about National Highways

		Environmental Movement Actors		
Project	*Period*	*Action*	*Goal-achievement*	*Influence*
A 67a	1958-1967	no	no	no
A 55	1958-1970	no	no	no
A 67b	1958-1970	yes	no	no
A 62a	1958-1971	no	no	no
A 75	1965-1972	yes	yes	yes
A 58a	1964-1973	no	yes	no
A 62b	1958-1974	no	yes	some
A 2/264	1968-1979	yes	yes	yes
A 58b	1967-1982	yes	no	no
A 62c	1968-1982	yes	no	no
A 62d	1968-1982	yes	no	some
A 69	1970-1983	yes	no	some
A 19a	1968-1984	yes	no	no
A 256	1967-1985	yes	no	no
A 19b	1968-1986	yes	no	yes

Action, Goal-Achievement, and Influence

Some findings are summarized in Tables 3 and 4. Table 3 provides information about:

1. the highway projects studied;
2. the period in which the decision-making processes about the projects occurred (until the decision to cancel the project or the moment the project was put out to contract);
3. the activities or lack of activity of EMAs ("action" whenever movement actors did more than present a point of view in the advisory council);
4. the SMA's degree of goal-achievement; and
5. the SMA's actual influence (was the outcome effected by the demands and activities of EMAs?)

A number of general observations can be made. There is a large difference between the movement's involvement before and after 1974. Before 1972, substantial SMA activity was very scarce. Traditional environmental and conservational organizations limited their input of the decision-making process to uncommitted recommendations in the advisory council. Even when projects cut across natural reserves, these organizations normally did not put forward fundamental criticism of highway construction projects. In only one instance, an attempt to save a nature reserve was found (A 67b). In this particular instance, the reserve was owned by the conservational organization represented in the council.

The situation changed dramatically at the beginning of the 1970s. In 1972, environmental groups organized the first campaign against the construction of a highway (A 75). From 1974 onwards, every single construction plan was subjected to fierce attacks by the SMAs. This new environmental movement, predominantly based in local environmental groups, was able to provide a counterbalance. When local actors were absent, the provincial federation took their places.

A second point of interest is that SMAs sometimes achieved their goals *without* exerting influence. Construction plans, with damaging consequences for the environment, were withdrawn by the government without an SMA being active (A 58a and A 62b). These decisions were made public in 1973 and 1974 which was all but coincidental. From 1971-1973, the Ministry of Transport and Public Works reconsidered its policy objectives drastically. Existing plans were critically reexamined. Population and mobility demographics were reevaluated. Attention was paid to the disastrous effects of uncontrolled growth of the motor traffic on (inner) city life. Issues of the environment and nature entered the politicians' and bureaucrats' agendas. The consequence was that the management of the central government bureaucracy rejected many plans that were previously accepted. Afterwards, the minister who took office in 1973 presented "his" new policy to the public.

This clearly suggests that changes in government policy were stimulated by general cultural changes. The value attached to the environment changed inside and outside of the bureaucracy. That means that there might be common causes for the rise of environmental movement activities as well as for the changes in government policy in the beginning of the 1970s. When the movement started to play a more important role in decision-making processes about highways, a number of important policy changes had already taken place.

Thirdly, in a number of decision-making processes the SMAs exerted influence but did not attain goals. In such cases, an SMA totally objected to the construction of a highway, or its proposed routing, or suggested the improvement of an existing highway as an alternative. This usually required additional investigations by the civil service to study the proposed routings. In the end, the minister sometimes chose a routing more favorable to nature and the environment, without fulfilling the movement's demands. Therefore, the SMAs did not achieve their goals but they certainly did exert influence.

A fourth, more general finding concerns the differences between the six decision-making processes in which traditional conservational organizations tried to influence government policy (A 67a, 55, 76b, 62a, 58a, 62b) and the

Table 4:   Most Influential Actors in Decision Making
About National Highways

Project	Decision	Most Influential Actors
A 67a	1967	National Civil Service
A 55	1970	National Civil Service
A 67b	1970	National Civil Service
A 62a	1973	Local Government
A 75	1972	National Civil Service
		Environmental Movement Actors
A 58a	1973	National Civil Service
A 62b	1974	National Civil Service
A 2/264	1979	National Civil Service
		Environmental Movement Actors
		Provincial Government
A 58b	1982	National Civil Service
		Local Government
A 62c	1982	Neighborhood Actors
		Local Government
A 62d	1982	Local Government
		National Civil Service
		Provincial Government
A 69	1983	National Civil Service
		Local Government
		Regional Government
A 19a	1984	National Civil Service
		Provincial Government
		Local Government
A 256	1985	Local Government
		National Civil Service
		Advisory Council
		Provincial Government
A 19b	1986	National Civil Service
		Agricultural Actors
		Environmental Movement Actors
		Local Government
		Provincial Government

nine processes in which the new environment movement was present (A 75 and all projects since 1975). The conservational organizations exerted influence in one of the six cases. This new environmental movement managed to exert influence in five of the nine cases. Thus, new EMAs were clearly more influential than the conservational organizations. At the same time, the chances of achieving movement goals were limited. In only two cases, SMAs achieved their goals. Whether these success scores led to the conclusion that decision making about highways in The Netherlands is of an elitist or a pluralist nature, depends on one's standards.

Table 4 reveals which actors actually did influence the decision of the Minister of Transport and Public Works. The actors mentioned are the national civil service (for the infrastructure, including national highways; Rijkswaterstaat), the advisory council on highways (Raad van de Waterstaat), local, regional and provincial government, EMAs, neighborhood actors (community groups) and agricultural actors that defended farmers' interests.

When all projects were considered, the decision making about national highways appeared to be dominated by the national civil service for transport and public works. In 13 out of 15 cases, Rijkswaterstaat played a major role. At the same time, it is clear that more actors managed to influence decisions since the beginning of the 1970s. This is primarily true for local, regional, and provincial governments. These government actors were influential in nine cases, while private actors were influential in only four cases. Of the four categories of private actors I distinguished, the EMAs were most influential (three cases). Neighborhood and community groups as well as organizations representing farmers' interests were influential in one case. Business organizations never had a decisive influence on policy outcomes.

Very remarkable is the lack of influence in this policy area of a political actor that is often considered very important: The parliament never played an important role. Parliament members often asked questions about the progress of projects but they never seized the opportunity to change policy decisions.

Explaining Influence

Which factors played an important role with respect to the influence in decision-making processes, that is, were the significant differences between cases in which EMAs were successful and cases in which the SMAs failed to exert influence?

A number of explanatory factors will be examined in this section:

1. characteristics of environmental movement actors:

   a. demands;
   b. resources (financial and human resources and expertise);
   c. strategy;

2. characteristics of the decision-making process;

   a. the presence of private allies and opponents;
   b. the presence of public allies and opponents;

3. changes in the political, economical, and cultural context.

The conclusions are primarily based on the analysis of the nine decision-making processes in which the new environmental movement was present.

Environmental Movement Actors

A more general argument about goals and demands can be put forward. In some cases, the SMA influence did not coincide with the SMA goal-achievement. More radical goals, such as the cancellation of a project, were not attained, but SMA activity in support of those demands in some cases, nevertheless, contributed to policy outcomes which were less damaging for the environment (A 19b, 62d) or contributed to the postponement of a damaging decision (A 69). This is in line with Tarrow's hypothesis (1983, p. 1) that the major outcome of radical protest is reform. The major outcome of demands for radical reform might be failure in terms of goal-achievement, but success in terms of political influence in the form of moderate reform. This is comparable to Everts' finding that radical proposals can create a space in which others can move in with more moderate and feasible proposals.

This means that doubts can be raised about the effectiveness of "the strategy of thinking small" (Gamson 1975). These doubts are supported by another result. The financial consequences of the proposals of EMAs did differ enormously. One might expect that "the strategy of thinking small" would be most effective. However, the comparison of the decision-making processes about the highway projects does not show that. The financial consequences were not decisive for SMA influence. In two cases, the SMA's suggested solutions, were much more expensive than competing proposals (A 2/264, A 58b). In one of these cases, nevertheless, SMAs succeeded in achieving their goals as well as influencing the outcome (A 2/264). The chosen A 2 solution was estimated to be a $f100$ million more expensive than the competing proposal ($\$1 = f2$; 1987).

Of course, the financial argument was not completely irrelevant in the decision making. In a number of cases, SMA proposals contained the construction of expensive tunnels in existing trunk roads (A 58b, 69, 256). These solutions were considered too expensive and this forced its adherents to search for cheaper alternatives. However, when they did manage to present a cheaper solution (A 256), their proposals were again rejected. Other aspects appeared to prevail. This indicates that the financial consequences of the SMA proposals were not the decisive factor for SMA influence.

The financial *resources* which the SMAs invested in influence attempts do not seem to matter. The highest expense an SMA exerted, was paid to have a consultancy firm investigate possible alternatives for the routing of highway A 58b ($f30,000$). Government authorities, however, refused to reconsider the project. A similar negative result was obtained by an expensive lawsuit against the A 69 project.

In general, it can be added that financial costs of organized campaigns were limited. When considerable financial resources were necessary, the financially strong provincial and national environmental organizations carried most of the burden.

ces are, almost by definition, important for public campaigns.
SMAs attempted to demonstrate, by organizing petitions,
and the like, that their objectives were supported by a
on of the population. SMAs managed to mobilize more than
four cases (A 58b, 62c, 62d, 69). Surprisingly, considerable
s to be unrelated to policy influence. In the four cases in which
s most successful, SMAs exerted less influence than in the other
vever, the mobilization of support was not totally irrelevant.
tion occurred in all cases in which SMAs were most influential
9b). When the demonstration of support failed completely, no
xerted.
ect of manpower appears to be relevant for movement influence.
poses the presence of a group of members to organize the
might influence political authorities. As can be expected, the
ch a group of active members relates positively to policy

, the *expertise* of these members appears to be important for
SMAs managed to present an alternative for the proposals of
e, this directly contributed to the policy influence the movement
never SMAs presented their own proposals, policy was influenced

When _ _*trategy* of SMAs is studied, the following strategies of influence
can be distinguished:[5]
- argumentation: presenting information and arguments, hoping to convince authorities;
- demonstration: adding to arguments the demonstration of considerable support;
- persuasion: offering explicit benefits or positive sanctions to authorities (money, electoral support, and so on);
- litigation: (trying to change policies through court decisions);
- contestation: the use of constraints, presenting negative sanctions or disadvantages to authorities. Forms of contestation are:
  - legal contestation
  - nonviolent illegal contestation
  - violent illegal contestation.

In the cases I studied, movements' efforts to influence government policy followed a similar pattern. Since the beginning of the 1970s, movement actors always argued, they tried to demonstrate, and they made use of litigation whenever possible. The other strategies were rare. Offering explicit benefits to political authorities is very uncommon in The Netherlands and contestation is only very seldom used by the environmental movement. In protest against highways in The Netherlands, the contestation strategy, was applied only once.

To stop the construction of the A 27, a forest near Utrecht was occupied, but this had no real effect upon government's policy (Grimbergen et al. 1983).

Strategy and movement influence appear to be less related than could be expected. Litigation, persuasion, and successful demonstration did not contribute to SMA's influence. Nevertheless, some public support had to be shown to influence government policy. Argumentation alone was insufficient.

Decision-making Processes and Context

With respect to the features of the decision-making processes, the following can be observed.

Three categories of *private* organizations were often present in the nine decision-making processes: community or neighborhood groups, agricultural organizations, and business organizations. In a number of cases, different neighborhood and agricultural organizations presented conflicting views.

The demands of EMAs were supported by neighborhood groups in five cases, by business organizations in one case. Opposition came from agricultural organizations in three cases, from neighborhood groups in five cases; and from business organizations in seven cases.

SMAs did not cooperate with all of their allies. In a number of cases, coalitions were viable between SMAs and neighborhood groups. Environmentalists and farmers did not coordinate their influence attempts. Farmers' distrust of environmental activists were insurmountable, which was harmful to both sides.

The influence of SMAs appears to be related to the number of opposing private actors. SMAs influence score is 75% in the three cases with no or only one opponent, and 40% in the other five cases. The number of supporting private organizations seems to be less important.

Two forms of alliances with *public actors* appear to be important:

- alliances with local and provincial government
- alliances with parts of the national civil service.

Local and provincial government were important for movement influence for two reasons. First, these government actors were influential themselves (Table 4). Their support for movement demands meant that the movement had an important ally in the decision-making processes.

Secondly, central government actors highly valued the local and provincial governments' points of view. When all local governments favored the same solution, the central government bureaucracy tended to support their point of view. When that unity was absent, the chances of success of any influence attempt on central government policy increased considerably. Important movement influence always coincided with the absence of an opposing unanimous bloc of local and provincial governments (A 75, 2/264, 19b).

A similar argument can be put forward with respect to bureaucratic actors at the national level. The Ministry of Transport and Public Works always negotiated with four other ministries about the construction of national highways. Usually, the Ministry of Finance and the Ministry of Economic Affairs agreed with the proposals of Transport and Public Works. More critical were the Ministry of Agriculture and the Ministry of Housing, Town and Country Planning and Environmental Control. The interests of nature and the environment were represented by three agencies inside those ministries: the agencies for nature conservation, for town and country planning, and for environmental control. When these potential allies of the environmental movement decided to oppose SMA demands, the movement's chances of success were minimized. In such a situation other bureaucratic actors could easily ignore SMA proposals.

Direct access to the agencies responsible for nature conservation, town and country planning and environmental control was no problem for the Dutch movement. Officials of the National Foundation for Nature meet their bureaucratic counterparts in many advisory bodies. The FNE thus could use this formal, and informal, network to defend the proposals of local and regional environmental groups and organizations.

The Ministry of Transport and Public Works was less accessible. Contacts with bureaucratic officials existed, but the amount of mutual distrust was considerable. This is not surprising given the main task of this department: the construction and maintenance of an adequate infrastructure (including national highways). The department image as a stronghold of "bulldozer-lovers" is exaggerated. However, the movement needed the support and pressure of other policy actors to be able to influence policy decisions in this area.

Alliances with parts of the bureaucracy appear to be more decisive for influence than alliances with national politicians and political parties. Ministers heavily relied on their civil servants and members of parliament made no serious attempts to change policy decisions. With respect to the issue of national highway construction, bureaucrats had the prerogative. Consequently, the third feature of the decision-making processes, the national political balance of power, seems unimportant. The bureaucratic balance of power was decisive.

When the changes in the political, economical, and cultural *context* of the decision-making processes are related to changes in movement influence, only one cultural factor appears to be important. Until 1972, the influence of EMAs was very small. SMAs were most influential from 1972-1976 and they managed to exert some influence in the following decade. In the years preceding the period with most movement influence, public opinion changed drastically. Nevertheless, the general attitude of the public towards the environment seems to be less important. Since 1971, a stable portion of the Dutch population supports the thesis that environmental protection is important and that the government has to take far-reaching measures in this policy area. Movement influence, however, clearly decreased after 1976. Another aspect of public opinion seems to be more relevant. In the beginning of the 1970s, the environmental problem was suddenly recognized as the *most* important problem of the country (Table 2). This recognition was related to movement influence. When the issue became less dominant, SMA's chances of influencing policy decreased.

CONCLUSION

This paper was an attempt to show that research on the influence of SMAs on government policy is difficult and time-consuming, but not impossible. It was suggested to collect information about decision-making processes in order to trace actual political influence. Research results on decision making about national highways served to empirically underscore the arguments. It was demonstrated that under specified conditions SMAs are able to influence policy-making. Influence does not necessarily restrict itself to goal-achievement. It was demonstrated that decisions can be influenced without achieving the stated goals. The opposite happened as well. In cases in which SMAs were absent, policy changes in accordance with environmental movement goals did occur. These findings cast doubts on research in which differences between goal-attainment and influence are ignored.

In addition, it was demonstrated that an open framework of explanatory factors can be used in the study of the influence of movement actors. Characteristics of SMAs, of decision-making processes, and of the context of these processes, were incorporated. The data presented revealed the importance of different factors for EMAs' influence.

To be sure, it is easier to present a framework with many explanatory factors than to use it in empirical research. Actual influence research concerns specific actors, activities, and decisions. The study of comparable sets of movement actors and political decisions will often reveal that some factors do not vary enough to make conclusions about the complete framework possible. As a consequence, we have to be careful in generalizing research findings. Nevertheless, the results presented here contribute to the literature on movement influence. The following theses make this contribution explicit:

1. Important policy changes occurred shortly before new EMAs started participating in the decision-making process. Therefore, these policy changes cannot be explained by movement activity. The changes as well as the growth of the movement might be explained by the sudden overall changes in the norms and values attached to nature and the environment.
2. EMAs in The Netherlands participated in governmental decision-making processes since the begining of the 1970s. They managed to exert

influence in five of nine cases but achieved their goals in only two of the cases.

3. Goal-attainment by movement organizations is served by the expression of moderate demands. Movement influence, however, appeared not to be limited by the expression of relatively radical demands. Proposals containing radical reform can contribute to the realization of moderate reform.

4. Persuasion and contestation, that is, the use of explicit positive or negative sanctions, were seldomly used by EMAs. In the context of highway construction, environmental groups and organizations limited themselves to the strategies argumentation, demonstration, and litigation. This contrasts with the emphasis new social movement literature places on the use of constraints as an important element of the strategy of EMAs.

5. Most characteristics of SMAs and activities (demands, resources, strategies) appeared to be unimportant for movement influence. Nevertheless, one resource contributed to SMA's influence: the expertise to present movement alternatives for civil service proposals.

6. Characteristics of the decision-making process appeared to be more important for movement influence than characteristics of movement actors and activities. Like actors outside the polity, different actors, within the polity, struggle about decisions to be made. Therefore, the balance of power between actors within the polity is vital for understanding the results of influence attempts by SMAs. When public actors were divided and the opposition of private actors was weak, SMAs were most successful.

7. Decision-making about national highways in The Netherlands was dominated by civil service agencies as well as regional and local governments. Movement influence attempts, directed at those actors, were much more effective than attempts to influence parliament and ministers. The role of the bureaucracy as well as its complexity and diversity are often underestimated. Bureaucratic opportunity structures might be more important for the success of influence attempts by movements than responsiveness of politicians and political parties.

8. Movement influence was connected with one characteristic of the cultural context. For a number of years, SMAs benefited from the public's recognition of the environmental issue as the most important problem of the country. Other characteristics of the political, economical, and cultural context were not related to movement influence.

9. Numerous local, provincial, and national public actors participate in complex, political decision-making processes. This makes a multilevel movement organization important for social movement influence. The

combination of local environmental groups, provincial federations, and a coordinating national foundation facilitated access of the Dutch environmental movement to relevant public actors.

ACKNOWLEDGMENTS

I am grateful for the useful comments on an earlier draft, given by Ernst Abma, Lex Huberts, Wim van Noort, Leo Rademaker and, in particular, the editor of this volume. I would also like to thank Martha Johnson and Lex Huberts for their help during my struggle with the English language.

NOTES

1. There are differences between social movements and pressure groups, as is often stressed in the literature. We have to realize, however, that movements often encompass established interest or pressure groups as well.
2. In Gamson's (1975, pp. 187-189) presentation of his basic codes and data, the distinction is made between four categories of groups. No information is given about the primarily public or private character of the challenges, but it seems plausible that occupational groups operate primarily in the private sector, while socialist, reform, and right wing groups are more government-oriented.
3. For example, the research on the influence of business on government policy. Braam (1973; translated in 1981) did research on the effects of influence attempts while network analysis revealed the network of relations between government and business (Fennema 1982; Zijlstra 1982; Stokman et al. 1985).
4. van Noort's results contradict Eckert and Willems' (1986, p. 140) conclusion that "youth protest of the 1980s had a minimal influence on political decisions." van Noort did research on decision-making processes, whereas Eckert and Willems gauged influence in terms of the goals of four youth movements (including the squatter movements in Berlin and Amsterdam).
5. This distinction is presented in van Noort et al. (1987). See also Berry (1977, pp. 253-285).

REFERENCES

Bachrach, P. and M.S. Baratz. 1970. *Power and Poverty. Theory and Practice.* London and Toronto: Oxford University Press.
Berry, J.M. 1977. *Lobbying for the People. The Political Behavior of Public Interest Groups.* Princeton, NJ: Princton University Press.
——— . 1984. *The Interest Group Society.* Boston and Toronto: Brown & Company.
Bos, J.M. and G.P. Braam. 1980. "Invloed van voetbalclubs op de gemeentelijke overheid" (The Influence of Soccer Clubs on Local Goverment). *Sociologische Gids* 27:453-483.
Braam, G.P.A. 1981. *Influence of Business Firms on the Government.* The Hague: Mouton.
Brand, K.-W., ed. 1985. *Neue soziale Bewegungen in West europa und den USA. Ein internationaler Vergleich* (New Social Movements in Western Europe and the USA. An International Comparison). Frankfurt and New York: Campus.
Brand, K.-W., D. Büsser, and D. Rucht. 1984. *Aufbruch in eine andere Gesellschaft: Neue soziale Bewegungen in der Bundesrepublik.* Frankfurt and New York: Campus (2. Auflage).

Browning, R.P., D.R. Marshall, and D.H. Tabb. 1984. *Protest Is Not Enough. The Struggle of Blacks and Hispanics for Equality in Urban Politics.* Berkeley, Los Angeles, and London: University of California Press.

Cloward, R.A. and F.V. Piven. 1984. "Disruption and Organization. A Rejoinder." *Theory, Culture & Society* 2:587-599.

Dahl, R.A. 1957. "The Concept of Power." *Behavioral Science* 2:201-215.

Eckert, R. and H. Willems. 1986. "Youth Protest in Western Europe: Four Case Studies." Pp. 127-153 in *Research in Social Movements, Conflicts and Change,* vol. 9, edited by K. Lang, G.E. Lang, and L. Kriesberg. Greenwich, CT: JAI Press.

Eisinger, P.K. 1973. "The Conditions of Protest Behavior in American Cities." *American Political Science Review* 67:11-28.

Everts, Ph.P. 1983. *Public Opinion, the Churches and Foreign Policy.* Dissertation, Leiden: Ryks Universiteit.

──────. 1985. *Controversies at Home. Domestic Factors in the Foreign Policy of the Netherlands.* Dordrecht: Martinus Nijhoff.

Fennema, M. 1982. *International Networks of Banks and Industry.* The Hague: Martinus Nijhoff.

Gamson, W.A. 1968. *Power and Discontent.* Homewood, IL: The Dorsey Press.

──────. 1975. *The Strategy of Social Protest.* Homewood, IL: The Dorsey Press.

──────. 1980. "Understanding the Careers of Challenging Groups: A Commentary on Goldstone." *American Journal of Sociology* 85:1043-1060.

Gamson, W.A. and E. Schmeidler. 1984. "Organizing the Poor." *Theory, Culture & Society* 2:567-585.

Goldstone, J.A. 1980. "The Weakness of Organization: A New Look at Gamson's 'The Strategy of Social Protest.'" *American Journal of Sociology* 85:1017-1042.

Grimbergen, C., R. Huibers, and D. Van der Peijl. 1983. *Amelisweerd: De weg van de meeste weerstand* (Amelisweerd: A Road of Resistance). Rotterdam: Ordeman.

Jenkins, J.C. 1983. "Resource Mobilization Theory and the Study of Social Movements." Pp. 527-553 in *Annual Review of Sociology 9,* edited by R.H. Turner and J.F. Short, Jr. Palo Alto, CA: Annual Reviews.

──────. 1985. *The Politics of Insurgency. The Farm Worker Movement in the 1960s.* New York: Columbia University Press.

Klandermans, B. 1986. "New Social Movements and Resource Mobilization: The European and the American Approach." *International Journal of Mass Emergencies and Disasters.* 4(2):13-39.

Lukes, S. 1974. *Power. A Radical View.* London and Basingstoke: Macmillan.

──────. 1979. "Power and Authority." Pp. 633-676 in *A History of Sociological Analysis,* edited by T. Bottomore and R. Nisbet. London: Heinemann.

McAdam, D. 1982. *Political Process and the Development of Black Insurgency.* Chicago: University of Chicago Press.

Marx, G.T. and J.L. Wood. 1975. "Strands of Theory and Research in Collective Behavior." Pp. 363-428 in *Annual Review of Sociology* vol. 1, edited by A. Inkeles et al.

Pickvance, C.G. 1973. "On the Study of Urban Social Movements." *The Sociological Review* 23:29-50.

Piven, F.V. and R.A. Cloward. 1977. *Poor People's Movements: Why They Succeed, How They Fail.* New York: Pantheon.

Raschke, J. 1985. *Soziale Bewegungen: Ein historisch-systematischer Grundriss* (Social Movements. An Historical and Systematic Introduction). Frankfurt am Main and New York: Campus.

Richardson, J.J. and A.G. Jordan. 1979. *Governing under Pressure. The Policy Process in a Post-Parliamentary Democracy.* Oxford: Martin Robertson.

Schattschneider, E.E. 1960. *The Semi-Sovereign People.* New York: Holt, Rinehart & Winston.

Schreuder, O. 1981. *Sociale bewegingen. Een systematische inleiding* (Social Movements. A Systematic Introduction). Deventer: Van Loghum Slaterus.

Sociaal en Cultureel Rapport 1986 (Social Cultural Report 1986). 's-Gravenhage: Staatsuitgeverij.

Steedley, H.R. and J.W. Foley. 1979. "The Success of Protest Groups: Multivariate Analysis. *Social Science Research* 8:1-15.

Stokman, F.N., R. Ziegler, and J. Scott, eds. 1985. *Networks of Corporate Power: A Comparative Analysis of Ten Countries.* Cambridge, MA: Polity Press.

Tarrow, S. 1982. "Social Movements, Resource Mobilization and Reform During Cycle of Protest. A Bibliographic and Critical Essay." Occasional paper No. 15. Cornell University, Center for International Studies, Ithaca, New York.

――――. 1983. "Resource Mobilization and Cycles of Protest: Theoretical Reflections and Comparative Illustrations." Paper presented to the annual meeting of the American Sociological Association, Detroit.

Tellegen, E. 1983. *Milieubeweging* (The Environmental Movement). Utrecht and Antwerp: Het Spectrum.

Tellegen, E. and J. Willems, eds. 1978. *Milieu-aktie in Nederland* (Environmentalism in The Netherlands). Amsterdam: De Trommel in samen werking met de Vereniging Milieudefensie.

Tilly, C. 1978. *From Mobilization to Revolution.* Reading, MA: Addison-Wesley.

Tilly, L.A. and C. Tilly, eds. 1981. *Class Conflict and Collective Action.* Beverly Hills and London: Sage.

Tilly, C., L. Tilly, and R. Tilly. 1975. *The Rebellious Century 1830-1930.* Cambridge, MA: Harvard University Press.

Turk, H. and L.G. Zucker. 1984. "Majority and Organized Opposition: On Effects of Social Movements." Pp. 249-269 in *Research in Social Movements, Conflict and Change,* vol. 6, edited by R.E. Ratcliff. Greenwich, CT: JAI Press.

Turner, R.H. and L.M. Killian. 1972. *Collective Behavior.* 2nd ed. Englewood Cliffs, NJ: Prentice-Hall.

van Noort, W.J. 1984. *De effecten van de kraakbeweging op de besluitvorming van de gemeentelijke overheden* (The Impact of the Squatters Movement on Decision Making by Local Government). Leiden: Centrum voor Onderzoek van Maatschappelijke Tegenstellingen.

van Noort, W.J., L.W. Huberts, and L. Rademaker. 1987. *Protest en pressie* (Protest and Pression). Assen: Van Gorcum.

van der Eijk, C. and W.J.P. Kok. 1975. "Nondecisions reconsidered." *Acta Politica* 10:277-301.

Webb, K. et al. 1983. "Etiology and Outcomes of Protest. New European Perspectives." *American Behavioral Scientist* 26:311-331.

Wilson, G.K. 1981. *Interest Groups in the United States.* Oxford: Clarendon Press.

Wood, P.A. 1982. "The Environmental Movement: Its Crystallization, Development, and Impact. Pp. 201-220 in *Social Movements: Development, Participation, and Dynamics,* edited by J.L. Wood and M. Jackson. Belmont, MA: Wadsworth.

Wrong, D.H. 1979. *Power. Its Forms, Bases and Uses.* Oxford: Blackwell.

Zijlstra, G.J. 1982. *The Policy-Structure of the Dutch Nuclear Energy Sector.* Dissertation, Universiteit van Amsterdam.

EFFECTIVENESS AND THE STRUCTURE OF NEW SOCIAL MOVEMENTS

Peter Gundelach

NEW SOCIAL MOVEMENTS AND EFFECTIVENESS

Ask members of a new social movement about the effectiveness of the movement and they will refuse even to address the question. Effectiveness is not what it is all about. Effectiveness is a concept relevant for companies not for movements. Movements, however, just as companies, are organizations and can, in principle, be judged by their effectiveness. The question raised in this article is whether the existing organizational structure of new social movements is effective in terms of reaching the goals of the movement. This is relevant because the structure is a tool in the hands of the participants and, the better the tool, the better the chance for obtaining the goal of the movement. Of course, the lack of interest in effectiveness does not mean that the participants are uninterested in the performance of the movement. The participants,

International Social Movement Research, Vol. 2, pages 427-442.
Copyright © 1989 by JAI Press Inc.
All rights of reproduction in any form reserved.
ISBN: 0-89232-964-5

however, are more apt to express themselves in terms of success and (reluctantly) failure than in terms of effectiveness. The concept of effectiveness connotates to a technical-economic rationality to use Habermas' (1981) concept. This is a type of rationality which is often very different from the ideology of the participants of the social movements who are more in favor of ecological and decentralized ideologies, a rationality rooted in a "moral-practic" rationality (Habermas 1981).

In this article I look into the relationship between the organizational structure and the effectiveness of new social movements. It will be argued that new social movements can be classified in two broad categories, which require different concepts of effectiveness. After I have introduced the two categories of new social movements, two different concepts of effectiveness are discussed. Subsequently, the two movement categories and the two conceptualizations of effectiveness are put together. The theoretical relevance of the question is to get closer to an understanding of the specific organizational structure of new social movements. It will be argued that, despite weaknesses of existing arrangements, new social movements actually are rather limited in their freedom to choose organizational structure.

A CLASSIFICATION OF NEW SOCIAL MOVEMENTS

New social movements can be classified in two broad categories. On the one hand, there are the movements which aim at transforming the society. Thus, the founding father of the modern study of social movements, Heberlé (1951, p. 6) wrote "The main criterion, then, is that it (the social movement) aims to bring about fundamental changes in the social order, especially in the basic institutions of property and labour relations." Heberlé goes on to argue that the more important social movements are communism and fascism.

Touraine ([1973] 1977, [1978] 1981) has used a similar approach. To him, a social movement is a central force in establishing a new social order (or to maintain the present one). Social movements fight to control the production of society.

Touraine has defined the labor movement as "the" movement in industrial society. Much of his recent work may be seen as an attempt to find the central movement of the "programmed" society he claims we are entering. This is a movement which, similar to the labor movement in the industrial society, fights for control over the development in society.

Analytically, such broad social movements may be placed at the one end of a continuum. At the other end are the movements which have much more narrow goals. Many such movements aim at influencing the political decision makers without changing the institutional context. This goes, for instance, for many citizen action groups, (see e.g., Boyte 1980) in Western Germany called "Bürgerinitiative" (see e.g., Mayer-Tasch 1976).

The objective of new social movements with more modest goals is to safeguard the interests of the participants. Those movements have, as potential participants, persons whose interests are threatened by some state initiative they fight against. The movements with broader goals, mentioned in the previous paragraph, fight over the production of society. In those movements, anybody outside the power centers are potential participants.

These two kinds of new social movements are ideal-types. One problem with the distinction is that some movements may intend to create small changes, but the effects of these may be more comprehensive. The cause-effect relationship is often opaque. This is also seen in the situation where a movement with general social goals has to try to obtain smaller objectives in order to win the big ones.

However, the distinction is a useful tool for analyzing the different new social movements in terms of their effectiveness. In the following paragraphs, I show that the two kinds of movements should be analyzed with two different concepts of effectiveness.

WHAT IS AN EFFECTIVE MOVEMENT?

The performance of a social movement can be analyzed in relation to two different bodies of social science literature. Using organization theory, the question to be asked is: Is an organization effective and has careful attention been given to a theoretical analysis of the concepts of effectiveness and efficiency? In the literature on social movements, performance is usually measured in terms of the goal attainment of the movement. This, however, is often difficult to evaluate because the goals may have a smaller or broader scope and/or be of a short or long term character.

I now turn to a closer inspection of these two parts of social science literature.

Organization Theory

A distinction between efficiency and effectiveness was introduced over 50 years ago by Barnard (1938) and organization theorists are still arguing about the relevance and definition of the two concepts. To Barnard, effectiveness meant an organization's economic goal attainment and efficiency, the satisfaction and cooperation of the members of the organization.

Etzioni (1961) gave a redefinition of the two terms using effectiveness as goal attainment, but efficiency as the relation between goal attainment and the amount of resources used to produce the output. Etzioni's definition, the so-called *goal approach*, has now become customary, even though it has been interpreted in various ways.

For instance, Etzioni's definition does not necessary mean that only one goal is considered. Steers (1975) has reviewed 17 multivariate models of organizational effectiveness. This illustrates the variations in the evaluation criteria in various studies. In general, however, these studies consider two different kinds of output of the organization: the economic performance and a psychological measure which usually stands for some estimate of the job satisfaction of the members of the organization.

The goals of the organization are measured in one or more of the following ways:

- the "official" goals as statements made by administrators or from annual reports,
- "operative" goals which reflect the activities performed within the organization,
- ordinary member's evaluation of the goals of the organization.

The measurement of resources is, in principle, simple, since it is possible to ascertain the amount of manpower, investments (machinery), and so on used to produce the output of the organization.

The result is a fraction: goal attainment divided by the resources used to obtain the goal. This can be used to judge the efficiency of an organization. While this fraction may be a questionable measure for a single organization, organization research generally argues that this concept of efficiency is relevant for comparisons among several organizations.

In the mid-1960s, the goal approach was strongly criticized. The argument was that organizations are not goal-oriented systems. Yuchtman and Seashore (1967) claimed that an analysis of the goals of an organization, as judged by observers, is incorrect because it is not based on the unit of analysis: the organization. Further, they argue that there is no consensus among members of an organization or among members and outsiders as to the goals of the organization.

This also means a rejection of the distinction between effectiveness and efficiency. What interested Yuchtman and Seashore (1967, p. 898) was effectiveness. They defined

> "the effectiveness of an organization in terms of its bargaining position, as reflected in the ability of the organization, in either absolute or relative terms, to exploit its environment in the acquisition of scarce and valuable resources."

The system approach, as described by Yuchtman and Seashore, and the goal approach have had conflicting evaluations of the concept and the measurement of effectiveness; in addition, other less important schools of thought have entered the field. Altogether, research in organization effectiveness has, at times, appeared extremely confused and fragmented. Some authors have even suggested that the concept of effectiveness should be abandoned altogether.

"We are arguing for a moratorium on traditional OE (organizational effectiveness) studies," wrote Goodman et al. (1983, p. 164). Others have tried empirically to compare the two approaches, but must conclude that "the two approaches measure separate, but related dimensions of organizational effectiveness" (Molnar and Rogers 1976, p. 412).

The result of the discussion has been that it has been proven fruitless to analyze organizational effectiveness and efficiency with any simplistic concepts of organizational goals.

While this conclusion may hold in relation to business organzations, one might wonder whether it is valid in the case of voluntary associations or social movements. Knoke and Wood (1981) conducted one of the few studies on the effectiveness of voluntary associations. Their analysis points to two kinds of performance measures: member ratings and the evaluation by a panel of knowledgeable community informants. The resources of the associations were measured by three variables: membership resource contribution (which was divided into: internal activity, leadership, infraresources and external activity), tolerance, and budget. By relating goal attainment to resources, Knoke and Wood claim to be able to measure the efficiency of the associations.

Within organization theory, there have been no attempts to measure the efficiency of social movements. The reason is that it is not possible to determine the denominator in the fraction which measures efficiency. The core resource of social movements is the participant's activities, but because of the unstable membership and unclear boundaries, movement resources are not a fixed quantity which can be established by the researcher. This means that the efficiency fraction cannot be calculated because the denominator—resources—cannot be measured exactly.

The system approach to effectiveness presupposes that a social movement attempts to improve its bargaining position. This concept can only be used for new social movements which act within the boundaries of the established political system. This corresponds to the new social movements with narrow goals. They aim at influencing the political decision making and are not interested in changing the political system as such. In this respect, the system approach from organization theory is relevant for an analysis of the new social movements.

Organization theory cannot be used for evaluating the new social movements with comprehensive goals, because organization theory does not consider the broader societal impacts of organizations.

Social Movement Theory

The impact of a social movement on the social order is a central theme in social movement literature. Often the question is posed: How does a movement bring about the changes it strives at? How does it succeed? These questions have been discussed from many different angles. Piven and Cloward (1977) offer an explanation which states that only mass insurgency can compel measurable concessions from the elites in society. They argue against organization building, but use a very narrow concept of organization, which to them is identical with bureaucracy. This simplistic conception of organization makes organization incompatible with insurgent action, but the argument made by Piven and Cloward does not hold if one has a broader definition of organization including loose, informal, network structures (Jenkins 1979).

In spite of their many differences, both resource-mobilization theorists and activists (e.g., Alinsky 1971) consider organization as an important tool for social change. Resource-mobilization theorists point to organization as a prerequisite for mobilization (Jenkins 1983) and, from this, it may be deduced that different kinds of organizational structures may have different capabilities to mobilize. To the people who organize actions, organization is clearly something they must constantly consider. To them, the proper use of an organizational structure is crucial to the success of collective action.

These theories more or less explicitly address the question of the relation between success and organization or, to put it in the terms so far discussed in this article: the relation between social change and organizational structure. To the extent to which the social changes it is striving for are obtained, a social movement is effective.

The problem with this conceptualization of effectiveness is that the changes a social movement is striving for vary a lot. If we use comprehensive and profound change in society as a success criterion, very few so-called social movements qualify as successful. However, as we will see more modest criteria are imaginable.

For those new social movements that demand more comprehensive and profound changes, social movement theory provides a more adequate frame to analyze a movement's effectiveness.

EFFECTIVENESS AND ORGANIZATION

The two kinds of new social movements should be analyzed with two different concepts of effectiveness. The movements with more narrow goals can be analyzed with organization theory because they aim at influencing the political decision makers. The movements with comprehensive goals must be studied from their impact on society and the participants which means drawing upon social movement theory.

Effectiveness and Influence of Political Decision Makers

The narrow definition of goals of a new social movement should, in principle, mean that it is easy to establish whether the movements have obtained their goals or not. However, this is rarely the case. Many obstacles are in the way of such an analysis. For one, the objective of a movement may be to prevent something, for instance, the building of a nuclear power plant. If the authorities do not build one, the question is whether it is the movement which has influenced this (non)decision or something else which has created the outcome (e.g., financial calculations).

In general, new social movements have limited success in influencing political decision makers. The measures they fight against will most often be carried through. The authorities win, the movement loses. However, as the movement activitists never become tired of saying, this does not mean that the movement has failed, since the fight has resulted in a consciousness-raising of the participants. Also, many movements have an important agenda-setting function, but this is seldom included in the stated goals of the movement.

To establish the effectiveness of new social movements it is necessary to have some other organizations to relate to. Political science treats social movements as a channel of influence just as other political organizations do, for instance, for political parties and pressure groups. In this context, I treat only the relation between the efficiency of pressure groups and social movements.

A social movement distinguishes itself from a pressure group because it is more dependent upon the activities of its members. A pressure group has other resources besides their members (e.g., funds, experts).

Recent literature on pressure groups has been able to show that many pressure groups actually take part in the agenda setting, the definition of the political problems, the decision making, and the implementation of the political decisions (Schmitter and Lembruck 1979).

In comparison with the well-integrated pressure group, with its hierarchical structure, the social movements are quite ineffective. Often the social movement is even unable to get into serious contact with political decision makers (Gundelach 1980). This may also be seen in historical analysis. For instance, of the 53 challenging groups from 1800-1945 in the United States, investigated by Gamson (1975), less than half had "a minimal acceptance relationship" to its antagonists.

One important drawback of the social movement compared to the pressure group, is its loose, flat, segregated structure. In order to negotiate with an organization, political decision makers demand that it has leaders who are able to control the members. The precondition for a political compromise is that it will hold. This includes that the leaders of the organization are able to control the members. One of the resources of the pressure group is that it may create social unrest if it is not given concessions. In order to be a reliable partner in negotiations, pressure groups must be able to secure that such unrest, in fact, does not occur after a compromise has been arrived at.

Often this is not possible for the leaders of the social movements. They are rarely able to guarantee that participants will follow the outcome of a compromise. The decentralized structure of the new social movement often means that the political impact, defined as political decisions favoring the organization, is much smaller than that of the pressure group.

This is as far as an "objective" analysis of the goal-attainment of the social movement may take us. Evaluation of the effectiveness of the organization can also be measured subjectively from the point of view of outsiders or insiders. Little research has been done of this. However, my general impression is that outsiders judge the effectiveness of their social movements even more negatively than what can be gleaned from research. Politicians and members of pressure groups often have a low opinion of the impact of social movements.

However, judged by insiders, even the defeat of the movement may be regarded as a success, for instance, because it may have improved the social network of the community in which the movement was operating (Jay 1979). This change of attitudes, however, is rarely a goal or an intended consequence of the movement. Rather, it should be analyzed as a psychological adjustment to a disappointing situation.

In sum, then, this kind of new social movement rarely obtains its stated goals. This is partially due to an organizational structure which puts more emphasis upon the participation of the members than on a hierarchy which enables leaders to control members, thus allowing for making compromises with public authorities or other groups. Compared to other political associations the effectiveness, measured as the degree to which the movement can influence political decision makers, is quite low.

Social Movements as Agents of Social Change

Analysis of effectiveness in social movement theory puts the emphasis on the societal impact of a social movement. The focus is on a change of society rather than political decision making.

In order to answer the question as to whether a social movement did succeed in promoting social change, it is necessary to determine the constitutive elements of the present society. There is, however, no agreed-upon opinion of what constitutes present society. Industrialism, urbanism, liberal democracy, capitalism are supposed to be the basic elements of modern society (Lee and Newley 1983). The central contradiction is that between labor and capital and the central agent for social change is the working class.

But, several authors are suggesting that the modern society is in the process of changing toward a programmed (Touraine [1969] 1974), a late-capitalist

(Habermas 1981), or a postfordistic society (Hirsch 1985). The present state of social analysis does not allow any clear conclusion as to the degree to which the characteristics of the modern society still exist. This implies that it is fruitless to judge the societal impact of a social movement in these broad terms. It seems more relevant to judge whether the movement has changed parts of society. This, in turn, can be analyzed in several ways. I shall limit myself to the following: political socialization, consciousness-raising, and the establishment of institutions.

In all these respects, the new social movements have made important contributions. The effects of the movement, of course, varies depending on which kind of movement one is discussing. I will illustrate my argument by discussing two important new movements: the womens' liberation movement and the ecology movement.

Traditionally, the major agent in political socialization has been the political party. This, however, has changed in several European countries. The political parties have been related to the class structure, but with the changes in the division of labor in society, the party structure has become less clear.

In Scandinavia, for instance, the party structure has been related to three classes: peasants, workers, and the bourgeoisie (Rokkan et al. 1970). The growth of the public sector and the differentiation of the working class has resulted in a fragmented class structure. This has weakened the social basis of the political parties. At the same time, the expansion of corporatist decision making has resulted in hierarchization of political parties and a tendency for party leaders to make compromises at the top with policymakers in other organizations and the state, resulting in weaker relations between the outcome of the political activities and the program of the party.

This sketch of the development of the political parties implies that they no longer play an important role as agents for political socialization. In its place, new social movements have become important as many young people have their first encounter with politics there, and there is some evidence that radicalism acquired in social movements does not disappear (DeMartini 1982).

One of the reasons for political socialization to occur increasingly in social movements is probably that movements provide more engaging and innovative opportunities than the political parties. The rallies, sit-ins, and squattings are just a few examples of the wealth of activities that social movements are generating.

The effects of consciousness-raising by new social movements are difficult to evaluate. This is not only because attitude surveys of the population, with regard to new social movements, are rare, but also because it is impossible to know whether attitude changes are produced by new social movements or not. The postmaterialistic values which, for example, a proportion of the Europeans appear to adhere to (Inglehart 1977), may be a precondition as well as a result of the new social movements, or have emerged simultaneously.

The construction of nuclear power plants has provoked many, often quite violent, demonstrations in Western Europe and in the United States. Pollution has increasingly become an item on the societal and political agenda.

The women's liberation movement has died, some feminists claim, but, at the same time, women all over Europe demand more women in parliaments, more women in highly-paid positions and, in the families, the changing role of women has had many consequences. The organizational center of the movement may have died, but the movement has changed the attitudes and the everyday life of the population (Dahlerup 1986).

Perhaps, more importantly, the new movements have succeeded to root changes in consciousness in new social institutions. They are often weak, some may die and others be born, but they exist in many places.

The environmental movement has tried to establish alternatives to the centralized energy production, for instance, with local initiatives like windmills, solar energy, and the like. Many of these alternatives have probably only been established because they are economically rational, but, even so, the idea of making energy in institutions which are different from the centralized plants does have social consequences differing from those of the centralized structure.

A similar argument can be made of institutions generated by the women's movement. Women's shelters can be taken as an example. Many that started out as feminist initiatives have been taken over by the state (Morgan 1981). However, they often function in a different manner than the traditional social security institutions of the state. Other kinds of less visible women's movement-inspired institutions are permanent women's groups in many formal organizations as well as associations.

In sum, although the new social movements have not been able to create changes in the social order on a large scale, they have been able to create changes in areas such as political socialization, public opinion, and the establishment of social institutions. This, however, should not be overestimated. The changes mentioned here are scattered and unstable. Social order has largely remained unchanged. Even where new social movements have had some success, the outcome of their activities has been modest and certainly much smaller than they had hoped for.

CAN MOVEMENTS BECOME MORE EFFECTIVE?

The new social movements have shown little effectiveness in the two meanings of the concept outlined above. They have only been able to influence few political decisions and they have only changed small parts of the social order. This conclusion may be too pessimistic, but the fact remains that, compared to the tremendous changes which the old social movements of the Western European countries have brought about, the changes wrested by the new social movements appear insignificant even if we take into account the much smaller span of time they have had. What, then, can the new social movements do about it? With regard to the impact on political decisions, one advice to the movements could be to organize in a way similar to the traditional associations. The organizational structure (Gerlach and Hine 1970) of the new social movements is not suited for the modern corporatistic decision-making structure. An organizational advisor of a new social movement would probably urge them to function in a fashion similar to that of the pressure groups. And, in fact, some of the new social movements—especially in the United States—have created such organizations. This, however, raises the question of the relation between the organizational structure of the social movements and the ideology of the participants.

Practically all research of the participants of the new social movements show that their attitudes are different from other parts of the population. Using the distinction Cotgrove and Duff (1980, 1981) make between dominant and an alternative paradigm of social values, they are more oriented towards the latter. The traditional paradigm stresses such values as economic growth, centralization, and rationality of means. The alternative paradigm has as its important elements self-actualization, harmony with nature, and participative structures.

The latter values are reflected in the SPIN-organizational structure of new social movements. The structure of the movement is the visible expression of the social values of the participants. The structure is not just a means of obtaining the goal of the organization. The goal is expressed in the structure which shows some of the social consequences of the values held by the participants. A core idea of many new social movements is to reject the dominant means-end rationality of the present society. The organizational structure of the movements is a reflection of the society they try to establish.

"We produce culture," activists of the Italian women's liberation movement said, when confronted with the question of their organizational structure (Melucci 1984).

This raises the question of how these alternative social values become rooted among participants of new social movements, because the answer may indicate whether or not it is likely that organizational structure of new social movements will change. Empirical research in different countries shows that new social movements are dominated by the so-called new middle-layers: civil servants in the social services, education, and health sectors (Brun 1978; Parkin 1968; Cotgrove and Duff 1980, 1981). Persons from the new middle-layers more often express alternative values and are more often members of new social movements.

Several explanations are suggested for the disproportionate adherence to alternative values among the new middle-layers: childhood socialization which may stress antimarket values (Parkin 1968), socialization/professionalization in the education (for an example see Jacobsen 1981), and, finally, "on the job" experience. Probably it is not very fruitful to try to sort out the relation between these factors. Important is that they are intertwined and work in the same direction. So the attitudes of participants of new social movements are solidly rooted in the socialization and work situation. As a consequence, they cannot easily be changed and probably these persons choose to become members of a new social movement rather than a political party because the activities and the organizational structure of the new social movements are more in accordance with their social values. Once they become activists of the movement and experience collective identity-formation (Weiner 1982), the alternative values are even more strongly integrated in their belief systems. Consequentially, people who have different views of the organizational structure of the movement are even more vehemently rejected. Very few members of the working class are participating in new social movements. This points to a cultural conflict between the alternative values of the middle class stressing participation and antihierarchy and the traditional values of the working class.

A Change of Structure?

Thus, it is not very likely that the participants of a new social movement will accept changes in the structure of the movement allowing it to become more effective in the way in which a pressure group is. From this, we may predict that new social movements do not become subject to the Weber-Michels iron law of oligarchy. They do not transform themselves into pressure groups because this would mean that most of the participants might feel that they would betray their values. As Zald and Ash (1966) have pointed out, the so-called iron law is not an inevitable process. From organization theory, they deduce that the movement may change in different directions, die, or even grow. One might add that the basic idea of the Weber-Michels analysis was to describe the workers' movements and there is no reason to assume that all movements, irrespective of the attitudes of their members and their goals, should develop in the same way.

Thus, it is not likely that a new movement will drastically change its organizational structure even after the first ambitious and innovative period. Probably the death of many movement organizations is due to the fact that they do not get political influence in the traditional political channels. They are unwilling to create a new hierarchical structure because they fear that the centralized structure will become a goal in itself, a goal which is in opposition to the general societal goals of the movement. This is probably a general dilemma for new social movements: join the power holders and change the structure (goal displacement) or keep your hands clean, but miss political influence.

One possible solution to this dilemma is to double-organize in the way which has been suggested by Wilson (1961) or Melucci (1980). The idea is to have two apparently competing movements or associations, a radical and a less radical one. The mixture of two movements fighting for the same goals, but with different activities, should give more power to the overall movement of which both are parts. This may work in some cases, but, in others, the method may be less effective, because it may not be possible for the two submovements to avoid rivalry and other unintended consequences of the competition (Wilson 1961).

In conclusion, there is not much hope for new social movements to become more effective in influencing the political decision makers because their organizational structure prevents it and it is not probable that the participants will accept changes in the structure because it expresses the culture of the movement rooted in the participants.

Given this, what will happen to new social movements? Most of them will die in the sense that they are no longer as visible as before (Melucci 1984). However, this, as mentioned, is often just the dying of formal core organizations of the movement. The network of the movement and its capacity of changing the attitudes of the population (resulting in, for instance, political decisions favoring the movement) may continue to exist. Moreover, former participants of a dying movement may become members of a new emerging movement.

Effective Movements

This is not to say that the new social movements are completely ineffective. In three different domains, they have proven to be effective, and that is where their structure turns out to be an advantage.

In the first place, there are the consciousness-raising activities. Here, new social movements do have success. New social movements are more effective in raising consciousness than other political associations. This may even be the most fundamental characteristic of a movement (Balle-Petersen 1986). The commitment process (Gerlach and Hine 1970) of the social movement means that the individual surrenders his old identity. It provides the individual with a new identity, new sense of group belonging, and even a new language. New values which become rooted in the individual's belief system will be of great importance in his future life.

The impact of the change in values is reinforced in the social institutions which some movements generate. Movement houses, meeting places, or stores are examples of institutions created by the movement. This is often combined with educational activities making for further changes in the participants' consciousness. To the individual, these changes may have the character of a bridge-burning act, an identity-formation process which is difficult to redress. In this regard, new social movements might be more effective than other associations.

Finally, the process of political socialization in new social movements may have created changes in the political system in the sense that it now is much more common and legitimate to use alternative political channels. Almost every group in society, from young to elderly, organize in order to get influence. The fact that such new social movements, which differ from traditional pressure groups, become much more common may be one of the most lasting consequences of the new social movements on the political systems in Western Europe and the United States even though it may be premature to state just how the changes will be in the long run (Barbrook and Bolt 1980).

EFFECTIVENESS AND STRUCTURE

In social science, there has been a trend from high hopes in new social movements to unclear and relatively small expectations. Following 1968, several theorists pointed to different new social movements for radical changes in society. Gradually, this has changed and some have even predicted the death of new social movements. There is no doubt that the movements in the 1980s differ from those of 15 years ago. They fight for new goals and the initial optimism has disappeared.

Even though the new social movements have so far not created major changes in the social order they have expressed new values and new kinds of political activities and have thus been important in making a new political culture. The specific organizational structure of new social movements has proved to be effective in mobilizing participants and it has reinforced the participants' attitudes thus making the organization stronger. In certain ways, the structure is better than other structures not just because it is tailored to the participants, but also because, in itself, the SPIN-organization has several advantages. The adaptability of the organization is great, it is flexible and can act quickly and above all the SPIN-organization creates committed participants. In the language of organization theorists, the organization culture is extremely strong. The bureaucratic procedures and control, however, are weak and this is the reason for the difficulty of the organization to coexist with, and carry out negotiations with, hierarchical organizations.

The SPIN-organization structure is constructed consciously by the participants. It grew out of the values and attitudes of the participants and is inspired by other movements. However, it is interesting to note that the SPIN-structure is also found at the top level of some multinational companies (Hine 1977). This may indicate that the structure is more effective than it sometimes is supposed to be even in organizations acting on an economic rationality.

The increasing number of studies of organizational culture (Alliare and Firsirotu 1984) in the last decade may result in more interest organizational theory in the SPIN-structure. Also voluntary associations may experiment with SPIN-like structures, for instance, by creating more engaging activities for their members and, on the whole, accept the expressive activities of the organization. The fact that the younger generation does not as readily accept bureaucratic control and that strong hierarchies have proved less effective may result in changes in many formal and voluntary organizations. This diffusion of the new social movements' organizational structure may become one of their more important long-term effects.

The new social movements have not invented the SPIN-structure, but they have demonstrated its superiority in a number of situations. Though not changing the social order, the introduction of SPIN-like organizational forms in other organizations may create greater effectiveness in those organizations.

REFERENCES

Alinsky, S.D. 1971. *Rules for Radicals. A Practical Primer for Realistic Radicals.* New York: Random House.

Alliare, Y. and M.E. Firsirotu. 1984. "Theories of Organizational Culture." *Organization Studies* 5: 193-226.

Balle-Petersen, M. 1986. "Everyday Rainbows: On Social Movements and Cultural Identity."*ARV Scandinavian Yearbook of Folklore.*

Barbrook, A. and C. Bolt. 1980. *Power and Protest in American Life.* Oxford: Martin Robertson.

Barnard, C.I. 1938. *The Functions of the Executive.* Cambridge, MA: Harvard Press.

Boyte, H.C. 1980. *The Backyard Revolution. Understanding the New Citizen Movement.* Philadelphia: Temple University Press.

Brun, R. 1978. *Der grüne Protest* (The Green Protest). Frankfurt: Fischer Taschenbuch Verlag.

Cotgrove, S. and A. Duff. 1980. "Environmentalism, Middle Class Radicalism and Politics." *Sociological Review* 28: 333-351.

_____. 1981. "Environmentalism, Values and Social Change." *British Journal of Sociology* 32: 92-110.

Dahlerup, D. 1986. "Is the New Women's Liberation Movement Dead? Decline or Change of the Danish Feminist Movement, 1970 till Today." Pp. 217-245 in *The New Women's Movement. Feminism and Political Power in Europe*, edited by D. Dahlerup. London: Sage.

DeMartini, J.R. 1982. "The 1960s Activists Today." Paper presented at The American Sociological Association Seventy-Seventh Annual Meeting, San Francisco.

Etzioni, A. 1961. *A Comparative Analysis of Complex Organizations.* New York: Free Press.

Gamson, W.A. 1975. *The Strategy of Social Protest.* Homewood, IL: Dorsey Press.

Gerlach, L.P. and V. Hine. 1970. *People, Power, Change. Movements of Social Transformation.* Indianapolis and New York: Bobbs-Merrill.

Goodman, P.S., R. Atkin, and F.D. Schoorman. 1983. "On the Demise of Organizational Effectiveness Studies." Pp. 163-185 in *Organizational Effectiveness. A Comparison of Multiple Models*, edited by K.S. Cameron and D.A. Whetten. New York: Academic Press.

Gundelach, P. 1980. *Græsrødder er seje!* (Grassroots). Aarhus: Politica.

Habermas, J. 1981. *Theorie des kommunikativen Handels Band 1-2* (Theory of Communicative Action). Frankfurt am Main: Suhrkamp.

Heberlé, R. 1951. *Social Movements. An Introduction to Political Sociology.* New York: Appleton-Century-Crofts.

Hine, V.H. 1977. "The Basic Paradigm of a Future Socio-Cultural Paradigm." *World Issues* 2.

Hirsch, J. 1985. "Auf dem Wege zum Postfordismus? Die aktuelle Neuformierung des Kapitalismus und ihre politischen Folgen" (On the Way to Post-Fordism? The Contemporary Formation of Capitalism and its Political Consequences). *Das Argument 151* 27: 325-342.

Inglehart, R. 1977. *The Silent Revolution.* Princeton, NJ: Princeton University Press.

Jacobsen, B. 1981. "Collection Type and Integrated Type Curricula in Systems of Higher Education." *Acta Sociologica* 24: 25-42.

Jay, A. 1979. *The Householder's Guide to Community Defence Against Bureaucratic Aggression.* London: Jonathan Cape.

Jenkins, J.C. 1979. "What Is To Be Done: Movement or Organization." *Contemporary Sociology* 8: 222-228.

————. 1983. "Resource Mobilization Theory and the Study of Social Movements." *Annual Review of Sociology* 9: 527-553.

Knoke, D. and J.R. Wood. 1981. *Organized for Action. Commitment in Voluntary Associations.* New Brunswick, NJ: Rutgers University Press.

Lee, D. and H. Newley. 1983. *The Problem of Sociology.* London: Hutchinson.

Mayer-Tasch, P.C. 1976. *Die Bürgerinitiativbewegung* (The Citizens Movement). Hamburg: Rowohlt.

Melucci, A. 1980. "The New Social Movements: A Theoretical Approach. *Social Science Information* 19, 199-226.

————. 1984. " An End to Social Movements?" *Social Science Information* 24: 819-835.

Molnar, J.J. and D.L. Rogers. 1976. "Organizational Effectiveness: An Empirical Comparison of the Goal and System Resource Approaches." *The Sociological Quarterly* 17: 401-413.

Morgan, P.A. 1981. "From Battered Wife to Programme Client: The State's Shaping of Social Problems." *Kapitalistate* 9: 17-40.

Parkin, F. 1968. *Middle Class Radicalism. The Social Bases of the British Campaign for Nuclear Disarmament.* Manchester: Manchester University Press.

Piven, F.F. and R.A. Cloward. 1977. *Poor People's Movements: Why They Succeed. How They Fail.* New York: Pantheon Books.

Rokkan, S., A. Campbell, P. Torsvik, and H. Valen. 1970. *Citizens, Elections, Parties. Approaches to the Comparative Study of the Process of Development.* New York and Oslo: David McKay Company and Universitetsforlaget.

Schmitter, P. and G. Lembruch., eds. 1979. *Trends Towards Corporate Intermediation.* London and Beverly Hills, CA: Sage.

Steers, R.M. 1975. "Problems in the Measurement of Organizational Effectiveness." *Administrative Science Quarterly* 20: 546-558.

Touraine, A. (1969) 1974. *The Post-Industrial Society. Tomorrow's Social History: Classes, Conflicts and Culture in the Programmed Society.* London: Wildwood House.

————. (1973) 1977. *The Self-Production of Society.* Chicago: The University of Chicago Press.

————. (1978) 1981. *The Voice and the Eye. An Analysis of Social Movements.* New York: Cambridge University Press and Maison des sciences de l'homme.

Weiner, R. 1982. "Collective Identity Formation and Social Movements." *Psychology and Social Theory* 3: 13-22.

Wilson, J.Q. 1961. "The Strategy of Protest: Problems of Negro Civic Action." *Journal of Conflict Resolution* 5: 291-303.

Yuchtman, E. and S.E. Seashore. 1967. "A System Resource Approach to Organizational Effectiveness." *American Sociological Review* 32: 891-903.

Zald, M.N. and R. Ash. 1966. "Social Movement Organizations: Growth, Decay and Change." *Social Forces* 44: 327-391.

International Social Movements Research

Companion Series to: **Research in Social Movements, Conflicts and Change,** Edited by **Louis Kriesberg,** *Department of Sociology, Syracuse University*

Edited by **Bert Klandermans,** *Vrije University, The Netherlands*

Volume 1. From Structure to Action: Comparing Social Movement Research Across Cultures
1988, 368 pp. $63.50
ISBN 0-89232-955-6

Edited by **Bert Klandermans,** *Vrije University, The Netherlands,* **Hanspeter Kriesi,** *University of Amsterdam,* and **Sidney Tarrow,** *Cornell University*

From structure to action is an attempt to bridge several gaps in the literature on social movements. Coming from different cultural and scientific backgrounds, the editors were surprised by the similarities between contemporary movements across cultures and the different directions taken by the European and American Approaches to studying them. More important, they were struck by the lack of comparative work in the social movement field. Struggling through the mass of American and European writings on social movements since the 1960's, they became more and more convinced that there was a blind spot between the two areas: in the dynamics that transform macrostructural developments into individual decisions to participate in social movement activities. The focal point of their interest became the formation and mobilization of consensus around social movement goals, and the networks, structures and subcultures supporting individuals' participation in movements.

CONTENTS: List of Contributors. Preface from the Series Editor. *Bert Klandermans.* **Preface,** *Bert Klandermans, Hanspeter Kriesi and Sidney Tarrow.* **Introduction. Mobilization into Social Movements: Synthesing European and American Approaches,** *Bert Klandermans and Sidney Tarrow.* **PART I. NETWORKS, SUPPORT STRUCTURES AND SUBCULTURES.** **Local Mobilization for the People's Petition of the Dutch Peace Movement,** *Hanspeter Kriesi, University of Amsterdam.* **Community Integration and Incentatives for Political Protest,** *Karl-Dieter Opp, University of Hamburg.* **Three in One: Currents in Milan Ecology Movement,** *Mario Diani and Giovanni Lodi, State University of Milan.* **Micromobilization Contexts and Recruitment to Activism,** *Doug McAdam, University of*

J A I

P R E S S

Arizona. **Recruitment Processes in Clandestine Political Organizations: Italian Left-Wing Terrorism,** *Donatella della Porta, European University Institute.* **PART II. CONSENSUS MOBILIZATION OR THE CONSTRUCTION OF MEANING. The Formation and Mobilization of Consensus,** *Bert Klandermans, Vrije University.* **Ideology, Frame Resonance, and Participant Mobilzation,** *David A. Snow, University of Arizona and Robert D. Benford, University of Nebraska.* **Political Discourse and Collective Action,** *William A. Gamson, Boston College.* **PART III. THE CREATION AND CAREERS OF COLLECTIVE ACTORS. From Peace Week to Peace Work: Dynamics of the Peace Movement in the Netherlands,** *Ben Schennick, University of Nijmegan.* **Old Movements in New Cycles of Protest: The Career of an Italian Religious Community,** *Sidney Tarrow, Cornell University.* **Themes, Logics, and Arenas of Social Movements: A Structural Approach,** *Dieter Rucht, University of Munich.* **Getting Involved: Identity and Mobilization in Social Movements,** *Alberto Melucci, University of Trento.* **The Independence of Structure and Action: Some Reflections on the State of the Art,** *Hanspeter Kriesi, University of Amsterdam.*

JAI PRESS INC.
55 Old Post Road - No. 2
P.O. Box 1678
Greenwich, Connecticut 06836-1678
Tel: 203-661-7602